D1234302

IBN SAUD

The Desert Warrior Who Created the Kingdom of Saudi Arabia

IBN SAUD

The Desert Warrior Who Created the Kingdom of Saudi Arabia

MICHAEL DARLOW
and
BARBARA BRAY

SKYHORSE PUBLISHING
A Herman Graf Book

First published in the UK by Quartet Ltd.

Skyhorse Publishing books may be purchased in bulk at special discounts for sales promotion, corporate gifts, fund-raising, or educational purposes. Special editions can also be created to specifications. For details, contact the Special Sales Department, Skyhorse Publishing, 307 West 36th Street, 11th Floor, New York, NY 10018 or info@skyhorsepublishing.com.

Visit our website at www.skyhorsepublishing.com

10 9 8 7 6 5 4 3 2 1

Library of Congress Cataloging-in-Publication Data is available on file.

ISBN 978-1-61608-579-7

Printed in the United States of America

Contents

Authors' Note

Details of many of the key events in the life of Ibn Saud are still disputed. In most instances where a dispute exists we have added an explanatory footnote rather than explaining in the main body of the text.

Spelling, etc

To make life easier for the reader we have tried to be consistent about the spellings and transliterations of Arab names, place names, words and expressions. However, a difficulty remains in that there is no universally agreed system of rendering Arabic names and words into English and writers in English about Arabia seem to adopt different approaches. On top of this, commonly accepted spellings and transliterations of common Arabic words and names seem to vary at different times. For instance, the spelling of Ibn Saud varies depending on who is writing his name and when. Similarly, common spellings for the name of Ibn Saud's father, Abd al-Rahman, include Abdur Rahman and Abdul Rahman. We have adopted Abd al-Rahman because we are assured by native Arabic speakers that it approximates most closely to his name as spoken in Arabic and is the spelling most acceptable among Arabs. A further complication arises from the use by Arabic speakers of familial and patronymic variations of names. We have therefore tried to adopt a single spelling and form of name for each person whenever they appear. However, there is a particular problem over the name of Ibn Saud himself. Ibn Saud only came to be widely referred to by that name after he had become the ruler of Najd. Prior to that various of his forebears had been commonly referred to by the family name Ibn, bin or al Saud. Before becoming ruler of Najd Ibn Saud was known as Abd al-Aziz, with or without the addition of his family name. Most of his Arab contemporaries continued to refer to him as Abd al-Aziz throughout his life. However, in the West once he had become the ruler of Najd he came to be widely and best known as Ibn Saud or bin Saud. So to avoid confusion we refer to him by the name Abd al-Aziz until the time when he became ruler of Najd and thereafter by the name Ibn Saud, the name by which he is now best known, especially in the West. We have clearly indicated in the text the point at which this change in the way he is referred to occurs.

An additional complication arises from the fact that a lot of different people bore the same name – for instance Faisal, Faysal or Feisal. In order to make it easier for the reader to distinguish between them we have wherever possible used accepted different spellings for each character – so the Saudi Faisal is spelt with an 'a' whereas the Hashemite Feisal is spelt with an 'e', and so on. For ease of reading we have also included a 'Cast List', giving the names of all the principal characters (with spellings as they appear in the text), together with a brief description of who each one is.

We have also provided a brief Glossary of the common Arabic and Muslim words that appear in the text.

Maps

Two detailed maps are included as end papers. One is political, and covers Arabia and the region immediately surrounding it, and also shows the location of the principal towns and cities in the story and of major international frontiers as they were towards the end of Ibn Saud's life. The other map shows the main physical features of the Arabian Peninsula together with the grazing areas of the main tribes that feature in the story. There are also smaller sketch maps at the beginning of each chapter showing the places or features relevant to that chapter.

Photographic Credits and Sources

The authors and publishers have made all reasonable efforts to contact the photographers and/or owners of all the pictures reproduced in this book, but in the event of any omissions or errors wish to apologise to the photographers, owners or copyright holders concerned. We are especially grateful to the following for permission to reproduce the photographs listed below:

THE ROYAL GEOGRAPHICAL SOCIETY for the following photographs by Captain Shakespear: Figs. 2, 5, 12, 15, 16, 17, 19, 20, 21 and 27, for the following photographs by Gerald de Gaury: Figs. 4, 13, 14, 28, 45, and for the following by unidentified photographers: Figs. 18, 38 and 42.

ST ANTONY'S COLLEGE, OXFORD, MIDDLE EAST CENTRE for the following photographs by Gertrude Bell: Figs. 24, 25, and 26, for the following photographs by H. St. J. Philby: Figs. 29, 30, 31, 32 and 35, and for Figs: 3, 8 and 22 by Sir George Rendel.

THE PITT-RIVERS MUSEUM, UNIVERSITY OF OXFORD for permission to reproduce Wilfred Thesiger's 'Interior of The Empty Quarter' (PRM 2004.130.12987.1) on the front cover and for Fig. 48 (PRM 2004.130.17416.1).

GETTY IMAGES for the following photographs: Figs. 33 and 50.

We wish to thank the DICKSON FAMILY for permission to use the following photographs by the late Harold and Dame Violet Dickson: Figs. 1, 9, 39 and 41.

We wish to thank the following photographers and artists for permission to reproduce their work: NOWFAL MOHAMMAD for Fig. 7, LARS BJURSTÖM and the members of the Saudi Caves project for permission to use Figs. 10 and 11, PETER MIDDLETON for Fig. 51, KATE BROOKS for Fig. 53, BROAD ARROW for Fig. 55 (GNU Free Documentation License) and MANAL ALDOWAYAN for permission to reproduce her works 'I am a Petroleum Engineer' and 'The Choice', Fig. 54.

A number of photographs reproduced in the book are either out of copyright, in the public domain or we have been unable to trace a copyright owner or person empowered to issue a reproduction licence. We list those photographs below and the sources from which we have reproduced them. We acknowledge our indebtedness to them all. THE LIBRARY OF CONGRESS in the United States for Fig. 43 and the UNITED STATES DEPARTMENT OF THE NAVY Fig. 46, ARAMCO (Geo Publishing Ltd) Fig. 44, RANDOM HOUSE Figs. 23 and 34, Constable & Co Ltd Figs. 36 and 40, ITHACA PRESS Fig. 37, CAMBRIDGE FORECAST (wordpress.com) Fig. 47, GLOBALSECURITY.ORG Fig. 49, SOLO SYNDICATION (The Daily Mail) Fig. 52, and FLICKR.COM (Creative Commons License) Fig. 6.

If the work of any photographer or copyright owner is featured in this book for which clearance has not been obtained the authors and publishers would be happy to pay the appropriate licence fee on establishment of such ownership.

Acknowledgements

This book was the brain child of Naim Attallah. It was he, with his characteristic enthusiasm and patience, allied with his personal knowledge of the Middle East and the Arab world, who overcame our initial lack of confidence over our fitness to take on the task of writing it. Throughout the almost three years of its gestation Naim has remained an unfailing source of advice, knowledge and encouragement. So our first and greatest debt of gratitude is to him. Thank you Naim. It has been fun.

We have also received unstinting help, advice and encouragement from numerous loved ones, friends, colleagues, scholars, historians, arabists, archivists, librarians and experts of all sorts. Although we already had an interest in Arabia and the Middle East as a result of stints of living and working there, our specific interest in Saudi Arabia and its founder, Ibn Saud, was first kindled more than thirty years ago by reading H. V. F. Winstone's pioneering 1976 book *Captain Shakespear*. Now, all these years later, Howard Winstone has generously allowed us to turn to him again for information and advice. In addition we have drawn extensively on the works of many other scholars more knowledgeable and learned than ourselves. Notes in the text cite specific instances and the Bibliography lists the principal published works on which we have drawn.

We wish to record our thanks to the staff of a whole host of libraries, archives and other institutions for their unstinting help. Among them we particularly wish to thank Debbie Usher of the Middle East Centre at St Antony's College, Oxford, Jamie Owen of the Royal Geographical Society in London, Philip Grover of the Pitt-Rivers Museum in Oxford, Kristen Wenger of the British Museum, Martina Oliver of Getty Images, and many members of the staff of the London Library who have been indefatigable in helping us to find material, old and very precious as well as new, in their magnificent collection of books, works of reference, newspapers and other publications dealing with Arabia, the Middle East, the history and personalities involved in our story. Not content simply to guide us in our research, they have themselves clambered repeatedly to the very top of the building and down into basements to search for and retrieve material for us. Through the London Library we have also had access to the JSTOR database giving us instant access to a great core of scholarly knowledge and journals from around the world and dating back for hundreds of years. As a result research which would previously have taken many months and involved repeated long journeys has become available to us at our own desks at the click of a computer mouse. In addition we would like to thank Jim Wolland and Carole Stone of Ex-Libris, our local independent bookshop in Bradford on Avon, who have been of enormous help in ordering us books and pointing us towards useful volumes on their second hand shelves.

We owe a special debt of gratitude to the family of the late Harold and Dame Violet Dickson who have granted us permission to reproduce a number of their photographs and to quote from their books and papers. We also wish to thank Kate Brooks for giving us permission to reproduce a photograph from her series for *Time Magazine* 'Saudi Women in Focus'. We are especially grateful to Manal AlDowayan, the Saudi photographic artist, who has generously given us permission to reproduce two of her works – 'I am a Petroleum Engineer' and 'The Choice'.

Various friends and colleagues have read our manuscript at different stages, providing us with encouragement and important suggestions for improvements and clarifications. Among them we would particularly like to thank Richard Moxon who read our manuscript as both a lawyer specialising in copyright and libel and as someone who knows Arabia and the Gulf from having worked in the oil industry there early in his career. We also wish to express special thanks to Sophie Balhetchet and Sophie Darlow. Sophie Balhetchet read the manuscript as an interested lay person with many years experience of reading and assessing manuscripts of all kinds but no first hand knowledge of Arabia. She wrote us a detailed appraisal of our manuscript which we found of great value in finalising and editing our book in preparation for publication. Sophie Darlow, who had spent sometime in Oman more than thirty years ago, read the manuscript in sections as we went along providing us with valuable insights, suggestions and encouragement as it developed.

Finally we wish to record our debt of gratitude to Debbie Slater. She not only read our manuscript at various stages and made numerous invaluable suggestions for improvements, she provided us with ongoing help during our research and then got our manuscript into a fit state for handing over to the typesetters. In addition to all this Debbie created the series of maps that appear as endpapers and at the start of each chapter.

Saudi Arabia, the kingdom which Ibn Saud created, is arguably *the* pivotal country in the Middle East. Much of what happens in the world in the next few years may well depend, to a greater or lesser degree, on what happens in and to Saudi Arabia. It not only contains the birthplace of the Prophet Muhammad and Islam's two holiest sites, it holds more of the world's proven oil reserves than any other country and is strategically positioned to control two of the world's most important trade and communications routes. The story of how Saudi Arabia was created and of the truly exceptional man who created it, Abd al-Aziz Ibn Saud, is remarkable. We, and the other people most responsible for producing this book, believe that story deserves, indeed needs, to be better known to a wider public.

MICHAEL DARLOW – Bradford on Avon
BARBARA BRAY – Paris
November 2009

Glossary

Abaya – cloak.

Agal – headcord used to keep a man's headcloth in place

Amir – a ruler or prince.

Caliph – successor of the Prophet Muhammad. A title latterly held by the Ottoman Sultans until 1924 when the Turkish Republic abolished the title.

Dirah – the grazing lands of a Bedouin tribe held in common by all members of the tribe.

Djinn – a local, usually malevolent, spirit.

Fatwa – an opinion or judgement given by a suitably qualified Muslim legal expert, a *mufti*, on legal or personal matters. The best known in the West is the death sentence pronounced on the novelist Salman Rushdie by Ayatollah Khomeini over his book, judged to be blasphemous, *The Satanic Verses*.

Ghazzu – a tribal raid, conducted according to strict rules and aimed at seizing property rather than taking life or inflicting physical injury.

Hadh – luck, as in a desirable attribute for a general or leader if they are to be successful.

Hadith – accounts of the deeds and sayings of the Prophet Muhammad compiled by scholars as an authoritative guide as to how individual Muslims and Muslim communities should live and act.

Hajj – pilgrimage to Mecca meant to be undertaken by every Muslim who is physically and financially able at least once in a lifetime as one of the 'five pillars' of Islam.

Hijra – the emigration, or 'withdrawal' of the Prophet Muhammad from Mecca to Medina in 622, the event which marks the start of Muslim history and the Islamic calendar. Also applied by the *Ikhwan* to their settlements – their 'withdrawal' from the community into their own ideal Muslim communities of the faithful.

Ikhwan – literally 'brothers' or 'brethren', the name adopted by members of a radical *Wahhabi* religious and social movement which became a powerful fighting force.

Imam – spiritual leader of a Muslim community and title of the person who leads prayers.

Jihad – literally to struggle or exert yourself in order to achieve a just or divinely ordered society, struggle against colonial or non-Muslim rule, 'holy war'.

Ka'aba – the cube at the centre of the Grand Mosque in Mecca in the side of which is the black stone, said to be part of what came down from heaven to provide light for Adam and Eve and which was subsequently rededicated to the worship of God by Abraham and his son Ishmael. Muslims perambulate around the Ka'aba during the *hajj* and ritually touch or kiss it.

Madrasa – Islamic religious school or institute of Muslim learning and sciences.

Majlis – a tribal council led by a *shaikh*, also a room or space in which meetings are held.

Muezzin – the person who makes the summons to prayer from the minaret of a mosque or a raised place near to it.

Mufti – a recognised Muslim authority on legal and religious matters. An opinion given by a mufti is a *fatwa*.

Shaikh – a tribal leader, elder or leader of a community.

Shari'a – Islamic legal code, rules and duties derived from the Qur'an, the *Sunnah* and *Hadith*.

Sharif – descendant of the Prophet Muhammad; Protector of the two Holy Cities of Mecca and Medina and the Holy Places of Islam, and for many years rulers of the Hijaz.

Sultan – literally 'he who has authority'. Title given to acknowledged rulers, notably to rulers of the Ottoman Empire but also to other rulers of Muslim states.

Sunnah – body of recorded sayings and practices of the Prophet Muhammad to become enshrined in Islamic law.

Surah – section or chapter of the Qur'an.

Ulema – learned men; authorities and guardians of religious and legal traditions of Islam.

Ummah – the worldwide community of Muslims.

Wadi – valley or channel of a watercourse which is dry except during the rainy season.

Wahhabism – uncompromisingly pure and strict form of Sunni Islam, inspired by a mid-eighteenth-century Sunni preacher, Muhammad al-Wahhab, who formed an alliance with the Al Sauds. The dominant form of Islam practised in Saudi Arabia.

Zakat – charity or alms giving, one of the obligatory 'five pillars' of Islamic faith incumbent upon every Muslim; also used to denote a tax.

Cast List

(Principal and recurring characters in the story)

THE SAUDS

Adb al-Aziz Ibn Saud, better known today simply as **Ibn Saud.**

Abd al-Rahman – Father of **Ibn Saud** and Amir of Najd.

Muhammad ibn Saud – Great-great-grandfather of **Abd al-Rahman.** Eighteenth Century ruler of Diriya and forebear of al Saud dynasty, the rulers of modern Saudi Arabia.

Turki Abdullah ibn Saud – great-grandfather of **Ibn Saud.** Ruler of Najd and much of the Arabian Peninsula during the early 1830s. Murdered in 1834 by his cousin Mishari.

Faisal, also known as **Faisal The Great** – son of **Turki Abdullah ibn Saud.** Ruler of Najd and surrounding region from 1840s to 1860s.

Sa'ad – younger brother of **Ibn Saud.**

Muhammad – youngest brother of **Ibn Saud.**

Nura – **Ibn Saud**'s favourite sister. One year older than him.

Wadhba – a daughter of the **Bani Khalid Tribe**, married to **Ibn Saud** in 1899 and mother of his son **Turki.**

Jauhara – much loved wife of **Ibn Saud.** Sister of his trusted cousin **Abdullah ibn Jiluwi.**

SONS AND GRANDSONS OF IBN SAUD

(Ibn Saud is known to have had at least 45 sons and probably an even larger number of daughters. He had hundreds of grandchildren and other direct descendants. Only those sons and other male descendants making multiple appearances in this narrative are listed.)

Turki – 1st son of **Ibn Saud** by **Wadhba,** born in Kuwait 1900. Died in 1919 influenza pandemic.

Saud – 2nd son of **Ibn Saud.** King of Saudi Arabia from 1953 to 1964.

Faisal – 3rd son of **Ibn Saud.** King of Saudi Arabia from 1964 to 1975.

Muhammad – 6th son of **Ibn Saud.** Voluntarily renounced throne of Saudi Arabia.

Khalid – 7th son of **Ibn Saud.** King of Saudi Arabia from 1975 to 1982.

Fahd – 11th son of **Ibn Saud.** King of Saudi Arabia from 1982 to 2005.

Abdullah – 13th son of **Ibn Saud.** King of Saudi Arabia since 2005.

Musaid – 15th son of **Ibn Saud.** Father of princes **Khalid ibn Musaid** and **Faisal ibn Musaid.**

Sultan – 16th son of **Ibn Saud.** Crown Prince since 2005.

Prince Bandar – son of **Ibn Saud**'s 16th son **Sultan.** Saudi envoy to USA.

Prince Faisal ibn Musaid – son of **Ibn Saud**'s 15th son, **Musaid** and younger brother of **Prince Khalid ibn Musaid.** Murdered King Faisal.

Prince Khalid ibn Musaid – son of **Ibn Saud**'s 15th son **Musaid.** Killed in demonstration against introduction of TV to Saudi Arabia.

'The Sudairi Seven' – the seven sons of **Ibn Saud** and Hassa bint Ahmad al Sudairi: **Fahd,** Nayif, **Sultan**, Salman, Ahmad, Turki, Abd al-Rahman.

OTHER MEMBERS OF THE WIDER SAUDI FAMILY

Muhammad ibn Abd al-Wahhab – Eighteenth century Muslim teacher and founder of the Wahhabi branch of Islam. Formed alliance with **Muhammad ibn Saud** giving rise to the spread of Wahhabism across the Arabian peninsula and creation of first Saudi-Wahhabi state.

'The Araif' (or 'Lost Ones', a Bedouin expression for a camel lost in one raid but recovered in another) – the grandsons of **Abd al-Rahman**'s elder brother Saud who remained unreconciled to their branch of the family's loss of the throne as a result of the bloody Saud family power struggle during 1870s.

Saud Al Kabir – member of rebellious **'Araif'** branch of the Saudi family, later married to **Ibn Saud**'s favourite sister **Nura.**

Abdullah ibn Jiluwi – courageous loyal cousin of **Ibn Saud** and hero of his recapture of Riyadh.

Musa'id ibn Jiluwi – brother of **Abdullah ibn Jiluwi.** Took part in recapture of Riyadh.

TRIBAL AND IKHWAN LEADERS

Sultan ibn Bijad – Ikhwan leader and head of the **Ataiba** tribe.

Faisal al Duwish – loyal follower of **Ibn Saud.** Ikhwan leader and head of first Ikhwan settlement (*hijra*) at Artawiya.

Abdul Aziz, known as **'Azaiyiz'**, **Duwish** – son of **Faisal al Duwish.**

Dhaidan Al Hithlain – leader of the **Ajman** tribe of Hasa.

Khalid bin Luai – Ikhwan leader in the Khurma region.

OTHER SAUDIS

Juhayman Ataiba – son of an Ikhwan warrior who had fought alongside **Sultan ibn Bijad** at the Battle of Sibilla in 1929. Leader of group that seized The Grand Mosque in Mecca in 1979.

Abdul Aziz bin Baz (or **Bin Baz**) – conservative Islamic judge in Al Kharj region. Later Rector of the Islamic University of Medina, Grand Mufti and from 1962 Head of the Council of Ulema in Saudi Arabia.

Juwaisir – camel trader with house opposite Rashid governor **Ajlan**'s fortress in Riyadh.

Muhammad bin Laden – son of a poor Yemenite who had emigrated to what became Saudi Arabia before the First World War, established a successful construction company and built a family fortune.

Osama bin Laden – son of **Muhammad bin Laden.**

Muhammad Abdullah al-Qahtani – claimed by **Juhayman Ataiba** and those who seized the Grand Mosque in Mecca in 1979 to be The Madhi.

Abdullah al Sulaiman – Ibn Saud's treasurer.

THE TRIBES

Al Murra – ancient and noble Bedouin tribe of southern central and eastern Arabia. Long-standing allies of the Sauds.

Bani Khalid – long-time rulers of Al Hasa region of eastern Arabia. Allies of Turks.

Mutair – tribe of north eastern Arabian peninsula close to modern Iraq and Kuwait borders. Allies of Sauds in abortive 1901 sortie against Ha'il.

Ajman – large and highly respected tribe whose grazing lands stretched from the Hasa region in the northeast of the Arabian peninsula all the way south to the Rub al-Khali. Allies of Ibn Saud in abortive 1901 sortie against Ha'il, but later betrayed him.

Ataiba – tribe with grazing areas south and west of Riyadh.

Duwasir – tribe from south and southwest of Riyadh close to the Rub al-Khali.

Muntafik – tribe with grazing grounds in northeast close to the river Euphrates.

Anaiza – large tribe, sections of which had grazing grounds in Hijaz north of Medina and in far north near the Euphrates in modern Iraq and Syria.

THE RASHIDS

Rulers of Ha'il and leaders of the Shammar Tribe.

Muhammad ibn Rashid – ruler of Ha'il and much of Central Arabia in late 19th century.

Abd al-Aziz ibn Rashid – young nephew of **Muhammad ibn Rashid** who succeeded him as ruler of Ha'il from 1897 to 1906.

Saud Abdul Aziz ibn Rashid – ruler of Ha'il from 1909 murdered in 1920 by a cousin.

Abdulla ibn Rashid – 18-year-old ruler of Ha'il from 1920 to 1921

Ajlan – Rashid governor of Riyadh 1891–1902.

THE KUWAITIS

Shaikh Muhammad – ruler of Kuwait in 1890s who allowed **Abd al-Rahman** and his family to settle and live as refugees in Kuwait.

Mubarak – half-brother of **Shaikh Muhammad** and ruler of Kuwait from 1906 to 1915. Friend and mentor of the young **Ibn Saud**.

Jabir Mubarak – eldest son of **Mubarak.** Ruler of Kuwait from 1915 to 1917.

Salim Mubarak – 2nd son of **Mubarak.** Ruler of Kuwait from 1917 to 1921.

THE TURKS

Colonel Hasan Shukri – Commander of Turkish force sent to subdue **Ibn Saud** in 1904.

Sayyid Talib – devious, untrustworthy, murderous intriguer and Basra politician. Sometime Turkish governor of Basra.

THE HASHEMITES

Family claiming descent from the Prophet Muhammad through his sister Fatima. Rulers of the Hijaz and Sharifs (guardians) of Mecca, Medina and Islam's holy places. Long-standing enemies of the Sauds.

Sharif Husayn – appointed Sharif of Mecca by the Turks in 1908.

Ali Husayn – **Sharif Husayn's** eldest son. Briefly succeeded his father as ruler of the Hijaz.

Abdullah Husayn – **Sharif Husayn**'s 2nd son. King of Transjordan 1921–51.

Feisal Husayn – 3rd son of **Sharif Husayn**'s son. King of Iraq 1921–33.

THE BRITISH

Herbert Asquith – Prime Minister 1908–16.

Gertrude Bell – Arabist, archaeologist and explorer. Assigned to British Army Intelligence Headquarters in Cairo in 1915 and later on staff of **Sir Percy Cox** in Iraq. After First World War played central role in drawing up the map of the modern Middle East.

Winston Churchill – politician and statesman who during his long career held many different cabinet posts. Those of most relevance to this story were: First Lord of the Admiralty 1911–15; Secretary of State for the Colonies 1921–2; Prime Minister 1940–5.

Sir Gilbert Clayton – British diplomat. One of architects of the Britain's First World War alliance with **Sharif Husayn.**

(Major, later Sir) **Percy Cox** – British Political Resident in the Persian Gulf 1904–14. High Commissioner for Iraq 1920–23.

Lord Curzon – Viceroy of India 1899–1905. Foreign Secretary 1919–24.

Harold Dickson – (H. R. P. Dickson) British colonial administrator, Arabist and author of authoritative books on Arab and Bedouin life, customs and mythology. British Political Agent in Bahrain 1919–20; British Political Agent in Kuwait 1929–36.

Violet Dickson – wife of **Harold Dickson.** Author, naturalist and authority on Arab and Bedouin life.

Lieutenant (later General) **John Bagot Glubb** – British army officer serving in Iraq during 1920s. Later Commander of the Arab Legion in Jordan.

Sir Edward Grey – Foreign Secretary 1905–16.

Colonel William Grey – Captain Shakespear's successor as Political Agent in Kuwait.

Field Marshal Lord Kitchener – Commander of British army which defeated the Madhi at the Battle of Omdurman in 1898. British High Commissioner in Egypt 1911–14; Secretary of State for War 1914–16.

Colonel Knox – Captain Shakespear's predecessor as British Political Agent in Kuwait.

Gerald Leachman – British Indian Army officer and Arabian explorer. Contemporary of **Captain Shakespear.**

H. St John Philby – British civil servant, colonial administrator, Arabist, author and business man. Enduring friend and confidante of **Ibn Saud.** Father of Soviet spy Kim Philby.

Captain William Shakespear – British Political Agent in Kuwait from 1908 to 1914.

Sir Mark Sykes – baronet, wealthy Yorkshire landowner, 'evangelical' Roman Catholic and Conservative MP. Described Arabs as animals, saw himself as a present-day crusader. With French politician **Georges-Picot** drew up 1916 Sykes-Picot Agreement which divided post-First World War Middle East between Britain and France.

Major Arthur Trevor – British Political Agent in Bahrain. Colleague and contemporary of **Captain Shakespear.**

Sir Reginald Wingate – Governor General of the Sudan and 'Sirdar' (commander-in-chief) of the Anglo-Egyptian army 1899–1916; High Commissioner of Egypt 1916–19.

THE OILMEN

Charles Crane – American millionaire philanthropist who in 1931 provided the services of **Karl Twitchell** to **Ibn Saud** to survey the Kingdom's oil, mineral and water resources.

Lloyd N. Hamilton – lawyer who represented the successful American company Socal in bidding for the first Saudi oil concession in 1933.

Major Frank Holmes – New Zealand-born oil prospector.

Stephen H. Longrigg – representative of Anglo-Persian Oil Company in bidding for the original 1933 Saudi oil concession. Later author of standard work on the history of the Middle East oil industry.

Karl Twitchell – American geologist and mining engineer sent, with his wife, by **Charles Crane** to **Ibn Saud** to survey his Kingdom's oil, mineral and water resources.

OTHERS

Saddam Hussein – Ba'athist ruler of Iraq overthrown in 2003 Iraq war.

Muslim Brotherhood – radical Islamic revolutionary movement active in Egypt, Jordan and other Arab countries, committed to establishing 'true' Islamic states governed in strict accordance with the teachings of the Prophet Muhammad and the Holy Qur'an.

François Georges-Picot – French diplomat who in 1916 negotiated secret Sykes-Picot Agreement with **Sir Mark Sykes** which divided post-First World War Middle East between Britain and France.

Sayyid Qutb – influential Egyptian writer on politics and social justice in Islam; one of the leaders of the **Muslim Brotherhood.** Executed in Egypt in 1966 for his revolutionary activities.

President Franklin D. Roosevelt – President of the United Sates 1933–45.

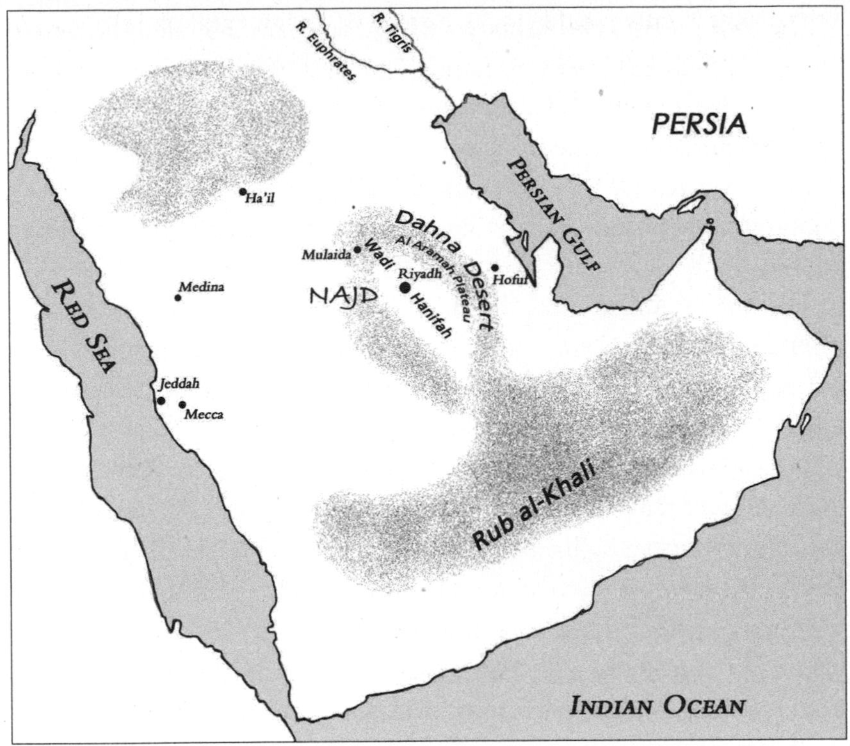

CHAPTER 1

Cast Out

'Wake up! Wake up!'

As the boy comes to he is aware of someone shaking him urgently by the shoulder. 'Get up. Now!'

Reluctantly he pushes the blanket down from over his head and opens his eyes. It is pitch black, dead of night. Yet the boy can distinctly hear hurrying feet and low, urgent voices elsewhere in the palace. The slave who has woken him, as black as the night himself, holds a lighted lamp close to his face so that the boy can see him. 'Your father says everyone must leave, now! The Amir says The Rashid is coming. With many men!'

The boy, young as he is, knows what this means. For all of his young life the Rashids have been his family's greatest enemies. Now they have sworn vengeance on his whole family. He rises hurriedly. Hastily pulls on extra clothes over the loose robe he is already wearing and prepares to leave. Meanwhile the slave is gathering together all of the boy's most important possessions and his bedding and tying them into one large bundle.

The boy is Abd al-Aziz ibn Saud, eldest surviving son of Abd al-Rahman, Amir of Najd, a poor, isolated province deep in the desert-surrounded heart of what we know today as Saudi Arabia. It is January 1891. Abd al-Aziz is ten years old.[1]

The room is cold. Outside it will be colder. Although for day after day in summer the temperature reaches more than 110° F (44°C), so hot that you can fry an egg by breaking it on to a rock, in winter there is often frost and sometimes even snow. The boy is bright, his father's hope for his family's future. He has been able to recite the whole of The Holy Qur'an from memory since he was seven and for the last two years has been receiving private instruction from the revered Islamic scholar Abd Allah ibn Abd al-Latif, grandson of Muhammad ibn Abd al-Wahhab, the founder of Islam's most austere creed, Wahhabism.

It is only three months since his father sent Abd al-Aziz with his uncle Muhammad and a delegation of Riyadh's citizens to negotiate an end to the years of hostility between his family and the Rashids. On first seeing Muhammad ibn Rashid, the head of the Rashid family, Abd al-Aziz had thought that he looked like the embodiment of pure evil. With the sharp eyes of a child Abd al-Aziz had seen that The Rashid's beard was flecked with grey hairs but that he had used dye to make it appear still black. In the words of an English traveller, Charles Doughty, who had visited The Rashid in his capital Ha'il a few years earlier, he was '... lean of flesh and hollow ... [his] looks are like the looks of one survived

1 The date of Ibn Saud's birth is not known for certain. The majority of sources tell us that he was born in 1880 (on November 26th according to some accounts) and other, circumstantial evidence points to that being the most likely date. However, some sources claim that he was born earlier, probably in 1876. Many years later, according to Faud Hamza, Ibn Saud made mention of an older brother, Faisal, who had died when he was about nine years old.

out of much disease of the world'.[2] To an English couple, the Blunts, who had met Rashid a few years later, he had appeared the very archetype of a villain, calling to mind: 'the portraits of Richard the Third, lean, sallow cheeks, much sunken, thin lips, with an expression of pain, except when smiling, a thin black beard, well-defined black knitted eyebrows, and remarkable eyes – eyes deep-sunk and piercing, like the eyes of a hawk, but ever turning restlessly from one of our faces to the other, and then to those beside him. It was the very type of a conscience-stricken face, or of one which fears an assassin.'[3] However, when The Rashid had spoken to young Abd al-Aziz he had shown him a more gentle and fatherly side of himself. He had consoled him on the recent death of his elder brother Faisal and said that perhaps God would cause him to grow into an able replacement.[4]

The previous spring, before Abd al-Aziz and his uncle's visit to him, The Rashid and his men had laid siege to Riyadh, the town where the Sauds lived, for more than forty days. They had cut down almost 8,000 of the palm trees that grew in the date groves that surrounded the town, had damaged and poisoned many of the wells on which the townspeople depended. Yet still the Sauds and the 10,000 people of Riyadh had refused to surrender. As a result, as the heat of summer had come on and still Ibn Rashid's men had seen no prospect of the town surrendering, they had started to tire of the drudgery of the siege and had begun to desert. So Ibn Rashid had had no alternative but to call for negotiations. And thus it had come about that Abd al Aziz had ridden out with his uncle to the The Rashid's camp to negotiate a peace. Agreement had quickly been reached. Rashid and his men had withdrawn, allowing

2 Doughty, Charles M., *Travels in Arabia Deserta,* Cambridge University Press, Cambridge, 1888.

3 Blunt, Anne, *A Pilgrimage to Najd, the Cradle of the Arab Race: A Visit to the Court of the Arab Emir, and our Persian Campaign*, John Murray, London, 1880. The German adventurer Baron Eduard Nolde, who met Rashid in 1883, confirms Doughty's and the Blunts' description, saying that his eyes were '... so sharp and piercing that occasionally they really have something of the look of a tiger'. Rashid himself told Nolde that he applied dye to his beard to hide the traces of grey hair and keep it looking jet black.

4 Winder, R. Bayly, *Saudi Arabia in the Nineteenth Century*, Macmillan, London, 1965.

Abd al-Aziz's father, Abd al-Rahman, to continue to rule in Riyadh and in return he had recognised Ibn Rashid as overlord of the whole of Najd and continued to accept a Rashid governor for the town.

However, a few months later a fresh alliance of tribes had risen against the Rashids in the north. There had been treachery, bloodshed and dishonour on both sides, ancient codes of chivalry and hospitality had been drowned in blood. Thousands of men had been drawn in to the struggle. For weeks one battle or skirmish followed another, but still neither side had gained the ascendancy. Seeing his chance to finally crush the Rashids, early in January 1891 Abd al-Rahman had once again marched out at the head of his fighting men to join the tribes opposing the Rashids. However, before he could join them news had reached him of a mighty battle near a place called Mulaidah, close to the vast rolling sands of the Dahna desert. Fifty, perhaps sixty, thousand men had been involved. Men were calling it the greatest battle in all of Arabia for more than a hundred years. At first the rebel tribes had appeared to gain the upper hand and The Rashid had seemed to withdraw. But then The Rashid turned. Having massed several thousand camels in the centre of his line he had tied bundles of brushwood to their backs and set fire to them. Terrified, the camels had stampeded headlong straight into the rebels' lines. Ibn Rashid's infantry had followed close behind. Finally, in the confusion he had unleashed his cavalry and mounted camel soldiers at the rebels' flanks. Many of the leaders and men of the rebel tribes had been killed or seriously wounded. The rebels had been routed

Learning of the defeat, Abd al-Rahman had turned and hurried back to Riyadh to prepare for a new siege. But the leading men of the town, hearing of what had happened, that Ibn Rashid had gathered a mighty army, that his blood was now up and he intended to show the Sauds and their subjects no mercy, had come to the palace and demanded an audience with Abd al-Rahman. Abd al-Aziz had seen the town's leading citizens arrive at the palace the previous evening, had sensed their agitation and seen them admitted to his father's audience chamber, the majlis. But Abd al-Aziz had not been allowed to sit in on his father's discussion with the leading citizens as he often was. Instead he had been sent to his bed. The discussion had still been going on when he had at last fallen asleep. Riyadh's leading citizens had told Abd al-Rahman that he and his family must leave the town. They had not had sufficient time to recover from the previous siege nor to gather in sufficient provisions to withstand another. They feared that this time Ibn Rashid would indeed show them no mercy. The Rashid and his men would not withdraw until they had crushed the town and taken vengeance.

Thus it was that later that night Abd al-Rahman roused his family and ordered that they must leave at once. Ibn Rashid's scouts had been spotted a few miles to the north west, making their way down the great Wadi Hanifah, through the outlying palm groves towards the town. There was no time to lose.

Leaving his room and walking down a corridor on to the balcony above one of the palace's inner courtyards, Abd al-Aziz immediately becomes aware of muted but purposeful bustle and activity down below. Dimly lit by oil lamps, more than a dozen of the palace's most reliable riding camels have been led into the courtyard. Under the direction of his father, 'amiable but austere', according to a European traveller, 'with an eagle eye and marvellously handsome, whole appearance ... suggesting a living episode of the *Thousand and One Nights*',[5] slaves are moving back and forth roping bundles of the family's clothes and most treasured possessions to the camels' backs. Yet despite the urgency, there is an almost studied calm about the actions of the people loading the camels. They work in silence, commands being given in whispers. It is vital to avoid communicating any sense of alarm to the camels because if they pick up a sense of panic from the human beings around them they too are liable to panic and are likely to start rushing round in ever diminishing circles, creating mayhem, and make it difficult for even the most experienced camel master to regain control over them. Nothing must be allowed to signal the al Saud family's impending flight. If word of it reaches The Rashid in advance he will set off after them and send out parties of men to cut off their escape.

Once the loading of the family's possessions is complete, the slaves start helping the women and children up on to the camels' backs. One lifts Abd al-Aziz off the ground and lowers him gently but firmly into a

5 Barclay Raunkiaer, *Gennem Wahhabiternes Land paa Kamelryg*, Nordisk Forl., Copenhagen 1913.

saddle bag secured with stout leather straps to the side of a large baggage camel. His sister Nura is lifted into the saddle bag which hangs on the opposite flank of the same camel. With their heads and shoulders poking out of the openings at the top of the saddle bags both children have a good view of everything that is happening around them. By being in saddle bags on either side of the same camel they will be able to talk to each other during the journey. Nura is a year older than Abd al-Aziz and is the daughter of the same mother, Sarah, daughter of Ahmad al-Sudairi, one of Abd al-Rahman's most powerful chieftains. Already Abd al-Aziz and Nura are the closest of friends and over the coming years will become closer still. Later in life, even after Nura is married, Abd al-Aziz will seek his sister's advice before taking any important decision and barely a day will pass without them meeting and talking together.

Once everyone is safely mounted Abd al-Rahman quietly gives a command and starts to lead the fugitives in single file out of the courtyard of the palace, along a narrow passage up to the solid square tower that houses the palace's main entrance. As they approach a sentry silently swings open the two heavy gates and the party files out under the arch and turns right into the main square of the dark, still-silent town. Keeping close in the deep shadow of the high palace wall and still in single file, the camels and their riders pad silently east up the full length of the deserted town square. More than fifty yards away over to the riders' left, stands a long row of shops and warehouses. So full of life, noise and bustle during the day, they all now stand shuttered and barred. Not so much as the glimmer from a single lamp is to be seen anywhere. It seems as if, except for themselves, the whole town is asleep. To their rear stands a colonnade, which in the heat of the day gives shade to sixty or more women who sell the citizens of Riyadh fresh bread, milk, dates, vegetables and firewood. This too now stands dark and still. Above the colonnade there is an enclosed private corridor which connects the family's quarters inside the palace to the town's great mosque. This also is now silent and deserted. Almost every day, usually five times a day, for as long as he can remember Abd al-Aziz has walked along that corridor on his way to pray in the mosque.

Having made their way silently, without mishap or drawing attention to themselves, over the more than one hundred yards length of the square, Abd al-Rahman leads his file of camels and their precious cargoes into a dark, narrow, slightly twisting street. At the end of it he turns left and then some twenty yards further on right into another long and twisting narrow street, coming eventually to one of the eastern gates in the high, thick, turreted town wall. The watchmen have been forewarned and upon Abd al-Rahman's approach un-bolt and slowly push open the two thick, wooden, studded gates which just a few months ago withstood the whole wrath of The Rashid and his army. After the last of the camels has passed safely through, the gates swing silently shut behind them.

Now outside the protective walls of the town Abd al-Rahman, his family and servants are fugitives, exposed and on their own. Quickening their pace and turning south, they cross the fifty or so dusty yards of open ground that separate the town's walls from its encircling palm groves. Although greatly depleted in number following The Rashid's siege six months ago, the remaining palm trees still afford the fugitives some protection from the prying eyes of enemies. But at the same time, once under the cover of the palm trees the fugitives face an extra hazard. They must avoid the many massive felled palm trunks and decaying foliage that litter the ground and impede their path. Yet the Saudi caravan must maintain its speed. To have any chance of escape they must be securely out of sight of the town and well clear of the many tracks leading to it well before the night sky begins to be streaked with grey ahead of dawn. Yet, as they twist and turn, picking their way between standing trees, felled trunks, damaged water wheels and poisoned wells, over the narrow irrigation channels, called *falaj*es, around the small fruit orchards and seed beds, which for generations have done so much to make Riyadh prosperous, Abd al-Rahman and his fugitive band must maintain the strictest silence. It is not only human ears they have to fear. Much of the ground they must cross is pasture for the small, broad tailed, Najdi Sheep of the central Arabian tableland, highly prized for their meat and fine, soft wool – regarded by many as the equal of Cashmere. The orchards and sides of the Wadi Hanifah are also home to numerous gazelle and game birds – partridge, quail, pigeon, even bustard. Any sudden sound or movement – the stumbling of a camel, a cursing voice, crack of a branch or animal crashing through fallen, decaying palm leaves – could cause game birds to fly clattering and clapping up into the sky, cattle to low in alarm, sheep or gazelles to bolt crashing through the vegetation and fallen trees, setting off a commotion which in the still night air will be heard for miles.

After more than an hour of picking their way through the ravished palm groves the file of camels and riders has covered barely two miles. Yet Abd al-Rahman judges that, still covered by the cloak of darkness, they have now reached a point sufficiently distant from the town walls to risk turning more towards the east. In doing so they begin to head out of the wadi bottom with its cover of trees, and gently upwards towards the wadi's steep and jagged eastern flank. In Arabia, even in January, a merchant travelling into town with his wares or a Bedouin caravan will be on the move early so as to have covered as much ground as possible ahead of the full heat of the day. Likewise the farmers and orchard owners will leave their beds long before sunrise in order to tend their animals, cultivate their fields and care for their palm gardens without having to endure the full energy-sapping glare of the Arabian sun. So Abd al-Rahman and his fugitive party must have ascended the steep zigzag path up the flank of Wadi Hanifah and disappeared from sight over the eastern skyline long before the first light of day can betray their direction of flight to anyone watching from either the town or travelling along the well frequented routes of the wadi floor.

As the file of riders begins to climb the ground becomes drier, the patches of pasture start to give way to stones and outcrops of hardened marl and rock. The tall palms give way to an increasingly sparse covering of smaller trees, until they in turn peter out, to leave only acacia, scrub and thorny brushwood clinging on among the loose stones and rocky outcrops of the wadi's increasingly steep side. As the camels pick their patient, sure-footed way upwards on the splayed pads of their generous hooves a still deeper silence seems to grip the entire caravan, the beasts too now seemingly as much in its grip as their riders. It is a silence to match the darkness and depth of fate at this blackest hour in the long history of the House of Saud.[6]

6 The description of the flight of Abd al-Rahman and his family from Riyadh in 1891 is drawn mainly from accounts written in the 1920s by those who met Abd al-Aziz and others who actually participated in these events rather than on accounts by those historians who gathered their material later and often at secondhand.

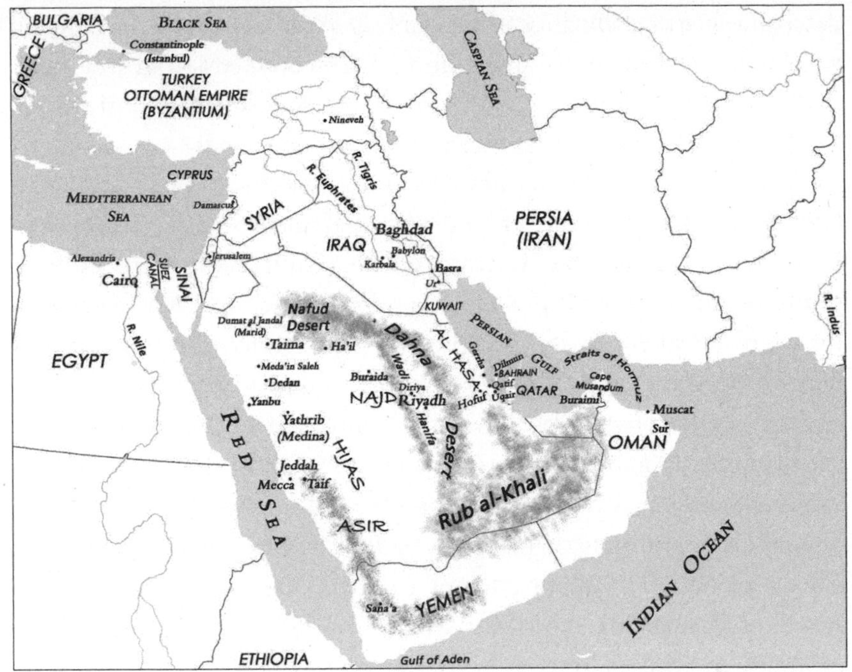

CHAPTER 2

Fugitives in the Land of Their Fathers

Having wound their way up more than three hundred feet of tortuous, steep and twisting track from the date gardens of the wadi floor, Abd al-Rahman and his small caravan come out onto a vast, stony, flat and featureless tableland that stretches steadily away ahead of them towards a still invisible horizon.

Without pause Abd al-Rahman heads south east. He plans to lead his family, servants, slaves and faithful retainers into and across the Dahna, a horseshoe of desert sweeping hundreds of miles up from the south west, around Riyadh and the Wadi Hanifah to the north and then down again to the east and south. The open ends of this vast desert horseshoe point south into the even more fearsome Rub al-Khali – the desolate desert furnace that fills almost the whole heart and centre of the Arabian peninsula. Until 1930 no European had even entered it and still today the Rub al-Khali, The Empty Quarter, remains one of the most feared, least charted great wilderness areas of the world.

There is now perhaps an hour left until dawn and Abd al-Rahman hurries onward. He and his fugitive band are now some two thousand feet above sea level on the Al Aramah Plateau and on the flatter ground, gently sloping east, Abd al-Rahman and his camels ought to be able to make greater speed. By the time the first pale smudge of dawn begins to lighten the sky above the horizon ahead of them they ought to have covered another five miles. Two hours after that they should start to catch the first glimpses of the soft, shifting sands of the Dahna Desert itself. Although it is barely more than ten miles across at its narrowest points, in the ordinary course of events no traveller would voluntarily choose to enter, let alone attempt to cross, the treacherous, reddish sands of the Dahna. Stories abound of whole caravans that have disappeared without trace into its fine, soft, shifting sands, endlessly moving, being shaped and re-shaped by even the slightest breeze, forever forming and re-forming into new unstable hills and valleys. Over the centuries the Dahna has given rise to a whole canon of wild Arabian tales of demons that carry off the wanderer and ghouls who devour unwary travellers. Yet for Abd al-Rahman these shifting sands offer the best hope of escape from his enemies. The shifting sand will quickly bury the prints of his caravan's camel hooves and the direction they have taken. He plans to head out straight into the desert, and then to cross it. Only after that, perhaps, he will move south and east, to the edge of the Rub al-Khali itself. Only there, where few men would dare to follow, will he, his family and the future of the Saud dynasty have a reasonable chance of escape from the revenge of the Rashids.

On the Al Aramah plateau, its marl and pebble surface broken only by some scattered brush and a few stunted bushes, Abd al-Rahman and his band are in the very heart of the Arabian peninsula. The shallow waters of the Persian Gulf are 250 miles in front of them to the east, beyond the Dahna and the fertile, undulating plains of Al Hasa. Behind them, to the west, the Red Sea is a thousand miles away, beyond the coastal mountains and the holy cities of Mecca and

Medina. A similar distance to the north are the great rivers Tigris and Euphrates, Mesopotamia and the legendary cities of the ancient Arab civilisations, Baghdad, Damascus and Jerusalem. To the south it is a full fifteen hundred miles, over the high mountains of the Hadramaut to the Gulf of Aden and the Indian Ocean. Modern Saudi Arabia is almost ten times the size of the UK, yet even today it still has less than half the UK's population. Put another way, Saudi Arabia occupies an area about a quarter of the size of the land mass of the United States but has less than one tenth of the number of inhabitants; it is about two thirds the size of India but has barely one fortieth of the number of people.

'In the dreary waste of Arabia a boundless level of sand is intersected by sharp and naked mountains and the face of the desert without shade or shelter is scorched by the direct and intense rays of a tropical sun. Instead of refreshing breezes the winds, particularly from the south-west, diffuse a noxious and even deadly vapour ... whole caravans, whole armies have been lost and buried in the whirlwind.'[1]

For centuries the land which we know today as Saudi Arabia had remained a land unknown and feared by outsiders. Gibbon, writing more than two hundred years ago had never visited Arabia, but his description, although not entirely inaccurate, accords almost exactly with the picture of Arabia in the popular imagination of Europeans until almost the present day. Although European and Asian seafarers had for centuries visited its shores, had established trading posts, built harbours and fortresses and even stationed garrisons around its coasts, even in Abd al-Rahman's day extremely few Europeans had ever ventured more than a few miles inland. Long after the Americas and Australia had been discovered and colonised, the great mass of the interior of the Arabian peninsula remained almost totally unexplored. In the whole of the nineteenth century, up until the time when Abd al-Rahman and the Sauds fled from Riyadh in January 1891, in a period of intense European exploration and imperial expansion in almost every other part of the world, only three Europeans penetrated into the heart of Arabia so far as

1 Edward Gibbon, *Decline and Fall of the Roman Empire.*

Riyadh. Najd and the whole of the centre of Arabia remained an impenetrable and forbidding mystery. To most outsiders the Arabian peninsula away from the coasts remained as it had more than two thousand years earlier to the Greek historian Herodotus, a land of mystery and legend, full of 'vipers and winged serpents'.[2]

Between two and three hundred million years ago the earth's tectonic plates and layers of rock had slowly drifted, spun, collided, buckled, folded and flowed over and under one another. A great volume of water teeming with both living and decomposing zooplankton, algae, trilobites (simple three sectioned creatures with rudimentary eyes or antenna) and pre-historic insects, was trapped between two large rock formations, known as the Arabian Shield and the Iranian Continental Block. Over time, as the earth's crust continued to buckle and bulge, the great mass of waterborne decaying biological matter settled into a vast layer of sludge more than twelve miles deep. This in turn was buried under further successive layers of heavy sediment. Trapped between the folds of rock, the organic sludge was subjected to greater and greater heat and pressure, slowly cooking and converting it into waxy hydrocarbons, tars and crude oil. Millions of years later these accidents of geology and the vast reservoir of crude oil which they created were to have a powerful effect on the life and destiny of the boy Abd al-Aziz and of the country that would one day be named after him, Saudi Arabia.

Successive ice ages, alternating with temperate epochs, came and went, and with them myriads of animal and plant species thrived or died, seas rose and fell. At the same time the earth's surface continued to bulge and flex, tectonic plates twisted, drifted, tore and revolved. The first mammals appeared and later primates. Twenty five million years ago a huge rectangle, more than two thousand miles long and over a thousand miles wide, was slowly ripped and twisted away from the north eastern flank of Africa, leaving a long, jagged 6,000 feet deep tear, or rift, in the earth's surface. In turn this was filled by the sea, creating the Gulf of Aden and the Red Sea. Seawater also filled the long hook shaped fold which had been left above the place where the Arabian Shield and the

2 Herodotus, *History*, tr. A. D. Godley, Cambridge, Ma, USA, 1926.

Iranian Continental Block had collided and buckled, creating the vast reservoir of crude oil, hydrocarbons and tars. This straggling, hook shaped length of water, the Persian Gulf and Straits of Hormuz, today divide Saudi Arabia and the Gulf States from Iran.

During the last of the great Ice Ages, the so-called 'Last Glacial Maximum', which began about twenty-five thousand years ago and lasted for about ten thousand years, while much of the earth to the north and south was submerged under great ice sheets, Arabia enjoyed abundant rainfall and rich fertility. It was this abundant age which almost certainly endured in the folk memory of the peoples of the region and, when it was over, gave rise to many traditional fables with which we are still familiar today – legends of lost paradises, the Garden of Eden, the Great Flood and the land of Gilgamesh.

Then, about fourteen and a half thousand years ago, the ice receded back towards the poles and the majority of the Arabian peninsula, except for some of the land around its shores and a few oases, underwent a harsh and dramatic transformation. Starved of water, vegetation died and the land was no longer gentle and generous, becoming instead harsh, arid, sun scorched and dust ridden. Verdant woodland and prairies were transformed into vast desert wastelands which covered most of the Arabian Peninsula, giving rise to yet more legends – of the anger of the gods which visited upon mankind drought, hardship, disease and death.

About 10,000 BCE, at the start of the Neolithic Age, fishermen and traders along the northern shores of the Gulf started using bitumen, found oozing up out of the earth from the great reservoir of tars, hydrocarbons and oil trapped below the surface millions of years earlier, to caulk their reed boats and make them more seaworthy. At about the same time an event occurred which did as much to shape the lives of the Arabs of the peninsula as any other in the next twelve thousand years – the first camels were imported to Arabia from Central Asia. In the more settled, still fertile, areas around the coasts and inland near oases and in places such as the Wadi Hanifah, domesticated sheep, cattle and goats appeared.

Around 4,000 years BCE, at the same time that Celtic tribes in western

Europe were constructing impressive arrays of stone megaliths and circles in places such as Carnac and Stonehenge, all across Arabia Arabs began doing the same. One particularly impressive stone circle, at a place called Eyoon some two hundred and fifty miles north-west of Riyadh, was discovered by the Victorian traveller William Palgrave, who claimed that if it were better known it would be as famous as Stonehenge or Carnac.[3] This period also saw the rise of the great civilisations of Mesopotomia and the Fertile Crescent – Sumeria, Assyria and Babylon – and the creation of the first real towns and cities along the banks of the rivers Tigris and Euphrates. The great ziggurat at Ur (Ur of the Chaldees in the Bible), which rose to a height of over one hundred feet, was dedicated to the moon god Nanna, or Allah, who decided the fate of the dead. According to the Book of Genesis Ur was the birthplace of the Jewish patriarch Abraham, or Ibrahim.

The greatest of the ancient cities was Babylon (the biblical Babel) which, according to the Greek historian Herodotus, was surrounded by great walls and towers which were reinforced by the use of asphalt. Asphalt, like the bitumen used by the gulf fishermen to caulk their boats, came from the great reservoir of tars and hydrocarbons trapped below the earth's surface millions of years earlier. The greatest of Babylon's kings was reputed to have been Gilgamesh who later legend claimed had been two thirds a god and one third a man. Although cursed in the Bible for their pride, it was nevertheless the Babylonians who through their great interest in astrology and the movement of the stars, gave us many of the concepts which we still use today – three hundred and sixty degrees in a circle, sixty seconds in a minute and sixty minutes in an hour. It was the Babylonians who, at Nineveh on the banks of the Tigris opposite present-day Mosul, drew together all the knowledge of the world into one great library, greater even than the later library at Alexandria.

In this period the east of the Arabian peninsula also enjoyed a boom as a centre of trade between the empires of the north and those of the Indus Valley (roughly the area which is today Pakistan). At the centre of this prosperity was the land of Dilmun which covered much of the fertile

3 In the years since Palgrave's visit the condition of the structure has deteriorated considerably.

land along the eastern shores of the Arabian Peninsula and had its capital on the island of Bahrain. According to one of the legends associated with Gilgamesh, Dilmun was the paradise where after the flood the gods settled Noah – a 'pure' and 'pristine' land where there was no disease, no ageing, no pain, where 'the lion did not slay, nor the wolf carry off lambs'. Four and a half thousand years later, this area would come to play an important role in many of the major events in the life of Abd al-Aziz.

The same period also saw rising prosperity in the west of the Arabian peninsula. Along the plain between the mountains and the shores of the Red Sea, prosperous caravan routes had opened up which linked the rich spice and aromatics producing regions of the south with the cities of the north. When the Queen of Sheba paid her celebrated visit to Jerusalem to test the wisdom of King Solomon, which if it actually happened must have been in about 950 BCE, it is probable that she and her large train of camels bearing the fortune in gold and spices, frankincense and myrrh which the Biblical account says she presented to Solomon, used this route to travel from her kingdom, Sheba or Saba in modern Yemen, in the far south west of Arabia to Jerusalem.[4] During her journey she would have passed through a succession of thriving oasis settlements which would have included Mecca and Yathrib (Medina). It was almost certainly along the same route that four hundred years later, after the First Temple of the Jews in Jerusalem had been destroyed by the Babylonians under Nebuchadnezzar, its most sacred object, the Ark of the Covenant, was secretly spirited away into the mountains of Yemen to afterwards disappear across the Gulf of Aden into Africa.[5]

In addition to the gold brought to him by the Queen of Sheba, the Bible tells us that King Solomon had access to large quantities of gold of his own. The source of this gold was traditionally believed to be the legendary King Solomon's Mines. Although over the years many different

4 Recent archaeological research supports this thesis.

5 Recent research by Professor Tudor Parfitt of London University's School of Oriental and African Studies, supported by genetic evidence, suggests that a priestly Jewish tribe or sect escaped with the Ark by this route through Mecca, into Yemen and thence to Africa.

locations, ranging from Pakistan to southern Africa, have been proposed as the likely site of this limitless wealth, long-standing tradition places the site near Mecca.[6]

But while all around Arabia's coasts and borders people became more settled and prosperous, its heart and centre remained untouched, unknown, mysterious, frightening. Its people, who according to one tradition were the descendants of Abraham's son Ishmael, remained mostly polytheistic nomads. However, they had gained a fearsome reputation as warriors. An Assyrian inscription dated 853 BCE tells of a certain 'Gindibu the Arab' who, with one thousand camels, fought alongside the armies of Syria and the Palestinians. Their style of fighting seems to have been little different from the style of fighting which Abd al-Aziz ibn Saud and his nomad armies would engage in almost three thousand years later.

However, the standing of women in Arabia in this period seems to have been very different from their standing in Abd al-Aziz's time and later. Assyrian records name five powerful queens of the Arab kingdom of Dumat Al-Jandal (Adumatu), an oasis region in today's province of Al Jawf in northern Saudi Arabia. One of these queens, Te'elhunu, was also the high priestess of Ishtar, the Sumerian goddess of fertility, love and war.

Over time the empires of the Fertile Crescent were one by one overthrown by Persia and then it, in turn, was defeated by Alexander the Great. Yet still, the deep heartland of the 'real' Arabia remained untouched. But in 324 BCE Alexander, having defeated Darius the Great of Persia and marched on to conquer large parts of India, turned and began preparing to invade and colonise Arabia. According to the Greek historian Arrian, the Arabs 'alone among the barbarians in these parts

6 Modern scientific exploration has revealed about one thousand sites in western Saudi Arabia showing signs of pre-modern mining activity. At one, Madh al-Dhahab (cradle of gold), near Medina, radio-carbon dating of residual charcoal slag shows that gold and silver mining and smelting was probably being carried out there as early as 950 BCE, i.e. during the period when King Solomon is reputed to have ruled Jerusalem. See *Arabia and the Arabs from the Bronze Age to the Coming of Islam* by Robert Hoyland, Routledge 2001.

had sent no envoys and had taken no other action reasonable or honorific to him ... The prosperity of the country was also an incitement, since he had heard that cassia grew in their marshes, that the trees produced myrrh and frankincense, that cinnamon was cut from the bushes and that spikenard grew self-sown in their meadows.'[7] One of Alexander's first intended prizes was to be the city of Gerrha. It was reputed to be inhabited by exiles from Babylon who built their houses of salt. According to the Roman historian Pliny its walls were five miles in circumference and had towers built of square blocks of salt. Although the precise location of the city of Gerrha has long been disputed, it stood somewhere in today's Saudi province of Al Hasa, once part of the ancient kingdom of Dilmun. But Alexander died before he could set out on his mission and the heartland of Arabia remained untouched for a further three hundred years.

The one serious attempt to conquer Arabia began in 26 BCE when the Roman Emperor Augustus, having subjugated Mesopotamia, defeated Cleopatra and taken possession of Egypt and its Red Sea coast, dispatched Aelius Gallus with instructions to cross the Red Sea and either win over the Arab nation as a client state or subjugate it by conquest. Augustus was motivated both by a desire to outdo the achievements of Alexander and by reports, going back over many generations, that the Arabs were very rich as a result of their trade in aromatics, gold, silver and precious stones. But Gallus's attempt to invade and conquer Arabia failed. Betrayed and misled by his locally recruited guides, his army became lost in the desert and was decimated by disease. Although they succeeded in capturing a number of settlements and laid siege to an important city in the south, 'for want of water' they withdrew. However, Gallus reported back to Rome that his expedition had been a success and on his return told the Emperor Augustus of the discoveries he had made. The nomads of Arabia, he reported, 'live on milk and the flesh of wild animals' and the rest of the tribes 'extract wine from palm trees'. They excelled as warriors and wore turbans or they went 'with their hair

7 Arrian, *Anabasis Alexandri*, edited and translated by P. A Brunt, Loeb, Cambridge, Ma, USA, 1976.

unshorn; they shave their beards but wear a moustache; others, however, leave the beard also unshaven'.[8]

One place where Roman influence seems to have taken hold was Meda'in Saleh (known also as Thamud after the people who inhabited it) in the northwest of the peninsula on the old spice route running up from the south along the Red Sea coastal plain through Medina. The Qur'an refers to the people of Meda'in Saleh as 'The Companions of the Rocky Tract'. Their city stood in a valley about 2,000 feet above sea level, cut into reddish and golden yellow rocks surrounded by sheer cliffs. Although many inscriptions and other artefacts have been found dating from earlier periods, today most of the tombs and domestic dwellings that survive at Meda'in Saleh date from between the second century BCE and the second century CE. Cut and elaborately carved into sheer rock faces of yellow stone, they positively glow in the sunlight. Behind elaborate doorways and classical porticos steps lead down into beautiful rooms and chambers painstakingly hammered, chiselled and fashioned out of the solid rock by highly skilled craftsmen. Recently designated Saudi Arabia's first UNESCO World Heritage Site, Meda'in Saleh has been described as the sister to Petra in Jordan. Were it not for the fact that many devout Saudi Muslims consider the place to be cursed and so will not visit it, it would surely be as famous as its sister city, Petra.[9]

By the year of the Prophet Muhammad's birth, 570CE,[10] the two dominant powers in the region, were Byzantium (formerly the Eastern Roman Empire) and Persia. They were locked in a debilitating struggle for control of Mesopotamia and all those territories to the north of Arabia which had once been home to the Assyrian, Babylonian and Sumerian civilisations. In the west the Byzantines controlled Egypt and Abyssinia, while Persia ruled the lands in the east. In the south the two

8 Pliny, *Natural History*, edited and translated by H. Rackham et al, Loeb, Cambridge, Ma, USA, 1942.

9 The Qur'anic curse relates to God's destruction of Thamud because its people refused to hear his Word and persisted in evil. See The Holy Qur'an, Surahs 7, 73–4; 9, 69–70; 29, 36–8; 41, 13–17; 51, 43–5; 89, 9–13. The prophet Salih, mentioned in some of the verses, was a prophet and predecessor of Muhammad.

10 Unless otherwise noted all dates from here in are CE.

empires vied with each other for control of the rich, fertile kingdom which had once been ruled by the Queen of Sheba. However, neither empire had any interest in the vast, empty wilderness at Arabia's heart. This continued to be thought of as a harsh, godless region inhabited by wild and dangerous tribes described by the Greeks as 'Sarakenoi', those who dwell in tents.

Both of the dominant regional powers had by this time adopted monotheistic religions. Byzantium was Christian, Persia Zoroastrian.[11] Under the Byzantines the land of Palestine had become largely Christian, although well established Jewish communities continued to live both there and throughout Mesopotamia, even in Arabia itself. However, for the majority of Arabs living away from the few cities spiritual life continued to be centred on the tribe. For nomadic peoples, living extremely hazardous, hand-to-mouth lives roaming the wastes with their flocks, searching for pasture and sustenance wherever they might find it, it was only through the tribe, through co-operation and absolute loyalty to the group, that they could hope to survive. All law and dedication was centred on the tribal group. The tribe itself, based on blood and kinship, was sacred. Notions of individual survival beyond the grave, of a personal afterlife, did not exist for these people. The only immortality a man or woman could hope for was through the on-going survival of their kin, their tribe. The result was a deep but dignified personal fatalism, an acceptance and stoic endurance of whatever chance, weather or other circumstance fate might bring. Often hungry, the nomad replaced the settler's concern for material possessions with an absolute dedication to the life and well-being of the group. The tribes could not afford to support castes of priests or shamans. Their role in tribal life was filled by the poets who sang or recited in verse, extolling the tribe's virtues and re-telling its time honoured stories. Poetry occupied an extremely important place in the life of all Arabs and poetry itself was often seen as magical; a

11 The Emperor Constantine had moved the capital of the Roman Empire east to Constantinople (Istanbul) in 330, shortly after he became a Christian. After the sacking of Rome by the Vandals and the fall of the Western Roman Empire a century later, the Eastern Empire survived for a further thousand years as Christian Byzantium.

poet in the act of reciting was commonly regarded as being possessed by the *djinn*, a supernatural spirit of the landscape. A curse uttered by an inspired poet might bring disaster upon an enemy. The Arabs of the desert viewed the new religions, the monotheisms adopted by the settled peoples of the north and far south, with deep suspicion.

However, to the Arabs living in the few cities those monotheisms, and the empires associated with them, represented progress, modernity, relative wealth and well-being. Yet, while many probably accepted that there was probably one god who was more important or powerful than others, at the time of Muhammad's birth most of the Arabs of the peninsula, even the city dwellers, remained nominally polytheists, their gods representing or associated with those forces which were most important to their lives: fertility, health, love, death, rain and so on. As with the Bedouin, illnesses or particular places might be associated with malevolent spirits, the *djinn* or with the displeasure of a god. By making votive offerings to the appropriate god or at a suitable shrine one could hope to influence that god in one's own favour. As well as places believed to be cursed or associated with evil spirits, there were also sacred places, trees, springs, valleys, rocks thought to be holy, to be associated with a particular god or legendary event. Archaic rituals were enacted at shrines erected in such places. The most revered of all such shrines was the Ka'aba at Mecca. Early in Muhammad's life this seems to have been formally dedicated to the powerful god Hubal, a god imported into Arabia centuries earlier from Mesopotamia. However, by Muhammad's time it was also probably associated with al-Llah, the High God of the Arabs. Many already believed that this god was the same god who was worshipped by the monotheists, Jews, Christians and Zoroastrians. The Ka'aba was surrounded by idols, effigies of pagan gods and large upright stones similar to those that had been erected in the region three thousand years earlier. There are reputed to have been three hundred and sixty of these – one, perhaps, for each day of the Babylonian year. Embedded in one corner of this shrine was a black stone, probably a meteorite. Tradition stated that this was part of whatever it was that had come down from heaven to provide light for Adam and Eve. It was believed that after the Great Flood this stone became hidden, but that the Angel Gabriel had revealed its whereabouts to Abraham and told him that he and his son, Ishmael, were to incorporate it into a shrine that they were to build, close to a sacred spring called Zamzam, to be dedicated to one all-powerful God. By Muhammad's time the land for twenty miles around this shrine had come to be accepted as a sanctuary, a place where all violence was forbidden.

Mecca was a thriving city, its success based on trade and its position at the intersection of two important trade routes – the one running along the western coastal plain from Yemen north into Syria, the other crossing it from the Red Sea to the Persian Gulf. However by around 600 the city had begun to suffer a kind of malaise, a loss of some of its valuable trade to other tribes. There was repeated fighting and feuds between leading clans and a loss of the traditional nomadic tribal values of community, cohesion and caring for weaker members of society. The citizens of Mecca sensed that, unlike the peoples to the north and south who had adopted one of the monotheisms, they could be regarded as unsophisticated, backward. While God appeared to have sent a prophet to every other people on earth, he had never sent a prophet to them.

Muhammad ibn Abdallah was a relatively successful Meccan merchant, the orphaned son of a respected local clan. By the time he was about forty he had gained a reputation for kindness to the poor and to slaves, and for the fact that despite his family's relative wealth he ensured that he and his family lived modestly. Muhammad had developed an annual ritual for himself. During the ninth month of every year, called Ramadan – 'the scorcher' – on account of the fact that it was the month when the sun was at its fiercest, he would withdraw from the town and his family and climb to a cave at the summit of a nearby mountain. There, in solitude, he would devote himself to prayer, fasting, giving alms to the poor and spiritual exercises. During Muhammad's annual spiritual retreat to the mountain-top cave in Ramadan 610 something extraordinary happened. He said that one night he had been visited by the Angel Gabriel, not some petty luminous, winged and robed ethereal being of the kind familiar in later Western art, but an overwhelming, towering presence. This figure commanded Muhammad to recite. When he refused, protesting repeatedly that he was 'not a reciter', the Angel simply overwelmed him by his presence, squeezing him until he heard himself proclaiming the first words of the Qur'an, 'the Recitation':

Proclaim! In the name of thy Lord and Cherisher, Who created,
Created man, out of a clot of congealed blood:
Proclaim! And thy Lord is Most Bountiful –
He who taught the (use of) the Pen –
Taught man that which he knew not.
Nay, but man doth transgress all bounds,
In that he looketh upon himself as self-sufficient ...

The Surah continues by threatening man with punishment unless he turns away from his conceit and sin, and calling on man to 'bow down in adoration, and bring thyself closer to Allah'.[12] By the time Muhammad awoke these words seemed to have been 'inscribed upon his heart'. Like some of the Old Testament prophets before him, Muhammad was not uplifted by his vision but terrified. Further visions followed. But Muhammad kept quiet about what had happened, confiding in no one except his wife and her cousin, a Christian. At first Muhammad feared he had been possessed by a *djinn*, but both his wife and her cousin were convinced that the revelations came from God.

It was not until 612CE, two years after his first vision, that Muhammad began to preach. Even then, he did not believe that he was founding a new religion but simply bringing the old faith in the One God to the Arabs. Most of the people Muhammad preached to already believed, as the Christians and Jews believed, that Allah, or God, had created the world and that on the last day He would judge humanity. God had sent the Christians and Jews their own scripture or revelation, now Muhammad had been entrusted to bring the Arabs their own scripture and revelation in their own language. Arabs referred to the Christians and Jews as the People of the Book but, as most of the Arabs to whom Muhammad preached were illiterate, the scripture God gave to them through Muhammad was delivered as an ongoing sequence of recitations (or Qur'an). The words that issued out of the mouth of Muhammad poured forth as a fount of the most beautiful and inspired poetry. Many who heard him were convinced of his Message by the

12 The Holy Qur'an, Surah 96, 1–7 & 19. A Surah is a Qur'anic chapter. They are not numbered in the order in which Muhammad received them.

sheer beauty of the words.[13] Over the next twenty-one years more and more of the divine Message continued to be revealed to Muhammad. These 'recitations', collected together, would come to form The Holy Qur'an. Later there would also come to be collections of *Hadiths*, reports of the deeds and sayings of Muhammad and his close companions. There would also come to be a series of *Sunnah*, sanctioned practices, procedures or actions.

The Qur'an did not seek to supersede or replace the other religions 'of the Book' but to bring the Word of the One God to Muhammad's people, the Arabs. His message was the same as that of Abraham, Moses, David, Solomon and Jesus, all of whom are specifically cited in the Qur'an. What mattered was not whether you were a Jew or a Christian but the quality and totality of your surrender to God. According to a well-known *Hadith* Muhammad declared that the faith he preached was based on five pillars. The first and most important was, and is, the submission by man or woman of their entire being to God, expressed in the prostrations on the ground that a Muslim is required to make five times a day together with the profession (*shahadad* or bearing of witness) to Islam's central tenet: 'There is no God but Allah and Muhammad is His Prophet'. The others relate to giving alms or charity, making the pilgrimage to Mecca and fasting during Ramadan. Some versions of *The Five Pillars* include another alongside prayer, *jihad*, which means 'exerting oneself in the path of God', by such acts as giving charity, freeing slaves, challenging oppression, armed struggle against injustice and creating space in which the Faith and Muslims may flourish.[14] The core teaching of what came to be called *Islam*, which literally means 'submission' or 'surrender' in the specific sense of to the will of God, was a call to social justice, practical compassion and a spirit of true community. In many ways Muhammad's message looked back to the old virtues of the nomadic tribal community, to values that seemed to

13 The sheer beauty of the words and poetry of The Holy Qur'an are inevitably lost in translation. Arabic scholars assure us that they can only be fully appreciated in the original Arabic.

14 See *Islam: The Key Concepts*, by Kecia Ali and Oliver Leaman, Milton Park, Oxon, UK, 2008.

have become lost in the urban life of Mecca. Unlike Christianity, where acceptance of a specific set of beliefs or doctrines were of central importance, in Islam, as in Judaism, the central requirement was that people live and act in a specific moral way and undertake a set of prescribed duties.

During the first three or four years in which he preached Muhammad seems to have been quite successful, winning many of his fellow Meccans to his reformed religion of the One God, Allah. However, trouble started in 616 when he specifically forbad his supporters from worshipping the other traditional Meccan deities and demanded that the Ka'aba be purged of totems and idols. This was an assault on tradition which seemed to many to jeopardise the prosperity and security of the city by antagonising the gods who had protected it. The leading families, who seem to have largely ignored Muhammad until then, now turned against him, accusing him of being a charlatan and a re-teller of fairy stories. By 622 relations between Muhammad and the leading families had become so bad that he and a small band of about seventy followers had to flee to Yathrib (Medina). Yathrib was a substantial agricultural settlement about 250 miles to the north of Mecca. There was already a sizeable community of Jews in Yathrib and so the concept of monotheism was not new to its citizens. However the area had become caught up in a series of bloody feuds and the settlement was in danger of disintegrating. So a delegation from Yathrib had approached Muhammad in the hope that he and his new monotheistic creed might bring them together again into one united community.

One of Muhammad's first actions on his arrival in Yathrib was to build a simple mosque (*masjid*, literally 'a place of prostration'). Yathrib would become Medina (*the City*) because it was the first place in which Muhammad could build the perfect Muslim community. A treaty was drawn up between the Arab and Jewish tribes of Medina. All were to bury their old enmities. Muslims, Jews and pagans were to live peaceably alongside each other and form what would effectively be a new tribe, with God as its head and source of security. Within this larger community the Muslims were to form their own single faith community (or *ummah*). The date of Muhammad and his followers' migration (*hijrah*) to Yathrib, in July or August 622, would come to mark the start of the Muslim era and of the first year in the 354 day Islamic lunar calendar.

For Muhammad to have left Mecca and led his followers to settle with alien tribes in Yathrib was regarded by the Meccan leaders as a grave insult. They vowed revenge. Over the next eight years a series of battles was fought between Mecca and the people of Yathrib, led by Muhammad. Eventually, in 630 Muhammad returned to Mecca at the head of a large army. Mecca quickly accepted defeat and opened its gates. As a result Muhammad was able to take the city without bloodshed or forcing any of its inhabitants to accept Islam. Having taken the city he destroyed the idols around the Ka'aba and re-dedicated it to the one God, Allah. He adapted the old pagan rites associated with the site to accord with the new monotheistic religion and gave them Islamic significance by linking them more firmly to the story of Abraham and his son Ishmael. Muhammad died two years later, in 632.

After Muhammad's death his followers elected his father-in-law, Abu Bakr, Caliph (*khalifah* – successor or representative). A number of tribes attempted to secede from the confederacy created by Muhammad but over the next two years Abu Bakr subdued their revolt and went on to unite almost all the tribes of Arabia. Now united in the Muslim *Ummah*, instead of fighting among themselves the Arabs moved on to achieve a series of astonishing victories. In 637 they defeated the army of the Persian Empire and in 638 captured Jerusalem. Within a hundred years of Muhammad's death they controlled an empire which stretched east across the former Persian Empire to the Himalayas and Central Asia, west across North Africa, north through Spain to the Pyrenees and up into France as far north as the river Loire at Tours. In the words of an anonymous Arab chronicler: 'The Moslems smote their enemies, and passed the river Garonne, and laid waste the country, and took captives without number. And that army went through places like a desolating storm ... For everything gave way to their scimitars. They rode at their will through all the land of Narbonne, Toulouse and Bordeaux.'[15] The leader of this formidable Muslim army was named Abd al-Rahman.

15 Quoted in *The Medieval Sourcebook*. Paul Halsall, www.fordham.edu. April 1996.

Al-Rahman's advance into Europe was only halted in 732 when a Christian army, reportedly numbering up to 60,000 footmen under the Frank Charles Martel, Charles 'The Hammer', decisively defeated Abd al-Rahman's even larger army of Saracen horsemen near Poitiers. Fourteen years earlier, outside Constantinople, the Arab advance into the Byzantine Empire and towards the Balkans had also been halted.

Although the Muslim advance into Europe had been checked the next hundred years saw a series of great cultural and scientific advances in the Islamic civilisation. Building on the example of the ancient Babylonians, astronomy, astrology, geography, cartography, engineering, mathematics, medicine, philosophy and poetry all flourished in Baghdad and the other major centres. Under the Qur'anic injunction to look, see, learn and understand, Muslim scholars made more scientific discoveries in this time than in the whole of previously recorded history. The works of the Greek scholars were translated into Arabic. The *Shari'a*, God's law revealed to guide humanity, was codified into a unified system and the *Hadith* and authoritative reports of the deeds and sayings of the Prophet and his close companions anthologised, so that together they would form a coherent body of Islamic law. But as trade and industry blossomed the elite increasingly came to live in luxury separated from the ordinary people. Now the rulers of a large empire, the Caliphs and their entourages lived in splendid isolation and elaborate pomp like absolute monarchs, with vast harems and courtiers kissing the ground whenever they came into the Caliph's presence. All this was in sharp contrast to the days of the Prophet when the only being in front of whom a man prostrated himself was God. But as more and more of what passed for normal became harder to square with the egalitarian ideals and religious message of Muhammad, tensions and splits began to appear inside the Muslim religious community. One in particular, which started in 644 over the appointment of the fourth Caliph, Uthman, resulted in a full scale civil war. Over time this led to a lasting division within Islam extending well beyond its immediate causes into a range of doctrinal, philosophical and administrative differences. This rupture, between the Sunni followers of Uthman, and the Shia followers of his rival Ali, has been likened by some commentators to the split between Catholics and Protestants in Christianity.

Over the centuries following the defeat of Abd al-Rahman at Poitiers, the lands of the Muslim *Ummah* became divided into separate kingdoms each under its own *amir*, thus weakening Muslim power still further. In 1099 the Christian army of the First Crusade re-captured Jerusalem, the third holiest city of Islam after Mecca and Medina, massacred 30,000 Jews and Muslims and established Christian kingdoms in Palestine and along the eastern fringe of the Mediterranean. Ninety years later the Muslims, under Saladin, retook Jerusalem. They were to hold it for the next eight hundred years, well into the lifetime of Abd al-Aziz. One of the weapons used by the Muslims which most terrified the Christians was burning naphtha, fired on arrows or lobbed in the form of primitive grenades. To the Christians it seemed to burn with an unnaturally intense heat and to cling to any object with which it came into contact. Naphtha was a solid distilled from the liquid tars found in Iraq and along the shores of the Persian Gulf. It was a forerunner of napalm.

Early in the fourteenth century a new Islamic power started to rise on the borders of Europe, the Ottoman Turks. Aided by a well disciplined slave army, the Janissaries, they seized most of the old Byzantine Empire and in the 1370s began to advance into the Balkans. In 1389 they defeated the Serbian army at Kossovo Field, sowing the seeds of a deep seated and on-going hatred of Muslims among Serbs. Over the next sixty years they annexed Serbia, laid siege to Belgrade and advanced up the Black Sea coast into the Crimea. In 1453 the Ottomans captured Constantinople itself, which would thereafter become known as Istanbul, and three years later they took Athens. Over the next century they went on to besiege Vienna and, although they failed to take the city, subjugated the whole of Hungary, much of Georgia, Moldova and the southern Ukraine. As a result there were now three major Islamic empires, the Safavid Shia Empire centred in Persia, the Moghul Empire in India and the Ottoman Empire ruling what is today Turkey, Syria and much of North Africa. There were also other lesser Muslim kingdoms further afield. The fact that the Safavid (Persian) Empire was composed mainly of Shias whereas the Ottomans were mostly Sunnis, greatly intensified the schism that already existed in the Islamic faith. This led to an intolerance and aggressive sectarianism between the Sunni and Shia that sometimes led to orgies of bloodshed by both sides.

As with earlier empires, the Babylonians, the Greeks and the Romans, still none of the three powerful Muslim empires had penetrated beyond the peripheries of the Arabian Peninsula itself. But in 1524, having conquered Egypt and seized the title of Caliph, the Ottoman Sultan Suleyman I (Suleyman the Magnificent) and his successor crossed the Red Sea, took possession of Mecca and Medina and also established their rule in the fertile eastern lands bordering the Persian Gulf, in what had once been the kingdom of Dilmun. Yet even then the Ottomans, by now probably the greatest power in the world, did not attempt to penetrate the interior of Arabia even though they laid claim to sovereignty over the whole peninsula.

In 1683 the Ottomans were back outside the gates of Vienna, but again they were repulsed. This defeat marked the start of a series of reverses. The other Islamic empires also started suffering setbacks. With the coming of the Enlightenment, the states of western Europe began growing in wealth, military strength, industrial and organisational know-how.

However in the early 1740s something stirred deep in the heart of that mysterious land which for millennia had remained unconquered and inviolate. That stirring, deep in the unpenetrated centre of Arabia, was to transform the fortunes of Abd al-Aziz's family, the Al Sauds, and profoundly affect the lives of all the peoples of the Arabian peninsula for generations to come.

By the early 1740s the Al Sauds, who had moved inland from the Gulf about two hundred and fifty years earlier, had become the amirs of Diriya. Diriya was a small urban settlement of small farmers, merchants, tradesmen, minor religious scholars and slaves consisting of about seventy families or perhaps seven hundred people in all. Lying about ten miles north of Riyadh in the southern half of Wadi Hanifah, Diriya was just one, and not particularly distinguished, among a number of similar small towns in Wadi Hanifah and the surrounding area. The wadi itself, notable for its many springs and wells, its abundant supply of good, clean ground water and fertile floor, runs for about eighty miles from northwest to southeast between steep, jagged, often precipitous, rock-strewn sides of varying height, in some places less than 300 feet high and in others more than 3,000 feet. Wadi Hanifah lies at the heart of the loosely defined region of central Arabia known as Najd.

The Sauds had moved inland from the Gulf Coast about two hundred and fifty years earlier and were quite possibly among Diriya's original founding families. As well as owning a number of wells, some cultivated land and date gardens in and around the oasis, the Sauds were merchants and small-time financiers, putting up the money to fund trading journeys by other local merchants. But these factors alone would not have been sufficient to gain them the level of respect needed for their fellow Diriya residents to accept them as their amirs. To be an amir was not a hereditary thing, an amir was not the same as a shaikh or tribal elder. An amir was the person a community, town, group of towns or small region was happy to accept as their leader. He was in effect the head of an entity amounting in modern terms to a political formation. So for a succession of members of the Saudi family to have become the amirs of Diriya they must, in addition to a certain wealth and material standing, have displayed distinct qualities of political leadership, skills in things such as mediation, a capacity to organise and the courage needed to lead the defence of their community against attacks by other neighbouring amirates or marauding tribes. However, the fact that the title of amir was not hereditary meant that the person holding the title was always open to challenge, both by other members of the same family who felt that they could gain enough support among other members of the community to hold the position or by outsiders. During the early years of the eighteenth century a number of Saudi amirs of Diriya had faced such challenges. For a few years they were actually deposed by members of a powerful tribe from way out to the east beyond the Najd altogether.

Ever since their defeat outside Vienna in 1683 the Ottomans' influence had started to decline. Nowhere was this more pronounced than in Arabia. Yemen had become completely independent. Mecca and the Hijaz, though still nominally under Turkish rule, had fallen under the control of various local noble families. The relative control and stability of Ottoman rule had been replaced by instability and increasingly rapacious demands made on the indigenous population by these local rulers. Money collected in taxes, instead of going to pay for the administration and security of an area, was increasingly confiscated for their own use by local sultans, district and provincial rulers. Landowners and merchants were frequently executed just so that a local official could confiscate their property. Because of the extortionate demands made upon them small farmers and peasants had begun to leave the land and abandon agriculture upon which so much of Ottoman prosperity had been built. With the land falling into disuse and decay, famine and disease became rife. Populations declined and large tracts of land, many villages and settlements became deserted. Raiding nomadic tribes came to dominate the trade routes, decimating not only the income of merchants but ruining the lucrative returns made by people living in Mecca and along the pilgrimage routes from pilgrims undertaking the annual *Hajj*. In the east, along the Gulf coast, even nominal Ottoman control was ended when the remaining Turkish garrisons were driven out by the most powerful local tribe, the Bani Khalid.

The loss of Ottoman authority, while not affecting the interior of the Arabian peninsula directly, nevertheless had a powerful destabilising impact. By the early 1740s the general loss of security in the surrounding areas, decline in trade with their neighbours and consequent loss of prosperity, repeated raids by nomadic tribes and a series of incursions from amirates to the east and west had combined to produce a strong sense of anxiety among the peoples of Najd. It was in this unhappy atmosphere that a new voice began to be heard.

The voice was that of Muhammad Ibn Abd al-Wahhab. A deeply religious young Muslim scholar, Ibn Abd al-Wahhab was the son of a distinguished family of local theologians and Islamic jurists. He had recently returned to Najd from an extensive journey around the Islamic Middle East studying with a range of highly respected Islamic scholars. He was an intense young man, a master of logic, a skilled and precise debater and an able and prolific writer. Returning home to al-Uyaynah, a small town about fifteen miles northwest of Diriya, he began to preach. His message was radical, but one which people in Najd, insecure and ill at ease, were ready to hear. He preached a return to the founding principles of Islam as originally preached by the Prophet Muhammad and to the ideals of the first Muslim *ummah*. The present ills of Najd and the wider Muslim world were, he proclaimed, the result of straying from the pure message of Muhammad, from absolute belief in the oneness of God and the doctrine of monotheism. The roots of the degeneration in the social order, of corruption, oppression and injustice, were to be found in a widespread departure from Islam's absolute and fundamental founding doctrines. Wahhab believed strongly in the importance of living one's religious beliefs in both one's public and private lives. He preached a return to Islamic concepts of social justice, to respect for women, the poor and protection for human life and property, the strict application of Islamic law and conformity with Muhammad's own religious practice. He attacked all forms of corruption, bribery, hypocrisy and oppression. The remedy for the current, essentially socio-political ills of Al-Uyaynah and the wider Najd, was a return to strict adherence to Islam's fundamental founding principles.

At first Wahhab's message was well received by the rulers of Al-Uyaynah and by its people. He seemed to be preaching a return to the values of community and justice that many people hankered for, with the result that Wahhab was able to enter into an agreement with the amir under which the amir would support Wahhab's call for a return to strict Muslim values and conformity to prescribed religious practice in return for Wahhab's support in the amir's drive to unite all of Najd under his leadership. All went well until Wahhab and the amir started to put some of his religious prescriptions into practice. The first clash with local people came about over the issue of sacred trees. Around Al-Uyaynah there were a number of special, or 'sacred' trees on which people would hang offerings or treasured possessions as a way of requesting a blessing or interceding for some particular favour from the deity. To Wahhab this was idolatrous, a serious and visible departure from the doctrine of there being only one God. So taking his example from the Prophet Muhammad, he sent his followers to start cutting the trees down. He reserved the most highly venerated of all the trees for himself and then very publicly chopped it down. This sent shock waves around the small community, appearing to signal a disturbing intolerance and extremism. He followed this by destroying, with the support of the local amir and his soldiers, a particularly cherished local tomb belonging to one of the original companions of Muhammad. To Wahhab this tomb breached Muslim doctrine because it honoured a human being rather than God. Both the tomb and the trees, he believed, might lead people into superstition, animist belief or the worship of objects, beings or spirits other than the One God, Allah. In committing these acts Wahhab was seen by people who did not accept his teaching as trampling on their own most sacred beliefs and traditions. He also seemed to many to risk antagonising the local spirits upon whom they relied for protection. Of course to his followers these acts by Wahhab were inspiring. They could be seen as akin to those of the Prophet when he destroyed the idols around the Ka'aba – the act which had led to Muhammad's exile from Mecca and the forming of the original *ummah* in Medina.

The final break between Wahhab and the people of Al-Uyaynah came about over a woman who confessed to repeated and unrepentant acts of adultery. After repeated questioning of the woman and her reasons, Wahhab finally responded to the urgings of the local *ulema* (respected Islamic scholars who fulfil a similar role in Islam to that played by the clergy in Christianity) and ordered that the woman be put to death by stoning in accordance with the example set by the Prophet Muhammad in a similar case.[16] By these three acts, the felling of the trees, the destruction of the tomb and now the stoning of the woman, Wahhab had antagonised a range of local leaders and ordinary people. By his actions and the acclaim he was now receiving from his followers he threatened to undermine the authority of both the religious leaders and the important men of the town. Alarm spread beyond the town to other powerful tribal leaders and Wahhab was forced to leave Al-Uyaynah and seek refuge fifteen miles away in Diriya.

Wahhab already had followers among some members of the ruling al Saud family and so knew that he was likely to receive a friendly reception in the town. As a result in 1745 Abd al-Rahman's great-great-grandfather, Muhammad ibn Saud, the Amir of Diriya, entered into an alliance with al-Wahhab. Muhammad ibn Saud was to remain Diriya's political leader but bolstered by the religious authority of al-Wahhab. In return al-Wahhab was to be recognised as the final authority in all religious matters. Together they would embark on a campaign of expansion,

16 There appears to be considerable uncertainty about the details of this story as regards the extent to which the woman did or did not act willingly both in having sex outside marriage, repeating the offence, advertising the fact to al-Wahhab and flaunting what she was doing publicly. Some commentators believe that the whole thing was intended in some way as a test of al-Wahhab's message of tolerance towards women and insistence on the strict implementation of Islamic law.

gathering more people within the fold of the reformed faith. Their alliance was to lead to the creation of the first Saudi theocratic state.

Their programme of expansion began by Wahhab inviting the leaders of surrounding communities to join his movement. Those who were willing to do so would enter into a formal alliance under which they and their followers accepted the doctrine of the absolute oneness of God and the leadership of Muhammad ibn Saud. If a community or its leaders rejected one or more invitations from Wahhab to join the movement and refused to enter into religious debate with him they would be declared 'unbelievers'. Only then could they become subject to *jihad*, holy war. The fighting force employed by Muhammad ibn Saud to make those who continued to refuse to join al-Wahhab's religious community submit was initially composed mainly of men aged between sixteen and sixty conscripted in Diriya and its immediate neighbourhood. As the Sauds and their religious movement (Wahhabis, as they came to be called pejoratively by their opponents),[17] grew in size and became stronger, increasing numbers of the leaders invited by al-Wahhab to join him did so voluntarily. As often as not this was not so much out of religious conviction as out of self-preservation and the knowledge that al-Wahhab and the Sauds together constituted what the Arabs called 'a House of Strength'.

But, despite their initial successes, al-Wahhab and Muhammad ibn Saud knew that if they were going to gain real control over the interior of Arabia they were going to need to enlist the nomadic Bedouin, who were regarded by most Arabs as the true, original Arabs from whom they had all sprung. Living as they did remote, harsh lives wholly dependent on the weather, chance, their own stamina and resourcefulness, Islam had made little real impact despite the fact that most of them were probably notionally Muslims. As one traveller who questioned the Bedouin he met during his travels on the outer fringes of Arabia recorded: 'They readily admit that Muhammad's religion was not created for them. They add, "How can we perform ablutions without

17 Al-Wahhab's followers referred to themselves as Unitarians (Muwahhidun) and their doctrine as The Religion of Unity (Din al-Tawhid).

water? How can we give alms, being not rich? Why should we fast in Ramadan after fasting all year round?" '[18] Or as the Victorian traveller to the interior of Arabia, William Palgrave, observed, 'Among the great mass of the nomadic population, Mahometanism during the course of twelve whole centuries had made little or no impression either good or ill.'[19] Palgrave concluded that for the Bedouin god was a chief, residing mainly in the sun. Guided mainly by the sun and the stars as they drove their flocks across the empty desert wastes in search of water and the scant, fast-fading patches of pasture that would spring into brief life following one of the very infrequent, short bursts of rain, it is not surprising that the Bedouin continued to place their faith in the tried and tested gods that they could identify with their needs and the universe that they knew and could see around them. Their spiritual values, commitment and ideas of the sacred continued, as they had for thousands of years, to be centred on the tribe. They preserved cults of the ancestors, would make sacrifices to them and seek their intervention and assistance when they needed help or a favour from the Almighty. They would still invoke the local *djinns* and seek guidance from magicians and clairvoyants before embarking on any hazardous undertaking. To al-Wahhab the Bedouin tribes were a prime target for conversion to his vision of pure Islam.

For Muhammad ibn Saud as well, in his quest for expansion by conquest, the Bedouin were a vital potential military resource. An essential part of sustaining life for the Bedouin was the *ghazzu* or raid. When a tribe ran short of food, as it often did, the men of the tribe would mount a raid on another tribe or settlement. Mounted on camels or horses, brandishing swords or guns and riding like the wind, throwing up great clouds of dust from under the animals' hooves, they would suddenly appear from out of the desert, behind a dune or hill, and fall without warning on some poor unsuspecting farmer, herdsman, group of travellers or settlement, swiftly drive off some of their livestock, snatch what they could of their possessions and disappear into the desert

18 Volney, C. F. *Voyage en Syrie et en Egypt, pendant les années 1783, 1784 et 1785*, Desenne, Paris 1787 as quoted by Vassiliev, Alexei in *The History of Saudi Arabia*, Saqi Books, London 2000.

19 Palgrave, William Clifford, *Personal Narrative of a Year's Journey through Central and Eastern Arabia (1862–3)*, Macmillan, London, 1871.

as fast as they had appeared. There was rarely any serious bloodshed or fatalities on either side as that would lead to a blood feud between the tribes involved and the aim of the raiders was to take enough of their opponents' possessions to sustain their own tribe's lives, not to kill the people they raided. The *ghazzu* was a recognised part of tribal life and had been raised almost to the level of a sport. The Bedouin were widely recognised throughout Arabia as its premier warriors.

The first military actions in Muhammad ibn Saud and al-Wahhab's expansion amounted in effect to nothing much more ambitious than a series of glorified *ghazzu*. A swift raid, an ambush by a few dozen men, some camels or sheep driven off or property looted. The proceeds would be distributed a fifth to Muhammad ibn Saud and the rest to those who had taken part in the raid. With the growing success, scale and frequency of these raids Muhammad ibn Saud was able to finance his nascent but growing state and reduce his reliance on other forms of tax or tithes. He was also able to start providing better support for the poor, reduce injustice and root out corruption. All of this was in line with al-Wahhab's interpretation of a return to Muhammad's uncontaminated message and also increased support for Muhammad ibn Saud and al-Wahhab's rule. The fact that the *ghazzu* were carried out in the name of 'purified religion' conferred upon them a prestige and air of authority which they could not otherwise have achieved. All of which facilitated Muhammad ibn Saud's ongoing expansion and helped to undermine resistance in those towns and tribes that he and al-Wahhab had not yet gathered into their fold.

All monotheisms can tend towards fanaticism simply by virtue of their exclusivity. If there is only 'one god' and 'one right way' then any other god, series of gods or system of beliefs must be 'wrong', 'sinful', would need to be purged and their adherents converted, punished or made to submit. The narrower the religious prescriptions of a particular monotheism or branch of that monotheism and the greater the rigidity of its religious practices the more prone it is likely to be to fanaticism and intolerance.[20] And so it quickly proved with the Wahhabis. They quickly

20 Similar tendencies have also been all too apparent in exclusive political creeds, e.g. Communism and Fascism, during the last century.

gained a reputation for being particularly harsh in their treatment of other sects or branches of Islam, such as the Shia. Wahhab regarded such people as polytheists and deviationists from the pure Muslim religion as laid down by Muhammad. If, having heard al-Wahhab's appeal, they did not respond they would be branded infidels and treated accordingly. Because Muhammad had said that other 'People of the Book' should be shown tolerance, Christians and Jews were usually treated more leniently than Muslims who refused to submit to Wahhabism. Although they were subjected to a tax, Christians and Jews were allowed to continue to pray in their own way provided that they did so in the privacy of their own homes.

As Wahhabi control was extended over a wider and wider area they gained a reputation, in part deserved but also much exaggerated by their opponents and detractors, for their cruelty and fanaticism. It was a reputation which would endure and spread well beyond Arabia. Whenever they invaded a place they would smash all the tombs, destroy the shrines of saints, chop down sacred trees, impose strict Wahhabi forms of worship and implement Islamic *Shari'a* law and punishments in all their rigour.[21]

Over the next twenty years almost all of Najd was incorporated within Muhammad ibn Saud's and al-Wahhab's religious-military confederacy through a combination of military conquest and alliances, often reinforced through intermarriage between members of the Saud family and members of the ruling families of the other amirates.

Despite continued resistance from some neighbouring towns, including Riyadh which was not brought into the Saudi confederation until 1773 when its amir was defeated in successive battles and forced to flee, the extension of the Saudi state accelerated under Muhammad ibn Saud's successors. By the mid-1790s his son Abd al-Aziz ibn Muhammad controlled most of the Arabian peninsula down to the borders of today's Oman and Yemen in the south, all of the eastern coastal region of Hasa bordering the Persian Gulf and had started harrying the Hijaz and the holy cities of Mecca and Medina.

21 *Shari'a* law is in Muslim eyes God's revealed law to guide and govern humanity in the correct path in both individual and communal life.

But as they continued their conquests, expanding still further the area they controlled, the Saudi Wahhabis came into steadily greater contact and, inevitably, conflict with the outside world. Isolated and largely insulated for centuries from the world beyond their fierce deserts and barren sun-scorched mountains, they could have little or no concept of the power and organisation of the emerging European empires, of their military might and modern weaponry, nor of the advances in science, industry, commerce and ideas wrought by the Age of Enlightenment. This ignorance, compounded by early successes against the Ottoman Turks who were distracted by insurrections closer to home, would engender in the Wahhabis a dangerous over-confidence. This growing belief in their own military invincibility was exacerbated still further by their religious zeal. The Wahhabi warriors were inspired by the conviction that their cause was holy, that they were engaged upon Allah's work of converting infidels, disciplining idolaters and enforcing God's law. Nowhere was this conviction greater than when they began their campaign against the Hijaz and the Ottoman Sultan's appointed ruler in the region, the Sharif of Mecca. They were outraged by the Ottomans' religious practices, their gaudy clothes and outward show, by the Ottoman nobility's way of life, their arrogance, arbitrary rule, corrupt courts and open sexual perversions.

In 1798, when Wahhabi attacks into Iraq and around Basra provoked the Ottoman Empire, the Governor of Baghdad sent a combined force of fifteen thousand troops and local tribesmen to attack the Wahhabi capital. But the Saudis succeeded in defeating the Governor's army outside the Hasa stronghold of Hofuf and two years later mounted a fresh series of attacks, this time in the south. In 1800 they seized the important oasis trading centre Buraimi and started attacking Oman, Qatar and Bahrain. But in doing so, they now threatened Britain's vital interests, control over the sea routes to their empire in India and their trade routes and commercial interests in the Persian Gulf and Persia. For the moment, distracted by the Napoleonic war in Europe, Britain did not respond. But in due time she would.

By now believing themselves more or less invincible, in April 1801, 10,000 Wahhabis attacked the Shi'ite sacred site at Karbala in Iraq and massacred 5,000 Shias, many of them women and children, and destroyed the ancient tombs, including the tomb of The Prophet Muhammad's grandson, Husayn. This horrified not only all Shias but many other Muslims as well. Later in that same year the Wahhabis further extended their control in the west, taking the city of Taif in the Hijaz and slaughtering its inhabitants. Then in April 1803 they seized Mecca itself. Tombs which had become the objects of Muslim pilgrimage were destroyed, new Wahhabi religious leaders installed, religious practices reformed, treasures from The Prophet's tomb seized, public prayers for the Sultan prohibited and pilgrimage halted for all Muslims except those who professed the Wahhabi doctrine. From now on, the Wahhabis proclaimed, responsibility for the holy cities of Mecca and Medina would be theirs and not the Sultan's.

By their acts in Mecca, Karbala and elsewhere the Wahhabis had now succeeded in outraging almost the entire Muslim world beyond the Arab peninsula itself. Not only had they antagonised the vast majority of the subjects of the Ottoman Empire, they had inflicted a grave insult upon the Sultan himself. As a result the Sultan, despite continuing problems nearer to his capital in Istanbul, immediately dispatched a force of Turkish troops to the Hijaz and had the Saudis ejected from Mecca. A few months later, in the autumn of 1803, the Saudi Amir himself was assassinated inside the mosque in Diriya by a man whose entire family had been murdered by the Wahhabis at Karbala.

Undeterred, the following year the Saudis returned to the attack in the Hijaz, extended their operations in the north and by the end of 1805 they had retaken Mecca and conquered the whole of the Hijaz all the way westwards to the shores of the Red Sea. By 1809–10 their armies had almost reached the gates of Baghdad and Damascus, advanced deep into North Yemen and had taken control of Oman. They even imposed duties on British ships of the East India Company trading across the Arabian Sea and through the Persian Gulf between Bombay and Basra. But now, sixty-five years after Muhammad ibn Saud and al-Wahhab had formed their original alliance their theocratic empire had reached its apogee. Not only had they amassed a greater area of territory than they could control, they had made a whole host of enemies, some of whom could exercise the kind of military power which the Najdis, shut off from the outside world for centuries, could barely imagine, let alone match.

Already alarmed by the threat posed to their interests by growing Saudi power, the British had dispatched warships to protect their trade routes in the Indian Ocean. In 1809, in an exemplary display of power intended to strike fear into anyone who contemplated allying themselves with the Wahhabis, the Royal Navy bombarded the Omani port of Ras al Khaima near the entrance to the Persian Gulf, landed troops, destroyed the shipyards, blew up the warehouses, razed the town to the ground and massacred its inhabitants.

In 1811 an Egyptian army of the Ottoman Empire landed on the Red Sea coast and captured the port of Yanbu. Although the Saudis immediately counter-attacked and defeated them, in 1812 a fresh Egyptian army invaded and seized Medina and early the following year took Jeddah, Mecca and Taif. Meanwhile in the south, the Wahhabis were routed and forced to withdraw completely from Oman. Although the Saudis mounted a number of successful counter attacks – one against the Egyptians in the west being led by a woman called Ghaliya whom the defeated Egyptians immediately branded a sorceress who had put the evil eye upon them – the Wahhabi success was short-lived.

The forces now aligned against them were simply too great and by 1815 Egyptian troops had regained control of most of Hijaz and Asir in the southwest. Finally in 1818 the Egyptians dispatched an army of almost 3,500 cavalry and 4,500 infantrymen, plus artillery, sappers and engineers against Najd itself. Regularly re-supplied with food, munitions and reinforcements, the Egyptians systematically subdued successive settlements and fortified towns across Najd and along the length of Wadi Hanifa until they reached Diriya itself. They surrounded and started to bombard it, killing many of the inhabitants including a lot of members of the al Saud family. Realising that their position was hopeless the Saudis surrendered. The Amir, Abdullah ibn Saud was taken to the Ottoman capital, Istanbul, publicly beheaded and his body thrown into the sea. The other surviving members of the al Saud family were exiled to Egypt. Diriya and all its fortifications were completely destroyed.

The destruction of the Wahhabi state triggered widespread rejoicing across much of the Muslim world. There were fireworks displays in Cairo and Istanbul. There was particular joy in the Shia heartland,

Persia, and even in parts of the Arabian Peninsula itself. Nowhere was this greater than in Mecca and Medina where the Wahhabi ban on Muslims, other than those professing their own puritan beliefs, had deprived people in the holy cities of much of their lucrative income from pilgrims making the annual *hajj* to the sacred sites. Many other tribes across Arabia, especially those who had allied themselves with the Sauds only reluctantly out of self-interest or self-preservation, were relieved to see the back of them and their stern religious and moral code.

However, the Egyptians rapidly squandered this reservoir of potential goodwill. They destroyed the walls and fortifications of every village and town in Najd. Members of noble families and the leaders of those who had fought on the Saudi side were killed all across Arabia, some being tied to the mouths of cannons and blasted apart, and their families' lands confiscated. Crops were uprooted, trees chopped down, possessions looted, all the horses stolen and unjust taxes imposed. As a British officer, Captain George Sadleir, who travelled across central Arabia in 1819 observed, the Egyptian commander's campaign amounted to a series of barbaric atrocities and violations of his sacred duties. Soon the Sauds' former subjects were wishing for a return to the stability and security, no matter how austere, they had enjoyed under the Wahhabis.

Captain George Foster Sadleir[22] of the 47th Foot arrived in Arabia in May 1819 on a mission. The British, having been alarmed at the growing power of the Saudi state were delighted to see it crushed but, in keeping with their policy of trying to make sure that no one power ever became strong enough to pose a serious threat to their interests, were now concerned to ensure that the Wahhabis did not make a comeback but also that Egypt and the Ottoman Empire would not now pose a new threat. Sadleir's mission was to carry a personal message of congratulation upon his defeat of the Wahhabis to the Egyptian leader, Ibrahim Pasha, from the Governor General of India, Lord Hastings, and to try to persuade the Egyptians to enter into an alliance with Britain. Under the treaty that it was Sadleir's mission to propose, the British navy and the

22 Sadleir's name is often spelled Sadlier, but this latter spelling is incorrect. See *Saudi Arabia in the Nineteenth Century* (page 40, note 3) by R. Bayly Winder, St Martins Press, New York, 1965.

Egyptians would work in conjunction to make sure that the Sauds and Wahhabis never again posed a threat to either of them. The British navy was to stamp out piracy in the waters around Arabia and ensure that no other power threatened the region's maritime trade routes, while the Egyptian army was to assist the British in establishing a series of strategically placed garrisons in ports along the Arab coast of the Persian Gulf and ensure that the Sauds and Wahhabis could never again come to exercise control over the Arabian mainland. Sadleir, a British imperialist of the old school if ever there was one, who insisted on wearing military uniform throughout and refused to conform to the local customs, did not speak a word of Arabic, believing that if he shouted loudly enough people would understand him and do as he ordered. Landing at Qatif, in the Persian Gulf, he set off for Hofuf in the Hasa believing Ibrahim Pasha to be there. On arrival in Hofuf he was informed that Ibrahim had moved further inland. Sadleir set off in pursuit in the company of a party of Egyptian troops, travelling mostly at night to avoid marauding Bedouin. Sadleir clearly despised the Arabs, describing them as 'turbulent barbarians' and commenting that their 'procrastination, duplicity, falsity, deception and fraudulence ... cannot be described'.[23] What he did describe was the appallingly gratuitous cruelty of the occupying Egyptians, the destitution they had wrought across the country, resultant collapse of order and moral disintegration. Arriving in Najd, Sadleir learned that Ibrahim had left for Medina two days earlier. When Sadleir did finally catch up with Ibrahim Pasha outside Medina in September their discussions came to nothing. So with no agreement reached Sadleir went on to Jeddah and finally sailed back to Bombay in January 1820. Although he had failed in his intended mission, Sadleir had in the process become almost certainly the first European ever to cross the whole Arabian peninsula and the first person to bring out a first-hand account of the people and life in the heart of Arabia since the luckless Roman general, Aelius Gallus, almost nineteen hundred years earlier. Arrogant but conscientious, the geographical and solar observations and descriptions recorded by Sadleir during his

23 Sadleir, G. F., *Account of a Journey from Katif on the Persian Gulf to Yanboo on the Red Sea*, Transactions of the Literary Society of Bombay, 1823, vol. 3.

frustrating journey across Arabia would remain for near on a century almost the only reliable source of information available to later travellers.

Although Sadleir's mission failed, its aims remained the basis of British policy in the region for the next hundred years and would play a major part in the life and fortunes of Abd al-Aziz. Unable to reach agreement with the Egyptians, over the next few years the British, through a combination of military action and treaties with local amirs, established a position of dominance throughout the Persian Gulf, in the Indian Ocean and along the southern coast of the Arabian peninsula. At the same time the Egyptians, having as they thought reduced Najd and the central regions of the Arabian peninsula to impotence, withdrew most of their forces. Now, while remaining in nominal charge of the whole area that had belonged to the Saudi state, they concentrated the remaining forces they kept in Arabia in the Hijaz, so ensuring their continued control of the holy cities, the safety of pilgrims making the *hajj* and the Ottoman Sultans' hold on the caliphate.

Over the next few years Najd and much of central Arabia was reduced to a state of virtual anarchy, riven by local wars and feuds within the families of many of the local amirs. But in 1820 Turki, a cousin of Abdullah ibn Saud the amir beheaded by the Turks, escaped from captivity in Egypt and began secretly to make his way to Najd. After living in hiding for a couple of years, in 1823 he began to make himself known to the people of Najd and started to build up a fighting force. Profiting from the unpopularity of the Egyptians, he quickly gained control of a number of settlements in and around Wadi Hanifa and by 1824 had succeeded in establishing himself in Riyadh which, following the destruction of Diriya, had become the Najdi capital. Turki would turn out to be the great-grandfather of the boy Abd al-Aziz. One of Turki's first actions on taking control in Riyadh was to build a new mosque and construct the strong town walls and palace from out of which Abd al-Rahman and his family were to escape almost seventy years later. With Turki now firmly in control, stability began to return to Najd and with it many of those who had fled. One of these returning refugees was the grandson of al-Wahhab. He strengthened Turki's authority still further by issuing messages to faithful Muslims throughout Najd that called upon them to reject the polytheistic practices of 'so-called Muslims' and return to the 'genuine Islam'. However, Turki was careful to ensure that the cruel fanaticism which had been associated with the first period of Wahhabi power did not re-surface.

By the 1830s Turki had re-established Saudi control over much of the territory ruled by his grandfather Muhammad ibn Saud except for the Hijaz and parts of the south. However he was weakened by growing dissension within the Saudi family and in May 1834 he was murdered coming out of Friday prayers in the mosque in Riyadh by assassins engaged by his cousin, Mishari, who then attempted to seize power. For nine long years after that Najd was wracked by civil war, during which time no fewer than four different members of the Saudi family displaced and replaced each other as rulers. For a period of three years, from 1838, the Egyptians returned and re-asserted their control. Finally, in 1843 Turki's eldest son, Faisal, succeeded in regaining undisputed ascendancy. One of his most loyal allies throughout these long war-torn years had been Abdullah ibn Rashid, who amongst his many other deeds had himself killed Mishari with his own sword. The Rashids were the leaders of the powerful Shammar tribe, whose capital was the ancient oasis city of Ha'il, almost five hundred miles northwest of Riyadh and an important stopping point on the caravan route from Iraq, Syria and Persia to the holy cities of Mecca and Medina. In recognition of Abdullah ibn Rashid's loyalty Faisal gave him rule of the whole Shammar region from the northern end of the Wadi Hanifah up to the great Al Nafud Desert bordering Iraq.

Over the next decade and a half Faisal set about regaining control over the rest of the territory that had been controlled by Abd al-Aziz ibn Muhammad forty years earlier. However, he was careful not to provoke an all-out conflict with either the British or the Ottoman Empire, continuing to pay nominal tribute to the Ottomans in the north and the Egyptians in the Hijaz. Although in the south his troops re-took Buraimi, he held back from attacking important ports along the Persian Gulf and Omani coasts which had recently been seized by Britain in order to be better able to protect her important trade routes to her growing empire in India and the Far East. Faisal was aware of the power of British arms and astute enough not to risk provoking their use against him.

Despite ongoing clashes with some of his tribal neighbours, Faisal brought about a return of stability and prosperity to his territory. People were once again able to go about their lives without fear for themselves or their property. He also developed a profitable international trade in exporting pedigree Arab horses to surrounding countries and beyond. But throughout the 1850s while Faisal was restoring the fortunes of Najd, the Shammar, though still Faisal's allies and still headed by the Rashids, were also gaining in strength. More distant, but no less significant, the British were establishing a virtual hoop of alliances, backed when needed by Royal Navy patrols, armed intervention and British military garrisons, with almost every ruler around the entire coastline of the Arabian peninsula from Oman in the south, round Cape Musandum at the mouth of the Persian Gulf and all the way up the east coast northwards almost to the mouth of the Euphrates. More ominously still, by the end of the 1850s dangerous rifts had once again started to open up within the al Saud family itself. The most serious was an increasingly bitter rivalry between Faisal's eldest son Abdullah, backed by Faisal's third son, Muhammad, and his second son, Saud. His fourth son, Abd al-Rahman (the future father of Abd al-Aziz) was only born in 1850 and so was still too young to be actively involved.

In 1862 William Palgrave, a Catholic with a penchant for disguises, who had undergone instruction in a Jesuit seminary after converting from the Church of England and now entertained ideas of converting Muslims and Jews to Christianity, became the first European since the luckless Captain Sadleir to succeed in reaching Riyadh. Son of the founder of the Public Record Office and younger brother of Francis Palgrave, compiler of *The Golden Treasury of English Verse*, Palgrave travelled into Arabia from Gaza on the Mediterranean coast of Palestine disguised as a Syrian travelling doctor or, as he put it, 'quack'. His purpose in making this, for a European, extremely dangerous journey was 'to fill up [the] blank' in European knowledge of the vast interior of Arabia, 'of its plains and mountains, its tribes and cities, of its governments and institutions, of its inhabitants, their ways and customs, of their social condition' and of 'how far advanced in civilisation or sunk in barbarism' they were.[24] Palgrave succeeded in his self-imposed task to an

24 *Personal Narrative of a Year's Journey Through Central and Eastern Arabia*

extraordinary degree, not only for his contemporaries but for generations to come. He has also provided us with a uniquely detailed and personal portrait of the Najd and Riyadh as it was in the last years of the reign the Amir Faisal (Faisal The Great, as he is often known) and as it still largely remained until well into the adulthood of Abd al-Aziz ibn Saud.

Having endured dust storms, thirst, dishonest guides and the threat of robbers during his journey across the Syrian desert, through the territory of the Shammar, into the Rashids' capital Ha'il and on southwards, Palgrave still expresses that special fear felt by Europeans at the prospect of entering Najd, cradle of Wahhabism and to the European imagination 'dark heart' of Arabia. Najd, 'the genuine Wahhabi country', he says, is 'to the rest of Arabia a sort of lion's den, on which few venture and even fewer return.' He quotes the words of an old man in Buraydah from whom he and his companion asked directions: 'This is Najd, he who enters it does not come out again.'

Once having entered Najd, however, Palgrave finds the people extremely hospitable, writing later that they are famed throughout Arabia and beyond 'in prose and verse for their hospitality and they really deserve their reputation'. He describes how Wadi Hanifah and the many smaller wadis dissecting it over its entire length, cut like sheer-sided fissures, often hundreds of feet deep, into the flat, hard, barren table lands that surround it. He marvels at the contrast between the arid plateaus above and the verdant date gardens and pastures in the wadis below. He remarks, too, on how everywhere the 'abrupt edges' of the wadis are 'furrowed by torrent tracks' caused by the sudden fierce rain storms of the short Arabian winter which 'rush over … and often turn the greater part of the gully below into a violent watercourse for two or three days, till the momentary supply is spent, and then pools and plashes remain through the months of spring while most of the water

1862–63 by William Gifford Palgrave, Macmillan, London, 1871. For many years doubts were cast on the accuracy of many of Palgrave's descriptions of Arabia, places and people, but more recent scholarship has suggested that in fact he was a much more accurate reporter than he has often been given credit for. In quoting from passages from Palgrave we have changed Palgrave's spelling of some Arabic names in order to maintain consistency with spelling in the rest of the book.

sinks underground, where it forms an unfailing supply for the wells in summer ... Hence the fertility of these valleys.' Approaching Riyadh he notes not only the wells and small windmills used for lifting their water to irrigate the date palms and gardens but also the abundant wild game, including partridge, quail, bustard, gazelles, wild boar and pigs and the domestic animals such as Najdi 'fat-tailed' sheep, camels and oxen. Palgrave is particularly struck by the thick walls that surround the small towns, saying of one a few miles from Riyadh that its walls and towers remind him of Conway, Edward the First's thirteenth-century fortress in North Wales built during his suppression of the Welsh. He notes that the only difference between the fortresses of Najd and those of medieval Europe is that rather than being constructed of stone the Najdi castles are built from sun-dried bricks. Palgrave's first sight of Riyadh was from a small hillock a quarter of a mile away: 'Before us lay the capital, large and square, crowned by high towers and strong walls of defence, a mass of roofs and terraces, where overtopping all frowned the huge but irregular pile of Faisal's royal castle, and hard by it rose the scarce less conspicuous palace, built and inhabited by his eldest son, Abdullah. Other edifices too of remarkable appearance broke here and there through the maze of grey roof-tops ... All around for a full three miles over the surrounding plain, but more especially to the south and west, waved a sea of palm trees above green fields and well-watered gardens; while the singing droning sound of water wheels reached us even where we had halted.' Entering the town through the town's northeast gate, in the shadow of whose towers lounged several be-robed sentries armed with swords, Palgrave finds himself in a broad street, lined on each side by large two-storey houses, wells for washing and mosques of various sizes, a few with fruit trees in their courtyards. He soon finds himself in the large rectangular open main square, over one hundred yards long and more than fifty wide, flanked on its southern side by the royal palace: 'Of recent and almost symmetrical construction, square in form, with goodly carved gates, and three storeys of windows one above the other.' Some sixty women sit in the shadow of the palace wall selling a range of goods and provisions including bread, dates, milk, vegetables and firewood. On the opposite, northern side of the square are bustling shops and warehouses and at the far, western end there is 'a long covered passage, upborne high on a clumsy colonnade' crossing the breadth of the square and joining the interior of the palace directly to the great mosque. This, says Palgrave, 'affords old Faisal a private and unseen passage at will from his own apartments to his official post at Friday prayers, without exposing him on his way to vulgar curiosity, or perhaps the dangers of treachery'. Palgrave reminds his readers that both Faisal's father and great uncle were assassinated during public worship and says that for this reason Faisal has become 'very timid'. The whole square is crowded with people, with 'camels, dromedaries, sacks piled up, and all the accompaniments of an Arab market'.

The Najdis themselves Palgrave finds more reserved than other Arabs, less prone to ostentation, to ornament or show in wealth or dress; not easily roused to anger but once roused 'firm of purpose, terrible in revenge, deep and implacable haters, and doubtful friends to all save their own immediate kindred'. He judges that because of their character, 'capacity for rule, organisation and perseverance' they are 'sure to triumph in the long run over their disunited and desultory neighbours' and will eventually absorb most of the Arabian peninsula under their own rule. They are both skilled agriculturalists and implacable warriors.

Palgrave finds Riyadh and the surrounding country under the oppressive control of a kind of religious police, whom he calls 'zealators' who are entitled to exercise arbitrary powers. They can beat or fine at discretion, without limit and on the spot. Among the offences for which they could exact punishment were failure to attend prayers five times a day at the public mosques, smoking tobacco, taking snuff, chewing or spitting, wearing silk or gold clothes or jewellery, singing or playing an instrument, children's street games, talking or having a lighted lamp in the house after night prayers, swearing by any other name than that of Allah or invoking any name but His and any other action which the 'zealators' may regard as suspicious or lacking in decorum.

Because of Palgrave's own religious zeal one should perhaps treat his observations on Wahhabism and Muslim religious practice with caution, but he does record one particularly enlightening conversation he had in Riyadh with a leading Wahhabi scholar who was married to a descendant of al-Wahhab himself. Palgrave asked the old scholar which were the 'great' sins and which the lesser ones. The old scholar said that 'The first and great sin is giving of divine honours to a creature'. Palgrave replied that 'Of course the enormity of such a sin is beyond all doubt. But if this be the first, what must be a second; what is it?' 'Drinking the shameful, smoking tobacco,' came the unhesitating answer.

'And murder, and adultery, and false witness?' Palgrave suggested.

'God is merciful and forgiving,' rejoined his friend; that is, these are merely little sins.

'Hence two sins alone are great, polytheism and smoking.'

Palgrave says that by 1862 the Amir Faisal had aged severely, was completely blind (probably as a result of trachoma contracted during his captivity in Egypt), corpulent and more or less incapable of active exertion. He had become extremely fearful, superstitious, bigoted and tyrannical. As a result he no longer appeared in person in front of his subjects with any regularity. Palgrave concluded that Faisal had effectively been reduced to being little more than a mere tool in the hands of his two eldest sons, his ministers and the religious authorities. Palgrave did, however, by virtue of the fact that he was masquerading as a doctor, come to be on extremely intimate terms with Abdullah, Faisal's eldest son. Abdullah, like his father, was 'short, stout, large-headed and thick-necked, a very bull in appearance', probably a family trait, reflects Palgrave. Abdullah's brother Saud, who Palgrave judged to be very close in age to Abdullah, was in contrast 'tall, slender, handsome, and with a strong trace of the careless Bedouin expression in his countenance. Open and generous, fond of show and horsemanship.' Saud is, according to Palgrave, 'a great favourite of the "liberal" party', whereas Abdullah headed the orthodox faction. Faisal's third son, Muhammad, 'much resembled his eldest brother and father', while the fourth, Abd al-Rahman, the future father of Abd al-Aziz, was 'a heavy-looking boy, who as yet inhabits his father's harem' who appears to Palgrave to be between ten and twelve years old and whose appearance suggests to him little 'promise for the future'. Eventually, after two or three months in Riyadh, people became suspicious of Palgrave and his companion and they had to flee east to the Hasa and the city of Hofuf.

Less than two-and-a-half years later Riyadh received three more British visitors who this time did not hide their true identity or purpose.

They were Lieutenant-Colonel Lewis Pelly, Her Majesty's Political Resident in the Gulf, and two Royal Navy officers, a Dr Colville and Lieutenant Dawes. They were members of the British government in India, based at the British Residence at Bushire on the Persian side of the Gulf. They landed in Kuwait in February 1865 and travelled on camels south to Riyadh. Taking care not to be observed they took bearings, estimated distances and collected plant and rock specimens as they went. Between leaving Kuwait and entering Najd, a distance of almost 400 miles, Pelly noted that they did not see 'a single fixed human habitation, and only one tree and one set of permanent wells'.[25] It being the Arabian spring, Pelly recorded, 'the grass and wild flowers were at their best, and just sufficient to give a light glow of green'.

Pelly's purpose in visiting Riyadh was to try to reduce what was perceived by the British as Saudi animosity towards them, negotiate a treaty with Faisal to assist in suppressing piracy and the slave trade in the Persian Gulf, and to warn him off making any further attacks on the Omani and Gulf Coast shaikhs with whom Britain had signed treaties of protection. Pelly found Faisal to be even more infirm than when Palgrave had met him two years earlier: 'I found the Imam seated at the upper end of the room, on a small handsome carpet, supported at his back by a heavy cushion.' When Pelly entered the room Faisal rose, 'but with difficulty; took my hand and felt slowly all over it ... He was quite blind, but his face was remarkable, with regular features, placid, stern, self-possessed, resigned ... His voice was well modulated, and his words calm and measured. He was dignified, almost gentle; yet you felt he could be remorselessly cruel.'[26] Pelly found Faisal pleasant, but while he was prepared to help in suppressing piracy he remained inflexible on the other major issues which were the central concern of Pelly's visit. He told Pelly that he wanted friendly relations with Britain but insisted that he had sovereignty over the whole of Eastern Arabia and the coast from Kuwait at its northern end all the way down to Sur on the Indian Ocean

25 *A Visit to the Wahabee Capital, Central Arabia*, by Lieut-Colonel Lewis Pelly, HM Political Resident, Persian Gulf. *Journal of the Royal Geographical Society*, No. 35, 1865.

26 *Report on a Journey to the Wahabee Capital of Riyadh in Central Arabia*, by Lewis Pelly, Bombay, 1866.

coast at the extreme eastern tip of Oman and beyond into Yemen 'which God has given us ... Be Arabia what it may, it is all ours.'[27] After one of their meetings Faisal invited Pelly to see the jail where he had incarcerated seventy hostages, leading members of different tribes held as a guarantee of their continuing loyalty. On another occasion Faisal told Pelly that he hated his religion and Pelly could not help but notice the suspicion with which he and his colleagues, as Christians, were regarded by some of the citizens of Riyadh, especially the religious leaders. Frustrated, Pelly left after three days to return to Bushire and report to his government that they should remain on their guard against further Saudi incursions into their and their allies' territory. Even during his short stay Pelly, like Palgrave, noticed the extreme, near open, hostility between Faisal's two eldest sons.

In December 1865 Faisal died and the state was plunged into long and bloody confusion as all four of Faisal's sons fought for his throne. Between April 1871 and the end of March 1876, Riyadh had no fewer than six different rulers, one following the other in violent and disorderly succession. As Faisal's sons, together with a greedy assortment of other branches of the Saudi family and ever-shifting alliances of neighbouring tribal leaders fought each other for supremacy, Faisal's former kingdom disintegrated.

As Saudi power became weaker neighbouring rulers seized their chance to become stronger. Subject tribes and local rulers seceded from Najd and became independent, formed alliances with other local leaders or placed themselves under the protection of more powerful leaders and tribes. Meanwhile the great powers increased their grip on the whole region. The opening of the Suez Canal in 1869 had rendered the region much more accessible to the European powers and greatly increased the strategic and trading importance of the entire peninsula. As a result, the Ottoman Empire, even though still riven with dissension and revolt much closer to home, re-asserted its authority in the area. In 1871 the Ottomans occupied Asir in the south-west of the peninsula, bordering Yemen and the Red Sea, and Hasa, bordering the Persian Gulf and almost as far north as the mouth of the Euphrates. Although the

27 Ibid.

Ottomans, wishing to conserve their military strength, pulled their forces in Hasa back to Baghdad a few years later, they appointed a governor, supported by the promise of their military backing, to rule for them.

During the 1880s the British, through their government in India, came steadily to exercise almost total control over the whole of the Persian Gulf, turning it in effect into a British inland lake. They also came to dominate the trade of the amirates and sultanates around all of southern and eastern Arabia. In 1882 the British sent troops to occupy Egypt.

Closer to Riyadh itself, it was the Rashids, rulers of the Shammar, who benefited most from Najd's collapse into civil war, integrating more and more of the surrounding territory and tribes into their domain. Now when western travellers like Charles Doughty and Sir Wilfrid and Lady Anne Blunt ventured into the Arab interior it was to Ha'il, rather than Riyadh, that they travelled to pay their respects to the Rashidi rulers, not to the Sauds. It is to these British explorer-adventurers that we owe the portrait that we have of the tyrannical but all-powerful leader of the Rashids during these years, Muhammad Al Rashid. Unlike the Sauds, faced with dissent and rebellion Muhammad Al Rashid crushed his opponents with a murderous authority that none of the warring Sauds had come near to matching. It was not for nothing that the Blunts compared the leader of the Shammar to Richard III. Doughty was told during his stay in Ha'il that Muhammad Rashid had 'committed crimes which before were not known in the world'. Yet he found that although they feared him his subjects respected his authority and the efficiency of his government.

Abd al-Aziz ibn Saud was born into the bloody chaos that was Riyadh in 1880, the second son to the Amir Faisal's youngest son Abd al-Rahman and Sarah Sudairi, a daughter of the Duwasir tribe from the south of Najd.[28] It was in the midst of this same anarchy that Abd al-Aziz spent his early years, with street fights outside, reports of spies and counter-spies, blood letting and pitched battles both in the town and out in all the country around. It was with bodies hung from battlements or left to be devoured as carrion by rats and birds that the young boy started to grow. His parents no doubt shielded him and their other

28 See note 1 Chapter 1 on Abd al-Aziz's date of birth.

children from the worst excesses so far as possible, bringing them up as devout Wahhabis. But there can be no doubt that the young Abd al-Aziz was aware of an all-pervading atmosphere of insecurity and sense of impermanence during his early years. Those were also the years when he learned to recite the Qur'an by heart, studied with a descendant of the great al-Wahhab himself, and, far more enjoyable to him no doubt, became adept at handling a sword. The people around Abd al-Aziz were probably not fully aware of the impact that these events must have been having on the child, but there can be little doubt that they had a crucial influence on the adult he was to become and on his future actions.

Throughout his adult life, most of those who were to meet Abd al-Aziz would remark on the fact that despite his great friendliness and charm, he somehow always seemed to keep some part of himself 'hidden'. But to a few, those who had the good fortune to get to know him intimately, he did reveal a number of important details about his childhood. One such person was Muhammad Asad, a remarkable and distinguished journalist-scholar who had started life as a Polish Jew but converted to Islam and in the 1920s came to know Ibn Saud well. Ibn Saud told Asad that it was his father's sister, more than even his own mother or any other adult, who had shown him the maternal love that any child needs in order to grow into a rounded, fulfilled adult and to achieve their true potential: 'She loved me, I think, even more than her own children. When we were alone, she would take me on her lap and tell me of the great things which I was to do when I grew up: "Thou must revive the glory of the House of Ibn Saud," she would tell me again and again, and her words were like a caress. "But I want thee to know, O Azayyiz,"[29] she would say, "that even the glory of the House of Ibn Saud must not be the end of thy endeavours. Thou must strive for the glory of Islam. Thy people sorely need a leader who will guide them in the path of the Holy Prophet – and thou shalt be that leader.' These words have always lived in my heart."[30]

29 Her affectionate diminutive for Abd al-Aziz.

30 Muhammad Asad records Ibn Saud saying this to him in the 1920s in his book *The Road to Mecca*, Max Reinhardt, London, 1954.

By the mid-1880s, when his aunt began instilling these ideas in young Abd al-Aziz's heart, his family's fortunes were reaching a new nadir. They had lost control of almost all of Najd and their other domains. The people in the towns and oases of Najd had become heartily sick of the long years of unending war, feuds, raids and bloodshed under the Al Sauds. They had become ready to accept the rule of one single strong leader and The Rashid, the ruler of Ha'il more than four hundred and fifty miles away to the north-east had seized his chance. Allying himself to the Ottoman Empire, he had wrested control of town after town from the Al Sauds. In 1887, when Abd al-Aziz was seven years old, yet another quarrel had broken out among the Al Sauds and Muhammad Rashid had seized his opportunity to swoop down upon Riyadh, take the town, cart off Abdullah, Faisal The Great's eldest son, to Ha'il, and hold him captive there as a hostage and 'honoured guest'. Determined to make sure that the Sauds did not try to re-assert their independence The Rashid had left behind a strong garrison in Riyadh and appointed one of his own most trusted and ruthless lieutenants as governor. He had also left behind Abd al-Aziz's father, Abd al-Rahman, and his family. Abd al-Rahman had a reputation as both a peacemaker and a devout Wahhabi. The Rashid hoped that Abd al-Rahman might exert his influence among the devout citizens of Riyadh to bring calm and stability to the area.

However, unknown to Muhammad Rashid, Abd al-Rahman nursed a strong sense of family pride and was determined that he and his sons would one day restore the Saudi empire to its former glory and had begun secretly to plan towards this end. In 1889 Abdullah, Faisal The Great's eldest son, fell seriously ill and Muhammad Rashid chivalrously, and no doubt also fearing that he might be accused of Abdullah's murder if he died in his custody, summoned Abd al-Rahman to Ha'il to escort his brother home to Riyadh. Shortly after arriving back in Riyadh Abdullah duly died.

In spite of the fact that Faisal the Great's third son, Muhammad, was still alive, Abd al-Rahman immediately proclaimed himself head of the Al Saud family and began secretly sounding out leaders among the neighbouring tribes to see who might be willing to try to launch a rebellion aimed at throwing off Rashid rule. As a result of the harsh rule, onerous taxes and punishments exacted by the Rashids and their governor since they took control of Riyadh, by the spring of 1890 Abd al-Rahman had gathered enough allies to seize back control of Riyadh and launch an open rebellion. Muhammad Rashid responded by dispatching a powerful force to attack Riyadh and retake it. But Abd al-Rahman was ready for him. He had strengthened the town's fortifications and laid in provisions for a siege. On top of which Abd al-Rahman and the people of Riyadh were proud and determined.

When the town refused to surrender, The Rashid laid siege and began chopping down the date palms, poisoning the wells, damaging the water wheels and destroying the crops growing in the fields and orchards around the town. But still Abd al-Rahman and the people of Riyadh refused to surrender. As the summer wore on and the temperature soared into the 100s for day after day, The Rashid's troops became disheartened and began to drift away to their homes and The Rashid had no option but to negotiate a truce.

Thus it was that young Abd al-Aziz, his elder brother having died a few months earlier, was sent in the autumn of 1890 by his father with his uncle Muhammad to the camp of The Rashid to witness the negotiation and start learning the skills he would one day need as a ruler. It was then he had seen how evil The Rashid appeared and been surprised when he had spoken kindly to him. A truce had been easily agreed. Abd al-Rahman had been allowed to continue to rule in Riyadh and the immediately surrounding area but subject to the authority of the Rashids and their appointed Governor. The siege was to be lifted and The Rashid and his army were to return to Ha'il.

However, revolt against the Rashids had soon been smouldering again among the tribes at the northern end of the Wadi Hanifah and Abd al-Rahman had again declared his support for the rebels. Muhammad Rashid, now determined to be rid of the Sauds for ever, sent secret orders to his governor in Riyadh. The day chosen by Muhammad Rashid for the final squaring of accounts was the festival of Eid al-Adha, the 'Greater Eid' or 'Feast of Sacrifice', which marks the conclusion of the annual *hajj* and commemorates the biblical sacrifice by Abraham of his son and God's miraculous last-minute substitution of a ram to take the place of the boy – for all devout Muslims a day of prayer, visiting and celebration.

In accordance with custom, the Governor of Riyadh was to pay a formal visit to Abd al-Rahman in the Al Sauds' palace in Riyadh to convey to him and his family his master Muhammad Rashid's traditional festive greetings. The Governor's most trusted guards and followers were to accompany him. But Muhammad Rashid had secretly arranged that, once all the Sauds had assembled in the audience chamber, upon a pre-arranged signal the Governor's companions were to seize the Al Sauds and slaughter them just as the ram had been slaughtered in the Bible story. However, a spy had found out about the plan and told Abd al-Rahman.

So Abd al-Rahman had devised his own form of sacrificial ritual, intended to foil the Governor's murderous plot and turn the Governor and his retinue themselves into sacrificial offerings. Accordingly, shortly before the appointed hour on the festive day Abd al-Rahman's courtiers, senior members of his council and, to allay suspicion even the ten-year-old Abd al-Aziz, accompanied by the same trusted personal slave who would awake him in the middle of the night a few weeks later, took up their accustomed places in Abd al-Rahman's *majlis*. The Governor and his retinue duly arrived, were shown into the chamber and greeted by Abd al-Aziz and Abd al-Rahman's courtiers. Then Abd al-Rahman himself arrived, went straight over to his honoured guest, the Governor, and offered him the traditional Eid al-Adha greetings. Abd al-Rahman then took his accustomed place and beckoned the Governor to sit in the place of honour on the cushions beside him. Once all the formal greetings were completed and everyone was seated in a circle on the luxuriously woven and embroidered cushions laid out around the chamber, slaves entered with the elegantly shaped, flamingo-necked and -spouted golden coffee pots and began pouring the strong, incense-spiced coffee. Then, as the polite conversation began to flow and all present appeared to begin to relax, Abd al-Rahman gave a discreet, pre-arranged sign to a servant standing by the door through which his guests had entered. Whereupon dozens of his henchmen rushed into the chamber with swords drawn from hiding places just outside each of the doors of the chamber and set upon the Governor and his companions. The Governor and those accompanying him, instantly spotting the danger and already awaiting a signal themselves, immediately leapt to their feet, unsheathed their own weapons and attempted to fight back. Now Abd al-Rahman, his counsellors and courtiers also leapt up from the elegant cushions, drew weapons they had concealed about themselves and joined in the slashing, cursing, blood-spurting confusion, as, wide-eyed, young Abd al-Aziz peered out from behind the large protective body of his trusted African bodyguard and slave. At last, with many bodies now writhing on the floor, groaning, screaming, oozing and spurting blood and a last one or two still slashing ever more wildly about them, the Governor was overpowered, bound hand and foot and hauled from the room. Outside in the courtyard he was dragged over to the well and pitched down it head-first to die.[31]

Those blood-soaked few minutes, intended by Abd al-Rahman to mark the end of the Al Sauds' subservience to the Rashids, in the event heralded the end of his own rule in Riyadh. When news of the murders reached Muhammad Rashid he flew into a great rage and sent out messengers with a summons to all the chiefs of the clans of the Shammar, the camels of the messengers draped over with black as a sign that to answer the summons was a debt of honour and that it would be a disgrace to fail to heed the call.

Soon The Rashid had assembled a great army amounting to tens of thousands of men with hundreds upon hundreds of camels and horses, and begun to march on Riyadh. Abd al-Rahman's allies in the north had sallied forth to meet them and for almost a month fought battle after battle without either side gaining a decisive victory. Abd al-Rahman, however, seemed strangely slow in marching out to join his allies. His warriors were probably wearied after the long years of war and disheartened by the accounts of the brutal carnage that had taken place in the palace in contravention of all the laws of traditional Arab hospitality. As a result he and his force were on their way north up the Wadi Hanifah when news of the great battle near Mulaidah, on the edge of the Dahna Desert, had reached them. Hearing that his allies had been utterly routed, Abd al-Rahman had hastily scuttled back to Riyadh to prepare for another siege.

However, the citizens of Riyadh, learning of the scale of their allies'

31 Accounts differ about the precise details of these events, some scholars doubting if they happened at all. But we believe that the balance of evidence suggests that they did and probably in much the way described.

defeat, the size of the Rashid army and with memories of the recent siege still fresh in their minds, sent a deputation of the town's senior citizens to Abd al-Rahman to beg him to surrender at once.

So thus it was that, with further resistance now impossible, Abd al-Rahman had roused his family in the middle of that January night in 1891 and led them furtively out of his capital, up and out across the arid table land into the red sands of the Dahna Desert, and that the ten-year-old Abd al-Aziz and his elder sister Nura had come to be riding in saddlebags on either flank of the same camel. And surely at some point in that long, dark night the words of his aunt when she had sat him upon her knee must have rung even deeper than ever in the boy's heart: 'Thou must revive the glory of the House of Ibn Saud, O Azayyiz. And even the glory of the House of Ibn Saud must not be the end of thy endeavours. Thou must strive for the glory of Islam. Thy people sorely need a leader who will guide them in the path of the Holy Prophet – and thou shalt be that leader.'

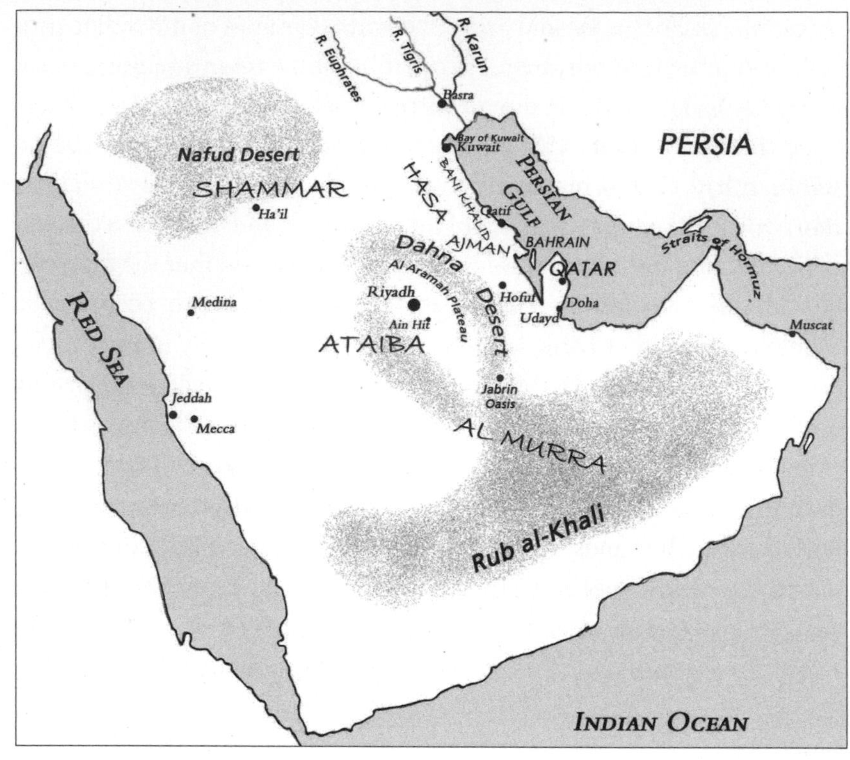

CHAPTER 3

Making of the Man

Having successfully made his escape from Riyadh, eluded Rashid search parties, led his small band of fugitives out over the hard al Aramah plateau and guided them safely across the treacherous red sands of the Dahna Desert, Abd al-Rahman had still by no means removed his family from danger. Apart from the continuing threat from the Rashids, they now faced the problem of survival in a harsh and alien landscape. Although for the moment Najd's winter rains had clothed large patches of the land they were crossing in a deceptively lush veil of green, dotted it with brightly coloured wild flowers, small fast-growing shrubs and dressed the skeletal desert bushes in brief but vigorous leaf, he knew this would not last. For some weeks it might feed their camels and a little later a flush of wild berries should provide some nourishment for their riders, the relief would be short-lived. Although for the moment Abd al-Rahman and his party can survive off camel milk, dried dates and the flat bread they can make over camp fires from the small supply of flour they carried away with them from Riyadh and the camels will do well enough from grazing the lush desert grass and shrubs, soon both men and animals will need water. Out here, away from the fertile Wadi Hanifah and its numerous springs and flowing irrigation channels, that means wells. In just a few short weeks the temperature will start to rise and a month or two after that the winter and spring rains will cease, the thin veil of plant life will wither and die and the harsh unrelenting sun will once more hammer the ground dry, hard and unforgiving. Then being able to find wells and draw sweet water from them will spell the difference between life and death.

'Most wells in the interior of the desert ... are exclusive property, either of a whole tribe, or of individuals whose ancestors dug the wells ... If a well be the property of a tribe, the tents are pitched near it whenever rain-water becomes scarce ... and no other Arabs are then permitted to water their camels there.'[1] The Swiss explorer of Arabia, John Louis Burckhardt, had written that seventy-five years earlier, but it still remained true. Also the wells would be among the places where the Rashids and their allies were most likely to be on the lookout for Abd al-Rahman and his fugitive family.

Abd al-Rahman and his fellow fugitives' most likely route to survival was, therefore, to attach themselves to one of the tribes of the region. Bedouin rules of hospitality were strict. They dictated that if a stranger, even an enemy, touched your tent that person became untouchable. Even to exact just revenge for a past wrong done to you by the stranger was deemed inadmissible, an offence against the laws of hospitality and an indelible disgrace: 'If a Bedouin agrees to share his bread and salt

1 John Louis Burckhardt, *Notes on the Bedouin and Wahhabys*, Colburn & Bentley, London, 1817, Vol ii. Quoted by Alexei Vassiliev in *The History of Saudi Arabia*, Saqi Books, London, 1998.

with a guest, nothing in the world can make him betray the guest.'[2] Normally the stranger did not even need to touch the Bedouin's tent, all he needed to do was to stop near the tent, slowly adjust his camel's harness and his potential Bedouin host would be obliged by the code to come out, greet him and invite the stranger inside. The host would then be obliged to share with his guest or guests all that he had. However, such hospitality would normally last for only three days. After that a host's polite enquiry as to his guest's intended destination was the signal that the guest should leave. Abd al-Rahman and his party seem to have stayed with a number of tribes and families in this way during the first part of their journey away from Riyadh. But they were not always welcome. Many of the tribes in the eastern part of the al Aramah plateau and on the fringes of the more fertile al Hasa had not always been friendly towards the Sauds and the leading tribe in the province had long been allied with the Turks against them. Also any tribe or family that harboured the Sauds risked placing themselves in danger of the vengeance of the Rashids and their allies. So Abd al-Rahman turned south, leading his family towards the great empty Rub al Khali.

In the Rub al Khali Abd al-Rahman knew he had one certain ally, the ancient and noble Al Murra tribe. Each Bedouin tribe has what it claims as its own range or *dirah*, the territory across which it will drive its camels and livestock each year in search of food. The Al Murra described their *dirah* as all the north, central and eastern areas of the Rub al Khali, a huge area stretching for hundreds of miles across the whole breadth of southern-central and eastern Arabia. The Al Murra is a large tribe with six different sections, each with its own sheikh. They are famed as wild and proud, and for their exceptional loyalty to each other and to those whose salt they have eaten or with whom they have sealed a treaty or promise of fealty. Almost twenty years earlier Abd al-Rahman had gone raiding with them, attacking the Bani Khalid who ruled the Al Hasa region along the eastern Persian Gulf coast on behalf of the Turks. They had shared the rich booty they had taken together. So it was to the Al Murra that Abd al-Rahman now turned.

2 C. F. Volney *Voyages en Syrie et en Egypte pendant les Anneés 1783, 1784 et 1785* quoted by Vassiliev op. cit.

Having managed to find the Al Murra, who always grazed their camels around the Yabrin oasis after the winter rains had come, Abd al-Rahman was not disappointed. His old friends and allies were happy to take him and his family in. However, as further security and to save them from the worst rigours of Bedouin life, Abd al-Rahman made arrangements for his womenfolk to be given sanctuary on the island of Bahrain in the Persian Gulf, the island which, more than 4,000 years before, had been home to the capital of the mythical land of Dilmun, the 'pure' and 'pristine' kingdom where God was reputed to have settled Noah after the flood. The boy Abd al-Aziz, however, stayed with his father. So it was that the young Abd al-Aziz was at a crucial stage of his childhood separated from the love of his mother and aunt and raised among the Bedouin Al Murra during the years of his early adolescence. It was from the Al Murra that he would learn many of the skills and gain the remarkable strength and powers of endurance that were to play such a vital part in his later success as the leader and creator of a new kingdom. It was from his years living the way of life of the Bedouin Al Murra in and around the Rub al Khali that Abd al-Aziz would inherit many of the tastes and habits that were to remain with him through life. Abd al-Aziz was briefly to be sent to Bahrain for medical treatment for rheumatism (Bahrain having gained a reputation for its medical services largely due to the presence there of foreign Christian missionaries), but having achieved some relief he soon returned to his father and life among the Al Murra.

With the Al Murra Abd al-Aziz learned how to set up the Bedouin black camel-hair tent with its open side always facing away from the wind, its central tent poles each held in place with two taut ropes, its ends each stretched out by three ropes at each end and how to hang, join and peg down or bury in the sand two long lengths of cloth so as to close off the back and ends of the tent while leaving enough material with which to close the front at night. Where and how to hang the dividing curtain to separate the men's quarters from the women's and children's, the cooking and storage areas. How to gather the firewood and dead shrubs that can nearly always be found in the desert, uprooted from the sand and tossed about, driven hither and thither by the desert winds, sandstorms and sudden winter torrential downpours; where to pile the firewood and the dried camel dung that will heat the coffee, where to hang the water skins and stand the shallow leather water trough.

It was from the Al Murra that Abd al-Aziz learned how to survive and find fulfilment in the hard nomadic life of the desert. For most of the year the Bedouin's food will consist of little other than camels' milk and a few dates each day. His clothes will be just a thin cotton smock (*dishdasha*) replaced only when it has become so ragged and worn that it is more or less falling from his back, together with an almost equally threadbare cloak and head cloth (*kaffiyah*) secured by a head cord (*agal*). For the average Bedouin these would be all the clothes he had to protect him from the harsh sun in summer and even harsher icy winds and rains of the desert winter. The harshness of their lives has bred into the Bedouin an exceptional hardiness, stamina and ability to survive even the worst privations. However, no matter how bad conditions become the Bedouin is unlikely to actually starve. His family and tribe, together with the system of affording anyone three days' hospitality, would rarely allow this. To have a member of your family or tribe die from starvation would, unless everyone else was dying also, be a grave dishonour upon those who permitted it to happen.

A Bedouin's fortune was in his animals, his camels, sheep and perhaps a few mares. They could double themselves in three years. Most of the ram lambs and male camels were killed for food or sold, only a few being kept for breeding and carrying the tents and baggage. Mares were never sold, while young stallions, if not killed shortly after birth and used as food, were sold to town-dwellers. To the outsider it might seem that the Bedouin drifted aimlessly about the open spaces following their animals. But in fact they followed a more or less strict annual pattern governed by the seasons, though dependent to some extent on specific weather conditions, trekking and driving their livestock from one well, oasis or area to another within their range or *dirah* where it was known there was likely to be grazing. While the men were responsible for the animals and hunting any other food, such as game, that they might chance upon, it was the Bedouin's wife who kneaded and baked the dough, made the coffee and boiled any meat. The daughters and other relatives drew the water, washed the clothes, wove and spun.

A family's possessions consisted solely of their animals, a tent, a few clothes, any jewellery worn by the women, harness for the riding and pack camels or horses, a portable coffee and spice mill, a large cauldron, one or more other cooking pans, a few mats, rugs or blankets and the men's weapons, a sabre, dagger or curved *hunjar*, a spear and perhaps a musket or primitive rifle.[3] But the Bedouin's most important single possession was his camel. It gave him mobility, its milk provided his staple food, its hide and fur the material out of which to weave his tent and some of his clothes, fashion water skins and floor coverings and at the end of its life provided him with meat. As a result of his years with the Al Murra Abd al-Aziz developed an ability which would endure into his old age to stay in the saddle of his camel for hour after hour without ever seeming to tire.

From the Al Murra Abd al-Aziz learned too the Bedouin's special sense of pride, or *sharaf*, something valued almost more than life itself. Abuse a Bedouin, call him names or make fun of him in front of others and he will be ready to kill you. Next to his pride and of equal importance stood his family honour, above all the good name of his wife, sisters and womenfolk. A Bedouin will guard his family honour with his life. Any woman whose honour becomes stained is likely to be killed. Next to his immediate family comes the honour of the wider family and then of the tribe. Kill a member of a man's family and you are likely to trigger a blood feud which will usually only be ended by the killing of the perpetrator or a near relative. On the other hand make a friend of a Bedouin and he will be a friend for life. He is a wonderful and generous host and has a ready sense of humour, love and understanding of jokes, provided only that you do not make fun of him. It is perhaps a part and measure of his pride in his family that a member of the Al Murra when asked about his ancestry will often be able without hesitation to list for

3 The British army's first proper breach-loading service rifle, which had been introduced in 1871 and used extensively by them in the first Zulu War, had started to be phased out in 1889 and many of these unwanted rifles made their way to Arabia. Many of these old guns could still be seen being carried by Arab travellers and men guarding important buildings in the interior of Arabia in the 1970s. (See also *The Last Corner of Arabia* by Michael Darlow & Richard Fawkes, Namara Publications & Quartet Books, London, 1976.)

you the names of ancestors running back in the correct order for more than twenty generations, that is back into about the thirteenth century.[4]

Palgrave, who during his crossing of the Dahna desert fell in with some of the Al Murra and described them as being in most respects 'mere savages ... Their hair was elf-locks, their dress rags, their complexion grime, their look wildness personified', readily conceded that they were good natured and extremely eloquent. Being mainly illiterate, story telling and the recitation of poetry played an extremely important role in the lives of all Bedouin. It not only provided enjoyment and escape from their harsh lives, it was the means by which the history, myths and values of the tribe were passed down from one generation to the next. General Sir John Glubb, who spent much time with Bedouin between the 1920s and the 1950s tells us that their poems were not the 'uncouth rhymes of peasants, but were governed by ancient artistic conventions, employed an extensive and varied vocabulary, and were both stirring and musical in their rhythm and diction'. He observes that, like the Bedouin himself, his poetry was outspokenly frank and lacked subtlety. It consisted mostly of heroic ballads about war, generosity, hospitality and love, 'couched in magnificently sonorous language', recited by the poet with 'great spirit and feeling'. Glubb quotes from one, reputed to date back to a time close to the birth of Islam itself, in praise of a young Bedouin woman called Umayma. Although in translation the magnificence of the original Arabic is lost, the sentiment still shines through:

> She charmed me, veiling bashfully her face,
> Keeping with quiet looks an even pace;
> Some lost thing seemed to seek her downcast eyes:
> Aside she bends not – softly she replies.
> Ere dawn she carries forth her meal – a gift

4 In *Kuwait and her Neighbours* H. R. P. Dickson records meeting a young al Murra tribesman in 1943 who, when Dickson asked about his ancestry and the history of his tribe, without a moment's hesitation listed off the names of twenty-two of his ancestors in their correct order. Lieut-Colonel Dickson was for many years in the 1920s and 1930s the British government's Political Agent in Kuwait and the Gulf. He travelled widely among the Arabs and Bedouin of Saudi Arabia, Iraq and other parts of the Arab world.

To hungry wives in days of dearth and thrift.
No breath of blame up to her tent is borne,
While many a neighbour's is the house of scorn.
Her husband fears no gossip fraught with shame,
For pure and holy is Umayma's name.
Joy of heart, to her he need not say
When evening brings him home, 'Where passed the day?'
Slender and full in turn, of perfect height,
A very fay were she, if beauty might
Transform a child of earth into a fairy sprite.[5]

The Al Murra were blest with a great many magnificent natural poets and the young Abd al-Aziz, who had acquired a love of poetry at his mother's knee, must have spent many evenings sitting around a fire deep in the desert with his father and the other men listening in rapt attention as one the Al Murra's revered poets recited one of the many heroic and romantic ballads of the tribe's past.

The Al Murra were famed, even among and above other tribes, as exceptionally fine trackers. Whereas guiding and finding your way across hundreds of miles of open desert depended on a perfect knowledge of the ground and of the stars, and was said by the Bedouin, especially of the best guides who were able to find their way even without sight of the stars, to be a gift akin to a fifth sense that was born into a man, tracking was the product of an uncanny, almost animal ability to read and follow the tracks of a man or animal. From a human or animal's tracks, scent or droppings a good Al Murra tracker could discern the exact type and condition of the animal or human he was following, where it had come from and how long ago. He could tell not only what kind of animal it was, but whether it was a pack animal, ridden or unridden, whether a camel was white, black or brown, male or female, in calf or not. The Al Murra were reputed to be able to tell if a woman whose tracks they came across was married or single, pregnant

5 Glubb, Sir John Bagot, *War in the Desert: An RAF Frontier Campaign*, Hodder and Stoughton, London, 1960. The poem he quotes is taken from *A Literary History of the Arabs* by R. A. Nicholson.

or not. They could identify a man and distinguish from each other a father and his son, even though they had never seen either. Similarly, they could link a particular camel calf to its mother.

To have good trackers among your number was vital if a group was to achieve success as raiders. The raid, or *ghazzu*, was an essential element in desert survival. It was quite distinct from tribal war, had its own rules and etiquette, almost as defined and complex as the rules of medieval chivalry or the joust. The object of a raid was not slaughter, the conquest of territory, subjection of the other side or seizing of a well or pasture, it was booty, livestock, possessions, equipment, sometimes perhaps slaves. It was a way of securing sustenance and the raiding group's survival. A small group of raiders who had perhaps endured a long period of hunger, crept up undetected at night on the camp of another group or caravan of merchants, silently un-hobbled a few of their camels and drove them off into the desert darkness, and perhaps seized some of their goods. Success in doing this might make the difference for the raiding group between survival and starvation or submission to another tribe and the permanent dispersal of the entire group. Although some tribes might decline or even disappear for ever as a result of suffering a period of repeated successful raids against its property and livestock and other tribes might grow strong and powerful as a result of raiding, on the whole and over time raiding tended to even out the differences in wealth between Bedouin groups. Raiding tended to advantage the camel-breeding Bedouin, the true nomads, over the semi-nomadic groups, those engaged primarily in sheep breeding or those living in small permanent settlements around oases and springs. These groups would often seek protection from the most powerful nearby Bedouin tribes, paying them tribute in return for protection from raiding. The Al Murra, being primarily camel breeders and fine trackers, were particularly good raiders.

Raiding was considered to be a noble occupation, a proof of manhood. To take part in a successful raid was a way in which a boy could demonstrate that he was now a man. It was a rite of passage, something close to a ritual 'blooding'. For a young man to be invited to take part in a raid was an honour, a signal that the men of the group thought he was coming to maturity. For a young man to refuse to take part in a raid was a dishonour and likely to get him branded as a coward, undeserving of the respect of his family and other members of the tribe. A young man might not be permitted to marry until he had 'proved himself' by performing some feats of valour or demonstrated his skill in a raid. Abd al-Aziz undoubtedly took part in raids during his time with the Al Murra, riding out, possibly for days and nights on end with a small group of men, picking up and following the tracks of another group of Bedouin or a caravan of merchants. Then, having come up closer to them, hiding out among nearby sand dunes, in hollows or behind rocks through the night. Early the next day he and his companions would creep up closer, untie the rope hobbles from the legs of some of their target's camels or, mounted on their own swift riding camels, sweep down on the tents of the still-sleeping or just-waking merchants' caravan and snatch some of their possessions. Then they would swiftly ride off over the horizon, carrying the booty they had seized across their saddles and driving the stolen camels before them, disappearing into the shimmering desert and vanishing as suddenly as they had appeared.

If you were raided you might raid someone else in turn, to make good your losses. But it was important not to kill anyone during a raid, especially not one of the women of the people you were raiding. A death was likely to spark a blood feud and real war between tribes. Then both sides were likely to lose more as the result of the war than they could possibly have gained or lost from a raid. Whole extended families or even tribes could perish either in the fighting or as a result of starvation following defeat. Strings of tribes had been known to decline, been forced to submit to other tribes or even disappear as a result of their losses in men, livestock and grazing grounds in tribal wars. So shedding blood during a raid was to be avoided. It simply was not worth the risk. A whole system of unwritten rules and etiquette governing raiding had developed over the centuries. If a raider saw that he was in danger of being captured during a raid he did not shoot or cut down the person who was likely to capture him, nor did those being raided shoot or stab the raiders. Raiding, although a serious undertaking, was not viewed in the same way as war but was treated more as a noble sport. Having overpowered some raiders, the people being raided were quite likely to invite their prisoners to sit and eat with them. Later, rested, fed and watered, the raiders would be allowed to make their way back home to their own tribe on foot, supplied with enough water and food to survive the journey and a rifle, plus possibly a dagger or two with which to protect themselves. But their camels and all their other weapons remained with the tribe they had tried to raid.

The true Bedouin seemed always to be dreaming of raiding and the plunder they might win. Stories of successful raids, the skill and prowess of successful raiders, were regular topics of conversation around the camp fire. Poets extolled the skills and virtues of revered raiders.

Raids were led by the tribal shaikh or, if he was too old, by his military commander. Plunder was shared out between the raiders, the shaikh receiving a special share even if he had not taken part in the raid – recognition that the shaikh had particular responsibilities for the welfare of the whole tribal group.

Raiding, the rules, tactics and techniques employed, was probably little changed since the time of the Prophet Muhammad or earlier. The fearsome Arab armies who had swept across the Ottoman and eastern Roman Empires, terrifying much of southern Europe between the seventh and seventeenth centuries, had been largely built upon the skills and techniques learned and passed down through generations of Bedouin raiders. Even Gindibu and his thousand camel warriors, immortalised by the Assyrians when they fought alongside their armies in the ninth century BCE, had probably acquired many of their military skills in prehistoric *ghazzus* or as nomadic raiders. The Al Murra's methods of fighting very rarely varied. They would entice their enemy into some remote piece of desert wilderness and suddenly turn about and launch a ferocious attack. Those same skills, plus the art of tracking, learned and absorbed by Abd al-Aziz as a teenager among the Al Murra, would help him develop into the warrior and military leader he was to become. His familiarity with Bedouin warriors, their strengths, weaknesses, codes of conduct, skills, tactics and techniques, gave him invaluable insights into the Bedouin character which he would employ later in the process of nation building.

Abd al-Aziz's time among the Al Murra, one of the poorest Bedouin tribes, helped him to understand the ways in which a Bedouin leader, a shaikh, who did not have money and whose tribe lacked wealth could still exercise his authority and successfully lead a thriving, well-ordered tribal community. A shaikh did not inherit the post simply because his father had been the shaikh before him and he was the eldest son. The shaikhdom did, however, normally remain within one family. The power and prestige of that family remained of paramount importance no matter which individual member was the shaikh. The shaikh and other senior family members would use marriages as a way of maintaining the family's wealth and enhancing its power and prestige. Upon the death of a shaikh the senior members of the family, plus possibly other leading members of the tribe, would agree between themselves who within the family was best suited to the role of shaikh and was likely to carry the tribe with him. During his lifetime a ruling shaikh would usually nominate a member of his family, often an eldest son but not automatically, to be his successor. However, other members of the family did not always feel obliged to accept his nomination. While the system had the virtue that it reduced the likelihood of someone completely unsuited to the role becoming leader, its drawback was that disputes could easily occur over who was best qualified to be leader. A shaikh's sons could fall out, as Abd al-Rahman's elder brothers Abdullah, Saud and Muhammad had in the 1870s after the death of Faisal the Great, leading to the fatal weakening of the Saudi family, the disintegration of the whole Najdi state, the loss of Riyadh and their subjection by the Rashids.

The shaikh had to be more or less literally the father to his people. He must be open and available to all of his people all of the time, be willing to receive and entertain them to coffee and refreshment in his *majlis* (the word *majlis* has a particular and uniquely Arab meaning, referring both to a ruler or influential person's sitting room, place for receiving guests or council chamber and to the council itself), to hear their petitions and grievances and to settle disputes between them fairly and in a way that they would accept. It was not his role to act as judge in matters of criminal and religious law. That was the role of the *qadis* or judges, religious leaders and those learned in the Qur'an and other works of scripture and Islamic law, the *ulema, muftis* and *faqihs*. It was important that the shaikh was not perceived as stingy. There was a specific Bedouin expression for those who were stingy – *bakh'il*, which had particularly pejorative connotations. No man who was *bakh'il* was likely to make a successful shaikh. The shaikh would normally be expected to throw an occasional feast, no matter how hard times were, for his fellow tribesmen, many of whom would hardly, if ever, be able to afford to eat meat. A camel would be slaughtered for such occasions or to mark a wedding, the arrival of an important guest or for other major ceremonies. The highest honour a member of the Al Murra could bestow on someone was to kill a young camel and boil it in its mother's milk for them to feast upon. A shaikh would often give presents to the families of members of the tribe who had fallen on particularly hard times. The chief wife or senior lady in a shaikh's family would be expected to perform similar services for the wives and womenfolk of the tribe. All of these things helped to maintain the shaikh's prestige.

To be successful a shaikh had to demonstrate that he had the necessary courage for the role, the qualities, charisma and force of personality necessary to exercise leadership and carry opinion with him. He could not simply announce an important decision, such as determining to go to war with a neighbouring tribe. He had first to consult other members of his family, the tribal elders and other influential men. Once a decision had been reached, however, the shaikh's authority was expected to be absolute. The other quality essential was *hadh*, luck. As H. R. P. Dickson put it, a successful general will also be a lucky general – it is no use being courageous and skilful if you do not also have a due quotient of luck. It is that quality of luck, *hadh*, that the Bedouin required in their shaikhs. It was a quality needed in a Bedouin shaikh not only in time of war but in peace, in the harsh daily round of a desert nomad tribe's existence.[6]

Abd al-Aziz had an opportunity to observe the operation of all those qualities which together made for a successful leader from his earliest boyhood onwards. He had seen how their absence had led to disaster in his own family. Then, during his time among the Al Murra, he saw how their presence, even among a poor tribe living in some of the most forbidding and difficult terrain in all Arabia, led not only to the Al

6 See H. R. P. Dickson, *The Arab of the Desert: A Glimpse into Badawin Life in Kuwait and Sau'di Arabia*, George Allen & Unwin, London, 1951.

Murra's survival, but to the maintenance and enhancement of its reputation as one of the noblest, most ancient and revered of all the tribes.

Palgrave had rated the Ål Murra as little better than 'sheer infidels', a godless lot barely touched by Wahhabism except for an occasional 'mangled prayer'. In fact the influence of Islam had had far less impact on many of the Bedouin tribes, particularly those living in the most remote areas, than it had among the settled populations of the towns and major oases. In northern Arabia, near the northern edge of the Nafud Desert, Palgrave had fallen in with some cheerful Bedouin who had regaled him with splendid and bawdy stories of romance and adventure. When he had ventured to ask one of his hosts 'What will you do on coming into God's presence for judgement after so graceless a life?' the young warrior had unhesitatingly and cheerfully replied, 'What will we do? Why, we will go up to God and salute him, and if he proves hospitable (gives us meat and tobacco), we will stay with him; if other wise, we will mount our horses and ride off.' Such a response would have been unthinkable from a Wahhabi or Najdi youth.[7]

Around the world peoples living in the harshest conditions, such as the wilderness areas of Arabia, are especially reliant for their continued survival on particular features of the landscape, such as the continued flow of water from a particular spring in a huge tract of land in which there is no other water, on a continued reliable rotation of the seasons, so that the long fierce heat of the Arabian summer will be followed by at least a few short cooler weeks of Arabian winter and some rain. Such people will tend to be particularly reluctant to abandon their faith in gods with whom they are familiar, the gods of the things upon which they are so utterly dependent. Why give up your belief in the goddess of the spring upon which you and your tribe rely for survival if, by ceasing to worship her and make her offerings, you risk her withdrawing her support and the drying up of the spring? People leading such a precarious existence tend to have little time for the grand abstractions of the great monotheisms, particularly if, by abandoning their prayers to the gods of the weather, or reliance on the movement of the stars and moon, they may endanger their survival and that of their whole tribe.

7 Palgrave, op. cit.

Such people will cling to the gods and the belief systems they already know and trust. Even as recently as the 1970s belief in the *djinn*, the often malevolent spirit beings whose eyes, instead of lying horizontally within their faces open vertically, was widespread. Coming down with an illness was often attributed to the malevolent actions of a *djinn*. Whenever one of the frequent small swirling dust storms, looking like miniature tornadoes or water spouts of dust, grit and dead dry shrubs rose curling into the air and raced, danced and spiralled across the hard desert floor, Arabs living in remote areas would routinely attribute it to the action of the *djinn*: 'There goes the *Djinn*', they would say, pointing at the swirling, dancing column of dust. 'Watch out that you don't attract his attention!' Although often said in a half-joking tone, there was nevertheless still a discernible undertow of continuing, genuine apprehension. Long-held beliefs die hard, especially if you live with the ever-present possibility of extinction.

According to the origins myth of the Al Murra, still current among members of the tribe well into the twentieth century, the Al Murra were descended from a *djinniyah*, a female *djinn*. The story goes like this: Many hundreds of years ago, long before the days of Abraham or the coming of Islam, there was a famous warrior who lived in the south of Arabia called Ali ibn Murra. One spring his camels became ill with the dreaded camel disease *jarab* – camel mange – and began to die. Unable to bear the sight of his beloved camels dying any longer, he took himself sorrowfully away deep into the Rub Al Khali. There, deep in the desert, he came upon a beautiful girl being ferociously attacked by a great wolf. He rushed to her aid and killed the wolf. In gratitude the beautiful girl promised to grant Ali ibn Murra any favour he asked. Ali replied that all he wanted was to marry her. For that, the beautiful girl replied, I will first have to obtain the permission of my father and my family. And they live down in the earth in the kingdom of the *Djinn*. It was then that Ali understood that the beautiful young woman was a *djinniyah*.

Seeing that Ali was sunk in sorrow she asked what was troubling him and Ali told her about his camels. 'Come with me,' said the *djinn* girl, 'I will take you to my father. He will know how to cure your camels and at the same time you can ask him for my hand in marriage.'

Telling Ali to close his eyes, the girl placed her hands over them, made a sign and a great cavern opened before them. Taking his hand, she led Ali ibn Murra down into the underworld, the land of the *djinn*. They were now in a beautiful country with flowing water and green grass everywhere. When he looked at the girl Ali saw that she now had vertical eyes not the horizontal ones she had had before. But in all other ways she was still as beautiful as she had been before.

Taking Ali to her father, who was the shaikh of all the *djinn* of this region, she told him the whole story, how Ali had saved her from the wolf, how his camels were dying and that Ali wished to marry her. The girl's father and her whole family were so grateful to Ali for saving their princess that they readily gave their consent, but on one condition: that he would never again say 'B'ism Illah' ('In the name of God'), but instead 'B'ism al Jin'un' ('In the name of the *Djinns*'). They warned Ali that if he failed to keep this promise a terrible thing would happen. Ali was deeply in love with the *djinn* princess and he readily agreed to her father's demand. They were married and after seven days of feasting and rejoicing the happy couple returned to the human world.

As they came out of the great cavern all of Ali's camels were waiting for them. All were restored to health. Turning to his wife Ali saw that her eyes were once again as they had been when he first saw her and she was as other human women, except that she was more beautiful than any other woman in the world. For seven years they prospered and Ali's *djinn* wife bore him a beautiful daughter. They lived as other Bedouin lived, in a black tent, moving with the camels according to the season from one patch of pasture and one well or spring to another. Then one day Ali had to go on a long journey. He was away for many days. Returning to his tent unseen by his wife, weary from his long journey, he pulled back the curtain dividing her part of the tent from the rest. There before him he saw his wife sitting with her back to him combing and cleaning her hair. But imagine his astonishment and horror as realised that she was holding the complete scalp in her lap and that her head was totally bald! Even after seven years marriage Ali did not yet he realise that this was common practice among the *djinn* and the normal way in which they combed and tended their hair. In his astonishment and horror Ali let out a cry 'B'ism Illah!'

Immediately there was a great clap of thunder and a flash. A gaping hole opened in the ground and Ali's wife, his tent and all his possessions disappeared into it, leaving just a huge cloud of smoke and dust. Hurling himself violently backwards Ali managed to save himself and rushed immediately to his daughter, grasping her and holding her tightly in his arms with all his strength.

The girl, saved by her father, grew up, married and had many children, becoming the ancestress of all the great Al Murra tribe which came to number many thousand souls.[8]

In Abd al-Aziz's time the Al Murra still clung to their share of old, pre-Islamic and pre-Wahhabi beliefs, the myth of their origin among them. For years to come the Al Murra were to boast that they inherited their great skill as trackers from the *djinn* and the spirits who live under the earth. Although he was to remain a devout and committed Wahhabi throughout his life, Abd al-Aziz perhaps learned during his time among the Al Murra that it might not always be necessary or expedient to require absolute submission to all the narrowest interpretations and injunctions of the strict Wahhabi code.

Abd al Aziz found a freedom among the Bedouin that might forever have remained unknown to him had he remained at home in Riyadh and among his family. Gerald de Gaury, the British army officer and explorer who travelled extensively in Arabia in the 1930s, records how whereas among the oasis dwellers of the Najd women were always strictly supervised by their menfolk, Bedouin women were often to be seen riding with their tribes on camel back unveiled and even to sing and take part in tribal dancing. He tells his readers of how the Bedouin women valued their independence and refused to surrender it, re-telling the story of one of the great-granddaughters of the Prophet Muhammad who was noted for her great wit, and beauty. When taken to task by her husband for never veiling herself, she replied that as God had blessed her with 'the stamp of beauty' she would under no circumstances veil herself so that

8 This myth is recounted in H. R. P Dickson's *Kuwait and her Neighbours*, George Allen & Unwin, London, 1956, in his section on the Al Murra, just one in his wonderful collection of stories, observations and accounts of Arab and tribal life in Kuwait, Iraq and Saudi Arabia between the 1920s and the 1950s.

the public should be able to 'view that beauty and thereby recognise God's grace unto them'.[9]

To understand what quality it was above all that the boy Abd al-Aziz took from his time among the Al Murra, one can do no better than repeat the words of the great Arabist and traveller, Wilfred Thesiger, who travelled extensively with the Bedouin in southern Arabia and the Rub Al Khali in the 1940s and 1950s. 'For untold centuries the Bedu lived in the desert; they lived there from choice ... All of them would have scorned [an] easier life of lesser men. Valuing freedom above all else, they took a fierce pride in the very hardship of their lives, forcing unwilling recognition of their superiority on the townsmen and villagers who feared, hated and affected to despise them. Even today there is no Arab, however sophisticated, who would not proudly claim Bedu lineage. I shall always remember how often I was humbled by my illiterate companions, who possessed in so much greater measure generosity, courage, endurance, patience, good temper and light-hearted gallantry. Among no other people have I felt the same sense of personal inferiority.'[10] For years to come Abd al-Aziz would return to the desert to relax and re-charge his batteries as well as to fight and win his kingdom; to ride for hours on end, to hunt and track, to sit around the camp fire, tell and listen to great stories of romance and adventure, to hear the tribal poets recite, to roll up in his blanket and sleep on the hard desert floor under the stars. For the rest of his life he would look back on his years in the desert with the Al Murra as the happiest years of his life.

Early in 1894, after he and his eldest son had been living with the Al Murra for getting on for three years, Abd al-Rahman received word that he and his whole family could now settle in Kuwait. Ever since they had been driven from Riyadh Abd al-Rahman had been seeking somewhere where he and his whole family could settle and live together, but nowhere had been prepared to take them. The rulers of all of the other small kingdoms and shaikhdoms in the region had been afraid of giving

9 de Gaury, Gerald, *Arabian Journey and other Desert Travels*, George G. Harrap, London 1950.

10 Thesiger, Wilfred, *Desert, Marsh and Mountain: The World of a Nomad*, William Collins, London, 1979

asylum to the Al Sauds for fear of angering either the mighty Rashids or the Turks, still the nominal rulers of the entire region. However, by 1894 the Turks were becoming worried that the Rashids were becoming too powerful and were starting to pose a threat to their dominance in the area. In order to maintain their power in the region the Turks had developed a strategy of playing one powerful tribe off against another, thus keeping all of them in a state of tension and potential conflict and ensuring that no one tribe or shaikhdom would achieve overwhelming strength. Turkey decided that it was now in their interest to give the Sauds a little support and encouragement in the hope that in this way they might distract the Rashids from pursuing conquests elsewhere. So they indicated to Shaikh Muhammad, the ruler of Kuwait, that they would have no objection if he allowed Abd al-Rahman and his family to settle in Kuwait.

Abd al-Rahman made arrangements to have his wives and other women-folk brought from Bahrain and together the family set up home in a small, single-storeyed house, with three rooms and a flat roof, built of sun-baked clay bricks around an open courtyard. It stood on a narrow, twisting street, little more than an alleyway, running down to the harbour and the foreshore. There the shipwrights built and repaired the traditional dhows of the Gulf, sail-makers plied their trade and pearl fishermen and trawler men hauled up their boats onto the shore to unload their catches and mend their nets. Kuwait, then as now, was for much of the year humid, stiflingly hot and debilitating. In those days it was still totally without sanitation of any kind. The town stank and was plagued by flies. The water closet, although it had been ubiquitous in the Indus Valley civilisation more than four thousand years earlier and common throughout the Roman Empire, remained unknown in 1890s Kuwait. The town's citizens simply defecated along the ample seafront and relied upon the tides to flush away their faeces. Although the wealthy had the use of modesty-preserving rickety wooden shacks perched on spindly legs above the water, the mass of the town's citizens had no alternative but to squat at the water's edge in full view. Huge rats were to be found in all the houses. Disease haunted the town's crooked streets, festering back-alleys and crumbling courtyards. There was no fresh water in Kuwait and its entire supply had to be shipped in from further up the river Euphrates. The water was then sold to the citizens for a few pence a gallon to be carried away to their homes in old tins.

In winter the town could become extremely cold. High winds would whip up fierce storms out in the bay, driving high waves in to break over the harbour wall. Winter would also give rise to sudden torrential downpours. When a particularly sharp downpour occurred water would sweep down straight through the mud-built houses near to the shore and on into the sea. Because the walls and ceilings of the houses were built of no more than sun-baked mud and poles of mangrove wood, shipped in from Africa, the walls could then soften so much that large parts of a house and its ceiling might collapse, burying its inhabitants and seriously damaging their few simple possessions. Barely a winter passed without one or more houses being damaged or totally destroyed in this way.

Yet Kuwait in the 1890s was a lively place, full of strange tongues, clashing colours, alien foods and unfamiliar noises, a bustling seaport, the Marseilles of the Persian Gulf. Even at night the town still seemed alive with the sounds of animals braying and coughing in the courtyards and from the small hours onwards the cockerels crowing and answering each other around the different quarters of the town. At the hottest time of year the sailors and longshoremen would often carry out the heaviest work at night so as to avoid having to do it during the heat of the day. Then the night air would be filled with the sound of their rhythmical songs as they dragged the heavy boats up onto the shore or stepped a mast. As dawn approached the noise would slowly ebb away until all was silent again, save for the occasional grunt of the animals. Then with the first hint of dawn the cocks would start to crow and with dawn itself the old muezzin's voice would float upwards and out across the town from the minaret of the old mosque near the harbour, rising and falling in the ancient call to prayer, ebbing away into the distance across the bay before finally becoming lost among the furthest inlets and sand dunes of the treeless shore. Now, for a few short minutes everyone and everything, even the animals and the seabirds, seemed to fall still and silent. But all too soon that holy silence would be gone as the movement and noise of the day proper began, creeping back first around the harbour and building until once again it engulfed the whole small, teeming, stifling town.

After the rarefied life of the palace in Riyadh, with its slaves, servants and deference, and afterwards the open spaces, clear, dry air, black tents, hunting, tracking, self-reliance and continuous closeness to the camels of his early adolescence in the desert with the Al Murra, the sweat, stench, bustle and continuous noise of Kuwait, the best natural harbour and largest seaport in all Arabia, came as a complete shock to Abd Al-Aziz.

Crammed together into their bare, tiny, dilapidated house near the foreshore, Abd al-Rahman and his family were now poor. Abd al-Rahman had been promised a small pension by the Turkish authorities, but it was rarely paid and they had to eke out their existence as best they could. With the Al Murra the fact that they were poor had not mattered, their hosts were poor also. A Bedouin did not think of himself as poor, he took pride in his existence and would not have chosen to have it any other way. But in the town everything was different. The communal life, collective endeavour and spirit of mutual support of Bedouin life were absent. Instead, even in a town as small and poor as the Kuwait of the 1890s, there was already much of the acquisitiveness and envy with which we, in our modern urbanised and Westernised societies, are all too familiar.

Kuwait was completely unlike anywhere else that Abd al-Aziz had ever known. Now almost fifteen, apart from his brief visit to Bahrain for medical treatment, he had never seen the sea, sea birds or ships, let alone all the other sights, sounds and smells of a bustling seaport. With its position at the head of the Persian Gulf, close to the mouth of the great Euphrates and Tigris rivers and the vital trade routes linking India and the East with the interior of Arabia, Syria, Persia, the rest of Mesopotamia and beyond with Turkey, the Black Sea, Russia and Europe, Kuwait remained the busiest and most important port in the entire Arabian peninsula. Although the opening of the Suez Canal in 1869 had provided Europeans with an alternative link with India, Australia and the Far East, Kuwait and the Persian Gulf still remained of vital strategic importance to the European imperial powers and the mercantile interests of most of the developed world.

Unused to encountering foreigners of any kind, in Kuwait Abd al-Aziz found himself jostling in the bazaars with sailors from China, Malaya, all over the East Indies, hanging about the port-side cafés listening to the strange tongues and alien conversation of skippers and traders, eavesdropping on bargaining between merchants from Aleppo and Bombay, Muscat and Damascus, of Armenians, Turks, Jews, Russians, Englishmen, Greeks, Frenchmen, Germans and Arabs from North Africa and deep inside the heart of Arabia. Merchant ships, now increasingly powered by coal and steam, berthed or set sail from here for ports around the Gulf, the coasts of southern Arabia, East Africa, Europe, India, Australia, the Far East and even sometimes the Americas. Abd al-Aziz began to see the reality of there being a wider world beyond Arabia. Here in Kuwait, that world was not just something you heard rumour of in stories, it was here and real, and now.

Now a young teenager, Abd al-Aziz, like many of his mother's family, had grown unusually tall for his age. But he had not yet filled out and become the strong adult he would be later. As a result he became the butt of other boys' jokes. They called him a freak and poked fun at him for being so tall and thin. Nevertheless, weather-beaten and toughened from his years in the desert, he hung about around the harbour, loafed in the cafés and got into minor scrapes with the other youths of the town. Yet he never forgot the goal inculcated into him by his father and aunt that one day he and his family must return to Riyadh, seize back Najd from the Rashids and build a new and even more powerful and respected Saudi shaikhdom than the one they had ruled before. Poor and feeling out of place, Abd al-Aziz would sometimes brag to his companions about what he planned to do, how one day he would seize Riyadh. But they would greet his boasts with mockery. Who was this boy, this tall, reedy freak from out of the desert with grandiloquent ideas but no money or strength? No one.

Kuwait embraced all the vices of any great seaport. Muslim it might be, but a sailor ashore from a long voyage could still readily find a harlot, boy or girl, or a brothel, gambling den or an opium house. Abd al-Aziz would grow into an extremely virile young man and was to enjoy sex and the company of women all his life. Whether he had his first sexual encounters as a youth in Kuwait we do not know – official accounts always firmly deny it – but we do know that one of those who befriended him early in his time in Kuwait was Mubarak, the half-brother of the Shaikh of Kuwait.

Mubarak was in his fifties when he first encountered young Abd al-Aziz. As the brother of the Shaikh, he was a well-known and well-liked figure about the town. Unlike his austere and skin-flint brother, Mubarak was generous and open-hearted. He was also licentious and something of a rogue. In his youth he had quarrelled with his brother and gone to live in Bombay. There he had wasted his inheritance in gambling, whoring and loose living. He was even reputed to have sold off his mother's jewels to pay off his debts. He had only recently returned home to Kuwait. Penniless, like the Sauds, he was now on the look-out for ways in which he might seize his brother's throne.

We do not know why Mubarak chose to befriend Abd al-Aziz. Young, willowy and something of an outsider though he was, something about Abd al-Aziz aroused Mubarak's interest. There was also probably some element of fellow-feeling. Abd al-Aziz was, like himself, the son of a ruling family who was currently down on his luck. Another consideration may have been that Mubarak calculated that in befriending Abd al-Rahman's eldest son and heir he might also serve his own wider purpose of replacing his brother as the ruler of Kuwait. Mubarak was said by one observer to have the calculating eyes, cunning, manipulative skills and ambition of a Richelieu. It would not have escaped him that, by sanctioning Abd al-Rahman's presence in Kuwait, the Turks were indicating that they had decided to give their backing to the Sauds in local inter-tribal power struggles – and the Turks were not only still the dominant imperial land power in the region, Kuwait was still part of the Turkish Ottoman Empire.

Because of its commanding strategic position at the head of the Persian Gulf, Kuwait had in recent years become a major focus of imperial power rivalries. The Ottoman Turks, who for centuries had liked to think of themselves as the dominant imperial power in the region, had recently begun to be seriously challenged by the other major nineteenth-century imperial powers, Britain, France and Russia. Weakened by rebellion and independence movements in the Balkans, the Ottoman Empire had become fearful of being dismembered and overthrown. In the previous twenty years the Ottomans had been defeated in war by the Russians, lost Bosnia, Bulgaria, Herzogovina, Montenegro and Serbia and since 1889 the Sultan had been facing calls for modernisation and reform from officers in his own imperial army and navy, 'The Committee of Union and Progress', the Young Turks. At the same time the rising imperial power in Europe, Germany, which by the end of the nineteenth century was probably the most productive and dynamic industrial economy in the world,[11] had started to look for ways of increasing its influence in Mesopotamia and the Arabian Peninsula. It had decided that the most effective way of achieving this was through an alliance with the Ottoman Empire.

In 1890 Bismarck, the 'Iron Chancellor', statesman and strategist who had ruled Prussia and Germany for more than thirty years, who had engineered Prussia's victorious 1870–1 war against France and masterminded the creation of the unified German nation-state, had been removed by the vainglorious, bombastically militaristic Kaiser, Wilhelm II. Wilhelm now wanted his own German overseas empire with which he could match the empires of Britain and France. He wanted this not simply as an outlet for Germany's massively increased industrial production but to satisfy his own vanity and lust for glory. To this end he initiated what he called his *Drang nach Osten* – pressure or intense desire towards the East. The centrepiece of this was to be a Berlin-to-Baghdad railway, with Kuwait as its intended eastern terminus. Along its route German schools were to be opened and German industrialists awarded concessions to exploit each region's mineral resources.

At the same time the Russians, who had fought the latest in a long series of wars against the Turks in the 1870s, had for generations sought an outlet into the Indian Ocean and entertained ambitions towards Persia. They also had a historic concern for the Eastern Orthodox Church and its holy places in Palestine and for the maintenance of their maritime southern door into the Mediterranean from the Crimea through the Black Sea and the Bosphorus. The Russians also were now actively involved in exploring the idea of a rail link with a western terminus on the eastern shore of the Mediterranean, probably at Tripoli,

11 America's economy was bigger in sheer size but had probably not yet achieved the full-scale transition from rural and agrarian economy to centrally organised manufacture and industrialism that had taken place in Germany during the latter third of the nineteenth century.

north of Beirut in Syria, and with its eastern terminus in Kuwait. If it could be built it would free them from having to use the British-controlled Suez Canal and might at last open their door to the Indian Ocean and beyond. The Tsarist Russian government also started a heavily subsidised shipping line to ply between the Crimea and Kuwait and in 1895 sent a survey vessel to the Straits of Hormuz, the narrow channel linking the Persian Gulf to the Indian Ocean.

The French, who had never really recovered from the humiliation of their defeat in the Franco-Prussian War of 1870–1, were also involved in the scramble for Empire. They were acquiring colonies all over the Far East, in Indo-China and Polynesia, and throughout Africa. In 1881 Tunisia became a French Protectorate alongside their existing territory in Algeria. They also acquired extensive colonial possessions in Central and West Africa. In East Africa they acquired French Somaliland and the major strategic port of Dijouti at the mouth of the Red Sea, and also Madagascar in the Indian Ocean. By the 1890s they had started to try to lure the Sultan of Muscat away from British protection with offers of lucrative trade deals.

Britain, however, the greatest imperial power of all, already had extensive interests in the region and was determined to see that its position was not undermined. Its warships regularly patrolled the Gulf, British-Indian merchant vessels dominated Gulf mercantile trade and a British steamship company, the Lynch Company, owned the concession for steam navigation on the Euphrates and Tigris rivers. The British government in India had established a series of protective 'trucial' agreements with shaikhdoms along each side of the Persian Gulf and around the southern Arabian coast which forbade their rulers from entering into any treaty with any other power without first obtaining permission from Britain. Britain controlled the Suez Canal and Egypt, held Cyprus and was preparing to take the Sudan. Britain operated a mail service between Iraq and India, and British-constructed telegraph lines linked India, Tehran, Baghdad and Istanbul. In recent decades British policy had aimed to maintain a balance of power between all of the major powers while leaving herself in a position to offer her support wherever she chose, thus altering the balance of power in her own favour and protecting her own position and interests. In pursuance of this policy Britain had in recent decades been content to leave the weakened Ottoman Empire – derided in much of the European press as 'the sick man of Europe' – to control events in the region. It was in Turkey's interests, as it was in Britain's, to ensure that no one shaikh or other local ruler gained too much power in the region or got into a position to threaten their interests. At the same time, although Turkey had been concerned about the extent of British power in the region it had been in no position to do anything about it. The British Navy remained invincible and while things remained as they were Britain had no interest in hastening the demise of the Ottoman Empire. However, in 1885 things changed.

In December 1885 the Turkish governor of Basra had informed the British that the Ottoman government intended to build a large fort at a place called Fao, a strategic point close to the confluence of the Tigris, Euphrates and Karun rivers and only a little inland from the head of the Gulf. The British protested and dispatched extra warships to patrol the Gulf. The Ottoman government responded that they were entitled to do as they liked in their own territory and intended to push ahead. Matters escalated, culminating in an incident in March 1890 when a party of British troops which had been landed at Fao from a British warship were fired on by Ottoman troops. Luckily no one was injured.

The dispute rumbled on for the rest of the decade. There was also a series of running disputes over the status of other petty shaikhdoms and ports along the Arabian Gulf coast between Kuwait and Bahrain. Further south still the Ottomans issued further challenges to Britain by stationing garrisons in their ports at Udayd and Doha. Yet more gunboats were sent to the Gulf by both sides. But both Britain and the Sultan continued to take care not to let matters escalate into open warfare. These disputes, together with evidence of the Ottoman Empire's growing closeness to Germany and plans for the Berlin to Baghdad and Kuwait railway, alarmed the British. From now on Britain, which had treated Turkey as an ally ever since the Crimean War of 1853–6, started to regard the Ottoman Empire as a potential enemy and to look for other allies in the region through whom to protect her interests.

In 1895, at about the time when Mubarak first started to befriend young Abd al-Aziz, he would have been keenly aware of the complex imperial power-plays taking place in the region. In taking the young man under his wing, inviting him to sit in on his discussions with his friends, supporters and contacts from overseas, he would have started to open his young protégé's eyes to the realities of international relations, the winning and holding of power. It seems probable that Mubarak also arranged for Abd al-Aziz to be given lessons in history, geography, English and mathematics, so broadening his education beyond the narrow study of the Qur'an, Islamic law and theology that he had so far received under the guidance of his strict Wahhabi father. Mubarak no doubt also opened the young man's eyes to other less weighty but more enjoyable matters.

Abd al-Rahman became concerned at the amount of time that his son was spending in Mubarak's company. To Abd al-Rahman's mind Mubarak was far too interested in the company of sinful women, fine silk clothes, the comforts of the flesh and the smoking of tobacco. To counter this dangerous influence his father arranged for a respected religious scholar to be brought to Kuwait from central Arabia to continue Abd al-Aziz's religious education and ensure that he continued in his strict Wahhabi faith. At around this time also his father arranged for Abd al-Aziz to be married for the first time. Unfortunately there seems to be no record of the girl's name nor even of what tribe she came from.[12] Sadly, about six months after their wedding, the young woman contracted one of the many diseases that were rife in Kuwait and died.

By May 1896 Mubarak was ready to act. One night he, a cousin and a trusted servant stole into his half-brother the Shaikh's palace at night, murdered him and another brother and declared himself ruler of Kuwait. Before carrying out his bloody coup, Mubarak had probably received secret assurances from the British that they would not intervene.[13] The murdered Shaikh's sons and other relatives fled to Basra and petitioned the Ottoman Sultan to depose Mubarak and punish him. But at the same time as the Shaikh's sons petitioned the Sultan so did Mubarak. He petitioned for recognition as Shaikh and governor of Kuwait but still

12 Philby tells us in *Arabian Jubilee* (Robert Hale, London, 1952) that the young woman's name was Bint al Fiqri, but more recent historians have tended to discount this evidence as to her name.

13 See Görkan Çetinsaya, 'Ottoman-British Relations in Iraq and the Gulf, 1890–1908', *Turkish Review of Middle East Studies*, 2004 – 15.

within the jurisdiction of the Ottoman Empire. As a gesture of loyalty he flew the Ottoman flag over Kuwait harbour. But to Mubarak's chagrin, for more than eighteen months the Sultan remained silent.

The murdered Shaikh had not been popular. He had taxed the town heavily but spent nothing on it or its people. As a result its inhabitants were delighted when he was replaced by his more generous, open-handed half-brother, Mubarak.

With Mubarak now the ruler of Kuwait it became more difficult for Abd al-Rahman to raise objections to his son spending time in his company. If Abd al-Rahman was ever to realise his ambition of throwing The Rashid out of Riyadh and winning back his shaikhdom, he was going to need Mubarak's support. So he dare not risk offending him. At the same time, perhaps to spare his father's feelings or to hide from him just how much time he was now spending with Mubarak, Abd al-Aziz did not always tell his father where he was going when he left the house.

From the moment he became ruler, Mubarak took Abd al-Aziz even more firmly under his wing, inviting him to sit in on his audiences, conferences and discussions with close advisers and confidants, explaining what he was doing and the reasoning behind it. In Mubarak's company 'he met foreigners of all sorts, traders, merchants, travellers, representatives of the French, English, Russian and German governments. He would see how Mubarak handled them and how the problems of the outside world affected him ... At audiences and conferences he would sit in a corner, his feet curled up under him, his brown Arab cloak drawn round him, playing steadily with the amber beads of a prayer chain, but watching always, alert, absorbing all that happened, learning always.'[14] Mubarak's long-term aim was his own and his tiny shaikhdom's total independence. In pursuing this goal he proved a master in the art of statecraft for a small power. He turned to maximum advantage the natural benefits enjoyed by Kuwait on account of its large, protected natural harbour, strategic position at the head of the Gulf, mouth of the great rivers of Mesopotamia and start point for the great trade routes

14 H. C. Armstrong, *Lord of Arabia: An Intimate Study of a King*, Penguin Books, Harmondsworth, Middlesex, 1938. Armstrong's description is based on the accounts of eyewitnesses he met in Riyadh and Kuwait in the 1920s.

into Arabia, the Mesopotamian hinterland and across to the shores of the Mediterranean. He was a wily politician, skilfully playing off one great power against another to the benefit of his own small state, offering friendship to each but never quite committing himself absolutely to any of them. Abd al-Aziz could not have had a finer instructor in the art of statecraft than Mubarak. He treated the young man almost as a son, sometimes actually allowing him to act as his secretary. Abd al-Aziz was to retain a deep respect for Mubarak for the rest of his life, always addressing him in letters as 'our respected father'.

Abd al-Aziz witnessed how, as soon as he had seized the throne Mubarak signalled his loyalty to the Ottoman Empire and petitioned the Sultan to be appointed governor of Kuwait under Ottoman jurisdiction, yet only a few months later and before he had received any reply from Istanbul, had also started to put out secret feelers towards the British. Like the Turks, the British also took a long time to respond. But unlike the Sultan, who chose to wait to see how events would unfold locally, the British inaction was the result of an internal dispute between officials in the Foreign Office in London and officials of the British government in India. Throughout the 1890s British policy in Arabia was bedevilled by the division of authority over policy in the region between London and India. It was as if an invisible line, drawn across the central courtyard of the Foreign Office building in Whitehall, matched by a similar invisible line drawn from north to south down the middle of the Arabian Peninsula, divided the realm of the Foreign Secretary on one side of the building from the realm of the Viceroy of India on the other and that never the twain should cross. As a result communications from British representatives on the eastern side of Arabia had to go first to the British government in India who might then either act directly themselves or, if they thought the issue warranted it, send the communication on to the India Office, lodged on one side of the building in London, for a decision. Similarly, a British representative dealing with an issue in the western side of Arabia would report not to India but direct to the Foreign Office, lodged on the opposite side of the same building in London. The result was endless delays, internal disputes over areas of responsibility and, all too often, bad, ill-informed or perverse decisions.

When Mubarak sent his message, via the British consul in Basra, indicating that he would welcome 'some sort of protective relationship' with Britain, his request went first from Basra to India and later to London. A long-drawn-out debate then began between Foreign Office officials in London and officials of the British government of India, with officials in London advising against any involvement with Mubarak while Indian officials advised in favour of it. A year passed with still no response. Then, in July 1897, rumours reached Kuwait that an Ottoman-backed military expedition was about to be mounted against Kuwait from Basra. Mubarak now repeated his request for a protective relationship and asked for an urgent meeting with a British representative. Two months later a British official did finally turn up in the Bay of Kuwait aboard a British vessel and sent a message ashore saying that he was authorised to explore Mubarak's request further. However, Mubarak remained on his guard. He did not want to risk causing the Ottomans any more offence than was necessary to achieve his own ends. He therefore refused to meet the British representative on board a British ship. As a result the British official had to be rowed ashore and the discussions with Mubarak were held there. Mubarak told his British visitor that he wanted to be taken under the same kind of British protection as the Shaikh of Bahrain and other small coastal shaikhdoms along the southern end of the Arabian side of the Gulf. The British official then told him that he would have to 'take instructions' and left without giving Mubarak any answer. Yet more deliberations then ensued between India and London until finally, a month later, the British government, not wanting to get drawn any further into the affairs of the Gulf than was necessary for the protection of their own interests, sent Mubarak a formal rejection of his plea.

Just weeks after this, fresh and more reliable reports reached Kuwait of an Ottoman-backed military expedition being launched from Basra upon Kuwait. This time as soon as the British Political Resident in the Gulf got to hear about it he telegraphed India, who telegraphed London, which this time instead of deliberating for weeks on end immediately authorised the sending of a gunboat. Days later a British warship steamed out of the Gulf haze into Kuwait Bay with orders to 'observe' and just weeks after that the Ottoman-Basran military expedition was called off. In December 1897, by which time it had become clear that no one except the murdered Shaikh's immediate family was going to actively intervene to remove Mubarak, the Sultan finally responded to Mubarak's original request, recognising him as both Shaikh and Governor of Kuwait, but in terms which served to further underline Mubarak's subservience to the Ottoman Empire.

From his privileged position as Mubarak's confidant, Abd al-Aziz witnessed at close quarters the way in which this whole great power minuet was played out. He saw how Mubarak played one great power off against the other and how the deployment of just one British gunboat had transformed the whole situation. For the first time he not only saw a British warship, he witnessed how just the threat of a modern industrial country's arms could deter not only an experienced local military leader like the ruler of Basra, but the mighty Ottoman Empire itself.

Abd al-Aziz gained further insights during his time in Kuwait from being able to watch at close quarters as Mubarak deliberately played off, all the time to his small statelet's advantage, the other great imperial powers, Germany, France and Russia, both against each other and against the British and Turks, as they competed for railway rights, trading concessions and privileged access to Kuwait and its harbour. All these were lessons which Abd al-Aziz was never to forget, with the result that he became equipped, as no other Saudi leader ever before, as the potential leader of his people.

At the same time as the British-Ottoman game of threat, bluff and counter-threat was being played out over control of Kuwait an event had occurred in Ha'il which would give Mubarak an opportunity to draw Abd al-Aziz and his father more directly into the realisation of his long-term aim of complete independence for Kuwait. The Rashid, who had driven the Sauds out of Riyadh, died. He was succeeded by his young nephew, Abd al-Aziz ibn Rashid, who was known to be a brave warrior, but inexperienced. Ha'il's new ruler took great pleasure in desert raiding and hunting, but had little time or patience for the slow, painstaking skills of diplomacy and compromise needed in a successful ruler. Where his uncle had been likened to the evil Richard the Third, he was soon seen as more like the courageous but foolhardy Richard the Lionheart.

As soon as news of the Rashid's death reached Kuwait Abd al-Rahman and his son became fired with a new determination and impatience to re-capture Riyadh and take back what they regarded as their birthright. Abd al-Aziz was now seventeen years old. He was no longer simply unusually tall. He had filled out and become both strong and broad shouldered. He was now more eager than ever to prove himself and the best way to do that was in battle. But still without money, the Sauds remained dependent on the support of Mubarak if they were to have any hope of realising their dream.

The Rashids were loyal allies of the Ottomans. With Ottoman support they now controlled all of central Arabia and had recently started to threaten Kuwait itself. So any action that was likely to weaken the Rashids was likely to improve Kuwait's security and serve Mubarak's own long-term ambitions. However, he was too wise to launch any sort of attack on them or to encourage the Sauds to do so on his behalf before they had a reasonable chance of success and before he had secured the support of one of the great powers to protect Kuwait from possible retaliation by the Ottomans. So throughout 1898 Mubarak and the Sauds had no alternative but to hold back.

However, by early 1899 things had begun to change. Discontent with Rashid rule had begun to grow among the tribes of central Arabia and the British, alarmed by increasing evidence of German and Russian designs on Kuwait and the ever growing closeness between Germany and the Ottoman Empire, decided that the time had come to shore up their own position in the area by offering Kuwait protection. The need for an agreement between Britain and Kuwait was lent further urgency when a major raid, backed by the Ottomans, was launched by the Rashids on tribes close to Kuwait itself. Urged on by the new British Viceroy of India, Lord Curzon, a secret agreement was quickly reached under which the British promised to protect Kuwait against attack by the Ottomans or anyone else and in return Mubarak agreed to have no dealings with any foreign power and not to cede any of his territory to anyone without first obtaining the agreement of the British.

However word of the agreement soon reached Istanbul. The Sultan responded by strengthening his naval flotilla stationed at Basra, ordering new improved telegraph links with his other outposts in the Gulf and instituting a clamp-down on the smuggling of arms into the interior of Arabia – smuggling which he suspected was being sponsored by the British. Later in the year the Ottomans re-asserted their authority over Kuwait by appointing a new Harbour Master. Mubarak, however, responded by refusing to allow the new Harbour Master to take up his post, ordering him out and forcing him to return to Basra. Before the Sultan could respond the British sent a warship to Kuwait, supported by a stiff note to the government in Istanbul saying that Britain did not recognise the Ottoman Empire's right to appoint such an official. After a further exchange of notes the Sultan decided to change tack, promoting Mubarak to the title of Pasha with an official salary paid in dates and presenting him with gold and silver Turkish Imperial medals.

Once again, Abd al-Aziz enjoyed a ringside seat and saw how, by skilfully playing both sides, Mubarak had been able to gain advantages and concessions for himself from both the British and Ottoman empires. Also in 1899, word reached Kuwait of the death of Abd al-Rahman's brother, Muhammad. Muhammad had remained behind in Riyadh after the rest of the Saud family had fled and had been appointed by the Rashids as nominal ruler of the town. Now the strong suspicion was that he had been murdered by the Rashids.

In 1899 also, Abd al-Rahman had found Abd al-Aziz a new bride. She was called Wadhba and came from the Bani Khalid tribe of the Hasa. A year later, in 1900, she bore Abd al-Aziz his first son, Turki.

With the British now not only guaranteeing the safety of Kuwait but actively encouraging him, Mubarak was ready to act against the Rashids. As a result, early in 1901 Mubarak, Abd al-Rahman and the twenty-year-old Abd al-Aziz, prepared for a major assault on the Rashids. With Mubarak leading his own force of Kuwaiti warriors and the Sauds heading their own small band of armed followers, they rode south out of Kuwait towards the Dahna Desert and into the territory of the Mutair tribe. On the edge of the Dahna they were met by large parties of warriors from their friends the Al Murra, the Al Murra's kinsmen the Ajman and warriors from the Mutair tribe itself. Altogether Mubarak and Abd al- Rahman now had a force of some ten thousand. The main body of this formidable army marched west towards Ha'il, while Abd al-Aziz, at his own request and after some reluctance from his father, was given a detachment with which to head south towards Riyadh and mount a diversionary attack.

Twenty years later Abd al-Aziz told a confidant that he left Kuwait that winter in a spirit of fatalism verging on despair; the death of his first wife and the news of his uncle's probable murder still so played on his mind that, in his words, he '... came to Najd seeking oblivion'.[15] He marched boldly down to Riyadh and with his warriors managed to scale the town walls, which the Rashids had allowed to fall into disrepair, and break into the town itself. Ajlan, the Rashid governor, withdrew with his small garrison and a plentiful supply of food and water into one of the town's two main fortresses, the Mismak, and a siege began.

Meanwhile Mubarak and Adb al-Rahman marched west with the main force. Sometime in early February, while they were still more than one hundred and fifty miles from Ha'il, on a bleak, salt-pan area on the edge of the Nafud Desert, they were met by the full force of Abd al-Aziz ibn Rashid and his Shammar warriors. Mubarak and Abd al-Rahman suffered a massive and decisive defeat, so devastating that, according to Philby, 'the rain mingling with the blood of the fallen flowed in a broad stream into the snow-white basin of salt'.[16] The remnants of Mubarak and Abd al-Rahman's force scattered and Mubarak and Abd al-Rahman with their own surviving followers fled back to Kuwait. When news of the defeat reached Abd al-Aziz in Riyadh, he lifted his siege and fled back to Kuwait as well.

Because of the approach of summer, when it would be too hot for campaigning, Abd al-Aziz ibn Rashid delayed mounting a counter-attack on Kuwait and instead set about wreaking bloody vengeance on the tribes and towns that had welcomed Mubarak and Abd al-Rahman, so laying up further enemies for himself if the Sauds should ever attempt to return.

Then, in September 1901 when the worst of the summer heat had ended, Abd al-Aziz ibn Rashid set out with his army of Shammar tribesmen to attack Kuwait. Mubarak countered by mustering a force of some ten thousand men from the town and surrounding tribes and, supplied

15 Rihani, Ameen, *Ibn Sa'oud of Arabia: His People and His Land*, Constable, London, 1928.

16 Philby, H. St John, *Heart of Arabia*, London, 1928.

with additional arms and ammunition by the British, prepared to defend the town. The Rashids reached al Jahra, a village on the Bay of Kuwait about twenty-five miles to the west of the town, and laid siege to it. Mubarak appealed to the British for assistance and a Royal Navy warship, steaming far up into the bay, took up position off al Jahra and began shelling Abd al-Aziz ibn Rashid and his Shammar warriors. Realising that he could no longer capture al Jahra, let alone Kuwait itself, without bringing down on himself the full might of Britain, Abd al-Aziz ibn Rashid withdrew inland and contented himself with raiding local shepherds and tribesmen, driving off their livestock and taking their goods.

Abd al-Aziz, meanwhile, remained eager to renew his attack on Riyadh and avenge the wrongs done to his family and people by the Rashids. Although he had proved, by succeeding in breaking into Riyadh and laying siege to the town's two fortresses a year earlier, that he was a brave warrior and could lead men, he was not content. Because he had not defeated Ajlan and captured the town, he felt that he had failed. He pleaded with his father and Mubarak for permission to try again by leading a small force on Riyadh immediately, while Abd al-Aziz ibn Rashid with his main force of warriors were still far away and preoccupied with raiding.

After deliberating Abd al-Rahman and Mubarak agreed and in October 1901 Abd al-Aziz, with about fifty well-armed relatives and retainers, including his younger brother Muhammad and his cousins Abdullah and Musa'id ibn Jiluwi, set out. They headed south into the fertile al Hasa so as to avoid the Rashids. Abd al-Aziz and his party gathered sympathetic tribesmen as they went and, once there were enough of them, began attacking tribes that supported the Ottoman Empire and the Rashids. Meanwhile the Ottomans, angered by the British shelling of their allies the Rashids and a growing number of reports of Abd al-Aziz's attacks on their supporters in al Hasa, protested to the British and their vassal governor in Kuwait, Mubarak. The British, who had no interest in an all-out war with the Ottoman Empire, put pressure on Mubarak to get Abd al-Rahman to recall his son.

But when his father's message reached him Abd al-Aziz ignored it. Instead of returning to Kuwait he headed south towards the lands bordering the Dahna sands and the Rub al Khali, ground familiar to him from his days with the Al Murra. But as the weeks passed the tribesmen he had gathered around him, having done well from the spoils of their raiding but with no desire to spend the winter in harsh and unfamiliar territory, returned home to their own tribes.

But still Abd al-Aziz did not give up. Employing all the skills in hunting and tracking he had learned with the Al Murra and keeping well away from all other tribes and people, he and the small band of followers with whom he had set out from Kuwait, seemed simply to disappear into the desert.

They spent most of the sacred Islamic lunar month of Ramadan, which in that year, 1901, started in December, in strict observance of the fast not far from the oasis of Jabrin, some one hundred and fifty miles south east of Riyadh. No group of men can ever have counted the days of the lunar month of fasting more anxiously, nor watched the waning of the moon more eagerly. As the days of the fast began to draw towards their end, early in January 1902, Abd al-Aziz and his forty to fifty men left the area close to the oasis and, moving stealthily and only at night, covering their tracks as they went and taking an indirect, zig-zag route to throw off all hint or suspicion of their presence or where they were heading, Abd al-Aziz began leading his small band towards Riyadh.

By 14th January, the last day of the fast, they had reached an ancient well called Ain Hit, a great gash or split in the horizontal strata of the limestone at the bottom of a cliff at the edge of some hills twenty-five miles south east of Riyadh. There, deep inside and under the cliff, where the roof of a water-worn cave had collapsed thousands of years ago and left a gaping giant underground pothole or cavern more than one hundred and fifty feet deep, they halted. With the setting of the sun and the first sighting of the new crescent moon in the cold winter air, the great feast and celebration of Eid al Fitr, marking the end of Ramadan, began. But for Abd al-Aziz and his small band of warriors it was to be only a short and poor feast. There would be time enough for celebration and feasting later, if they succeeded in their desperate mission. If they failed he, and probably most of his companions, would be dead.

Leaving a small group to keep watch and guard the camels, shortly before nightfall Abd al-Aziz and his companions duck inside the gash in the rockface. They begin to scramble down a steep zig-zag path inside, over crumbling, loose stones and rough, worn steps cut into the rock used by generations of shepherds, camel drivers and other thirsty travellers over many centuries. The last rays of the soon-to-set sun throw a shaft of golden-red light deep into the cavern, lighting Abd al-Aziz and his dusty travel-worn companions as they pick their way ever deeper and deeper into the pit, around huge sharp-edged boulders left from the time when the roof of the cavern collapsed. As they near the bottom they disturb a flock of birds that have made their roosting places on ledges of rock high in the pit's domed roof, sending them flying up, angry at this intrusion so late in the day, beating their wings, squeaking and twittering like some dread augury.

At last, almost one hundred and fifty feet down, Abd al-Aziz and his men reach water. Cool, deep and sweet, it is a gently flowing underground river, formed out of the generous rainfall of the centuries before the last Ice Age, before Arabia became dry and barren. Here, in the manner laid down in the Muslim ritual with which they have been familiar all their lives, they wash their hands three times, the right hand first and then the left, take water into their mouths three times and spit it out, draw water into their noses three times and then expel it, wipe their faces and hair with the water, their ears, forearms, feet and all the places where dust and mud from their journey could have clung to them. Thus refreshed and prepared, they fill their water skins and skins for the camels and then climb back to the surface.

Once Abd al-Aziz and his warriors are all assembled again at the mouth of the cave they kneel to face towards Mecca and say the prayers for the end of Ramadan, prostrating themselves on the stony ground. Their prayers done, they rise, and in low voices exchange the traditional Eid greetings. Then they take a few dates from their saddle bags, cram them down, drink a little of the water they have carried up from the underground river and allow their camels to drink as well. Then they remount their camels and silently ride off into the night.

Now they move fast. They have much ground to cover before the first hint of day. The night is cold and the thin crescent moon throws barely enough light to see the ground ahead of their camels' well-splayed hooves. They know that tonight of all nights they are unlikely to be seen. Everyone is inside, celebrating the Eid feast with their families, their doors tightly closed and their windows firmly shuttered against the cold.

By daybreak they have covered more than twenty miles and have reached the edge of the Aramah Plateau, a little north east of Riyadh above the Wadi Hanifah. They now halt on the same plateau up to which Abd al-Aziz and his sister Nura had been carried in the saddle bags of the camel on that night eleven years earlier, when their father and their family had made their hurried escape from Riyadh. For the whole of the next day, as below them the inhabitants of Riyadh celebrate, exchange presents and greet each other, Abd al-Aziz and his companions lie low in one of the plateau's many shallow valleys. Abd al-Aziz knows better than any of his companions how desperate the throw they are about to take is and he spends the day in mental preparation – better to die honourably in trying to restore the Al Saud birthright and fulfil the destiny staked out for him so clearly by his aunt than that his family be forced to meekly suffer still further humiliation and dishonour at the hands of the Rashids!

With the coming of nightfall they pray and then, once it is completely dark, begin to pick their way silently down from the plateau into the Wadi below. They are now perhaps an hour and a half's walk from Riyadh itself. Here, close to the first of the outlying palm groves Abd al-Aziz halts. From the fifty or so who are still with him, he picks a striking force of forty men. He tells them to take their weapons but to leave everything else. Turning to the others, he tells them to wait, keeping out of sight as best they can with the camels and baggage, until the evening of the next day. Then, if they have still heard nothing from him and his companions, they are to make their way as fast as they can back to Kuwait.

Abd al-Aziz now leads his forty hand-picked armed men into the palm groves and towards Riyadh. Avoiding known paths, he and his followers pick their way as quietly as possible through the trees, over the many irrigation channels and around the numerous wells and water wheels, giving a wide berth to any small houses, huts and animal enclosures so as not to wake any of the dogs or other livestock that could betray their presence. After about an hour and a half they start to make out the silhouette of the town wall about a hundred yards in front of them through the last of the trees. Abd al-Aziz knows from his brief presence in the town eleven months earlier that the walls are still likely to be in a bad state of repair and that the people of the town have become tired of the Rashid occupation and the harsh treatment meted out to them by the Rashid governor, Ajlan. He guesses that their plight will have been made still worse by reprisals taken by the Rashids against those who welcomed his earlier brief return. But he also knows that now he will not be welcome in the town unless he can first defeat and kill Ajlan and drive out his garrison. He also knows that his only hope of achieving this will be by taking Ajlan by surprise.

Keeping just within the shelter of the trees Abd al-Aziz and his men creep round to the north of the town to opposite a place where he knows that the wall is in a particularly bad state of repair. Next they hunt around for one of the palm trees cut down by the Rashids as punishment for the help given to the Sauds and prepare its trunk for use as a rough scaling ladder. That done, Abd al-Aziz selects just six of the men, including his cousin Abdullah ibn Jiluwi, and prepares to creep forward towards the wall itself. The rest of the warriors he leaves behind at the edge of the trees under the command of his younger brother Muhammad, telling them to wait for the command to join him inside the town. If, however, they have heard nothing from him by noon the next day they are to return to the camels and make their way as best they can back to Kuwait as he and his six companions will be dead.

Abd al-Aziz and his six companions now creep forward carrying the tree trunk. Having first made sure that there are no watchmen nearby, they lean the trunk gently up against the lowest part of the wall, quickly scramble up it to the top and drop silently down on the other side into the darkness of the town. Once all six are over they creep forward, their swords and rifles bound securely in their cloaks to hide them from view and muffle any sound. Heading into the deep shadow of the street directly in front of them, Abd al-Aziz and his six companions are relieved to find that the doors of all the little baked-mud houses are tightly shut. All is quiet. There are no more than two or three houses where even a single glimmer from a lamp shows through a crack in a door or window shutter where someone is still awake or a child needs re-assurance through the darkness of the long, cold night. It seems that, with the Eid feast done, every family in Riyadh has taken early to their beds.

In single file and hugging the deepest shadow at the side of the streets, Abd al-Aziz and the six warriors glide silently forward, stopping at each bend or turning so that their leader can peer round the corner into the length of street that they are about to enter. Having checked that there is no one there, he beckons his companions to follow and moves on. They are heading for the centre of the town and the Mismak fortress where they know that, for his own protection, Ajlan goes to sleep each night.

Standing in its own small square, a little down the main thoroughfare from the rambling old palace which was Abd al-Aziz and his family's former home, the Mismak fortress stands like the grim and imposing inner keep of some European medieval castle. Built only forty years earlier, during a previous period of Rashid occupation, it is square, with thick, high walls and four powerful, forty five feet tall, crenellated round towers at each corner. Slit windows in each of the four towers provide the garrison with an excellent field of fire onto any attacking force. There is just one gateway into the fortress, situated in the centre of its western wall. This gate is constructed out of four-inch-thick palm and tamarisk trunks. In the centre of the gate there is a tiny postern, placed some three feet off the ground so that anyone trying to get through will be forced to more or less pull themselves through head first, thus offering their necks as an excellent target for any sword-wielding guard stationed just inside.

Opposite the gateway to the fortress there stands a row of houses. The middle one, directly opposite the gate itself, is slightly larger than the rest and appears particularly strongly barred and shuttered. This is the house where Ajlan's wife and family live. Two doors along there is a smaller house belonging to a livestock trader and his family, called Juwaisir. It is to this house that Abd al-Aziz and his companions head. He hopes to be able to hide up in the house until morning and then, when the fortress gate is thrown open and Ajlan comes out, Abd al-Aziz hopes to be able to take him and the garrison by surprise. Such is the rough plan, in so far as Abd al-Aziz has worked out any plan at all. He knows, however, that much will depend on chance and so far he has not told his companions in any detail what he has in mind.

It is now near midnight. While his companions hang back in the shadows, Abd al-Aziz goes up to Juwaisir's door and knocks softly, hoping that Juwaisir himself will answer. At first no one answers and then, after some seconds that seem to Abd al-Aziz and his companions like long, slow minutes, a girl's voice answers. 'Who are you?' asks the girl anxiously.

Now, suddenly recalling that Juwaisir has two daughters, Abd al-Aziz replies, 'I am sent by the Governor, the Amir Ajlan, to inquire about buying livestock. I must speak with your father.'

'Go away,' says the girl firmly. 'This is no time of night to come knocking at a house where there are women.'

'Open up,' says Abd al-Aziz with a voice of authority, 'or the Governor shall hear of it in the morning and then not only you but Juwaisir will be in trouble.'

Overhearing this threat, Juwaisir himself now hastily begins to unbar the door. As soon as the door starts gingerly to open, Abd al-Aziz and his six companions spring out of the shadows and force it right open. All bundle inside, overpower Juwaisir and his terrified daughter and, putting their hands over their mouths to silence them, hastily shut the door securely behind them.

Once the warriors are inside and the light falls on to their faces, the girl and her father recognise Abd al-Aziz as the son of their former ruler, Abd al-Rahman, and greet him. After moving deeper inside the house to reduce the risk of being overheard, the other members of Juwaisir's family are called and they too welcome Abd al-Aziz and his six companions. Abd al-Aziz inquires about Ajlan, his whereabouts, daily routine and movements. Juwaisir and his family explain that he never goes anywhere without his guards, that he always sleeps in the fortress where there is at all times a garrison of between sixty and eighty men. But that in the mornings, at between half an hour and an hour after sunrise, Ajlan always comes out of the fortress with some of his guards and either mounts his horse to go for a morning ride or crosses the square to his wife's house to take breakfast with her. Unlike the fortress, although it has secure locks and is well barred at night, Ajlan's wife's house has no guards.

Abd al-Aziz now goes up on to the roof of Juwaisir's house with his companions and, having rapidly surveyed the roofs of the adjoining houses, formulates a rough plan of action. Stealthily, he and his six companions leap across on to the roof of the next-door house. Softly lifting a trap-door in the roof they creep into the house and down a rickety ladder to the bedroom where they find a man and his wife asleep in bed. Swiftly binding and gagging them with their bedclothes, they swear the man and woman to silence, promising to return and slit their throats if they utter a single sound. Now Abd al-Aziz returns to the roof and crouches, listening. He is now on the roof of the house almost directly opposite the entrance to the fortress and right next to the house of Ajlan's wife. There is silence. The alarm has not been raised and he and his companions appear to have remained undetected. Relieved, he now instructs two of his companions to return the way they have come and summon the men he has left in the palm grove just beyond the town wall to come and join him.

An hour or so later, after everyone has assembled safely in Juwaisir's house, Abd al-Aziz leads his men across on to the roof of the neighbouring house. Ajlan's wife's house is a full storey higher than the others and so, in order to gain access to its roof, the men have to climb up onto each other's shoulders. Once sufficient men have made it up on to the roof of Ajlan's wife's house, they force open the door leading down into the house itself and Abd al-Aziz leads his men down the stairs. Sending some men further down to secure the cellars, overpower the servants and lock them inside, Abd al Aziz silently slides a bullet into the breech of his British made Martini-Henry service rifle. Then with his cousin Jiluwi following him with a lighted candle, Abd al-Aziz heads for the bedrooms. In what appears to be the largest bedroom they find two figures bundled up under heaps of bedclothes. Abd al-Aziz tiptoes over to them. Jiluwi raises the candle and they peer down into the small sections of faces that can be seen poking out from the heaps of bedclothes. Neither face belongs to Ajlan. Both are women. One Abd al-Aziz recognises as Ajlan's wife, a Riyadh girl called Mutliba whose father had worked for Abd al-Rahman in the palace. The second woman is her sister.

The two men prod them awake and immediately gag them to silence their screams. Abd al-Aziz accuses Mutliba of being a slut for marrying a Rashid to which she spiritedly responds that she only married Ajlan in order that her family should survive after Abd al-Rahman and his family had fled and deserted them.

Having now secured all three houses facing the fortress gate across the small square, Abd al-Aziz posts men to watch the prisoners and make sure that none escapes or succeeds in raising the alarm. He also posts men a little back from the upstairs windows with orders to keep watch on the square and the fortress gates and let him know if they see any movement. There are now about four hours remaining until dawn.

Juwaisir manages to find each man a little food and brings them water so that they can drink and cleanse themselves before the morning prayer. Then all settle down to wait. Some quietly pray. Others recite short passages from the Qur'an to themselves. Each man knows that in a few short hours he may be dead and that, if things go badly, not only he but all his companions will probably be dead also. None of them is more aware of this than Abd al-Aziz himself, nor of the weight of responsibility that he bears, not just to his own family and himself but for each one of the men he has brought with him to this place and to each one of their families. It is the responsibility that any man who has led others into battle and mortal danger bears and feels most heavily. It is the responsibility that many men who have borne it will tell you makes a man a man and more than that, if he can bear it well, a leader of men. This then, is the moment of Abd al-Aziz's final testing. Through these last four hours before morning he senses, as perhaps he has never sensed before nor ever will again, that he knows his own destiny. Can he now live up to that destiny?

As the moment of dawn arrives, at that moment laid down when the white thread can first be distinguished from the black laid beside it, the voice of the muezzin in the old mosque beside the palace where Abd al-Aziz passed the first years of his boyhood begins to rise in the age old chanted call above the still-sleeping town. All the men, having first cleansed themselves in the prescribed manner, form themselves into two orderly lines behind their leader and facing west towards Mecca, bow down and prostrate themselves before their Maker, each praying quietly as he has been taught since he was a boy.

Now the morning light begins slowly to creep across the night sky, turning it to grey and then starts to filter into the square. Each man is now armed with sword, spear or rifle. Abd al-Aziz has posted four of his best shots at upstairs windows where they have a good line of sight straight down onto the fortress gate itself and can command a good, broad arc of fire down into much of the square as well. The rest he has told to be ready, on his command, to charge behind him out into the square, their aim being to overpower Ajlan and his guards, kill him and seize the fortress by any means they can. Abd al-Aziz himself now seems totally, almost serenely calm. He has removed the headcord from his *kaffiyah* (his head cloth), pulled the ends of the head cloth tightly round and over his head and back around his neck, tying them together so that they cannot fall loose. In similar fashion he has also tied the flapping ends of the billowing sleeves of his smock (*dishdasha*) behind his back. Thus, fully prepared for action, he waits, alert but still, for the moment when Ajlan will appear.

After what seems to his companions like an eternity of minutes of waiting, each man tense with muscles and nerves keyed up ready for action, there comes the distant sound of horses' hooves being led towards the square. Now there is movement inside the fortress as well. Abd al-Aziz relays his final whispered instructions to the four riflemen stationed at the windows: they are to hold their fire until he orders otherwise or he and the others become involved in fighting in the square, when they are to try to shoot Ajlan and as many of his men as possible.

At last the Governor's horses come into the square led by some of Ajlan's grooms. The heavy wooden gate of the fortress starts to swing slowly open and after a few moments Ajlan himself appears, his guards behind him, walking confidently out into the square towards his horses and his wife's house. But where is he heading? Into the house to see his wife or to the horses? It is still not clear and the fortress gate is starting to swing closed again behind him. Deciding he can wait no longer, Abd al-Aziz leaps down the steps to the door, letting out a mighty roar to his companions to follow him and to the riflemen in the windows to open fire.

Racing out into the middle of the square, Abd al-Aziz makes straight for Ajlan, continuing to bellow as he does so, and the other men pile out of the house after him. Taken by surprise, Ajlan whips round, drawing his sword as he does so, to face his assailant, and takes a mighty slash at him. Abd al-Aziz raises his rifle to parry the blow and launches himself straight at Ajlan, crashing headlong into him and knocking him to the ground. Startled, Ajlan's guards start to run, some helter-skelter back towards the fortress, others to protect their master. Abd al-Aziz's men race after them. In no time the small square is full of shouting, struggling men, rifle shots and the, clattering hooves of frightened, neighing, bucking horses. The guards on the fortress ramparts are now firing down on Abd al-Aziz's men in the square as others still pour from the house.

For some moments Abd al-Aziz and Ajlan grapple, rolling and sprawling on the ground in the dust. One of Abd al-Aziz's companions sees what is happening and races to his master's aid, but before he can reach him is felled by a rifle shot fired from the ramparts of the fortress. Now Ajlan succeeds in freeing himself sufficiently to jump to his feet and turn again for the fortress gate. But Abd-al Aziz is up in an instant also, launching himself headlong after Ajlan, discharging his rifle as he does so and hitting him in the arm so that he drops his sword. But Ajlan still plunges forward headlong towards the fortress gates and the tiny postern which is still open even though the fortress gates themselves are now almost closed. Abd al-Aziz again grabs Ajlan around the waist and legs and attempts to pull him back from the postern, but Ajlan succeeds in thrusting his head and shoulders through the postern and his guards on the inside grab his arms and shoulders and try to pull him through into the fortress. But Abd al-Aziz still holds him tight around the waist and legs and will not release his hold. Now one of Ajlan's guards who is still outside the fortress, seeing what is happening aims a mighty sword blow at Abd al-Aziz. But in that instant his cousin, Abdullah Jiluwi, spotting what is about to happen just in time, cuts the man down with one mighty thrust of his spear. Jiluwi then aims another mighty thrust at Ajlan, but just missing his target, buries his spear head so deep into the wooden beam beside the postern that he cannot wrench it out again without breaking off the spearhead.

Now, thrashing with his legs and writhing, Ajlan gets one leg free and kicks out at Abd al-Aziz's crotch. Caught with the full force of Ajlan's leg straight in his crotch, Abd al-Aziz is doubled up in pain, retching, crying out and winded. With the loosening of Abd al-Aziz's grip, the guards inside the gate are able to pull Ajlan free, dragging him tumbling headlong into the fortress. But before the guards can slam the postern closed Jiluwi comes diving head first through after Ajlan. In the confusion those inside the gate fail to see the danger in time and miss their chance to cut him down. Jumping quickly to his feet, Jiluwi grabs a sword and starts slashing and cutting wildly at all about him. More of Abd al-Aziz's men pile through the postern, joining Jiluwi amid the bloody confusion of twisting, shouting, swirling, slashing bodies, blood, swords, arms and heads. From inside and out yet more of Abd al-Aziz's men push and pull, forcing the heavy fortress gates fully open. From up above on the rampart walls men of the garrison hurl down rocks and fire upon the struggling men below. Abd al-Aziz too, quickly recovering his breath and pulling himself back upright, comes swarming into the fortress, eager to be back in the fight. In these few minutes, even though outnumbered two to one, Abd al-Aziz and his small band of warriors, after all the months of pent-up anticipation, the weeks of mental preparation while they kept out of sight in the desert and then the last hours of tense waiting, are near invincible. Ajlan and his unprepared garrison are no match for them. Soon Ajlan has been cut down and many of his men with him. Swarming, discharging their rifles and cutting their way up on to the battlements, Abd al-Aziz and his men now steadily force the remainder of the garrison back into one small room, shut them in and force them to surrender.

With the fortress now his, Abd al-Aziz sends messengers throughout the town proclaiming what has happened and that Allah's will has been done. With morning now brightening into full day, the citizens of Riyadh come out of their homes and acclaim Abd al-Aziz as their liberator.[17]

17 There are numerous accounts of Abd al-Aziz's seizure of Riyadh in January 1902 and all vary to some extent. We have relied mainly on accounts based on those given by Abd al-Aziz and others who themselves took part in these events. Abd al-Aziz was often asked by visitors to repeat the story of what had happened and even his own accounts differ, apparently depending to some extent on his mood when he was telling the story or the person to whom he was telling it. The same is true, though to a lesser extent, with other eye-witness accounts. In a sense, it might be fair to say that this story quickly took on much of the same character as the tribal myths and heroic Bedouin stories that were re-told around the camp fire when Abd al-Aziz was a teenager among the Al Murra. However, we believe that our account adheres pretty faithfully to the known and attested facts.

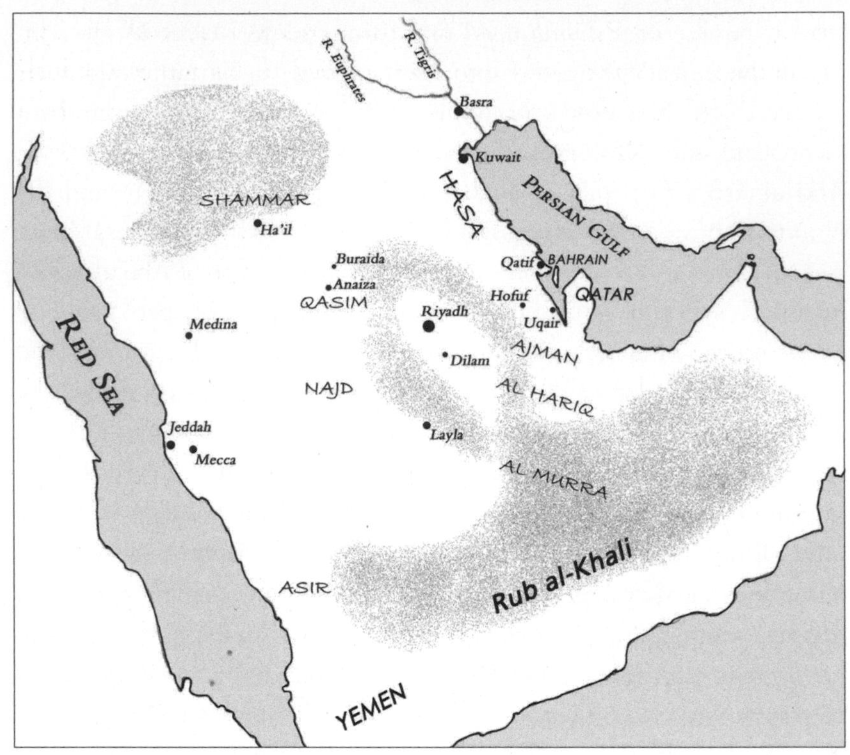

CHAPTER 4

Shaikh Amid the Imperialists

From the time of his capture of Riyadh on January 15th 1902 onwards Abd al-Aziz ibn Abd al-Rahman ibn Faisal Al Saud, meaning Abd al-Aziz son of Rahman son of Faisal of the family of Saud, to give him his name in something nearer to its full version and in a form that might have been used by many of his Najdi contemporaries when referring to him, began to become known beyond the confines of Najd and Kuwait. People, particularly those not well versed in Arabic and Arab names, began to refer to him simply as Ibn Saud – Son of Saud. 'Ibn Saud' also conveyed the idea of something akin to a title of the kind applied to the head of a clan or family, as in 'The MacLeod of MacLeod' or 'The Macdonald'. Ibn Saud, as a title, had applied to his father, Abd al-Rahman, and his grandfather, Faisal, before that. Accordingly, from here on in this narrative we shall refer to Abd al-Aziz ibn Abd al-Rahman ibn Faisal Al Saud simply as 'Ibn Saud'.

January 15th 1902 marked the beginning of a new era in the history of Najd, of the Arabian peninsula, indeed, one might say of the whole of Arabia. But on that cold January morning in Riyadh it was far from clear what that new era might hold.

Ibn Saud was twenty-one years old and, whatever his potential as a future leader of his people, his sole concrete achievement to date was that he had captured one small and not particularly significant town in the middle of a largely barren land into which few if any outsiders ever ventured. Exceptionally tall, at six feet four inches he was almost a foot taller than most of his fellow Najdis, he was broad shouldered and exceptionally strong, possessed great charm, had a sweet smile and unless roused to great physical exertion, generally deliberate in his movements. People who met him remarked on his steady, penetrating gaze and yet noted a certain reserve except when roused to one of his not infrequent bursts of great anger. People who got to know him talked of there being something veiled or forever unknown within him. Yet no one who met him, however fleetingly, doubted that he possessed genuine charisma.

The one quality required of any leader if he is to be successful, a quality highly prized by the Bedouin, and that Ibn Saud could perhaps be credited with on that first January morning in Riyadh was *hadh*, luck, in the sense that a successful general must possess it. In capturing the town he had shown that he had courage, could lead and inspire a small group of hand-picked men in a guerrilla operation and had absorbed many of the skills he had encountered during his adolescent years with the Al Murra. To have captured Riyadh in the way he had amounted to a considerable achievement. But beyond that single achievement Ibn Saud had so far proved nothing.

Could he hold the town against the inevitable counter-attack that would come, possibly within days, from the Rashids? Could he hold the loyalty of the people of Riyadh and the surrounding countryside, particularly when they had experienced so many years of hard Rashid rule and knew too well the terrible price in vengeance that the Rashids were likely to exact from those they suspected of disloyalty? Had this young man the patience or capacity for the long slow grind of government, diplomacy, compromise and statecraft needed of a successful ruler rather than just the taste and appetite for action? Had he really learned from watching Mubarak and could he put what he had learned into practice? On that January morning the real test for Ibn Saud was still to be taken.

Having taken the Mismak fortress there was still much to do. Ibn Saud knew that he and his warriors could ill afford to rest. No sooner had the remainder of the garrison of the Mismak surrendered than he dispatched parties of warriors to go around the town forcing the surrender of other buildings which Ajlan had fortified or where he had posted guards. When these other Rashidi soldiers heard that the Mismak had fallen and that Ajlan was dead most were ready enough to surrender. Those that were not, Ibn Saud's men overpowered and killed. Even when all resistance had finally been crushed Ibn Saud still did not rest. He immediately set about surveying the town walls and putting in hand the urgent repair of all those sections of it that had fallen into the worst state of disrepair. He was determined that no Rashid counter-attacking force should be able to get into the town with the ease with which he and his men had done twice within one year. At noon on that first day he led the people of the town in prayer and afterwards received their greetings and allegiance. That afternoon he dispatched a messenger to his father in Kuwait, telling him what had happened and asking him to come immediately, with the other members of the family, to join him. Only with the coming of nightfall, and after a strong complement of sentries had been posted around the still-depleted town walls, were Ibn Saud and his surviving men able to rest their weary and bruised limbs a little and start to make up for a part of the Eid Festival that they had forgone. Yet the knowledge that two of their number, fellow warriors and companions in the last three months of shared deprivation and danger, were dead and others wounded must have weighed heavily upon them, dampening any appetite for celebration.

One other major event had occurred during that day, probably in the hours immediately before he had charged out into the square to launch himself upon Ajlan. Although Ibn Saud did not yet know it, back in Kuwait his wife, Wadhba, had given birth to his second son. This son would be called Saud ibn Abd al-Aziz.[1]

During the next days, while Ibn Saud waited for the arrival of his father, work continued feverishly on repairing Riyadh's walls. There was no way of knowing how soon a Rashid army might appear and attempt to storm the town.

During the days immediately after Ibn Saud's recapture of Riyadh, another altogether stranger event is reputed to have occurred. Mutliba, Ajlan's wife, summoned Ibn Saud and begged him to accept a present from her, a mattress and cushion which she had made herself. Had she forgiven Ibn Saud and Jiluwi for slaying her husband and now intended to demonstrate her loyalty to Ibn Saud as Riyadh's rightful ruler? Whatever Ibn Saud may have thought privately about Mutliba's gesture, he accepted her present. What Mutliba had not told Ibn Saud was that inside the pillow she had placed some special objects, magic writings, needles, coloured threads and so on. She had taken advice from a woman reputed to be skilled in magic and the casting of spells. If Ibn Saud laid his head on the pillow it would kill him and in this way she intended to take her revenge on him for killing her husband. The spell is reputed to have had no effect for some days, but then one night Ibn Saud and one of the other warriors who had helped him to recapture Riyadh, Manahi ibn Mijlad of the Ajman tribe, placed the pillow between them while they slept and leaned on it. Manahi, the story goes, quickly became sick and died. Ibn Saud also is said to have been struck with an agonising pain in his head and eyes. He was only saved from death by a famous breaker of spells, one Hitlan al Dausari, who released him from the spell. In the process of the spell being broken a large quantity of small black worms or caterpillars came out of his nose and many small white worms were discharged from his throat. Upon discovering who had been responsible for casting the spell upon him, Ibn Saud is said not to

1 There appears to be some doubt about the precise date of Saud ibn Abd al-Aziz's birth, but Leslie McLoughlin in *Ibn Saud: Founder of a Kingdom*, Macmillan Press, London, 1993, claims that this is the most likely date.

have ordered Mutliba's punishment but had her sent back to her husband's family in Ha'il.[2]

As soon as he received his son's message Abd al-Rahman slipped quietly out of Kuwait with Ibn Saud's younger brother, Abdullah, and a small group of loyal followers. They had to make their departure as unobtrusive as possible and, once out of Kuwait, keep away from any of the main tracks and well-used routes. Hearing of Ibn Saud's capture of Riyadh the Rashids were likely to be on the look-out for other members of the Saud family trying to make their way to Riyadh. As a result Abd al-Rahman's journey from Kuwait to Riyadh took some weeks.

Ibn Saud used the time before his father's arrival in making a start on the complex but vital task of re-establishing Saudi control in the area around Riyadh. He began by paying visits in person to the inhabited places and Bedouin areas to the south and east of the town, winning over both the people and their leaders with hospitality and persuasion – he had no money to buy their support even if he had wished to. By these methods he aimed to demonstrate the sharp contrast between Saudi rule and the harsh rule and punitive taxation imposed on them by the Rashids. When one tribe, the Qahtan, proved recalcitrant, he mounted a lightning raid against them, seizing their goods and driving off many of their animals – rather in the manner of a large-scale Bedouin raid or *ghazzu* – in a demonstration that he intended to rule in fact as well as name.

When Abd al-Rahman arrived in Riyadh Ibn Saud laid on a triumphal welcome for him, receiving his father with great deference and re-submitting himself to his authority. In consultation with the *ulema*, the leading Wahhabi scholars and arbiters of religious doctrine and law in the town, together with senior members of the other leading families, father and son agreed that Abd al-Rahman was to remain Imam – head of the Saudi dynasty, spiritual leader of the Wahhabis and formal head of state. But henceforth Ibn Saud was to be the Shaikh, the day-to-day leader who performed the duties of running the state and being its

2 This story was told to Violet Dickson more than thirty years later by an elderly shaikh of the Ajman tribe, the tribe of which Manahi ibn Mijlad had been a shaikh and the tale, Violet Dickson tells us, was widely believed by all Bedouin, especially among the Ajman. Violet Dickson recounts the story in her book *Forty Years in Kuwait*, George Allen & Unwin, London, 1971.

military commander. He had demonstrated that he possessed courage and good fortune, *hadh*. But as Shaikh Ibn Saud would be expected to make himself freely and regularly available to his people and other senior members of the community in his *majlis*. If he was to maintain his position and be a successful ruler he would need to retain the consent and support of those he ruled. In an important symbolic demonstration of the hand over of day-to-day authority to him, all the leading religious specialists in Riyadh and the surrounding area assembled after Friday prayers to take a sacred oath of allegiance to him, the *bay'a*, in a ceremony which had its roots in the pact entered into by Muhammad ibn Saud, the ruler of Diriya, and Muhammad Ibn Abd al-Wahhab in 1745. During the gathering at which they swore the *bay'a*, Ibn Saud addressed the religious leaders in these words: 'You owe nothing to me. I am like you, one of you. But I am appointed to direct the affairs of our people in accordance with the book of Allah. Our first duty is to Allah and those who teach the Book of Allah, the Ulema. I am but an instrument of command in their hand. Obedience to God means obedience to them.'[3] For the rest of his reign Ibn Saud would regularly be seen at public prayers, kneeling before God alongside his subjects.

In a further gesture bolstering Ibn Saud's authority, Abd al-Rahman publicly presented his son with the historic sword which had belonged to Muhammad ibn Abd al-Wahhab and had been handed down since the time of his death from one generation to the next of Saudi rulers.

In practice the new arrangement would come to mean that for much of the time Abd al-Rahman, in addition to undertaking the ceremonial and formal functions of the Imam and head of state, stayed behind in Riyadh dealing with all the things related to the central administration, while Ibn Saud was out in the field, fighting wars and bolstering loyalty among the tribes and outlying regions.

From this time on, until his father's death in 1928, whenever he was in the same place as his father, Ibn Saud would visit him each evening to receive his guidance and counsel, while every Friday, after prayers, his father would pay a formal visit to his son. Ibn Saud was to remain

3 Ibn Saud's words are recorded in Ameen Rihani's *Ibn Sa'oud of Arabia: His People and His Land*, Constable, London, 1928.

extremely respectful to his father and defer to him for the rest of his father's life. Other members of the family were also given important roles, particularly Ibn Saud's brother Muhammad, who had been with him during the re-capture of Riyadh, and Abdullah Jiluwi, the cousin who had saved his life and forced his way into the Mismak fortress. Members of the family would often accompany Ibn Saud on visits to the tribes and outlying areas to demonstrate the solidarity and cohesion of the Saudi family both as fighters and as a dynasty.

Within weeks of recapturing Riyadh Ibn Saud had sent a message to the Ottoman governor in Basra, assuring him that in recapturing Riyadh he was only seeking to retrieve the dominions of his ancestors from Rashid usurpers and that he was definitely not seeking to oust the Ottoman Empire. His message went on to assure the Sultan that he intended to rule his recovered domain as a 'loyal subject' of the Ottoman Empire. Considering that the Wahhabis had always regarded the Ottomans as infidels and that there had been more than a century of quarrels and wars between the Sauds, the Ottomans and their subjects the Rashids, this apparent reversal in attitude, especially considering it followed a victory rather than a defeat, was remarkable. Ibn Saud, it seemed, was seeking to profit from the example set by his mentor Mubarak, who immediately after he seized Kuwait in 1896, had dispatched assurances to the Sultan of his loyalty and as a gesture of that loyalty hoisted the Ottoman imperial flag over Kuwait harbour.

While Ibn Saud was writing to the Sultan to assure him of his loyalty, Abd al-Aziz ibn Rashid was also sending the Sultan messages. Unlike Ibn Saud who was seeking to avoid Ottoman intervention, Rashid's goal was to provoke it. He requested Ottoman assistance in suppressing 'the revolt in Najd' and, in an attempt to up the stakes and inflame Turkish fears, accused the British of being behind Ibn Saud's capture of Riyadh. The British, Rashid suggested, intended ' … to establish themselves in portions of Arabia which dominate the Ottoman possessions of Hasa and Qatif by means of Mubarak and Ibn Saud'.[4] However, while the

4 Ibn Rashid to The Grand Vizier, March 2nd 1902 quoted in Jacob Goldberg *The Foreign Policy of Saudi Arabia: The Formative Years 1902–1918*, Harvard University Press, Cambridge, Ma., USA, 1986.

Ottomans were suspicious of British intentions in the region, Ibn Saud's seizure of Riyadh suited their own policy of divide and rule in the area. As long as Ibn Saud and the Rashids both continued to recognise Ottoman suzerainty, they were quite content to have the Sauds keeping the Rashids busy, so helping to prevent the Rashids from becoming a dominant power in the area. The Ottomans therefore rejected Abd al-Aziz ibn Rashid's request and, on the contrary, resumed payment of an annual pension to Abd al-Rahman.

By March 1902 messages and communiqués were positively flying around the region between local imperial representatives, their local protégés and their governments in London, India, Istanbul and Moscow. As early as February 1902, the British Political Resident in the Persian Gulf reported to his bosses in India, who had in turn reported his message back to London, that sometime 'about the middle of January an event of great importance occurred in the capture by Abd al-Aziz Ibn Saud of Riyadh, the old Wahhabi capital'. The Resident went on to inform his bosses that while Ibn Saud had 'gained many supporters', the Rashids had so far taken 'no active measures' against him, adding laconically that the Saudis' 'ultimate defeat by ibn Rashid would seem to be probable'.[5]

In May Ibn Saud wrote to the British Political Resident and, citing the protection Britain already extended to others in the Gulf, sought similar protection for himself – 'May the eyes of the British government be fixed upon us.' Hoping to 'up the ante', so to speak, he described how he had been approached by the Russians requesting a full account of the 'ill-treatment' he had received at the hands of the Turks 'and the help they have given to Ibn Rashid'. However, he went on, 'I did not see fit to go to other than your Government. I request of your benevolent Government to consider me as one as their protégés.' By deliberately flagging up both the Russian and the Turkish interest in him and Najd in this way, he no doubt hoped to increase Britain's incentive to intervene in the area on his behalf. However, while control of the Gulf was of major importance to Britain, that interest did not extend to Central Arabia. In fact, from

5 British Political Resident in the Persian Gulf, C. A. Kemball, to the government of India, February 19th 1902.

Britain's point of view becoming involved in the affairs of Najd or the Sauds was likely simply to lead to a further deterioration of relations with the Ottoman Empire. So Ibn Saud's letter went unanswered. Indeed, the British Government in India took an even tougher line, demanding of London that Ibn Saud be given no encouragement and putting pressure on Mubarak not to offer assistance to Ibn Saud nor encouragement to 'any action'[6].

For months Abd al-Aziz ibn Rashid appeared remarkably unconcerned by Ibn Saud's recapture of Riyadh. When first told the news of Riyadh's capture by Ibn Saud he is reported to have responded blithely: 'The rabbit is in the hole and the caravan is waiting around it.' By August 1902 Ibn Saud had fortified the town and won the support of almost all the neighbouring tribes in southern Najd. He had also succeeded in purchasing a considerable quantity of rifles and ammunition from Kuwait and engaged the services of a number of Kuwaiti marksmen. These he instructed personally in the tactics he hoped to employ to defeat Rashid when he did at last take the field against him. Ibn Saud knew full well that until he had himself defeated Abd al-Aziz ibn Rashid in open battle his own position would remain precarious and the people of Riyadh and the tribes of central Arabia would continue to fear that at any moment the Rashids might return and drive him out, leaving them at the mercy their cruel vengeance.

Finally, in the early autumn of 1902, Abd al-Aziz ibn Rashid sent out scouting parties. They were given instructions to go out to the tribes to the south and east of Riyadh, which had pledged their loyalty to the Sauds, and spread fear and disaffection among them. These tribes included the Sauds' friends the Al Murra. But this Rashid ploy met with little success. Ibn Saud responded by immediately sending his brother Muhammad and his cousin Jiluwi to reassure them and as a result most of the tribes remained loyal.

6 From Foreign Office and Government of India papers quoted by Jacob Goldberg in *The Foreign Policy of Saudi Arabia: The Formative Years, 1902–1918*, Harvard University Press, Cambridge, Ma., USA, 1986

With this accomplished, Ibn Saud could concentrate all his efforts on inflicting a decisive defeat on the Rashids. The first thing he did was send members of his family to the tribes to recruit additional warriors. This he did in exactly the same way as tribal leaders throughout Arabia had done through the centuries, promising spoils to those who joined him and making it clear that it was a call of honour and that to fail to answer that call would bring lasting shame upon their families. Next, having assembled a substantial force, Ibn Saud marched out of Riyadh, leaving it under the command of his father and well defended behind its rebuilt walls. Embarking on a series of feints and diversionary moves, plus a little light skirmishing, he aimed to draw Rashid and his army away from Riyadh and to disguise his real intentions. Finally, in November 1902, Ibn Saud succeeded in luring Rashid to battle on ground of his own choosing about fifty miles south of Riyadh at an oasis called Dilam.

Unknown to Rashid, Ibn Saud had arrived with the main body of his force at Dilam the previous night and concealed his Kuwaiti marksmen and other warriors behind their camel saddles among the palm trees. The next morning when Rashid advanced with his army towards the palms, instead of simply blasting away with their guns and charging out into the open to attack the Rashids, Ibn Saud's men stayed concealed and held their fire. Then, when the Rashid troops were almost upon them and so close that they could not miss, Ibn Saud ordered his men to open fire. The intensity and concentration of the Saudi fusillade, together with the total surprise, resulted in the Rashids suffering far more casualties in just a few minutes than was usual in the whole of a normal tribal desert battle. As the Rashid troops began to retreat in confusion, Ibn Saud launched his own cavalry against them. The Rashids turned and fought back bravely, resisting for much of the rest of the day. But in the end the number of casualties they had suffered during the first few minutes of the battle when they had come under the withering fire of the Saudis, together with the fact that Rashid had not expected to encounter such a large Saudi force, meant that the Rashids had no choice but to flee into the night. The next morning, when Abd al-Aziz ibn Rashid saw that ibn Saud and his cavalry were still pursuing him, he withdrew with the battered remnants of his army out of the area completely. Had Abd al-Aziz ibn Rashid known that with that first decisive fusillade of concentrated fire Ibn Saud had almost exhausted his entire supply of ammunition and that he did not yet possess enough money to purchase more, he might not have decided to withdraw. But as it was, Ibn Saud had won his first major battle over the Rashids and shown that he was not quite such a 'rabbit' as Abd al-Aziz ibn Rashid had supposed. Ibn Saud had won his victory at Dilam by introducing a new tactic into desert warfare, the kind of tactic employed by the imperial armies of Europe. The fact that he had introduced such a tactic was probably one more result of his studies under the tutelage of Mubarak in Kuwait. But whether Ibn Saud thought up the tactics he employed at the battle of Dilam himself or whether he had learned them from a European military textbook in Kuwait, it was unlikely that Abd al-Aziz ibn Rashid would ever again make the mistake of under-estimating him.

Over the succeeding months Ibn Saud continued harrying and pursuing the Rashids wherever he found them or their supporters. As a result, by the time the campaigning season ended in the summer of 1903 he had achieved control over a wide swathe of territory both north and south of Riyadh and was ready to begin expansion outward, into territory that had not been controlled by the Saudis in more than a generation.

While Ibn Saud had been consolidating his position in the centre of Arabia the tensions between the imperial powers in the region had been growing. In March 1903 both Russian and French warships had arrived in the Gulf. While the British were concerned about the intentions of their old adversaries the French, they were even more perturbed by the actions of the Russians. Already involved against Russia in the so-called 'Great Game', the ongoing imperial rivalry over territory in Central Asia, the British now feared that by building up his military strength in the Persian Gulf and surrounding area the Tsar intended to extend the Great Game to Arabia and the Gulf. British fears over the possibility of a Russian railway line running from North Africa to an outlet in the Gulf, so giving them a gateway to India and the East, re-surfaced. They were given fresh impetus in 1903 when reports began reaching London from the British Government in India that a Russian warship was engaged in making calls at ports down the whole length of the Gulf and that the

Russian officers and crew were engaging in 'purposeful socialising' in Muscat and Kuwait. Reports soon began to circulate that the Russians were planning to 'purchase the Straits of Hormuz'.[7] If they succeeded this would enable them to close the Gulf to British shipping. With hindsight the posturings of the imperial powers during this period, both in Arabia and further afield, can be viewed as symptomatic of their coming decline. In recent years British rule in Southern Africa had been seriously challenged by the Boer settlers. Britain was also facing increasingly vocal independence movements in India and elsewhere, plus serious social unrest at home, strikes (in 1900 the trade unions had created their own political party, the Labour Party) and ever more strident calls for women's suffrage. During the same period Tsarist Russia had embarked on a disastrous war with Japan in the Far East while also trying to suppress growing unrest at home. The year 1905 saw the first, ultimately unsuccessful, revolution in Russia and a serious mutiny on board the battleship *Potemkin*, a capital ship of the very fleet whose warships were causing the British such consternation by their presence in the Persian Gulf. The Turks meanwhile, having already lost many of their territories in the Balkans together with much of their prestige, now also faced an increasingly vigorous reform movement at home.

Just how aware of all these internal convulsions, power-plays and imperial posturings Ibn Saud was is unclear, but certainly he was more aware of the imperial powers, their roles, aims, relative strengths and weaknesses than most of their rulers, senior statesmen and regional representatives would have given him credit for. To most of them he was little more than a temporarily successful minor 'native' chieftain, likely in the long run to prove no more than another Arab hick from the desert sticks, little better than a savage. Yet his time with Mubarak had made him appreciate the importance of the imperial powers in Arab affairs and from that time on he had gone out of his way to keep himself informed about developments well beyond the shores of Arabia. As we have seen from his actions immediately after recapturing Riyadh, Ibn Saud had formed the clear view that in order to succeed in his goal of recapturing the lands

7 See Leslie McLoughlin, *Ibn Saud: Founder of a Kingdom*, Macmillan Press, London, 1993, p 28.

that had been the Sauds' and Wahhabis' a century earlier, he needed the goodwill and protection of the British. At the same time he knew he must also avoid provoking armed intervention against him by the Turks.

Accordingly, as the campaigning season ended in the early summer of 1903 Ibn Saud and his brothers Muhammad and Saud made their way to Kuwait, arriving in time for the visit to Kuwait of a Russian warship. Invited aboard with his mentor Mubarak, Ibn Saud politely declined (as had Mubarak, for fear of offending the Turks back in 1897 when the British had invited him aboard one of their warships). However, when Mubarak organised meetings for him with the Russian consul on-shore, Ibn Saud not only went along, he enthralled the Russian official with a blow-by-blow account of his capture of Riyadh, with details of the current political situation in central Arabia and also flagged up his fear of Turkish intervention. Mubarak played his part too, at one point telling the Russian consul with a great display of emotion, how impressed he was by his protégé's success. At one point, according to the Russian account of the meeting, Mubarak flung off his head-dress and swore that he wished to become Ibn Saud's servant. Ibn Saud would later say that the Russians offered him guns and money to enable him 'to retain the support of the tribes since Ibn Rashid received money and support from the Ottomans'.[8] However, he remained careful, while sounding polite and interested, not to actually accept the Russian offer. Following these meetings Ibn Saud took the earliest opportunity to inform the British about them, highlighting the Russian offer of money and arms. The fact that he highlighted the offer of money and arms led one British official to doubt that the offer had been made and to suggest that Ibn Saud had invented this as a way of providing the British with a further inducement to offer him support. However, other sources available to the British told them that such an offer had been made. Whether the offer was in fact made or was simply an embellishment invented by Ibn Saud himself, it does show his acute

8 Quoted from a report of the British local representative contained in British Foreign Office Papers included in Jacob Goldberg's *The Foreign Policy of Saudi Arabia: The Formative Years, 1902–1918*, Harvard University Press, Cambridge, Ma., USA, 1986.

awareness, even this early in his career, of the nature of great power relations in the region and his readiness to play off one power against another to achieve his own ends. But clever ploy though it was, Ibn Saud was rebuffed once more. The British, still determined to do nothing that might finally push the Turks into the arms of the ever more stridently militaristic Germans, far from acceding to his request reminded him that they would regard it as highly undesirable should any 'foreign European country interfere in the affairs of Najd'.[9] In May 1903 Britain spelled out its position over the Gulf even more clearly when Lord Lansdowne, the Foreign Secretary, issued the following warning in a statement to the House of Lords: 'We should regard the establishment of a naval base or a fortified port in the Persian Gulf by any other power as a very grave menace to British interests and we should certainly resist it with all means at our disposal.'

Receiving news that Ibn Saud was away in Kuwait, Ibn Rashid seized his chance to mount a fresh attack on Riyadh. He marched rapidly south and, arriving undetected on a hilltop overlooking the town, set up camp for the night in preparation for launching a full-scale assault at dawn next morning. However, unfortunately for him, his army had been spotted by some Bedouin who sneaked into Riyadh and raised the alarm. Abd al-Rahman and the citizens promptly took up positions on the town's rebuilt ramparts and prepared to repulse Rashid. Furious at being foiled, Ibn Rashid vented his frustration on some of the palm groves and any luckless peasants he found round about and then the following day, after a little desultory fighting outside the walls, withdrew back northwards towards Ha'il.

Ibn Saud's continuing success was by now throwing the two established great powers in the region, Britain and the Ottoman Empire, into considerable confusion. Officials in both administrations had begun to argue amongst themselves about the best way for their respective governments to proceed. Ottoman officials in Basra and Iraq sent messages back to Constantinople urging the Sultan to take a stronger line with Mubarak and the British, who they suspected of covertly supporting Ibn Saud, and to authorise the sending of Turkish troops to support the Rashids and

9 Ibid.

quash Ibn Saud. Their opposite numbers in Constantinople, on the other hand, urged a more conciliatory approach. Turkish officials in Basra were particularly concerned, probably with considerable cause, that Kuwait and other Gulf ports were being used by gun runners to smuggle arms to Ibn Saud and that the British were deliberately turning a blind eye.

Meanwhile Ibn Saud issued a third appeal to the British, intended to appeal to their special concerns in the region – the security of British interests along the Gulf Coast. He did this by sending an emissary to see the British Political Agent in Bahrain. The emissary informed the British that, after he had completed the task of defeating Ibn Rashid, Ibn Saud intended to eject the Ottoman garrisons from the Hasa as he wished to restore that region, as well as the whole of Najd, to the Saudi state. However, he would only embark on this plan if he knew in advance that the British were prepared to offer protection to the coast of Hasa against any possible future Ottoman attempt to invade and recapture it. The British Political Agent's response was evasive: it would, he said, be 'inappropriate' for the British Government to 'intrigue' against a 'friendly state'. Nevertheless, behind the scenes British officials were interested. Ibn Saud was becoming more powerful and they did not want to discover too late that they were 'backing the wrong horse'. Lord Curzon, the new Viceroy of India, began to wonder if maybe some British officers should be sent on a secret mission, 'in disguise if need be', to Riyadh. However, other voices were raised against the idea and the Government finally vetoed it, anxious about further arousing Ottoman suspicions about Britain's aims in the region.

Instead Lord Curzon staged, as only he, the epitome and embodiment of British imperial supremacy and pomp, could, a great imperial show. In November 1903 he sailed in full vice-regal regalia together with a large entourage of be-plumed, be-medalled and magnificently uniformed officers and imperial officials up the Gulf, accompanied by an escort of not just one but eight Royal Navy warships. Calling at various ports along the Arabian coast he and his escorts, together with a gold-and-silver throne, were ferried or carried ashore on the backs of an army of native bearers to hold court and address the assembled shaikhs, sultans and amirs. In a series of ringing speeches he told them that the British had been in the region for longer than any other power: 'We found strife and we have created order.' Claiming that Britain had saved them 'from extinction at the hands of your neighbours', he told them that British intervention in the Gulf amounted to a century of costly, triumphant and benevolent enterprise – 'the most unselfish page in history'. Such was Britain's, and Curzon's own, imperial self-confidence and arrogance that at the time when he spoke those words Curzon almost certainly believed them. 'The peace of these waters,' he declared not simply to the assembled shaikhs but to the Russians, Turks, French, Germans and anyone else who might still have not grasped the point of this whole display of imperial might, 'must still be maintained; your independence will continue to be upheld; the British government must remain supreme.'

With the start of the 1903–4 campaigning season the Rashids and Saudis once more took to the field, but this time to the north of Riyadh. Over the succeeding months Ibn Saud and his allies advanced into Qasim, the territory midway between Riyadh and Ha'il. In March Ibn Saud captured Anaiza, an important trading post on the caravan route across Arabia between Kuwait and Medina. Among those who took part in the battle for Anaiza on the Rashid side were three grandsons of Ibn Saud's uncle, Abd al-Rahman's elder brother Saud, one of those who had been involved in the bloody contest for the throne in the 1870s following the death of Faisal the Great. Saud's descendants had never become reconciled to their loss of the throne and so had never returned to live in Riyadh. After capturing them Ibn Saud, in a characteristic gesture of magnanimity towards former opponents, granted them an unconditional pardon, offering them the choice of either joining him or returning to Ibn Rashid in Ha'il. They accepted his offer of reconciliation and hospitality. From this time on Ibn Saud would refer to them jokingly as the 'Araif' – a Bedouin word for camels taken by an enemy in a raid but later recaptured. Three of the 'Araif' joined Ibn Saud's immediate family circle when he gave them the hands in marriage of three of his own sisters. The head of the group, Saud Al-Kabir, the grandson of Abd al-Rahman's second eldest brother Saud, received the hand of Ibn Saud's favourite sister and life-long companion, Nura. However, even this would not be the end of Ibn Saud's difficulties with the Araif.

One catches an interesting glimpse of Ibn Saud as a man and war leader at this time in two descriptions he gave of the battle for Anaiza and of his feelings. The first is in a letter which he wrote to his mentor and guide Mubarak immediately after the battle. In it he says: 'When it was the fourth hour of the night we bestirred ourselves and came to Anaiza ... And after we had said the morning prayer, we sent against them Abdullah ibn Jiluwi, with him a hundred men of the people of Riyadh to assist. We marched against Majid [the opposing commander], and when he saw the horsemen, God lifted his hand off his men and helped us against them. And we broke them and slaughtered of them three hundred and seventy men. And God restored to us our kinsmen of the family of Saud who were prisoners in their hands ... And by Almighty God, but two Bedouins on our side were slain. We then returned to the village of our friends.' The other glimpse of Ibn Saud comes in a recollection of the battle and his killing of one of Ibn Rashid's brothers, as he recalled it some years later: 'I struck him first on the leg and disabled him; quickly after that I struck at the neck; the head fell to one side, the blood spurted up like a fountain, the third blow at the heart, I saw the heart which was cut in two palpitate like that ... It was a joyous moment. I kissed the sword.'[10]

When the citizens of the nearby town of Buraida, a town previously captured from its own rulers by the Rashids, learned of Ibn Saud's capture of Anaiza they sent a delegation to him asking for his assistance and permission to attack their town's fortress, which was garrisoned by Rashid soldiers. Ibn Saud promptly dispatched a detachment of his warriors to Buraida who successfully entered the town and laid siege to the fortress. But the one hundred and fifty strong Rashidi garrison resisted strongly, holding out for two months into the heat of the summer. Finally in June 1904, exhausted by the heat and their growing shortage of food and munitions, they surrendered. Ibn Saud treated them, as he had others, with clemency and respect, allowing them to return to Ha'il with their weapons.

However, Ibn Rashid's repeated appeals to the Turks for assistance, coupled with his allegations that Ibn Saud was acting with covert British

10 Quoted from India Office Papers in Alexei Vassiliev, *The History Of Saudi Arabia*, Saqi Books, London, 1998 and Robert Lacey *The Kingdom*, Hutchinson, London, 1981.

support, together with the Turks' own concern that Ibn Saud's successes might cause them problems by upsetting the balance of power in Central Arabia, at last bore fruit. The Ottomans despatched a force of two thousand four hundred men and six field guns under the command of a Turkish colonel, Hasan Shukri, to confront Ibn Saud.[11] Realising the danger, Ibn Saud made a further urgent appeal to the British. The news that the Turks were sending troops against Ibn Saud did indeed concern the British. They responded by sending a series of strongly worded notes to the Turks, urging them to abstain from any action likely to worsen tensions in central Arabia and spelling out that the 'tranquillity' of the area was 'a matter of interest' to the British Government. But beyond that the British still did nothing.

Before setting out against Ibn Saud, Colonel Shukri sent him a letter warning that there would be grave consequences if he continued to attack Ibn Rashid. The Great Caliph, he wrote, had heard about 'the sedition in Najd, directed by foreigners' hands. Therefore he sent me here to prevent bloodshed'. Accusing Ibn Saud of supporting Mubarak and the 'infidel' British, Shukri told Ibn Saud that he still had a chance to benefit from the benevolence of the Ottoman Empire in the same way that Ibn Rashid did, provided that he desisted from his attacks on the Rashids and re-submitted himself to Ottoman authority. But Ibn Saud, worried by these threats though he was, remained defiant. He replied: 'We do not accept your advice or recognise your suzerainty. If you do not want bloodshed, your had better leave this country. If you attack us, we shall undoubtedly treat you as an aggressor. If you were free and objective, you would note that the cause of my disobedience is mistrust of you.'[12] He concluded by warning the colonel that if he moved his troops into the region which he controlled he would regard them as aggressors and treat them accordingly.

Unimpressed by Ibn Saud's threat, Shukri marched his troops, many of them conscripted peasants from the gentler climate and greener

11 Estimates of the precise number of Ottoman troops and field pieces put into the field against Ibn Saud vary, possibly in part because they also had an unknown number of Rashid troops fighting alongside them.

12 From exchange of letters quoted by Alexei Vassiliev in *The History of Saudi Arabia*, Saqi Books, London, 1998.

landscapes of Anatolia, in thick uniforms and with cumbersome and heavy equipment unsuited to fighting a campaign in the intense heat of full Arabian summer, together with all their kit, stores and ammunition, and their field guns slung between mules, south from Basra into the desert to confront the upstart young shaikh and teach him a lesson. On reaching Qasim Shukri was joined by Rashid's citizen army from Ha'il and the warriors of two Bedouin tribes. It was now July and the daytime temperature was regularly reaching well over 50°C. For a few weeks Ibn Saud and his warriors devoted their time to dodging the Turkish troops. They would pop up in one part of the desert and then, as the Turkish troops wheeled round and started to make towards them, disappear again, only to re-appear a few minutes later somewhere else. As a result the Turkish troops were continually on the move. By these tactics Ibn Saud hoped not only to avoid a direct confrontation with the better-armed Turks but also to give the intense heat of the central Arabian desert a chance to do his work for him, to wear down the Turkish troops unused and ill-prepared for desert warfare in temperatures so extreme.

But on July 15th the two armies at last came face to face in a region of undulating sandhills and salt flats called Bukairiya about twenty-five miles west of Buraida. Both armies had camped overnight in comparative security a mile or so apart, but still within sight of each other, among the extensive palm groves. Ibn Saud had placed his men in defensive positions ready for the Rashid and Turkish attack which he expected soon after dawn. But the attack did not materialise. Instead the Turkish soldiers had formed themselves into a defensive square with their artillery, holding the Rashid and Bedouin tribesmen in reserve. When the attack did not come Ibn Saud launched the main body of his men against the Turkish square. But his snipers and mounted swordsmen, ill-equipped and unsuited to the task, could make little impression upon it. Therefore, as morning advanced and the sun rose to full strength, they withdrew back into the cover of their encampment among the palm trees to wait out the heat of the day.

At midday, in the full heat and glare of the July sun, the Turks suddenly fell upon them, blasting them with their artillery and then charging in amongst them. Many of Ibn Saud's Bedouin were terrified by the noise and explosions of the bursting Turkish artillery shells.

Shellfire was something they had never so much as heard of before, let alone been subjected to. Confused and terrified, they scattered, fleeing in all directions. Ibn Saud was seriously wounded in a hand and leg when an artillery shell fell and burst beside him. It was only due to luck that he was not killed. Streaming with blood, he lost consciousness and had to be helped away from the fighting. However it was now, when in extremis and facing the imminent threat of total defeat, that he proved the true depth of his resilience and determination. Coming to and with his wounds roughly bandaged, he returned to the thick of the fighting and, moving among the mayhem, among the dying, shooting, shouting and frightened men, going from group to group, he rallied his warriors, urging those losing heart back into the fray. Nevertheless, the day was lost, and he knew it. By this time he and his men were doing no more than fighting a rearguard action. As soon as darkness began to fall and they were able, they beat a retreat away into the protection of the trees and quickly deepening gloaming.[13]

But unknown to both the Turks, Rashids and the Sauds, one contingent of local Bedouin from the area around Anaiza who were allied to Ibn Saud had early on in the battle managed to avoid the advancing Turks and, moving around the flank, had fallen on the Rashid Bedouin held in reserve in the rear. They surprised them and overran their camp. The Rashid Bedouin had scattered in terror and the men from Anaiza, true to the form of a Bedouin raid or *ghazzu*, instead of pursuing the Rashid men or re-joining the main battle, had stayed behind to loot the camp they had overrun.

In their turn too, having forced Ibn Saud and the main body of his force to retreat, the Turks and Rashids set about plundering the Saudi camp. However, as they were gathering their loot they were suddenly surprised to see a new force of apparently well-armed and -provisioned Arabs advancing upon them from behind. The Turks and Rashids scattered in confusion, abandoning their loot as they went. What they did not know was that the Arab force that had appeared to be about to

13 Accounts of this first phase of the battle conflict but this seems the most likely order of events. However, there is much less disagreement about what happened next.

attack them in the rear was in fact the Anaiza men returning to camp with the booty they had looted from the Rashid Bedouin. The Anaiza men were no less astonished than the Turks and Rashids when, on entering what they thought was Ibn Saud's camp they found it full of Turks and Rashids. They were further alarmed when, entering the camp from which the Turks and Rashids had just fled, they discovered that the camp was empty and that there was no sign of their leader, Ibn Saud. So, already nearing exhaustion after a long day of fighting and looting in the intense heat, they in turn also fled.

The next morning revealed the true cost of this confused and in many ways ridiculous battle, so typical in many ways of the often chaotic nature of Bedouin warfare. More than a thousand blood-covered, broken-limbed bodies lay on the battlefield beneath the intensifying sun, each visible patch of skin, congealed blood or exposed flesh submerged under its own canopy of angry, buzzing, crawling, ravening desert flies. As the sun rose and grew hotter the bodies began to swell until, by the time the sun reached its zenith and the desert heat reached its hottest, the shimmering air for miles around was filled with the unmistakable putrid sweet stench of human corpses. Arab chroniclers say the conscripted Turkish soldiers had lost between one thousand and one thousand five hundred killed, Ibn Saud and his allies a thousand, the Rashids and their allies between three and five hundred. These figures are almost certainly exaggerated, but the Turks and Rashids had certainly lost more than a hundred and Ibn Saud twice that number.

That morning, despite their losses, Colonel Shukri's regular troops remained the only credible military force in the field. Because of their better discipline and organisation they ought to have been able to follow up their victory and defeat Ibn Saud for good. But they didn't. They were already exhausted by the heat, continuous marching and action of the last few weeks. Then disease started to take its toll as well. Cholera broke out among Rashid's warriors and the Turks retired to their own defended encampment, hoping that their tactical victory might be enough to undermine Ibn Saud's support among the tribes and force him to withdraw back to Riyadh.

Thus spared immediate and total defeat, Ibn Saud nevertheless still faced potential disaster. The tribes had always been fickle, unreliable allies and, after his mauling by the Turks it seemed to many as if Ibn Saud's star might be waning. With this, plus the summer heat of July and August when the campaigning season would normally be over until the cooler weather of autumn returned, and now with the added threat that cholera might spread from the Rashid ranks, many of Ibn Saud's allies drifted away back to their villages and tribes. Soon only those warriors who were residents of Riyadh remained with Ibn Saud.

But Ibn Saud was never better than when facing defeat. Though still limping and weak from loss of blood as a result of his wounds, he roused himself, riding out to the east and south to rally support among the tribes and sending his most-trusted relatives and henchmen to more distant parts to contact the Mutair, Ataiba and Duwasir tribes in the south and the Muntafik and Anaiza in the far north close to the Euphrates. He countered their doubts with his warmth and conquered their pessimism with his optimism. He cajoled and encouraged the shaikhs, dealing with their quarrels, pride and tetchiness with infinite patience. He told them that they must all come together to fight the Rashids as they had brought the Turks into their land and that close behind them, unless they were halted now, would come their allies the Germans and all kinds of other infidels and imperialists who would take from them their freedom and their land forever.

In a matter of weeks Ibn Saud had brought together a new force. Finally late in September 1904, by which time the continuing summer heat, together with their unsuitable kit and equipment, had taken a further toll of Colonel Shukri's peasant conscripts, the two armies came face to face about forty miles south west of Buraida, on the sandy floor of a broad wadi near a village called Ar Rass. For almost a month the two armies had sat in their camps watching each other, doing little more than send out scout parties and sometimes engaging in a little inconclusive cavalry skirmishing. These weeks of inactivity told much more heavily on Colonel Shukri's army than on Ibn Saud's. The continuing summer heat had taken a further toll on Shukri's un-acclimatized Turkish troops and Ibn Rashid's Bedouin cavalry had become restive. Unable to pasture their camels beyond the narrow confines of the camp for fear of Saudi raids, they started to sneak out of the camp with their animals at night and make for home. With their army threatened by disease, hunger and now desertion, Ibn Rashid urged Shukri to mount an immediate attack on Ibn Saud. When Shukri refused, fearing that an attack was premature while the heat persisted and so many of his men were debilitated, Ibn Rashid flew into a rage and shot him dead. But Rashid still could not order the Turkish soldiers to attack and so he was forced to split his forces into two. Ordering his Bedouin to load up their booty and round up their animals, ready to move that night under the cover of darkness, he and his men started to move out of the camp towards the north west, in the direction of Ha'il and their homes. Meanwhile the Turks, fearing that they were being deserted, formed up into a square, ready to break out next day and head north east, towards Basra.

Whether Ibn Rashid intended by this action to lure Ibn Saud out of position and then launch a combined attack upon him with the two wings of his army we will never know. But the next morning, September 27th, discovering that the Rashids had stolen away, Ibn Saud also hastily split his army. Detaching a body of his cavalry, he sent them in pursuit of Ibn Rashid. Quickly overtaking Ibn Rashid and his Bedouin, Ibn Saud's warriors immediately charged down upon them. Laden with booty and caught unprepared, the Rashids were no match for Ibn Saud's men and were quickly scattered, abandoning their booty as they fled.

Meanwhile Ibn Saud and the main body of his army launched themselves against Shukri's surviving Turks and some remaining Rashid infantry. Having learned from the mauling he had received two months earlier when he had sent his men against the Turks when formed up into a defensive square, Ibn Saud now knew that in order to succeed against them he must get his swordsmen and cavalry warriors right in amongst them. Once fighting was taking place at close quarters and hand-to-hand the Turkish artillery and concentrated rifle volleys would be ineffective.

Mounted on his horse, backed by his bodyguard and shouting the name of his favourite sister, Nura, he led his full force in a headlong charge straight at the centre of the Turkish line. Startled and confused by the blind foolhardy courage of Ibn Saud, the sheer weight and speed of his army's charge, and deprived of the protection of their own cavalry, the Turks failed to repulse the charge. Ibn Saud and his warriors burst right through the Turkish line, cutting men down as they went. Then wheeled about and charged back in among them again from the rear. The Turks broke and began to scatter, then tried to reform and make an orderly fighting retreat. But the Saudi warriors kept at them, harrying them as they retreated until nightfall. The retreat turned into a rout and the field was Ibn Saud's. The Turkish artillery, most of their equipment and ammunition, and even the Turkish pay-chest, full of gold coins, fell into his hands. He had achieved a total victory over a full force of regular Turkish troops.[14]

As Saudi historians and chroniclers would later agree, this battle above all cemented Ibn Saud's position in Najd. It greatly enhanced his reputation amongst the tribes, seriously undermined the Rashid ascendancy and weakened Ottoman influence across Arabia. The victory outside Ar Rass in 1904 was as important as Ibn Saud's earlier seizure of Riyadh.

For Napoleon and Hitler it was the Russian winter as much as the Tsarist and Red armies that defeated them, so with Colonel Shukri and the Ottoman army it was the Arabian summer that had defeated them as much as Ibn Saud. In victory Ibn Saud was once again magnanimous. He showed mercy to those he had captured, offered hospitality to many and allowed the survivors among his defeated foes to return home. In this he once again highlighted for the peoples of Arabia the contrast between Saudi rule and the rule of the Rashids. Of the two thousand four hundred Turkish troops who had marched into Qasim just four months earlier, only seven hundred survived. All through that autumn small groups of exhausted, often injured, Turkish soldiers could be found limping towards home across Arabia. Many were set upon and killed for whatever possessions they still carried by scavenging tribesmen

14 The many accounts of this battle more or less agree, although the detail about Ibn Saud using his sister Nura's name as his war cry occurs in only one so far as we know, that by H. C. Armstrong, *Lord of Arabia: An Intimate Study Of A King*, Penguin Books, Harmondsworth, Middlesex, 1938. Armstrong paid many extensive visits to Saudi Arabia from the early 1920s onwards and interviewed many of the participants in the events he described, including Ibn Saud himself, and says that before including any account he always tried to obtain corroboration from more than one witness. The account of Ibn Rashid's shooting of Colonel Shukri is contained in David Howarth's *The Desert King: The Life of Ibn Saud*, William Collins, London, 1965.

and poverty-stricken peasants, but some survived to make it home to their families in Anatolia and tell their stories. It is from those survivors that we know the story of Colonel Shukri and his murder by Ibn Rashid.

Back in Riyadh the *ulema* and Wahhabi leaders, learning of Ibn Saud's victory, became boastful and full of war talk. They urged Ibn Saud to build on his success and extend the war on the Ottoman 'heretics', to push on towards the goal of complete Arabian and Wahhabi independence. But Ibn Saud and his father were more realistic. Whatever their long-term ambitions, they knew that if really roused the Ottoman Empire could mass huge forces against them and crush them. So early in October Abd al-Rahman sent a grovelling letter to the Sultan via the Turkish governor in Basra which opened: 'My family has of old been known to be loyal to the State and especially to the Commander of the Faithful.' He went on to blame 'intriguing Ottoman officials, egged on by the tyrant Ibn Rashid' who had falsely accused the Sauds, deceived the Ottoman government and brought about the dispatch of Ottoman troops against Najd. He claimed that Ibn Rashid had mounted a series of unprovoked assaults against Najdi and Qasimi villages and citizens and that in repelling the Rashid invasion of their territory, his son had done everything he could to confine his military operations to repelling the Rashid forces and to leave the Ottoman troops unmolested. But Ibn Rashid had responded by deliberately moving his troops in amongst the Turkish soldiers, thus making it impossible for Ibn Saud to attack the Rashid troops without involving the Turks. Finally, Abd al-Rahman pointed out that after Ibn Saud's victory in Qasim he had gone out of his way to prevent 'the Muslim population of Najd from molesting the [Ottoman] troops'. He ended by tendering his and his son's continuing loyalty to the Sultan, adding that he was 'Ready to perform any service to the State and guarantee on oath the security of the roads and pilgrims. I beg that my submission may be accepted and that we may not be left in despair.' Finally he asked the Sultan to resume paying him a pension.[15]

15 Quotations from Abd al-Rahman's letter are from 'The Foreign Office Files Confidential Print (Eastern Affairs)' held at the Public Record Office in London and reproduced in Jacob Goldberg op. cit.

The Sultan was understandably suspicious of Abd al-Rahman's protestations of loyalty, believing them to be insincere. So, still harbouring grave misgivings about Ibn Saud's and his father's real intentions, he ordered the mobilisation of a much larger force of Ottoman troops, half of whom were to come from Mesopotamia and half from Medina – sixteen battalions amounting to seven thousand troops in all. Simultaneously, the Sultan instructed his representatives in the region to invite Ibn Saud to a meeting to see if the dispute could be settled peacefully. Letters went back and forth until finally, in February 1905, a series of meetings was held outside Kuwait between the Turkish governor of Basra and Abd al-Rahman, accompanied by Mubarak. At the meetings it was agreed that Abd al-Rahman was to be made governor of the area of southern Najd around Riyadh and his pension, backdated to 1903, was to be restored. Qasim, however, was to be ruled directly by the Ottomans and an Ottoman garrison installed to prevent both Ibn Rashid and Ibn Saud attempting to seize it again. Finally Najd was to become a mere sub-region within the jurisdiction of the governor of Basra.

When news of this agreement reached Riyadh the *ulema* were outraged, accusing Ibn Saud of treason. 'Our ancestors would be ashamed of us', they protested. In their eyes the agreement amounted to submission to Ottoman heretics. But Ibn Saud recognised that by this agreement he had secured Ottoman recognition for the re-establishment of the Saudi state. The alternative would have been almost certain defeat at the hands of the Turkish military machine. He had bought himself time to find other means of freeing himself and his people from Ottoman shackles.

Two months later an Ottoman garrison entered Qasim, Ottoman flags were hoisted, salutes fired and prayers said for the Sultan. However, behind the scenes and unbeknown to Ibn Saud, the Turks continued to put together a much larger expedition intended to put him down for good.

But before that much larger force of Turkish soldiers could begin to make their advance into Najd, a rebellion broke out in Yemen in the far south west of the Arabian peninsula – that strange and mountainous region from which the Queen of Sheba was said to have come. As a result, in the autumn of 1905 the large force of Ottoman soldiers which had been put together to deal with Ibn Saud instead marched down into the Yemen and never came back to settle the Sultan's scores with the Sauds. By then, too, the Turkish garrison in Qasim was in dire straits. The local shaikhs who had turned out in a show of welcome when they first arrived came to resent their presence. What they really wanted was what they had always wanted, independence to run their affairs as they chose, independence from the Turks and above all from the harsh rule of the Rashids. Far from their home base, from money and supplies, resented by the local people, the Turkish troops began to starve. Covertly Ibn Saud worked to worsen their plight, encouraging the local people not to supply the Turks with food or other goods. By late summer the Turks were on half rations and disease had once again begun to take its toll. As their commander wrote to the Governor of Basra, they could not even afford to buy shrouds for their dead. More and more men began to desert and stumble their way back north. The following year, with the force down to less than half its original number, the Ottoman garrison was recalled.

When the new campaigning and raiding season came round in early 1906 Ibn Rashid returned to Qasim to try to reassert his control. To Ibn Rashid and his followers this meant caravan raiding as much as conquering and re-establishing harsh Rashid rule among the town and oasis dwellers. Ibn Saud also returned to Qasim, hoping that he might catch Ibn Rashid and defeat him for good. On April 12th Ibn Rashid and his men swooped down on a caravan in the sand desert some twenty miles north of Buraida. As it happened the luckless camel drivers were carrying supplies to some of the last Turkish troops. It is unlikely that Ibn Rashid and his men knew this, although even if they had it is unlikely that this would have stopped them. Having scattered the camel train and seized the goods it was carrying, Ibn Rashid and his men retired to a nearby oasis village called Muhanna to divide up the spoils and rest for the night, confident that Ibn Saud was many miles away and that no one would disturb them.

But Ibn Saud, who had been trying to find Ibn Rashid, was only a few miles away. The master of the looted caravan found Ibn Saud and appealed to him for help. Ibn Saud immediately called his warriors together and set off on foot into the darkness to hunt Ibn Rashid down.

Early the next morning before sunrise, a wind got up, raising a swirling sand storm. Taking advantage of the darkness and driving sand to cover his approach, Ibn Saud and his warriors crept up undetected on the barely waking Rashid camp. They then charged in upon them, cutting them down and scattering them as they rose and grabbed their weapons in confusion. A group of Ibn Saud's men managed to seize the Rashid banner and raised it in triumph. But Ibn Rashid, seeing what had happened, waded towards the banner through his panicking, disorientated men, shouting Shammar battle verses in his native dialect to rally them. Ibn Saud's men, realising who this brave but foolhardy warrior must be, shot him down. With their leader dead, the Rashid troops fled back to Ha'il and their own tribes, abandoning their loot as they went. Ibn Saud ordered that Ibn Rashid's head should be severed from his body and paraded on a pole around Buraida, Anaiza and the neighbouring villages to show the people that he was dead and demonstrate that Ibn Saud was now their ruler. It was then thrown to the dogs.

The death of Abdul Aziz ibn Rashid triggered a long, blood-soaked feud between the leading members of the Rashid clan. Abd al-Aziz ibn Rashid was succeeded by his son, but within a year he had been murdered by a cousin who, in turn, was murdered nine months later by another of Abd al-Aziz ibn Rashid's sons. The battle for the Rashid succession would continue in various forms up to the outbreak of the First World War in 1914 and beyond, spreading outwards and infecting the outlying regions and tribes that had been under Rashid control. As a result the Rashid and Shammar power was seriously undermined, enabling Ibn Saud to turn his attention eastwards, towards the fertile lands and Gulf ports of Hasa. He was also able to devote more time to the government of Najd and Riyadh and to re-inforcing his authority within it.

Ibn Saud had had his eyes on Hasa ever since he seized Riyadh. In order to support and feed his people and so secure his rule, he knew he needed both access to Hasa's fertile land and abundant crops and to a seaport and the lucrative trade of the Gulf. Before taking the field against the Rashids early in the spring of 1906 he had addressed another appeal to the British in much the same terms as the appeal he had made late in 1903. He repeated that it was still his intention to eject the Ottomans from Hasa and re-establish Saudi rule across all those parts of Arabia which his family had long believed was their ancestral and religious heritage. But he added that, with his recent defeat of Ibn Rashid and the Ottoman weakness, he now believed he was in a position to achieve his goal of removing the Ottomans from Hasa and their fortified port at Qatif. When he had briefly entered Hasa six months earlier to re-assert Saudi authority in those regions not garrisoned by the Turks and effect a reconciliation between some of the warring tribes he had intended to visit Qatar and some other Gulf ports that had once been Saudi possessions. But the British had let him know in no uncertain terms that if he should attempt to interfere with any of the Arab tribes allied to Britain the British government would regard this as an unfriendly act and take 'suitable measures' against him. As a result Ibn Saud had been left in no doubt that if he meddled with British interests he would risk bringing down the full military might of the British Empire on his head.

So now in February 1906, in this the sixth overture Ibn Saud had made to Britain, he tried to offer them a sweetener. He told them that he wished to enter into a treaty with Britain. He would eject the Ottomans from Hasa and Qatif and, in return for British protection against a possible Ottoman counter-attack from the sea, would allow the British to station a political agent in Hasa or Qatif. However, at the same time Ibn Saud sent yet another missive to the Sultan, reiterating that he remained his loyal and obedient servant ready to render him any service. The British once again turned Ibn Saud down.

In fact the British knew all along that each time Ibn Saud had approached them for support he had at the same time sent a further missive to the Sultan pledging his continued and unswerving loyalty to the Ottoman Empire. Britain's network of agents and informers throughout the region made sure that little of importance could occur without them getting to hear about it. It was perhaps lucky for Ibn Saud that rather than regarding his behaviour as unacceptable and incurring their wrath, sophisticated British officials in the region regarded such blatant duplicity as naivety and so rather charming. Later that same year, 1906, after the death of Ibn Rashid at Muhanna, Ibn Saud made two further overtures to the British. These were also rejected.

However, Ibn Saud's continuing success and his repeated overtures were beginning to cause some rather more far-sighted British officials to have second thoughts about their government's policies in the region. Notes started to fly between officials in charge of the British imperial outposts in the Gulf, the Imperial Government of India and the Foreign Office in London. Sometimes the officials concerned and their attitudes seemed like characters out of a Gilbert and Sullivan opera yet many of them were fine Arabists with a real concern for Arabia and the Arabs. One such official was Percy Zachariah Cox. Tall, slim, ramrod-backed and utterly imperturbable, he had been appointed British Political Resident in the Persian Gulf in 1904 at the age of forty on the recommendation of Lord Curzon himself. He was strict in his unswerving adherence to diplomatic protocol and, as was to be expected of a British Indian civil servant educated at Harrow and Sandhurst, always utterly correct in his dress, even to the point that when venturing into the full heat of the desert he would dress in Homburg hat, impeccably creased black and white striped trousers, tightly buttoned, thick dark jacket, white shirt, starched collar and precisely knotted bow tie. In the autumn of 1906 Cox wrote to his superiors in the Government of India urging them to reconsider their policy towards Ibn Saud. For as long as the Arab amirates had continued to neutralise each other and none had become dominant, the British Government's policy of avoiding entanglements in central Arabia had served it well. But once the Arabs found a leader, as Cox believed they now had in Ibn Saud, that policy would no longer suffice. However, by reaching an understanding with Ibn Saud the British would provide reassurance to Gulf coastal chiefs anxious about Saudi intentions towards them and enlist Ibn Saud in their own fight against piracy in the Persian Gulf. In any case it seemed likely that, with Ibn Saud continuing to extend the area he controlled, the British Government would at some point be compelled to reach an understanding with him, in which case the earlier such an understanding were reached the better. However, to continue to neglect Ibn Saud's overtures was to risk making an enemy of him, in which case there was a danger that he would turn to some other power in his struggle to free himself from interference by the Ottoman Empire. Cox stressed that he was not advocating that Britain should make Najd a protectorate, as it had a number of the amirates along the coast of the Persian Gulf, but rather that in future British policy should favour an independent central Arabia.

Young Colonel Knox, on the other hand, the British Political Agent in Kuwait and another fine Arabist, argued that if Ibn Saud succeeded in conquering Hasa he would be bound to turn to the British for protection from the Ottomans, in which case Britain would be in an unassailable position to dictate the terms of any protection agreement. However, to the most senior of all the British representatives with an interest in the power struggles of the region, the British ambassador in Constantinople Sir Nicholas O'Conor, while Ibn Saud's defeat of Ibn Rashid had made him a more important player in Arabia that only meant that Britain must watch his relations with Kuwait and the Gulf amirates more carefully. Nothing about Ibn Saud's military skill or administrative ability had to date convinced Sir Nicholas that he would ever become sufficiently powerful to free himself from the power of Ottoman arms and interference in his territory. For Britain to do anything that implied its approval for a consolidation of Saudi-Wahhabi power would only serve to antagonise the Ottoman Government and that was to be avoided at all costs.

The Foreign Office in London accepted Sir Nicholas's arguments and instructed the British Government of India and its representatives in the Gulf to continue to avoid involvement of any kind with the affairs of central Arabia. This had been Ibn Saud's ninth attempt since his seizure of Riyadh five years earlier to ally himself to Britain and his ninth rejection. So he concluded that he had better abandon his efforts at allying himself to Britain and, for the time being at least, put off ideas of conquering Hasa. Instead he turned his attention elsewhere.

* * *

In 1907 Ibn Saud married Jauhara, sister of his loyal cousins and brothers-in-arms during the seizure of Riyadh, the Jiluwis. Of all the wives Ibn Saud would have during his life, Jauhara would be the one with whom he fell most deeply in love. He would write her glowing love poems. Years later he would tell a confidant: 'Whenever the world was dark around me and I could not see my way out of dangers and difficulties that beset me I would sit down and compose an ode to

Jauhara; and when it was finished the world was suddenly lighted, and I knew what I had to do.'[16]

All marriages were arranged. As might be expected in the capital of Wahhabism, marriage ceremonies in Najd, even in the ruling family, were very simple. The parents of the bride and groom gathered at the bride's house and the prescribed form of words was pronounced by a shaikh or judge. Some days later guests and visitors would gather in the house of the bridegroom to be entertained to coffee, tea, sweetmeats, to be sprinkled with perfume and fanned with incense. After prayers in the mosque, they would go with the bridegroom to the home of the bride's parents and be entertained in the same way as in the house of the bridegroom's parents. The bridegroom was then led to a private room where he met his bride for the first time. After consummating the marriage he would usually live with his new wife for two or three days in her parents' house, after which he would take her to his own house. Ameen Rihani described one Saud family wedding he was allowed to witness in the old palace in Riyadh in the 1920s. This followed the same formula as for a wedding between two lesser families except that the number of guests was larger – no fewer than three thousand according to Rihani. Both the parents and other relatives of the couple being married slaughtered a total of eighty sheep and thirty camels for that one feast. Because the number of guests was so large the meal had to be eaten over four or five sittings and the guests divided between three of the palace's open courtyards and all the refectories. The guests, mixed together at random without regard to individual class or rank, were seated on the ground in large circles around steaming platters piled high with spiced rice and meat, many large enough to hold a whole camel, carried in by an army of servants. After Ibn Saud had said a short prayer: 'Think of Allah and Allah will think of you', and then a brief pause during which every poised hand was held still, the guests, their flowing sleeves tucked carefully up so as not to fall into the food, began to eat, tearing and plucking at the meat with their right hands and rolling the rice into round balls between their fingers. Westerners often think that eating only with

16 Quoted by M. Almana in *Arabia Unified: A Portrait of Ibn Saud*, Hutchinson Benham, London, 1980.

the right hand, without the aid of cutlery, must be a messy and inelegant business, but in fact among practised Arabs and Bedouin it is as elegant and sophisticated a ritual as in any well-mannered western household.

Marriages being arranged, marriages 'for love' were almost unknown, but marriages which came to involve love, love real and deep between the two partners, were far from unknown. A number of Ibn Saud's marriages came to involve deep and lasting love. Often so fierce in public and to other members of his family, including his own sons, Ibn Saud seems to have revealed a much gentler side of his nature to his wives. One of his wives once told one of Ibn Saud's sons that with his wives he was a different man from the one that his sons so frequently saw. No one seems to know for certain exactly how many times Ibn Saud married during his lifetime. Some accounts suggest he had twenty-two wives but the true figure was almost certainly many times that. Ibn Saud himself told one tribal shaikh that he had married over one hundred women, while in the 1930s Philby records Ibn Saud telling a small evening gathering of his intimates that he had 'married no fewer than one hundred and thirty-five virgins, to say nothing of "about a hundred" others' but that he had decided to limit himself in future 'to two new wives a year'.[17] He had forty-three sons by his marriages and more than fifty daughters. In addition to his wives he had countless concubines.

The Qur'an refers to marriage as a 'solemn covenant' and states that God 'created for you spouses from among yourselves that you might live in peace with them, and planted love and kindness in your hearts'.[18] It also states that a man may marry 'two, three or four' women but only in so far as he is able to support them properly and be just to all of them.[19] As can be adduced from the number of women Ibn Saud married, divorce was also easy, requiring little more than that the man formally repudiate his wife. Men were also permitted, within certain limits, to remarry ex-wives. Upon marriage a man was required to give the wife a dowry and, except where the wife had committed some breach in the

17 H. St John Philby, *Arabian Jubilee*, Robert Hale, London, 1952.

18 Qur'an 30:21. Translated by N. J. Darwood, Penguin Classics 50th Anniversary Edition, Penguin Books, London, 2006.

19 Qur'an 4:3.

code of wifely behaviour, she was permitted to keep her dowry even after divorce.

Ibn Saud was extremely fond of women but for him marriage was also a political tool. He used marriage as a means of consolidating his power, cementing his alliances and, when he married the former wives or daughters of those he had recently defeated, as an extension of his domination of that family. Because of his frequent divorces, marriage was not necessarily a reliable means of building a lasting alliance, but because of the children a marriage might produce it was often a valuable means of creating inter-connected networks of familial relationships and so bringing his disparate and disunited state closer to becoming a homogeneous entity. Ibn Saud's use of marriage as a political instrument extended well beyond his own marriages. As we have seen in his treatment of the 'Araif', he frequently arranged marriages between members of his own extended family and members of families with whom he wanted to make or cement an alliance or reduce tensions, as a means of ending inter-tribal or inter-family disputes or as a way of bringing together previously disparate groups and tribes into his emerging unified and interdependent Saudi state.

Traditional tribal loyalties were very important in central Arabia. It was because of such traditional tribal loyalties that Ibn Saud had little difficulty in bringing the peoples of the southern Najd to his side after his recapture of Riyadh in 1902. But when he moved north into Qasim such traditional loyalties were far less strong. One of the means of making the people of Qasim his allies was through going raiding together and giving his new allies an equal share of the spoils. Arranging marriages between members of his own family and the leading tribal families of the region was another. In Qasim Ibn Saud's policy of showing mercy to those he had conquered and forgiving those who had sided with his enemies was also important in building new and lasting alliances. In Qasim Ibn Saud's generous policy stood in sharp contrast to the harsh treatment the tribes had often received from the Rashids. As a result when Ibn Saud advanced into Qasim he was able to form alliances from among the local tribes whereas the Rashids had to turn to outsiders, the Ottomans, for assistance. Ibn Saud showed that he could exact the harshest retribution upon those who persisted in their treachery, arriving in a place, having his warriors lay it waste, bringing the offending leaders before him and having them executed. But generally after conquering a town or region he would send the leaders home, appoint the head of one of the town or region's leading families governor and perhaps arrange one or more marriages between himself or members of his own family and a member or members of the families of his vanquished opponents. Where he was less certain of winning the loyalty of the place by these means alone, he might appoint one of his close relatives or trusted lieutenants as the governor. But always he tried to make sure that the inhabitants of a place that he had conquered were treated justly, rather than having them brutalised and humiliated.

Another essential element in Ibn Saud's rule was his partnership with Najd's Wahhabi religious leadership, publicly acknowledged in the sacred oath of allegiance, the *bay'a*, taken by the area's leading religious leaders and scholars after Friday prayers in Riyadh's main mosque shortly after his seizure of the town in 1902. By their public submission to him, as manifested in their taking of this sacred oath, the religious leaders had conferred upon Ibn Saud's rule an enormous additional authority. From that moment on Ibn Saud and his advocates had been able to lay claim to the idea that by submitting politically to Ibn Saud's authority a person, tribe, town or region was also submitting themselves to God. Ibn Saud's conquests became in effect religious conquests. The concept of partnership between the political leader and the religious ritual specialists went back to the roots of Wahhabism and the partnership between Muhammad Ibn Abd al-Wahhab and Muhammad ibn Saud out of which Wahhabism and the first Saudi state had been born.

The respective spheres of authority of the religious specialists, the *ulema* (religious scholars who in the Sunni and Wahhabi traditions were the only people who had sufficient learning to interpret the Qur'an – the 'final' word of God) and *mutawwa'a* (the Najdi term for religious enforcers or, as Palgrave had called them 'zealators'), and of Ibn Saud were quite distinct. The *ulema* and *mutawwa'a* were given sole and absolute responsibility for interpretation of Islamic law and the sacred texts, for enforcing strict observance by all Ibn Saud's subjects of the Five Pillars of Islam – bearing witness ('There is no god but God, and Muhammad is His witness'), prayer five times a day and mosque attendance at the prescribed times and in the correct form, payment of *zakat* (religious taxes or charity based on a proportion of an individual's wealth), making pilgrimage to Mecca (*hajj*), observance of the Ramadan fast. The *mutawwa'a*, wearing what Rihani described as 'white turbans' and carrying long sticks, patrolled the streets of Riyadh and the other places subject to Ibn Saud's rule, enforcing these rules and the other Wahhabi prohibitions, such as the ban on smoking and injunctions against singing and music. They also ensured observance of the rules on modesty and 'chaste behaviour', lowering of the gaze in the presence of members of the opposite sex, correct dress and for women the covering of the hair, legs, arms, face and of any adornments. Punishments for even quite minor breaches of the codes could be severe. In the 1920s Ameen Rihani recorded watching a man who had been found guilty of smoking a cigarette being made to lie face down on the ground in front of a crowd of onlookers and given sixty lashes with canes by two *mutawwa'a*. Ibn Saud would sometimes encourage the *mutawwa'a* and religious scholars to move into an area that he planned to conquer to re-invigorate people's commitment to the observance of Wahhabi codes and rituals ahead of him as a preparation for their acceptance of his political authority.

Ibn Saud not only renewed the original partnership between religion and the state established by Muhammad Ibn Abd al-Wahhab and Muhammad ibn Saud but in some ways developed it. Where previously the *mutawwa'a* had been unpaid, living off charity or, if they were lucky, by farming or operating as merchants, Ibn Saud gave them salaries, paid either in cash or in kind. In return for this and his recognition of their absolute authority in all religious matters the religious leaders legitimised Ibn Saud's rule, underwriting his absolute discretion in political matters. This dual authority was to prove fundamental to the functioning and development of the Saudi state.

The other vital element of Ibn Saud's rule was his *majlis* or council. Senior *ulema* and other religious leaders frequently took part in the discussions in Ibn Saud's *majlis* and the smaller evening sessions always began with readings by a religious scholar from an appropriate religious text, followed by discussion and interpretation of its meaning and significance. The morning session of the *majlis*, lasting two hours, was the one where members of the public could bring their disputes to Ibn

Saud, as their Shaikh, for settlement, lay petitions before him, seek redress for perceived injustices, and generally bring their problems to him to seek his help. Observers agree that it was at these sessions that he was to be seen at his very best. His imposing stature and personality, seated at the centre of his subjects with only his closest advisers or the most senior members of his own family and any particularly honoured guest accorded the privilege of a reserved space beside him, added to his aura of authority. Patient with the over-awed and shy, firm with the belligerent or over-loquacious, a pithy interjection from him could quiet even the most over-heated arguments between whole families or villages of disputants, cutting through a maze of conflicting and confusing facts and narratives, bringing clarity to confusion, sifting the relevant from the irrelevant and reducing complexities to their essentials. He would make his judgements, issue his commands, refer some complex point of law to the experts in *shari'a* (the Islamic legal code), or recommend a compromise between disputing petitioners. Philby records him saying of the Bedouin, who frequently brought their disputes to him for settlement, that he had 'brought to bear on them a method unknown to the rulers of Arabia before me. I have made it my aim to be patient with all men. Be patient with God, and be patient with the stiff-necked; for these will either repent and be cured, or come out in their true colours openly, when they can be struck down once and for all.' [20]

Later in the morning Ibn Saud would conduct a much smaller meeting with his advisers at which more complex or confidential matters of state were discussed and decisions reached. When not out fighting wars, Ibn Saud frequently made tours with his entourage to different parts of his domain. This was a way of making his authority tangible to all his subjects. The whole court would ride out on camel back, making frequent stops at oases or villages for rest and refreshment. At each stop Ibn Saud would hold a *majlis*. Local shaikhs and Bedouin would come in, present themselves, renew their allegiance to him and make him gifts of local produce. He would hear grievances and settle disputes. He would distribute gold and silver coins to the poor and needy from a special purse he always carried on these occasions. Those who came to

20 H. St John Philby, *Arabian Jubilee*, Robert Hale, London, 1952.

the *majlis* would also be invited to enjoy his hospitality, not only to drink coffee but at the appropriate times to feast on lamb and rice which he provided. Important guests would also be perfumed with incense before they left. Whole tribes of often hungry Bedouin would come in from the desert to camp outside major towns where Ibn Saud stopped so that they could enjoy his hospitality. Word of Ibn Saud's generosity and power would spread far and wide, so reaching even those who had not themselves seen their ruler or attended his *majlis*. In this Ibn Saud's method of rule and spreading his authority was in sharp contrast to that of other powerful shaikhs like the Rashids who ruled and imposed their authority through harsh punishments and the extortion of punitive fines and taxes.

While Saud was expanding and consolidating his domain in central Arabia events were happening far from the Arabian peninsula's shores that were to have a huge impact upon its fate. In 1904 France and Britain had entered into an agreement, the Entente Cordiale, aimed at controlling German power in Europe. The Entente put an end to Britain and France's centuries of enmity. Under it France agreed to give up all her claims on Egypt and allow Britain a free hand there, while, in return, Britain agreed to back France's claim to Morocco. In 1907 Russia joined the Entente and agreed to divide Persia into British and Russian spheres of influence. In the following year, 1908, oil was discovered in Persia.

Meanwhile the Ottoman Empire had grown still weaker as a result of continuing insurrections and, at the same time, grown even closer to Germany. On July 23rd 1908, following a military mutiny and under increasing pressure from the reformist Young Turks, the Sultan restored the liberal constitution which he had suspended thirty years earlier. Across the Empire rejoicing people came out into the streets carrying banners that hailed the end of autocracy and the dawn of a new age of political and religious freedom. Palace spies were banished and a new free press was born. Elections were called.

Later that year the Sultan deposed the ruling Sharif of Mecca and replaced him with another member of the same family, Husayn Ibn Ali. Husayn was a member of the Hashemite clan and, like his predecessor, claimed direct descent from the Prophet Muhammad through the Prophet's daughter Fatima. For more than eight hundred years the post of Sharif, Protector of the Two Holy Cities and the Holy Places, had always been filled by a member of the Hashemite family.[21] The Sharif, who was also appointed Amir of the Hijaz, was expected both to protect The Cities and Holy Places of Mecca and Medina and to oversee the annual *Hajj* pilgrimage. But in the continuing struggle between the Sultan and the Young Turks the sultan's appointment of Husayn as Sharif was controversial. For the Young Turks, by appointing Husayn, one of his own supporters, the Sultan appeared to be trying to bolster his own power. The appointment was not universally popular inside Arabia nor in the wider Muslim community. The Hashemite clan, like so many of the peninsula's ruling families, had long been riven by its own deep internal disputes and feuds. Just how significant Husayn's appointment was in the wider struggle between the Young Turks and the Sultan it is hard to be certain, but less than six months later, in April 1909, the Sultan was deposed.

Husayn, however, continued in his post and, because of continuing strife within the Ottoman Empire, soon came to exercise considerable autonomy. As time passed he came to entertain ever greater ambitions until, finally, he came to see himself as a future King of all the Arabs.

By April 1909 Ibn Saud was occupied by more pressing matters than the possible dreams of the new ruler of the Hijaz. A year earlier a dreadful drought had begun in central Najd, around Riyadh. As the crops failed and the people started to go hungry they began to lose faith in Ibn Saud. Perhaps the drought around his capital was a sign of Allah's displeasure? But further north, in the Jebel Shammar, close to Ha'il, the rains were more abundant than ever. People and tribes began to move north in search of food and water. Some now also shifted their loyalties towards the Rashids.

Around Ibn Saud's domain rebellions and uprisings became ever more frequent. In February 1909 a revolt broke out a hundred miles to the south east in a district called Al Hariq. Ibn Saud hurried southeast with a force of loyal followers and over two months and a series of battles

21 The title 'Sharif' was more correctly 'Grand Sharif', as all descendants of The Prophet are called 'Sharif'. However, in popular usage the word 'Grand' is usually omitted.

restored order. By which time there was fresh trouble to the north of Riyadh, in Buraida. Ibn Saud dashed north and dealt with this too. Across his domain old tribal rivalries and family feuds which Ibn Saud hoped he had put to rest for ever flared anew. During the years 1908 to 1910 Ibn Saud seemed to be almost continuously in the field dealing with a new revolt here, a challenge there, a defection somewhere else. The series of battles he fought, the continuously shifting loyalties and alliances were endlessly confusing, probably even to many of the people who found themselves caught up in them. Many of the Bedouin who took part in the battles of this period must often have been unsure on whose side they were fighting and confused as to who was supposed to be their ally and who their foe. Yet throughout Ibn Saud seemed to be tireless, dashing from one trouble spot to the next, often across hundreds of miles of desert and scrubland, appearing in person at the head of his forces, urging his allies on and himself plunging deep into the heart of the battle. He was not always victorious and was often injured. But nothing seemed to stop him. After a setback he would pick himself up, rally his supporters and try again. Repeatedly pressing forward, he mounted new attacks and campaigns, until at last he was successful. In each place that he re-conquered he personally appeared to restore order, right wrongs, listen to grievances and dispense justice. Although he could be stern when the occasion demanded, he persisted in his policy of showing mercy to those he defeated. Even when the governor he had himself appointed after his original capture of Buraida had led a revolt against him, after defeating him Ibn Saud restored him to his post. Even when the same governor defied him a second time and Ibn Saud again recaptured the town, he did not have the governor beheaded as the governor and townspeople might have expected, instead he dismissed the governor and allowed him to go and live in exile in Iraq. By such means Ibn Saud steadily and painstakingly built up a fund of goodwill and loyalty towards himself and his growing infant state.

However, there were some challenges and types of disloyalty that Ibn Saud believed could only be eradicated by exemplary punishment. One such challenge arose early in 1910 when some of the 'Araif' whom he had pardoned after he captured them at Buraida six years earlier, mounted a major challenge to his rule. One in particular, Saud Al Kabir had been given one of Ibn Saud's own sisters, Nura, in marriage. At the start of 1910 the Araif began fomenting rebellion among tribes to the south disaffected by the continuing drought, arguing that Ibn Saud's hereditary right to rule was inferior to their own. One of the tribes in which they succeeded in rousing a number of clans to revolt was the Ajman, one of the largest and most revered tribes in all Arabia whose grazing territory stretched from the Hasa in the north east of the peninsula southwards almost to the Rub Al Khali. Egged on by the Araif, this section of the Ajman began plundering among the towns, farmers and oases a hundred and fifty miles south of Riyadh. Among the places where the flag of rebellion was raised was a town called Layla, astride the ancient trade route from Saba, the kingdom which had been the home of the Queen of Sheba, to Uquair on the Gulf coast, the site of the ancient city of Gerrha and land of Dilmun. Ibn Saud had put down a revolt in this area two years earlier. Then, having systematically driven the rebels southwards out of the area they had held, he had surrounded them in Layla and started a siege. But the town, secure behind its own strong high walls had seemed impregnable against the primitive armaments available to him, so Ibn Saud had resorted to a ruse. Making a great show of digging and earth moving outside the town walls, Ibn Saud had put the word about that he had driven a mine deep under the town walls and was ready to blow up the walls and a great part of the town with them unless the defenders surrendered at once. The ruse had succeeded and the town's leaders, all members of the Hazzani family, had surrendered. Instead of punishing them, Ibn Saud had taken the Hazzani and other ringleaders of the revolt back to Riyadh and detained them there as his guests. After some months they had been allowed to return home.

Now many of the same people had risen against him a second time. This time Ibn Saud was merciless. Marching south with a much larger force, he sent out parties of men to systemically loot and raze to the ground each pocket and centre of revolt along his route. As before the rebels retreated before him, many of the Araif leaders fleeing to safety in Oman or with Husayn in the Hijaz. Those that remained, the Hazzani and the most senior of the Araif, Saud Al Kabir, again attempted to lock themselves in behind the high protective walls of Layla. But this time, with the citizens less united in their defiance and with the help of the governor he had appointed to rule the area after the previous revolt, Ibn Saud had little difficulty in forcing the town to surrender.

Nineteen of the ringleaders of the revolt, including his brother-in-law and cousin Saud Al Kabir and the senior members of the Hazzani family, were caught and paraded before him. Ibn Saud condemned each man to death but gave each of them twenty-four hours' grace before the sentence was carried out. In the twenty-four hours that followed, while the men returned to their prison to make peace with their maker and say farewell to their families, Ibn Saud sent messengers throughout the town and surrounding region summoning the people to attend him next morning outside Layla's main gate.

When the people began to approach the gate next morning they found that immediately in front of it carpenters had erected a sturdy wooden platform and arranged a short row of chairs on it. At the appointed hour, by which time a large crowd had assembled in front of the platform and stood talking among themselves in subdued puzzlement and expectation watched over by some of Ibn Saud's warriors, Ibn Saud himself appeared, striding purposefully through the town gate, accompanied by his bodyguards and senior shaikhs. He mounted the platform and took his seat in the centre of the row of chairs, his face dark, brooding and implacable. When the senior shaikhs had taken their seats on either side of him and his bodyguards had grouped themselves behind him and to the sides, Ibn Saud rose and in a strong, deep voice that could be clearly heard at the back of the large crowd, he commanded that the traitors be brought before him.

Moments later the nineteen condemned men were marched out of the town gate in pairs with halters round their necks. In turn each man was made to kneel at the foot of the platform holding the ritual bowl which was to catch the unclean blood from his neck after his head had been struck off. Then Ibn Saud, standing above him, in a voice like cold steel said to each in turn: 'There is no Might nor Power save in Allah.' Having spoken these words he gave the sign whereupon a tall, immensely powerful African slave, the executioner, bare from the waist upwards and drawn sword in hand, stepped forward. In a technique reminiscent of an expert slaughterman intending to kill an animal in one clean blow, the executioner, swinging the mighty curved blade deliberately upwards and outwards in a forehand arc, pricked the neck of the man about to be executed with the point of the sword and then, as the man instinctively stiffened and stretched in a reflex of fear, brought the sword down again in a mighty backhand arc, slicing clean through the man's neck, sending blood fountaining into the air from the prisoner's still-pumping heart and his head tumbling and rolling through the hot air into the dust on the ground. Eighteen times this happened, coldly and deliberately, with no joy or exultation in the deaths of the vanquished foe. All the while Ibn Saud looked on, erect, stern, his face unchanging, the embodiment of implacable unbending justice. The last man to kneel before him was Saud Al Kabir, his cousin and his sister Nura's husband. He had been made to stand by watching as one by one each of his fellow conspirators had had their heads struck from their bodies. Now he knelt as his implacable cousin towered above him. The executioner again stepped forward, sword-blade wiped clean of the last man's blood, gleaming in the sun. But as the executioner began to raise his blade Ibn Saud halted him. Looking down on Saud Al Kabir he gave him this choice: either he could remain and become Ibn Saud's loyal follower or he could go to join his fugitive brothers under the protection of Husayn in the Hijaz. Saud Al Kabir chose to stay with Ibn Saud.

With the executions done Ibn Saud spoke to the people. His voice rolling like thunder he told them of the sin of rebellion and how they had witnessed its just punishment. Then, speaking more quietly and drawing them closer around him, he addressed them as his beloved subjects. Promising them that, so long as they remained loyal to him he would ensure that they would be protected and live in peace, he told them to go back to their communities and recount what they had seen, to tell all they met how they had seen his justice and of the promises that he had made to them. Then he sent them home with his blessing.

Word of what had happened duly spread through the villages and oases and around the Bedouin camp fires not only in the region around Layla but far beyond around much of central Arabia; of Ibn Saud's justice, of his mercy and of his power. More and more came to believe that he was, indeed, the man, the warrior and amir fit to be their ruler.

Ibn Saud's pardoning of Saud Al Kabir at Layla turned out to be a wise decision. Saud Al Kabir served Ibn Saud loyally for the rest of his life and grew to be one of the most respected and honoured members of the House of Saud. In fact the pardon was probably inevitable because Ibn Saud could hardly have executed the man who was both his cousin and arguably his senior in the line of succession but also the husband of his favourite sister, Nura, without bringing great dishonour, and probably new dissension, to his own family. In fact the arranged marriage between Saud Al Kabir and Nura seems to have developed into a deep and lasting love affair, giving rise to stories of Saud Al Kabir slipping back home at night when out campaigning in order to creep into his house to spend the night with Nura.[22]

Family honour and brotherly affection also played an important role in another crisis that beset Ibn Saud that same spring. Ever since being appointed Sharif of Mecca, Husayn had been trying to draw the Ottoman Empire into supporting him in an assault on Ibn Saud. Eager to curry favour and demonstrate his value to them, early in 1910 Husayn had marched into the far south with his army to put down an uprising against the Ottomans in Asir. At about the same time Ibn Saud had sent one of his younger brothers, Sa'ad, into the lands which he had previously conquered to the west of Riyadh to recruit more warriors for his campaign in the south against the Araif. Sa'ad and his small force had inadvertently marched straight into the arms of Husayn and his army as it was returning home from putting down the uprising in Asir and Husayn, hardly able to believe his luck, had taken Sa'ad prisoner. Immediately Husayn dispatched a messenger to Ibn Saud demanding not only a six thousand rial ransom for Sa'ad's safe return but an acknowledgement from Ibn Saud that he accepted Ottoman suzerainty over Qasim and northern Najd. If the ransom and the acceptance of Ottoman suzerainty were not forthcoming Husayn would take Sa'ad

22 There is some dispute as to whether the man pardoned was Saud Al Kabir or another of the Araif who was married to another of Ibn Saud's sisters (Robert Lacey in his book *The Kingdom* claims that it was another Araif brother with the name Saud). However Philby and H. C. Armstrong, both of whom knew Ibn Saud and had ample opportunities to question him in the 1920s, less than two decades after the events, both claim that the man pardoned was Saud Al Kabir. There is also some doubt as to whether he was made to kneel before Ibn Saud and the executioner before being pardoned but it seems probable.

back to Mecca as his prisoner and hand him over to the Ottomans as proof of Ibn Saud's obduracy. Ibn Saud set about trying to negotiate with Husayn, but Husayn was not prepared to compromise. So rather than lose his brother, Ibn Saud agreed to Husayn's humiliating terms. Sa'ad was released and returned to Riyadh.

Here, as in other important decisions, Ibn Saud had determined his course of action based on a large degree of statesmanlike calculation, but also out of strong bonds of family affection and a powerful sense of family honour. Ibn Saud had saved his brother out of love and also because to have surrendered him without a fight would have brought dishonour not only upon him but upon the whole Saudi family. To have allowed his brother to be handed over to the Turks as a prisoner by Husayn would have risked provoking a fresh feud inside his own most immediate family. In any case, Ibn Saud was well aware that he was not yet strong enough militarily to take on Husayn successfully and that, even if he were to defeat Husayn in battle and rescue his brother in that way, doing so would almost certainly bring down the full military might of the Ottoman Empire upon him. So Ibn Saud put off his intended show-down with Husayn but in the clear knowledge and determination that one day, when he had built up his own military strength to a sufficient extent, that show-down would come.

In fact Ibn Saud never paid any of the ransom money to Husayn, claiming that his agreement to pay was not binding because he had been forced to accept the agreement under duress. Nevertheless Hausayn returned to Mecca in triumph. Not only had he crushed the rebels in Asir but, as he trumpeted far and wide, he had humiliated the Sauds.

So in just those few months in 1910 Ibn Saud had both greatly increased his power and prestige in the south, not only by putting down the revolt fomented by the Araif but also by the way in which he had dealt with the ringleaders. At the same time he had suffered a serious humiliation at the hands of Husayn when he had not only allowed his brother to be captured by him but had then been forced to pay a ransom and accept his subservience to the Ottomans in order to obtain his brother's release. This had brought Ibn Saud into great discredit among the tribes to the west and north of Riyadh, the tribes that were already more vulnerable to the Hashemites and Rashids.

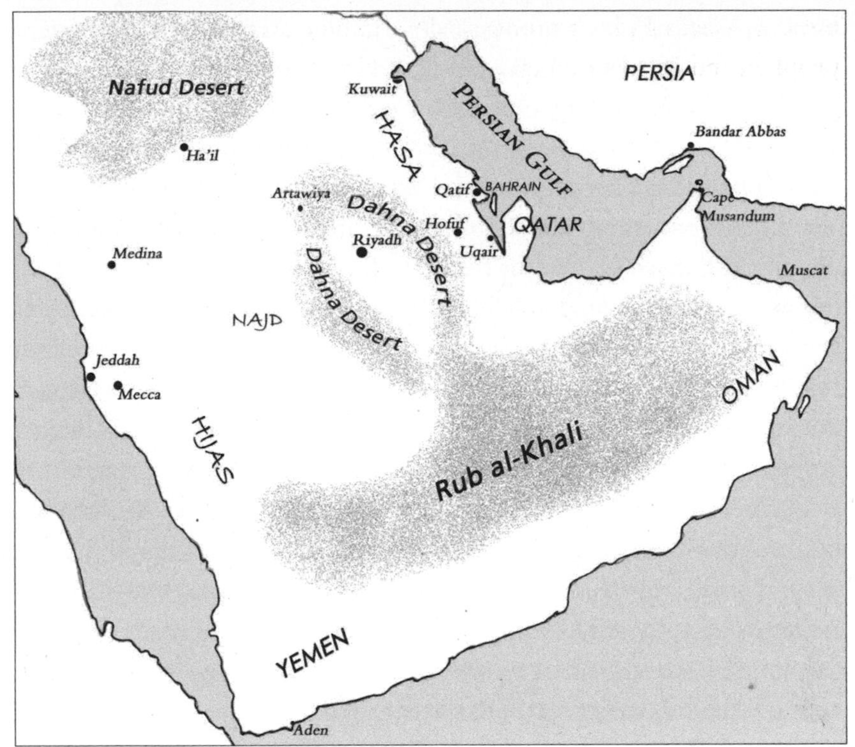

CHAPTER 5

Shakespear, the Ikhwan and the Coming War

The spring of 1910 saw a third event just as significant for Ibn Saud as either his suppression of the Araif revolt or humiliation at the hands of Sharif Husayn. On February 28th he was introduced for the first time to Captain William Henry Irvine Shakespear.

Shakespear had succeeded Knox as Britain's Political Agent in Kuwait in 1908. He was just two years older than Ibn Saud, but despite his youth he had already packed enough colourful adventure into his life to furnish the plot of one of the plays of his illustrious namesake (a distant forebear). Like the sons of most British middle-class servants of Empire, Shakespear had spent much of his childhood away from his parents at boarding schools in England. Of his mother Annie's three sons it was above all her eldest, William, into whom she had channelled all her own strong character, intense emotional loyalty and ambition. Commanding and elegant but wholly undemonstrative, in the way demanded of well-mannered English women of the period, Anne, known throughout her life as Annie, had taught William to read and write long before he started attending school. By the time he was six she had ensured not only that he had an exceptionally wide English vocabulary but spoke fluent Punjabi as well, the language of the family's Indian servants. William's father, a mild-mannered and retiring man, worked for the Government of India Forestry Department. By the time he was seventeen William had been captain of his school's cricket eleven and his house rugby XV and an acclaimed athlete. After officer training at Sandhurst, William had been posted to his first regiment in India at the age of nineteen. Over the next five years he had been promoted progressively to the rank of acting Captain, mastered two further Indian languages and Arabic, distinguished himself by his energetic and extremely effective handling of a horrific outbreak of plague (which as the Black Death had ravaged medieval Europe) in the city of Bombay. He had become a fine cavalry-man and marksman, commanded a squadron on exacting manoeuvres, passed the Staff Corps examination and come to the favourable attention of his superiors, including the Viceroy himself.

However, by the age of twenty-four, seemingly set for further rapid promotion, Shakespear was thirsting for even more responsibility and action. So, restless and ambitious by nature, he had applied for a transfer to the Viceroy's Political Department and been posted as deputy to the British Political Resident in Persia, Percy Cox. As a result Shakespear, at just twenty-four years of age, became the youngest consul in the British Administration of India.

Cox and Shakespear could hardly have been more different. Although like Shakespear an army officer, the forty-year-old, tall, slim Cox had from the moment he had joined the British Civil Administration of India become a civil servant *par excellence*, donning his pinstripe suits and stiff wing collars as though born to them. Cox was a stoic, exceptionally abstemious, patient and tolerant, never allowing any hint of frustration to show no matter how perverse the commands of his government or the actions of the people he sometimes had to deal with. Young Shakespear, on the other hand, often appeared bristling and impatient, remaining first and foremost a soldier and man of action. He had arrived to take up his post in Bandar Abbas, on the Persian side of the Gulf Straits directly opposite Cape Musandum, in full army uniform, complete with topee and gaiters, bearing the largest Union Jack he had been able to lay his hands on. Already older looking than his twenty-five years, Shakespear had a hair line that had started to recede to reveal his high domed forehead. He had darkened his youthful light brown hair with pomade and tamed his potentially unruly military moustache with wax. However, his dark eyes, strong straight nose and powerful, pronounced chin, revealed the determined and intense character that lurked within.

Not a man for the dull disciplines and self-effacing tact of civil service office routine, Shakespear found it hard to sit in the same chair for more than five minutes at a time. He would argue forcefully, expressing his views and feelings about issues, policies and politicians with no regard for his own junior position or diplomatic niceties. Yet Cox quickly spotted that this young man, while unlikely ever to make a conventional diplomat, was more than usually alert and extremely well-informed. Privately Cox often agreed with Shakespear's outspoken opinions and a genuine friendship and respect quickly sprang up between the two men.

Shakespear rapidly came to hate Bandar Abbas. The people around him bored him and the climate was 'pestilential'. He took to escaping as often as he could, undertaking journeys of exploration up into the Persian hinterland or making short tours in a small boat around the islands of the Gulf, crossing to Muscat and the shaikhdoms along the Arab coast where he would practise his Arabic among the traders in the souks.

In 1906 Russia had also appointed a Government representative to Bandar Abbas and he and Shakespear had taken an instant dislike to each other. The last thing that Cox or the British government wanted at that moment, when relations between Britian and Russia were already extremely tense, was some kind of confrontation with the Russians in the Gulf on account of a mutual dislike between their two local representatives in Bandar Abbas. So Cox, eager to retain Shakespear's considerable talents but needing to get him out of harm's way, had posted him to Muscat on the south-east Indian Ocean coast of Arabia. There Shakespear had quickly demonstrated that he was adept at getting onto good terms with local leaders and sorting out disputes between them. As a result he was given a succession of similar brief postings and troubleshooting missions.

During this time Shakespear also developed a reputation as an intrepid pioneer motorist. In 1907, before even learning to drive let alone master the intricacies of car mechanics, Shakespear took delivery of a single-cylinder Indian and Colonial model eight-horsepower Rover costing £250. Just weeks later he set out to drive overland from Persia to England, his car loaded with twenty two-gallon spare cans of petrol (filling stations were still unknown). He also carried oil for the head-lamps, eight spare tyres and two spare wheels, a jack, pick, shovel, axe, yards of rope, coils of wire, spare accumulator batteries, blankets, groundsheet, copious tins of food and a small stock of whisky and wine with which to see himself through the cold desert nights, his plate camera and photographic materials, tripod, sextant, compass and mapping instruments. Shakespear's family were distantly linked by marriage to Fox-Talbot, the early pioneer of photography, and Shakespear was an extremely enthusiastic and accomplished photographer. Despite all the dangers and hardships of his epic trip, on top of the hazards of passing through lands where there were no roads, motorcars were unknown and Europeans often regarded with deep suspicion, all the privations, accidents and breakdowns, the mountains, deserts and flooded rivers that had to be crossed and the many difficult and dangerous situations, Shakespear was truly happy during this journey. He was a natural adventurer who thrived on conquering difficulties, on testing his determination and using his ingenuity to get himself out of tight situations. He loved to beat the odds, even though he had been responsible for getting himself into the difficulties in the first place.

While passing through Switzerland on his epic journey Shakespear met and became deeply attracted to a young woman called Dorothea Baird. She, like Shakespear, had spent part of her childhood in India. She also shared his deep interest in and knowledge of Arabia. During his leave in Britain after the journey the couple had spent as much time as they could in each other's company and when Shakespear returned to the east at the end of that summer he and Dorothea continued to keep in touch through frequent letters.

The following year, when Shakespear had once more been in England to spend Christmas with his family, he made time to fit in another visit to Dorothea's family in Scotland. By then both families were well aware of the bond between Dorothea and William ('Shako' or 'The Consul' as he was known by Dorothea's family) and expected that they would become engaged. Yet Christmas and the New Year passed and no engagement was announced.

In selecting Shakespear to follow Knox as the Political Resident in Kuwait, Percy Cox had deliberately chosen someone who, like Knox, was a good Arabist, who he knew had the strength, stamina and interest to undertake frequent journeys into the heartland of Arabia to keep tabs on developments that might impact on Britain's interests. He had also chosen Shakespear because of his proven ability to win the confidence of local leaders and because he knew that Shakespear shared many of his own views on British policy in the area. On top of which, Kuwait was one of the few places in the Gulf where there was probably little likelihood of him coming up directly against the representatives of Turkey and antagonising them.

Shakespear arrived in Kuwait at a difficult moment. In London, where Herbert Asquith had recently become Prime Minister, he and his new Foreign Secretary, Sir Edward Grey, were obsessed by the possibility of war in Europe. The result was an even greater fear of allowing anything to happen in the Middle East and Gulf which might provoke Turkey into becoming more hostile towards Britain. Towards the end of his time in Kuwait Knox had repeatedly been ordered to warn Shaikh Mubarak that if he provoked the Turks he would get no help from Britain. In this climate relations between the Foreign and India Offices had descended into something nearing open conflict.

Shakespear, impatient and outspoken, was very different from the punctilious and reliable Knox. Shakespear arrived in Kuwait as he had earlier in Bandar Abbas, in khaki army uniform and carrying in his baggage the same enormous Union Jack. This he immediately raised on the flagpole on the seafront in front of the British Agency building. A little later his trusty Rover arrived in Kuwait as well, causing much stir among the populace. Soon Shakespear's yacht was also to be seen bobbing at anchor a few yards off shore in front of the Residency Building.

Colonel Knox and Mubarak had got on well together largely due to the fact that for most of the time they left each other alone. Shakespear and Mubarak, on the other hand, got off to a bad start together, resulting in a series of angry disagreements. Fortunately, however, their arguments led fairly quickly to a friendship between them as they grew first to respect, understand, then to trust each other.

Before he arrived in Kuwait Shakespear had read much about Ibn Saud and his growing power in central Arabia in the numerous reports of British representatives in the region. He had also been told a lot about him by Percy Cox. His already deep interest in Arabia, Najd and its rising shaikh had been intensified still further as a result of his intense friendship with Dorothea Baird and her voracious reading about the subject. He had therefore been surprised on his arrival in Kuwait to receive a copy of a memorandum which had been written by the recently deceased British ambassador in Constantinople, Sir Nicholas O'Conor. This suggested that rather than Ibn Saud being the coming man in the region, the Rashids were likely to remain the dominant family in northern Arabia and that the Sauds would become 'merely notable as hereditary amirs of the Wahhabis'. Shakespear suspected that O'Conor had been biased in favour of the Rashids, perhaps on account of the Rashids being loyal to the Turks and O'Conor, as ambassador in Constantinople, being committed to the British policy of appeasing the Turks. Shakespear decided to discover what Mubarak made of O'Conor's opinion. As he expected, Mubarak rubbished O'Conor's judgement, telling Shakespear that Ibn Saud had the support of 'the majority of the tribes' and was 'the more powerful leader'. But, he said, he lacked money and supplies. It was dangerous for the British to allow the Turks to continue to arm the Rashids without doing anything to help Ibn Saud. When Shakespear reported Mubarak's opinion to his superiors and urged them not to allow Arabia to fall under the control of the Rashids, his superiors in both India and London became alarmed. Cox was told to warn his new man in Kuwait about his duty, which was to 'stand firm' by Britain's policy of non-interference in the affairs of 'Turkish Arabia'.

Shakespear quickly became a familiar and respected figure in both Kuwait and the surrounding hinterland. Nearly always in uniform, never attempting to disguise himself in Arab dress as many other Europeans had done and still did, and speaking perfect Arabic, he quickly proved himself as strong and self-reliant as the hardest desert Arabs. In his spare time his main hobby became sailing, but he also frequently ventured out into the wild hinterland around Kuwait, both in the Rover and on camel back. On these excursions he always went armed with his camera, tripod and plates, sextant, compass and mapping equipment, plus a small disguised store of bottles of wine and whisky. He acquired a hawk and a pack of salukis, the ancient hunting dogs of the Middle East sometimes known as Gazelle Hounds. With characteristic determination, he set about mastering the art of hunting with them, soon becoming almost as proficient as the Arabs he moved amongst. Many areas inland from Kuwait and along the Hasa coast were still unmapped. Shakespear diligently set about filling in the gaps, taking bearings, noting details of the terrain and the correct Bedouin name for each place and feature in the landscape, meticulously logging his progress. Soon the British military authorities in India were sending their secret maps of the area to Shakespear for correction and updating.

Shakespear also photographed avidly as he went. Many of the Arabs he met had never seen a camera before and regarded it with fear or worse. He always sought people's agreement before taking out his small box camera or setting up his heavy wooden and brass tripod and mounting his heavy plate camera on top of it, draping the black cloth over his head and peering through the lens. Some people ran away and hid from 'the evil eye' but many stayed to be photographed and in this way he built up a unique and timeless collection of photographs of Arabia and its people before the intrusion of the modern world, a collection which to this day remains a treasure trove for all those interested in Arabia, its history and people.

Shakespear also used his trips into the hinterland to learn more about what was happening in the interior of Arabia. Unlike most other European travellers before him, Shakespear approached the Arabs he met openly, respectfully and as himself. Unlike other Europeans, many of whom were frightened of the men of the desert and either regarded them as dangerous savages or looked down on them with a kind of lofty Christian charity, Shakespear had a genuine liking for the Bedouin because, as he said, 'they were men'. When he approached parties of Bedouin in the interior he would almost always receive a warm and hospitable welcome, and usually be invited to join them in their guest tents and often to travel with them and take part in their sports, hunting and racing bareback across the harsh terrain. In this way, too, in unhurried conversation about the things that mattered to them, the weather, the grazing and the benevolence of Allah, he came to be regarded as a friend, respected by them for his skill and endurance in the necessary ways of the desert. In this way, too, he picked up much valuable information about what was happening deep in the interior of Arabia, about which shaikhs were in the ascendant, of new alliances and feuds between tribes and leading families. Shakespear was truly himself and fulfilled in the desert. He came to spend more and more time there rather than in the dull routines of the Residency.

His first major journey into the interior, a circuit of almost two hundred and fifty miles to the south and west of Kuwait, was in November 1909. He followed this with a much longer journey of exploration towards the edge of the Dahna desert, in January and February 1910. One night when hundreds of miles from Kuwait, and after Shakespear and his small party of retainers had pitched their tents for the night in a depression in the semi-desert, they were raided by a group of dishevelled-looking Mutair tribesmen. During the exchange of shots Shakespear's most trusted guide was killed.

As Shakespear and his small disconsolate band of retainers returned towards Kuwait they received news that Ibn Saud and two of his brothers were in Kuwait visiting Mubarak and were anxious to meet him. On the day he arrived back at the Residency Shakespear received an invitation to dine with Mubarak in his palace that very evening. Tired, dirty and still angry at the death of his favourite guide, Shakespear said he would go, snatched a few hours' sleep, washed, shaved and downed a stiff whisky. He then set out for Mubarak's palace and his first encounter with the Arab leader he had so long wanted to meet, Ibn Saud.

Ibn Saud and Shakepear took a liking to each other almost immediately and when the meal ended Shakespear invited Ibn Saud, his brothers and Mubarak to dine with him at the Residency next day. When he returned home after that first encounter he noted: 'Abdul Aziz, now in his 31st year, is fair, handsome and considerably above average Arab height ... he has a frank, open face, and after initial reserve, is of genial and courteous manner.' Although they were similar in appearance, Ibn Saud's brothers seemed to Shakespear 'dour and taciturn'.[1]

The following day, when Shakespear entertained Ibn Saud, his brothers and Mubarak he laid on a typical English meal for them: roast lamb with mint sauce, roast potatoes and tinned asparagus. After apparent doubts at first, Shakespear's guests had enjoyed the meal. Soon they were talking freely and seemed to warm to this young Englishman who, in little more than a year, had mastered Najdi Arabic and gained such a good knowledge of the desert. He seemed unusually sympathetic towards them and their hopes. Even Ibn Saud's brothers dropped their reserve and started to join in the conversation freely.

As he was leaving Ibn Saud turned to Shakespear and told him, 'As a true friend of Mubarak you are my friend.' Shakespear thanked him and asked if he might the next day take some photographs of him and those he had travelled to Kuwait with and Ibn Saud said 'Yes'. A new and important friendship had been born.

The photographs taken by Shakespear, the first of Ibn Saud, his brothers and Mubarak, happily have survived and show clearly not only his imposing physique, height, broad shoulders and open good looks, they also give some hint of Ibn Saud's powerful presence. As well as taking photographs Shakespear recorded his impressions of those first meetings with Ibn Saud and his brothers, in the process revealing not only a lot about his guests but also about the then common view of most Europeans about Arabs. Ibn Saud was, Shakespear recorded: ' ... particularly intelligent ... a broad-minded man and straight man who could probably be trusted further than most Arabs ... His reputation is that of a noble and generous man who does not descend to mean

1 Quoted in *Captain Shakespear: A Portrait* by H. V. F. Winstone, Jonathan Cape, London, 1976.

actions.' Shakespear was clearly surprised and relieved to discover that Ibn Saud displayed none of the xenophobia or narrow-minded fanaticism commonly associated with Wahhabis. Even though Ibn Saud's brothers were 'dour' and 'taciturn' in manner all three he found 'Despite their Wahhabi reputation [were] ... much interested in the ways of foreigners and the outer world. They dined with me, appreciated a Western table and menu, and even submitted to the camera.' Even when Shakespear brought the topic of their conversation round to 'matters of doctrine, custom and religion, which are held to be anathema by the Wahhabi sect' Ibn Saud always answered his questions with 'calm and intelligent reasoning without a trace of fanatical heat'. Shakespear assured his superiors that he had not discussed politics with his guests beyond Ibn Saud having said that 'he thanked God there were not Turks nearer his capital than Al Hasa, and that the English, as friends and brothers of Mubarak, were themselves his brothers and friends'.[2] Before they parted, Ibn Saud invited Shakespear to visit him in Riyadh.

A year later the two men met again, this time out in the Hasa, the province which stretched from the Dahna Desert to the Persian Gulf coast. They met on a day of pouring rain in an area known as Al Gerrha. Ibn Saud had come to Hasa with his brothers, eldest sons and a large number of his followers for a meeting with two shaikhs from the Hasa who were loyal to him rather than the Ottomans. Although the area where Ibn Saud and Shakespear met bore the same name as the ancient city of Gerrha, it was almost certainly not the site of the fabled city of the same name to which the exiled Babylonians were reputed to have fled after incurring God's wrath for their pride in building the Tower of Babel, or which Alexander the Great had failed to conquer. That ancient city had almost certainly been about a hundred miles further to the east, on or near the coast. Yet the remote spot where they met had been on one of the major ancient trade routes along which merchants had carried their valuable cargoes of spices, frankincense and myrrh from the prosperous kingdoms of South Arabia northwards to

2 From Foreign Office Papers in a dispatch from Shakespear to his colleague, the Political Agent in Bahrain, Arthur Trevor, quoted in Goldberg, op. cit. Also H. V. F. Winstone op. cit.

the cities of the Babylonian empire and to Gerrha itself. Shakespear, eager to explore the area for evidence of its fabled past, did indeed find fragments of inscriptions and ruins dating to the period of Gerrha's greatest prosperity close to the place where he and Ibn Saud held their meeting. Before returning to Kuwait Shakespear took photographs and made extensive notes about both the ruins and inscriptions.

During their first meeting in Kuwait Ibn Saud and Shakespear had talked of meeting again, but in a place where they could talk without others present or being interrupted. By the time of their meeting at Gerrha in March 1911, both men had further pressing reasons to want to talk. Ibn Saud had become eager to make another approach to the British about entering into some form of alliance with them. Shakespear's masters in Delhi and London were eager to learn from Ibn Saud his own account of his recent clash with Husayn which Husayn was now claiming had resulted in Ibn Saud being utterly defeated and his acceptance of Ottoman suzerainty.

Knowing of Ibn Saud's habits on forays away from the Najd, Shakespear took his pack of salukis and his hawk with him. When Shakepear and his small party of trekkers and servants rode up to Ibn Saud's remote camp, in the pouring rain, the two men greeted each other like old friends. Ibn Saud invited Shakespear and his small party to join him and ride out with him and his followers the next day. The next morning the by now large caravan of Saudis, Hasa shaikhs and their followers rode out behind Ibn Saud's war flag northwards. Halting in a spot where there was good grazing for the animals, Ibn Saud and his English guest spent most of the day in friendly, general conversation over copious cups of coffee. Much of the time the two friends were alone. At others they were joined by members of Ibn Saud's family, especially his favourite sons, Turki, Saud and Faisal. Later that same day they went off hunting with their hawks, exercising Ibn Saud's war mares and competing against each other in tests of marksmanship. Apparently so different in background and life experience, the two men had found in each other an almost perfect friend and companion. Both were sportsmen who enjoyed challenging and testing each other in skill, strength, speed and courage. Both were spirited and resourceful, determined to remain true to themselves and their beliefs, to take on and overcome the most challenging odds and situations. Both were fearless and able to remain cool in the face of danger.

It was not until the evening of the second day that the two men began to talk seriously. By then Ibn Saud's sons and many of his followers had gone to bed and the two Hasa shaikhs had withdrawn to their tents for the night. Sitting alone in Ibn Saud's majlis tent, except for the slave who kept them supplied with fresh cups of coffee, Shakespear, Ibn Saud and the brother he had rescued from Husayn, Sa'ad, talked far into the night. Ibn Saud told Shakespear the story of his family, of the repeated rise and fall of its fortunes, of his relations with the Ottoman Empire, of his determination to restore the kingdom and fortunes of the Al Sauds and his great hope and wish for an alliance with the British. 'We Wahhabis hate the Turks only less than we hate the Persians,' said Ibn Saud, 'for the infidel practices which they have imported into the true and pure faith revealed to us in the Qur'an.'[3] He told Shakespear how deeply he and all good Wahhabis resented the Ottoman occupation of the Hasa, of how his faith forbade him from accepting the Ottoman Caliphate. Yet, he told Shakespear, for him and his people to rise against the Turks would be pointless as the Turks could bring in whatever reinforcements they needed to crush a revolt. Although there was ongoing talk between many of the rulers in the Arabian peninsula about combining to rid their lands of the Turks, for the time being, Ibn Saud told Shakespear, to even mount an expedition to drive the Ottomans out of Hasa, which had always belonged to the Sauds and had been their richest province, would be fruitless because the Turks could easily bring reinforcements to the Hasa by ship through the Gulf. For one hundred years, Ibn Saud continued, the British had maintained the peace in the Persian Gulf and prevented anyone who wanted to make war from sailing on it. Surely, he urged, it was no less important now to stop the Ottomans from bringing their troops to the Gulf to wage war against the Arabs?

Shakespear protested that he had not come to see Ibn Saud to discuss politics and that, in any case, he did not have the authority to explore

3 The words spoken and reported from the discussions between Ibn Saud and Shakespear in March 1911 are drawn from H. V. F. Winstone and Goldberg op. cit.

political matters with him. Yet they talked for three whole days. Shakespear told Ibn Saud how Husayn had spread the story of his overwhelming victory over Ibn Saud and his brother, of how he had 'surrendered' to Husayn and of how he and all the tribes of Najd had afterwards submitted to Ottoman suzerainty. He explained too that Husayn's account of what had happened had been believed and reported in newspapers in Britain, Egypt and Constantinople. Ibn Saud and Sa'ad protested at this. Husayn's account was untrue. This was not the way that things had happened at all! He, Ibn Saud, would have called forth all his forces and crushed Husayn had it not been that Sa'ad had had the misfortune to fall into Husayn's hands. But for this he would never have accepted Husayn's or the Turks' terms. But he had to rescue his brother, both because he loved him and for the sake of his family's honour. He swore that the day would come when he and his family would be revenged on Husayn and drive his family, and the Turks as well, out of Arabia for ever. And, said Ibn Saud, he had never submitted to being a vassal of the Ottoman Empire. Sa'ad eagerly confirmed all that his brother said.

Shakespear warned his friend once more. Although they talked simply as friends, he said, it would be his duty on his return to Kuwait to tell his government all that had passed between them. Ibn Saud, far from being put out or offended by this information, simply told Shakespear, 'I expected that my friend.'

Turning to the subject of Ibn Saud's ambitions for his family and the future of Arabia, Shakespear warned his friend not to underestimate the power of his enemies, the Rashids, Husayn, the Hashemites and above all the Turks. He repeated his warning not to expect anything from Britain. The British had always restricted their interests in the Persian Gulf to the coast and had repeatedly held back from interfering in central Arabia. His government, Shakespear told Ibn Saud, wished to maintain its friendship with the Ottoman Empire. Ibn Saud responded that he was not seeking British help in driving the Turks out of Hasa, all he sought was that after he had thrown them out he would be protected by Britain against any Ottoman attack by sea. He was simply asking for the same kind of relationship with Britain that she had extended to Kuwait and other coastal shaikhdoms of the Gulf. His desire was for no more than an agreement with Britain that would cause the Ottomans to pause before attempting 'to oppress us or interfere in our affairs'. In return he would be happy to accept the posting of a permanent British Resident in Riyadh or the Gulf port of Qatif.

Shakespear promised his friend to pass on his request to his superiors. But he repeated his warning that he should not hold out too much hope of a favourable response. Ibn Saud replied that he would rather hear the truth, however unpalatable, from the English than the deceitful half-truths he had come to expect from the Turks. As Shakespear prepared to leave, Ibn Saud warned his friend of the danger he was putting himself in by always travelling in the desert in British uniform and urged him to go dressed as an Arab. 'You are in great danger', he told him, 'and I shall not always be there to protect you.'

'Why?' asked Shakespear. 'Am I not among friends?'

Although Ibn Saud did not know it, Shakespear had by now become his most enthusiastic advocate among the British. Upon his return to Kuwait he wrote a full report of his meeting with Ibn Saud to his boss, Percy Cox. His praise of Ibn Saud's character and attributes as an Arab leader was even more glowing than he had given in his report of their first meeting a year earlier. He repeated and endorsed Ibn Saud's version of events surrounding his clash with Husayn and of Sa'ad's capture and subsequent release. He reiterated all that Ibn Saud had told him of the hatred felt by the tribes towards the Turks and their occupation of their lands; of Ibn Saud's ambition to drive out the Turks and re-establish in full what he regarded as the Sauds' rightful inheritance. He also passed on what Ibn Saud had told him about consultations between Arab rulers from across the length and breadth of the peninsula and a span of branches of the Islamic faith about uniting to raise an Arab Revolt against the Ottoman Empire and liberate their lands. Such an alliance and combined Arab uprising was, Shakespear claimed, not only possible but probable and would 'be welcome by every tribe throughout the peninsula. From all I can learn hatred of the Turk seems to be the one idea common to all the tribes and the only one for which they would sink their differences.'[4] Shakespear urged his superiors to give serious consideration to Ibn Saud's

4 Report of Shakespear to Cox, April 8th 1911. Public Records Office.

request for British protection if he should attempt to retake Hasa, repeating his request for a treaty similar to those that Britain had with the other Gulf shaikhdoms and his offer to accept the posting of a British Resident in either Qatif or Riyadh. With Ibn Saud in control of Hasa, Shakespear suggested, Britain's position in the Gulf and the wider region would be considerably strengthened.

Cox tended to agree with Shakespear and would much prefer to have to deal with Ibn Saud as ruler of Hasa than the Ottomans. In passing Shakespear's report on upwards to the Government of India, Cox pointed out that Britain had very good reasons 'for maintaining cordial relations with Ibn Saud; at any rate, for not wishing to create in him a feeling of soreness and ill-will towards us'. In return for only a nominal subsidy Ibn Saud was likely to be willing not only to uphold British control of the Gulf but to 'prohibit the import of arms by sea'. But Cox was also a realist as regarded Britain's strategic policy in the region as a whole and conceded that for as long as Britain's relations with the Ottoman Empire remained more or less satisfactory it was 'no more in a position now' than it had been five years earlier to enter into any understanding with Ibn Saud 'which would envisage the expulsion of the Turks from Hasa'.

Throughout the summer of 1911 correspondence flowed back and forth between Cox and his superiors in Delhi and London about Shakespear's proposals and the policy Britain should adopt toward Ibn Saud. Officials in London remained fearful not only of antagonising the Ottomans but of the possibility that if Ibn Saud drove the Turks out of Hasa he might himself become a danger to British interests in the region and advance south into Muscat. In the end, despite Cox's continued advocacy and the support of a few more far-sighted officials in the Indian and London governments, Britain's concern to maintain good relations with Turkey as a protective buffer between Europe and Asia and against any German, French or Russian designs on Britain's Indian Empire, together with on-going fears in London and India of taking any step which might be perceived as antagonistic towards Turkey and the Caliphate and so serve to inflame anti-British sentiment among Muslims in India, prevailed. Ibn Saud's request for some form of alliance or protective agreement with Britain was to be politely rejected. From

Britain's point of view Ibn Saud, despite his successes and growing power, remained no more than the minor ruler of an out of the way, strategically and economically unimportant minor statelet.

This was the tenth time in the nine years since his recapture of Riyadh that Ibn Saud's overtures towards the British had been rejected. As the revolts against him in the previous two years had demonstrated, his small state, despite his recent conquests and growing power, remained fundamentally unstable. Local and tribal loyalties remained a far more powerful influence than any idea of loyalty to the state. Now it was also clear that he could not look to the British for help or protection either in securing what he had already gained or in his quest to extend his state still further. So, if he was to secure what he had already gained, increase it still further and eventually realise the ambitions for the Saudi dynasty which he had so recently outlined to Shakespear, he was going to have to look to the intrinsic resources of Najd itself and of his own people.

As we have seen, Ibn Saud had a strong sense of his family's destiny. He was also aware that his family had achieved its greatest success, in the years from about 1770 until 1811, through its alliance with Muhammad Ibn Abd al-Wahhab and through harnessing the loyalty and fighting qualities of the Bedouin. A hundred years earlier the state's identification with Wahhabism had given it a cohesion and dynamism which it had not enjoyed before nor since. It was upon this identification, his own Wahhabism, deep knowledge of the Qur'an and of the Bedouin that Ibn Saud would now start to draw.

In the years before Ibn Saud's meeting with Shakespear at Al Gerrha a movement for religious revival and a return to the strict observance of the tenets of Wahhabi doctrine had begun to emerge among certain religious scholars and leaders in Riyadh. This religious movement was not unlike the one led by the 'zealators' described by Palgrave during his visit to Riyadh in 1862. 'The Arabs of the desert are the worst in Unbelief and hypocrisy, and the most fitted to be in ignorance of the command which Allah has sent down to his Messenger,' warned the Qur'an[5] and so, as well as trying to win adherents in Riyadh itself, the leaders of this new movement started to send preachers out to proselytise among the

5 The Holy Qur'an, Surah 9, 97.

Bedouin tribes. As a result, heeding the Qur'an's dire warnings of eternal damnation for those who persist in unbelief and the promises of 'everlasting felicity' to those who repent and embrace the one true faith, late in 1912 or early 1913 a group of about fifty men from two of the noblest Bedouin tribes, the Mutair and Harb, together with their families and some of the leaders of the new revivalist movement, started selling up their horses and camels, disposing of their other wealth and separating themselves from their tribes. Together they established a community settlement based on agriculture, communal life and mutual support, strict adherence to the articles of the Muslim faith and Wahhabi doctrine. This settlement, or *hijra* – the word used by Muslims to describe the withdrawal of the Prophet Muhammad and his followers from Mecca in 622 and establishment of the first truly Muslim community in Medina – was seen by its members as a return to the original values of Islam. The members of this new community became known as the Ikhwan, or brethren. As well as a strict observance of the rules and disciplines of the Muslim faith, the brothers were required to demonstrate commitment to the community and their fellow 'brothers'. This new community was intended to mark a return to the early Muslim ideal of equality between all true believers. If one member of the community fell upon hard times the others were expected to support him and the members of his family. The brethren were required to live the simple life, to avoid ostentation and display and be without personal wealth. As a sign that they had abandoned their nomadic way of life, all new members of the Ikhwan had to wear a simple white turban instead of the *aqal*, or head-cord, over their headcloth. A result of the insistence on simplicity of dress was that 'the brothers' often appeared poor and ragged. They would not return the traditional *salaam* greeting when encountering another Arab who was not a member of the Ikhwan and if they came across a European or an Arab from Iraq or one of the Gulf states they would turn away and cover their faces with both hands.

A simple, unadorned mosque with a low, square minaret was constructed at Artawiya, an oasis area on the Al Aramah Plateau about 140 miles north west of Riyadh, and became the focal point of the first Ikhwan settlement. Nearby the mosque a town square, including a market and stables, was built and around them a tight-packed cluster of austere two-

and three-room mud-brick houses, most with their own well. Beyond them were tents for the former Bedouin who did not yet have a house. All was surrounded by a wall and watchtowers. Outside this were their fields, other cultivation and grazing areas. Discipline in the *hijra* was strict and life highly regimented. Men and women were obliged to attend the mosque for each of the five daily prayers and sermons, which could sometimes last for as long as two hours each. Absentees were beaten with twenty strokes and a man who absented himself for days on end without a valid reason might be publicly executed. The evening meal had to be eaten at least one hour before sunset so as to allow time for religious reading and instruction before going to bed. In the words of one contemporary commentator, 'In this city men are more interested in the next world than they are in this one.'[6] Like the original followers of al-Wahhab and Muhammad ibn Saud, the Ikhwan quickly started to gain adherents. Artawiya grew and more *hijras* were established. Also like the original followers of al-Wahhab, because of their stern discipline and rigid enforcement of the five articles of the Muslim faith, the Ikhwan soon started to inspire fear and provoke opposition.

All well as being zealous in the service of their faith and commitment to their own community, the Ikhwan were committed to the service of their leader, the Imam, Ibn Saud, and his state. They believed also that it was their duty to bring others to repent of their mistaken ways and come to the true path of strict obedience to the five articles of Wahhabi Islam. But they went further, they believed it was their duty to impose a similar adherence to their vision of monotheism upon all those who were not prepared to embrace it voluntarily. This meant that the Ikhwan believed that they were called, if need be, to impose submission to Allah and 'the one true faith' by force of arms. In doing so they believed they would be following in the footsteps of the Prophet Muhammad himself, who as well as being a successful military leader, had returned to Mecca at the head of a large army to force its surrender. His immediate successors, 'the rightly chosen ones' in the century after Muhammad's death, had conquered a large empire. The Ikhwan, fired by religious zeal, their courage fortified by faith, accustomed to rigid discipline and marching

6 Paul W. Harrison, *Moslem World 8*, 1918.

under the banner of the one true faith, had the potential to become a formidable and unique desert fighting force. For many a former Bedouin, settling down to the life of prolonged toil entailed in becoming successful farmers was to prove difficult, and many were to fail. So to such men, the prospect of devoting themselves to a life of proselytising and 'fighting for monotheism' must have seemed far preferable to having to spend their time labouring in the fields and date orchards, or tending the settlement's cattle. The Ikhwan and *hijras* have unmistakable similarities to revivalist movements and communities in other religions where there has been a concentration on brotherhood, egalitarian values, discipline and purity of faith, combined with an enthusiasm for agriculture and its settled, timeless values. One thinks of some of the Puritan settlements in Cromwellian England and some early settler communities in America, of similar movements among Indian Buddhists and Hindus, also in China and Japan and some kibbutzim in Israel. The same phenomenon became familiar to the great secular faiths and political movements of the twentieth century – the young Communist pioneers in Soviet Russia and Maoist China and the SS in Nazi Germany. Some of these communities and organisations were also to create and supply some of their respective regimes' most feared and fanatically effective military formations.

Despite the Ikhwan's forbidding manner, severity and narrow-mindedness there was evidently much about them which many people found engaging. H. R. P. Dickson, the British diplomat and colonial administrator who some years later came to know many of the Ikhwan well, records a sneaking admiration for them. 'There is a curious charm about men who are so truthful, are earnest believers in one god, and, according to their lights, are out to cleanse religion of abuse ... I found very little difference between them and other good types of Badawin Arab elsewhere. They were just as fond of their women, their children, their camels and their mares as others were, while their attractive ladies had the same delightful characteristics as one finds among their sisters all over Arabia.'[7]

It was a mark of Ibn Saud's perceptiveness as a leader that he was

7 H. R. P. Dickson, *Kuwait and Her Neighbours*, George Allen and Unwin, London, 1956.

quick to recognise the potential of the Ikhwan as a force for stability and unification in the emerging Saudi state. Communities of settled farmers, especially when their new lifestyle was underpinned by the authority of religion, were likely to put a much higher value on stability than Bedouin, eking out an existence through the traditional ways of nomadism and raiding. So in order to speed the process of Bedouin settlement Ibn Saud started to make grants of money, seed, equipment and building materials to new *hijras* and helped in finding land suitable for settlement. He also established a system for making grants to established settlements and paid for additional preachers and religious instructors to be sent to them. He started sending preachers out among the Bedouin tribes to try to encourage the creation of further settlements. In return he would start to expect them to supply him with conscript units for his wars. There was just one voice that counselled Ibn Saud against placing too much reliance upon the Ikhwan – his loyal cousin Abdullah Jiluwi, the hero of the seizure of Riyadh. But for the moment that voice and its warnings seemed irrelevant.

The year 1912 saw a fresh round of unrest, revolt and war in the Ottoman Empire. Italy had declared war on the Ottoman Empire in the autumn of 1911 and attacked Libya. With this war still raging a fresh round of dissent began at home in Constantinople and a group of military officers forced the resignation of the government. Weeks later, in October 1912, an alliance of Balkan states, Montenegro, Serbia, Bulgaria and Greece, declared war on the Ottoman Empire and within weeks had succeeded in driving the Turks more or less completely out of the Balkans and most of their few remaining territories in Europe.. The Bulgarian army was only finally halted a few miles outside Constantinople itself. Meanwhile Italy seized the Dodecanese Islands. When the crisis began Sir Edward Grey, the Foreign Secretary, had told Parliament that Britain would not allow any alteration in the status quo as regarded the Ottoman Empire's dependencies and Britain's interests but in the event, as so often in these years, Britain stood aside as Turkey faced successive defeats. Faced by these difficulties and without outside help, the Ottoman Empire withdrew many of its troops from Hasa, Basra and Baghdad to bolster its defence of Turkey itself.

In December 1912 Ibn Saud received reports of a European travelling in disguise as an Arab approaching Riyadh from the north. He immediately sent out scouts and had the mysterious stranger brought to him. As soon as he was brought before Ibn Saud the stranger revealed his true identity. He was Gerald Leachman, a British Officer serving in Mesopotamia who had previously undertaken intelligence missions in Arabia and now hoped to make a journey of exploration into the Rub al-Khali. On learning the traveller's identity Ibn Saud welcomed him enthusiastically and immediately started plying Leachman with questions. He wanted to know everything Leachman could tell him about what had been going on in Turkey and about the Ottomans' difficulties and defeats. Leachman was astonished to find that Ibn Saud, far away from all the main capitals and trade routes in the remotest part of central Arabia was so well informed about recent events in the world beyond the desert. Ibn Saud continued questioning Leachman until he had discovered everything that Leachman could tell him about the insurrections and wars being conducted against the Ottoman Empire and was clearly pleased to learn of the Ottomans' losses. Ibn Saud told Leachman that the Ottoman Empire's troubles were 'the judgement of Allah' on a people who had 'neglected their religion, oppressed their subjects, embezzled religious endowments, broken every ordinance of the Qur'an and subverted the Caliphate'; their misfortunes proof that Allah had abandoned them. After Leachman left, Ibn Saud wrote to his friend Shakespear to ask for further detailed information about Ottoman losses. At the same time he dispatched spies to Hasa and its capital Hofuf to discover more about reports of Turkish troop withdrawals and the dispositions of the remaining troops.

Shortly afterwards, at the end of December 1912, Ibn Saud announced a general mobilisation of his Bedouin and settled Najdi warriors and marched north with them into Qasim. Among them for the first time was a small group of the Ikhwan. Upon hearing that Ibn Saud had amassed a large force of warriors in Qasim, the Turks dispatched emissaries to ask his intentions, warning that if he moved against any Turkish possessions they would send an army to crush him. Ibn Saud replied that he only intended to deal with a recalcitrant tribe near Kuwait, adding cheekily that if the Turks were intent on attacking him he would make it easier for them by moving nearer to Kuwait.

In Kuwait Shakespear was put out when he learned of Leachman's visit to Riyadh. He disapproved of Leachman's habit of travelling in the desert in disguise, believing that it was likely to sow distrust of the British amongst the Arabs. But he was also jealous. He had himself begun planning an epic journey right across Arabia from east to west via Riyadh and was dismayed to discover that Leachman had got to Riyadh before him. Excursions by British officers into the desert had been banned by London for fear of antagonising the Turks while Britain was trying to negotiate a comprehensive treaty with Turkey intended to establish once and for all who controlled which territories along the Gulf Coast. But Cox, not wishing to curb the enthusiasm of talented officers like Leachman and Shakespear or deny himself the intelligence that they might gather, had turned a blind eye to Leachman's excursion, allowing his officers to know that anyone intending to undertake such a journey should not tell their superiors about it in advance.

Shakespear had been specifically instructed not to have any further contact with Ibn Saud before the treaty with the Turks had been signed. But in late February 1913 he collected together his small caravan of faithful servants and headed out of Kuwait towards the Dahna sand belt. At that moment Shakespear's emotions were probably in greater turmoil than usual and as a result he was probably in less of a mood than ever to heed the instructions of his superiors in London and India. Since his first meetings with Dorothea six years earlier they had continued to meet when he came home to England on leave and to correspond regularly. Yet despite members of their families and their friends continuing to expect them to become engaged no announcement had been forthcoming. Shakespear's growing devotion to desert exploration and to the cause of Arabia and the Arabs, which had played such a powerful part in bringing them together, had by now become a problem. If Shakespear had been willing, like other officers serving in Arabia, to return to India and continue his service there at the end of his tour of duty in Kuwait Dorothea would have been able, and almost certainly eager, to join him as his wife. But there was no way in the circumstances of the time that she could have joined him as his wife in his work and exploration in Arabia. The result was that by the start of 1913 they had not met for eighteen months, since his last home leave in

London, and Dorothea had become engaged to another army officer, one who was serving in India. Perhaps this news, coupled with his disappointment that Leachman had reached Riyadh before him, plus the fact that the Viceroy of India had recently turned down flat a request from him for permission to import and assemble a flying machine with which, as he told his superiors, he would be able to get around the Gulf more quickly, together with his ever mounting frustration over Britain's policy towards his friend Ibn Saud, meant that at that moment he did not really care whether he incurred official displeasure by travelling into Arabia or not. However, the biggest element in Shakespear's mood of obstinate and frustrated fatalism at that moment was almost certainly his loss of Dorothea. He was to carry her photograph with him at all times right up to the moment of his death. Years later Dorothea was to say that she had had no choice but to give him up: 'I lost him to the desert.'

By now it was late March and although there were still heavy showers which briefly reduced the desert to a combination of quagmires and short-lived raging torrents, the temperature even in the shade was rising into the 80°s F. Marching swiftly, Shakespear and his small party crossed the eastern arm of the Dahna Desert which, with its deep red and orange sand and teeming gazelle, lived up to the expectation he had had of it from his and Dorothea's extensive reading, and marched out onto the Al Aramah Plateau above the northern end of Wadi Hanifah. Reaching a fertile and well-cultivated area he and his party rested in a small town called Majmaa. There Shakespear learned that Ibn Saud and his warriors were encamped about sixty miles to the south. Ignoring his specific instructions not to contact Ibn Saud, Shakespear and his small party immediately hurried south and after three days hard-going over jagged hills and crags arrived in Ibn Saud's camp. Ibn Saud greeted his friend warmly. With the formalities of Arab desert hospitality completed, the two friends became locked in private conversation which lasted with little more than interruptions for sleep, the obligatory five rounds of daily prayer and meals, for the whole of the four days that they were together.

Ibn Saud inquired of Shakespear for any further news of Turkish defeats or successes and their troop movements, but Shakespear was able to do little more than confirm what he already knew. Unlike during their previous conversations, Ibn Saud did not ask Shakespear to use his good offices with his government to secure a treaty of protection for him from the British. He knew from the previous rejections he had received that this would be futile and that he now had to act on his own initiative to secure the future of his state and alter the status quo in the Gulf. So instead he asked Shakespear what Britain's reaction would be if he drove the Ottomans out of Hasa. Shakespear responded by warning his friend that if he attacked the Turks in Hasa he could expect no help whatsoever from Britain and reminded him, as he was bound to do, that he had no power whatsoever to help his friend other than being able to relay his friend's views and requests to his own government. Ibn Saud did not display any anger or disappointment at this response beyond telling Shakespear that the Turkish governor of Hasa had treated its inhabitants with such harshness that they were ready to rise against the Turks without assistance from him or anyone else. He also reiterated his family's historic right to dominion over Hasa. He told Shakespear that the Turks were continually pressing the Arab leaders to accept Turkish titles, send their children to be educated in Turkey, to serve in the Ottoman army. He also told him that the Turks demanded to see all their correspondence with any foreign government, so demonstrating their intention to dictate the affairs of Arabia and negate any British influence. When Shakespear repeated his warning to expect no help from Britain Ibn Saud responded calmly that 'some day you will be forced by circumstances to take up my case'.

Shakespear left Ibn Saud's camp on April 4th 1913 with a gift of fresh baggage camels from Ibn Saud and repeated avowals of their ongoing friendship. Shakespear was now in little doubt that Ibn Saud had made up his mind sooner or later to attempt to conquer Hasa. He also knew, from his inside knowledge of the treaty discussions between Britain and the Ottoman Empire, that his own government was determined to continue its policy of supporting the dominance of the Ottoman Empire in the Gulf and Arabia. He seems at this point to have been in something close to despair. On all his previous desert travels he had taken his bearings and written up his logbook with immaculate care. Now he travelled fast and only hastily scrawled a few rough notes, giving up doing even this during the last few days of his return journey to Kuwait. On his return he was in no hurry to report what he had discovered to Cox. When he did file a report for Cox, on May 15th 1913, he told him that hatred of the Ottomans was growing in the desert and that unless they changed their policies towards the Arabs they would be faced with an uprising and defeat. He told Cox that for Britain to reject Ibn Saud's overtures would undoubtedly cause resentment 'which may react upon our interests along the whole Arabian littoral of the Gulf'. He repeated his earlier assessment of Ibn Saud as a man and ruler 'of the best Arab type and his personality is one which is likely to lead Arabia should any extensive combination come into being among its tribes, an event which to me seems exceedingly probable in the near future ... As soon as some such combination occurs and perhaps even before, I do not think that there is the least doubt that Bin Saud's first move will be on Hasa and Katif, and when that happens it seems to me that we shall be forced into relations with the Amir of Najd, however much we may desire to avoid them.'[8] When Shakespear's report reached the Foreign Office in London it provoked an angry reaction. He had disobeyed orders and his assertion that to reject Ibn Saud's overtures might cause resentment and harm Britain's interests throughout the Gulf was rejected as 'nonsense'. He received an official reprimand.

The speed with which Ibn Saud now acted took everyone, including Shakespear and his enemies, by surprise. No sooner had Shakespear left his camp and gone far enough not to discover what he was doing, than Ibn Saud began to march his warriors eastwards. His spies having by now reported back to him the numbers of Turkish soldiers left in Hasa and where they were camped, he crossed the Dahna sandbelt and headed towards Hofuf, Hasa's capital. A few days later, sitting on a sand dune with the walls of the town and its powerful citadel, the Kut, in sight, Ibn

8 Letter from Captain W. H. I. Shakespear, Political Agent Kuwait, to the Political Resident in the Persian Gulf, May 15 1913. There is some doubt about exactly what was said between Ibn Saud and Shakespear during their meeting, but we have based our account principally on the Foreign Office and Government of India Papers in the Public Record Office and the accounts in Winstone's *Captain Shakespear*, Goldberg's *The Foreign Policy of Saudi Arabia* and Christine Moss Helms's *The Cohesion of Saudi Arabia*.

Saud was, as he told a traveller years later, 'heavy with indecision as I weighed the advantages and dangers' of what he planned to do. Hofuf he knew was a well-fortified town garrisoned by about twelve hundred Turkish soldiers, almost as many as his own entire force. 'I felt tired; I longed for peace and home; and with the thought of home the face of my wife, Jauhara, came before my eyes. I began to think of verses which I might tell her if she were by my side – and before I realised it, I was busy composing a poem to her, completely forgetting where I was and how grave a decision I had to make. As soon as the poem was ready in my mind I wrote it down, sealed it, called one of my couriers and commanded him: "Take the two fastest dromedaries, ride to Riyadh without stopping and hand this over to Muhammad's mother (Jauhara)." ' As the messenger disappeared on his camel into a cloud of dust thrown up by its hooves, Ibn Saud continued, 'I suddenly found that my mind had made a decision regarding the war: I would attack Hofuf and God would lead me to victory.'[9]

That evening, May 4th 1913, Ibn Saud called his warriors together and sought their approval for his decision. The Turks, he said, had created chaos in Hasa, traders were not safe to travel across it because of fear of being robbed by armed gangs. Those responsible for these outrages had been allowed by the Turks to take refuge in Hasa as had criminals fleeing justice in Najd and, he continued, the leaders of the community had asked him to step in and restore order and justice. The assembled warriors hailed his decision and he then selected three hundred of the most loyal and fearless of them to lead the assault. Next he ordered some palm trees to be cut down from a nearby date grove and prepared them for use as rough scaling ladders. A small scaling party was chosen from among the three hundred and issued with well-ropes of the kind habitually carried by travellers in Arabia. Two hours after midnight the scaling party moved stealthily forward to the town walls. The palm trunk ladders were carried across the moat, avoiding those lengths of it that were filled with water, and laid silently against the walls. A first group of men then scrambled hastily up the palm trunk

9 As told to Muhammad Asad and recalled in Asad's book *The Road to Mecca*, published by M. Reinhardt, London, 1954.

ladders to the top of the walls, secured their well-ropes to the battlements and lowered them down the other side into the sleeping town. They then slid swiftly down them and dropped silently to the ground. The remainder of Ibn Saud's hand-picked three-hundred-strong assault party then followed. Ibn Saud and his men had taken the Turks completely by surprise. Next the few sleepy sentries that had been posted that night were quickly overpowered and killed before they could raise the alarm. While most of the assault party spread out through the town a small group headed for the gate in the town wall nearest to where the remainder of Ibn Saud's force was waiting out of sight in the shadows. They overpowered the men guarding it and threw the gate open. Now the main body of over a thousand of Ibn Saud's warriors poured into the town, firing their rifles and shouting their war cries as they went to add to the garrison's confusion, to their fear and the impression that they were hopelessly outnumbered. Because of the speed and suddenness of their assault, Ibn Saud's warriors succeeded in breaking into the Kut fortress before the main body of the garrison billeted there could collect their wits and secure it. In the confusion the garrison commander and his men hastily withdrew into the sanctuary of the mosque within the fortress and barricaded themselves inside.

With dawn the people of the town poured from their houses to welcome Ibn Saud and his warriors. After receiving the townsfolk's greetings, Ibn Saud began preparing to drive a mine under the mosque where the governor and his men were sheltered. At the same time a captured Turkish soldier was sent into the fortress with a surrender demand to the garrison commander – either he and his men surrendered immediately, in which case Ibn Saud would have them escorted safely to the coast, or he would detonate the mine. The garrison commander chose to surrender. So he and his men were then marched out of the town, under an escort headed by one of Ibn Saud's distant relatives, and conducted to the coast. There some boats were commandeered and the Turkish soldiers were shipped out to the island of Bahrain. Meanwhile Ibn Saud and the main body of his men raced to each of the other places throughout Hasa where Ibn Saud's spies had reported that garrisons of Turkish soldiers were stationed and seized them.

A few days later the Turkish commander decided to try mounting a counter-attack and dispatched a landing party of soldiers to the port of Uqaïr in an attempt to land and retake it. But Ibn Saud was ready for them, rounded them up before they could take the port and took them into captivity. Unable to land, the main body of the Turkish force was forced to return to Bahrain. Ibn Saud also secured the other harbour close to Bahrain Island, Qatif, dismissed the Turkish customs officers and sent them packing to Bahrain as well. By his lightning action Ibn Saud had conquered the whole of Hasa in just a few days and now controlled the whole Arab coast of the Persian Gulf from Kuwait southwards to the Qatar peninsula, a distance of almost four hundred miles. He slashed the customs dues exacted by the Turks by almost two-thirds and made the trade routes into and across Hasa to Najd and the rest of Arabia safe again. He appointed his most trusted cousin, Abdullah Jiluwi, who he had made governor of Qasim after its recapture, governor of the Hasa. Jiluwi, thin faced, cold-eyed and sallow, had a well-justified reputation for being hard and cruel except when in the presence of Ibn Saud. Then his face would soften and his love and respect for his cousin would positively shine out of him.

Hasa had long been home to a large population of Shia who were traditionally hostile to the Saudis; while the Saudis, as Wahhabis, regarded all Shia as heretics. So the new governor of Hasa, Jiluwi, with Ibn Saud's active agreement, instituted an extensive programme of active re-education amongst the Shia. He instituted reforms of the courts in Hasa to make them operate in strict accordance with *Shari'a* law and began the Shia's systematic repression and conversion. By this action and his active encouragement of the Ikhwan movement Ibn Saud who, although he had been brought up as a strict and believing Wahhabi, had shown little overt concern with religious issues since seizing power in Riyadh, demonstrated that he intended his emerging state to be identified with a Wahhabi renaissance.

Within days of sending his dispatch to Cox telling him of his meeting with Ibn Saud near Majmaa Shakespear was writing to his boss again telling him of the news reaching him in Kuwait of Ibn Saud's capture of Hasa, news which confirmed that his forecasts of what would happen in Hasa had been correct. Perhaps the Foreign Office in London would now sanction reaching some sort of agreement with Ibn Saud?

Ibn Saud had chosen this moment to attack Hasa rather than his more immediate opponents the Rashids in part out of strategic calculation and in part for economic reasons. Ever since seizing power in Najd Ibn Saud's state had been dogged by its shortage of money. To have succeeded in defeating the Rashids and taking Ha'il at this stage would probably only have exacerbated this problem as Ha'il, like Najd, lacked natural resources and had little or no source of other revenue. By overrunning Hasa on the other hand, Ibn Saud had not only captured twelve field guns, two machine guns, a large quantity of rifles and ammunition and a substantial sum of money which had been held in the citadel in Hofuf, he had gained control of all the Hasa's fertile land, abundant crops and date palms and, perhaps most significant of all, two of the main ports in the Arabian Peninsula, Uqair and Qatif, a long length of the Persian Gulf coast and all its customs revenues. He had doubled his state's income at a stroke and provided himself with the basic economic lifeline that he needed if he was to achieve his further ambitions.

But he had also made a political and military calculation. With the Ottoman Empire beset closer to home and its garrisons in Arabia and Mesopotamia reduced, the Ottomans were less likely to be able to mount an effective and immediate counter-attack against him. His meetings with Leachman and Shakespear had been important not only because of the information they had provided him with about the extent of Turkey's problems but also because, despite Britain's repeated refusal to offer him protection from attack by the Turks from the sea, when he had questioned Shakespear about how the British would react if he re-occupied Hasa Shakespear had not said that Britain would view such a move with disfavour, only that he could expect no help from Britain if he did. As he had been told repeatedly by British representatives, the reason that Britain would not extend the same protection to him as she offered to other amirates along the Gulf Coast was that Najd, not being a coastal state, lay outside their area of concern. Britain did not wish to become entangled in affairs inside central Arabia and wanted to maintain its friendly relations with the Ottoman Empire. So he had been caught in a kind of Catch-22 situation: Britain would not offer him protection because he was not in control of any of the Gulf Coast, but he could not hope to succeed in an attempt to secure control of any of the Gulf Coast until he had Britain's protection. But now, in the spring of 1913, because of the Ottoman Empire's domestic upheavals and wars near to home, Ibn Saud had seen his opportunity to break out of the vicious circle. He had calculated that, as he told Shakespear, if he seized Hasa and a length of the Gulf coast, Britain would be 'forced by circumstances to take up my case'.

Immediately after he had completed his conquest of Hasa Ibn Saud contacted the Ottoman authorities, telling them what he had done, but at the same time stressing that in occupying the province he had not mounted an insurrection against them. On the contrary, he had been acting in the Ottomans' interests and in answer to appeals by the local inhabitants for action to be taken against the oppression and maladministration of Turkish officials in the province. In any case he had done no more than restore the position to what it had been before the Ottoman occupation of Hasa in 1871. Giving his personal assurance that he remained 'an obedient servant of the Sultan', he promised to maintain order in the province and stated his willingness to become its governor on behalf of the Sultan. Shortly after dispatching this letter he wrote to Sir Percy Cox. He told him, as he had told the Turks, that he had recovered his 'forefathers' ancestral dominions' in Hasa but assured him that in doing so he had no intention of attacking or interfering with the coastal amirates with which Britain had treaties and nor would he do so in future. Now, he said, he wished to enter into relations with Britain such as would deter the Turks from mounting an attack on him. If Britain was not willing to preserve its former friendship with him, he went on, then he wished to be informed 'so that I may look to my own interests'.[10]

At that moment Britain had reached the critical stage of negotiations, begun more than two years previously, with the Ottoman Empire, aimed at resolving the longstanding issues between the two governments over a whole range of matters, including those in the Persian Gulf. These issues included defining British and Ottoman territories and spheres of influence along the entire length of the Gulf, customs

10 Ibn Saud to Sir Percy Cox, June 13th 1913.

duties and terms for the completion of the long-projected Baghdad railway. One of the issues that had been provisionally resolved between the two sides was the question of Najd, which was to be recognised as an Ottoman province and to include Hasa. So Ibn Saud's sudden seizure of Hasa and the renewal of arguments from British Officials in the Gulf and India, including both Cox and the Viceroy, for reaching some kind of agreement with Ibn Saud, were greeted in London with dismay. Sir Edward Grey, one of the longest-serving but least-travelled Foreign Secretaries in British history, had little knowledge of the world beyond Whitehall. He spoke no foreign languages and had never travelled further than France. One highly respected contemporary described him as so ignorant of the lands beyond Europe that 'he hardly knew the Persian Gulf from the Red Sea and Europe'.[11] At that moment Grey was far more concerned with the worsening situation in Europe, the threat of war with Germany and trying to prevent Turkey from joining the German camp, than any developments inside a far-off country of which he knew nothing. He was, in any case, as the result of briefings by his officials, far from convinced that Ibn Saud would be able to hold on to Hasa in the face of the might of the Ottoman Empire. On top of which he knew that there was already a strong suspicion in Constantinople and other European capitals that Britain had been complicit in some way in Ibn Saud's successful attack on Hasa. So Grey was more opposed than ever to any move that might appear to give substance to such suspicions or might in any way risk worsening Britain's relations with Turkey. He, therefore, repeated his prohibition on all contact with Ibn Saud and the continuation of a policy which, in the words of the senior Foreign Office civil servant responsible for the region, amounted to 'pretending that Saud does not exist'.

This unsatisfactory state of affairs persisted through the remainder of 1913, into 1914 and the outbreak of the First World War. Under the Anglo-Ottoman Treaty, signed at the end of July 1913, it was agreed that Britain should have excusive rights to oil exploration in Persia, that

11 See Blunt, Wilfrid Scawen, *My Diaries: Being a Personal Narrative of Events, 1888–1914, Part Two 1900 to 1914*, Martin Secker, London 1920 for contemporaries' comments on Grey.

Najd, including all of Hasa, remain part of the Ottoman Empire and that Kuwait, Bahrain and Trucial Oman were British Protectorates. Ibn Saud, however, was not informed of the terms of the treaty. So he continued to try to placate the Turks by swearing his continued loyalty to the Sultan and at the same time draw the British into a treaty of protection. This he did by a combination of implied threats to British interests in Qatar and Oman and promises of willingness to facilitate British trade in his territories, uphold British control of shipping in the Gulf and assist in suppressing piracy and illegal arms trafficking. Meanwhile Turkey tried to push Ibn Saud into accepting closer Ottoman control over his territory. They demanded the right to re-introduce Ottoman garrisons into the Hasa ports and to direct control of his relations with foreign powers, including supervision of all his correspondence with any other country. They increased their pressure on him by sending large quantities of arms to his Rashid foes and reinforcing their army in Baghdad. At the same time British officials in the Gulf and India still pressed London to recognise the reality on the ground. They asked to be allowed to make contact with Ibn Saud and to approach the Ottoman Empire with an offer to mediate a solution to the areas of disagreement between them whereby the Ottomans would recognise Ibn Saud's control over Hasa but as a servant of the Ottoman Empire and under their control.

By December 1913 London, fearful as the senior civil servant in charge of the India Office admitted in private, that Cox and Shakespear were involved in all manner of schemes aimed at gaining recognition for Ibn Saud, had relented to the extent that it had allowed the Gulf officials to sound out the Ottomans. The Ottomans, for their part, while they raised no specific objections to British officials sounding out Ibn Saud, said that they were already in touch with him and dealing with these issues. At the same time the Ottomans made it clear that they wanted much tighter controls on Ibn Saud than he was likely to accept.

As a result London told the authorities in India and Cox that it saw no objection to 'an amicable exchange of views' with Ibn Saud and Cox wrote to Ibn Saud to suggest a meeting. It was the first time that the British had approached him to arrange a meeting and Ibn Saud was exultant. It seemed that his decision to attack Hasa and so force the

British into entering into to some kind of agreement with him had paid off. Unknown to Ibn Saud however, further discussions were still going on between Britain and the Ottoman Empire aimed at agreeing a final division of their areas of control throughout the whole of Arabia. Cox, very unhappy at the way in which the discussions seemed to be going and the concessions that his government seemed to be prepared to make to the Ottomans, decided that he should not attend the meeting with Ibn Saud. So he persuaded London to let him send Shakespear in his place, together with Major Arthur Trevor, the British Political Agent in Bahrain. Reluctantly, and reiterating its instructions that the two British officers were to adhere strictly to the brief that Cox had drawn up for them, London agreed.

So on December 15th 1913 Shakespear and Major Trevor arrived in the port of Uqair for two days of formal meetings with Ibn Saud. They carried with them Cox's strict instructions as to the topics to be discussed and the British position on each of the issues to be covered. They knew that as far as the British Government was concerned Ibn Saud, despite his capture of Hasa, remained no more than the 'Amir of southern Najd'. The meeting was given an added personal significance for Shakespear because his tour of duty in Kuwait was due to end early in 1914 and he knew that this formal meeting with his friend Ibn Saud was likely to be his last major task in that post.

Ibn Saud greeted his friend and Major Trevor warmly. When they settled down to business Ibn Saud gave an outline of the history of his family and its historic rights, branding the Ottomans as intruders and foreign usurpers. He was, he said, concerned above all with his family's honour and the preservation of their ancestral rights. This was the reason that he was seeking the support of the British Government. Shakespear and Trevor asked what kind of support he was seeking and he told them that what he wanted was an assurance from the British Government that it would maintain the peace in the Gulf and along the Hasa coast, and recognise him as Hasa's *de facto* ruler. As the British well knew, such an assurance would have the effect of protecting him from invasion from the sea by the Turks and enable him to gain his independence. Shakespear and Trevor told him that they were not empowered to give him any such assurance and, sticking to their brief, that their Government because of its friendship with the Ottoman Empire and the fact that the Ottomans would regard any such move as a hostile act on the part of Britain, would not be willing to do so either. Ibn Saud responded by repeating his earlier offers of facilitating British trade in his territories, upholding British control of shipping, assistance in the suppression of piracy and illegal arms trafficking, adding that he would be happy to consult the British government on all important matters of policy and agree not to enter into relations with any other government without prior British consent. He also reminded them that turning down his request might have certain undesirable consequences for British interests. He was, he told them, at that moment being pressed by the Ottoman government to accept an agreement which would give him a large degree of autonomy on condition that he agree to the return of Ottoman garrisons to Hasa, the appointment of judges in his territory and control of his relations with foreign powers by the Sultan, the ending of concessions to foreign merchants and exclusion of all foreigners from territory under his control. If the British were not to agree to his request he would have no alternative but to accept the Ottomans' terms. As Shakespear and Trevor knew, there was a further implied threat in what Ibn Saud had said. He could plausibly claim that both the Qatar peninsula on the Gulf coast and parts of Trucial Oman, both important to British interests, were a part of his ancestral dominions and that he was now almost certainly capable of overrunning them from Hasa at any time.

As soon as he began alluding to the penalties for Britain of not acceding to his request Ibn Saud detected an immediate change in Shakespear's attitude. The Ottoman conditions, the British officers said, would be damaging to British interests especially in the matter of the exclusion of British subjects from Hasa and Britain's right to have direct relations with whoever controlled the province. Their government would have to take up this matter with the Ottomans directly. Ibn Saud pressed them to take a stand on his request immediately as he was under pressure to make an early response to the Ottoman terms.

Shakespear and Trevor's reply to this was to ask Ibn Saud to delay any response until after the British government had had an opportunity to study their report of the meeting. Ibn Saud readily agreed. He would defer any response until he could meet the Turks face to face in the spring. This would give the British government three months in which to react to his proposal.

Despite the seriousness of their discussions there was a certain light-heartedness to the meeting. Outside the formal sessions Ibn Saud spent a lot of time discussing Shakespear's plans for a crossing of the whole of Arabia from east to west the following spring and a visit to Riyadh during the journey. Ibn Saud agreed to supply him with letters of introduction to friendly shaikhs on his projected route and guarantees of safe passage across all the territory under his control. After the two days of talks were concluded Shakespear and Trevor left with promises of meeting again in Riyadh in the spring.

After Shakespear and Trevor had left, Ibn Saud returned to Riyadh. Months went by and still he received no reply from the British to the requests he had made through Shakespear and Trevor. The Ottomans continued to press him for a response to their terms and at the same time increased the pressure on him by openly stepping up preparations for an attack and bringing fresh troops into the region. Ibn Saud played for yet more time and continued to press the British for a response. Unknown to him, while this was going on the British and Ottoman governments had continued to negotiate and in March 1914 reached an agreement dividing the whole Arabian peninsula between them. All the lands south of a straight line drawn across the peninsula running south west from Qatar in the east, across the Rub al-Khali and along the northern borders of Yemen and the Aden Protectorates in the south west to the Red Sea were to belong to Britain and everything to the north of the line, including all of the Hijaz, Najd and Hasa was to be part of the Ottoman Empire. The wishes of the peoples, rulers and governments of all the territories concerned were not considered and their rulers were not even consulted.

At the beginning of February 1914 Shakespear left Kuwait at the start of his long-planned journey across Arabia. For many months the British authorities had refused him permission to attempt his crossing. But in late January 1914, after receiving letters backing his request from Cox and the Viceroy himself in which they had stressed the valuable military intelligence he would be able to obtain during his journey and the mapping of uncharted areas that he would undertake, the Foreign Office had grudgingly relented, subject to him paying all his own expenses and the warning that the Ottoman authorities could not guarantee his safety and that the Hijaz was closed to him and all other non-Muslims.

The last few days before Shakespear's departure had been hectic as he cleared up the Agency and handed over its affairs to his successor, Colonel William Grey. The two men had taken an instant dislike to each other. Grey was an unbending stickler for protocol and a fusser. Shakespear described him dismissively as an old woman. Shakespear feared for Britain's future relationship with Kuwait when left in Grey's hands and for his handling of relations with the other desert shaikhs, including his friend Ibn Saud. Shakespear bequeathed Mubarak his salukis and his hawk as it would be impossible to take them with him on his long journey and went round the town saying his farewells. During his five years in Kuwait Shakespear had become a popular and much talked about figure not only in Kuwait but throughout the Gulf. On his last night Shakespear gave a party in the agency for his local friends. It lasted all night long and he did not get to bed until 6.30 a.m. An hour and a half later he was up and on his way.

Shakespear's small caravan when he left Kuwait consisted of eleven men, himself, personal servants, guides and camel minders, riding on seven riding camels and eleven baggage camels, together with four sheep. As they set out the weather was wet and cold and after three days one of the guides deserted them, terrified that he 'was being taken to the end of the world'. Shakespear travelled, as he always had, in army uniform and topee to keep the fierce sun off his neck. As was his custom, he took accurate readings of height, bearings and meteorological information as he went, noting geographic details and the precise location of settlements and other features, marking them on maps and meticulously writing up his diaries and log books every night. He also took his camera, taking many photographs along the route. These he developed each night in a minute darkroom set up in a corner of his tent. He also took a hunting rifle, supply of ammunition and a hip bath, a subject of much wonder and amusement to his Arab companions, which he set up when water was available in a special bathroom section which he had constructed for his tent. He also carried a plentiful supply of Moselle carefully hidden among his baggage for drinking at night with his dinner in the privacy of his tent. Over his years of desert exploration Shakespear had made progressive improvements to the comfort of his tent. These included a verandah next to the bathroom section, divided by an embroidered curtain sewn by an old Bedouin woman, where at night after the others in his party had gone to bed he could sit and read or write up his diary and logs while finishing his bottle of Moselle. Finally he would turn in to sleep, unless it was raining or a storm was blowing, in the utter quiet and peace of the desert, when the stars seem so close that you could reach up and touch them and the heavens will suddenly be enlivened by a shooting star. The pull of the desert seems to exert a special power on all Englishmen.

By March 10th Shakespear and his nine remaining companions were nearing Riyadh. As they approached along the same track that Palgrave had taken more than fifty years earlier, Riyadh still presented much the same picture as it had then: '… large and square, crowned by high towers and strong walls of defence, a mass of roofs and terraces' and all around 'a sea of palm trees above green fields and well-watered gardens' together with the sound of 'singing droning' water wheels. Shakespear would leave no matching picture in words of the city for he was no poet with words like Palgrave or T. E. Lawrence, although he would leave notebooks full of topographical descriptions and details. However, he would take many photographs of the old town as it was before the arrival of modernity and still little different from the way it had been when Ibn Saud's great-grandfather, Turki, had established himself in Riyadh in 1819 after the destruction of Dariya by the Egyptians.

That evening he and his companions set up camp in the date gardens outside the town and Shakespear sent his head guide into the town to warn Ibn Saud of their arrival. Ibn Saud was suffering from a cold but immediately dispatched a party of men and ponies out to escort his guests into the town and bring them to him. Shakespear's diary records being taken in the moonlight 'through the East gate along a wide road, past a lot of ruins and some big houses … ' to the palace where he was 'greeted warmly by Abdul Aziz (Ibn Saud) and Sa'ad (his brother) and then taken to the library or office. Tea, coffee and sweets and talk until evening prayer and then again afterwards until nearly 9.30.' Ibn Saud invited his friend to stay in the palace but Shakespear declined as he wanted to return to the peace of his tent to write up his maps and diaries.

Next morning, while Ibn Saud conducted his majlis, Shakespear took coffee with Ibn Saud's father Abd al-Rahman. Then he explored the town taking photographs. Shakespear noted that Palgrave's plan of Riyadh had been 'extremely good' except that the Rashids had demolished many of the Saud family's palaces, which Ibn Saud was now reconstructing. 'Quite a third of the town is taken up by the homes of the Saud family', Shakespear noted.[12]

During his stay in Riyadh Ibn Saud and Shakespear spent many hours in conversation, both in Riyadh and Shakespear's camp, sometimes alone, sometimes with Ibn Saud's father and brothers. Ibn Saud and Shakespear also played with Ibn Saud's young children. It was for the most part a happy and carefree time, except that Ibn Saud repeated to Shakespear his frustration that he still had not received any answer to the requests he had passed through him and Trevor to the British government and how he still believed that his country's future lay in some form of alliance with 'the Great Government' (Britain).

During Shakespear's stay in Riyadh Ibn Saud had been mustering his warriors, in part in preparation against any direct Ottoman attack or Ottoman, instigated attack by the Rashids. On March 12th Ibn Saud and his warriors set out on a great *ghazzu* (raid) with the green and white war banner of Riyadh at their head with the words 'There is no God but Allah' inscribed on it and the war cry 'Victory is God's: success is near'. Shakespear and his party brought up the rear, the first time that an Englishman had travelled under the war banner of the Sauds. It was a new high point in Ibn Saud's friendship with Shakespear.

For two days Shakespear and his party marched north with Ibn Saud's raiding party and in the evenings were invited to join the discussions in Ibn Saud's *majlis*. Shakespear talked to Ibn Saud and his followers about modern warfare, wireless, warships and other new European inventions of war. Ibn Saud and his shaikhs listened with close attention and thought. They also talked of religion and politics. Before his friend left

12 The quotations from Shakespear's diary are taken from H. V. F. Winstone's *Captain Shakespear*, op. cit.

them Ibn Saud presented him with three new and experienced guides to help him on the next, least-explored and most dangerous part of his great journey. Before they parted to go their separate ways Ibn Saud told Shakespear once more of the special nature of their friendship.

Ten days later Ibn Saud received a letter from Major Trevor telling him that Britain was trying to come to an arrangement with the Ottoman Empire that would meet his needs. Ibn Saud's confidence rose enormously. At last the British were intervening on his behalf with his enemy the Turks, or so it seemed.

Three weeks later, in mid-April, Ibn Saud got a message from his old friend and mentor Mubarak requesting him to meet him some five miles inland from Kuwait. Mubarak stressed that it was urgent. Ibn Saud sent a note to Major Trevor telling him he was going to Kuwait and hoped to be able to meet British officials when he got there. So, with his hopes so raised, his consternation and anger were all the greater when he arrived to find not Mubarak but a group of Ottoman officials, including a former Ottoman governor of Hasa and one Sayyid Talib who they intended to install as the next Governor of Hasa. The Ottomans had brought a treaty with them, drawn up and ready for Ibn Saud to sign. With his friend Shakespear no longer in Kuwait to turn to, Ibn Saud demanded to see Colonel Grey. When Grey reluctantly appeared Ibn Saud told him that he had no wish to sign the Turkish treaty and asked him what he should do. Grey, terse and unfriendly, told him that the Ottomans had rejected Britain's offer to mediate in his dispute with them and there was therefore nothing that Britain would or could do. He was free, Grey told him coldly, to negotiate with the Ottomans on his own. 'You can expect no help or guidance from Britain.' In fact the British had been complicit in the whole affair. With London determined to reach an agreement with Turkey which would, Sir Edward Grey believed, protect Britain's oil installations in Persia, keep the Germans out of the Persian Gulf and safeguard communications with India, Colonel Grey and other British representatives in the region had helped to engineer the whole event. By tricking Ibn Saud into coming to Kuwait and then cornering him they planned to force his submission and so meet the provisions of the still-secret Anglo-Ottoman Treaty which had been signed between the two countries nine months earlier.

Ibn Saud was furious. But realising that he had been cornered he knew he would have to come to some kind of deal with the Ottomans. When he met the Ottoman delegation again they demanded that he surrender all the forts in Hasa to them, that their garrisons be reinstated and that their arms be returned to them. In return the Ottoman Empire was willing to allow him to rule Hasa as their governor and to collect taxes, but he was to have no dealings with any foreign power. However, they would also allow him to capture the Trucial States of Oman when and if he chose.

After much intense negotiation and argument Ibn Saud agreed to each condition except one – the reinstatement of the Ottoman garrisons. This was the sticking point. Tension rose. Ibn Saud, normally so calm, had an anger which when roused was terrible to behold. Many times it had struck fear into his enemies and those around him. When one of the delegation, the Ottoman Chief of Staff in Basra, threatened Ibn Saud, telling him that if he did not accept the garrisons he would be made to, Ibn Saud rose from his chair starting to draw his sword. He ordered the Turk to leave the room. For a few moments it looked as if the negotiation would become a fight. Luckily calmer counsels prevailed and the negotiation was suspended. Ibn Saud hastily withdrew to Riyadh and mobilised his warriors while the Ottoman delegation returned to Basra. Neither side wanted a war at that moment. Ibn Saud had had his warriors mobilised for almost three months, the summer was upon them and the warriors wished to return home. The Ottomans, still beset at home and in the Balkans, were in no state to mount a full-scale invasion of Najd and Hasa. So ten days later a face-saving compromise was reached. Ibn Saud would accept a token Ottoman garrison in Hasa in return for recognition of his autonomy in Hasa and Najd. At the end of May 1914, the Ottoman governor of Basra and Ibn Saud's agent in the town signed a document which would become known as the Saudi-Ottoman Treaty.[13] Later Ibn Saud would say that he had been

13 There are slightly varying accounts of the negotiations over the treaty and we have based our account on a combination of the account as later told by Ibn Saud to Shakespear and the Ottoman records as outlined in Goldberg's *The Foreign Policy of Saudi Arabia*, op. cit. The treaty itself bears two dates, May 15th and 29th 1914.

forced into the agreement under duress and that, as he himself had not signed it, it did not count.

While all this was going on Shakespear had been out in the uncharted deserts of northern Hijaz and so knew nothing of what had happened until he arrived in Egypt. On his arrival in Suez, having covered more than 1800 miles, two thirds of it unmapped, he had written to Ibn Saud to tell him of his safe arrival and thank him for all the help that he had provided. Ibn Saud replied, congratulating him, adding 'Our friendship will never be affected by being away from each other because it is based on respect and sincerity.' His letter ended with the words 'God bless and Guard you.'

In Egypt Shakespear updated the British military and intelligence authorities on the situation in Arabia and what he had discovered during his crossing. Before sailing to return to Britain he met General Sir Reginald Wingate, soon to take over from Kitchener as Consul, and with Field Marshal Lord Kitchener himself, the British Consul General in Egypt, who was soon to become Secretary of State for War and whose face would soon be seen staring out of posters all over Britain telling its citizens: 'Your Country Needs You'. Shakespear found the 'local bigwigs' had only 'sketchy information on Central Arabia' and an inflated opinion of the influence of Sharif Husayn.

On June 28th 1914 in the Bosnian capital, Sarajevo, Gavrilo Princip, a Bosnian widely suspected of being a member of a Serbian nationalist terrorist group, the Black Hand, fired his pistol at Archduke Franz Ferdinand, the heir to the throne of Austro-Hungary and killed him. Over the next five weeks the world, led by blinkered and arrogant men, tumbled into an avoidable and horrific war.

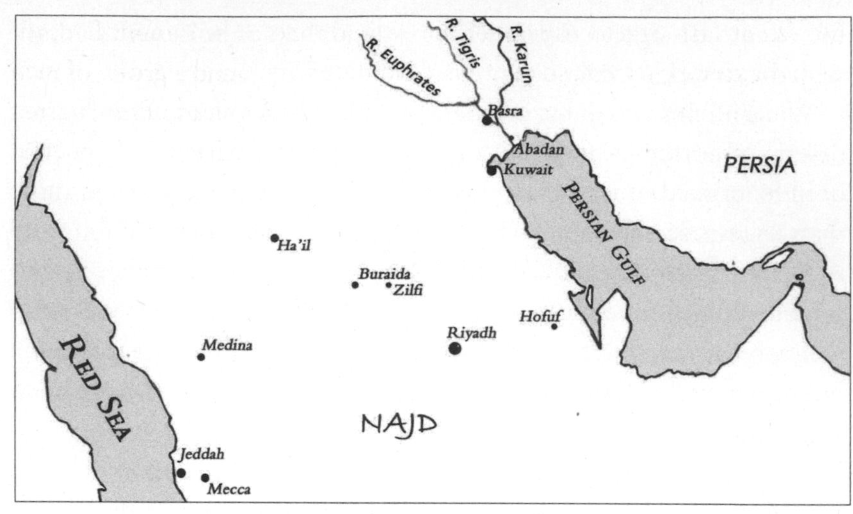

CHAPTER 6

Death of an Englishman

On August 4th 1914 Shakespear was in London which, with Dorothea now married and in India with her new husband, seemed empty and claustrophobically hot after the clean dry air of Arabia. He had been to see Sir Arthur Hirtzel, the Permanent Secretary of the Political and Secret Department in the India Office, to urge the Government to change its policy *vis-à-vis* Ibn Saud and the Ottoman Empire, but to no avail. He had accomplished his great Arabian ambition of recent years, his crossing of the peninsula, had written up his notes, given a lecture to the Royal Geographical Society and presented the collection of plants he had made during his crossing to the Natural History Museum. But now both his diplomatic and his personal lives seemed to have reached an impasse.

His life had become empty and so it was with more than just patriotic zeal that with the declaration of war he immediately reported to an army recruitment office. However, although he was a trained army officer, no one seemed interested in him. August dragged by and then in September he was at last sent to Aldershot. Having arrived he still found himself without specific orders, so on his own initiative he found a group of men and began preparing himself and them for active service in France.

Back in Arabia as the European crisis had deepened Ibn Saud had been following events closely. He knew that with the outbreak of a war, with Britain, France and Russia probably on one side and Germany and Austria, perhaps with the Ottoman Empire, on the other, he might be presented with the chance to secure the independence which he had so long waited for. But equally, he realised, that if the wrong side won or he mishandled events, they might spell disaster for him. However, as August turned to September and the Ottoman Empire continued to remain neutral, his hopes began to rise. Suddenly countries which had for years treated him with disdain began beating a path to his door. Even before the war had begun the Ottoman Empire had sent him instructions on the role he was to play if war came. According to these he was to end his long-standing dispute with the Rashids, advance north with them to Zubair on the Euphrates and prevent any British assault on Basra. Arms, ammunition and Turkish officers would be sent to him and the Rashids with which to attack the British and any tribes that chose to support them. As an inducement the Turks had also sent him money, a sum amounting to almost one and a half times the annual taxes and customs duties he was now levying as a result of his occupation of Hasa. But Ibn Saud was much too astute to rush into things until he saw how matters might turn out. So he took the Ottomans' money but sent them a non-committal response: he could not enter into any binding commitment at this time as he dare not antagonise the British. However, he would do nothing to prevent Najdi merchants from supplying Ottoman armies with food. For the time being his prime responsibility had to be to look to his own defence. At the same time as sending this message to the Ottomans Ibn Saud also sent a message to the British, telling them about the Ottoman approach.

Before making any further move Ibn Saud decided to consult his old friend and mentor Mubarak. Despite the way he had treated him only a few months before by helping corner him into making the treaty with the Ottomans, Ibn Saud still respected him as a wise counsellor. The two men met in the desert outside Kuwait. Mubarak, now an old man with hennaed hair and beard, arrived at their meeting place in style with a large entourage of rifle-toting outriders. The old man's advice to his young protégé was that he should try to stay out of any war but also attempt to make a treaty with the British. Ibn Saud saw at once that in advising him in this way Mubarak had his own interests at heart as much as his – for Mubarak it was vital that the British should win any war so that they could continue to protect him. At the same time he needed to avoid doing anything that might provoke the Ottomans to retaliate against him if the British lost. Much the same considerations applied for Ibn Saud. However, with greater forces than Mubarak, he might by helping the British be able to improve their chances of frustrating any Ottoman attack on the Arabian peninsula or shores of the Gulf. So once again Ibn Saud listened to the advice respectfully but did not commit himself to anything.

Ibn Saud's next move was to approach all the Arab leaders to try to get them to agree to a joint Arab alliance under which they would all agree to remain out of Europe's war and use their neutrality to force the imperial powers to guarantee the self-determination of all the Arab peoples. But the Rashids refused even to discuss this idea – they told him they would fight against anyone whom the Ottomans fought and make peace with those with whom the Ottomans made peace.

Ibn Saud did, however, hold a meeting with one of Husayn's sons, Abdullah. They met in the desert on the border between Najd and the Hijaz, but were unable to reach any agreement either. Husayn was already entertaining greater ambitions for himself than being merely one in an alliance of Arab leaders who would gain their own individual independence. He had begun to conceive visions of himself as the independent leader of all the Arabs. As soon as war had broken out between Germany and Britain in August 1914, while Kitchener was still in Egypt prior to being recalled to London to become Secretary of State for War, he had sent Husayn a personal message of greetings. Husayn had responded by sounding out Kitchener over the British attitude to a possible Arab uprising led by him against the Ottomans. No conclusions had been reached but the seeds of an idea had been planted.

The British, of course, having helped to engineer it had been well aware since the summer, months before war with Germany had been declared, that Ibn Saud had entered into a treaty with the Ottoman Empire. Britain was also aware of German efforts to bring the Ottoman Empire into the war on its side. If Germany succeeded, Germany and Austria together with the Ottoman Empire would present a serious threat to Britain and her allies. The Ottomans, sitting astride the Bosphorus, could block access for British and French shipping to their ally Russia through the Black Sea and prevent the Russian Black Sea fleet from entering the Mediterranean. Turkey could also act as the launch pad for a German-Ottoman 'second front' against Russia from the south. The Ottoman Empire, with its subject dominions in Mesopotamia and the northern Arabian peninsula, would pose a serious threat to the British oil fields in Persia and be in a position to block British communications and shipping through the Suez Canal, Red Sea and Persian Gulf to India and the British colonies in the Far East and Australasia. For Britain, with a relatively small professional army and a much smaller pool of trained reservists than the other combatants, this was a particularly serious threat. Her military strategy depended heavily on having a ready supply of Empire troops to bolster her forces. The Ottoman threat to Britain's Persian oil fields presented an additional threat for the British fleet which was in the process of rapid conversion from coal to oil firing for its boilers. Last, but by no means least, the British authorities in London and India had long feared that if the Ottoman Empire entered the war and the Caliph proclaimed *Jihad* (holy war or war against enemies of God) this might unite the whole Muslim world against Britain and her allies. In India this could trigger a massive revolt of Muslims, resulting in widespread bloodshed and mutinies in Britain's imperial Indian army.

From the Ottoman standpoint the potential gains to be had from allying herself to Germany and Austria included the military support of Germany and Austria in a campaign aimed at regaining Ottoman territories lost over recent years to Balkan nationalists and a bolstering of her strength in Mesopotamia. Most of the Turkish army officers who in 1913 had seized control of the Turkish government had been trained in Germany and were strongly pro-German.

From the German point of view the benefits of inducing the Ottoman Empire to fight on her side were the obverse of the dangers to Britain. For the German Kaiser, with his heart long set on acquiring an Empire not simply to match but to eclipse Britain's, an alliance with the Ottoman Empire offered the prospect of being able to advance into Persia and India.

Britain was well aware of all these dangers and had prepared contingency plans. Immediately after the declaration of war with Germany an additional warship had been sent to the Gulf and an Indian brigade sent to the head of the Gulf to occupy the Persian oil installations at Abadan and protect Basra and Kuwait. It was also decided that a special messenger should be sent to Ibn Saud, his task to ensure that if war with the Ottoman Empire did break out Ibn Saud and the tribes of central Arabia would support Britain but that unless and until war was declared Ibn Saud and the tribes would do nothing precipitate. The obvious man for this mission was Shakespear. Late in September he was found, still at Aldershot, and ordered to report to the India Office in Whitehall. Suddenly this officer who so long had been seen in London as a disobedient, wrong-headed irritant was in demand.

During the days of briefings that followed Shakespear's return to London, he repeated to the same officials in the Foreign, India and War Offices who only months before he had been trying in vain to get to see the true situation in Arabia, that Britain's best hope remained to recognise and support Ibn Saud, to give him a binding guarantee of independence under British suzerainty and provide him with the arms with which to take on the Ottoman Empire's allies in the region, in particular the Rashids. But this was still much too radical a shift in policy for the British Government. Sir Edward Grey, the Foreign Secretary, remained far from convinced that Ibn Saud's seizure of Hasa was more than an aberration, some kind of flash in the pan. He did not believe it would be permanent and expected the Turks to turn him out as soon as they had a mind to. Kitchener, now Secretary of State for War, still retained his over-inflated confidence in the potential of Husayn. Despite the briefing he and Wingate had received from Shakespear when he was passing through Cairo at the end of his crossing of Arabia, Kitchener still harboured the idea that Husayn, as the Sharif of Mecca and therefore a figure with enormous prestige throughout the Muslim world, could lead and inspire a general uprising of all the Arabs against the Ottoman Sultanate. Back in January 1914 Kitchener had met with

Husayn's son, Abdullah, in Cairo and been impressed by both him and the account Abdullah had given of his father's influence. Shortly after the war had begun Kitchener had sent his message of personal greeting to Husayn and instigated further secret discussions with his son, Abdullah. The purpose of these discussions was to explore the possibility of a concerted Arab uprising against their Ottoman masters. Kitchener had inquired whether Husayn and the Hashemites would be 'with us or against us' in the event of Turkey entering the war on the German side. In his personal message to Husayn he had spoken of what he called 'the Arab Nation' and of the possibility of 'an Arab of the true race' assuming the Caliphate. He had also given a clear hint that Britain would approve if Husayn were to assume the Caliphate and become the recognised leader of 'the Arab Nation'.

But that was to look ahead. In the meantime immediate steps had to be put in hand to deal with the situation on the ground in Arabia and repair Britain's relations with Ibn Saud after the way in which Colonel Grey and the British had treated him just six months earlier, when they had tricked him into coming to Kuwait and more or less compelled him to sign a treaty with the Ottomans. So Shakespear was ordered to return to Arabia immediately as Political Officer on Special Duty, and report directly to his old chief and mentor, now 'Sir' Percy Cox.

The result was that early in October 1914 Ibn Saud received a message from Colonel Knox. It said simply: 'Your friend Captain Shakespear is on the way' and added that he would have an urgent message for him from the British Government. With Knox's message came a fresh message from Mubarak. Mubarak told him that the war between Britain and Germany was Germany's fault and that the Germans were inciting the Ottomans to come into it on the German side. Cursing both of them, Mubarak warned Ibn Saud that if the Turks did enter the war the Germans would hand the Turks control over all the Arabs. This would include both of them. His and Ibn Saud's interest, Mubarak said, was to go along with whatever the British asked of them.

However, after the treatment Ibn Saud had received from the British only six months earlier when he had sought their help with the Turkish delegation in Kuwait and been brusquely told by the iron-faced Colonel Grey to expect no help or guidance from Britain, Ibn Saud remained wary. His reply, carried by his faithful cousin Jiluwi, except for a routine reference to the 'love and friendship' between Britain and the Sauds, contained no hint as to his attitude in the event of a war between Britain and the Ottoman Empire. He said simply that he would expect Captain Shakespear. When Mubarak showed this reply to Colonel Grey he misread it entirely and jubilantly wired Knox in Bahrain: 'Ibn Saud is with us.' In a separate message to await Shakespear's arrival in Arabia, Ibn Saud advised him that he must travel in disguise so as to avoid the Turks finding out about their meeting.

On October 10th 1914 Shakespear sailed aboard the S.S. *Arabia* for Bombay, from there to tranship to Bushire on the Persian coast of the Gulf. His orders were: 'As soon as possible to place himself in personal communication with the Amir of Najd and exert his influence on that chief with the object of 1. Preventing our proceedings from causing disturbance among the Arabs. 2. In the event of war with Turkey, to make certain of Arab goodwill.'[1]

On October 31st 1914, following a deliberate act of war by the Ottoman Empire in which Turkish battleships, recently acquired from Germany, attacked Russian shipping and ports in the Black Sea, Britain and the Ottoman Empire went to war. Britain immediately ordered the ships carrying troops which it had sent to Bahrain to set sail and begin the liberation of Basra from the Ottomans. A British proclamation was issued to all the rulers in the Persian Gulf who, in the words of the proclamation, 'have sought freedom from the Ottoman oppressor'. It urged them to preserve order and reject Ottoman calls to '*Jihad*'. This was followed the next day by a second British proclamation which guaranteed to protect the holy places of Arabia and Iraq from attack. Two days after that Knox, on behalf of the British Government, invited Ibn Saud to co-operate with Britain and with Mubarak in the liberation of Basra by preventing any Ottoman reinforcements from reaching it before the British arrived. In return Britain promised to protect Ibn Saud from Ottoman attack by sea, recognise his independence and enter into a

1 Instructions from Sir Edward Grey, Foreign Secretary, to India Office and British Government of India, October 9th 1914.

treaty with him. On November 5th Britain issued an official Declaration of War on the Ottoman Empire and Sir Percy Cox issued a formal proclamation to all the Arabs of the Euphrates and Tigris estuary (the Shatt al Arab) which said that Britain had 'with great regret been forced into a state of war by the persistent and unprovoked hostility of the Turkish Government instigated by Germany for her own ends'. The proclamation went on to say that Britain had no quarrel with the Arabs and that, provided they did not harbour Turkish troops, they had nothing to fear from Britain. The Ottomans responded by proclaiming a *jihad* against Britain, France and Russia, a solemn declaration that it was now the sacred duty of all Muslims to fight the enemies of the Sultan-Caliph.

Ibn Saud was now faced with an immediate dilemma. While he wished for the total defeat of the Ottomans, this was still far from guaranteed. An Ottoman victory, especially if he had sided with Britain, might well spell total disaster for him and end his hopes of independence for ever. However, as the British and Ottomans were already at war, there appeared to be no great hurry for him to do anything other than to play for time and see how the war developed. Nevertheless, in order to avoid antagonising the Ottomans, especially in light of the instructions he had received from them during the summer about his role in any war with Britain, he did need to explain his inaction. His solution was to send them a courteously worded message saying that, at least until he was sure that the Rashids would not exploit any opportunity that might be provided by his troops' absence from Najd to mount an attack on him, he must continue to retain his warriors in Najd and to look to the defence of his own domain. He was, therefore, unable to advance northwards towards Basra and the Euphrates until he knew for certain that the Rashids' forces were fully engaged elsewhere.

Ibn Saud's response to the letter from Knox presented him with an even greater problem. The British appeared to be offering him more or less exactly what he had repeatedly asked from them ever since 1902 – protection and a guarantee of his independence. On the other hand he dare not accede to Knox's invitation to take an active part in the liberation of Basra. Also, what would happen once the war was over? Even if Britain defeated the Ottoman Empire, might she not once again enter into a treaty with the Ottomans? What Ibn Saud needed, therefore, was to obtain from the British promises of independence and protection but without actually committing himself to doing anything active at all. He therefore delayed making any reply to Knox until November 28th, by which time the British, with some assistance from Mubarak, had captured Basra themselves. Then, when he did reply, he confined himself to telling Knox that he remained one of 'the great helpers of the British' and that his trust in God and 'the Glorious Government' remained strong that Britain would prevail. However he continued, 'I am a person who desires to remain quiet and in repose so that my state may not become impaired. As for the war, I hope God will give victory to those from whom advantage comes to us.' For the rest, he told Knox, he was looking forward to meeting Shakespear and discussing the British proposals with him.[2]

Meanwhile Shakespear had arrived in the Gulf and received further detailed instructions from Cox, who was now with the British forces advancing north up the Euphrates towards its confluence with the Tigris. Shakespear's brief was now, in furtherance of the instructions he had received from Sir Edward Grey in London, to link up with Ibn Saud, remain with him as a permanent emissary and induce him to commit his forces to the British campaign in Mesopotamia. On his arrival in Kuwait, on November 18th, a letter had been waiting for him from Ibn Saud. It told him he should travel south along the same route he had taken on his earlier journeys into the desert and that Ibn Saud and his men would find him. Ibn Saud's letter continued: 'My hopes are strong that matters may be resolved so as to protect our religion, and please God when our meeting takes place, the real objectives will be disclosed on both sides.'

In Kuwait Shakespear also learned that Sayyid Talib, the Ottomans' intended governor of Hasa who had been present when Ibn Saud had been tricked into agreeing to the Saudi-Ottoman Treaty in Kuwait in May 1914, had just left the town for Riyadh on a mission to Ibn Saud on behalf of the Ottoman Empire. During his service in the Gulf Shakespear had come across Talib a number of times and knew him to be an extremely dangerous and devious man. As he had warned officials in the India Office in London during briefings before sailing for the Gulf: 'The

2 Ibn Saud to Knox, November 28th 1914.

man is a strong, wilful, utterly unscrupulous character usually heavily in debt and therefore importunate.'[3]

Sayyid Talib came from a family of Basra merchants, but had become a gang leader and gun runner. He was known also as a wily, totally unscrupulous and cruel politician who had repeatedly shown that he was prepared to serve anyone so long as doing so promoted his own advancement and accumulation of wealth. Along the way he had been involved in at least one murder committed in pursuit of his own enrichment. He had spent a lot of time in Constantinople and taken on various roles under the Ottoman Empire. In 1902 he had been appointed the Ottoman governor of Hasa but his rule had proved so harsh and corrupt that two years later the Ottomans had been forced to recall him to Constantinople. There, amid the political turmoil, Talib had managed to ingratiate himself with each ruling clique as it had come to the fore. As a result in 1912 he had returned to Basra and been involved in a whole series of failed schemes, plots and missions, including a putative plot to foment an Arab revolt against the Turks with Ibn Saud as its proposed figurehead. In 1913 he had briefly acted as Ottoman governor of Basra and had made a number of approaches to the British (including an offer of his services to Kitchener) before becoming heavily involved in the Anglo-Ottoman scheme which had pressured Ibn Saud into signing the Ottoman-Saudi Treaty of May 1914.

Setting out on his mission to Ibn Saud on behalf of the Ottoman Government in November 1914, the devious Talib had called in at Kuwait and approached Colonel Grey. He had told Grey that he was on his way to Ibn Saud on the Caliph's behalf to persuade him to answer the call to *jihad* and rise against Britain. Nevertheless, he told Grey, he would prefer to serve Britain. But, he continued, in return Britain would have to offer him better terms than those being given to him by the Ottomans. This meant that he required an annual retainer, a large sum of money up front on account, a guarantee that he would be able to retain all his properties in and around Basra after the war and an undertaking that he would be appointed governor of Basra. Of course, Talib said, if the

3 See H. V .F. Winstone *The Illicit Adventure: The Story of Political and Military Intelligence in the Middle East from 1898 to 1926*, Jonathan Cape, London, 1982.

Ottoman Government discovered that he was making this offer to Britain the lives of his family, who were still in Basra, would be in danger. So he needed British protection for them as well as for himself.

However, before Grey could pass on Talib's offer to his superiors and receive an answer, Talib, probably fearing for his own safety if he stayed anywhere for too long while the outcome of Britain's advance on Basra was uncertain, had disappeared without warning into the desert with his henchmen and begun making his way to Ibn Saud. When, on arriving in Kuwait, Shakespear learned of Talib's mission he sent a message post-haste to Ibn Saud, warning him about Talib and his history of deceit.

When Sayyid Talib arrived in Najd he was accompanied by a gang of almost fifty retainers and armed men, plus four *ulema* (scholarly religious instructors). Immediately on reaching Ibn Saud's territory these *ulema* began busying themselves in preaching and instructing his subjects on their obligations as good Muslims, telling them that it was their duty to obey the Caliph's call to '*jihad*' in the face of the Christian foe. They were reminded that the Caliph was 'the successor of Muhammad'. Ibn Saud's reaction to the *ulema*'s intrusion into his territory was to detain them and place them in honourable confinement. However, Sayyid Talib could not be dealt with quite so easily.

By the time he had reached Riyadh news of Britain's seizure of Basra and continuing successes were the talk of the town. As a result, by the time he came to deliver his Ottoman masters' message, Sayyid Talib was in an extremely awkward and potentially dangerous position. If he failed to carry out his instructions from the Turks he risked antagonising them and incurring their wrath. On the other hand, if the British continued to be victorious and captured him they might also decide to exact revenge upon him rather than take him into their service. But Ibn Saud also continued to face something of a dilemma. The fall of Basra was encouraging and if the British success continued and they succeeded in defeating the Ottomans he might at last secure his total independence. On the other hand there was still no guarantee of this or that, once the war over, the British might not again enter into a treaty with the Ottomans. So Ibn Saud politely but firmly reiterated to Sayyid Talib what he had said to the Ottomans in his earlier message: that he could not advance northwards towards Basra until he was certain that the Rashids would not use his absence to mount an attack against Najd.

Happily (and perhaps it was no coincidence?) Ibn Saud had just received information that his old foes the Rashids had indeed sent raiding parties out into his domain in northern Najd. As a result he was able to inform Talib that further discussion must be deferred while he hurried north to confront the Rashids. In fact, seemingly unknown to both Talib and Ibn Saud, the Rashids, who had already received extra arms from the Turks, were at that moment also trying to avoid committing themselves to sending their forces north to support them. So they had sent all the able-bodied men they could muster out into the desert in order to evade an impending visit to Ha'il by an Ottoman recruiting mission. It seems probable, therefore, that the Rashid raiding parties that provided Ibn Saud with his excuse for breaking off discussion with Talib were the able-bodied men the Rashids had sent into the desert. Alternatively they may have been nothing more than a series of local tribal *ghazzu*, of the kind that always occurred at that time of year. Unfortunately for Ibn Saud the loquacious Sayyid Talib was not so easily fobbed off and insisted on travelling with him as he and his warriors headed north to confront the Rashids.

Meanwhile, as Ibn Saud and his party of warriors were leaving Riyadh, Shakespear was still in Kuwait trying to speed up preparations for his journey. His meetings with the British High Command in Basra had served to convince him of their incompetence and he felt that if he had to serve under them he would be court-martialled within a week. When Cox asked Shakespear to hang on in Kuwait for long enough to meet the Viceroy, who was due to arrive on a visit, Shakespear declined. Fortunately at that moment he had received a response from Ibn Saud inviting him to join him in the desert and he was able to plead that he needed to be on his way.

After what he had seen in Basra and the continuing refusal of the British authorities to recognise what he believed to be the true potential of Ibn Saud, Shakespear was in a less than buoyant mood as he set out southwards into the desert, three weeks behind Talib, on December 12th 1914. It was more than just the low opinion he had formed of the British High Command in Basra that had depressed him. He had been disgusted by the unhelpful attitude of his successor in the Kuwait agency, Colonel Grey, and by the extent to which, in just the few short months that he had been in post his aloof and unfriendly attitude had soured the local Arabs' feelings towards the British. Shakespear had had difficulty keeping his temper with Grey – more than once having to leave a room when Grey was in it to avoid an open row. Grey seemed to have deliberately re-deployed all Shakespear's old retainers and guides to other duties so that they would be unavailable to accompany him on his desert mission to Ibn Saud. As a result Shakespear had had to borrow camels from Shaikh Mubarak and find a new team to accompany him. As he soon discovered, the new cook he had taken on was useless and, as he wrote to his younger brother a few days into his journey, 'has almost done for my stomach'.

Yet Shakespear's greatest concern as he headed south into the desert to meet his old friend was the continuing vacillation of his own government and its inability to recognise who were its potential friends and who its foes. Shakespear knew too that his mission was, in view of the battle that now seemed likely to be fought between Ibn Saud and the Rashids, likely to be both protracted and dangerous. With these considerations all weighing in on him, before leaving Kuwait he had put his own affairs in order, making his will and leaving with Colonel Grey a handwritten note and letters to his family in case he should 'get snuffed out in the desert'. The closing words of his note to Grey were: 'I think I have left everything squared up so as to give as little trouble as possible, anyway I have tried to.'[4]

It was December 31st 1914 when Ibn Saud's scouts found Captain Shakespear and his small caravan and brought the two men face to face again in Ibn Saud's camp on the Al Aramah Plateau north of Riyadh. Ibn Saud's greeting for his friend was, in contrast to their earlier meetings, distant and restrained. Shakespear sensed at once that something was wrong. One cause for the change in Ibn Saud's demeanour became obvious almost at once, the hovering, self-ingratiating presence among the small group of onlookers and Ibn Saud's intimates of the ever-

4 Note from Shakespear to Lieut-Colonel Grey, dated December 11th 1914, from facsimile in H. V. F. Winstone, *Captain Shakespear: A Portrait*, op. cit.

loquacious Sayyid Talib. But the greatest reason for the change in Ibn Saud's attitude to Shakespear became apparent once the formalities of Arab hospitality had been sufficiently observed and they fell to serious conversation in Ibn Saud's tent. Ibn Saud was angry. He was still bitter at the way he had been treated by Colonel Grey and the British when he had called for their help when confronted by the Ottoman delegation outside Kuwait eight months earlier. He felt he had been tricked and deserted by Britain and even by his old friend and mentor Mubarak. Now all of Ibn Saud's pent-up anger exploded out towards Shakespear, the Englishman he had trusted as no other. It took a long time for Shakespear to calm him down. But once he had and got Ibn Saud to listen, Shakespear told him that he still had friends in the 'Great Government', that he and Sir Percy Cox were still his allies.

That night when Shakespear retired to his tent and began to pound out on his typewriter his first set of notes and report to Cox, he was nearly as angry as Ibn Saud himself. He was furious at the behaviour of Colonel Grey and the manner in which he had treated Ibn Saud and deeply dismayed at the stupidity and duplicity of his own superiors. 'It is unnecessary for me to recall what passed between Bin Saud and Grey', he wrote. On his arrival, he continued, he had found Ibn Saud 'completely detached from the British Government'. Ibn Saud had, as Cox well knew, 'trusted the British Government as no other'. But now Ibn Saud found himself in a difficult position. The government that six months earlier had let him down and told him when faced by 'his most powerful and bitter enemies' that it 'could not intervene on his behalf and left him free to do a deal with the Turks' was now asking him to 'commit himself to open war' with those same powerful, bitter enemies.

It had been clear to Shakespear even before the discussions he and Major Trevor had held with Ibn Saud back in December 1913 that he would and could not commit himself to any form of binding agreement with the British cause until he had a watertight written commitment of protection from the British Government. It also seemed extremely unlikely that any meaningful discussion of any treaty or agreement with Britain would take place as long as Sayyid Talib remained in Ibn Saud's camp. Ibn Saud was clearly anxious about Talib's presence and had himself asked for Shakespear's help to have him removed. Shakespear had advised him to send a note to Cox, telling him about Talib's mission and explaining that while Talib was present he dare not commit himself to any kind of agreement with Britain for fear of Ottoman retribution.

In fact, as news of the continuing British advance up the Euphrates north of Basra had continued to arrive in Ibn Saud's camp Talib himself had become increasingly uneasy and begun to look for further opportunities to ingratiate himself with the British. So when Shakespear, recognising that a means of getting rid of Talib had to be found immediately, had advised Ibn Saud to send him to Cox in Basra, Talib was ready to go.

Having disposed of the problem of Talib, Shakespear and Ibn Saud, sometimes joined by his brother Sa'ad and cousin Jiluwi, got down to three days of intense discussions. Ibn Saud put to Shakespear six conditions for entering into an agreement with Britain: He, Ibn Saud, and his heirs would be recognised as the independent rulers of Najd, Hasa and Qatif; Britain would defend all his territories from all external aggression; in any boundary dispute between himself and other rulers under British protection (such as the Gulf amirates) the resolution should be in accordance with ancestral rights; Britain would not habour refugees from Saudi lands; Britain would treat all his subjects within her territories with the same consideration as her own subjects; *Shari'a* law would apply to all Muslims in Ibn Saud's territories, whether they were his subjects or not. In return, Ibn Saud would have no dealings with any other power nor offer any outside government any concessions except with prior British agreement; he would protect trade within his own territories, but prohibit the arms traffic, provided only that he could acquire the arms which he needed through the British government; he would protect British subjects and protégés in his ports. In order to exert additional pressure on Shakespear and his British masters to accept his terms, Ibn Saud reminded him of Talib's mission and told him about the *ulema* he had placed in honourable confinement. In view of Talib and the *ulema*'s mission and the ongoing threat to him presented by the Ottomans' allies, the Rashids, Ibn Saud said in a note which accompanied Shakespear's report to Cox, 'I fear force of circumstances may drive me to give some overt demonstration of my intention to side with the Ottomans'. Throughout his discussions with Shakespear Ibn Saud remained careful not to commit himself to undertaking any active part in British military operations in the region, other than such actions as might at the same time serve his own ends.

While these discussions were still going on a messenger from Husayn's son Abdullah arrived in the camp. Abdullah wanted to know if Ibn Saud was going to answer the Caliph's call for *jihad* and obey the Ottomans' instructions to attack the British around Basra. On Shakespear's advice, Ibn Saud sent the messenger back to Abdullah saying that he should play for time but agree to nothing and sent with him a copy of a promise from the Viceroy of India that Britain would protect the Holy Places. Shakespear also penned a warning to the British authorities about the dangers of a *jihad* being proclaimed by a figure as influential as Sharif Husayn.

After three days of intense discussion Shakespear dispatched a draft of the treaty he had agreed with Ibn Saud to Cox. With it he sent not only Ibn Saud's own note to Cox, but a letter of support for the treaty from the self-seeking Sayyid Talib, plus a letter of his own pressing Cox and his superiors in the British Government of India and in London to agree to Ibn Saud's terms. In the letter Shakespear told Cox that Ibn Saud would not 'move a step further towards making matters either easier for us or more difficult for the Turks as far as the present war is concerned, until he obtains ... some very solid guarantee of his position, with Great Britain practically as his suzerain. Granted this he can be relied upon to use all his resources and immense influence in Arabia on our side.' Shakespear, aware that Ibn Saud was unlikely to commit himself to the active support that Britain had asked for in her military operations around Basra and further north even after he had got the treaty and guarantee of British protection that he sought, tried to convince Cox that a treaty along the lines he and Ibn Saud had drafted still offered Britain and its military campaign huge benefits. 'The co-operation Ibn Saud has furnished by his own attitude and his influence with other Arab chiefs has been of no less value than the active support asked for.'[5]

5 Quotations from Shakespear's and Ibn Saud's letters to Cox dated January 4th 1915 and draft treaty from India Office Papers quoted in Winstone op. cit. and Goldberg *The Foreign Policy of Saudi Arabia,* op. cit.

Cox received Shakespear's letter and the draft treaty five days later and immediately sent the treaty on to his superiors in India with a supporting letter of his own urging its acceptance. In order to make the treaty more palatable to the British authorities Cox added a number of suggested modifications: that Ibn Saud receive a permanent British political agent in Riyadh or Hasa; that he cooperate in the suppression of piracy in the Gulf, allow British merchant vessels to use Hasa's ports, protect pilgrims passing through his territory to Mecca and permit the building of post and telegraph offices in one of the Hasa ports. Cox told his superiors that in agreeing to protect Ibn Saud against aggression it was running little risk as Britain was already at war with the only likely source of such aggression – the Ottoman Empire. A few days later Sayyid Talib appeared in Cox's office saying he wanted to discuss his terms for working for the British. Cox promptly detained him and had him sent to India. The Caliph's call for *jihad* had recently started to gain a response among Arabs living along the banks of the Tigris and Euphrates and the last thing Cox was going to risk at this juncture was having Talib change sides again and start promoting the idea of a *jihad* among the Arab tribes. The military situation along the Euphrates had worsened and the military command, on the orders of the authorities in India, had ordered a halt to the British advance up the Euphrates at a place called Kurna, just north of its junction with the Tigris, on the grounds that they did not have sufficient troops to sustain any further advance. Unfortunately for Cox, even after he had dispatched Talib to India it was still not to be the last he would hear of him. Shortly after arriving in India Talib started preaching *jihad* to the Indian Muslims. Years later still Talib would turn up and trouble Cox in Iraq.

Meanwhile, when the authorities in India received the draft treaty and Cox's recommendations their reaction was extremely cautious. They foresaw huge difficulties over such issues as defining Ibn Saud's borders, over refugees, the application of *Shari'a* law and the clauses on the arms traffic. A full two weeks after Shakespear had dispatched his draft the authorities in India sent the draft treaty on to London, together with their own advice. As the time factor was important and resolving the problems which they foresaw was likely to take a long time, the Indian authorities recommended that Cox be authorised to negotiate a preliminary agreement with Ibn Saud pending later agreement on a comprehensive treaty. This preliminary agreement would recognise Ibn Saud as ruler of Najd, Hasa and Qatif subject to certain conditions and provide him with protection in the event of unprovoked aggression by a foreign power.

During all the time that Ibn Saud and Shakespear had been negotiating their draft treaty the war drums had beaten almost continuously except for the five breaks each day for prayer and for a few hours in the dead of night when the warriors slept. Every day more Bedouin warriors had been arriving in the camp as leaders of the Ajman, Mutair and other tribes of the north east came riding out of the desert at the head of columns of their own warriors. Now, almost two weeks after the draft treaty had been dispatched to Cox, some six thousand men had been assembled and thousands of camels had started to be brought in from the winter grazing grounds beyond the Al Aramah Plateau. Now at last the drumming became less insistent. For days the warriors had worked themselves up into a fervour for battle. Now, as the time approached for them to be sorted into their fighting groups and allocated with fresh camels, they seemed to become listless. Perhaps they had waited too long or perhaps, as the prospect of battle and bloodshed had approached, the Bedouin had become more introspective in their thoughts. Small groups sat on the ground brooding in silence or talking listlessly.

Saud ibn Rashid, the young ruler of Ha'il who six years earlier had murdered his cousin and played a part in other murders in the long-running blood feud that had gripped the House of Rashid ever since Abd al-Aziz ibn Rashid had been killed and defeated in battle by Ibn Saud, was reported to be marching south east from Buraida towards Zilfi with a large force. Ibn Saud, now buoyed up with the hope of an imminent treaty with Britain, had decided to bring him to battle and, he believed, make an end of the Rashids for ever. Shakespear too, once the draft treaty had been agreed with Ibn Saud and dispatched to Cox, had seemed briefly to regain his optimism. He had written to Gertrude Bell, who had made an epic journey to Ha'il a year earlier at about the same time as he had been making his crossing of Arabia. They had never met but had, as fellow Arab travellers and explorers, corresponded. Shortly after dispatching the draft treaty Shakespear wrote to her from Ibn

Saud's camp. Ibn Saud, he told her ' ... is as pleased as possible. He is making preparations for a big raid on Ibn Rashid with a view to wiping him out practically and I shouldn't be surprised if I reached Hail in the course of the next month or two as BS's [Ibn Saud's] political adviser.'[6]

Two weeks later, while the draft treaty was still making its measured way between Cox, the authorities in India and the Government in London, Shakespear's mood, like that of the warriors, had begun to darken again. He wrote a long, hastily composed letter to his brother, telling him that he was encamped with Ibn Saud in the desert and that there were 'some 6,000 of his men' with them 'in tents and thousands of Badawin [sic] all round and in a couple of days we should make a move for a biggish battle with the other big chief of Central Arabia, Ibn Rashid. From all accounts he hasn't anything like the same force so the result ought to be pretty certain, but' he added, 'there is never any knowing what these Badawin will do; they are quite capable of being firm friends up to the battle and then suddenly changing their minds and going over to the other side in the middle of it.'

Shakespear seemed to sense that the British Government's interest in a treaty with Ibn Saud had waned following their military successes north of Basra and he increasingly feared that his advice would be disregarded and that the officials in London and India would continue to prevaricate. He told his brother: 'They will probably go on messing about until they make Bin Saud so utterly sick that he will chuck his present friendly attitude.' If so, he added, 'Heaven knows what trouble may be in store for us and all the petty chiefs along the coast.' By now Ibn Saud knew for certain that Saud ibn Rashid was encamped with his Ha'il and Shammar tribesmen warriors between Buraida and Zilfi and was preparing to march out to attack him. Ibn Saud asked his friend to leave for his own safety but Shakespear refused, telling him that he intended to accompany him to the coming battle. As he told his brother, 'Bin Saud wants me to clear out but I want to see the show and I don't think it will be very unsafe.'[7]

6 Letter from Shakespear to Gertrude Bell quoted in H. V. F. Winstone's *Gertrude Bell*, Jonathan Cape, London 1978.

7 Extracts from Shakespear's letter to his brother Lieut-Colonel H. T. Shakespear dated January 14th 1915 quoted in H. V. F. Winstone *Captain Shakespear*, op. cit. and *The Illicit Adventure*, op. cit.

A week later, on January 22nd 1915, Ibn Saud and his army set out northwards towards Zilfi. The pale desert winter sunlight was clear but cool, not so fierce yet as to heat the grey cold desert rocks. Ibn Saud, a be-robed and commanding figure on a fine black mare and Shakespear, in khaki British desert uniform riding beside him on a camel. Above them fluttered the green and white war banner of the Sauds bearing the timeless words: 'There is no God but God.' The Amir and his English friend were at the head of a motley throng of upwards of eighteen thousand men, some six thousand of Ibn Saud's camel-mounted townsmen and enlisted tribesmen, ammunition bandoliers across their chests, rifles to hand before them on the pommels of their camels' saddles, and behind them some twelve thousand Bedouin tribesmen of the north-east, the Ajman, Mutair, Sbei and Bani Harb. For much of the time as they rode Ibn Saud and the Englishman were locked in low, intense conversation. They went once again over the agreement they had made, speculated on how Shakespear's superiors might respond and on the possible actions of the Ottomans. But there were other topics of conversation also, subjects which were also near to their hearts – their friends, hunting, sports and loved ones. On this last subject there was a lasting hole in Shakespear's heart, the hole where Dorothea had been, the hole he himself had made by his failure to speak out nor to relax the hold his love of Arabia had over him even so far as to allow him to consider service for a while in a place where he and Dorothea could set up home together. Now she was married to someone else and he was left with just his one true love – Arabia.

For much of the time as they rode the muffled scuff of the thousands of camels hooves, the gentle slap of their harnesses and the clanking of some of the field guns that Ibn Saud had captured from the Turks as they were dragged along by pack-camels, were almost the only sounds that broke the desert silence. At others one or more of the thousands of Bedouin would raise their voices in tribal chants – chants such as had over thousands of years spurred on the camels and broken the monotony for Arabs as they had travelled across the great deserts and open spaces of Arabia in search of fresh pasture or in long caravans carrying goods from the coasts to the towns of the interior – chants such as could have been heard by the Queen of Sheba as she travelled with her great train of camels bearing her gold and precious spices from her southern kingdom to Jerusalem to test the knowledge of King Solomon, chants such as would have been raised by the desert warriors of Gindibu as they journeyed to fight alongside the Assyrians three thousand years earlier. This was a timeless scene such as few Englishmen had been privileged to witness let alone be part of, for no Englishman other than Shakespear had ever before been permitted to ride with the Amir to battle at the head of his warriors beneath the war banners of the Al Saud.

The next day, January 23rd, they camped near Zilfi. Through the day Ibn Saud's scouts brought in more and more reports confirming that Ibn Rashid was twenty-five miles to the southwest in the direction of Buraida and that he had with him an army of some seven hundred Ha'il townsmen and eight to nine thousand Shammar Bedouin warriors. Confident of victory, Ibn Saud and his warriors prepared to do battle with the Rashids next day.

That night, preparations for the next day's battle now made, Ibn Saud went to Shakespear's tent and once again begged him to leave. His friend should go now with his own young son to the safety of nearby Zilfi from where he and the boy could rejoin Ibn Saud after the battle was over. But Shakespear again refused. They argued back and forth and at one point one of Shakespear's servants heard him tell Ibn Saud: 'If I go now, I desert not only you but my own country. I cannot do that.' Seeing that his friend's mind was set, Ibn Saud again asked Shakespear that, if he must stay, then at least he should wear Arab dress. But Shakespear again refused. He had worn British uniform during all his travels into the desert and now above all he could not descend to the deceit of disguise. Not only was he now in the desert with his friend, Ibn Saud, he was in the desert on the business of his own Government. He could not, therefore, don disguise because his friend was going into battle against the ally of his government's enemy, the Rashid. Later, as Ibn Saud was walking back towards his own tent, a messenger appeared out of the desert, accompanied by one of Ibn Saud's scouts. He had serious news: hearing of the coming battle Sharif Husayn's son, Abdullah, was at that moment heading with a Hashemite army out of the Hijaz towards Najd and was even now encamped at a place called Shara, less than two hundred miles to the west of Riyadh. Ibn Saud nodded and thanked the man who withdrew. As he walked the rest of the way back to his tent

Ibn Saud was deep in thought: perhaps the final showdown with his enemies which he had so long expected was now at hand?

The next morning, January 24th 1915, Ibn Saud's camp was astir early, well before the first rays of the sun appeared over the red sands of the Dahna and the eastern horizon. Shakespear too was woken early by his servant. Sitting at the mouth of his tent eating a hearty breakfast as Ibn Saud's army prepared for battle he watched as the fast war camels were saddled up and the Arab chargers untethered from where they were grazing. Each charger was led by his warrior master on a halter and loosely tied to the girth strap below the saddle of the warrior's camel. The chargers had neither bridle nor saddle, their only harness being the halter. In battle the warriors would ride them bare-back, guiding and driving them on with only their knees, their legs and the rope halter.

Shakespear ordered his servants to furl the tent, pack their belongings and prepare to leave. He checked his revolver, gathered his spare ammunition, slipped on his field glasses and picked up his small camera and spare rolls of film.

When all was ready and the war banners unfurled, Ibn Saud, watched by Shakespear, rode out at the head of his cavalry. Then Shakespear himself, with one trusted retainer, mounted his camel and followed after the infantry and field guns. A small body of Ibn Saud's men was left behind to mind the baggage and pack camels. The warriors were now out on a flat level plain surrounded by sand dunes. To their left, sweeping away westwards and below them towards Buraida was the dry, salt-caked floor of the great Wadi ar Rummah, behind and to the east beyond the sunrise lay the Hasa and distant shores of the Gulf. The battle would be fought near Muhanna, the village close to which Ibn Saud had nine years earlier surprised Abd al-Aziz ibn Rashid, defeated and killed him in battle, so setting off the long-running Rashid blood-feud from which Saud ibn Rashid had now emerged as Ha'il's blood-stained ruler.

Ibn Saud and his cavalry, together with the mounted warriors of the Ajman, Mutair and Bani Harb fanned out to the left along the north bank of the wadi, while the Bedouin infantry spread out to the right behind the sand dunes with the field guns to wait for the approaching Rashids. One section of the Ajman tribe were given the task of protecting the line of Saudi infantrymen from any direct assault by the Rashid cavalry.

Shakespear, in his Indian Army khaki uniform and wearing his topee, took up position at the top of a small sandhill near to one of the field guns, which was manned by one of Ibn Saud's gunners named Husayn. The Englishman prepared his camera, took some pictures of the Saudi infantry and guns in their positions on the tops and behind the sand dunes and then began to scan the western skyline through his field glasses for the first sign of the approaching Rashid army riding and marching towards the rising sun. The place where Shakespear stood was known as Al Jarab.

It was six in the morning. The minutes passed as the pale sun began to rise in the east behind the Saudi army. At last the silence was broken by the faint but growing sloughing and muffled clatter of an approaching multitude of camels and horses hooves. Then the western horizon began to be broken by a steadily growing cloud of grey-brown dust that rose gently into the first rays of the morning sun. Minutes later, into and below the cloud, a bobbing sunlit and ever-growing multitude of the spotted kaffiyas, heads, and war banners of the Rashids began to appear above the horizon. Soon thousands upon thousands of warriors and Bedouin, some mounted on camels, hundreds on horses and thousands more on foot, rifles in hand, their chests crossed with bandoliers of ammunition and with sharp, curved *khunjars* tucked into their belts, could be clearly seen steadily and inexorably advancing eastwards, the sun on their faces, towards the waiting Saudis. Ibn Saud, sitting erect on his great war charger, the war banner of the House of Saud fluttering gently above him, waited patiently in the morning sun. When the right time came, but not a moment before, he would give the sign that would begin the battle.

While the rest of the army waited in silence, all eyes watching their amir and the inexorably advancing Rashid horde, among the sand dunes the inexpert Saudi field gunners swung and heaved their guns around so that their barrels pointed directly at the heart of the Rashid line. They then began to try to gauge the exact range and angle of elevation for the barrels to ensure that their first shots would fall among the advancing Rashids and not in front of or behind them. On his dune-top vantage point Shakespear was peering through his camera towards the advancing Rashid horde. More minutes passed and the shutter of Shakespear's camera was heard to click open and shut. The waiting Saudi infantrymen and gunners saw him lower the camera from his eye, methodically wind on the roll of film, raise the camera again and click. Then again, three or four more times. Then he carefully put his camera back into its leather case and began calmly shouting instructions to the nearest of Ibn Saud's novice artillerymen, Husayn.

More minutes passed and then the advancing phalanxes of bobbing, marching, trotting Rashid warriors began to quicken their pace. As their trot developed into a run and then a gallop Ibn Saud gave the signal and his field gunners opened fire. Most of their shells missed their targets and as the gunners paused to hastily reload, Ibn Saud's riflemen, pressing their bodies still deeper into the sand dunes began to fire indiscriminately. As the Rashid gallop developed into a wide, wild charge Ibn Saud, at the head of his own cavalry, gave a further signal and led his own cavalrymen in a charge into the advancing enemy's flank. The cry *Allah akbar* rose all around, amid the crackle of the rifle fire, pinging and whistling of the bullets, thudding and booming of artillery shells, the drumming of thousands of hooves. As the Saudi camels reached full speed, the chargers galloping beside them still tied by their halters to the camels' saddle girths, Ibn Saud's warriors loosened the chargers' halters and leapt, halter in one hand and rifle in the other, straight from the camels' saddles onto the bare backs of the horses, spurring them on headlong into the flanks of the enemy, firing as they went. Unlike the Saudi warriors who were spurred on with cries of religious exhortation and promises of Paradise, the Rashid cavalrymen were spurred on by Shammar tribal war cries shouted by beautiful girls riding camels, their hair flowing behind them in the wind and their faces uncovered.[8] As the battle reached its peak the sounds of gun fire, shouted commands, galloping hooves and slashing *khunjars* were joined and mixed with a growing crescendo of cries, screams, grunts and whinnies as men and animals were wounded, trampled, slashed, torn, blasted and killed.

8 The detail about the beautiful Rashid girls shouting tribal war cries is, so far as we have been able to ascertain, contained in only one published account of the battle, that of Alexei Vassiliev op. cit. and so may be of dubious veracity. However, all the published accounts of the battle are based on second-hand information, much of which is at best questionable. We have relied mainly on those accounts which seem likely to be the most reliable, namely those of H. V. F. Winstone in *Captain Shakespear* and *The Illicit Adventure*.

The advancing Rashid line, hit by the charge of the Saudi warriors and camels in the flank, wavered, seemed about to break and began to disintegrate into a swirling, struggling and confused mass of men, charging and rearing horses and loose camels. But a section of the Rashid's Shammar cavalry on the furthest flank of their line, spotting the danger in time, wheeled and then charged straight at the Saudi infantry and guns which were firing at them from behind the dunes. Riding low and fast, firing as they came, to the tribesmen cowering in their path behind the sand dunes they were a terrifying sight. Many of the Saudis became seized with fear and were ready to break and run. At this moment the Ajman, beginning to fear that the battle would be lost, instead of moving in among the Shammar cavalry to break up their charge, wheeled and joined in the charge themselves, thus fulfilling the prophecy of treachery made by Shakespear in his letter to his brother a few days earlier.

Shakespear himself, still standing erect on the sandhill, continued to shout instructions to Husayn and such other gunners as could hear him. Husayn shouted up to him to remove his topee and get down. Shakespear removed the topee but continued standing, giving instructions and calling out ranges. But by now the Ajman's act of treachery had broken the resolve of the remaining Saudi infantry and field gunners and they too, obeying the first rule of Bedouin warfare, began to flee towards the cover of the Wadi ar Rummah. Husayn, hastily trying to bury his gun in the sand, called out to Shakespear to flee and save himself as well. But Shakespear drew his revolver and prepared to stand his ground in the face of the rapidly closing enemy. Shakespear was hit first in the arm and then in the groin. He went down and as the advancing Shammar and Ajman cavalry swarmed over and past him he was shot in the back of the head. The Ajman then rode on to loot the Saudi baggage train which had been sheltered in trenches dug some five hundred yards behind the Saudi line. The battle of Al Jarab was lost.

Shakespear's cook, Khalid (who Shakespear told his brother 'has almost done for my stomach'), having been taken prisoner by the Rashids managed to escape and two days later, after hiding under a bush in the Wadi ar Rummah, returned to the battlefield and found Shakespear's body. 'Everything had been stripped from his body except his ganji [Indian] vest'. A wandering Bedouin later found his compass and gave it to Ibn Saud, who in turn returned it to Major Trevor, the British Agent in Bahrain.[9]

Shakespear had died because he had disregarded one of the fundamental rules of traditional Bedouin warfare: that he who fights and runs away, lives to fight another day. It was a rule founded on the fact that for thousands of years for nomadic Arabs most warfare had been regarded as little more than an extension of the traditional *ghazzu*, a heightened form of sport. For Shakespear, a true military son of the high tide of nineteenth century British imperialism, such an idea was completely alien. Even if he had been able to after receiving his wound in the thigh, to have followed the gunner Husayn's shouted advice and run away to save himself when the others fled in the face of the Shammar charge would have been impossible. Shakespear, because of all his years of upbringing and training, simply could not have turned and run. So he stood his ground, firing his revolver at point-blank range, at the galloping, shooting, slashing Shammar cavalry. Some people have speculated that by deliberately standing his ground as he did, Shakespear deliberately committed suicide. But this seems unlikely and seems wholly out of character. Yes, he was depressed both by the intransigence and stupidity of his own government, by the incompetence that he had discerned among the British High Command in Basra and by the destructive effect on relations with the Arabs of the actions of some British officials in the region such as Colonel Grey. He was also still deeply affected by the ending of his relationship with Dorothea Baird.

9 The various accounts of the Battle of Jarab vary widely, one might almost say wildly. According to some accounts the total numbers involved on each side amounted to no more than 1,500, in others to more than four times that number. The number of deaths varies greatly as well, from one – Shakespear – to many hundreds. According to some accounts Shakespear did not take an active part in the battle, but simply observed and took photographs; according to others all of Ibn Saud's field artillery was under his command. Some accounts, including those contained in Intelligence Reports compiled for the British Indian Army, record that Husayn's field gun jammed during the battle and that Shakespear was trying to get it working again when he was overrun by the Shammar charge and killed. We have tried in our account to set out the most probable course of events. Colonel Grey, according to H. V. F. Winstone in *Captain Shakespear*, op. cit. in a typically pedantic act of small-mindedness insisted that Shakespear was killed by a stray bullet in a small tribal skirmish.

Perhaps the cumulative effect of all these factors did at that moment make him more careless for his own safety. But to be careless for one's own safety is a long way from amounting to a deliberate intention to commit suicide. It is equally likely that in standing his ground and continuing to fire his revolver at the oncoming enemy Shakespear was committing an act of pure, selfless courage.

Whether, by dying as he did at the Battle of Jarab in January 1915, Shakespear altered the subsequent course of the war in Arabia and history of the Middle East, for years to come and possibly to the present day, remains one of the unanswerable questions of history. Would Shakespear, by his presence and persistence, have been able to persuade the British Government to enter into a treaty with Ibn Saud more quickly; to back and support him more effectively? Would he have been able to persuade Ibn Saud to enter more fully into the war on the British side? Would the British and their French allies have adopted a different military strategy and tactics in achieving their eventual defeat of the Turks in the Arabian peninsula and Mesopotamia? Would the subsequent division of the Middle East into separate, competing and often unstable countries have occurred? Quite probably. But who knows?

Had Shakespear not died when he did, he would almost certainly not have vanished for so many years from the pages of history.[10] But whether, had he lived, he would have achieved the fame accorded to some of his contemporaries seems doubtful. Shakespear lacked the instinct for self-promotion essential for success in that hall of distorting mirrors filled with the drifting smoke of exaggeration, half-truth, distortion, publicity and suppression that is fame. He lacked T. E. Lawrence's gift of poetic words and striking public gestures. He possessed neither the instinct nor taste for being an actor in some scenario of his own or others' devising. He was, in short, too honest, too nice, too straightforward to become famous.

But one thing we do know for certain – for years afterwards, when asked who was the greatest Englishman he had ever met, Ibn Saud would answer without hesitation: 'Shakespear!'

10 Shakespear's name was to remain almost completely unknown except to a few historians of the region until 1976 when H. V. F. Winstone published his pioneering biography *Captain Shakespear*, op. cit.

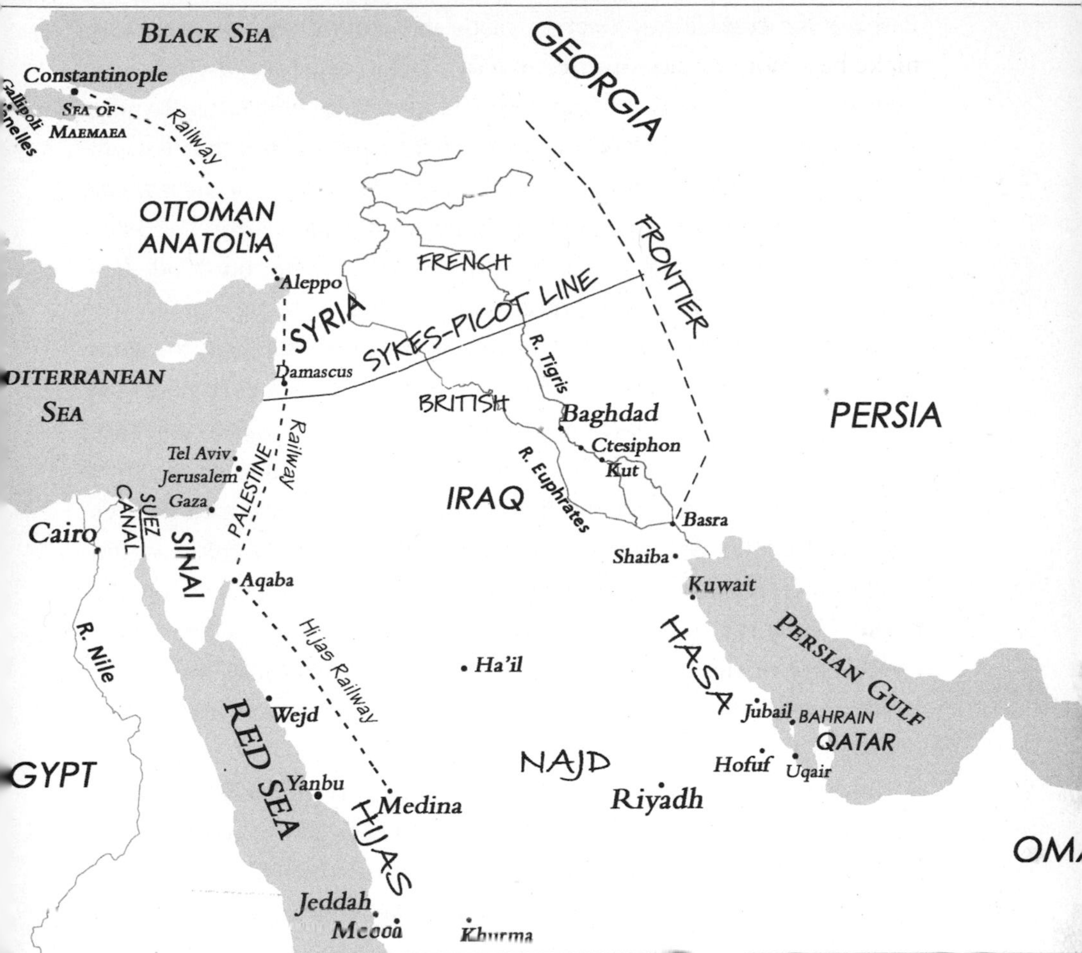

CHAPTER 7

War and Revolt

The Battle of Jarab was neither a decisive victory nor a crushing defeat for either Ibn Saud or Saud ibn Rashid. Like so many Bedouin battles, its outcome was inconclusive and confused. Yet its effects, especially for Ibn Saud, were to be profound.

After the mauling they had received in the battle Ibn Saud's army was in no condition to continue his campaign against the Rashids and so he gathered them together as best he could and headed back to Riyadh. Learning that Ibn Saud and his army were returning and that Riyadh would be defended, Abdullah ibn Husayn decided to withdraw his Hashemite army back to the Hijaz. Saud ibn Rashid's army had been almost as badly mauled at Jarab as Ibn Saud's and he too decided to discontinue his campaign and return home to Ha'il.

One of Rashid's fighters had found Shakespear's topee in the sand close to where he had fallen. He retrieved it and gave it as a trophy to Saud ibn Rashid. Ibn Rashid in turn sent it on to the Turks as evidence of how he was abiding by his part in their agreement and using the arms they had supplied him. The finding of the topee, by seeming to provide evidence that Ibn Saud was allied to the British, also reinforced Ibn Rashid's case for delaying sending his troops to support the Turks in the north. The Turks, in turn, sent Shakespear's topee on to Medina where it was hung on the gates to reinforce the message that those, like the Al Sauds, who did not answer the Caliph's call to *jihad* were in league with Britain and so were enemies of Islam.[1]

Although the result of the Battle of Jarab was inconclusive, it did amount to a very considerable setback for Ibn Saud. It was not only that he had failed to achieve the overwhelming victory he had hoped for, it marked the end of the run of almost uninterrupted successes that he had achieved ever since he had defeated and killed Abd al-Aziz ibn Rashid at Muhanna in 1906. Jarab undermined Shakespear's argument to his superiors that in Ibn Saud the Arabs had found a leader who stood head and shoulders above all others and was the only Arab leader who might be able to unite all the Arabs in a successful revolt against the Ottomans.

1 The story about Shakespear's topee is based on the account in Robert Lacey's *The Kingdom,* Hutchinson, London 1981. Unfortunately, while he rightly dismisses as groundless the account given to him by Shaikh Zaidan that Shakespear's head was displayed on the gates of Medina, Lacey provides no corroborating source for his assertion that Shakespear's topee was hung on the gates. However, Lacey's version, even if it is based only on his own surmise, does seem reasonable so long as one accepts that Shaikh Zaidan's account was not entirely an invention but was based on something.

Jarab also seriously damaged Ibn Saud's standing among the Arabian peninsula's tribal leaders, resulting in a loss of support for him and a growing number of revolts against his rule.

Immediately on returning to Riyadh Ibn Saud wrote to Cox to express his deep regret over Shakespear's death. In his letter he presented the battle of Jarab not as a defeat or as inconclusive, but as a victory. At the same time he asked either for another British officer, 'familiar with Arabic', to be sent to him to finalise the draft treaty he had negotiated with Shakespear or that Cox himself complete the treaty negotiations with him by mail. Meanwhile, the British Government in India and London, having now received and considered Shakespear's draft and the modifications proposed by Cox, but still unaware of Shakespear's death, dispatched instructions to Cox to authorise Shakespear to conclude an amended interim treaty with Ibn Saud pending the agreement and ratification of a comprehensive treaty. Once news of Shakespear's death and Ibn Saud's request had reached them the British authorities appointed Captain Gerald Leachman as Political Officer on Special Duty in Arabia in Shakespear's place. As the Viceroy of India, in a note dated March 26th 1915, commented: 'Captain Leachman has travelled considerably in Arabia, sometimes in disguise. While not of the same calibre as Shakespear, he may do well under Sir Percy Cox.'[2]

However, by March 1915, the British authorities' desire to enter into an agreement with Ibn Saud, which had in any case never been a particularly major concern in their list of priorities, except as a way of securing their communications and supply routes through the Persian Gulf, had been demoted still further by events elsewhere in the Middle East and the wider war. In France the war, which had been supposed to be 'over by Christmas', had become hopelessly bogged down in the trenches and mud of Flanders and casualties were continuing to mount alarmingly. On the Russian front the German advance was inflicting massive casualties and Bolshevik agitators had begun to sow the seeds of revolt. Britain had suffered its first air raids by German Zeppelins and in Singapore there had been a major mutiny of Indian Army Sikhs. In

2 Note from Viceroy dated March 26th 1915 minuted in Foreign Office Papers quoted by H. V. F. Winstone in *Captain Shakespear*, op. cit.

Mesopotamia, however, the British advance up the Tigris and Euphrates rivers had resumed and Ottoman soldiers were surrendering to British and Indian troops in such numbers that British soldiers had taken to referring to the enemy soldiers as 'Catch'em alive'o's'. However, on the night of February 3rd 1915, in a daring secret dash by twenty thousand Turkish troops commanded by German officers across Sinai, the Turks threw three pontoon bridges over the Suez Canal and attempted a mass crossing. The crossing was repulsed by Indian troops stationed in Egypt and commanded by British officers, supported by a bombardment by warships of the Royal Navy and the guns of an armoured train. Nevertheless, the Turkish attack on Suez, coupled with an attempt by them to foment an anti-British insurrection by Muslims in Egypt, served to underline for Kitchener, the Secretary for War in London, and his erstwhile colleagues in Cairo the strategic importance of securing the territories bordering the eastern end of the Mediterranean and the Hijaz coastline, which ran almost the entire length of the Red Sea's eastern shore. These considerations prompted a renewed British examination of a proposal for a general Arab revolt against the Turks, led by the Hashemites in the name of Husayn as Sharif of Mecca, the proposal which had been first floated in 1914 by Husayn's son Abdullah with Kitchener while he was still in Egypt. This proposal, which had been followed up by Kitchener in his message to Abdullah in September 1914, and pursued on and off ever since, now began to receive more urgent consideration.

The large number of Turkish casualties and prisoners in the Suez action had also served to reinforce a growing and dangerous attitude of contempt among the British for the fighting qualities of the Turks. This had been further re-inforced by a sense of moral superiority engendered by reports of atrocities committed by the Turks and their Arab allies. With the war deadlocked or going badly elsewhere, the possibility of being able to mount a decisive blow directly against the Turkish mainland and knock her out of the war seemed not only more and more attractive but increasingly feasible. As a result on February 19th 1915, the ill-fated, inadequately planned and under-resourced Allied naval attack on Gallipoli and the Dardanelles was launched. Initiated by Kitchener, enthusiastically backed by Churchill and, after much discussion, endorsed by the British cabinet, the plan was for a flotilla of Royal Navy ships to force the Dardanelle Narrows, cross the Sea of Marmara and force the Turkish army to withdraw from Constantinople. Thereafter, the ships were to pass through the Bosphorus, enter the Black Sea and provide relief to Britain's ally Russia. This action was to be the 'magic bullet' which would lead, by naval action alone and without the need to withdraw any troops or munitions from the Western Front, to a *coup d'etat* in Constantinople and the capitulation of Turkey. Thus, as Lloyd George put it, by 'knocking out the prop' of Turkish support, we would achieve the defeat and surrender of Germany.

But by mid-March the British plan had begun to go disastrously wrong. It was decided to divert a substantial force of Australian and New Zealand troops who were in Egypt on their way to fight on the Western Front, plus contingents of British and French troops, to make a landing in the Dardanelles Straits at Gallipoli. Kitchener was confident that the Australians and New Zealanders who were to lead the attack would be quite adequate to this 'cruise in the Marmara'. They would then sail on to Constantinople, take on and defeat what he and the other British generals still believed were the vastly inferior soldiers of Turkey. Again inadequately planned, prepared and generalled, the Allied attack started on April 25th. After a promising opening, it quickly ran into serious and very costly difficulties.

Meanwhile, two weeks before the start of the Allied landings at Gallipoli, a British and Indian force had defeated a Turkish force of almost twice the size at a place called Shaiba a few miles south of Basra. All these events, together with the setback suffered by Ibn Saud at Jarab and the death of Shakespear, combined to distract the British from finalising their treaty with Ibn Saud and to relegate him in importance in their planning. As a result it was not until mid-April 1915 that Ibn Saud received a reply from Cox to the draft treaty he had negotiated with Shakespear. With his reply Cox enclosed a modified version of the draft negotiated by Shakespear which he urged Ibn Saud to sign. Within days Ibn Saud had been through the new draft, added some amendments and corrections curtailing the amount of control which Britain would be allowed to exercise over Saudi affairs while limiting his own commitment to fighting on Britain's behalf in the war, signed it and dispatched it back to Cox with a note reiterating his friendship and goodwill. Now, at last, with some security from the possibility of an Ottoman attack, Ibn Saud could turn to other more pressing matters.

Ibn Saud had not forgotten and would never forgive the Ajman's treachery at Jarab. So in the spring of 1915, when he received a report from Mubarak that the Ajman had attacked and robbed several tribes living under his rule and asked Ibn Saud to punish them, Ibn Saud determined to use this as the pretext to settle his scores with the Ajman for good. However, before setting out to do so he had first to secure his rear from any renewed attack by the Rashids. Accordingly he sent an emissary to Saud ibn Rashid in Ha'il to try to reach a mutually acceptable understanding over the areas and tribes under each side's control and an undertaking by both sides not to attack the other. After some negotiation, in June 1915 Ibn Saud and Saud ibn Rashid reached agreement. Under it the land and tribes in the southern half of Najd and southwards, right down to the Rub Al Khali, plus those to the east including the Hasa as far north as Kuwait and up to the shores of the Persian Gulf, fell under Saudi influence, while those in northern Najd, around Ha'il, the Jabal Shammar, northwards through the Nafud Desert to the borders of modern Jordan and Iraq, and westwards to the borders of the Hijaz came under Rashid control.

With his rear and flanks now secured, Ibn Saud set out in the full heat of the Arabian summer with his brother Sa'ad and three hundred warriors to exact his punishment against the Ajman. As he passed through each tribal domain on his way east more and more local warriors joined him. By mid-July he had reached a hilly area some thirty miles west of Hofuf, near to where the Ajman had recently been raiding. Soon his scouts were bringing in reports that the Ajman were encamped a few miles away at an oasis village called Kinzan. Ibn Saud decided to make a night march and take them by surprise immediately after sunrise the next morning, in much the same way that he had swooped down, surprised and killed Abd al-Aziz ibn Rashid at Muhanna in 1906.

All seemed to be going well. He and his fighters, having marched east through the night, sighted the fires of the Ajman camp exactly where the scouts had foretold. He and his fighters crept closer and having apparently remained undetected, settled down to wait for sunrise.

With the first signs of dawn each fighter, after silently praying the morning prayer, took up his position or mounted his camel and upon Ibn Saud's signal swooped down on the Ajman camp. But at that moment the Ajman appeared behind and all around them. They had fallen into a carefully prepared ambush. Now, rather than Ibn Saud and his fighters falling upon the Ajman, the Ajman swooped down into the first rays of the morning sun and started slaughtering the Al Sauds. At least three hundred of Ibn Saud's fighters, including his much-loved brother Sa'ad, were killed and Ibn Saud himself received a bullet wound in the thigh. Ibn Saud and his surviving fighters made their way as best they could to the relative safety of Hofuf whither, once they had regrouped, the Ajman followed them.[3]

In the immediate aftermath of the battle, while Ibn Saud lay in his tent struggling to overcome the pain and regain the mobility he had lost as a result of his wound, word began to go round among his already demoralised fighters that the bullet that had wounded Ibn Saud, as well as damaging his thigh had taken away something far more important, his manhood. Upon learning of this rumour, Ibn Saud at once ordered that one of his men go to the nearest village and bring him back a new bride. Ibn Saud had some time since established the practice, by use of the easy Muslim divorce laws, of making sure that at any one time he was never married to more than three current brides. So when the man he had sent returned with a suitable young woman, Ibn Saud immediately, and in front of his warriors, married her. He then retired with her to the sleeping quarters of his tent. His demoralised fighters, meanwhile, withdrew and started waiting a respectful distance away outside the tent, but still within earshot. A few minutes later the sounds and cries that began to reach them from the tent were unmistakable. Immediately the dejected warriors began to straighten up, their solemn gloomy faces transformed by broad smiles. Clearly, the bullet had not done the reported damage. Ibn Saud's virility was obviously un-

3 Reports of the battle of Kinzan are confused. According to some, the Sauds and Ajman had been trying to negotiate a settlement to their dispute but the Sauds, possibly at the instigation of Sa'ad who had a reputation for impetuousness, had treacherously attacked them.

diminished, his vigour unimpaired. Morale was restored! The story of Ibn Saud's wound and the virgin bride may be just that, a story. But even if it is no more than that, it is a story that grew as tales of what had happened at Kinzan were passed on over the years among groups of men gathered in the evenings around their camp fires. It tells us something about Ibn Saud and the reputation that he inspired. And in any case, it is far too good a story to be excluded from this narrative.

Although battered and depleted Ibn Saud and his fighters managed to hold out in Hofuf until Abd al-Rahman had put together a new force of fighters and dispatched them to Hofuf under the command of Ibn Saud's brother Muhammad. Outside Hofuf this new force was joined by two hundred of Mubarak's fighters from Kuwait, commanded by his son Salim. Together Muhammad's and Salim's warriors succeeded in dispersing the Ajman besieging Hofuf and released Ibn Saud and his men.[4] Nevertheless for all the months that Ibn Saud and his fighters had been holed up in Hofuf the Ajman had had the unfettered control of Hasa and all its lucrative trade routes. As a result they had been free to plunder and raid at will.

In fact by December 1915 the British and the Saudis both needed to get the treaty that had been negotiated by Shakespear finally sorted out and signed. Ibn Saud because he was now in urgent need of British protection against possible Ottoman, Hashemite or Rashid attack and because he needed British arms and money to deal with tribal revolts inside his territory. For their part, the British needed the treaty with Ibn Saud because they had been suffering a mounting series of defeats. At Ypres on the Western Front the Germans had used gas for the first time. On the Eastern Front the Germans continued to push forward inflicting appalling casualties on the Russians, while the Dardanelles campaign, far from being the cruise up the Sea of Marmara to Constantinople promised by Kitchener, was turning into a disaster. The Allied landings

4 There is some dispute about how long Ibn Saud was trapped in Hofuf, exactly when the battle of Kinzan took place and the date on which Muhammad and Salim relieved Hofuf. But Ibn Saud and his men were certainly trapped in Hofuf for at least three months and some authorities suggest that it may have been for as much as six months. See Vassiliev op. cit., p. 239.

at Gallipoli had barely advanced beyond the beaches and degenerated into a hard-fought and extremely costly stalemate. In May Asquith had been forced to form a coalition government and Churchill, the most vocal political advocate of the Dardanelles campaign, had been made to relinquish his seat in the cabinet. By November the British Government had ordered the evacuation of all British troops from the Dardanelles. Later in the same month, British troops were routed by a larger Ottoman force close to the ancient city of Ctesiphon and the British advance north up the River Tigris halted twenty-two miles short of Baghdad. More than four thousand British troops, half of their advancing army, many of whom were Indians, were killed. The remainder then began a hasty retreat back down the river to the fortress town of Kut Al Amara. There the Turks surrounded them and a protracted siege began. At about the same time the British got wind of the Turks collecting troops together in western Mesopotamia – they were reported to have purchased forty thousand camels to carry their warriors and supplies – in preparation for a fresh and much larger assault on Egypt than the one they had mounted earlier in the year. The British therefore needed the treaty with Ibn Saud not because they any longer thought that he would or could march north to support their troops in Mesopotamia but to ensure that he did not join the string of other Arab amirates which had allied themselves with the Turks. If he did join the Turks he and the Rashids together would present a serious threat to British forces and their supply routes strung out along the Euphrates and Tigris rivers, to Britain's oil supplies in Persia and to Britain's communications and protectorates along the Persian Gulf.

Sir Percy Cox had tried to arrange a meeting with Ibn Saud to finalise and sign the treaty some months earlier but Ibn Saud had been unable to get to the proposed meeting because of his difficulties with the Ajman. But finally, on Boxing Day 1915 Ibn Saud and Cox, Cockus as the Arabs invariably called him, met. For over a decade the two men had been hearing about each other. They had exchanged countless messages and official letters, but this was the first time that they had met face-to-face. Their meeting took place at Darin on the island of Tarut in a bay off Al Qatif, a little north of Bahrain in the Persian Gulf. Neither man was to be disappointed in the other. Ibn Saud, although still limping a little from his wound, was still a commanding figure. He was now thirty-five years old and in the prime of his life. Almost six and a half feet tall, broad shouldered and clearly extremely strong, his high forehead visible below the *kaffiya* (headcloth) and double-stranded princely *agal*, piercing, slightly hooded brown eyes that looked directly into the eyes of the person he was talking to, strong straight nose, neatly trimmed moustache and beard, and quiet smile, made him a figure who commanded attention and respect from the moment he entered a room. Cox was now fifty-one years old and also tall, although not as tall as Ibn Saud. He was slim, straight backed and, as ever, impeccably dressed in suit, tie and stiff, usually wing, collar. His grey hair, parted slightly to the right of centre above the deep forehead and piercing eyes in a long archetypically aristocratic face, straight but broken nose pushed slightly to the right above a firm mouth and strong pronounced chin, presented a contrasting but equally strongly defined character. Cox, a product of Harrow and Sandhurst, was typical of the best type of British colonial administrator. Always quiet and controlled, he had been a studious boy, with a keen interest in natural history, and had grown into a fine, resourceful and brave officer, before opting to transfer to the government of India's Political Department. Like many of the best British Colonial Administrators he had always taken a great interest in the people he ruled and made a number of studies of tribal history, customs and genealogy. He was a good Arabic speaker, so much so that he always drafted official letters and announcements addressed to Arab leaders first in Arabic and only later translated them into English for his secretary to pass on to London and Delhi. Cox and Ibn Saud liked and respected each other from the moment they met.

The treaty was soon agreed and both men signed it. Under the treaty the British formally acknowledged Ibn Saud and his successors as the rulers of Najd, Hasa, Qatif, Jubail and all their dependencies and undertook to protect Ibn Saud and his territories from outside aggression or interference. In return Ibn Saud agreed not to sell or lease to any other power any part of any of his territories or enter into any agreement, treaty or correspondence with any foreign power without Britain's prior agreement and to follow Britain's advice in all his dealings with other countries provided only that that advice did not conflict with his own interests. He also agreed not to attack or interfere with the British protectorates of Kuwait, Bahrain, Qatar and the Omani coast and to keep his ports and roads open to British traders and pilgrims making their way to Islam's holy places. In return for signing the treaty Ibn Saud was to receive a monthly subsidy of £5,000 and a thousand rifles, other weapons and ammunition. In the event Ibn Saud only received just over three hundred and seventy rifles because the British needed them elsewhere. Cox also agreed to advance Ibn Saud an immediate British loan of £20,000. So almost a year after he and Shakespear had hammered out the treaty in the weeks before the battle of Jarab, Ibn Saud had the agreement and promise of British protection that he had striven to achieve ever since he had seized power in Riyadh in 1902. What was more, he had achieved this agreement without committing himself to taking any direct or active part in Britain's war against the Ottoman Empire.

The only time that Cox and Ibn Saud's meeting became tense was when the discussion turned to the subject of Ibn Saud co-operating with Husayn. It was clearly in the British Government's interest that all their Arab allies should work together to defeat the Turks. But, especially since Husayn's recent incursion into Khurma, Ibn Saud was resentful of any suggestion of co-operation with the Hashemites, let alone of any implication that he should be in any way subservient to them. His resentment was further heightened by Cox speaking of 'Arabia as a whole', seeming to imply that Britain might envisage Husayn as its possible future leader. As we have seen, the idea of Arabia as a single state entity had always been wholly alien to the ideas and culture of most Arabs and to most Arab leaders, who saw themselves in terms of tribes and families rather than of areas of land with fixed boundaries, centralised institutions and government administrations. Despite his increasing amount of contact with Britain and the British, Ibn Saud was still a long way from thinking in such an essentially Western and imperial way. In any case, Ibn Saud, despite his current difficulties, still had his eyes firmly fixed on restoring his family's historic domination to the whole of the Arabian peninsula and was certainly not willingly going to allow himself to be thwarted by a man like Husayn. He, in common with many Muslims, dismissed Husayn as an Ottoman placeman unworthy of the office Sharif and Guardian of Islam's Holy Places. Privately Cox also had very considerable misgivings about Cairo and London's confidence in Husayn and his potential as a leader of all the Arabs. Cox believed that Ibn Saud, in spite of being a Wahhabi, was far more in touch with Arab sensibilities than Husayn and had already amply demonstrated his ability as a warrior-leader. But, unlike Shakespear, Cox was far too good a diplomat and loyal servant of the Crown to betray his private opinions to Ibn Saud.

This one area of discord apart, Ibn Saud and Cox's first face-to-face encounter went well and the two men parted with heightened respect and liking for each other. On his departure Ibn Saud repeated to Cox his assurances of goodwill and friendship towards Britain.

But the setbacks at Jarab and Hofuf, the most severe Ibn Saud had suffered in all the thirteen years since he had seized Riyadh, had resulted in a whole range of tribal leaders, including not only the Ajman but his old protectors and friends, the Al Murra, becoming emboldened to reassert their independence and resume raiding. But now, at the start of 1916, with his treaty with Britain at last in place and with fresh British arms and money, Ibn Saud was in a position to deal with such rebels. This he set about doing by a combination of means. First he invited all the tribes to re-affirm their loyalty to him and pay all due taxes (*zakat*). Those that did so were duly rewarded but any that refused became the target of punitive expeditions by him, his loyal lieutenants and warriors. He also continued to make judicious use of marriage between members of his own family and his most trusted lieutenants and the families of the subject tribes. Perhaps most interesting and controversial of all, early in 1916 he issued an order that all Bedouin tribes, whether they wanted to or not, must join the Ikhwan. Jiluwi again warned him of the potential danger of this move, but Ibn Saud calculated that this was likely to be the most effective way of bringing traditionally rebellious and independent tribes under his central control as the Ikhwan's leader and Imam.

Any tribal leader who was not immediately willing to submit and join the Ikhwan received a summons to Riyadh. There Ibn Saud would confront him and tell him in the bluntest terms that he and his tribe were ignorant and had no religion. The offending shaikh would then be ordered to attend the school attached to the great mosque in Riyadh run by the leading religious scholars, doctrinal and legal authorities, the *ulema*, who were, in the words of the Prophet, 'the heirs of the prophets'.[5] There the offending shaikh would undergo an intensive course of study in the correct understanding and practice of his Wahhabi faith. As for all Muslims, this consisted above all of the worship of one God and the brotherhood of all believers. The second of these meant loving one's country, absolute obedience to the Imam (Ibn Saud) and the giving of financial and material help to all other true Muslims. While the shaikh was away in Riyadh undergoing this course of religious instruction, a group of *ulema*, carefully selected by Ibn Saud himself and led by a loyal and fanatical Ikhwan leader, would visit the shaikh's tribe to preach to the people, to rouse enthusiasm and belief that Ikhwanism, and with it loyalty to Ibn Saud, was the only true and authentic path to the Muslim faith. Thus Ibn Saud added many more thousands of Bedouin to the ranks of the Ikhwan and created in the process a very substantial and formidable armed force of warriors who were fanatically loyal to himself.

By this combination of means Ibn Saud had by the high summer of 1916 largely subdued the revolts inside his territory. However, by then Britain had suffered a further series of humiliations in the wider war, especially in her war with Turkey. After their disastrous attempted invasion of Turkey through the Dardanelles, which had cost them almost fifty thousand dead, a further 200,000 wounded or missing, and huge quantities of abandoned arms and ammunition, the British and their Australian, New Zealand and French allies had completed their ignominious evacuation from Gallipoli at the beginning of January. As a result the Turks were able to divert some thirty thousand additional troops to the campaign in Mesopotamia and the siege of Kut. By April, after repeated British attempts to relieve Kut had failed, the besieged British and Indian troops had used up all their food and they and their cavalry animals had been reduced to starvation. With Kitchener and the War Office's approval Captain T. E. Lawrence was dispatched with another officer from Cairo to Kut to offer the Turkish commander in charge of the troops besieging it a bribe of £1 million in return for the

5 Words ascribed to the Prophet Muhammad in *The Hadith*. See also H. R. P. Dickson, *Kuwait and Her Neighbours*, George Allen & Unwin, London, 1971.

safe release of the British garrison. When Sir Percy Cox, who was by then the Chief Political Officer in the region, learned of the proposal he refused point blank to have anything to do with it, pointing out that if news of the offer came out, which it surely would, Britain's authority in the entire region would be undermined for years to come. But Lawrence, on London's orders, continued with his mission. His initial offer of £1 million was contemptuously turned down by the Turkish commander who told Lawrence 'We are gentlemen' and would not sell our honour in such a way. Lawrence promptly increased his offer to £2 million. The Turkish commander rejected this too. As a result, on April 29th, the surviving 11,600 British and Indian troops in Kut surrendered. Over the next few months more than a third of these survivors died as they were driven and beaten like cattle northwards into captivity in a series of forced death marches, often being stoned by the inhabitants of the villages they passed through. By now, less than two and a half years into the campaign, more than 29,000 Indian troops had been killed in Britain's operations in Mesopotamia. As news of the series of British defeats and the attempted bribes at Kut spread, Britain's standing among the Muslims and Arabs of the Middle East reached an all-time low.

By June, therefore, with the British Government unable to spare any extra troops to bolster the campaign in Mesopotamia on account of the heavy demands of the war in France (the life-and-death struggle at Verdun had raged for months and the Battle of the Somme was about to begin), Britain desperately needed a fresh means of attacking the Turks in the Middle East and drawing Ottoman troops away from their continued harassment of Britain's forces in eastern Mesopotamia. The most obvious means of achieving this was through employing Britain's allies in the Arabian Peninsula, Ibn Saud and Husayn.

Since 1914, even before Turkey had entered the war on Germany's side, British agents based in Cairo had, with Kitchener's personal encouragement, been holding secret discussions with Husayn and his sons about the possibility of the Hashemites leading a general Arab uprising against the Ottoman Empire. By early 1915, with the death of Shakespear and his humiliation at the hands of the Ajman at Jarab and Hofuf, Ibn Saud had become a much less credible figure as a potential ally in the eyes of British policy makers, especially those in Cairo on the western side of the great British administrative divide in Arabia. In 1916 this view was further reinforced by a damning assessment of Ibn Saud in a review of all Britain's potential allies and leading personalities in the region circulated by the organisation responsible for co-ordinating British intelligence in the Middle East, the Arab Bureau. The Bureau, based in the Savoy Continental Hotel in Cairo, was largely the creation of the British diplomat and arch-backstage string puller, Sir Mark Sykes. The intention behind the creation of the Bureau was to end the damaging competition in the formation of British policy in the region and to act as a single, expert and impartial source of intelligence and advice upon which Britain's leaders could draw in determining policies in the area. Formally established early in 1916, it was composed of a small group of brilliant, mainly academic, Arabists and enthusiasts for Husayn's cause, many of whom had worked together on an informal basis since shortly before the war. They were, according to one military man who observed them at work, 'A queer mixture of brilliant men – too greatly influenced by the ebb and flow of events, they mostly forgot the rest of Arabia.'

The review and assessment of Ibn Saud, published and circulated in the Bureau's regular secret intelligence update, *The Arab Bulletin*, among Britain's leading policy makers and military strategists in 1916, was penned by someone who had not even met him, the traveller Gertrude Bell. Given the task of making an assessment of Ibn Saud as a potential British ally, Bell based her opinion on the word of a Dr Paul Harrison, a Dutch Reformed minister serving as a doctor with the American Mission in Kuwait, who a few months earlier had paid a brief visit to Riyadh to treat Ibn Saud for a minor ailment. The resultant portrait and assessment of Ibn Saud, to modern eyes at least, betrayed almost as much about the moral and cultural prejudices of Gertrude Bell and Dr Harrison as it did about its subject. Harrison, and Bell, described Ibn Saud as a 'great kingly-looking man like an Assyrian picture' possessed of great personal charm. But, the report continued, 'He says, seemingly with pride, that he has been married 65 times, each wife lasts about three days; he divorces each one, giving them to his shaikhs or his ordinary followers.' Then, while conceding that his internal policies were 'good and strong', Bell accused him of pursuing an external policy which 'consists in flirting with the Sharif of Mecca, and in punishing Ibn

Rashid whenever he can'. Then she came to the really damning bit, 'When the war broke out Ibn Saud sat on the fence. Captain Shakespear brought him back to our side but when Captain Shakespear was killed in a skirmish, Ibn Saud behaved badly and created the impression that he was unreliable.'[6] The *Bulletin*'s editor and head of the desert intelligence service in Cairo, Lieutenant Commander David Hogarth, concluded from Bell's report that it would be 'in the last degree undesirable that we should be drawn into Central Arabian politics'. Ibn Saud was, in Hogarth's opinion, far less powerful than Husayn and less able to bring influence to bear in the area that would be advantageous to Britain. He even floated the idea of Britain attempting to get a treaty, similar to the one she now had with Ibn Saud, with the Rashids, apparently discounting the fact that to do so risked driving Ibn Saud to give up his alliance with Britain and side with the Turks.

Prejudices such as Bell's and Harrison's, coupled with inaccurate or inadequate information such as Hogarth's, served to reinforce valid strategic arguments for backing the Hashemites ahead of Ibn Saud. By 1916 these strategic arguments had become more or less overwhelming. Britain's defeat in the Dardanelles, the renewed Turkish threat to the Suez Canal, together with the Hashemites' Hijaz shoreline that ran almost the entire length of the Red Sea, their proximity to the Suez Canal, Egypt and the eastern Mediterranean, made retaining Husayn's loyalty and preventing him from throwing in his lot with the Turks vital. Only a year earlier Husayn had made the most thinly veiled of threats that if Britain did not back his ambition to lead an Arab uprising, aimed at full Arab independence under his leadership, he would join the Germans and Turks against Britain and seek Arab independence by that means. In the days before his death at Jarab, Shakespear had himself warned of the danger of Sharif Husayn declaring a *jihad* against Britain

6 Quoted by H. V. F Winstone in *Gertrude Bell,* Jonathan Cape, London 1978. Looking at Bell's assessment of Ibn Saud today and remembering that much of the information that it was based on was supplied to her by the Dutch Reformed Church missionary Dr Harrison, one cannot but suspect that there is kinship between the attitude that informed his judgement of Ibn Saud and the role and attitudes of members of the Dutch Reformed Church in the creation of the apartheid regime in South Africa barely a generation later.

and entering the war on the Turkish side. In addition to these military and diplomatic considerations there was the immense prestige attached to the position of Sharif throughout the Muslim world. Even though Husayn had been appointed Sharif by the Ottomans and was widely derided as an Ottoman placeman, his status as Guardian of the Holy Places of Islam meant that a call from him to Muslims for an Arab revolt against Ottoman Turkish rule was likely to carry an authority throughout Arabia and the wider Muslim world that could not be matched by any other Arab leader. This element in Britain's calculations weighed even heavier because many of the Ottoman troops who had defeated the British in the Dardanelles, at Ctesiphon and at Kut had been both Muslims and Arabs. All these considerations taken together helped to blind the British authorities to Husayn's shortcomings of character and temperament. A difficult, arrogant, tactless old man, he was likely to antagonise those who should have been his allies. The age-old British division of responsibility for Arabia between the India and Foreign offices and the history of disputes between them also helped to deafen the British Government in London to the well-founded reservations about supporting Husayn and his proposed Arab revolt voiced by Cox, by those working with Arabs on the eastern side of Arabia and by the authorities in India.

The upshot was that Britain adopted a policy, which in later years came widely to be seen as disastrous, of backing Husayn. As a result, by early 1916 Britain was actively encouraging Husayn to instigate an immediate Arab revolt, had promised him military support, arms and money and had assured him that 'Great Britain is prepared to recognise and uphold the independence of the Arabs in all the regions inside the frontiers proposed by the Sharif of Mecca.'

With the war going badly in Europe and elsewhere, Britain's government and generals agreed this policy on the basis of short-term and immediate military needs and without any regard to its possible long term consequences. In any case most of them had no real intention of honouring any of the longer-term promises to Husayn about Arab independence. Even the British officials and officers on the ground in Egypt and the Hijaz knew this. Even T. E. Lawrence, who was to play such a large part in leading the Arabs in the Revolt, knew that the promise of Arab independence was in practice 'a dead letter'. As he wrote, 'We are calling them to fight for us on a lie.' He and some others were secretly ashamed of the deceit and yet they continued to practise it. Lawrence knew that even if the Revolt was completely successful, Britain would never allow it to lead to the kind of single unified Arab state envisaged by Husayn. At best it might lead to a series of small competing countries and shaikhdoms over which Britain and France would continue to exert control.

However, at that very moment behind the scenes and shrouded in secrecy even from Lawrence and most of the other senior British officers and officials on the ground in the Middle East, an even bigger deceit of the Arabs was being negotiated on behalf of their governments by the British and French diplomats and politicians François Georges-Picot and Sir Mark Sykes. Sykes, the sixth baronet Sykes, was the son of a wealthy Yorkshire landowner and squire. An energetic busybody who at this period seemed to have his finger or nose into everything that was happening anywhere connected with Britain's war effort, especially in the Middle East, it was Sykes who had been largely responsible for creating the Arab Bureau. Sykes was a devout Catholic of the kind who today would probably be considered an evangelical. Before his death he created a monument to himself and his closest friends on which he had himself pictured as a Crusader knight. Sykes's attitude to Arabs was one of general contempt. He considered them cruel, bigoted, fanatical and told Gertrude Bell that they were 'animals'. Under negotiation during all the time that the British officials had been discussing with Husayn plans for the Arab Revolt, the Sykes-Picot Agreement, signed in May 1916, was kept secret. The Agreement meant that, far from the Arabs being given full independence as promised, the French were to be given control of all the land and peoples south from the borders of modern Turkey and north of what is today the southern border of Lebanon and thence eastward to the borders of Persia. Everything to the south of this, excluding Kurdistan, but including the whole of modern Iraq, was to be under British control. Sykes and his fellow negotiator, Picot, exemplified the bare-faced opportunistic cynicism of so many of the British politicians and diplomatic instigators of the Arab Revolt.

Unaware of what had been going on behind their backs, and after some hesitation during which they tried to placate the Turks and deceive them about their real intentions, on June 5th 1916 Husayn's sons Feisal and Ali, accusing the Turks of manifold crimes against Islam, proclaimed the independence of the Arab people from Ottoman rule. A few days later Husayn himself issued a flowery declaration proclaiming that through this Arab revolt, led by him, 'Our independence is complete, absolute, not to be laid hands on by any foreign influence or aggression. Our aim is the preservation of Islam and the uplifting of its standard in the world.'

Husayn's sons, leading an Arab force of 50,000, of whom only 10,000 had rifles, launched an immediate, enthusiastic but ill-executed attack on Turkish troops outside Medina. The Arabs were swiftly driven off. On the same day a small group of British military advisers, who included Captain T. E. Lawrence, landed in the Hijaz at the Red Sea port of Jeddah. Over the next ten days, supported by two British warships and three British seaplanes dropping bombs, the Hashemite troops, having quickly learned from their experience outside Medina, outnumbered and out-gunned the small Turkish garrisons at Jeddah and Mecca and seized both. However their success was short-lived. The Turks rushed reinforcements down the Hijaz railway line and by October 1916 the revolt was in serious trouble. Far from relieving hard-pressed British forces as intended, it began to look as if additional British troops and supplies would have to be diverted to the Hijaz to prop up Husayn and his revolt.

Two weeks after Husayn proclaimed the start of the Arab Revolt, Cox sent Ibn Saud a message urging him to unite with Husayn in his struggle against their common enemy, the Turks. But Ibn Saud remained deeply suspicious of both Husayn and his ultimate designs on Najd. At the same time, however, he was anxious not to impair his relations with the British. So, calculating that some sort of demonstration of loyalty was now required, he sent a token gift of 'camels and high-bred horses'[7] to Husayn and at the same time dispatched a large force to attack the

7 Words of *Arab Bulletin*, No. 29, November 8th 1916, quoted in Haifa Alangari, *The Struggle For Power in Arabia, Ibn Saud, Hussein and Great Britain, 1914–1924*, Ithaca Press, Reading, 1998.

Rashids close to their capital, Ha'il. The result of this second gesture was immediate and of real benefit to the British. The Rashids were forced to withdraw the forces that had been assisting the Ottomans in Mesopotamia and mount a defence of Ha'il. As a result Ibn Saud and his troops around Ha'il were now outnumbered and he was forced to withdraw them and send a hasty appeal to the British for assistance. In a note to Cox, Ibn Saud said that he would not be able to pursue an all-out campaign against the Rashids unless he was provided with a lot more arms and ammunition. At the same time, as a safeguard in case Husayn and the British were ultimately defeated, he continued to maintain secret contacts with the Turks and to turn a blind eye to traders smuggling arms to Turkish troops fighting in the Hijaz.

In August, with his revolt now in serious trouble because of the Turkish reinforcements, Husayn sent Ibn Saud the first of a number of direct appeals for assistance. Ibn Saud replied by reminding Husayn of their 'past misunderstandings'. He informed Husayn that he would co-operate with him but only on condition that Husayn first undertake not to interfere in the internal affairs of Najd or renew his attacks on his territory: 'If you are desirous of our services and co-operation, then we desire you to give us a promise so that our mind may be at rest in regards to your attitude.'[8] At the same time Ibn Saud informed Cox of Husayn's approach and his response. He stressed to Cox that he would not even have entertained Husayn's request but for the fact that he knew that Britain wished him to co-operate with him.

Husayn, standing on his dignity in the face of possible defeat and more puffed up with self-importance than ever because of the overt backing given to him by the British, responded to Ibn Saud's letter by returning it to him 'so that you may reflect on what you wrote'. He accompanied this with a deliberately insulting note, calculated to offend any Muslim let alone the leader of the ultra-puritan Wahhabis. He told Ibn Saud that no one but a drunk or someone 'bereft of reason' would have written a letter requesting such an undertaking. Ibn Saud, instead

8 Ibn Saud to Husayn, 13th August 1916 contained in Foreign Office Papers and quoted in Goldberg, *The Foreign Policy of Saudi Arabia*, Harvard University Press, USA 1986.

of replying in kind, made a copy of Husayn's note and sent it on to Sir Percy Cox.

Cox hastened to reassure Ibn Saud that Britain had not reneged on its promises to him of support and re-confirmed Britain's recognition of him as the independent ruler of Najd. He also told him that he had reminded Husayn of these facts. Cox went on to say that while the British did wish Ibn Saud to support Husayn's revolt he should do so in whatever way he felt able. Britain would be quite satisfied if he did this either by attacking Ibn Rashid or by winning him over to the British side. What action to take and how would be left entirely to his discretion.

Cox having thus restored Ibn Saud's confidence in Britain's promises, Husayn promptly threw everything back into confusion and angered Ibn Saud still further. Just days later, on November 5th, he had himself proclaimed 'King of the Arabs'.

With the quarrel between Ibn Saud and Husayn now set to escalate still further, desperate to forestall this, Cox hastily organised a new face-to-face meeting with Ibn Saud. It took place six days later on November 11th 1916 at Uqair on the Hasa coast opposite the island of Bahrain on the Persian Gulf. On the vexed question of Husayn's new self-proclaimed title, Cox told Ibn Saud that Britain had insisted that Husayn make a formal admission that he claimed no jurisdiction over any other independent Arab ruler. Somewhat mollified, Ibn Saud told Cox that nevertheless what Husayn had done meant that any co-operation between him and Husayn was now impossible. However, he said, he was willing to send one of his own sons with a small token force to support the Arab Revolt provided that Husayn first send him a friendly request to do so.

During the meeting at Uqair Cox invited Ibn Saud to attend an Imperial Durbar in Kuwait being staged by Britain to celebrate the accession of Shaikh Mubarak's eldest son, Jabir, as ruler of Kuwait (Mubarak had died almost a year previously). During the Durbar, largely intended to seal Jabir's continuing friendship with Britain, Jabir was to be invested as a Commander of the Order of the Indian Empire. Ibn Saud accepted the invitation.

The Durbar was held ten days after Ibn Saud's meeting with Cox at Uqair, in front of a great assembly of Arab chieftains and Ibn Saud was delighted to be informed that Britain wished to invest him also as a Knight Commander of the Empire of India. In addition he was presented with a bejewelled ceremonial sword of honour. Ibn Saud responded to these honours by making an impromptu speech 'as spontaneous as it was unexpected' to the assembled shaikhs, Arab chieftains and ceremonially dressed British officers and officials. In it he said that the Turks had estranged themselves from the true Islamic faith by their manifold injustices towards their brother Muslims. The way in which they had sought to divide and weaken the Arabs contrasted with the way that Britain had encouraged them to unite. He even went on to praise the action of Sharif Husayn, urging 'all true Arabs' to co-operate with the Sharif in advancing the Arab cause.

From Kuwait, the British took Ibn Saud on a warship up the Shatt Al Arab to Basra. This was Ibn Saud's first trip on a modern British warship and he was clearly impressed. But, it happening to be a Sunday, he was even more impressed when, after requesting to be allowed to attend the Christian shipboard service, he witnessed the reverence of the sailors attending the service. He was impressed above all by the fact that, the chaplain being absent, the service was conducted by the ship's commander, Rear-Admiral Wake.

In Basra the next day he was taken on a visit to see the British army in Mesopotamia as they were building up in preparation for a major new offensive against the Turks. For much of this visit he was shown around by a woman, the woman who less than a year earlier had penned the disparaging report on him for the Arab Bureau, Gertrude Bell. This was probably the first time that Ibn Saud had met an unveiled European woman who spoke to and treated him as an equal. He was quick to notice that the British officers and officials around them treated Bell not simply with respect as a woman but as an equal, in many cases as their superior. Such a thing was almost certainly completely outside his experience, yet, as Cox observed, 'He met Miss Bell with complete frankness and sangfroid as if he had been associated with European ladies all his life.'[9]

During the visit Ibn Saud was shown machine guns, witnessed a

9 Comment by Cox in *Letters of Gertrude Bell, Vol 2*, Pelican Books, Penguin Books, London, 1939.

heavy artillery barrage and the firing of anti-aircraft guns. Overhead he saw an aeroplane for the first time. He was taken on a railway train, was shown around a military hospital and when Gertrude Bell put her hand inside an X-ray machine he followed suit, seeing the bones inside his hand for the first time. He was clearly impressed by almost everything he saw, but by no means overawed. He took a lively interest in everything he was shown and asked lots and lots of intelligent questions, clearly eager to learn all he could. After his visit Bell wrote a series of much more accurate and complimentary reports of her meeting with Ibn Saud, for publication in *The Arab Bulletin*, for her friends and family and for circulation among senior British officers and officials in Cairo and London: 'We had an extraordinarily interesting day with Ibn Saud who is one of the most striking personalities I have encountered. He is splendid to look at, well over 6ft 3, with an immense amount of dignity and self-possession ... carrying himself with the air of one accustomed to command ... His deliberate movements, his low sweet smile and the contemplative glance of his heavy-lidded eyes, though they add to his dignity and charm, do not accord with the Western conception of a vigorous personality. Nevertheless reports credit him with powers of endurance rare even in hard-bitten Arabia. Among men bred in the camel saddle he is said to have few rivals as a tireless rider ... he is of proved daring, and he combines with his qualities as a soldier that grasp of statecraft which is yet more highly prized ... We took him in trains and motors, showed him aeroplanes, high explosives, anti-aircraft guns, hospitals, base depots – everything. He was full of wonder but never agape. He asked innumerable questions and made intelligent comments. He is a big man ... Politician, ruler and raider, Ibn Saud illustrates a historic type. Such men are the exception in any community, but they are thrown up persistently by the Arab race.'[10] During his visit to Kuwait and Basra Ibn Saud had shown all those British officials who cared to face the facts that he was definitely not the narrow-minded

10 Quotation compiled from extracts from accounts written by Bell in the days immediately after Ibn Saud's visit to Basra contained in W. H. V. Winstone's *Gertrude Bell,* op. cit. and Georgina Howell's *Daughter of the Desert: The Remarkable Life of Gertrude Bell*, Macmillan, London, 2006.

Wahhabi fanatic so commonly imagined by Europeans who had never met him.

Although he was far too wise to show it, the impression made on Ibn Saud by Gertrude Bell was a great deal less flattering than the one he had made on her. For years after his visit to Basra he would have the guests in his *majlis* in stitches with his comic impressions of Bell. He would mimic her shrill voice, her feminine chatter and forceful attempts to get his attention: 'Ya Abdul Aziz, ya Abdul Aziz! Look at this! What do you think of that?'[11]

During the meetings in Kuwait and Basra Ibn Saud promised the British that he would keep four thousand men in the field against Ibn Rashid with the purpose of keeping his forces tied up and preventing them from assisting the Turks in Mesopotamia. In return the British agreed to put further pressure on Husayn to adopt a more reasonable attitude towards Ibn Saud and Britain's other Arab allies on the eastern side of the Arabian peninsula. They also agreed to give Ibn Saud three thousand rifles, ammunition, four machine guns plus a monthly subsidy of £5,000. They also trained four of his men to fire the machine guns.

After the celebrations and meetings in Kuwait and Basra were over Husayn acceded to British pressure and telegraphed Ibn Saud his congratulations and apologised for past slights. However, when Ibn Saud returned home he had the machine guns put into storage in the citadel at Hofuf where they were to lie unused in their crates for over a year. In that time three of the four gunners the British had trained to use the machine guns died and the fourth forgot how to use them. Still with no permanent British envoy in Riyadh to goad him into action, Ibn Saud remained in his capital placating both the Turks and the British but not actually committing himself to any overt military action against the Turks or Rashids apart from an occasional expedition to quell one or other of his own unruly tribes.

Meanwhile on January 7th 1917 the new British offensive in Mesopotamia which Ibn Saud had seen in preparation in Basra began. The British force, now commanded by the able General Maude and greatly reinforced to a total of 150,000 men and properly re-supplied, was soon

11 H. St J. B. Philby, *Arabian Jubilee*, Robert Hale, London, 1952.

advancing rapidly. By late February they had retaken Kut, taking 1,730 Turkish prisoners in the process. By March 6th they had captured Ctesiphon and on March 11th they captured the Mesopotamian capital, Baghdad. At the same time, while the war in France ground remorselessly on with its ever-mounting toll of deaths and revolution broke out in Russia, the British began to steadily drive the Turks back out of Persia. To the west, on the other side of Arabia, a replenished British army in Egypt had launched a renewed thrust across Sinai towards Gaza and Palestine. Simultaneously a small commando force of Husayn's Arabs, commanded by a British officer, blew up the Damascus-to-Medina railway north of Aqaba, interrupting the flow of Turkish reinforcements to the Hijaz. In the Hijaz itself an Arab force commanded by Husayn's son Feisal, supported by three British warships, had captured the port of Wejd towards the northern end of the Red Sea. As news of these successes spread, tribes in the west of the Arabian peninsula, who had previously hesitated to ally themselves with Husayn, began to join the Revolt. After helping Husayn's son Feisal to re-organise the Hashemite troops into a series of small, fast-moving and effective guerrilla units, on July 6th T. E. Lawrence, leading a small force of these Arab fighters, seized the port of Aqaba, thus preparing the way for the British to fight their way out of Sinai and into Palestine and opening the road for an allied advance towards Jerusalem and Damascus.

With all this other activity going on it was not until October 1917 that the British got round to sending a permanent emissary to Ibn Saud. That emissary was Harry St John Philby, a junior civil servant and one of Sir Percy Cox's assistants. He travelled to Riyadh with another British officer, the British Agent in Kuwait, Colonel Hamilton. But within a week of their arrival in Riyadh Philby, who could be amongst the most difficult and self-opinionated of men, had quarrelled so seriously with Hamilton that Hamilton had left in disgust to return to Kuwait. Philby, like so many British colonial officials sent to Arabia, was to fall in love with it and develop into a fine Arabist, traveller and naturalist. He was to become besotted with Ibn Saud, and over time develop into the most prolific of writers about both him and Arabia. Philby was to remain with Ibn Saud on and off for most of the rest of his life and came to be regarded as one of the most controversial figures in the history of Saudi

Arabia. Philby was later to adopt the Muslim faith and take as his second wife a Muslim girl given to him by Ibn Saud. He was also to be the father of Kim, who nearly fifty years later would be unmasked as a Communist double agent working for the Russians.

The purpose of Philby's mission to Riyadh was to get Ibn Saud to take a more active role in the war by making the attack on the Rashids that he had promised and prevent them from attacking the potentially exposed southern flank of the British advance into Palestine. The other half of Philby's mission was to calm the still edgy relations between Ibn Saud and Husayn and heal the rupture that had recently opened up in relations between Ibn Saud and the new ruler of Kuwait, Mubarak's second son Salim.[12]

When he arrived in Riyadh, on a deathly still day at the end of November 1917, Philby was warmly welcomed into Ibn Saud's *majlis* by Abd al-Rahman: 'a little old man, somewhat inclined to stoutness, sharp-featured and bright-eyed'.[13] For some time he did not even notice Ibn Saud who, in deference to his father, was sitting humbly and self-effacingly in a corner of the room drawing no attention to himself. But once he had spotted Ibn Saud and explained his purpose in coming to Riyadh they quickly got down to business. Philby found Ibn Saud quite prepared to resume more active operations against the Rashids but only on condition that he receive sufficient arms, ammunition and money. After some bargaining between the two men, Philby agreed to recommend to the British authorities that Ibn Saud be supplied with four 'siege or field guns' plus an adequate supply of ammunition for them and some trained gunners, preferably Arab prisoners who had surrendered from the Turkish armies fighting in Mesopotamia and Palestine. Philby also recommended to his superiors that Ibn Saud be provided with 10,000 modern rifles and ammunition, £20,000 to buy pack and transport animals for the campaign and a monthly subsidy of £50,000 for three months. As Philby noted, this was but a tiny fraction

12 Salim's elder brother, Jabir, had died suddenly barely a year after assuming the throne.

13 From Philby's description of his first meeting with Abd al-Rahman and Ibn Saud contained in McLoughlin op. cit.

of the amount being lavished by the British on Husayn for his campaign, but it would greatly improve Ibn Saud's capacity to mount effective operations against the Rashids.

One day while Philby and Ibn Saud were still negotiating in the palace they were interrupted by the sound of shouts and whoops of joy coming from outside in the courtyard. The *ulema* in Riyadh and the growing Ikhwan movement had always been much more concerned about purging the Hijaz and holy cities of Mecca and Medina of what they saw as the sinful and irreligious practices of Husayn and the Hashemites than they had about attacking the Sauds' old enemy, the Rashids. The gunshots and celebrations in the palace courtyard were a reaction to the news that a group of preachers sent, quite possibly with Ibn Saud's secret knowledge and approval, by the *ulema* to the disputed border area around Khurma had been successful. The inhabitants had responded so enthusiastically to the call to return to the true path of Wahhabism preached to them by the *ulema*'s missionaries that they had ejected the governor appointed by Sharif Husayn and proclaimed their allegiance to Ibn Saud.

This new development threatened to precipitate a new round of fighting between Husayn and Ibn Saud and rendered the second part of Philby's mission to Ibn Saud, the repair of the relations between the two rulers, even more urgent. So, while his recommendations about the arming and supply of Ibn Saud were wending their slow way to British military headquarters in Baghdad and were then discussed by the various functionaries and committees that had to decide how much, if any, of the materials and money requested to send to Ibn Saud, Philby decided to act on his own initiative. Far exceeding his official brief, he set out with a small bodyguard of Wahhabi fighters provided by Ibn Saud, across the desert to the Hijaz. Husayn having previously refused permission for a British official from Egypt to travel across the Hijaz to Riyadh to talk to Ibn Saud on the grounds that it was not safe, Philby intended to confront Husayn himself and try to broker better relations between the two leaders that way. Philby's decision to leave Riyadh and Ibn Saud at this critical moment was motivated as much by his own personal ambition as by any commitment to his mission. Philby secretly longed to become a famous explorer and desperately wanted to become one of the handful of Europeans who had crossed Arabia from coast to coast. The journey to meet Husayn would provide him with an opportunity to achieve this.

Having made his way to Jeddah without mishap Philby found the always conceited and contrary Husayn was in no mood to compromise. Extremely put out that Philby had succeeded in making his way through the whole of Ibn Saud's domain, into and across the Hijaz and the whole way to the coast without mishap, and without seeking his assistance, his protection or even his permission, he was not going to be persuaded by Philby to adopt a less aggressive attitude to Ibn Saud. Worse, Husayn was deeply suspicious that Philby's mission was fresh evidence of Britain's continued interest in and protection of Ibn Saud. Philby, every bit as difficult and contrary a character as Husayn, spent the next two days in furious argument with him. By mid-January, he had achieved nothing other than to infuriate Husayn and embarrass Britain's official representative at Husayn's court. That official happened to be none other than the member of the Arab Bureau staff in Cairo and editor of the *Arab Bulletin*, Lt. Commander David Hogarth, who had concluded from Gertrude Bell's first report on Ibn Saud that it would be undesirable to enter into any kind of treaty with him. Philby, having achieved less than nothing, decided to return to Riyadh. However Husayn, by now thoroughly enraged, responded by flatly refusing him permission to travel directly back overland to Riyadh the way he had come, forcing him instead to make a massively time-consuming detour across the Red Sea to Cairo, thence by sea to Bombay and only after that back overland from the Gulf to Riyadh.[14]

In the meantime Philby's recommendations for the supply and re-arming of Ibn Saud had become the subject of yet another interminable argument between the various British authorities in Baghdad, India, Egypt and London with the result that by the time Philby got back to Riyadh in mid-April 1918 events in the wider war had changed Britain's

14 There is some doubt as to whether the British official Philby embarrassed at Husayn's court was Hogarth, as stated by Philby in *Arabian Jubilee*, or Ronald Storrs who had been sent by the British authorities in Egypt to try to broker an end to hostilities between Husayn and Ibn Saud and was due to meet Ibn Saud in Riyadh as well.

strategic priorities in Arabia almost beyond recognition. On the Western Front a new series of offensives by British and French troops had ended in failure, becoming bogged down in the mud, gas and mass slaughter of Passchendaele. Anti-war feeling had grown ominously in London and wholesale mutinies had broken out among French troops. In Russia the revolution that had begun in March 1917 led on November 7th 1917 to the seizure of power by Vladimir Ilich Lenin and the Bolsheviks.

The very next day, Arthur Balfour, the British Foreign Secretary in Lloyd George's coalition government, wrote to Lord Rothschild, the leading British Zionist: 'His Majesty's Government views with favour the establishment in Palestine of a national home for Jewish people and will use their best endeavours to facilitate the achievement of this object', adding the caveat that 'nothing shall be done which may prejudice the civil and religious rights of existing non-Jewish communities in Palestine'. Balfour asked Rothschild to bring this undertaking, which was to become known as The Balfour Declaration, to the knowledge of the Zionist Federation. The Declaration was the result of a growing intensification of Zionist lobbying which had begun following the first Zionist conference in Basel back in 1897. Although the Arabs who already lived in Palestine had not been consulted, the Declaration was intended to encourage Zionist guerrilla groups who had been assisting the British and Arab advance in Palestine by mounting attacks on Turkish troops and communications. It was also hoped that the Declaration might be a means of securing the continued support for the war of the new Russian government. To many British politicians, steeped in the nineteenth-century Christian imperial tradition which saw it as Britain's destiny to bring about the realisation of God's kingdom on earth, the return of the Jewish people to their biblical Jewish homeland was a necessary pre-condition for the Second Coming. To not a few others who were deep-dyed anti-Semites, the establishment of a Jewish homeland in Palestine was a means of getting the Jews out of Europe. So overall, the Declaration was every bit as much an act of cynical political calculation as it was of idealism. For the majority of Arabs including Husayn, to whom in future years the Declaration would become the source of much anti-British recrimination and bloodshed, the assurance contained in the Declaration that nothing would be done that would prejudice the civil and religious rights of the people already living in Palestine was for the moment sufficient reassurance to forestall any immediate backlash. Even so, for many of the more far-sighted, including Ibn Saud, distant alarm bells began to sound.

Just days later new and much louder alarm bells sounded. The new Bolshevik government in Russia had found a copy of the secret Sykes-Picot Agreement in the deposed Tsarist government's archives. They sent it to the Turks who passed it on to Husayn as proof of his British and French allies' bad faith. When he, understandably incensed, asked the British to explain the document they hastened to assure him that it was a forgery. Husayn, although still not entirely convinced, decided that his own interests were likely to be better served by fighting on on Britain's side than by withdrawing his troops or changing sides to support the Turks.

Days later the tally of military and diplomatic disasters confronting the British and French mounted still further when, in one of its first acts, the new Bolshevik Russian government issued The Decree of Peace and sent four million copies to its soldiers fighting on the front line calling for the end of all hostilities. On December 2nd a Bolshevik delegation, led by the new Bolshevik Commissar for Foreign Affairs Leon Trotsky's brother-in-law Leo Kamenev, began negotiating the terms of a humiliating peace treaty with Germany at Brest-Litovsk. To the new Bolshevik government in Russia this was an imperialist war being fought in the interests of the capitalist ruling class. The workers and ordinary people of all the countries on both sides had more in common with each other than divided them, so they should stop fighting and unite to overthrow their rulers and end their oppression. To millions of war-weary people facing years more bloodshed and suffering it was an attractive message which Bolshevik sympathisers in all the combatant nations enthusiastically began spreading among the soldiers and civilians. The theatre of war where this message was likely to have least appeal was in the Middle East where the people were still largely un-urbanised and continued to be inspired by Islam and so were unlikely to be attracted to a new atheist, materialist creed such as Marxism with its roots in industrial Europe.

By the beginning of December 1917, with setbacks and disasters multiplying on all the other fronts, the only theatre of war where Britain was enjoying continuing success was the Middle East. General Allenby, Lawrence and the Arab forces of Husayn's son Feisal, having taken both Jaffa and the Crusader town of Lydd (by tradition the home of St George, slayer of the dragon) close to modern Tel Aviv, were now advancing through the Judean Hills to within a few miles of Jerusalem. Lloyd George was hoping that the Holy City would be captured by Christmas to act as a much-needed morale-boosting Christmas present to the hard pressed British people. On the morning of Sunday, December 9th, two British soldiers out foraging for something to eat for breakfast were on almost exactly the same spot that the English Crusader King Richard the Lion Heart had reached just over seven centuries earlier in his failed attempt to capture the Holy City and bring back to Europe the most sacred relic in all Christendom, The Holy Cross. Looking up from their search for eggs the two British privates were astonished to see a small crowd of people, some civilians, some in Turkish uniform, coming towards them from the direction of the city bearing a large white flag. They were the Mayor, priests, imams and rabbis of Jerusalem coming with the keys of the city to surrender. The Turkish troops had pulled back to the north and Jerusalem fell without a shot being fired.

Two days later on December 11th 1917, acting on strict instructions from the government in London, General Allenby, with T. E. Lawrence at his side, heading a large column of Arab, British, Australian and Indian Muslim troops, rode up to the ancient Jaffa Gate of the old city. Out of respect and as a gesture of his humility before its sanctified status as the home of the sacred places of the three great Abrahamic religions, Allenby dismounted and walked through the gate and into the city. Allenby was the first Christian conqueror to enter Jerusalem at the head of a victorious army since the First Crusade in 1099. On that occasion the victorious Christians had massacred thirty thousand of the city's Muslim and Jewish inhabitants. During their advance through Palestine and the Biblical Holy Land towards Jerusalem many of the soldiers in Allenby's army had felt themselves to be Crusaders, followers in the footsteps of their Christian forefathers. But the British authorities were anxious to avoid any echo of that earlier conquest or hints of Christian triumphalism. They had therefore given Allenby precise directions, devised and orchestrated behind the scenes by the ubiquitous crusading Christian Sir Mark Sykes, as to how the British entry into the city, the victory parade and subsequent administration were to be stage managed. An official proclamation, promising goodwill and respect for all the religions, was read out in English, French, Russian, Arabic, Hebrew and Greek. No Allied flags were to be flown over the city and guards placed on all the holy places; in the case of the Dome of the Rock, the site of Muhammad's ascent into heaven, Allenby ensured that the guards were Indian Muslims. However, the effect of all this was somewhat marred when as part of the victory parade, taken by Allenby standing on the steps of the city's ancient citadel with Sykes discreetly behind him, rank after rank of the be-plumed, helmeted Australian Light Horse Brigade trotted past on their huge horses in a show that evoked images of ranks of mounted Crusader knights in earlier centuries. They were greeted by the hysterical cheers of Christians and Jews in the crowd. Further embarrassment followed when, in his victory speech, Allenby referred to the capture of Jerusalem as the completion of the Crusades and promised its fall would bring a new era of Christian rule.[15] The assembled Muslim leaders in his audience promptly walked out. The desired Muslim reaction was muted still further when reports started to reach the Middle East that the bells of St Peter's in Rome, the Catholic cathedral in London and churches elsewhere in Allied Europe had been rung in celebration.

The fall of Jerusalem captured imaginations across the Christian Allied world and *Punch* magazine summed up the mood when it published a cartoon showing Richard the Lionheart saying 'At last my dream come true!' To Lawrence and other British soldiers and officials who were there that day, this was the supreme moment of the war. Some Muslims even took comfort from the fact that the name Allenby resembled the Arabic words Al Neby – the prophet.

The effect of Allenby's successes together with the fact that after their capture of Baghdad Maude's army had continued to fan out and had occupied most of eastern Mesopotamia meant that by mid-April 1918,

15 See Armstrong, Karen, *Muhammad: A Biography of the Prophet*, Victor Gollancz, London, 1991.

when Philby at last got back to Riyadh, the threat presented to the British flank and operations in Mesopotamia by Ibn Rashid had largely disappeared and Britain had better uses for any surplus arms, ammunition and money than giving them to Ibn Saud. As a consequence Ibn Saud's last opportunity to become an active participant and ally in Britain's victorious war against the Ottoman Empire, and to participate in the benefits that were likely to flow from that participation, had gone. Ibn Saud was furious, with the British and with Sharif Husayn who he saw as responsible. The result seemed likely to be that Ibn Saud would launch a fresh series of attacks on Husayn. The second part of Philby's brief on behalf of the British authorities had been to improve the relations between Husayn and Ibn Saud, so he now decided on his own responsibility to make Ibn Saud a loan of £20,000 that had been put at his disposal for use during his mission, on condition that he mobilise for an attack on Ha'il and the Rashids. Ibn Saud, in desperate need of the money, agreed. In July, having waited for the end of Ramadan, Ibn Saud dispatched his son Turki with a force of warriors to the Rashid frontier. Ibn Saud with his main body of warriors set out after him in August and by the end of September, the Rashids having withdrawn ahead of them to the protection of the walled city of Ha'il, Ibn Saud began to besiege it. But, denied the four siege guns that Philby had requested the British to supply him with, Ibn Saud could not take the town. He therefore withdrew to Buraida, taking as much booty, including 1,500 camels and thousands of sheep, as he could with him.

Meanwhile further trouble had broken out on the border between Najd and the Hijaz. Husayn's son Abdullah had appeared with a large force and re-occupied Khurma. Three days later the local Ikhwan leader and his followers gathered outside and drove Abdullah and his troops out. Abdullah attacked Khurma twice more but each time the local Ikhwan leader and his followers threw him out. The third time Abdullah attacked, the local Ikhwan leader sent a message to Ibn Saud warning him that if he continued to allow his subjects to be attacked by Abdullah he would send a virgin out from Khurma, unveiled and bareheaded, to rouse all the tribes of Najd to launch a great attack on Sharif Husayn. Enraged and alarmed, Ibn Saud immediately had a message conveyed to the British that he would go to war against Husayn unless Britain at once honoured the pledge made to him during his visit to Basra almost two years earlier to restrain their ally Husayn from further provocations against him and his people. This Britain promptly did and the attacks ceased.

By now the war was coming to an end. On October 1st the Australian Light Horse Brigade, having ridden 400 miles in twelve days, charged into Damascus with swords drawn and galloped onwards through the streets to the main barracks where thousands of Turkish troops were stationed. For a moment the Turks hesitated and the cavalry rode straight on at them. Then every Turkish soldier laid down his arms and surrendered. A spontaneous burst of cheering, clapping and rifle shots loosed into the air as the relieved citizens burst out of their houses in wild celebration. However, the doubts of some Muslims about the Christians' intentions towards them were deepened when the commander of the French troops who entered Damascus marched up to the tomb of Saladin and announced: 'Nous revenons, Saladin.'[16]

Meanwhile on the Western front, despite the Germans being able to deploy tens of thousands of extra troops to it from the Russian front as a result of the Russian capitulation, the arrival of the growing flood of fresh, well-armed American troops, over a million in all, meant that the balance of forces had been tipped decisively in the Allies' favour. As a result the German assaults of the summer had been held and British, French and American armies were now driving forward towards the Siegfried Line and borders of Germany. Inside Germany itself dissent was increasing and calls for an end to the fighting growing louder. The Kaiser was stripped of most of his powers and it began to look as if Germany, like Russia before it, might dissolve into chaos and revolution. In Warsaw patriots declared the establishment of a 'free and independent Polish state'. On October 23rd the Austrian army in Italy mutinied and two days later a Hungarian National Council was set up in Budapest, making the eventual separation of Hungary from Austria inevitable. On the same day Allenby and Husayn's forces reached Aleppo, within forty miles of the Turkish frontier and the day after that a delegation from the Turkish Government began armistice talks on board a British warship anchored in the Aegean. In the following days, as the talking and fighting

16 Armstrong, Karen, op. cit.

continued, Bosnians, Croats, Serbs and Slovenes came together to create a new independent, sovereign state of the southern Slavs – Yugoslavia. Czechs and Slovaks also declared for their own independent state, Czechoslovakia. The Austro-Hungarian Empire had disintegrated.

At noon on October 30th Turkey officially surrendered. Under the terms of the armistice Turkey had to demobilise all its forces, release all prisoners, accept Allied occupation of the Dardanelles and Bosphorus and evacuate all its Arab provinces. The Ottoman Empire ceased to exist.

On November 3rd Austria surrendered and on 4th November all fighting ended in Italy. On November 9th the Kaiser abdicated and across Germany revolutionaries seized railway stations and other vital centres. The next day the German Government accepted the Allies' armistice terms and at 11am on November 11th 1918 the guns fell silent. The First World War was over.

* * *

The war had been a worrying, frustrating, sometimes confusing experience for Ibn Saud. As he took stock of his own situation in November 1918 it would have been difficult to say if overall he had gained or lost from the war. Among the gains was the fact the Ottoman Empire was no more, although the Caliph, the spiritual leader of the Muslim world, still remained with his seat in Constantinople. Another plus for Ibn Saud was the treaty of protection he now had with Britain Also the Ikhwan, by their success in resisting Abdullah at Khurma, had demonstrated their potential as a military weapon. But against those gains had to be set the loss of his friend Captain Shakespear and the fact that he had not played an active part in Britain's victory and so was unlikely to get the benefits that now ought to accrue to Britain's wartime allies. Although the Rashids had lost their sponsor and protector, Turkey, Husayn was now firmly allied with Britain. Ibn Saud's treasury had been seriously depleted by the loss of trade across his territory due to the war, the customs dues he had not been able to levy and loss of income as a result of fewer pilgrims making the annual Hajj journey across Najd to the holy cities. Finally, and still unknown to Ibn Saud, he had lost his most high-ranking advocate with the British Government,

Sir Percy Cox. Cox had never had any stomach for the prospect of becoming the British administrator who would be responsible for implementing the Sykes-Picot Agreement and had requested a transfer to another post.

The post-war world that Ibn Saud was now going to have to confront would be very different from the one in which he had seized Riyadh and expanded his kingdom in the previous sixteen years. It was not just the changed international situation, or that Britain, with to a lesser extent France, was now the only real imperial power left in the region, it was also all the technological changes that had been hastened by war – radio, the growth in volume and importance of motor vehicles, the developments in aviation of all kinds, the huge increase in range, destructiveness and accuracy of weapons of all types, developments in medicine and the growth of new political structures and systems such as socialism and Communism. And there was the emergence of America, untested as yet and still largely unknown in the region, but already clearly the coming power in the world.

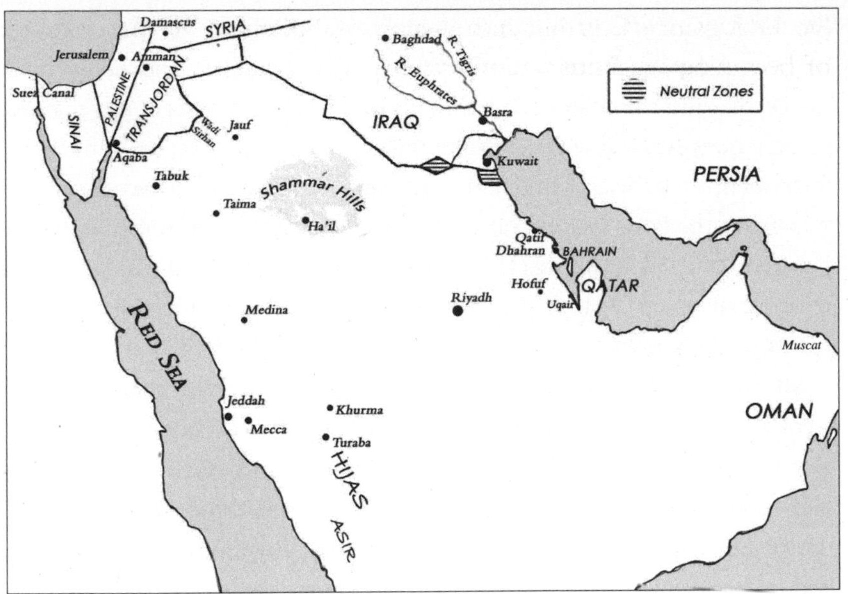

CHAPTER 8

Unleashing the Ikhwan

'The Paris of the Peace Conference ceased to be the capital of France. It became a vast cosmopolitan caravanserai teeming with unwanted aspects of life and turmoil, filled with curious samples of races, tribes, and tongues of four continents ... An Arabian Nights touch was imparted to the dissolving panorama by strange visitants from Turkey and Kurdistan, Corea and Azerbeijan, Armenia, Persia, and the Hedjaz – men with patriarchal beards and scimitar-shaped noses, and others from the desert and oasis, from Samarakand and Bokhara. Turbans and fezes, sugar-loaf hats and headgear resembling episcopal mitres, old military uniforms devised for the embryonic armies of new states on the eve of perpetual peace, snowy-white burnouses, flowing mantles, and graceful garments like the Roman toga, contributed to create an atmosphere of dreamy unreality ... Then came the men of wealth, of intellect, of industrial enterprise, and the seed-bearers of the ethical new ordering, members of economic committees from the United States, Britain, Italy, Poland, Russia, India and Japan, representatives of naphtha industries and far-off coal mines, pilgrims, fanatics and charlatans of all climes, priests of all religions, preachers of every doctrine, who mingled with the princes, field-marshals, statesmen, anarchists, builders-up and pullers-down.'[1] So wrote an eyewitness of the Paris Peace Conference which convened in Versailles on the outskirts of Paris on January 18th 1919. Its self-appointed task was to so re-order the world as to make good the promise of the leaders of the Allied nations that the Great War would be 'The War to End all Wars'.

Sharif Husayn, as an active ally of the Allies, was represented at Versailles by his son Feisal, but Ibn Saud, despite all of the promises made to him by Britain under the various agreements and understandings they had negotiated since he and Shakespear had reached that first agreement on the eve of the Battle of Jarab, was not even invited. By the end of the war his reputation with the British stood lower than at any time since his first meeting with Shakespear back in 1910. Because of his repeated failure to act decisively in the British cause during the war he was seen as vacillating, ineffective and unreliable. The result was that neither he nor any representative of his was present among all the great throng of rulers, would-be rulers and representatives of vested interests who gathered at Versailles to settle the peace and divide up and devise a new world order.

Two years earlier the idealistic American president, Woodrow Wilson, had told the US Senate that peace must be founded on the equality of nations big and small and based upon 'an equality of rights'. At Versailles in 1919 President Wilson became the dominant force in the deliberations of the Peace Conference. He presented the Conference with his own manifesto for enduring peace, 'The Fourteen Points'. Number 12 stated that 'The non-Turkish nationalities of the Ottoman Empire [are] to be assured of autonomous development' and the Conference accepted that the principle of self-determination should apply for each nation state. With all these lofty ideals accepted, it was not unreasonable for Sharif Husayn and his representative at Versailles, Feisal, to assume that Britain's 1916 promise to him that in return for instigating the Arab Revolt she

1 *The Inside Story of the Peace Conference* by Dr E. J. Dillon, Harper, New York, 1920.

would be prepared 'to recognise and uphold the independence of the Arabs in all the regions inside the frontiers proposed by the Sharif of Mecca', would now be honoured. In his eyes this meant the creation of one unified Arab kingdom under his control stretching from the small British protectorates in the south and east of the Arabian peninsula all the way to the Red Sea in the west and north along the eastern shores of the Mediterranean to the borders of Anatolia and Turkey to include all of Mesopotamia. But what about the promises that Britain had made to Ibn Saud? His exclusion from Versailles probably encouraged Husayn to believe he would be allowed free rein to overrun Najd. And what about the no-longer-secret Sykes-Picot Agreement dividing control of the former Ottoman territories in Arabia and Mesopotamia between Britain and France? Or the Balfour Agreement, with its promise of 'a national home for the Jewish people' in Palestine? How were all these conflicting promises and agreements to be squared? The Versailles Peace Conference conjured up an ingenious, idealistic, but in practice conflict-inducing, solution: 'Mandates under the League of Nations'.[2] Under the Mandate system the new and emergent nations of the Middle East which had formerly been part of the Ottoman Empire were granted provisional international recognition while at the same time remaining under the 'instruction' or control of a nominated Mandatory power until such time as they were judged sufficiently strong and developed to survive unaided as full, independent states. As a result, with the blessing of the Versailles Peace Conference and League of Nations, Britain and France, as Mandatory Powers, divided the Middle East between them almost exactly as they had previously agreed under the terms of the Sykes-Picot Agreement. Syria and Lebanon became French Mandates. Iraq, Palestine and Transjordan, a newly created state to be carved out of the east of Palestine, became British Mandates. Britain also took on responsibility for facilitating the creation of a national home for the Jews in Palestine without at the same time prejudicing the rights of the indigenous Arabs who had been living there continuously for millennia.

2 The League of Nations, a creation of the Versailles Peace Conference, was the forerunner of the United Nations. The League proved ineffective particularly because a number of important powers refused to join it or were excluded.

In June 1919, after five months' labour in Versailles, the assembled statesmen, representatives of vested interests and embryonic new states announced that they had reached a peace agreement. They had, they claimed, 'made the world safe for democracy'. Their critics jeered that, on the contrary, all they had done was to 'make the world safe for hypocrisy'. Time would prove the critics right. The men gathered at Versailles had sown the seeds from which, twenty years later, would grow the next, even bigger, world war, plus many other smaller wars, revolutions, uprisings and genocides which continue to this day.

To most of the Arabs the Mandate agreements looked like old-fashioned British and French colonialism under a different name. Husayn felt that he had been cheated by Versailles. But no sooner had the Versailles Conference ended than Ibn Saud went to work to find a means of realising his long-term ambitions under the new circumstances. For him the mandate system appeared to do little more than replace the two imperial powers which had for centuries encroached upon his borders and attempted to interfere in his affairs, Britain and Turkey, and to leave just one in their place, Britain, with France on the periphery to the north. Whereas before he had been able to play Turkey and Britain off against each other as he had been taught by Mubarak, from now on he was going to have to find ways of manipulating Britain alone so as to prevent her from intervening in his affairs and frustrating his long-term goal of bringing the whole Arabian peninsula under his control. The proposed Jewish homeland in Palestine did not impinge on Ibn Saud directly. But it seemed to him, as to the majority of other Arabs, to be an affront, an imperial imposition that was likely to displace thousands of innocent Palestinian Arab families.

Determined to make his presence felt immediately, but unable to leave Riyadh for fear of fresh insurrections or that, with the war over, Husayn might make a further attempt to regain Khurma, in July 1919 Ibn Saud obtained Britain's agreement to his thirteen-year-old third son (there had been another son born shortly before Faisal but he had died in infancy), Faisal, making an official visit to London on his behalf. Faisal, a good-looking, gentle child of a rather sickly disposition, had recently begun to be groomed by Ibn Saud to take charge of his foreign policy. Faisal's task in London would be to convey his father's congratulations to the British

Government on its victory and at the same time make plain his father's views about Sharif Husayn and the still-unresolved dispute over Khurma.

Faisal set off accompanied by eight retainers of various kinds plus two older and more experienced companions, Abdullah al Qosaidi, one of Ibn Saud's commercial agents, and a distant cousin, Ahmad al Thaniyan, who had been trained as a diplomat in Constantinople. As this was an 'official' Saudi visit the party's arrival and itinerary had been agreed with the British in advance and a British representative from their Political Staff in Baghdad, Humphrey Bowman, was detailed to accompany the Saudis on their journey to Britain. On the Saudi party's arrival in Plymouth, in mid-October, Bowman's duties were taken over by their old friend, H. St. John Philby, who accompanied them on the train to Paddington and then took them in three cars to the Queen's Hotel in Upper Norwood, a fashionable address near the site of the Crystal Palace. The hotel, a large neo-classical pile, had previously played host to a range of important official guests including Kaiser Wilhelm just a few months before the outbreak of the First World War and the French writer Emile Zola. However, the next morning it became all too apparent that the British government's arrangements for their Saudi guests had been catastrophically bungled. The hotel manager informed Philby that the Government Hospitality Department had booked the Saudis' rooms for only one night and they would have to vacate them that morning. Philby immediately set about making a series of desperate phone calls to the government officials responsible for the visit but could find no one in their office who was able to deal with the problem. Next he tried ringing round all the suitable hotels he could think of, but to no avail. All were fully booked. Eventually, with the help of an officer in the India Office, Philby managed to find his charges accommodation in the King's Indian Orderly Officers' House, behind Victoria Station. This was a house set aside as the London living accommodation of Indian Army officers who, as part of their training and development, were posted four at a time to London to undertake royal guard duties. But unfortunately, while this solved the immediate problem of providing the Saudis with somewhere to sleep at night, it did not solve the problem of feeding them. The Officers' House was unable to provide meals so Philby had to shepherd his Arab charges thrice daily, in full Arab dress, through the rain-sodden autumn London streets from their sleeping accommodation to the Grosvenor Hotel beside Victoria Station, to eat.

Inevitably, the spectacle of the small party of be-robed Saudis walking regularly through the wet London streets from the Officers' House to the Grosvenor Hotel for their meals quickly attracted the attention of the London press. *The Times* came out with a strongly worded article headed 'Our Guests From Arabia' attacking this regrettable 'lapse of Government hospitality' while the *Daily Graphic* went still further, denouncing what it called 'A Government Bungle' which had condemned the Saudis to becoming 'Wandering Arabs'. As a result of the newspaper articles the Saudis' plight and the government's breach in diplomatic protocol came to the attention of King George V. He immediately intervened, having a number of officials ranging from Lord Curzon himself downwards hauled over the coals and himself invited young Faisal to meet him, the Queen and Princess Mary in the Throne Room at Buckingham Palace.

Young Faisal was a charming boy and in spite of knowing only a few words of English, which he had learned specially for the occasion, made a very favourable impression on both the king and queen. Faisal presented King George with an ornamental, jewel-encrusted sword in a solid gold sheath. In return the King presented the boy with two signed photographs, one of himself and one of his wife.

Faisal also made a very favourable impression on the hardened British press corps – the Arab boy prince from deep inside the mysterious deserts of Arabia, slighted by the Foreign Office and braving the cold and wet of the English autumn in the smoke encrusted streets of Victoria with his bodyguards, was, from the point of view of newspaper editors, too good a story to let pass – and they duly played it to the hilt.

When not carrying out his official duties young Faisal was able to do a lot of boyish sightseeing. He visited the London Zoo, the Natural History Museum, the Bank of England, both Houses of Parliament, where he remarked on the difference in dress between the members of the Lords, with their top hats and frock coats and the more ordinary suits of the Commons, to Greenwich Observatory, Cambridge, various horse-racing stables and studs, an arms factory in Birmingham, to Dublin and a South Wales steel-works. He even set off to walk up Snowdon, only to be caught in a sudden snowstorm and forced to return hastily to his hotel. He went to the Savoy Theatre to see *The Mikado* and *Patience*, was filmed for the newsreel, saw telephones, a typewriter, inspected a captured German submarine and an aeroplane. However, when his hosts proposed that he should be taken up for a flight in a Handley Page bomber his guards angrily prohibited it. He took a boyish delight in all he saw, showing his father's keen interest in the inventions of the developed world. Still a child, in spite of the responsibility that had been thrust upon him by the visit, Faisal seemed most entranced of all by the new escalators at Piccadilly Underground station. In his moments off he rode down and up, down and up, down and up, time after time.

A child he might be, but Faisal knew when he was being patronised. When he went with Ahmad al Thaniyan to meet the newly installed British Foreign Secretary, Lord Curzon, to discuss the main purpose of their visit, his father's dispute with Sharif Husayn and the Khurma affair, Curzon offered the boy a boiled sweet. The old imperialist treated Thaniyan with similarly lofty disdain and their discussion got nowhere. The two Saudis left seething with suppressed rage at having been treated 'like children'. Afterwards Faisal's companion, Thaniyan, told Philby that if the British officer who had accompanied them to their meeting with Curzon ever came to Najd he would cut his throat.

The Saudi party travelled on to France, visiting the First World War battlefields before going on to Paris. There they were again snubbed by the British. Persuaded by them against his better judgement to meet Husayn's son Feisal, who was still in Paris to represent his father in the run up to the ratification of the peace agreement, al Thaniyan was subjected to further insults. When Feisal made derogatory remarks about the Ikhwan, Feisal's and al Thaniyan's bodyguards had to intervene to prevent the two men from laying into each other with their swords. Faisal and al Thaniyan also went on to make visits to Strasbourg and Cologne.

Faisal and his party did not return to Arabia until February 1920. After travelling by sea to Bahrain, Faisal and his companions rode inland to Hofuf where his father was waiting to welcome him home. Ibn Saud was almost pathetically pleased to see his son returned to him so obviously fit and well. The boy had much to tell his father not only about his meetings in London and Paris but about all the strange and wonderful things he had seen. When he handed his father the personal letter that King George had written to him Ibn Saud asked for Lt. Colonel Harold Dickson, Britain's recently appointed official agent in Bahrain, to translate and read the King's letter to him. Ibn Saud seemed so pleased by the King's personal greetings and warm wishes that he immediately asked Dickson to read the letter to him again twice more. However, Ibn Saud's mood rapidly changed when al Thaniyan told him about the meetings he and Faisal had had with Lord Curzon in the Foreign Office and Feisal in Paris. Al Thaniyan spelled out the ways in which his son and he had been repeatedly belittled by the British and left in no doubt that the British regarded them, and by implication Ibn Saud himself, as inferior and less important than Sharif Husayn. Ibn Saud was both angry and cast down by this news. Why, he asked Dickson with a mixture of anger and profound sorrow, could the British not see the truth about Sharif Husayn? That he was a broken reed whose days were numbered?

This placed Dickson, as his government's official representative in the region, in a difficult position. He was new in his post and this was the first time he had met Ibn Saud. He had heard great things about Ibn Saud from Cox and other colleagues, yet he knew that he was expected to follow the British Foreign Office's 'pro-Husayn' policy as regarded the competing claims of Sharif Husayn and Ibn Saud to the Arabian peninsula. Dickson was to some extent still feeling his way in his new post in Bahrain and now at his first meeting with Ibn Saud he was thrust into the thick of the politics of the interior of the Arabian peninsula. The son of a British Middle East diplomat, Dickson was through-and-through a British imperial diplomat in the finest tradition. He had been born in Beirut and lived in the Middle East for much of his life. Now just turned forty, he was a fine Arabic speaker and Arabist, taking a great interest in all aspects of Arab life. Dickson would go on to become a great authority on the different Arab tribes, tribal life, customs, traditions and legends, later writing a number of books on them. He was newly married and his wife, Violet, shared all these interests and herself also became an authority on traditional Arab architecture and the region's flora and fauna. The Dicksons were to devote their whole lives to Arabia and the Arabs, living on in Kuwait after their retirement until their deaths.

This fresh evidence of Britain's continuing belief in Sharif Husayn's superiority over Ibn Saud was all the more surprising because nine months earlier Ibn Saud's Ikhwan had inflicted a new and crushing defeat on the Sharif's forces. In March 1919 Sharif Husayn's fat, braggart eldest son, Abdullah, after much ostentatious preparation and boasts about his coming success, had with the full knowledge of the British marched south from Medina towards Khurma. He had under his command more than eight thousand seasoned fighters armed with modern rifles, ammunition, machine guns and artillery.[3] Curzon had said repeatedly that if it came to a showdown between Husayn and Ibn Saud, Husayn was certain to win 'hands down' over Ibn Saud's 'Wahhabi rabble'. This looked as if it could be that showdown. The previous year, when he had agreed to call off the Ikhwan following Britain's request during the earlier dispute with Husayn and Abdullah over Khurma, Ibn Saud had made it absolutely clear that if Husayn or Abdullah attacked again he would do whatever was necessary to defend his honour. So now, hearing that Abdullah was again on the march, he too began to prepare. On receiving news that Ibn Saud was preparing to repel Abdullah, the British authorities in Cairo and London conferred and agreed a note must be sent to Ibn Saud ordering him to allow Abdullah to restore his father's territory in Khurma and warning that if he refused they would render Abdullah 'all assistance' and might reduce or cut off completely the subsidy they were paying him. The threat of rendering Abdullah 'all assistance' was in practice meaningless as the British had no intention of getting involved in any military adventure in the middle of Arabia so soon after the war, whether on Sharif Husayn's part or anyone else's. The only part of the British threat that carried any

3 Estimates of the numbers involved on both sides in this encounter, as in so many others throughout the history of the region during this period, vary widely. The numbers we have used conform to the most reliable modern sources.

weight was the threat to cut off Ibn Saud's subsidy and Ibn Saud seemed to know it. He replied to the British note by protesting that the territory had long been part of his family's birthright and was also part of the long-established grazing area of tribes loyal to him. He told the British that he did not deserve such treatment. But, he said, 'Success comes from God alone.' If Britain did cut off its subsidy to him so be it: 'My honour, God be praised, will remain untarnished. I shall be free to act according to the dictates of my honour.'[4]

On May 21st 1919 Abdullah arrived in Turaba, about sixty miles to the southwest of Khurma, plundered the town and set about dealing with local inhabitants suspected of disloyalty to his father. Abdullah boasted that after he had captured Khurma he intended to press on to the east, drive Ibn Saud out of Riyadh, retake all of Najd and sweep on through Hasa to the shores of the Gulf. He would, he told all around him, start the Ramadan fast in Riyadh and celebrate the end of it, *Eid-al-Fitr*, on the far shores of Hasa.

Word of what was happening had by now reached Khalid bin Luai, the local Ikhwan leader who had inflicted the series of defeats on Abdullah a year earlier. He and his followers were furious and swore terrible vengeance. This time, unlike a year earlier, Ibn Saud openly encouraged an Ikhwan attack on Abdullah and headed out with his own force from the wells where he was encamped some five or six days' march to the east. But before he could reach Turaba and just three days after first learning of Abdullah's seizure of the town, an Ikhwan force of some 4,000 men from three different Ikhwan colonies, led by bin Luai and another powerful Ikhwan tribal leader, Sultan ibn Bijad, converged a few miles outside Turaba. They had approached so rapidly that Abdullah was still totally unaware of their arrival. However, refugees who had fled into the surrounding desert from the town had spotted the Ikhwan's arrival and were eager to give them precise information as to the whereabouts and layout of Abdullah's encampment. Still unaware of the Ikhwan's approach, and even more over-confident and puffed up

4 See *Lord of Arabia* by H. C. Armstrong, Penguin Books, Harmondsworth, Middlesex, 1938. Armstrong first met Ibn Saud shortly after these events and heard about many of them directly from Ibn Saud and others who had taken part in them.

following his easy capture of Turaba, Abdullah had not even bothered to erect proper defences around his camp or post sentries.

The moon was in the third quarter. It was a pitch-black night except for the barely moving banks of mist that clung to the ground following a sudden desert rainstorm a few hours earlier. As Abdullah and his eight thousand men slept unaware of the encroaching danger, bin Luai and ibn Bijad's thousands of Ikhwan crept stealthily around their camp and encircled it. Barely a camel or horse's hoof had clicked against the ground, nor voice or clank of metal from sword or gun travelled through the misty air to alert any light sleeper during those dark hours. Any eye that had opened and spied ghostly white-clad figures as they glided through the darkness could hardly have distinguished them from the gently dissolving and reforming patterns of the mist itself – mist, or dream, or nothing. So Abdullah and his eight thousand men slept on until, upon a signal, the Ikhwan fell upon them. Abdullah and his men were suddenly wrenched awake to find themselves enveloped in a confusing tsunami of darkness and slashing, hacking blades, of howling, ululating white-robed Ikhwan chanting their nightmare war cry: 'The winds of heaven are blowing!' The Ikhwan, heedless of death for themselves, killed every Hijazi they saw. They gave no quarter, showed no mercy. For the Ikhwan, Abdullah, Sharif Husayn and all Hijazis were sinners and unbelievers. They deserved death.

Abdullah was lucky to escape alive in the darkness and confusion. Without any thought for the men under his command he rushed from his tent in the loose nightshirt in which he had been sleeping, leapt onto his horse and galloped away. He is said to have galloped all the way to Mecca without stopping, where, still in his nightshirt, he ran straight into the palace and straight up to his father. Without pausing for breath, shaking and jabbering, he blurted out all that had happened, how the Ikhwan had fallen upon them at night without warning, murdering and killing in a frenzied orgy of death and blood.

Of the eight thousand men who had been with Abdullah at Turaba only a few hundred escaped. All their weapons and ammunition, including their machine guns and artillery, fell into the Saudis' hands. When Ibn Saud arrived two days later, the ground around the remains of Abdullah's shattered and looted camp was still soaked with dried and blackened blood, strewn with thousands of mutilated, decomposing bodies and swarming with flies. Walking among the dead on the black, hardened blood, amid the unceasing hum of millions of flies and the stench of the decomposing human flesh of his slain enemies, Ibn Saud wept. 'This is the burden with which Allah has burdened me. Upon me is the responsibility of bringing the *mushrekin* [those who invoke saints in their prayers] back to the straight path ... Would I were a common soldier fighting for the cause of Allah.'[5]

With Abdullah's army destroyed, Mecca and the rest of the Hijaz lay at Ibn Saud's mercy. Mecca was barely two days' march to the northwest and the Ikhwan wanted to press on and take the holy city. But Ibn Saud refused and, after allowing them to extend his territory southwest into Asir, ordered them back to Riyadh and their settlements. He understood, although they could not, that the British were not yet ready to allow their protégé and ally in the recent war, Sharif Husayn, to be destroyed. And he was right. When news reached London of what had happened, together with fresh appeals from Husayn for help, Curzon and his aides again conferred in the Foreign Office. An ultimatum was dispatched to Ibn Saud saying that His Majesty's Government was 'astonished' to learn that he had advanced into the Hijaz and taken Turaba and that if he did not 'immediately withdraw his forces from the Hijaz' and Turaba area they would regard this as a hostile act against Britain herself. In which case his subsidy would be immediately withdrawn and the treaty of December 1915 treated as null and void. The British also dispatched a flight of war planes from Egypt to strengthen Sharif Husayn's position. Ibn Saud responded by saying that he was willing to return to Najd and submit to arbitration provided that Sharif Husayn gave him a satisfactory guarantee that he would refrain from all aggressive acts against him. Husayn refused to submit to arbitration and again refused London's envoy, Philby, permission to travel across the Hijaz to hold discussions with Ibn Saud in Riyadh. Ibn Saud's willingness to compromise and defer to British wishes as compared with

5 Quoted by Ameen Rihani in *Ibn Sa'oud of Arabia: His People and His Land*, Constable, London, 1928, as told to him by one who was close by Ibn Saud on that day.

Sharif Husayn's intransigence were beginning to have an effect on opinion inside the British Government. At a departmental Foreign Office meeting a few weeks later one official spoke of Husayn being 'difficult and unreasonable' while another described him as a 'pampered and querulous nuisance'.[6] When Gertrude Bell had suggested during a meeting in the Foreign Office a few weeks earlier that unless Sharif Husayn was given his way he might abdicate, Lord Curzon had responded that he contemplated Husayn's 'complete disappearance not only without apprehension, but even with satisfaction'.[7] Privately Curzon admitted that there was now nothing that anyone could do to prevent Ibn Saud from eventually taking the whole of Arabia. It was, therefore, doubly surprising that only weeks later when young Faisal and Al Thaniyan had visited London and Paris as Ibn Saud's official representatives, they should have been treated with a disdain amounting almost to contempt by Curzon himself and nearly all the other British officials that they met.

Part of Ibn Saud's purpose in inviting Harold Dickson to meet him in Hofuf at the same time as he welcomed home his son Faisal from his mission to London and Paris was to try to impress upon him, as Britain's new representative in the area, his continuing loyalty and friendship towards Britain. Ibn Saud complained to Dickson that by her actions Britain was making his position difficult with his own people. They were angered by the news that Britain was planning to make Husayn's sons the new rulers of territories astride their traditional trading routes in the north and felt aggrieved that Britain had denied them the fruits of their victory over Husayn at Turaba. Ibn Saud also told Dickson that Arab nationalists in the new territories created under the British and French mandates in the north had sounded him out about joining a possible anti-British and -French *jihad* but that he had loyally refused to co-operate. Dickson reported to his superiors after the meeting that he had been struck by Ibn Saud's 'affection for everything British, and his almost

6 From Foreign Office departmental minutes dated July 9th 1919, quoted in Troeller, Gary: *The British in Saudi Arabia: Britain and the Rise of the House of Sa'ud*, Frank Cass, London, 1976.

7 British Government papers June 17th 1919, quoted in Troeller op. cit.

pathetic trust in HM's Government'. Ibn Saud was, he said, 'head and shoulders finer than any Shaikh I have ever met'.[8]

The second part of Ibn Saud's purpose in inviting Dickson to Hofuf was to try to allay the growing fears of the British Government over the Ikhwan. These fears had been aroused by reports that had reached them of the fanatical violence shown by the Ikhwan during their victories over Abdullah and by the veil of secrecy that seemed to surround the movement. Aware that they were feared by the authorities in London as fanatics over whom Ibn Saud had little control, Dickson was intent on discovering as much as he could about the Ikhwan during his time in Hofuf. He concluded that the Ikhwan was not the entirely bad movement that it had been made out to be. It seemed, Dickson wrote later, to be 'a genuine religious revival of the old type of Wahhabism, an attempt on the part of the masses of central Arabia to improve themselves morally and religiously'. Intended to purify Islam of the evils brought by contact with the outside world it had, believed Dickson, been born of distrust of foreigners and 'a deep-down determination to retain at all costs Arabia, and Najd in particular, for the Arabs'. Ibn Saud told Dickson that today, old Wahhabism, with the new impetus of Ikhwanism, 'is the purest of all religions in the world'. Seeing that Dickson was still concerned, Ibn Saud assured him, 'O Dickson, don't worry. I am the Ikhwan – no one else.'[9]

It became clear to Dickson during his time in Hofuf that while Ibn Saud was quite capable when it suited his purpose of espousing beliefs every bit as fanatical as the most fanatical Ikhwan zealot, for instance on the eve of battle so as to inspire the Ikhwan warriors, he was never himself, even in battle, seized of the same religious frenzy displayed by his Ikhwan followers. A demonstration of the contrast between Ibn Saud's true beliefs and the face he sometimes chose to show to the Ikhwan or to impress foreign visitors actually occurred during Dickson's visit to Hofuf. One day shortly after his arrival when a number of Ikhwan leaders were present with Ibn Saud in his *majlis* he warned

8 Dickson to Cox February 10th 1920 quoted in Troeller op. cit.

9 See H. R. P. Dickson, *Kuwait & Her Neighbours*, George Allen & Unwin, London, 1956.

Dickson that tobacco was *harám*, a deadly sin and that anyone using it was breaking the law and could be punished. However, suspecting that Dickson like most Europeans he had met enjoyed a cigarette, later that day he had one of his trusted inner circle come to Dickson's room after dark with a gift of two tins of the best Egyptian cigarettes. Handing him the present, Ibn Saud's messenger requested that Dickson smoke them only in the privacy of his own room.

Ibn Saud explained to Dickson that by persuading Bedouin tribes to establish Ikhwan settlements and spend part of each year tilling the land he had given these nomads a stake in the land, making them more secure and making his domain and the tribes within it easier to control. By 1920 when Dickson met Ibn Saud in Hofuf there were fifty-two Ikhwan settlements and, as Dickson concluded, the skill with which Ibn Saud had inspired and cajoled the Bedouin tribes to embrace Ikhwanism showed him to be no ordinary leader.

The months immediately after the end of the First World War, as well as bringing Ibn Saud serious troubles as a leader, also brought him great personal sadness. The worldwide influenza epidemic, which began during the closing months of the war in 1918 and eventually killed more millions than were killed in the war itself, struck Arabia late in 1918. At the height of the outbreak in Riyadh the death rate reached one hundred a day. So bad did it become that, recorded Dr Harrison, who had been urgently summoned to Riyadh from Bahrain, 'the whole town was sick, so much so that the bodies were carried out on donkeys and camels – two to a donkey and four to a camel'.[10] At least one person in every ten of the population of the town died. One of the reasons that the thirteen-year old Faisal had been sent as his father's emissary to London was that Faisal's eldest brother Turki, who was nineteen and being groomed by Ibn Saud as his heir, had died in the influenza outbreak in January 1919. Two of Faisal's younger brothers also died and Ibn Saud's favourite wife, Jauhara. Ibn Saud had been married to Jauhara since 1907 and he loved her as he loved no other of his wives. It was she who had inspired

10 India Office Records quoted by Robert Lacey in *The Kingdom*, Hutchinson, London, 1981.

him when he had been sitting before the strongly fortified walls of Hofuf six years earlier wracked by doubts and indecision, tired and longing for peace and home. As he told Muhammad Asad many years later, it was the vision of her face that had inspired the poem he had composed to her and led to his clear knowledge that he must attack Hofuf and that God would give him victory. For two months after Jauhara's death Ibn Saud shut himself away from company for hours on end and seemed to those around him to be locked in a deeply private grief which made him appear absent even when he was in the room with them. Years later he could still not mention Jauhara's name without a catch coming into his voice and tears welling up in his eyes.

But Ibn Saud was not allowed to give himself over to grieving for his lost wife and sons for long. In the months since he had prevented the Ikhwan from marching on to Mecca after their annihilation of Abdullah's army at Turaba, discontent among them had been rising. Ibn Saud knew that if he delayed finding a means of distracting them for too long the Ikhwan might cease to be loyal and turn on him. He therefore needed something that would appease them by satisfying their lust for conquest in the name of bringing more Muslims into the fold of true Wahhabi belief. But in identifying a new infidel enemy for the Ikhwan he had to be sure that he did not antagonise the British.

Months went by and the Ikhwan became ever more restless. An increasing number of voices began to be heard criticising Ibn Saud's subservience to the British. Then in September 1920 news reached Riyadh that Salim Mubarak, the new young ruler of Kuwait, was building a fort on the coast of the Persian Gulf well to the south of Kuwait and far inside territory that was the traditional grazing ground of tribes loyal to the Saudis. Ibn Saud immediately ordered his loyal henchman Faisal al Duwish with a large body of Ikhwan of the Mutair tribe from the original Ikhwan *hijra* at Artawiya and other local Ikhwan tribal leaders to drive Salim and the fort builders out. Duwish marched into the area, launched a surprise dawn attack on Salim and his force, seized a large quantity of camels and other booty, and sent them scuttling back to the walls of Kuwait itself. Salim had suffered 200 deaths among his men in the battle, while Duwish and the Ikhwan, with typical disregard for their own lives, had lost 1,200. Nevertheless,

Kuwait was now in imminent danger of capture and Salim appealed to the British for help.

While waiting for the British response Salim ordered all able-bodied inhabitants out of the town to dig defences. A massive defensive trench and fortifications were dug. Duwish meanwhile sent a messenger into the town to demand that the townspeople submit to strict Wahhabi religious observance and become Ikhwan. Salim replied that while he was a good Muslim and would be happy to ensure that his subjects adhered to strict Muslim religious observance in public he could not control what his people did in the privacy of their own homes.

The British response to Salim's call for help was to instruct their Political Agent in Kuwait to get the two sides together to thrash out a settlement to the dispute and at the same time to order planes from an RAF base in Iraq to drop thousands of leaflets among the Ikhwan encamped around Kuwait. The leaflet said that while the hostilities between Salim and Duwish had been confined to the desert and grazing grounds outside Kuwait they had not felt obliged to do more than try to get the parties to come to an amicable settlement of the dispute, but now that Duwish was threatening the town of Kuwait itself, and with it British interests and subjects who resided there, Britain was bound to intervene, with military force if necessary, to honour the pledges she had made to the Shaikh of Kuwait. Britain was confident, the leaflet continued, from the repeated assurances given to the British Government by Ibn Saud that the current Ikhwan action had not been carried out with his knowledge or on his orders – as Ibn Saud would doubtless make clear as soon as he heard what had happened. The appearance of British military aircraft coupled with the threat of British armed intervention appeared to have the desired effect. Ibn Saud disowned all knowledge of the attack and the Ikhwan forces withdrew from the immediate vicinity of the town. A series of protracted discussions between the two sides began under the aegis of the British.

Meanwhile in the newly created British Mandated state of Iraq an insurgency had broken out as a gaggle of aspiring would-be leaders, among them the egregious Sayyid Talib – now freed by the British from his enforced detention in India – competed for supremacy. The insurgents, led by the Shia majority, were inspired by a combination of

President Wilson's promises of self-determination and anti-colonialist rhetoric emanating from the Bolshevik leadership in Russia. They were also provoked by the evidence that despite Iraq's newly proclaimed status as a Mandated state, the British intended to continue to rule it in exactly the same way as they had ever since driving out the Turks and establishing military government during the war. The British soon found themselves struggling to maintain control and sections of the press and public in London, sick of wars, fighting and high taxation to pay for them, began to raise a clamour for immediate and total British withdrawal. The confusion grew still worse as a series of different Ikhwan tribes began raiding into the country across the newly created border.

On June 6th 1920 Ibn Saud's old friend Sir Percy Cox, now running the British administration in Persia, received an urgent summons from the Foreign Secretary, Lord Curzon, to return by the fastest route to London. He was to become the first British High Commissioner of Iraq, charged with the task of establishing a provisional Arab government. Returning to London, Cox accepted the new post but on one condition, that he would not be called upon to serve two or more masters as he had in the past when he had been subject to often conflicting orders from both the India Office and the Foreign Office, and latterly the War Office as well. His condition was accepted and he set sail for Baghdad, taking with him as a member of his staff Ibn Saud's friend Philby.

Cox broke his journey for two days in the Persian Gulf to meet with Ibn Saud in the Hasa port of Uqair. As well as seizing the opportunity of this unexpected meeting with Cox to try to resolve the difficulties over the Ikhwan action around Kuwait, Ibn Saud voiced his serious concern over fresh rumours that the British were planning to offer the crown of the newly created Mandated Kingdom of Iraq to Sharif Husayn's son, Feisal. Cox tried to reassure him – nothing would be decided before he had had a chance to study the situation in Iraq for himself and then make his recommendations to London. Privately Cox was against the idea of giving the crown of Iraq to Feisal, despite the fact that his claims were being strongly advocated by T. E. Lawrence. By the time their discussions were over and Cox re-boarded his ship for the remainder of his journey to Baghdad, Ibn Saud felt considerably reassured. This was not only because of what Cox had said about Feisal Husayn and the

Iraqi throne, but because with Cox back in a responsible position in the region he knew that he would have a sympathetic British ear to turn to in times of trouble.

Cox arrived in Baghdad shortly before sunset on Monday October 11th 1920. Gertrude Bell was amongst the crowd of people waiting on the quayside to greet him: 'He came out in white uniform and after shaking hands with the C. in C. stood at the salute while the band played "God Save the King". I thought as he stood there in his white and gold lace, with his air of fine and simple dignity, that there had never been an arrival more momentous – never anyone on whom more conflicting emotions were centred, hopes and doubts and fears ... '[11] Once the formalities were over, Cox got down to work at once. He issued a proclamation stating that he had returned to Mesopotamia to 'assist the leaders of the people to create a National government' and called upon the insurgent leaders to stop fighting and commence talks with the new British administration.

Meanwhile back in London Lloyd George's government made good the promise Lord Curzon had given to Cox by creating a new cabinet post of Secretary of State for the Colonies, who was to combine the responsibilities previously exercised by the India Office and Foreign Office for policy in Arabia and the Middle East. The first incumbent was to be Winston Churchill. He was seen by many Middle East experts as knowing little about the intricacies of the Middle East's history and politics: 'I really think you might search over history from end to end without finding poorer masters of it than Lloyd George and Winston Churchill', Gertrude Bell told her father shortly after the appointment was announced.[12]

However Churchill was determined to make up for his lack of knowledge. He appointed two wild, romantic and often unreliable characters of the kind that he was to tend throughout his career to promote, as his Arabian advisers, T. E. Lawrence and Colonel Richard

11 *The Letters of Gertrude Bell, Vol II*, edited by Lady Bell, E. Benn, London, 1927.

12 Ibid. (quoted in H. V. F Winstone, *Gertrude Bell*, Jonathan Cape, London, 1978).

Meinertzhagen. Lawrence was by then pursuing publicity for himself as the fountainhead of all knowledge in the Middle East and chief begetter of British success in the Middle Eastern war, in part in order to further his championship of the Hashemite cause, while at the same time feeling ashamed and embarrassed by his craving for attention. Churchill's other Arabian adviser, Colonel Richard Meinertzhagen, was in some ways an even more complicated and confused character than Lawrence. A convinced imperialist with a glowing but violent reputation for having maintained the British imperial interest in East Africa, a convinced Zionist who was not a Jew nor even a conventional Christian, he had been known to express anti-semitic views but claimed to be much influenced by 'the Divine promise that the Holy Land will forever remain Israel's inheritance'. Even Lawrence regarded Meinertzhagen as odd. With these two already deeply prejudiced characters as his guides, Churchill immediately got down to a thorough study of the issues involved, his aim being to achieve a stable future for the region that would at the same time reduce government spending in the area and meet Britain's strategic needs. The region remained important to Britain as its gateway to India, the Far East and East Africa – in addition to the well-established sea and land routes through the region, air routes were now being developed. It also remained important as a source of vital raw materials, especially cotton and oil. Britain's continuing presence in the region also helped to guarantee her on-going position as a Mediterranean and world power. For some British politicians there was the additional moral obligation of establishing a national home for the Jews and for Churchill's adviser, Lawrence, there was the need to honour the promises he and others had made to Sharif Husayn and the Arabs.

After only a few days in his new post Churchill told Lloyd George that the more he studied the Middle Eastern problem the more convinced he became that it was impossible to deal with it except as a whole: 'The Arab problem is all one ... Feisal or Abdullah, whether in Mesopotamia or Mecca, King Husayn when at Mecca; Ibn Saud at Najd, [Ibn Rashid] at Ha'il; the Shaikh of Kuwait; and King Samuel at Jerusalem [a reference to Sir Herbert Samuel the British Zionist politician who had been sent by the government to administer Palestine] are all inextricably interwoven, and no conceivable policy can have any chance which does not pull all the strings affecting them.'[13] Muddle, failure and discredit, Churchill said, were certain with any plan which did not take this fact as its starting point.

At the strong urging of T. E. Lawrence and other members of the Arab Bureau, the British Government had for a time been contemplating putting Sharif Husayn and his family on the thrones of the various kingdoms which it intended to create under Mandate in the Middle East. But a week after his letter to Lloyd George, Churchill was beginning to appreciate the potential weak spot in this proposal. Writing to Sir Arthur Hirtzel, the Head of the Political Department in the India Office, he said that 'I had not appreciated the weakness inherent in King Husayn's position. He is only a member of the Sharifian family selected by the Turks on political grounds ... Will not Ibn Saud be offended if a son of King Husayn is made ruler over Mesopotamia, or will he not care? Will not the selection of Feisal or Abdullah strike him as a hostile act on our part? From the papers you have sent me it would seem that Ibn Saud is much the strongest figure in the Arabian Peninsula.'[14]

Six weeks later Churchill convened a conference of 'practically all the experts and authorities in the Middle East' in Cairo. Over the course of a fortnight some thirty-five Englishmen, most of them military, Churchill's two advisers on Arabian affairs, plus Gertrude Bell, Sir Percy Cox and two aides of Sharif Husayn's son Feisal, but no representative of Ibn Saud, mapped out what they intended to be the future of the Middle East and parcelled it out between Sharif Husayn and his sons. The future state of Iraq was sketched out, according to Churchill, on a piece of paper in the 'course of a Saturday afternoon' and Husayn's son Feisal placed on its throne. A new state was carved out of the land east of Palestine on the far side of the river Jordan, to be called Transjordan, and Abdullah, the son of Husayn who Ibn Saud had defeated at Turaba, was appointed its Amir. The frontiers of the new states were determined

13 Churchill to Lloyd George, January 12th 1921, in *Winston S. Churchill, Vol. IV Companion, Part 2, Documents July 1919– March 1921*, by Martin Gilbert, William Heinemann, London 1977.

14 Ibid. Note: for consistency and to avoid confusion we have changed the spellings of the names from those used by Churchill so as to make them conform to the spellings used elsewhere in this book.

with little or no regard to the pre-existing religious, tribal and ethnic divisions within them – an oversight which in years to come was to result in massive problems. Sharif Husayn was confirmed as King of the Hijaz and the commitment to a homeland for the Jews in Palestine with a guarantee for the democratic rights of the Palestinian Arabs already living there, re-confirmed. The practical impossibility of both creating a homeland for the Jews in Palestine and guaranteeing the democratic right to self-determination for the Palestinians was recognised by many of the participants in the conference but Churchill decided to simply ignore the problem. Probably most important of all for Lloyd George and the Government back in London, the conference announced that as a result of its decisions it would be possible to begin immediate British troop reductions in the region and slash administrative costs. When Ibn Saud got to hear about the decisions made by the British at the Cairo Conference he raged that they had surrounded him with his enemies.

Even Churchill seemed to appreciate that Ibn Saud could easily wreck his plans. As he wrote to Lloyd George from Cairo as the conference neared its end, Ibn Saud, if he chose, could easily plunge the whole of Iraq 'into religious pandemonium.' He therefore proposed that he should be bought off by increasing the subsidy Britain paid to him to £100,000 per year 'paid monthly in arrears, conditional upon his maintaining the peace with Mesopotamia, Kuwait and the Hijaz'.[15] Lawrence also prevailed on Churchill to extend Palestine southwards to the head of the Red Sea at Aqaba so as to create a protective wedge between what he regarded as the growing threat presented by Ibn Saud and British Egypt. As more than one participant at the Cairo Conference commented, Churchill seemed throughout to hero-worship Lawrence and seemed almost pathetically in awe of him.

Ibn Saud accepted the British subsidy and bided his time, awaiting his chance to break the ring of hostile states and amirates around him. The weak link in the ring seemed to be Ibn Rashid and Ha'il. The previous spring Saud Ibn Abdul Aziz Ibn Rashid, who had ruled since 1909, had become the latest in the line of Rashid rulers to be murdered by another member of the Rashid family. While out shooting with his

15 Ibid. Churchill to Lloyd George, March 20th 1921.

cousin the cousin, instead of aiming at the target, had taken a pot shot at his head. The murderer had been instantly cut to pieces by Ibn Rashid's slaves, and another cousin, suspected of being involved in planning the murder, was thrown into prison. As a result a struggle for power had broken out between a number of claimants and the throne had devolved onto the eighteen-year-old son, Abdulla Ibn Rashid, of one of Ibn Rashid's slaves-girls.

So, Ibn Saud, seeing his chance, did as he had earlier around Turaba before defeating Abdullah. He sent his Ikhwan preachers into the Shammar hills around Ha'il to preach the pure doctrines of Al Wahhab to the desert tribes. The harsh unyielding doctrines of Wahhabism seemed to stir something deep within the hearts of the true men of the desert and the Shammar tribes were no exception. Soon they were afire with religious zeal, a zeal that displaced previous loyalties to the Rashids and their shaikhs. With this 'diplomacy' (*siasa*), as he described it, Ibn Saud began to undermine Abdulla's remaining power. After the Turks had been defeated Abdulla's father, Ibn Rashid, had allied himself with Sharif Husayn and hoped for his protection, but Husayn was facing growing problems of his own in the Hijaz on account of his unjust and ineffective rule. The British too had their hands full with the still unresolved insurrection in Iraq, trouble with nationalists in India and Egypt and problems with Turkey and its former colonies. The weakness of Abdulla and Ha'il was further demonstrated by the fact that a Syrian shaikh had led a party of raiders down to the important oasis town of Jauf in the far north of the Rashids' territory and seized it and Abdulla and his Shammar warriors had been unable to throw them out.

Realising that his moment had come. Ibn Saud acted with lightning speed. Duwish was sent ahead with 2,000 Ikhwan to engage the Rashid army while he stayed behind to gather the main body of his warriors, tribesmen and Ikhwan. He took the old Turkish cannons captured at Hofuf out of storage, gave each contingent of his army its orders and, at the beginning of October 1921, set off, with war banners unfurled at the head of a great desert assembly of ten thousand warriors. Both Sharif Husayn and his son, the new ruler of Iraq, Feisal, appealed to the British to help Abdulla, but they refused. This was a dispute between two rulers of the inner desert and so no concern of theirs. As Ibn Saud and his army marched reports began to come in of the Shammar tribes, their loyalty to the House of Rashid weakened by the Ikhwan preachers, surrendering to Duwish and declaring their loyalty to Ibn Saud. Others were reported to be fleeing across the border into Iraq. Young Abdulla panicked and released the cousin who had been implicated in the murder of his father from prison. But the freed cousin, instead of supporting him, immediately turned on him. Abdulla fled to Ibn Saud's advancing army and threw himself upon Ibn Saud's mercy.

The treacherous Rashid cousin now rallied some Shammar tribesmen to fight a large but indecisive battle against the advancing Saudi army and then fled back behind the great walls of Ha'il itself. When Ibn Saud had last approached Ha'il in 1916 he had been unable to capture it for lack of British artillery. Now, having had his old Turkish cannon drawn over rough tracks and stony deserts more than four hundred miles from Riyadh to Ha'il, he had them wheeled into position with much show and trained them on the town. However, he did not fire them, perhaps because his gunners had long since forgotten how to operate them and because to fire them after such a long period of disuse and lack of maintenance would probably have presented more of a danger to those attempting to fire them than to the people and walls that they were firing at. Ibn Saud knew that the sight of the guns and the threat that they presented was likely to be enough to strike fear into the already disunited and demoralised citizens of Ha'il.

The walls of Ha'il had three main gates into the town, each guarded by a separate detachment of the Rashid's men. Ibn Saud's representatives approached the commanders of each of these guard detachments and offered them bribes. After three weeks, with the townspeople becoming more hungry and despondent, one of the guard commanders weakened and opened his gate to Ibn Saud's men. Silently they flooded in and took the town with barely a fight. Abdulla's usurping cousin fled to the town's citadel fortress and with a few trusted supporters barricaded himself inside. There he held out for a further month before he and his followers also surrendered. Ha'il and the land of the Shammar was now Ibn Saud's and his family's long-time enemies were fnally vanquished. Ibn Saud then sent his son north and west to take the remaining parts of the Rashids' lands which had not already fallen to Duwish.

As ever, Ibn Saud was magnanimous in victory. Despite the complaints of the Ikhwan warriors against showing any tolerance towards people they branded as 'infidels', Ibn Saud issued strict orders that there was to be no looting and had stores of food from his own army distributed to the now starving citizens of Ha'il. The inhabitants of Ha'il who were Shia were particularly frightened that they would suffer violent reprisals at the hands of their Ikhwan conquerors, but Ibn Saud issued a special ordinance guaranteeing their safety. He married the murdered Saud Ibn Abdul Aziz Ibn Rashid's most favoured widow, adopted the orphaned Rashid children as his own and took the rest of the Rashid family members to Riyadh to live out the rest of their days in comfort within his own court as his honoured guests. Ibn Saud gave the other two wives of the murdered Rashid as brides to his eldest surviving son, Saud, and to his own younger brother. The most important officers, elements of the Rashid army and the three commanders of the detachments who had guarded Ha'il's gates were absorbed into his own army – the two who had resisted bribes being promoted faster than the one who had accepted.

Ibn Saud returned to Riyadh in triumph. Before his father, Abd al-Rahman, the *ulema* and other religious leaders, all the shaikhs and other members of his family in the great *majlis* chamber of the palace he was formally proclaimed 'Sultan', literally 'he who has authority' over all of Najd and its dependencies.

Ibn Saud was now the master of territory stretching twelve hundred miles from the borders of the new Mandate states of Transjordan and Iraq in the north, south to Asir and the British protected Sultanate of Muscat and Oman, and six hundred miles from Kuwait and the coast of the Persian Gulf with its handful of tiny British-protected Trucial Amirates to the disputed borders of Husayn's Hijaz. It was a vast territory, larger than Britain and France combined but with only a fraction of the population of either. Yet, as could be seen in his generous treatment of his vanquished Rashid enemies and their dependants, he continued to rule as he had since the day he seized Riyadh. Marriage, as evidenced by him marrying his Rashid enemy's principal wife and giving in marriage the other widowed Rashid womenfolk to other close members of his own family, continued to be an important instrument in his exercise of power. His eldest surviving sons, Saud and Faisal, were now growing into men and he gave Saud command in some of the military campaigns he waged while Faisal, following his visit to London and Paris, was encouraged to play a role in relations with countries outside the Middle East. However, Ibn Saud continued to handle relations with immediate neighbours, such as Iraq and Kuwait, himself.

The Lebanese-American writer and scholar, Ameen Rihani, arrived in Riyadh for the first time one afternoon shortly after Ibn Saud's return from the capture of Ha'il. He has left this description:

> Even as we go through the principal street to the Palace square the men look up incuriously, as we pass, and the children gape in silence. There were crowds, squatting along the walls or just visiting in the street; but there was no bustle and no visible sign of business. Even the square, which in the morning is a busy scene, was at that hour almost empty, except that part of it immediate to the Palace gate.
>
> There, was a spectacle – the first of its kind I had seen in Arabia.
>
> Along the Palace wall were clay benches in double tiers filled with people … not until I had inquired did I know the intent and purpose of these people sitting solemnly outside the Palace and in the court and corridors within. They were waiting, not meekly or beggarly, but like personages who had an appointment with their sovereign lord. Indeed, some had the mien of princes; others, whose rags were most conspicuous, were dignified enough with the inevitable bamboo stick … Thus, about five hundred people, mostly Bedu, came to the Palace twice a day in the morning and in the afternoon for two square meals. Some of them carry, concealed under the *abas*, kettles or wooden platters for the purpose of taking some rice or lamb to their kith and kin outside the city. These people have nothing to do in times of peace; they form a part of the sultan's standing army, as it were, whom he has to feed and cloth and keep content. And there are many among them, who, moreover, receive an allowance of money…[16]

16 Ameen Rihani, *Ibn Sa'oud of Arabia, His People and his Land*, Constable, London, 1928.

All were waiting to see Ibn Saud. All would be received by him in his *majlis* as was their ancient right. Each one would be listened to by him, his complaint, request or dispute dealt with by him in person as he had always done and as Arab rulers before him had done down the ages. Each would greet him by his first name and be welcomed as though as an equal, each would be sent on his way after his case or concern had been heard and attended to with a gift, usually a ceremonial cloak, sometimes with money or other goods if they were in need. Foreigners and other important visitors would receive more elaborate gifts, jewelled daggers, swords, horses, rings or occasionally slave girls. No one, no matter how lowly, ever thanked him, for the giving of such gifts by the ruler was in accordance with time-honoured desert custom. If Ibn Saud should withhold the giving of a gift to any person received in his *majlis* it was to be taken as a sign of grave displeasure. All were fed at his expense and many given food for their journeys home. As his kingdom grew in size and the number of his subjects increased he spent more and more time in his *majlis* until it was taking almost all his time except when he was away from Riyadh on campaign. His detailed knowledge of the families of all his subjects was phenomenal and this time-honoured means of direct rule through his subjects' unfettered access to him was to remain his principal source of authority and rule throughout his long reign no matter how large and complex his kingdom became. Rihani noted that outside the back door of the palace there was also a swarm of beggars and ill people. They, too, received daily helpings of food from Ibn Saud. Unstinting traditional Arab generosity, even when the funds available to his exchequer were strained, was an important element in Ibn Saud's popularity among his people. Strength of character, determination, unflagging stamina, self-confidence, courage, that quality of luck so prized among Bedouin leaders, and skill as a commander in the field had won him his domain. But his continuing accessibility and generosity remained among his principal means of maintaining the power he had won.

Beyond Riyadh he ruled through the governors he appointed and through the tribal shaikhs, each appointed by their respective tribes by the traditional means. They, like he, came to power and stayed in it only through tribal consent, arrived at among the heads and most influential members of each of the most powerful and prestigious families. As the kingdom grew bigger, more complex and the number of his subjects greater, Ibn Saud began to appoint a number of advisers, mostly foreigners with experience of the wider world beyond Arabia. But they remained just that – advisers. Real power continued to be exercised by him, using the traditional methods and in consultation with the religious authorities, *ulema* and most trusted members of his own family.

With their victories at Turaba and now Ha'il, the Ikhwan seemed to be developing a growing taste for conversion to the strict tenets of Wahhabism through conquest and for indoctrination by intimidation. Their thirst for further victories, for inflicting punishment upon 'infidels' and coercing more into acceptance of the true faith now began to threaten Ibn Saud's relationships not only with Britain's Hashemite puppet rulers but with Britain herself. The potential for trouble had been greatly exacerbated by Britain's insistence on establishing clearly defined frontiers between each of the new mandated states and the newly enlarged Najd. For the tribes, economically dependent for their survival upon being able to move freely between different areas of grazing for their animals and on raiding, the creation of permanent boundaries between the different new states and territories was not only a wholly alien concept, it was a fundamental threat to their way of life and even to their very survival. On top of these problems there was also the existence of a series of age-old feuds between the leaders of various tribes on either side of the newly established borders of Iraq, Trans-jordan and Najd, the enmity between Ibn Saud and the Hashemite rulers of the new territories and the issue of traditional rights to tax (*zakat*) collection. Conflict, therefore, seemed inevitable. So even if Ibn Saud foresaw it (he was later accused of not only foreseeing trouble but actually encouraging it), he would probably not have been able to prevent it, even if he had wanted to.

So, in March 1922, only weeks after Ibn Saud had returned from Ha'il to Riyadh in triumph, a large detachment of Ikhwan from the north-eastern Mutair and Zafir tribes led by Duwish, spurred on by elements of each of the above motives, carried out a massive raid over the border into Iraq. Their target was the camp of a new tribal force recently set up by the British Mandate authorities to guard the Iraqi border, the Iraqi Camel Corps, which had recently itself carried out a raid on the Zafir. The result was that on March 11th the Ikhwan surprised the members of the Camel Corps in their camp and massacred nearly all of them together with some members of Iraqi tribes who happened to be camped nearby. The British responded by calling in RAF planes from their airfield at Hinaidi in Iraq to bomb and strafe the Ikhwan raiders. Ibn Saud immediately ordered the Ikhwan raiders to withdraw from Iraqi territory and the hostilities came to a temporary halt. Later, to remove one of the causes of tension between the tribes loyal to Feisal and those loyal to Ibn Saud, the British disbanded the Camel Corps. The Corps' commander then fled to Riyadh and offered his services to Ibn Saud. But Ibn Saud rejected the man's offer of services and dispatched him back to Iraq laden with gifts.

Cox knew that the lull in hostilities would be short-lived unless a permanent solution was found. So he persuaded Ibn Saud to send representatives to meet a British delegation in the tiny independent Shaikhdom of Muhammara beside the confluence of the Tigris and Euphrates, on the Shatt-al-Arab south of Basra. The British insisted that a permanent border must be established between Najd and Iraq. Ibn Saud's representatives responded that any border had to be based on traditional tribal grazing grounds. The idea of fixed borders remained alien – as the Arab saying went, 'The only borders are the borders in men's hearts'. However, on May 5th 1922 an agreement of sorts was reached. Subject to ratification by the British High Commissioner in Iraq, Cox, and Ibn Saud, the tribes, or sections of tribes, whose principal traditional grazing grounds were inside what the British designated as Iraq were to be regarded as Iraqi and those whose principal traditional grazing areas lay inside the area that the British accepted as Najd were to be regarded as Najdi subjects. The tribes affected were sections of the Anaiza and the Zafir, members of which had taken part in the recent raid on the Camel Corps led by Duwish. The treaty also laid down that any tribe that carried out a cross-border raid was to be punished. Any tribe moving its animals peacefully across the border into the territory of a state to which it was not assigned under the treaty was in future going to have to pay a fee for the privilege. In addition the treaty provided for the protection of the traditional routes for those making the annual *hajj* pilgrimage to Mecca and Medina. However, when the wording of the treaty reached Ibn Saud he refused to sign it on the grounds that the Zafir and their leader had already rejected submission to Feisal and Iraq, and had sought his protection and that he had agreed to give it.

Ibn Saud almost certainly knew that the treaty of Muhammara would be unworkable and that it was likely to be the cause of more trouble than it was worth. Evidence of the truth of this was provided only weeks later when a different force of Ikhwan started advancing north-west into Transjordan, up the ancient trade route of the Wadi Sirhan, in the area where three thousand years earlier in Assyrian times generations of powerful queens had reigned in the cities of Adumatu and later the Romans had held sway in cities such as Taima and Meda'in Saleh. The Ikhwan seized Jauf, then moved west and took Taima and Tabuk, in each place converting and massacring people, claiming territory and getting the tribes to swear allegiance to Najd, and also collecting *zakat* taxes in the name of Ibn Saud and Riyadh. Having advanced along the eastern borders of Husayn's Hijaz, they moved north again up the strategically vital Wadi Sirhan into Transjordan until they were only fifteen miles from Adbullah Husayn's capital, Amman, and almost on the border of French mandated Syria. They now threatened not only Amman but were driving a wedge between the two British mandated territories of Transjordan and Iraq and cutting Britain's strategically vital projected rail link, oil pipeline and east-west communications corridor linking her Persian oil fields, Mesopotamia and the northern end of the Gulf with the Mediterranean. RAF planes and armoured columns based in both Transjordan and Iraq attacked them. Suddenly faced by noisy machines which attacked them from the sky with explosives and bullets, the Ikhwan, many of whom had never seen a machine of any kind before, turned tail and fled.

Among the RAF officers posted to Iraq at this time was a thirty-year-old named Arthur Harris. He would later become better known as Air Chief Marshal Sir Arthur Harris, 'Bomber Harris', the World War Two head of RAF Bomber Command who masterminded the mass bombing of Nazi Germany. In November 1922 he took over command of RAF Number 45 Squadron based at Hinaidi, north of Basra. Over the next three years in dealing with the Ikhwan and uprisings in Iraq and Kurdistan, Harris, along with other RAF colleagues, began to develop new techniques of 'policing by bombing'. One of his innovations was to rig up improvised bomb racks and bomb-aimer sights in slow-flying transport planes. Flying at under 70 m.p.h. these planes could pinpoint their targets and achieve a much higher degree of accuracy when dropping their bombs. As a result the number of casualties they inflicted was greatly increased, terrorising the Ikhwan raiding parties.

Ibn Saud, realising that the latest Ikhwan raids had seriously jeopardised his relations with Britain and risked bringing down the combined might of Britain, Sharif Husayn and all his sons plus the families of all the tribes among whom the Ikhwan had carried out massacres, was furious. He summoned the leaders of the Ikhwan tribes who were responsible to Riyadh, arrested them and threw them in jail for three months. At the end of that time, before releasing them, he had them brought before him: 'Think not, ye Ikhwan,' he said in a crushingly dismissive tone and with his face set like granite, 'that we consider you of much value. Think not that you have rendered us great service and that we need you. Your real value, ye Ikhwan, is in obedience to Allah and then to us. When you go beyond that you will be punished. And do not forget', he thundered, 'that there is not one among you whose father or brother or cousin we have not slain. Aye *billah*! [in the name of God] it was by the sword that we conquered you. And that same sword is still above your heads. Beware, ye Ikhwan. Encroach not upon the rights of others. If you do, your value and that of the dust are the same ... We took you by the sword, and we shall keep you within your bounds by the sword, *inshallah*. [if God wills].'[17]

The British knew that a permanent solution to these border disputes and raids had to be found and in September Cox had sent Harold Dickson, who had recently married and been transferred from Bahrain to serve as a political officer in charge of a region of Iraq, back to Bahrain on a special mission. His task was to make contact with Ibn Saud and persuade him to come to Uqair, the Hasa port where he had met Cox two years earlier, and meet face-to-face with Cox once more.

17 Quoted by Rihani, op. cit. who was present when Ibn Saud made this speech.

Shortly after arriving in Bahrain Dickson was informed that a certain Major Frank Holmes, a mining engineer, and a Dr Alex Mann, a Jewish physician who had once been on Cox's staff and so was known to Dickson, who had attended Ibn Saud in Riyadh and recently been appointed by Ibn Saud as his representative in London, were due to arrive shortly in Bahrain. Both Holmes and Mann were now in the employ of a company called The Eastern and General Syndicate Limited of London. They were travelling on Ibn Saud's instructions on a planned visit to the Arabian interior. Ibn Saud had requested that the Dicksons put up the visitors during their brief stop-over in Bahrain in the same official Saudi guesthouse where Dickson and his new wife were staying and also feed them. Dickson happily agreed. His suspicions about the visitors and the real purpose of their visit had been aroused and having them to stay in the house would give the Dicksons a good chance to quiz them. At the same time, as soon as he received the news of Holmes and Mann's visit he wired his boss, Cox, in code. Two years previously, while he had been Britain's Political Agent in Bahrain, Dickson had heard repeated rumours of there being an oil seepage at a site some six miles north-east of the port of Qatif, inside Saudi territory at a place known as Dhahran. An oil seepage was often a sign that below ground there was a reservoir of oil. On his days off during his service in Bahrain Dickson had made a number of visits to the Dhahran area and ridden all over the reported site several times on a camel. But he had failed to find any trace of any oil seepage. However, a local shaikh on a small island just off Dhahran had shown him a copy of an official Turkish report, dating from the time before Ibn Saud had seized control of Hasa, which stated categorically that an oil seepage was known to exist at a site close to Qatif. Dickson now suspected that Ibn Saud had got wind of this same Turkish report and had invited Holmes and Mann to carry out a search in the hope of finding oil.

The very next day, following Dickson's coded wire to Cox, Holmes and Mann disembarked in Bahrain from the slow mail boat which plied a regular mail delivery and passenger service between the various ports and landing places up and down the Persian Gulf. Holmes, decidedly tubby and perspiring, presented a strange sight and soon had Dickson and his wife, Violet, suppressing their laughter. As well as wearing a tightly buttoned suit he carried a large white umbrella lined with green material and wore a white pith helmet of the type issued by the French to their troops stationed in Africa. Over this and hanging down across his face he had attached a large piece of fine green gauze as a veil. Dickson commented, he looked like a tourist on his way to visit the Pyramids in Egypt. The Dicksons also marvelled at 'the amazing number of presents Holmes had brought for Ibn Saud. There must have been over fifty cases, leather bags, boxes and guns.'[18]

The Dicksons quickly discovered that Holmes was an unusually interesting and amusing guest, effusive and full of stories. He was a New Zealander who spoke English with a New Zealand accent peppered with words and phrases of New York slang. Trained as an engineer, he had lived in America, had worked for Herbert Hoover in China before the war, served with the British as a Royal Marine during the war and travelled widely in the Middle East but did not speak Arabic. He exuded charm, seemed to have met everyone and had contacts everywhere. But, as the Dicksons soon discovered, he had bladder trouble. How, he wondered aloud to the Dicksons, was he going to manage the journey by camel to Hofuf and possibly beyond to meet Ibn Saud? Dickson, who had made the journey a number of times while he was stationed in Bahrain, was able to provide him with a number of tips.

A week later the Dicksons were surprised by the arrival of two motorised dhows which drew alongide and moored on the quayside in front of the house where the Dicksons and their guests were lodging. Over a traditional British bacon-and-eggs breakfast before their guests' departure, Harold Dickson asked Holmes why he needed two dhows. 'Ah,' he replied, 'one is for Dr Mann, who goes via Uqair, and the other is for me, for my journey takes me via Qatif.'

Dickson was surprised. 'But you are a sick man,' he said. 'Why ride a hundred miles by camel when, by the Uqair route, you will only have to cover a bare fifty?'

Holmes, Dickson later recalled, immediately became 'mysterious'. 'Dickson, I am a butterfly collector, and I have been told that a

18 H. R. P. Dickson, *Kuwait and her Neighbours*, George Allen & Unwin, London, 1956.

wonderful black variety, known nowhere else in the world, is to be found in the Qatif oasis. I have already called it the Black Admiral of Qatif and am out to get a specimen. Then my name will be famous.'

Violet Dickson, who had been quietly getting on with her bacon and eggs, looked up and barely pausing between mouthfuls, said quietly: 'Major Holmes, this is the first time I've heard of an oil seepage being called by the name of a butterfly.'

The effect was electric. Holmes jumped up from his chair saying, 'What on earth do you mean, Mrs Dickson?'

'Exactly what I have said.'

Holmes, now clearly taken aback, rushed round the table and clasped Violet Dickson's hand. 'My God, you are a wonderful woman!' he exclaimed. 'I shall telegraph today to the curator of the Zoological Gardens in London and ask that you be made a Fellow of the Zoo.'

Holmes and Mann departed in their two dhows and shortly afterwards, to her surprise, Violet Dickson received a letter from the Zoological Society of London informing her that she had been elected a Fellow.[19]

* * *

The Eastern and General Syndicate Limited of London, the company for which Major Holmes and Dr Mann worked, was a company set up by a small group of speculators two years earlier to search out and acquire the rights to potential oil and mineral concessions which, lacking the funds to develop and exploit them itself, it then sought to sell on at a profit to larger companies. When Dickson, accompanying Sir Percy Cox and his aides, arrived in Uqair a few weeks later, on November 21st, for the long-sought meeting with Ibn Saud intended to resolve the various border disputes, he found Major Holmes was already there. It seemed that he had met Ibn Saud in Hofuf and then travelled down to Uqair with him. He had pitched his tent between the large white tents that Ibn Saud had had put up for the British and those Ibn Saud had had erected for his own large party. Ibn Saud's entourage included a personal bodyguard of three hundred men and Saud Al Kabir, his Araif cousin

19 Based on the account of H. R. P. Dickson, op. cit.

and husband of his favourite sister Nura, who he had spared from execution outside the walls of Layla after the 1910 Araif revolt. Another member of Ibn Saud's party was a trusted Najdi merchant and Basra banker, Abdul Latif Pasha al Mendil, who he had brought with him to provide commercial advice during the negotiations. Also present at Uqair was Ameen Rihani, who had contrived to get himself taken on by Ibn Saud as an interpreter and general adviser. He would later write a colourful, blow-by-blow account of those parts of the negotiations at which he was present. While he was waiting for the British to arrive at Uqair Ibn Saud had told Rihani: 'People think that we are receiving large sums of money from the Inglaiz. But of a truth, they have only paid small sums considering our services in their behalf. What we have done for the Inglaiz during the war and after no other Arab could do. And we will keep faith with them, even through loss and injury, so long as they keep faith with us ... Be assured, the Inglaiz are my debtors. But I make no claims. And yet see what they have done to me – to Ibn Saud their friend and ally. They spin, and spin – spin nets for me. They have surrounded me with enemies – set up states which they are supporting against me.' Raging against the calumnies heaped upon his head by Sharif Husayn and his sons, Ibn Saud had finished, 'We will not concede a jot of our rights. And we ask for nothing that is not ours, which our forbears have not always enjoyed. Let the Inglaiz know that.' Then striking the carpet in front of him with the long cane he always carried, he added, 'And let the Sharif and his sons know it.' And he struck the carpet again. Ibn Saud knew what he was about to get into by coming to Uqair to meet Sir Percy Cox and he also knew what his long-term goals were.

Among the people Sir Percy had brought with him was the head of a section of the Anaiza tribe, Sabih Beg, to represent the newly created mandate state of Iraq, and Major Trevor, the officer who had met Ibn Saud with Captain Shakespear at Uqair nine years previously, when Ibn Saud had sought in vain for British protection if he should seek to free himself from Turkish subjection. Major Trevor was now himself the British Agent in Kuwait, as Shakespear had been in 1913.

The conference got down to business the next day. After various polite speeches by all sides Sir Percy explained that as a friend of Iraq and Najd, His Majesty's Government wished that there should be an amicable settlement of the border disputes between them. He then turned to Sabih Beg and asked him to say what he thought would be a fair boundary line. Beg jumped to his feet and said: 'Since God created the world and history began to be written, Iraq's boundary extends south to within twelve miles of Ibn Saud's capital, Riyadh. It runs west to the Red Sea, so as to include Ha'il, Medina and Yanbo, and east to include Hofuf and Qatif on the Persian Gulf. As God is my witness, this and only this is the true boundary and cannot be disputed.'

Ibn Saud rose and roared back, 'I know nothing about creation, but I do know that from the days of Abraham, my great-grandparent, the territories of Najd and the Bedouin world have extended as far north as Aleppo [in the north of the French Mandate area of Syria] ... and included the whole country on the right bank of the Euphrates from there down to Basra on the Persian Gulf.'[20]

For the next five days the conference continued in this vein, with both sides being completely intransigent. Ibn Saud implied that by agreeing to any boundary at all his representative at the earlier Muhammara conference had disobeyed his instructions. He refused to accept any boundary based on a line drawn on a map and insisted that the dispute could only be resolved by accepting the right of tribes to enter and graze across all the territory and around all the wells within their traditional grazing areas. This meant that certain tribes loyal to him must be granted access annually right up to the river Euphrates. Since the days of Abraham each tribe had known which wells were its wells, which grazing grounds its grazing grounds and which wells were common property. This, he insisted, was an issue of life and death for the members of these tribes. The boundary must be based on these territories and the common wells and grazing grounds should be declared neutral.

By the sixth day, although the two sides had modified their demands somewhat they were still a long way short of any workable compromise. On top of which, Major Trevor had so far said almost nothing about the minimum demands of Kuwait. Telling both sides that the way they were going it would be a year at least before anything would be settled, Sir Percy then summoned each of the leaders in turn to meet him in private.

20 H. R. P. Dickson, op. cit.

He started with Ibn Saud. With only Harold Dickson present to act as interpreter (although Cox's Arabic was good his vernacular Arabic was not as good as Dickson's), Sir Percy confronted Ibn Saud, scolding him for his childish attitude over the frontiers and his arguments about tribal boundaries. It was astonishing, as Dickson later wrote, to watch the Sultan of Najd being 'reprimanded like a naughty schoolboy'. He, Sir Percy, would now himself decide on the line and type of the frontier. Ibn Saud seemed almost to break down. Sir Percy was his father and mother, he said pathetically, who had made him and raised him from nothing to the position he now held. He would surrender half his kingdom, nay the whole, if Sir Percy ordered him to.[21]

After this Ibn Saud seemed to withdraw from the conference for the rest of the day, leaving it to Sir Percy and Abdul Latif Pasha to decide the frontiers between them. Calling all the other delegates to the conference together, Sir Percy took a red pencil and very carefully drew a line on a map of Arabia from the Persian Gulf to a point close to the frontier of Transjordan. This gave Iraq a large chunk of the territory that Ibn Saud had claimed for Najd, but then Sir Percy drew a second line, taking nearly two-thirds of the territory claimed by Kuwait and gave it to Najd, saying that the power exercised over this desert region by Kuwait was now much less than it had been before the war in the days of the Anglo-Turkish Agreement. Next Sir Percy drew two diamond shapes, one to the west and one to the south of Kuwait. These, he declared, were to be known as the Iraq Neutral Zone and the Kuwait Neutral Zone. When Abdul Latif Pasha interrupted, saying that there was no need for a Kuwait Neutral Zone, Sir Percy responded that the tribes of Kuwait also needed their grazing grounds. But Abdul Latif Pasha was still not satisfied. Whereupon Sir Percy asked him sharply: 'Why, pray, are you so anxious that this area go to Najd?'

'Quite candidly', Abdul Latif Pasha replied, 'because we think oil exists there.'

Cox and Dickson exchanged a surreptitious glance. 'That', retorted Sir Percy, 'is exactly why I have made it a neutral zone. Each side shall have a half-share.'

21 See Dickson, op. cit. p. 274.

Later that evening Ibn Saud sent Sir Percy a message asking to see him alone. Taking Harold Dickson with him, Sir Percy went to Ibn Saud's great reception tent. There they found him alone, standing in the centre of the huge tent, a picture of grief and dejection.

'My friend,' the great warrior Sultan moaned, 'you have deprived me of half my kingdom. Better take it all and let me go into retirement.' Then he burst into tears. Distressed, Sir Percy seized Ibn Saud's hand and began to weep as well. There they stood in the gently flickering lamplight, the great Arab warrior and the veteran British diplomat, grasping each others hands, tears rolling down their checks, magnificent together in grief.

'My friend,' Sir Percy said through their sobs, 'I knew exactly how you felt, and for this reason I gave you two-thirds of Kuwait's territory. I don't know how Ibn Sabah [the new ruler of Kuwait] will take the blow.'

As Dickson commented many years later, both were great men – and great actors too.[22]

The boundary lines drawn by Sir Percy earlier that afternoon stood and remained unchanged until long after the end of the Second World War. The imposition of this Western-style boundary line restricted the traditional annual movements of the tribes and their animals for almost the first time in more than ten thousand years, since the era in which camels and domesticated agricultural animals were first introduced into the region. Although the lines on the map and the borders they delineated stood, they did not end the trouble with the Ikhwan.

Signing the Uqair Protocols was almost Sir Percy's last public act before retirement. A similar conference to try to resolve the border problems with Transjordan held in Kuwait a year later, after Sir Percy had retired, ended in failure.

During all the time that the emotional discussions about borders were being played out directly between Sir Percy, Ibn Saud and Sabih Beg, another drama was also being played out in the camp at Uqair which involved Major Frank Holmes. Holmes' presence at Uqair was an embarrassment to Sir Percy, especially since Dickson's suspicion that his real purpose in coming to the region was to obtain the Qatif-Dhahran oil concession had been shown to be correct. Sir Percy knew

22 See Dickson, op. cit.

that the Anglo-Persian Oil Company, which had been working the oil fields in Persia productively since 1908 and in which the British Government held a large shareholding, was at that very time also actively interested in obtaining the concession to search for oil in exactly the same area. More embarrassing still for Sir Percy, Sir Arnold Wilson, the man he had replaced as Britain's senior representative in Iraq after the British Government had decided that Wilson's high-handed policies could have helped to provoke the revolt in Iraq, was now the Head of Anglo-Persian's Middle Eastern operations. During the course of the negotiations at Uqair Sir Percy had received a letter from Wilson in which Wilson had said that he was planning to visit Ibn Saud shortly and 'maybe we can strike a deal about oil'.[23]

Sir Percy could hardly refuse to use his good offices with Ibn Saud on Sir Arnold's behalf over the granting of the Qatif-Dhahran oil concession, especially as the government which he himself served as its senior representative in the region had a major stake in Sir Arnold's company. So when Holmes approached Sir Percy for his advice and help over obtaining the concession for Eastern and General Sir Percy advised him to 'Go slow about the concession. The time is not yet ripe for it,' adding that the British Government was not in a position to 'afford your company any protection'.

On the same day as the emotional outburst between Sir Percy and Ibn Saud, Holmes approached Ameen Rihani as 'a friend at court' and asked for his advice about obtaining the oil concession. Rihani was not forthcoming, telling Holmes only that he believed, 'The less a company applying for a concession has to do with politics the better for the Sultan.' The following day, during a private conversation with Sir Percy and Dickson, Ibn Saud himself raised the question of the oil concession and sought Sir Percy's advice on whether he should grant it to Eastern and General. He told Sir Percy all about Holmes's visit to Hasa and that Holmes had now applied to him to be granted an immediate concession. Would His Majesty's Government have any objection, he wanted to know, if he granted Holmes and Eastern and General the concession?

'No,' said Sir Percy, 'go ahead.' But, he warned, Eastern and General

23 Rihani op. cit. p. 84.

is not an oil company. They will probably sell the concession on to someone else. Ibn Saud thanked Sir Percy and then called in Major Holmes. Holmes restated his case and his belief that there was a strong possibility of finding oil and maybe copper as well, outlining on a map the concession area that he wanted. Sir Percy did little to disguise his dislike of Holmes or that he thought he had no business intruding on an inter-governmental conference and negotiation in the way that he had. Later Sir Percy wrote out a letter in pencil for Ibn Saud to send to Holmes refusing his request for the concession, requesting that Ibn Saud have the letter copied out and that he sign it, and send him a copy. Three times Ibn Saud declined to be dictated to in this way, but in the end, fearing that if he did not he might lose his annual British subsidy, he did have the letter copied and signed it.

However, four months later, Britain announced that it was ending all subsidies to rulers in Arabia and the Middle East. Frank Holmes immediately set out for a fresh meeting with Ibn Saud and this time, with Ibn Saud desperate to make up the shortfall in his income, Holmes got his oil concession. However, Eastern and General did little with the concession. They, like Dickson, failed to find the oil seepages reported by the Turks. The natural and continuous shifting of the sand dunes under pressure from the winds had buried them. After a few years Eastern and General stopped paying their rent and the concession lapsed.

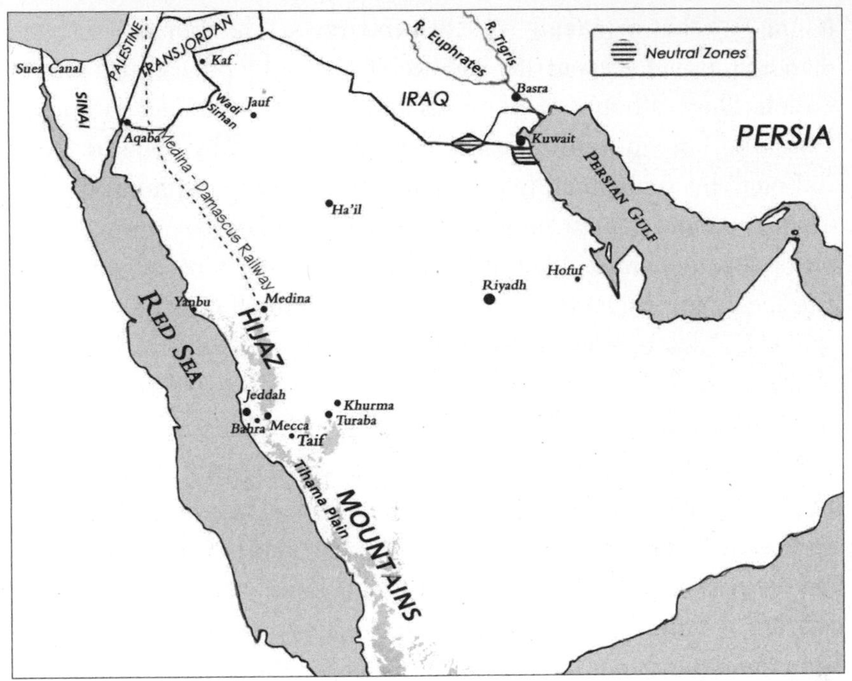

CHAPTER 9

'Calif Out'

'Calif Out' read the headline above the article in *Time Magazine*.

On March 3rd 1924 Ataturk, the new charismatic nationalist leader of Turkey, and the Turkish National Assembly abolished the Caliphate and sent the Caliph and his family into exile. Henceforth Turkey was to be a secular state. As *The Times* of London commented in its leader two days later: 'Of all the vast changes wrought by the war ... no single change is more striking to the imagination than this and few, perhaps may prove so important in their ultimate results.'[1]

Two days later Sharif Husayn proclaimed himself Caliph, the leader of the world's Muslims – all 220 million of them. He founded his claim

1 *Time Magazine*, March 17th 1924. *The Times*, March 5th 1924.

on the fact that his family were descendants of The Prophet and more than a thousand years earlier had been Caliphs. By proclaiming himself Caliph, Husayn hoped to boost his authority and prestige, both in the Hijaz and abroad. But his claim had the diametrically opposite effect. Although his sons dutifully proclaimed their loyalty to him as the new Caliph and that of their subjects in the new mandated states over which they ruled, millions of other Muslims all around the Muslim world were outraged. No man had the right to proclaim himself Caliph, least of all, perhaps, Husayn, who had proved himself an appallingly bad guardian of the Holy Places. Corruption and bribery were rife throughout his state and government. He had imposed ever higher taxes on his own subjects and on the pilgrims who came to the Hijaz to make the *Hajj*. Far from protecting the pilgrim routes he had allowed robbers to prey upon them with impunity. He had allowed all kinds of extortionists and crooks free play among them, turning a blind eye when they fleeced the pilgrims for food and accommodation. He did not provide even the most basic sanitation or medical services for the pilgrims. On top of which Husayn had become ever more vain and unreasonable. Even his sons were now tiring of his interference in their affairs, of the way he treated them as his vassals, issuing them with orders and telling them what policies to pursue in the countries over which they ruled. The British too, were becoming weary of him, of his waywardness, vanity and unreasonable demands. He steadfastly refused to ratify the Treaty of Versailles even after the British had sent T. E. Lawrence to reason with him, his grounds being that Syria had not been handed to him and his sons but had been passed over to French control and that Palestine had been made a British mandate. Another problem for the British was that, as the rulers of millions of Muslim subjects, especially in Egypt, the Indian subcontinent and the Far East, they were now finding their continued support for Husayn a growing liability.

Nowhere was Husayn's assumption of the Caliphate more resented than in Najd, among the Wahhabis and by Ibn Saud. The Ikhwan above all were incensed. In this, in the dwindling support of the British, the resentment of Husayn's bad stewardship of the Holy Places and the H*ajj*, and the reaction to his assumption of the Caliphate, Ibn Saud saw his opportunity – the opportunity he had been waiting for for so long –

the opportunity to overthrow Husayn, conquer the Hijaz and retake the Holy Cities. Immediately news reached him of Husayn's assumption of the Caliphate he sent him an open message publicly warning him that he would never accept him as Caliph unless he was elected by all Muslims everywhere.

Yet characteristically Ibn Saud did not rush headlong into action. Instead he moved cautiously, testing the ground each step of the way and building his support. He also took longer to act because he had been unwell. A skin disease producing ulcers had affected the area around his left eye. His own doctor's treatment had only made the condition worse and by the time a properly qualified doctor had been brought from Egypt it was too late. He had lost most of the sight in his left eye.

He began preparing the ground against Husayn, as he had before earlier campaigns, by sending preachers among the tribes of the eastern Hijaz to fan their discontent with Husayn's rule. At the same time in order to maintain his good relations with the British he severely punished any errant Bedouins who mounted a *ghazzu* across the frontier into Iraq. Then, on June 4th 1924 he called a great assembly of all the tribal, military, religious and Ikhwan leaders in the great covered courtyard of his father Abd al-Rahman's palace. This was a religious matter, affecting Muslims in all countries rather than just an issue facing the ruler of Najd and Ibn Saud persuaded his father to preside over the great assembly. Ibn Saud sat humbly to one side, listening to the debate but taking very little part. Flanked by the *ulema*, Abd al-Rahman, shrewd and alert as ever but with the added dignity of his great age and experience, called upon the leaders one by one to speak their minds on what was to be done about the usurper Caliph, Husayn, and the Holy Sites of Islam. Leader after leader spoke out against Husayn, calling for the Hijaz to be attacked, the Holy Cities taken and Husayn deposed. For two years Husayn had prevented Ibn Saud's subjects from undertaking the *Hajj* on the grounds that he feared what members of the Ikhwan might do if they were allowed to enter Mecca. So it was the Ikhwan who were now most eager for immediate action.

But at this point Ibn Saud himself entered the debate to counsel caution. The Holy Sites did not belong to the Wahhabis alone but to all Muslims. They must therefore seek other Muslims' sanction before making any move. The Ikhwan leaders were impatient with this approach. For them good Muslims were Wahhabis and all those who were not Wahhabis were guilty of heresy. To them their duty was clear, to follow their consciences and act now. But bit by bit, through patient argument, Ibn Saud quietened them. Finally it was decided to send a message from this conference of the Wahhabi faithful to Muslims all over the world, seeking their agreement to action. The message detailed all the sins of Husayn and cited the doctrine known as 'the General Islamic Mandate' which decreed that Mecca must be protected and the pilgrimage and Holy Sites kept open for all Muslims.

The message met with few responses. But among those who did reply were the leaders of the sixty million Muslims of India. They were enthusiastic for action. With their support it now seemed less likely that if Ibn Saud did act and launch an attack on Husayn and Mecca the British would intervene against him. But still he did not move. On July 13th, during *Eid al-Adha*, the festival which marks the end of the pilgrimage season and commemorates the sacrifice by Abraham of his son, a season when gifts are distributed to the poor and large-scale community prayers said, Ibn Saud called a further conference. This time he confined those attending mainly to the Ikhwan and *ulema*. As a result and with their support a 'Green Book' was circulated among all the Islamic nations and communities explaining the decision to invade.

Now, having tested the ground, marshalled his support, justified his action and waited to see who, if anyone, would oppose him, Ibn Saud moved. But still he did not mount a direct frontal assault on Mecca. Instead, staying behind in Riyadh himself so that he could still disown the attacks if the British intervened, he sent out five separate columns of Ikhwan to probe what opposition they would encounter and confuse Husayn about where the main attack would fall. He had Ibn Bijad and his Ataiba warriors mount a series of raids up and down the eastern frontier of the Hijaz. Another column went north towards the border with Iraq but did not cross it, a third was sent northwest to cut the railway line linking Medina and Damascus, a fourth north through the Wadi Sirhan from Jauf into Transjordan, so making it more difficult for the British or Abdullah and Feisal to come to their father Husayn's aid. The Ikhwan who raided, looted and murdered inside Transjordan were eventually driven back across the border not by Husayn's sons but the aircraft of the RAF, but the other columns advanced unopposed.

The fifth and largest column of Ikhwan, under Khalid bin Luai, pushed west through Khurma in the direction of Mecca. As they marched, more and more fighters, eager to be rid of Husayn and hoping to benefit from the loot they might capture, joined them as they went. By late August they were approaching Taif, high among the greenery and granite of the Hijaz mountains and less than fifty miles south-east of Mecca itself. Almost five thousand feet above sea level, Taif's cool and sparkling climate had for centuries made it the ideal summer retreat from the intense heat and humidity of Mecca for the city's rulers and wealthy merchants. A place of generous gardens set behind high stone walls, well-proportioned houses and interesting narrow streets and alleys, Taif was not a large city, yet it contained the summer palaces of successive rulers of Mecca. That August as bin Luai and his Ikhwan neared Taif they heard that Husayn's son Ali was staying in the town. It seemed too good an opportunity to let slip. So with Ibn Saud still in Riyadh, a good two weeks camel ride away, and with no time to await his orders, bin Luai sent urgent word to Ibn Bijad, calling on him and his Ataiba warriors to join him and prepare to attack the town.

At the beginning of September, as soon as Ibn Bijad had reached bin Luai, they and their men approached the town and prepared to attack. Ali and his force were better armed than their attackers and should have been able to defend Taif which, as well as having strong stone walls, had a well-appointed fortress and generous reserves of food. Yet on the night of September 4th Ali, who was no soldier and had been passed over during the war by Lawrence and the British in favour of his brothers Abdullah and Feisal as leaders of the Arab Revolt, fled the town under the cover of darkness. Most of his soldiers followed him, leaving Taif and its inhabitants to their fate.

After making a truce with bin Luai and Ibn Bijad the townspeople opened the gates and the Ikhwan marched in. What happened next is still disputed. The Ikhwan later claimed that they were fired on from a police post, but whether provoked or not, what had been a bloodless victory was suddenly transformed into an orgy of blood-letting. The Ikhwan rampaged from house to house, smashing the doors down, looting valuables and killing every man and boy they found. Taif's *ulema* and religious leaders fled into the mosque, but the Ikhwan followed them, broke in and murdered them. The mosque contained a number of domed tombs which to the Ikhwan made it a place of idol worship. They smashed the tombs and desecrated the mosque. All night long they raged through the town killing and looting while families cowered in their homes behind barricaded doors and windows. It was not until morning that Ibn Bijad and bin Luai restored order among their followers. But by then more than three hundred of Taif's citizens were dead. Ibn Saud is said to have wept when he was told what had been done in the name of Allah in Taif. Although not as bloody in bald numbers, this seemed ominously like an echo of the massacre that had occurred in the same city when the Wahhabis had last seized it in 1802.

The town's surviving inhabitants were allowed to go free to Mecca. On the road some of the survivors caught up with stragglers from Ali's retreating army and murdered them in revenge for deserting them to their fate in Taif. At last, on the precipitate edge of the foothills overlooking Mecca itself, Ali and the remnants of his army turned to fight bin Luai and Ibn Bijad's pursuing Ikhwan. But the Ikhwan did not so much as pause. They rushed straight at Ali and his army, broke through their hastily prepared line, scattering them and sending them fleeing headlong in the direction of Mecca. Terrified for their lives, many of Ali's men and the refugees from Taif did not even pause when they reached Mecca but instead bypassed it and headed straight for Jeddah and the Red Sea coast. Reaching the coast, many boarded boats and fled across the sea, only halting when they reached the eastern coast of Upper Egypt and the Sudan.

Mecca now lay at the mercy of Bin Luai and Ibn Bijad's Ikhwan, its inhabitants paralysed by fear. As refugees from Taif had poured into the city they had brought with them horrific tales of the slaughter carried out by the Ikhwan. As those tales passed from mouth to mouth they grew in each re-telling until blind terror held every corner and pocket of each house and alley, and every man, woman and child in the entire city of Mecca was held in its unyielding, cold iron grip.

Ali had rushed back to Mecca but his father had refused even to see him, accusing him of cowardice and having him chased out of the palace. He told him to be gone to the safety of Jeddah.[2] Raging up and down in his palace the old man barked out his orders, summoning the Hijazi tribes and swearing that he would resist. He also sent urgent messages to the British for assistance. But by the time Taif had fallen the people of the Hijaz had become so heartily sick of Husayn 'that they would welcome almost any change'.[3] As a result the tribes did not answer Husayn's call and the British failed to respond. Even his own soldiers and servants began to leave. Outside the palace a crowd began to form, shouting for him to go. Some were for storming the palace and killing him, others for capturing him and handing him over to the Ikhwan in return for their own safety. A delegation of the Hijaz's nobility, his own wider family, leading merchants and the *ulema*, all by now convinced that getting rid of Husayn was their only chance of saving themselves from the wrath of the Ikhwan, came to the palace and begged him to abdicate in favour of his son Ali. Yet still the old man refused, dismissing them with the words that he was no coward and he would fight. Eventually it was his Turkish wife, believed to be the only person who could get him to see reason when he was angry, who persuaded him to leave while there was still a chance of saving his skin. So at last, on October 3rd 1924, he signed the abdication document and his son Ali was proclaimed ruler in his father's place.

Yet still the old man did not leave. Three more days passed as rumours spread of frantic activity going on inside the palace. The reason became clear on October 6th when a column of Husayn's six motor cars, the only motor cars that he had allowed to be imported into the kingdom, drove out of the palace. Each one was piled high with his most valuable possessions and all the members of his immediate family who had

2 According to some accounts, e.g. H. St John Philby, *Sa'udi Arabia,* op. cit., Ali dared not face his father, but after fleeing from the battle by-passed Mecca and fled straight to Jeddah. According to others, e.g. Robert Lacey, *The Kingdom*, op. cit., it was Ali who persuaded his father to abdicate.

3 Bullard, Sir Reader, *Two Kings in Arabia: Sir Reader Bullard's letters from Jeddah*, Edited by E. C. Hodgkin, Ithaca Press, Reading, England, 1993. Bullard was a member of the British Legation's staff in Jeddah and expressed this opinion in a letter home to his family at the time.

remained with him. Husayn himself, maintaining a kind of dignity to the end and showing not a morsel of fear, rode by himself in the lead car, surrounded by his personal bodyguards who stood on the car's running-boards. As Husayn and his pathetic entourage drove through the city and out on to the road to the coast, sullen crowds lined the streets watching in silence as he passed. At Jeddah Husayn personally supervised the loading of the contents of the cars onto the old coaster which he called his royal yacht. Amongst the possessions which he saw loaded were several tightly sealed and soldered petrol cans. These contained the fortune in gold coins which he had amassed out of his wartime subsidy from the British and the taxes which he had extorted from his subjects and the pilgrims making the *Hajj*. On October 16th his so-called yacht set sail. Yet even then fate seemed to hesitate about letting Husayn go. Just hours after setting sail his ship ran aground on a reef. But a few hours later fate seemed to change her mind. The tide and wind floated Husayn's ship clear and it then sailed on without further mishap to Aqaba. Later the British allowed him to settle in Cyprus. Six years later he had a stroke and was permitted to return to Transjordan to live with his son Abdullah. He died there shortly afterwards. To sum up in the words of H. C. Armstrong, Husayn had been 'to the end a pig-headed, irascible, preposterous old man, yet clean living and devout, without fear and also without common sense'.[4]

Meanwhile Ali had returned to Mecca and again attempted to make some sort of truce with Ibn Saud or get assistance from the British. But both turned him down. For the British this was now a religious dispute and therefore none of their business. Ali set up a representative council of the nobility and for a few brief days the Hijaz became a kind of dilute constitutional monarchy. Ali did not claim the Caliphate which lapsed and to this day has never been restored.

Bin Luai and Ibn Bijad had continued to advance on Mecca and had made camp on the road just outside the city. As soon as he had heard of what had happened in Taif, Ibn Saud had sent messengers on two of

4 The precise details of Mecca's fall, Husayn's abdication and departure, and of what happened next in Mecca, remain unclear, differing slightly in every account. Yet the broad outlines remain clear.

his fastest camels to bin Luai and Ibn Bijad bearing the strictest of instructions that when the Ikhwan entered Mecca there was on no account to be any repeat of the massacre and looting that had taken place in Taif.

Ali, no fighter and still with no additional reinforcements from the other Hijazi tribal leaders, decided that resistance was pointless and withdrew from Mecca, taking with him the members of Mecca's police force. Having reached the coast he barricaded himself behind the strong, well-fortified walls of Jeddah.

The day after Ali left Mecca the Ikhwan leaders sent forward four of their men on camels, unarmed and dressed in the plain white robes of pilgrims. The four rode slowly through the empty, shuttered streets of the city and at each deserted market place and major meeting point they halted and called out in loud voices, proclaiming a promise of security for each and every inhabitant: 'The people of Mecca – The Neighbours of God – are under the protection of God and Ibn Saud', they cried. The people of the city, cowering behind locked doors and peering through cracks in the shuttered and barred windows, heard and saw the four men, but remained afraid.

The following day bin Luai and Ibn Bijad, at the head of two thousand men, all of whom had purified themselves in accordance with Islamic ritual practice and were wearing white, entered the city riding camels but carrying rifles and swords in contravention of the sacred prohibition on carrying arms inside Mecca. They prayed and circled the Ka'aba with all due reverence. Some domed tombs were smashed and ornaments inside the mosques destroyed, musical instruments were broken and pictures of human beings defaced. But no looting took place and no one was killed. After these acts of 'purification' bin Luai, Ibn Bijad and their men returned peacefully to their camp outside the city. A few days later some of the Ikhwan warriors are reputed to have broken into Husayn's palace and led a donkey into what had been Husayn's *majlis* and, placing one of Husayn's old turbans on the donkey's head, tied it in the place where Husayn had had his seat. Later these same men are said to have driven the donkey around the town, still with Husayn's turban on its head, to have kicked one of Husayn's bejewelled Constantinople-tailored coats and his state umbrella through the town into the market place and sold them there for a few pence each.[5] Slowly, as the days passed and the Ikhwan did no further violence in Mecca, the citizens' fear started to ease and they began to re-emerge from their houses. The hated Husayn had gone and life in the city began to return to normal.

Having conquered Mecca without a fight, bin Luai, Ibn Bijad and their armies spread out across the surrounding country. Tribe after tribe and village after village offered their submission until the only significant places in the whole of the Hijaz which held out were the ports of Jeddah and Yanbu, and Medina, more than two hundred miles away to the north. Still Ibn Saud did not hurry to Mecca to claim his conquest of the Holy Places, instead he held back in Riyadh and in answer to anxious inquiries from governments around the Muslim world about the future governance of the Holy Cities by the Wahhabis (Muslims were all too aware of the brutal way in which the Wahhabis had imposed their own customs and doctrines when they had last controlled Mecca a century earlier), he sent out a proclamation designed to reassure his fellow Muslims. Ibn Saud knew his own family's history well – how the last time they had captured Mecca and imposed their will upon it, it had led to the loss of their own capital, Dariya, and the destruction of the whole Wahhabi state. He had no intention of repeating his family's earlier mistakes. So now he issued a solemn statement for circulation throughout the whole Islamic World. His sole purpose, he declared, in invading the Hijaz was to guarantee the freedom of the Pilgrimage and evict the blasphemous false Caliph, Husayn, and his family. He had no intention of annexing or dominating the land of the Holy Cities. He would leave the nature and style of their and the Hijaz's governance to be determined by the Muslim world itself.

It was only after issuing this declaration and other reassurances that, in mid-November 1924, Ibn Saud set out for Mecca. He rode at the head of an army said to number 50,000.[6] Yet still he did not hurry. It took

5 The story of the donkey, Husayn's coat and state umbrella were told to Eldon Rutter, an English Muslim convert who visited Mecca while making the *Hajj* one year later, by a Meccan citizen who had been in the city when it fell. When Rutter asked his informant if he had actually witnessed these events the man confessed that he had not but had heard it from others who had. See Rutter, *The Holy Cities of Arabia*, Westminster Press, London 1928, p. 142–3.

6 This number may well have been greatly exaggerated.

him all of twenty-three days to travel a little over six hundred miles. As he rode, tribe after tribe and village after village came out to pledge their fealty to him and as he began to near Mecca itself couriers from the consulates of various foreign countries based in Jeddah rode out to meet him and assure him of their countries' neutrality. When he reached the gates of Mecca itself, on December 5th 1924, he did not take up residence in Husayn's palace but instead pitched camp outside the city. He then unbuckled his sword, took off the gold headropes, and shed his normal robes. Finally, having donned the simple white robes of the pilgrim, he entered the city bareheaded and in all humility, repeating over and over again the age-old words of the pilgrim: 'Here am I, Oh God, at Thy command. Thou art One and Alone. Here am I' – the last and only member of his family to have entered Mecca since his forebear Saud ibn Saud had made his last *Hajj* in 1812. He entered the Great Mosque and with the Ikhwan and other pilgrims pressing around him, circled the Ka'aba seven times, drank water from the Well of Zam-Zam, ran seven times between the hills of Safa and Marwa and had his hair shaved in the last of the acts of the ritual purification – thus performing each of the acts of the lesser pilgrimage, the *Umra*.

While Ibn Saud was tied up in organising the new government of the Hijaz, more than a thousand miles away to the north-east on the border with Iraq, Duwish and his Mutair Ikhwan started raiding again. In mid-December the twenty seven-year-old John Bagot Glubb, a lieutenant in the Royal Engineers then serving as an intelligence officer with the British Army in southern Iraq, heard that the rains having so far failed over their normal grazing grounds close to the river Euphrates to the north-west of Basra, a number of Bedouin desert tribes had moved their flocks south to benefit from the abundant rains and fresh green covering of new season grass and herbs on grazing grounds fifty to sixty miles to the south. These grazing grounds lay close to the Neutral Area between Iraq and Najd, created two years earlier under the Uqair Protocols. Upon hearing news of the shepherds' action, Glubb became alarmed. In the three years he had served with the British Army in Iraq he had got to know many of the Bedouin shepherd tribes and had developed a considerable affection for them. He knew that, despite the Uqair Protocols, by moving south they were putting themselves in danger of being raided by Ikhwan from over the border in Najd. Having tried to warn the shepherds of the danger and failed, on December 24th Glubb rode out at his own expense with a party of four local camelmen and an African servant to try to find the shepherds and bring them back to safety.

On Christmas Day 1924 Glubb came upon what seemed to be 'a whole shepherd nation' fleeing northwards with their animals. Moments later he and his companions were surrounded by a group of men 'some on foot and some mounted, their faces wild with terror and excitement. All shouted together, some pausing for a second only as they ran past, others pushing up to us and jostling our camels or seizing the reins. "The Ikhwan! The Ikhwan! A battle! A battle! The Ikhwan!" were all we could distinguish. Then others, seeing me in uniform, cried out, "Where is the government now? Why don't they save us? Oh officer! Have you brought help? The Ikhwan! The Ikhwan!" '

The pursuing Ikhwan were Duwish and the Ikhwan members of his Mutair tribe, who were stealing the shepherds' goods, rounding up their animals and murdering without mercy as they went. Glubb described the tragedy he witnessed as he and his companions passed through innumerable little groups of fleeing shepherds, their donkeys laden with all their worldly goods – 'a couple of cooking pots, a few little bags of rice or dates, a goat skin filled with water, and the rolled up tent. The convoys of donkeys were urged on by the women, running bare-footed behind them, frantic with fear, many carrying babies at the breast, pushing and beating their tiny donkeys ... ' As they ran these refugees constantly looked over their shoulders in terror, moaning and calling upon their saints. As Glubb explained, to be overtaken by the Ikhwan meant not only the loss of everything they owned in the world but the death of their fathers, brothers, sons and husbands. The Ikhwan were reputed to wrench the babies from their mothers' arms and, if they were boys, cut their throats and toss them into the dust, but to return the girls to their mothers. These raids carried out by the Ikhwan were a long way from the traditional *ghazzu* undertaken by the Bedouin since time immemorial and taken part in by Ibn Saud while he was growing up among the Al Murra more than thirty years earlier.

Unable with just four unarmed companions to offer the fleeing Bedouin shepherds effective help, Glubb and his companions rode as hard as they could all through the night and a violent, icy rainstorm, much of the way through sand desert, to the nearest telegraph station to call for military assistance. The following day, Boxing Day, they reached the Baghdad-to-Basra railway line and the tiny station at Jaleeba. From there they tapped out an urgent message to British headquarters, calling for planes to be sent immediately to attack the raiders. All day Glubb waited in mounting frustration for some action. But for operational reasons, and perhaps because it was Boxing Day and half the RAF squadron at the nearest airfield were due to take ship back to England the next day, all that actually happened was that late that afternoon a single plane landed near the station to pick up the exhausted and infuriated Lt. Glubb. The following day, December 27th, he took off as the observer in one of only three aircraft which the RAF had available, to try to find and bomb the raiders. They flew south, low over miles of dead bodies, dead horses and debris along the route taken by the retreating shepherds until they spotted in the distance hundreds of tiny figures, spread over an area two miles by three, separated into small groups, each driving whole flocks of sheep and donkeys. They were Duwish and his Ikhwan, heading back south to the Najdi border with the livestock and booty they had stolen from the Bedouin shepherds. Circling above them, the RAF planes bombed them, causing panic and scattering the Ikhwan but, so far as Glubb could see, killing none of them. As Glubb ruefully concluded, as soon as the planes broke off the attack, the raiders would have re-formed, rounded up the flocks and continued to drive them south. The following day a whole squadron of RAF planes attacked the raiders again and did manage to inflict some casualties. However, Duwish and most of the Ikhwan succeeded in crossing the border back into Najd with their booty, where under the Uqair Protocols the RAF was forbidden to pursue them.

Over the following days the RAF flew further sorties against other parties of Ikhwan in the area until finally all had been driven back across the Najdi border. When Ibn Saud learned of what had happened he issued strict orders forbidding the Ikhwan from making further raids into Iraq and shortly afterwards charged Duwish with a mission that would take him and his Ikhwan far away from the Iraqi frontier. Although the RAF continued to fly daily patrols along the Iraqi frontier in case of further

Ikhwan intrusions, the cross-border raids had now been stopped and for the rest of that year there were no more Ikhwan frontier violations.

Nevertheless, the effect of what Glubb had witnessed was to have far-reaching consequences for the Ikhwan. Years later he wrote: 'My experiences on Christmas Day, 1924, had stirred me deeply. The terror of the women in their flight, the anguish depicted in the faces of the children, the miserable donkeys laden with the few pathetic possessions of the shepherd families – all these and much else had aroused my compassion and made me boil with indignation that such misery could be inflicted on human beings who relied for their protection on the government of which I was a servant. With youthful passion, I vowed that I would devote all my energies to put an end to such abominations.'[7] Glubb, who would later become famous as General Sir John Glubb, Commander of the Arab Legion, had a well-known craving for action. He came from a military family and had served with distinction in France during the First World War. He had won the Military Cross and been wounded three times, once almost fatally. He had had part of his jaw shot away and remained disfigured for the rest of his life, earning him the nickname among the Arabs *Abu Hanaik* – 'Father of the Little Jaw'. Physically small – 'cherubic' according to some – he spoke in a high-pitched voice, had a famous temper, proven courage and spoke fluent Arabic. By their actions over Christmas 1924 the Ikhwan had made for themselves in Glubb a powerful and implacable enemy.

Meanwhile back in the Hijaz, Ibn Saud still had his hands full. In January 1925 he established temporary consultative councils, *Majlis al Shura*, made up of the heads of the leading families, religious leaders and the most successful merchants, to rule with him in Mecca and Taif. He had said that he did not intend to incorporate the Hijaz into Najd or impose any government upon it without the acquiescence of its leading citizens. The councils, which were to operate until such time as Ali and the last of the Hashemite resistance had been defeated, were his way of honouring that promise. At the same time he kept the control of security in his own hands.

7 Glubb, Sir John Bagot, *War In The Desert: An RAF Frontier Campaign*, Hodder and Stoughton, London, 1960.

Ali had retreated to Jeddah which, in addition to its walls, he had surrounded with barbed wire and minefields. Ibn Saud knew that a lot of foreign nationals were still living in the port city and that its garrison did not consist only of Hijazis loyal to Ali but also included several hundred Palestinians, Egyptians, Syrians and Yemenis. So he convened a meeting of his own military and Ikhwan leaders to determine what to do. Bin Luai and a prominent Hijazi tribal leader, Humayd, pressed him to order an immediate assault on the city, but Ibn Saud feared for the effect on his relations with other countries, in particular Britain, if the result was that a number of their nationals were killed. So he decided instead to persuade his military commanders to begin a siege and early in January 1925, 5–6,000 of Ibn Saud's fighters surrounded Jeddah and began besieging it.

Ali had few forces capable of mounting any kind of effective counter-attack, but he did succeed in recruiting several young White Russians. More enthusiastic than competent, they commandeered two or three ancient aircraft they found abandoned close to the city and attempted to mount a series of bombing raids on the besieging Wahhabis. Unfortunately one of the would-be air aces taxied his plane into a wall and wrote it off completely while another, who was sent off with a home-made bomb to drop on the enemy, blew himself up in the air.

Yet even after these provocations Ibn Saud still refused to order a general assault, preferring simply to maintain the siege. Nevertheless, his troops did succeed in finding one means of retaliating directly. In their haste to flee Mecca Ali's troops had left behind some small field guns and the Saudi warriors besieging Jeddah managed to make some of them work and fired a few salvoes into the city. The very first shell they fired crashed through the roof of the British Consulate and landed on the bed of the British Consul, Reader Bullard. Fortunately for subsequent Anglo-Saudi relations the shell failed to explode.[8]

In fact Ibn Saud had by now become so confident that so long as he maintained the siege, Jeddah would eventually fall without serious bloodshed, that during the *Hajj* season in June 1925 he permitted a substantial part of his army besieging Jeddah to leave and undertake that year's pilgrimage.

8 Philby, H. St John, *Forty Years in the Wilderness*, Robert Hale, London 1957.

Back in February 1925 when Ibn Saud had ordered Duwish and his Mutair Ikhwan to leave the area near the Iraq border he had sent them to besiege Medina. With the order Ibn Saud had also sent Duwish strict instructions not to actually take the city unless he specifically ordered him to. He was fearful that if the Ikhwan assaulted the city and entered Medina they might damage or deface the tomb of the Muhammad and destroy other holy sites. Ibn Saud ordered yet another force to besiege the port of Yanbu, again with instructions to avoid bloodshed.

Ibn Saud also began preparing for that year's *Hajj* pilgrimage. He made arrangements for effective policing of the event and the prevention of the kind of extortion and wholesale theft from pilgrims that had been rife under Husayn. The locally recruited guides that each party of pilgrims was required to hire to conduct them to and from the shrines, many of whom in Husayn's time had abused their positions to extract huge additional payments from pilgrims and in some instances made profit-sharing deals with gangs of robbers to lead their pilgrims along remote routes where the robbers could more easily attack them and relieve them of their possessions, were dismissed and replaced with more trustworthy guides.

He issued a decree stating that as the main Red Sea pilgrim ports of Jeddah and Yanbu were closed owing to the continuing sieges, new pilgrim entry facilities were being created in three Red Sea fishing villages to the north and south of Jeddah. With the knowledge that a war was still going on between Ibn Saud and Ali in the Hijaz, relatively few pilgrims braved making the *Hajj* that summer, but amongst those who did were a substantial number of Muslims from the Indian subcontinent and the English Muslim convert Eldon Rutter. Rutter left a fascinating and detailed account of making the *Hajj* and seeing Ibn Saud in that first year when the Holy Sites of Islam were under Saudi control.[9] Rutter described how Ali had sworn to blockade Ibn Saud's new pilgrim entry ports with his navy, 'a decrepit steam launch armed with a small gun', how easy it was to 'run' this so-called blockade and how Ibn Saud's Wahhabi police, dressed like the pilgrims in simple white robes, rode on dromedaries amongst the crowds of pilgrims watching for any signs of

9 Eldon Rutter, *The Holy Cities of Arabia,* Westminster Press, London, 1928.

theft or other 'misdemeanours such as smoking'. He watched as one Hijazi, who had been caught stealing from a pilgrim and had just suffered the Islamic punishment for theft, the cutting off of the robber's right hand, came running down the street streaming blood from the stump of his right arm and holding the right hand and the severed section of his right arm in his left hand. Seeing a stallholder selling hot meatballs, the wretched robber had thrust the bleeding stump of his right arm into the cauldron of boiling fat which the stallholder used for cooking his meatballs. After holding it in the boiling fat for a few moments he had withdrawn it and run away – 'just in time to escape the impending blows of the stall-holder. As he scuffled away, a gruesome object, which was suspended about his neck with a piece of string, swung from side to side. It was his severed hand.'

With exemplary and very public punishments such as this being exacted against criminals it was hardly surprising that theft and robbery during the *Hajj* almost completely disappeared. During his stay Rutter heard countless testimonials from Hijazis of the transformation Ibn Saud had wrought to his subjects' personal safety and the security of their property. He heard of a money-changer who had travelled alone carrying four hundred pounds in gold coins from near Jeddah to Mecca without being attacked, of someone who had unwittingly dropped valuable possessions on the road into Mecca and upon discovering the loss had returned to look for them and found them untouched where they had fallen. Such things would have been impossible under Husayn or the Turks and were now the cause of much wonder and praise for Ibn Saud among the Hijazis. Ibn Saud had succeeded in persuading the Ikhwan to take a more relaxed attitude towards the behaviour and customs of the pilgrims from overseas and treat them with courtesy as guests.

There was, however, one clash between members of the Ikhwan and a group of Egyptian pilgrims and soldiers who were bearing the traditional black-and-gold cloth sewn by craftsmen in Egypt each year for ceremonial draping over the Ka'aba. As the group of Egyptians bearing the cloth, known as the Mahmal, was approaching Mecca a group of Ikhwan was spotted eyeing them with suspicion. To the Ikhwan the Mahmal and the ceremonious way in which it was carried smacked of idolatry. The

Egyptians accompanying the Mahmal included ceremonial buglers and when one of them sounded his bugle the Ikhwan rushed towards the sinful sound hurling stones and angrily demanding that the music be stopped. Some Egyptian soldiers, seeing the Ikhwan charging at them, opened fire. Panic broke out. Luckily Ibn Saud's son Faisal chanced to be nearby and on hearing the commotion galloped to the scene and restored order in time to prevent a dangerous situation from becoming really ugly. Even so, a number of people had been killed and the Egyptian government severed diplomatic relations with Ibn Saud for the next ten years.

During the final stage of the *Hajj* Eldon Rutter joined the crowds who were flocking to offer Ibn Saud the traditional greetings marking the end of the festival. The green flag of Najd flew above the entrance to the large reception tent that had been set up for Ibn Saud to receive his guests. At the entrance stood two black slaves, armed with curved Arab swords with massive silver hilts, dressed in the cloaks and headdresses of Bedouin. When Rutter eventually reached the front of the crowd he saw Ibn Saud, unarmed, barefoot and dressed in the simple white robes of a pilgrim, a plain yellow robe and red-and-white headcloth held in place with a black headcord threaded with silver wire. He sat on a chair at the centre of a small semi-circle of leading citizens and military commanders. He was wearing sunglasses to lessen the glare of the desert sun and rose smiling to greet and return the salutations of each of his hundreds of guests. Each visitor shook hands with him, a few also kissed him on the forehead, the shoulder or the back of his hand. Ibn Saud was now forty-five years old and Rutter described him as 'considerably over six feet in height, well and even gracefully proportioned. The features of his long Arab face are large and strong, the mouth somewhat coarse and thick-lipped, the eyes a trifle on the small side. His beard and moustache – the latter cropped short, the former in length a hand's breadth in the Wahhabi style – are inclined to sparseness. He speaks remarkably well, in an easy well-modulated tone, and uses slight graceful gestures of the hands.'

Rutter also met Ibn Saud a number of times during his visit when there were fewer people present. He found Ibn Saud a good conversationalist interested in a whole range of topics and not at all fanatical. When Rutter told him that he was thinking of writing the story of his life, Ibn Saud seemed genuinely pleased and told Rutter he was greatly obliged to him. One of Ibn Saud's first acts on taking over Mecca had been to establish an official news-sheet which published official decrees and provided information about what the new government was doing for the people. Although he had lived most of his life cut off from the outside world of popular newspapers, the spread of modern systems of communication and, more recently, the birth of radio, Ibn Saud seemed to have an instinctive understanding of the uses of information and even propaganda.

In spite of the recent imposition of Wahhabi rule with its strict sanctions and codes of personal behaviour, Rutter found that in private the people of Mecca remained remarkably relaxed, hospitable and not a little cynical about the new puritanism. While visiting the home of one Meccan, his host rolled a cigarette and offered it to him. When Rutter declined, saying 'God bless you, but I am a Wahhabi', his host replied smiling, 'Good, then you may smoke in the house as the pious Wahhabis[10] do, but not in the street. That is to say, the act of drinking smoke is not unlawful. The unlawful is for a man to let people see him smoking.' So for the sake of their friendship Rutter agreed to smoke the cigarette.

Although only relatively few Muslims from overseas made the *Hajj* in 1925, when those pilgrims who had made the trip returned home they spread word of the transformation that Ibn Saud had brought about in the Hijaz, of the thoughtful and hospitable way in which they had been treated. His international reputation soared, largely dispelling the fear and revulsion which had spread following the massacre at Taif.

By October Ali's position in Jeddah was becoming hopeless and the British realised that it was now becoming urgent for them to enter into binding agreements with Ibn Saud over the southern frontiers of their mandated territories in Palestine, Transjordan and Iraq. So they dispatched one of the original architects of the Arab Revolt and Britain's war-time alliance with Husayn, Sir Gilbert Clayton, with an assistant

10 Rutter uses the Arabic word 'Mudayyina' which means 'pietists' and was used to refer to Wahhabis.

well versed in Arab tribal history, George Antonious, to Jeddah to contact Ibn Saud. While passing through Jeddah Clayton had one brief meeting with Ali, from which he concluded that Ali was as good as beaten both morally and physically and that Ibn Saud was capable of seizing the three towns held by Ali and his supporters more or less whenever he wanted to. Clayton was then driven out of Jeddah up the road towards Mecca in a Mercedes sent by Ibn Saud. After crossing the fertile Tihama plain they started to climb up into the foothills of the granite mountain wall that runs the entire length of western Arabia. About twenty miles into their journey, perched on the side of a wide wadi, they passed through the deserted ruins of a village called Bahra, destroyed a few months earlier during the fighting. A couple of miles further on they saw a large collection of tents some two miles away on the far side of the wadi. This was Ibn Saud's camp. After turning and beginning to drive down the side of the wadi to reach it, it soon become clear that the ground was too rough for the cars to cross and Clayton and Antonious were forced to get out and walk the last two miles. On reaching the camp they were warmly received by Ibn Saud and that evening treated to an elaborate feast which, as Clayton noted in his diary, included 'three or four sheep roasted whole and stuffed with rice, almonds, raisins, etc'.

The next day, once the formalities were over the discussions began. Clayton, who was meeting Ibn Saud for the first time, took to him at once. However, much of the actual negotiation was with two of Ibn Saud's new lieutenants, Hafiz Wahba, a fugitive from the British authorities in Egypt where he had been a journalist and political activist, and Yusuf Yasin, an argumentative Syrian refugee from Palestine. These two, Clayton complained, were typical 'pinch-beck oriental politicians whose methods consist in arguing every small point, employing a certain amount of low cunning, and resorting at all times to a policy of consistent obstruction. Ibn Saud, on his side, has the natural shrewdness of a Bedouin but is obstinate and devoid of all sense of logic as we know it.' But Clayton could not help conceding that although Ibn Saud was 'obstinate and self-willed – [he] is a fine type of the true desert Arab and possesses all his good points'. It was almost solely due to Ibn Saud's unflagging charm and consideration for his guests that, although the negotiations frequently reached the point of impasse, they did not actually break down.

Clayton and Antonious's lives in Ibn Saud's camp quickly took on an almost monotonous routine. As Clayton recorded in his diary: 'About 5 a.m., before it is light, one of our temporary retainers steals into my tent with a large bowl of camel's milk, freshly milked. It is a favourite food of Ibn Saud, and I am, therefore, expected to consume large quantities. I like it in moderation, and I usually drink a cupful when it is brought in fresh and warm. As the first glimmering of light appears the musical call to prayer goes up and the whole camp turn out to the morning prayer. At about 6.15 a.m. the flies appear, so I get up and have a cup of tea and a biscuit ... At about 8 a.m. breakfast appears, consisting of three diminutive Hijaz eggs, lightly boiled, which I break into a cup, with some bread, followed by some native cheese [this would probably have been made from sheep's milk] and occasionally a preserved apple from Taif.' The British representatives would start their first meeting of the day, usually with Ibn Saud as well as his advisers, at 9 a.m. and it would last until 11 a.m., after which the two Englishmen would go back to one of their tents and have a secret gin and tonic. Lunch with Ibn Saud's advisers and various guests was at 12.30 and was, as Clayton noted with approval, 'always very well cooked'. It was a large meal consisting of soup, followed by chicken and a course of pieces of meat, with onions, rice, gherkins and many herbs and spices. This was followed by a sweet, bananas, pomegranates and unsweetened Arab coffee. Each afternoon, at about 5.30 p.m. Clayton and Antonious would take a post-prandial stroll accompanied by an armed slave called Idris, during which they would seek out a vantage point above the surrounding ground from which to watch the sunset before returning to the camp for further negotiations after the most intense heat of the day had abated. This was followed by dinner, at which there were always small pieces of ice to put in the water, made with a small portable ice machine which had been brought by Ibn Saud's retinue from Mecca.

One afternoon on their stroll Clayton and Antonious strayed near to some tents beyond the limits of the camp. They were approached by two 'fanatical looking Arabs who began gesticulating and obviously cursing us roundly as dogs of Christians'. Clayton and Antonious walked on affecting to take no notice, but Idris, seeing what had happened, started remonstrating with the two Arabs and threatening them, whereupon a crowd gathered and the situation looked ominously like turning into a brawl or something worse. Luckily, with the two Englishmen by now out of the way, things calmed down. However, Clayton thought it politic to write a note of apology to Ibn Saud for having caused the trouble by being where he should not have been. But Ibn Saud, far from reproving his guests, immediately had the two 'fanatical' Arabs found and brought before him. As they entered Ibn Saud's tent they greeted him with the customary words: 'God greet you with prosperity, O Abd al-Aziz.' To which Ibn Saud roared back, 'God greet you with dung in your faces, you curs. Who are you who dare to insult my guests?' Whereupon they were each given thirty lashes in his presence and then immediately sent to Mecca to be thrown into jail.[11]

After three weeks of hard negotiation an agreement had been hammered out. Aqaba, which British troops had occupied during the summer to protect their lines of communication between Egypt, Transjordan and Iraq, was ceded by Ibn Saud to Transjordan. In return he was given all of Wadi Sirhan, stretching north like a dagger pointed at the heart of Transjordan to include the town of Kaf, only seventy miles southeast of Transjordan's capital, Amman. The rights of tribes from either side to cross the Transjordanian and Iraqi frontiers with Najd and the Hijaz were restricted and arrangements made for resolving disputes. Eighteen months later a further agreement was reached at Jeddah which guaranteed the protection of pilgrimage traffic and suppression of the slave trade. By these agreements Britain tacitly accepted Ibn Saud's right to act as he saw fit within his own enlarged borders.

Ibn Saud could now turn his attention to ending the sieges at Medina, Jeddah and Yanbu. For months they had continued in a desultory fashion, sometimes descending to the almost farcical, as when Ali's Russian émigré pilots had attempted to bomb the Saudi besieging force.

11 The account of Sir Gilbert Clayton's meetings and negotiations with Ibn Saud and with Ali Husayn are taken from *An Arabian Diary* by Sir Gilbert Falkingham Clayton, edited by Robert O. Collins, University of California Press, Los Angeles, 1969.

On another occasion Ali's troops had tried sallying forth against Ibn Saud's encircling forces in armoured cars which had been knocked together by a Syrian entrepreneur out of old American army trucks and iron sheeting, only to have their armour riddled by rifle fire.[12] No doubt Ibn Saud could, as Clayton had reported, have captured the three towns much sooner had he been prepared to authorise direct assaults on them. But his main concern had been to preserve as many lives within them as possible, particularly in Jeddah where there were a lot of foreign nationals. So, apart from lobbing a few shells into each city, his troops had done little more than maintain cordons around them. When people began to starve in the besieged cities Ibn Saud even arranged to have food smuggled in secretly to reduce the number who died.

The defenders of Medina had started putting out feelers about bringing the siege there to a peaceful end back in October and on December 5th the city did at last surrender to Ibn Saud's son Muhammad. Ibn Saud issued direct instructions to Muhammad to make sure that the Ikhwan were not seen to take too prominent a role in the town's fall and that killing, looting and the defacement of Islamic monuments were prevented. On entering the city Muhammad prayed at the tomb of the Prophet Muhammad in the prescribed form and had food distributed to the hungry citizens. As a result the Ikhwan spared the tomb of the Prophet, a site which was especially sacred to Shia Muslims, even though it was anathema to any good Wahhabi. However, from then on sentries were posted at the tomb to make sure that people did not kneel before it or use any other form of prayer there except the one that was prescribed. The other tombs in Medina, however, were destroyed.

On December 21st Yanbu surrendered and the leading citizens and merchants of Jeddah, suffering by this time not only from hunger but from the loss of their trade as an important seaport, went to Ali and tried to prevail upon him to surrender. Realising that his position was hopeless, Ali agreed and shortly afterwards sailed away on a British warship to

12 Bullard, Sir Reader, *The Camels Must Go: An Autobiography*, Faber & Faber, London 1961.

take refuge with his brother Feisal in Iraq. Meanwhile a deputation of the leading citizens of Jeddah, accompanied by the British Consul to Jeddah, had ridden six miles out of the town to meet Ibn Saud and negotiate surrender terms. He agreed to grant an amnesty to all of Ali's supporters, the continued employment of his civil servants and safe conduct without loss of pay for his soldiers. With surrender terms agreed, on December 23rd Ibn Saud rode into Jeddah on horseback and received the homage of its citizens. On December 25th an official announcement was made that the war between Najd and the Hijaz was at an end. Two weeks later, on January 8th 1926, Ibn Saud was proclaimed King of the Hijaz and Sultan of Najd and its Dependencies and, following midday prayers, the leading shaikhs, heads of the leading families and other important citizens came to pledge him their allegiance. In Jeddah too, Ibn Saud prevented the Ikhwan from indulging in any orgy of killing and plunder, but they were permitted, as they had been in Mecca and Medina, to impose their own austere codes of religious practice. So all ostentatious dress, the wearing of gold and silk, drinking of alcohol, music and smoking were prohibited, and tombs destroyed or defaced, including the tomb a mile north of the town believed to be that of Eve, the first woman, a site customarily visited by women when they wanted to conceive. Eve was reputed to have been one hundred and eighteen feet tall and the tomb was almost four hundred feet long, but only ten feet wide with three small mosques or temples interspersed along its length. However, the tomb continued to be visited after the Ikhwan had defaced it, until in 1928 Ibn Saud's son Faisal had it sealed so as to stop the offence given to Wahhabis by Shia and some other Muslims who continued to pray at it.

A month after the fall of Jeddah the Soviet Union, an avowedly atheistic state, became the first country to grant Ibn Saud, the head of a state owing its primary loyalty to God, formal recognition as King of the Hijaz. Comrade Kerim Hakimoff was appointed as the USSR's minister to Jeddah. On arrival in Jeddah Hakimoff donned full Arab dress, robes and head-cloth, which he wore from that time onwards until the end of his posting. Over the following two months Britain, France, the Netherlands and all the leading Muslim countries followed suit by appointing diplomatic missions to Jeddah. The young Dutch consul, Daniel van der Meulen, wrote down his impressions of the Jeddah he arrived in by steamer in the spring of 1926. Jeddah, or 'grandmother' as he noted the name meant, appeared to stand out 'like ivory in the heat of a scorching sun and wind-blown desert, in front of a line of blue rocky hills. With her protective walls around her Jeddah looked like an old cameo in a gold and toquoise setting.' But van der Meulen noted that once he stepped ashore 'the spell was broken ... Seen at close quarters the town was neither serene, lifeless nor clean. It seemed to be crumbling into ruins and overhung by a penetrating odour. The smell, peculiar to Jeddah, arose chiefly from the sewage which was allowed to seep through the walls of houses. The streets, too, were dirty and unswept and used as a common latrine by both man and beast. Jeddah had an age-old smell.' Was it, van der Meulen wondered, the dirt from the camping gounds of generations of pilgrims who had landed at Jeddah on their way to the *Hajj*?[13]

For the first time since the end of the ascendancy of the original Saudi-Wahhabi alliance over a century earlier, a single Arab ruler now reigned over the entire Arabian Peninsula from the Persian Gulf to the Red Sea, from the borders of the ancient lands of the Sumerians and Israelites in the north to the mountains shielding the ancient kingdoms of Sheba and Oman in the south. In June 1926, before the start of the annual *Hajj*, Ibn Saud invited the leaders of all the Muslim countries to attend a great congress of Muslim leaders in Mecca to discuss and determine the future government of Islam's Holy Places. Sixty-nine people attended including leaders of Muslim organisations from India, Turkey, Egypt, Palestine, Lebanon, Syria, the USSR, the Sudan, Afghanistan and Yemen. Ibn Saud had promised before he conquered the Hijaz that he would not impose any form of government upon it without the agreement of the Hijazis and Muslims worldwide. However, when the Muslim leaders convened in Mecca, Ibn Saud made it clear that, while he would care for and protect the Holy Places in accordance with their wishes and look after the safety and welfare of all pilgrims, he would not tolerate any interference in the affairs of the Hijaz. Whereupon a number of delegates to the congress walked out. However, Ibn Saud set about charming all those who remained, going out of his way to meet delegations and foreign consuls who had been posted to look after their government's

13 D. van der Meulen, *The Wells of Ibn Saud*, John Murray, London, 1957.

interests in Jeddah. All were captivated and impressed by him, by his wisdom, knowledge, smile, level-headedness and lack of fanaticism. By the end of the congress, although many remained critical of him for allowing himself to have been proclaimed King of the Hijaz, all had accepted the new reality – that from now on it was Ibn Saud who would control and protect Islam's Holy Places.

That year, 1926, with the reputation for security achieved in the previous year, more people made the *Hajj* pilgrimage than ever had before. In the process they swelled Ibn Saud's state coffers with customs duties and taxes as had never happened before in the twenty-four years since he first seized Riyadh.

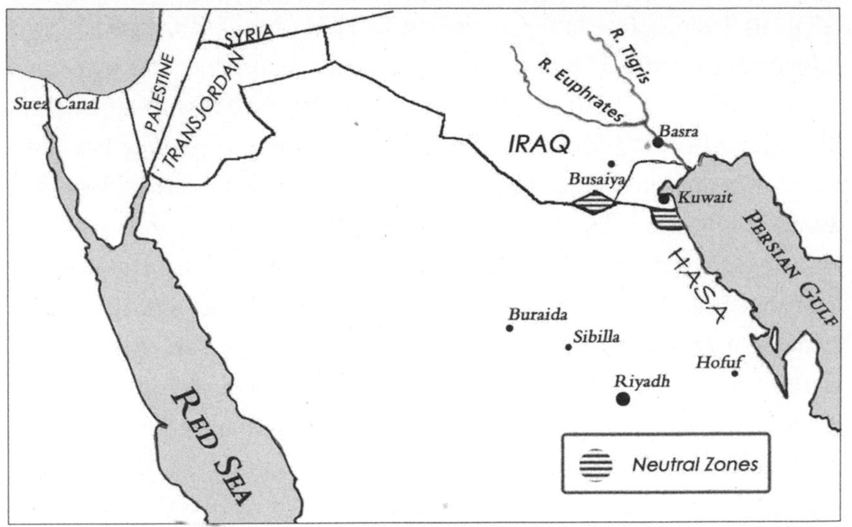

CHAPTER 10

Rebellion

The Ikhwan, the hammer with which Ibn Saud had largely forged his new state, now began to turn against him. As was evident from the attack by the Ikhwan on the Egyptians bearing the black and gold *Mahmal* cloth during the *Hajj* in 1925, their despoiling of the Tomb of Eve after the fall of Jeddah and the treatment of Sir Gilbert Clayton and George Antonious by the 'fanatical Arabs' during their evening stroll, the Ikhwan remained deeply hostile to anything with which they were unfamiliar or regarded as un-Islamic. The conquest of the Hijaz in particular confronted the Ikhwan with a whole host of things with which they were unfamiliar, regarded as sinful or un-Muslim. On capturing Taif and Mecca they had set about smashing mirrors, items they considered blasphemous or signs of vanity, self-adornment or urban luxury. On capturing Mecca bin Luai had ordered the burning of large quantities of tobacco which were found in the storerooms of wealthy Meccan import merchants. But it was not simply a matter of the Ikhwan considering many Hijazis heretics on account of their religious beliefs and lax practices, the Hijaz had been much more subject to the influence of the outside world than Najd and the other inland regions of Arabia from which most of the Ikhwan came. For centuries Muslim pilgrims had been visiting the Holy Sites, bringing with them the knowledge and customs of the outside world. Husayn's wartime alliance with the British had seen the introduction into the Hijaz of all kinds of modern inventions and devices which the Ikhwan regarded as godless or 'contrary to Allah's Will' – things such as motor vehicles, telephones, the radio, gramophones, ciné film, aeroplanes. In the opinion of leading Ikhwan religious scholars aeroplanes flew contrary to Allah's will, radio and even the bicycle were inventions of the Devil and on at least one occasion members of the Ikhwan, on seeing a lorry for the first time, set fire to it and were only persuaded with difficulty to refrain from subjecting its driver to the same fate.

On the other hand, as he had demonstrated by the interest he had shown in the modern weapons, medical innovations and the X-ray machine he had been shown by the British during his visit to Basra in 1916, Ibn Saud could see the value of such modern inventions and recognised that if his kingdom was to prosper he would need to embrace them. So while he slowed down the introduction of some modern inventions, especially in regions where the Ikhwan were particularly influential, he never made any secret of the fact that while he based his rule on the Qur'an and the traditions of Muhammad, he did not believe that these stood in the way of or forbade progress. In what could be seen as a public demonstration of his attitude to such new inventions, he had actually returned to Riyadh from the *Hajj* celebrations in 1926 in a motor car.

Yet at the same time he knew that if he was to avoid his kingdom disintegrating into chaos, into inter-tribal and inter-community strife and prevent the Ikhwan from turning against him, he was going to have to make some concessions to them. As a first step he needed to find a means of bridging the divide between the Ikhwan religious leaders and the religious leaders of the Hijaz. He therefore persuaded the *ulema* of Riyadh and Najd to hold a series of discussions with their counterparts from the Hijaz with the aim of reconciling their doctrinal and practical differences. After protracted and sometimes difficult discussions the two sides reached an agreement that stated that there were no substantial fundamental differences between them. This was, in fact, something of a fudge and the differences between them were soon to resurface. However, it did suffice to paper over the doctrinal rifts for the time being.

As a concession to the Ikhwan, and to stop them from taking the law into their own hands, Ibn Saud introduced a series of strict Wahhabi regulations into the Hijaz and set up a body called The League for the Encouragement of Virtue and Denunciation of Sin. Two *ulema*, who were descendants of the Al Wahhab family, were appointed to head the League which soon came to act as a kind of religious and moral police. Later the League became a department of the Saudi Directorate of Police.

With the League in place it became the duty of the Ikhwan to report all acts which in their view were not permitted by the faith to the League rather than taking action against the alleged perpetrators themselves. The League, not the Ikhwan, then decided whether a breach had been committed and, if so, what punishment was to be exacted, how and by whom that punishment was to be administered. As well as bringing to bear the full rigour of *Shari'a* law and its punishments for such crimes as robbery and murder, it also became a punishable offence to fail to attend the mosque, not to observe the fast, or to smoke, sell or consume alcohol, fail to pay *zakat* taxes, violate the *Hajj* or cheat customers in the market. For missing a prayer time an offender could be fined or sent to prison for anything between one and ten days. Drinking alcohol was punishable with both a fine and a month in jail – a repeat offence got you two years in jail. It also became an offence to attend an unauthorised meeting or spread false information and 'harmful ideas'. The latter measures were clearly aimed not so much at preserving the purity of the faith as at protecting the Sauds' own hold on power.

However, discontent among the Ikhwan and their leaders was not based solely on their disapproval of the irreligious practices and lax moral standards of the Hijazis and of the Shia in Hasa, nor on their fear of the unfamiliar and condemnation of 'un-godly' devices such as motor cars and radio communications. It was in large part a result of their sense of grievance over the fact that they had not received what they regarded as their fair share of the spoils of victory in the Hijaz and of their own worsening economic situation. It was based, too, on the thwarted ambitions of some of the Ikhwan leaders and on tribal enmities going back generations. All these things together helped to fuel a sense of grievance against Ibn Saud. Duwish had hoped to be elevated to the rank of Amir after the conquest of the Hijaz and rewarded with the governorship of Medina. Ibn Bijad had hoped for a similar preferment in Ta'if and to be appointed General Commander of all the Saudi forces. But Ibn Saud had appointed to these posts either members of his own immediate family or loyal henchmen who were not tribal shaikhs and who therefore lacked a tribal base from which to start to build a centre of power which might one day come to rival his own. In the autumn of 1926 the two disappointed and disgruntled Ikhwan leaders and their followers withdrew to their tribal homelands.

Another potent source of the growing discontent with Ibn Saud was the treaties he had signed with Britain and the prohibition he had placed on cross-border and inter-tribal raiding. Down the ages the *ghazzu*, or raid, had been an important element in Bedouin survival when times were hard and food and pasture short. By co-operating with the British in outlawing cross-border raids against 'infidels' in Transjordan, Iraq and Kuwait, in the name of religion but for the purposes of plunder, Ibn Saud was depriving poor Bedouin who had few alternative sources of sustenance and poorly developed agriculture, of a prime means of staving off poverty and starvation. In 1926 matters were exacerbated further by a severe drought which reduced many Bedouin to begging. The introduction of motor transport was also beginning to damage another long-established source of Bedouin income, camel breeding. The result of all these problems was that when the Ikhwan leaders accused Ibn Saud of the 'sin' of consorting with British and other foreign 'infidels', they found a ready audience of Bedouin prepared to join in the chorus of condemnation. The last 'offence' of consorting with infidels was highlighted further in August 1926 when news spread that Ibn Saud had sent his two eldest sons on overseas missions, Saud to Egypt to make arrangements for Egyptian pilgrims making the *Hajj*, and Faisal to England to conduct talks with the British Government.

In October 1926 ibn Bijad and Duwish convened a meeting of the Ataiba, Mutair and Ajman Ikhwan in the original Ikhwan settlement at

Artawiya to draw up a 'charge sheet' against Ibn Saud. Among their complaints against him were his relations with the 'infidel' British, his introduction into the Muslim land of inventions of the Devil and products of witchcraft such as motor cars, the telegraph and telephone, his imposition of new and 'illegal' taxes and customs duties on his subjects, his willingness to allow tribes from Iraq and Transjordan to graze their animals on Ikhwan lands and his failure to impose the Wahhabi faith upon the Shia of the Hasa. The meeting called upon him to declare *jihad* against the infidels of Transjordan and Iraq and to force the Shia of Hasa to become Wahhabis or, if they refused, to kill them.

After learning of the Ikhwan meeting at Artawiya, in January 1927 Ibn Saud summoned ibn Bijad, Duwish and the other rebellious Ikhwan leaders to a conference with himself and the *ulema* in Riyadh. Ibn Bijad, unlike other Ikhwan, refused to go to the conference, but Duwish, albeit reluctantly, rode to Riyadh at the head of three hundred of his warriors. When Duwish arrived in the courtyard of Ibn Saud's palace in Riyadh, accompanied by his fully armed warriors, Ibn Saud came out to confront him alone and unarmed. It was a moment charged with danger. Duwish, a small, wiry, slightly hunchbacked man, described by some who met him as like the wicked dwarf in a children's fairy story, backed by his three hundred fully armed men stood, bristling with righteous anger, before Ibn Saud, calm, powerful and towering above him. Duwish, a fearless, ruthless and inspiring leader of men, his courage proven over the course of many successful battles, was perhaps unprepared to be confronted by Ibn Saud on his own and unarmed in this way. So he blustered, angrily listing the Ikhwan's charges against their ruler. Ibn Saud, on the other hand, said little, and what he did say he said slowly and quietly in contrast to Duwish's torrent of loud and angry words. As time passed and Ibn Saud went on passively listening, Duwish's flood of words began to slow, until eventually all the bluster and anger had drained out of him.

Once that had happened and the immediate danger had passed, Ibn Saud called together all the other Ikhwan who had come to Riyadh in answer to his summons, together with Najd's leading *ulema*. Once everyone was assembled – more than a thousand men in all – he bade Duwish and the Ikhwan to lay their grievances before the full assembly, telling them that the *ulema* and religious scholars, as experts in matters of faith and the Islamic law accepted by all, should resolve the conflict between himself, Duwish and the Ikhwan.[1]

Duwish and the other Ikhwan presented their 'charge sheet' against Ibn Saud and then the *ulema* retired to deliberate. They decided to uphold the Ikhwan criticisms of the irreligious practices of the Hijazis and recommended that all tombs of the dead should be destroyed. They also recommended that the Shia in Hasa should either be made to embrace Wahhabism or be thrown out of the country (Wahhabis regarded Shia Muslims as not being Muslims at all). The *ulema* demanded that Egyptian and Syrian pilgrims to the Holy Sites be made to stop un-Islamic practices such as playing instruments and chanting and told Ibn Saud that Shia tribes from Iraq should be prevented from grazing their livestock on 'Muslim land' inside Najd and the Hijaz. They insisted that any 'unlawful' taxes collected by Ibn Saud should be returned, even though Ibn Saud pointed out that it was not he who benefitted from the collection of taxes but the thousands of his poorer subjects who he supported from them. The *ulema* did, however, decree that even if Ibn Saud had collected taxes not sanctioned under Islamic practice, this was not sufficient reason to rebel or threaten the unity of Ibn Saud's Muslim state. On the issue of new and 'ungodly' innovations such as the telegraph, the *ulema* remained uncommitted. Crucially, the *ulema* laid it down that only Ibn Saud, as the Imam, could proclaim a *jihad*. So compromise was reached and a final rift between Ibn Saud and the Ikhwan forestalled. That there could be no doubt that those who had taken part in the conference judged it a success was demonstrated when, at the end of proceedings all those present unanimously proclaimed Ibn Saud 'King of the Hijaz and Najd and its dependencies', thus raising his status in Najd to the same level as he enjoyed in the Hijaz.

The final seal seemed to be set on Ibn Saud's total hold on his new enlarged kingdom when in May 1927, in answer to a number of concerns that Ibn Saud had raised with the British, Sir Gilbert Clayton returned to Jeddah at the head of a new mission to negotiate a new

1 Some accounts state the total number of people attending the conference as 3,000 but this seems unlikely.

seven-year treaty of 'friendship and good will'. This treaty, which became known as 'The Treaty of Jeddah', replaced the treaty of protection that Ibn Saud had signed with Sir Percy Cox back in December 1915. Under the new treaty Britain for the first time recognised his and his kingdom's 'complete and absolute independence'. In return Ibn Saud recognised Britain's special relations with its Gulf amirate protectorates. He agreed to observe, although he did not formally recognise, the new frontiers between the Hijaz and Transjordan and undertook to help to stamp out the slave trade. At the end of the negotiations, after both he and Sir Gilbert Clayton had signed the new treaty, Clayton asked Ibn Saud who was the greatest European he had ever met. Without a moment's hesitation Ibn Saud replied 'Captain Shakespear'.

However, the new agreement with the British and the success of the conference in Riyadh had not eliminated all the sources of opposition to Ibn Saud. In the summer of 1927 a plot was uncovered in which both Ibn Saud's younger brother Muhammad and the son of his loyal cousin Jiluwi were implicated. The intention of the plotters was to murder both Ibn Saud's eldest son Saud, who during his father's absences had been deputising for him in Riyadh, and Jiluwi himself, who was still Ibn Saud's governor in Hasa. Muhammad was known to be particularly sympathetic to the Ikhwan and their grievances against Ibn Saud and was also resentful of what he saw as Ibn Saud's preferment of his own sons as his deputies over himself. Many of the people of Hasa hated Jiluwi because of his harsh rule and were deeply resistant to the new drive to impose Wahhabism upon them. Fortunately the plot was discovered before it could be put into effect. However, rather than punishing his two kinsmen for their alleged involvement in the plot, Ibn Saud allowed them to go free. To have punished them would have been to run the risk of creating a major and destabilising rift within his own immediate family.

It was the British who inadvertently struck the spark which eventually led to an open uprising by the Ikhwan against Ibn Saud and to the worst crisis he had faced since immediately after the death of Shakespear. In September 1927, belatedly acting on the recommendation of Lt. Glubb after he had witnessed the Ikhwan attacks on the shepherds on Christmas Day 1924, the British authorities in Iraq had sent a party of twelve workmen, escorted by seven Iraqi policemen, to construct a police post near some important wells at a place called Busaiya, eighty miles north of the Iraq-Najd border inside south-east Iraq. As soon as Ibn Saud learned of this he sent a strongly worded protest to the British accusing them of a breach of the agreements he had entered into with Sir Percy Cox at Uqair five years earlier which stated that 'The two governments mutually agree not to use the watering places and wells situated in the vicinity of the border for any military purpose, such as building forts on them, and not to concentrate troops in their vicinity.' He demanded that the police post be demolished. But to British and British-trained Iraqis there were no grounds for Ibn Saud's protest: eighty miles from the Najdi border was not, to their minds, 'in the vicinity of the border'; policemen were not soldiers and a police post was not a military installation. But, as Glubb himself later conceded, what seemed so clear to someone schooled in the customs and culture of Europe appeared very different to Ibn Saud, to a Najdi shepherd or to a member of the Ikhwan. For them there was no distinction between a policeman and a soldier and the concept of frontiers as delineated on a map was meaningless. The only frontiers that counted were still 'the frontiers in men's hearts'. So the building of a police post within what was regarded as a traditional grazing area of Najdi shepherds was an affront and tantamount to military occupation. As Glubb commented after the event: what 'in normal times could doubtless have been solved by negotiation' lit the fuse to a chain of events which were to lead to British military intervention and a full-scale rebellion inside Najd.

To Duwish the building of the police post was clear evidence that Ibn Saud had sold his country's rights to the infidel British. So ignoring the fact that Ibn Saud had protested to the British, at around midnight on November 5th–6th 1927 about fifty members of the Mutair Ikhwan, led by one of Duwish's lieutenants, stormed out of the darkness on to the workmen's tents and slaughtered them. Twelve workmen, one civilian official, one woman and six policemen were killed. Just one policeman, who happened to be on duty at an outlying post at the time the raiders swooped, managed to escape and make his way to the nearest British army post some twenty miles to the north and raise the alarm. By then the Ikhwan had vanished back across the border and in any case, the

RAF patrols and other measures that Glubb had put in place after the raids two years earlier had been disbanded in response to British Government demands for cost savings after the signing of the Bahra and Hada agreements by Ibn Saud and Clayton the previous year.

However, the British were not to be deterred from the construction of the police post and less than two weeks after the massacre at Busaiya a fresh party of workmen, escorted by police but also by a detachment of RAF armoured cars, was dispatched to the site to complete the task.

This served to provoke the Ikhwan to even greater fury and two weeks later a much larger band of Mutair raided deep into Kuwait. The Kuwaitis appealed to the British for protection and RAF patrols once more began to operate. However, with none of the pilots left in Iraq who had gained experience of attacking the raiders in the hostilities two years earlier, the RAF was at a considerable disadvantage. Five days after that first Mutair raid into Kuwait an RAF routine patrol over the Neutral Area came under heavy fire from the ground and a radio operator was wounded. The RAF had stumbled upon a large party of Ikhwan, led by Duwish himself, at the very moment when it was attacking a tribe of Iraqi shepherds. The RAF crews, with no previous experience of this kind of warfare, did not recognise what was happening in front of their eyes on the ground immediately below them. So they turned to fly home to their airfield deep inside Iraq without attacking the raiders or taking any action to protect the defenceless shepherds. Later that day another flight of RAF planes returned and did attack the raiders. However, their attack was at best only a partial success and Duwish and most of his men got safely back across the border into Najd with their loot. In any case, the attack by the RAF planes was no deterrent to Duwish and his warriors and just days later they mounted another raid, this time over the border into Iraq. They killed forty Iraqi tribesmen and drove off twelve thousand sheep, fifteen hundred donkeys and carried off more than one hundred tents and their contents.

By mid-December the Iraqi police post at Busaiya had been completed but, following the Ikhwan attack, instead of being occupied by the Iraqi police it was garrisoned by an Iraqi army unit which included two sections of armoured cars. At the same time the British Government in London gave the RAF permission to pursue any Ikhwan raiders back over the border into Najd. As a result, the RAF moved a lot of additional aircraft into the area and established a forward operational airfield close to the ruins of the ancient Sumerian city of Ur of the Chaldees. Yet still the Ikhwan raids continued. The weather was particularly bad that winter, making flying difficult, let alone the accurate bombing or machine-gunning of Ikhwan raiders. Simply finding the raiders in the great expanses of desert was difficult enough for the aircrews flying in open, often unreliable and flimsy biplanes, with none of the aids to navigation, target identification or bad-weather equipment which became common in military aircraft during the Second World War. When the planes did attack what they thought were the Ikhwan they frequently turned out to be mistaken and as a result probably killed as many innocent Iraqi shepherds, their wives and children as they did Ikhwan raiders. Even when they did correctly identify Ikhwan raiders and attack them they were themselves often subjected to withering rifle fire from the ground with the result that quite a lot of the RAF planes crashed. In order to make it easier for the RAF to identify raiders all the Iraqi shepherds were ordered back seventy-five miles inside the Iraqi frontier to the north. But there was not sufficient grazing in this area at that time of year which was the reason why the Iraqi Bedouin shepherds were in the habit of moving south either into the Neutral Zone or over the border into Najd. The result was that those tribes that obeyed the order to remain back seventy-five miles behind the Iraqi frontier lost many of their animals through malnutrition, while many of those who disobeyed the order and moved south with their livestock early in 1928 were subjected to attack by the Ikhwan.

However a raid on January 27th 1928 by three hundred and fifty Mutair camel-riders and fifty horsemen only sixty miles west of the town of Kuwait pointed to a possible way of defeating the Ikhwan raiders. When news of the raid reached Kuwait that evening all the serviceable cars in Kuwait, mostly Model-T Fords, were commandeered, loaded with eight or nine men in each and ordered to race ninety miles to the south west in an attempt to cut off the raiders return route into Najd. Of the twenty-five cars commandeered fifteen made it across the desert through the darkness – there were no roads – and the next morning surprised the raiders. Better armed than the Ikhwan and taking them by surprise, the Kuwaitis, even though outnumbered three-to-one, inflicted heavy casualties on the raiders. The sudden appearance of the motor cars, probably the first that many of the Ikhwan warriors had ever seen, served to greatly increase the raiders' surprise and confusion. The result was that those who were not killed or seriously wounded by the Kuwaitis' fire fled, abandoning most of their booty and stolen livestock as they went. Over the next two days the RAF pursued the fleeing raiders across the border into Najd inflicting further casualties. Glubb was amongst those who noted this success and drew the correct conclusions from it – accurate information about the raiders' whereabouts rapidly followed by an assault by a fast-moving ground force supported from the air could defeat a much larger force of raiders mounted on camels or horses.

Another person who was learning the lessons of bombing through his operational experience in Iraq at this time was the young commander of 45 Squadron RAF, Arthur Harris. He quickly came to realise, from his experience during these years in Iraq, that bombing when employed against a stationary target, such as the villages of Iraqi Kurds who rebelled against the imposed rule of a Hijazi, Feisal, could be a very effective deterrent. Arabs, he said, quickly come to understand that 'within 45 minutes a full-sized village can be practically wiped out and a third of its inhabitants killed'. Accordingly he advocated dropping 'one 250lb or 500lb bomb in each village that speaks out of turn'. These recalcitrant Arabs would then quickly come to heel. All that had to be discovered now was how to apply this doctrine to moving columns of Ikhwan warriors.

There was little doubt that in mounting raids across the border into Iraq and Kuwait and by attacking Iraqi Bedouin who crossed the border into Najd to graze their flocks, Duwish and the Mutair were deliberately signalling their defiance of Ibn Saud. The Iraqi Bedouin who moved their livestock into Najd for seasonal grazing were willingly paying Ibn Saud the taxes that had been agreed with the British under the various treaties he had signed with them. So by mounting cross-border raids Duwish and his Ikhwan were deliberately breaching the terms of the treaties he had signed and their prohibitions on cross-border raiding. But at the same time their actions placed Ibn Saud in a very difficult position. Duwish was well aware that over the previous decade the Ikhwan had become the most powerful weapon in Ibn Saud's military armoury and had been the principal instrument by which he had enlarged his kingdom. In attacking 'non-believers' in Iraq – in Wahhabi eyes Shia were 'non-believers' – Duwish and the Ikhwan could claim to be acting in accordance with the dictates of the true Muslim faith and so had religious justification on their side. So if Ibn Saud tried to prevent them from mounting their attacks he would be guilty of preventing them from doing their religious duty and would, therefore, be guilty of siding with unbelievers against believers. This could in turn undermine his standing with his Wahhabi subjects and might be seen as rendering him ineligible to rule over the true Wahhabi state. Thus, by their actions, Duwish and his Ikhwan had got Ibn Saud caught in a double bind. He dared not risk bringing down the full military might of Britain upon himself by joining with Duwish and the Ikhwan in attacking Iraq and Kuwait and he dared not take effective action against Duwish and the Ikhwan for fear of increasing the numbers of devout Wahhabis who sided with Duwish against him. So early in 1928 Ibn Saud had hurried back from the Hijaz to Riyadh and made his strong protest to the British about the construction of the police post at Busaiya. Afterwards, however, he took no further action against either Duwish and the Ikhwan or against Iraq and the British. For the moment he appeared paralysed.

By the early spring of 1928 the amount of plunder being garnered by Duwish and the Mutair from their raids was attracting other tribal leaders to join Duwish. One especially, Ibn Bijad, presented a particular threat to Ibn Saud. He had been one of the most effective military commanders in Ibn Saud's conquest of the Hijaz and had been one of the most aggrieved by Ibn Saud's refusal to let him and his Ikhwan reap what they believed were the rewards due to them in plunder from that conquest. Late in February Ibn Bijad unfurled his war banners and at the head of a force said to number twelve thousand Ikhwan, left his tribal base at Ghat Ghat west of Riyadh and started marching north to join Duwish. The avowed intention of the two Ikhwan leaders was to join forces and together declare *jihad* (holy war) against Iraq.

Hearing that they were coming and that the intended target might be Basra, the British stepped up their air patrols over the approaches to

Iraq. But the British knew all too well that if the Ikhwan forces of Ibn Bijad and Duwish did combine and make a determined push into Iraq there was little likelihood of them being able to force them to a halt before they reached the Euphrates. Throughout March and into April the RAF flew repeated patrols over the desert expecting every day to see a fearsome army of white-robed, camel-mounted warriors riding inexorably northwards. But day after day passed with the pilots scanning the distant horizons, but still the tell-tale cloud of dust that would betray the approach of a massive Arab army never materialised. What had happened?

We will probably never know for certain. Ibn Bijad had met up with Duwish in his Ikhwan headquarters at Artawiyah late in March, but three days later they had abandoned their plan for an immediate joint attack on Iraq. Perhaps increased patrolling by the RAF had deterred them – thousands upon thousands of leaflets had been dropped all along the northern borders warning that any tribesmen seen in the area would be bombed repeatedly and without mercy until they withdrew. Perhaps Ibn Saud had dissuaded them from mounting their attack. He had sent bin Luai and a leading cleric to Ibn Bijad to reason with him and try to talk him out of attacking Iraq. Also, by this time Duwish's Mutair Ikhwan warriors, having secured for themselves ample amounts of plunder, were for the moment weary of raiding. On top of which by April the searing summer heat had returned, drying out the desert water pools and shrivelling the pasture, making it near impossible for a large army to march across hundreds of miles of desert and launch an attack on Iraqis armed with modern British weapons and backed by air-power. So for whatever reason, or more probably out of some combination of all of them, the planned attack in 1928 by the Mutair and Ataiba Ikhwan on Iraq never materialised.

In May Ibn Saud went back to Jeddah for another meeting with the British to try to resolve the issue of the Iraqi police posts. The arrival of the British delegation in Jeddah coincided with yet another attack by British bombers on a group of innocent Najdi tribesmen, giving Ibn Saud yet another justified cause for complaint against the British.

The British delegation was again headed by Clayton, but among his lieutenants he had brought the recently promoted Captain Glubb. Glubb was meeting Ibn Saud for the first time and, like so many others, was immediately impressed by both Ibn Saud and his followers. The British party had arrived in Jeddah a few days before Ibn Saud and Glubb had noted the town was 'cosmopolitan, with a flavour of Egypt ... [and] certainly nothing to suggest Najd or bedouins'. However, the moment Ibn Saud arrived all that changed: 'Suddenly Najd had come. The staircases and passages of the house where he was staying were full of Bedouins and negro slaves.' Ibn Saud seemed younger than Glubb had expected but 'He wore spectacles at all times. He was extremely smiling and pleasant when talking to Sir Gilbert.'

Later that first evening there was a state dinner with over two hundred guests including many Europeans who were resident in Jeddah. But as Glubb observed, 'It was curious to see the old king walking barefoot, amid so many diplomats in dinner jackets and patent leather shoes – a contrast that seemed to epitomise the divergence between two such vastly different cultures. One could not but admire the fact that no Najdis tried to imitate European dress.'[2]

Glubb concluded that at root the cause of the differences between the British and the Najdis over the border issue and the police posts was a reflection of the differences between their two cultures. On the Najdi side it was a product of the mindset that saw the only real borders between men as being the borders in their hearts. The deserts of Arabia were, in a sense, like the sea. In the same way that, as Glubb suggests, the north Atlantic states would object if the United States were to annex half of the north Atlantic Ocean, so to Ibn Saud and the Bedouin it was impossible to contemplate the artificial division or annexation by one power or group of powers of large sections of the desert. The desert was like a sea over which the Bedouin roamed at will like mariners. Ibn Saud himself, and his loyal followers, regarded him as the monarch of all the Bedouin and so, in much the same way that in the old days the nation with the strongest navy and commanding the greatest loyalty amongst those sailing upon an ocean, might have command of that ocean yet still not own it, so Ibn Saud, because he had the strongest desert army and commanded the

2 Glubb, Sir John Bagot, *War in the Desert: An RAF Frontier Campaign*, Hodder and Stoughton, London, 1960.

greatest Bedouin following, expected that he and his loyal Bedouin would continue to be able to roam the desert at will no matter what notional borders or lines were drawn upon it by Christian statesmen or in treaties drawn up by Europeans. Now the British, having apparently agreed in the Uqair Protocols that there would be no forts in the desert, were insisting that they had to build forts in order to control both the Najdi and the Iraqi Bedouin. To Ibn Saud and his colleagues this seemed incomprehensible. During the negotiations at Jeddah the British team were repeatedly asked by the Saudis: 'Why do you people in Iraq want to control Bedouin tribes? Town Arabs do not understand anything about them. Ibn Saud is the king of all nomads.' A contention which, Glubb admitted privately, had much truth to it. Talking to the British delegates informally outside the negotiations Ibn Saud spoke more than once of 'government by despotism or by force' being no good. This, although the British did not seem to recognise it, could be seen as a criticism of the imposition by the British upon the Arabs of Iraq of rule by the Hashemite Feisal. 'A despotic government may appear to hold its subjects in a band of iron, but in a crisis or in war, if the iron were to snap, the whole structure falls to pieces. Government by consent is like a thread. A thread is sometimes stronger than iron.' He also expressed his disapproval of the kind of despotism being imposed in Italy by Mussolini.[3]

The negotiations were made much more difficult because of the deep mutual distrust between Ibn Saud and Feisal Husayn, the new British-appointed king of Iraq. Ibn Saud believed that almost every suggestion made by the British team was in fact part of some devious plot being devised by Feisal and the British to get the better of him. Ibn Saud's suspicions were being fuelled by the Egyptian and town Arab advisers that he had again employed to carry out the detailed negotiations on his behalf, who saw fuelling such suspicions as a way of increasing their own influence over him. The result was that the negotiations dragged on for three weeks without making any progress and the participants got steadily more frustrated and despondent. Ibn Saud seemed to get more depressed and bitter with each passing day. One evening, about ten days

3 Notes of conversations with Ibn Saud made by Glubb and included in *War in the Desert*, op. cit.

into the negotiations, Ibn Saud burst out to the British: 'When the English first came to Iraq, I congratulated my people. They were surprised and asked me why. I had always abused the Turks as unbelievers, they said, yet here were people who were even worse, because they were not Muslims at all. I told them that the English were honest, and were my friends. Now I must admit that we have despaired of the English and their hair-splitting. At Uqair I understood from Cockus that the protocol meant no forts in the desert. Now you say the wording of the agreement does not mean that. How do I know? I am a Bedouin and that was what Cockus told me and I trusted him.'[4]

Glubb recognised the sincerity of Ibn Saud's outburst and felt sorry for him. Clayton, on the other hand, more used to the ways of Egyptians, town Arabs and the likes of Feisal and Husayn than to the unsophisticated honesty of the Bedouin, did not and made an evasive reply. Glubb believed that the best chance of reaching an agreement would be for Clayton to cut out Ibn Saud's advisers and speak with him on his own honestly and as man to man; to accede to Ibn Saud's demand for the dismantling of the forts so that he could return home and confront the Ikhwan with a diplomatic victory and say to them in effect, 'You tried to get rid of this police post by raiding, even though I advised you against it. Your raids did not produce a result, but by talking to the English I have succeeded.' With this success behind him Ibn Saud would, Glubb hoped, be able to re-establish his unchallenged control over his kingdom.

But Clayton, Feisal and the Iraqis would not agree. To demolish the police post at Busaiya would amount to a surrender to the Ikhwan who had massacred a group of innocent Iraqi workmen and would be taken as a sign of British and Iraqi weakness. So the negotiations failed, even though Glubb feared failure would result in the spasmodic Ikhwan raiding escalating into full-scale war and would lead to the ultimate fall of Ibn Saud and the relapse of Najd into chaos.

So the two sides headed home. Glubb to devise new tactics for defeating the Ikhwan and Ibn Saud to try to avert an all-out Ikhwan

4 Words of Ibn Saud reported in diary entry made by Glubb and quoted in *War in the Desert*, op. cit.

uprising against him and the descent of his kingdom into civil war. Ibn Saud returned to Mecca where just weeks later news was brought to him that his seventy-eight-year-old father, Abd al-Rahman, had died in Riyadh. Muhammad Asad, the Polish Jewish convert to Islam who had travelled to Mecca in 1922 and become an intimate of Ibn Saud's, happened to be in the room when the news was brought to the king. 'I shall never forget the uncomprehending stare with which he looked for several seconds at the messenger, and the despair which slowly and visibly engulfed the features that were normally so serene and composed; and how he jumped up with a terrible roar, "My father is dead!" and, with great strides, ran out of the room, his *abaya* trailing on the ground behind him; and how he bounded up the stairway, past the awe-struck faces of his men-at-arms, not knowing himself where he was going or why, shouting, shouting, "My father is dead! My father is dead!" For two days afterwards he refused to see anyone, took neither food nor drink and spent day and night in prayer.'[5] Ibn Saud had always loved his father. He also looked up to him, depending on him for advice at the most difficult moments in his career; reliant upon him because of the immense respect and reverence in which he was held by so many of his subjects. Now, with Ibn Saud facing possibly the greatest crisis of his career, his father was dead. During the next few months Ibn Saud was probably more lonely than at any time in his entire life.

That summer, while Ibn Saud was locked in grief over the death of his father, a secret deal was being struck in Ostend in Belgium between the leading American, British, Dutch and French oil companies – Jersey Standard Oil (which later became Exxon),[6] Anglo-Persian (later known as BP), Royal Dutch Shell and the French company later known as Total. Under the deal, which was negotiated with the active consent of the companies' respective governments, it was agreed that all the crude

5 Asad, Muhammad, *The Road to Mecca*, Max Reinhardt, London, 1954.

6 Standard Oil of New Jersey was the holding company of the original Standard Oil Company founded by John D. Rockefeller in 1863 and broken up in the 1920s under Anti-Trust legislation into a series of smaller companies all with names including the words Standard Oil together with some other word such as the name of a state. One, Standard Oil of California (SOCAL), was shortly to start playing a central role in Ibn Saud's story.

oil produced anywhere in the Middle East between Egypt and Iran, would in future be divided equally between the four companies concerned. In dividing up the oil in this way, the governments of the countries from which the oil was to be extracted were not so much as consulted. The agreement, which followed the discovery of an immense new oil field in northern Iraq, became known as the Red Line Agreement because during the negotiations it transpired that none of the negotiators was exactly sure where the pre-war frontiers of the countries concerned had been and so one of the negotiators, Calouste Gulbenkian, took out a red pencil and, working from memory, drew a line on a map of the Middle East defining the area to be covered by the agreement. Britain, in particular, in all its negotiations and decisions since the end of the First World War about the future shape and control of the Middle East – especially with regard to Iraq – had always been extremely clear about the importance of oil. Even before the war ended Sir Arthur Balfour, the Foreign Secretary, had told the British Dominions Prime Ministers: 'I do not care under what system we keep the oil, but I am quite clear it is all-important for us that this oil should be available.'[7] Although barely noticed at the time it was drawn up, 'the Red Line Agreement' was to have enormous and long-lasting consequences for all the countries concerned, not least for Ibn Saud and Saudi Arabia.

By October 1928 it was clear that the full-scale rebellion led by Duwish and the Ikhwan, which Ibn Saud had tried to head off and Glubb had feared following the failure of the talks with Clayton in Jeddah, was now inevitable. More Ikhwan, including Dhaidan Al Hithlain, the chief of the Ajman tribe of Hasa, had joined Duwish. Duwish, Ibn Bijad and Al Hithlain had now agreed to overthrow Ibn Saud and divide up the kingdom between themselves – Duwish was to rule Najd, Ibn Bijad the Hijaz and Dhaidan Al Hithlain Hasa. It was also now clear that Feisal Husayn and his brother, Abdullah, the British-appointed ruler of Transjordan, had, as Ibn Saud suspected, been egging on the rebels and supplying them with money. Yet even now Ibn Saud still had to move

7 Quoted by James A. Paul in *Great Power Conflict over Iraqi Oil*, in Global Policy Forum, October 2002.

with caution. He dare not immediately launch a punitive attack on the rebels on the grounds that they had defied him by raiding Iraqi heretics and breaching the terms of the treaty he had signed with British non-believers, for fear that by doing so he would alienate even more of his devout Wahhabi subjects and drive them too into the arms of the rebels. Before making any move he had to carefully prepare the ground.

Ibn Saud's first move was to once more summon the leaders of the Ikhwan, the Bedouin tribes, the townspeople and the *ulema* – some 800 people in all – to a new conference in his palace in Riyadh. All except ibn Bijad and Dhaidan Al Hithlain answered Ibn Saud's summons. Duwish sent his twenty-five-year-old eldest son Azaiyiz (the diminutive for Abdul Aziz) in his place. However, Ibn Saud refused to see Azaiyiz and demanded Duwish's presence in person. He also sent messengers to ibn Bijad and Dhaidan Al Hithlain to repeat his summons and delayed the start of the conference to give them time to make the journey to Riyadh. But they still refused to attend.

The conference began on December 6th 1928[8] in the great courtyard of the Royal Palace in Riyadh. Ibn Saud sat on the steps to the palace with the members of his family around him. Below them all the 800 Bedouin shaikhs, leading townsmen, religious leaders and Ikhwan chieftains sat, row upon row, filling the entire courtyard from side to side, from end to end and overflowing through the great doors out into the market square beyond. Over the previous months all had heard many things said against Ibn Saud, not a few themselves had complaints against him and some were openly hostile. All sat watching him, waiting to see how he would handle them, knowing that this might be the final and greatest test of his personal power and influence over them and that if he mishandled them this might be the end of him. Ibn Saud knew this better than any of them.

He started by greeting them as his subjects and his brothers. He placed himself in their hands, asking for their opinions, advice, criticism and decisions. He reminded them of his family's ancestral rights and of their history. He told them that the repeated Ikhwan raids on the frontier with Iraq had resulted in the construction of the police posts. Then he

8 According to some accounts it began on November 5th.

said: 'Might belongs to God alone. You will remember that when I came to you I found you divided amongst yourselves, killing and plundering each other. All those who God caused to rule over you, whether Arabs or non-Arabs, intrigued against you. They sowed divisions amongst you so that you should become disunited and have no power or importance. When I came to you I was weak. I had no strength save in God, for I had no more than forty men with me, as you all know. Yet I have made you into one people, a great people.

'I did not call you here out of fear of any man. As in time past I stood alone and had no help, save in God. As I did not fear the armies of my enemies then and God gave me victory, so it is only in the fear of God that I have summoned you now. It is in the fear of my God lest I may fall into the sin of vanity or pride.

'I have heard that some of you harbour grievances against my governors and amirs. I wish to know about those grievances so that I may discharge my duty towards you and stand absolved before God.

'But first, if there are any among you who have good cause against me, decide now amongst yourselves, whether you wish me to continue to lead you and whether you wish to appoint someone else as your leader in my place ... I will not surrender my authority to anyone who would challenge me or wrest power from me by force, but I will surrender my authority and right to rule into your hands of my own free will. I have no wish to rule over a people who do not wish me to lead them.' Then gesturing towards the members of his family who were sitting on either side of him Ibn Saud said: 'See, here in front of you are the members of my family. Choose one from amongst them and whoever you chose and agree on I will loyally help and support. And I give you my promise before God that I will not punish anyone who speaks out against me in this matter either now or in the future, because, I thank God, I do not believe that I am indebted to anyone for my rank except to God who granted it to me.'[9]

Ibn Saud then stood in silence and waited to see if anyone would speak

9 Based on extracts of the speech of Ibn Saud to the Ikhwan and *ulema* as reported in the India Office Records 'Political and Secret Department Separate Files 1902–1931' included in H. C. Armstrong, *Lord of Arabia*, op. cit. and Christine Moss Helms, *The Cohesion of Saudi Arabia*, op .cit.

out to call for his abdication. In making his dramatic offer of abdication it has been suggested by most commentators that Ibn Saud knew full well that no one would speak out against him and that by making his offer in this dramatic way he was making a carefully calculated gesture that would have the effect not of undermining his power but of greatly enhancing it. That may well be true. Ibn Saud was nothing if not a shrewd politician. Yet the gesture probably also contained more than a grain of sincerity. At that moment, still reeling from the loss of his father and the repeated slights and rebuffs of the British despite his best efforts to conciliate them and win their friendship, with his eyesight failing and the physical strength of his youth beginning to ebb, a part of him might well have welcomed the prospect of being able to shed the day-to-day burden and worry of rule over a deeply divided and unruly kingdom that seemed surrounded on all sides by enemies.

But the silence in the palace courtyard did not last for long. It was only for a few seconds that the assembled leaders sat stunned as they tried to take in what their king had said, to understand that he had offered to stand down, to abdicate if that was what they desired. But then, almost as one, the eight hundred called back to him: 'We are all agreed. We desire no one other than you to lead us!'

So the moment of supreme crisis passed. Then Ibn Saud, having been confirmed by them as their ruler, invited them, each and every man, to speak freely, to voice any concerns, make any criticisms of him or his rule or of any of his governors, officials and lieutenants; he reminded them of their duty before God only to speak the truth and to hold nothing back. He asked them to voice any criticism that they had heard others voice.

He also turned to the *ulema* and charged them with explaining the proper duties of the ruler towards his people and of the people towards their ruler in accordance with Islam and the laws of the world, to explain to them 'the things in which the ruler has to be obeyed and those in which he is to be disobeyed'. Where there might be differences between them, he promised to follow the course which was nearest to the teaching of the Qur'an, the *Hadith*, respected Islamic tradition and the most respected scholars. Finally he charged them not to conceal anything in the hope of pleasing him. Reminding them that 'He who conceals a matter which he believes is contrary to the *shari'a*, is cursed by God', he charged them to tell the assembly what was right, to explain it and to speak out.

The assembly was now seized with a great spirit of liberation and all the people present spoke out with great candour and with a strong sense of relief. Every problem, every grievance, old and new, was aired. The discussions continued for many days. Among the issues discussed were their mistrust of Ibn Saud's dealings with non-believers and heretics, his friendship towards the British and his tolerance towards the lax practices of the Hijazis, especially in Mecca. The members of the Ikhwan who took part in the assembly had three key demands – one concerning the issue of taxes, a second over the introduction of new devices not sanctioned by the Qur'an, such as motor cars and the wireless, and the third the destruction of the Iraqi frontier posts. Ibn Saud made concessions on the first. To the second he responded that he believed that many of these new inventions offered real benefits to good Muslims but, he said, he was willing to destroy all the motor cars, telephones and wirelesses that he possessed if in return the Ikhwan would destroy all their guns and ammunition. These, much as any of the other things, were the inventions and products of infidels. After much discussion it was decided by the religious leaders that all these things were equally lawful.

The third Ikhwan demand was the most troublesome. In the end all that Ibn Saud could do was to get the Ikhwan to agree to keep the peace until he had made one final attempt to persuade the British and Iraqis to demolish the police posts themselves. If, however, they still refused he, Ibn Saud, would be with the Ikhwan 'heart and soul' in attacking them.

Throughout the conference Ibn Saud refused to let the assembled leaders discuss the quarrels between themselves or between one tribe and another. He would deal with these himself, as their ruler, at a later date. Throughout the weeks that the conference lasted Ibn Saud was tireless in speaking to people, entertaining and feeding them, moving among them, listening, talking and making friends. When at last the discussions ended, the amirs, men of God, townsmen and Ikhwan leaders returned to their followers, their tribes, their families and their settlements with their loyalty to their leader re-invigorated. Ibn Saud had achieved what he needed to achieve. His right to rule had been re-confirmed and he had split the Ikhwan, isolating the rebels, Duwish, Ibn Bijad, Dhaidan Al Hithlain and those other minor sub-sections of Ikhwan tribes that supported them, from the rest of the Ikhwan and all his other loyal subjects. Now he could strike against the rebels without the risk of dividing his kingdom and plunging it into chaos.

No sooner had the conference ended than news arrived that a group of Ibn Bijad's Ataiba Ikhwan had attacked a group of defenceless camel merchants near Buraida. These merchants were loyal Najdi citizens and Buraida was one of the most devoutly Wahhabi towns in the kingdom. This attack was no *ghazzu* or raid conducted to the ageless rules of Bedouin raiding. Not only had the attacking Ataiba Ikhwan driven off the merchants' livestock, they had massacred each and every one without mercy or reason. These were not unbelievers or foreigners, they were good Arabs and faithful Wahhabis. This was not only a breach of every rule of Muslim Arab brotherhood, chivalry and hospitality, it was an open challenge to Ibn Saud's legitimacy and authority. Ibn Saud's loyal subjects, Ikhwan, Bedouin and townsmen alike, were outraged by what the Ataiba Ikhwan had done. All now wanted Ibn Saud to crush the rebels once and for all.

Further attacks followed. Each of the groups of rebel Ikhwan made long, stabbing raids into Iraq, Kuwait and the neutral zones, massacring groups of defenceless shepherds and driving off their flocks. In one in the north of the territory of Kuwait, carried out by Ajman Ikhwan led by Dhaidan Al Hithlain, not only were six shepherds massacred and hundreds of sheep and donkeys driven off, an American missionary, called Henry Bilkert, was killed. On the morning of the raid Bilkert chanced to be driving from Basra to Kuwait in a car accompanied by another American, a millionaire former United States ambassador to China, called Charles Crane. They happened to be passing just as the Ikhwan swooped upon the defenceless shepherds. Seeing the car, an invention of the devil and the two godless white men in it, the Ikhwan opened fire. Bilkert was killed but fortunately, although the car was hit, Crane survived unscathed and was able to make his escape. A few years later Crane was to play an important part in the life of Ibn Saud and the fortunes of his country.

By this time Glubb had succeeded in establishing the rudiments of a method of dealing with the Ikhwan. He had set up the beginnings of a spy network that would give him advance warning of the intended movements of the Ikhwan and a system of armed mobile military columns backed by planes of the RAF. On the evening of December 16th 1928 one of Glubb's spies arrived in his camp in the Iraqi desert just north of the Neutral Zone and warned him of an impending Ikhwan raid led by a minor shaikh of the Mutair tribe. Glubb consulted with a number of Bedouin with long experience of this area of desert and, knowing where the various groups of shepherds that they might attack were, calculated the most likely target and date of their first raid. Glubb immediately sent a long radio message asking for RAF planes armed with bombs and machine guns to mount patrols over the area of desert concerned. The next day Glubb himself made his way to an RAF landing strip and flew as observer in one of the RAF patrol planes. Late that day, spotting a group of shepherds Glubb landed nearby and warned them that the Ikhwan were in the area. However Glubb persuaded them not to flee immediately but to camp and light their fires as if everything was as normal, but then to sneak away in the night leaving their fires burning.

Next morning Glubb took off again and flew with two other aircraft to the fertile hollow where the shepherds had been. Flying high over the desert they at first could not make out anything. Then he spotted two moving black specks. Straining his eyes and circling in the plane he made out first two camels and then a hundred camels grazing in the place where yesterday the shepherds had been grazing their sheep. Could this be the Ikhwan? He circled again. There were certainly a hundred camels or more but there were no men to be seen. Then he spotted just two men. If these were indeed the Ikhwan there should have been a hundred men. Yet there were no small camels and if this were a flock of grazing camels there should be young camels amongst them. These camels were all fully grown. Might it be a large caravan or merchants travelling across the desert to a place where they could sell their camels?

Glubb tapped the pilot on the shoulder and passed a hastily scribbled note asking him to fly lower. Lower and lower they circled until they were down to only five hundred feet. In they came again roaring over the camels with Glubb straining over the side of the aircraft peering at the ground. Now he saw it. Every camel had a saddle on its back and yet there were no riders. Glubb scribbled another hasty note, tapped the pilot on the shoulder and passed it to him. It read: 'Raiders. Shoot.'

Climbing again, turning and banking, the plane dived straight towards the camels, releasing a stick of bombs and firing as it went. Suddenly, as the ground all around was pitted with puffs of dust and smoke where the bombs and bullets struck, every camel had a rider on its back and was galloping wildly away from the scene. They scattered, fleeing in panic in every direction. Before the first bombs dropped the Ikhwan warriors must have been crouching motionless close by their camels, their cloaks camouflaging them against the desert. Round and round the three planes went, dropping bombs and firing their machine guns until they were out of bombs and ammunition. For the first time Glubb had beaten off and routed a party of Ikhwan before they could carry out any attacks.

Meanwhile Ibn Saud had made a new appeal to the British to remove the police posts and for help in dealing with the Ikhwan. The British agreed to submit the issue of the police posts to arbitration and to supply him with rifles, machine guns and ammunition. Ibn Saud also sent messages to the amirs of all the towns and villages and the tribal leaders, commanding them to come to Riyadh with their men armed and marching under flags of *jihad.* As it was then the middle of the Ramadan fast he absolved the men of having to observe the remainder of the fast. By issuing this command and absolution Ibn Saud, as their lawful leader, made it a sin for any man to refuse to answer his summons and continue the fast. Some of the warriors rejected his call and determined to continue with the fast but Ibn Saud, in line with the strict prescription of Wahhabi religious law, ordered those that refused the call and continued with the fast to be stoned. However, he ordered that any stonings were to be symbolic only, the aim being to shame them into obedience and above all not to kill them.

By now, as the rebels strove to stir a general revolt against him, much of the tranquillity that Ibn Saud had striven so hard to bring to each of the areas that he had conquered was fast disintegrating. Muhammad Asad, who was in the country at this time, would later describe the changed atmosphere: 'Central and Northern Arabia became the scene of widespread guerrilla warfare; the almost proverbial public security of the country vanished and complete chaos reigned in Najd; bands of rebel Ikhwan swept across it in all directions, attacking villages and caravans and tribes that remained loyal to the king ... Mysterious emissaries rode on fast dromedaries from tribe to tribe. Clandestine meetings of chieftains took place at remote wells ... '[10]

At last, the weapons and ammunition he had requested from the British arrived from India and Ibn Saud set out northwards with a great army made up of fifteen thousand warriors from all over his kingdom. He travelled on the first leg of his journey from Riyadh to Buraida not on a camel, as he had travelled on all his previous campaigns, but in an open car, at the head of a small fleet of cars, his personal bodyguards riding beside him standing on his car's running-boards. The fact that he decided to travel by car was in itself tantamount to a challenge to the Ikhwan. It was emblematic of the benefits of the modernity that Ibn Saud wanted to bring to his people as opposed to the closed-minded and backward looking Qur'anic literalism of Duwish and his fellow Ikhwan rebels.

Ibn Saud travelled north at a leisurely pace, stopping frequently in the villages and oases along the way. In each place where he stopped he held a large assembly of local shaikhs and tribesmen, entertaining generously and giving them ample opportunity to speak freely to him and express their opinions. He moved amongst his guests, smiling and joking, seemingly carefree and unworried by the danger posed by the rebels. So as he travelled he increased still further his stock of goodwill among his people, the number of his allies and the size of his army. The assemblies and talk amongst all ranks and kinds of his subjects also increased his stock of intelligence about the rebels. As Muhammad Asad, who travelled with Ibn Saud, wrote: 'Each tribesman ... might give an opinion about the strength and whereabouts of the enemy or allegiance of a particular tribe or tribal section [and] in this way the King gained a mass of information.'[11]

Having reached Buraida and made sure that it was secured, Ibn Saud rode out at the head of his army eastwards in the direction of Duwish's settlement, the first of the Ikhwan settlements, at Artawiya. With battle

10 Muhammad Asad, op. cit.
11 Ibid.

shortly to be joined and the terrain beyond Buraida largely impassable for a car, Ibn Saud now rode on one of his specially selected war camels. The rebels Duwish and Ibn Bijad, who had been raiding in the north in the Neutral Zone and further west near the Iraqi frontier, now turned and marched south, leaving Dhaidan Al Hithlain in the north ready to counter any move by Ibn Saud's loyal cousin Jiluwi to advance on the rebels from Hasa. By the third week of March 1929 the armies of Duwish and Ibn Bijad had linked up on a plain a few miles south of Artawiyah near some wells at a place known as Sibilla. By March 24th Ibn Saud had reached a spot just four miles away from them. Both sides now dug in and prepared for battle.

Yet even now Ibn Saud tried one last time to settle his dispute with the rebels by peaceful means. He had brought with him two of the most learned and respected of the *ulema* and sent a message to Duwish and Ibn Bijad suggesting that they come and lay the case for what they had done and all their grievances before them. He undertook to be bound by whatever judgement the *ulema* might come to under Islamic law. Duwish responded by sending his son Azaiyiz as his intermediary to negotiate with Ibn Saud. Azaiyiz is reputed to have been fair-haired, suggesting that his mother or one of his other forebears may have been a northern slave-girl. In contrast to his father, he was also possessed of considerable charm. Back and forth between the two sides Azaiyiz went as Ibn Saud tried repeatedly to get the two rebel leaders to talk rather than fight until finally Duwish agreed to meet Ibn Saud alone and unarmed. Yet still neither Azaiyiz nor the inducements offered by Ibn Saud could persuade Ibn Bijad to meet the *ulema* or Ibn Saud except with sword-in-hand.

A tent with four openings, one at each corner, was pitched on ground an honourable distance in front of Ibn Saud's camp and then, on the evening of March 28th, eight men of Duwish's bodyguard went out, swords in hand, two to each corner of the tent and simultaneously lifted the flaps to the four openings. Having in this way checked that the tent was indeed empty and that Ibn Saud had not had an assassin concealed within it, the eight bodyguards returned to Duwish. Then Duwish and Ibn Saud rode out alone from their two armies to the tent. As the sun set they prayed together in the time-honoured fashion of all Muslims. Then they sat talking alone for most of the night. After many hours of talking through the darkness Duwish agreed that henceforth he would live in peace under Ibn Saud. He would return to his camp and try to persuade Ibn Bijad to do the same. If Ibn Bijad agreed they would return together next morning for a further meeting with Ibn Saud. 'But', Duwish said, 'I warn you that if we do not come our absence will mean war.'[12]

However when Duwish returned to his own camp it seems that rather than really trying to persuade Ibn Bijad to return with him the next morning to Ibn Saud's tent, he told him and the other Ikhwan leaders that Ibn Saud's army was full of fat townsmen, 'cooks who know nothing except sleeping on mattresses ... We will defeat this false God at dawn'. In battle, Duwish sneered, these men will be 'about as much use as camel bags without handles'.[13] So, fired by the belief that Ibn Saud and his army would be no match for them, and convinced that Ibn Saud himself had gone soft and now preferred talk and easy living to fighting, Ibn Bijad and his fellow rebel leaders determined to have done with negotiation and attack Ibn Saud immediately. In a mood of contempt for their opponents, the two rebel leaders and their warriors now hastened to prepare for battle. Once the sun had risen and the time of morning prayer had passed, Ibn Saud too, seeing that Duwish and Ibn Bijad had not returned to the tent, commanded his army to prepare for battle.

Exactly what happened in the hours immediately after that remains uncertain. Accounts given by eyewitnesses differ greatly according to the sympathies and prejudices of the witness. In his book Harold Dickson, the British diplomat and Arabist, faced with these conflicting accounts abandoned describing the course of events in detail and settled instead for simply describing Sibilla as 'A Rather Mysterious Battle'.[14] That seems in many ways the wisest course. Yet from what we know of the characters and state of mind of the leaders on both sides, of the make up of their respective armies, of their habitual

12 Words attributed to Duwish by M. Almana in *Arabia Unified*, London, 1980, quoted in McLoughlin, op. cit.

13 Quoted from an Arabic source in Christine Moss Helms, *The Cohesion of Saudi Arabia: Evolution of Political Identity*, Croom Helm, London 1981.

14 H. R. P. Dickson, *Kuwait and Her Neighbours*, Allen & Unwin, London, 1956.

methods of fighting and dispositions on the day, as well as the various accounts we do have it seems to us possible to piece together the most likely course of events.

Once his men were in arms and all was prepared Ibn Saud bent down and scooping up a handful of sand hurled it in the direction of the enemy in the traditional gesture, reputed to have been used by the Prophet Muhammad himself, to signal the start of a battle. Leaving a substantial force of men armed with rifles and machine guns concealed behind two lines of sand dunes on either side of the shallow valley at the far end of which waited Duwish, Ibn Bijad and their rebel army, Ibn Saud started to lead his men forward down the valley towards them. The rebels, seeing their despised enemy advancing towards them, instead of holding their fire until Ibn Saud was within easy range as planned, ordered all their eight thousand warriors to charge at them immediately. So the combined forces of the Mutair and Ataiba tribes and their allies began to charge headlong straight at Ibn Saud and his much larger army. Immediately ahead of them the rebels drove the unique emblem and special weapon which had helped to make the Mutair such a formidable fighting force, the *al Shuruf* – The Honoured Ones – a herd of three hundred specially bred black camels, kept apart, trained and revered down the centuries. In the battles of the Mutair these black camels were the rallying point for their warriors. In attack the *al Shuruf* charged at the head of the warriors, driven as one trained, compact phalanx straight at the heart of the enemy line and upon impact scattered the Mutair's opponents in all directions. Following close behind the *al Shuruf* on their war camels with their horses galloping on loose leads close beside them, the Mutair warriors galloped forward ready to leap from their camels onto the backs of their horses and spur them on behind the *al Shuruf* into the heart of the enemy line and put their foes to the sword.

But on the field of Sibilla that morning few of the Mutair and Ataiba warriors actually reached their enemy's line. Once the rebels were committed, exposed out in the open and charging in a cloud of earth-shattering camel and horses hooves, swirling dust, streaming war banners, screaming war cries and brandishing their rifles above their heads, charging headlong towards their enemy, Ibn Saud calmly signalled to the machine gunners and riflemen concealed behind the dunes on either side of the shallow valley to open fire. Suddenly caught between the withering cross-fire of Ibn Saud's British-supplied machine guns and modern rifles, up to a thousand of the Mutair and Ataiba warriors and *al Shuruf* were mown down in just a few seconds. In those first few seconds of surprise, confusion and bloody mayhem the Mutair and Ataiba warriors wavered and then many turned and began to flee. Even the *al Shuruf* seemed dazed and confused, some galloping onwards towards Ibn Saud's line, others breaking and running wildly across the desert in all directions. Then, with the rebels confused and broken Ibn Saud ordered his own warriors to charge, breaking the last charging remnants of the rebel army and driving them too into headlong flight. Among those seriously wounded in those first few seconds was Duwish himself, shot through his ample paunch. Ibn Bijad was among those who fled.

That night when the fighting and pursuit were over for the day and Duwish had been carried back to his settlement at Artawiya by loyal supporters to recover, Ibn Bijad went to him and urged him to continue the fight. But Duwish refused. Ibn Bijad stormed out, swearing to continue the fight with Dhaidan Al Hithlain and such allies as the rebel Ikhwan had left. Next morning Duwish offered his surrender to Ibn Saud in accordance with time-honoured Arab custom by sending six veiled women – his own daughter, two further members of his immediate family and three others – in camel litters under the care of one of his most trusted lieutenants, to Ibn Saud's tent to ask for sanctuary. But Ibn Saud hesitated before responding to their request. First he called together his *ulema* and sought their advice. They told him that the killing should end – the bloodshed had gone far enough. But, they agreed, there should be conditions. Duwish and his warriors must surrender their weapons, camels, horses and rifles, and all the loot they had seized from Ibn Saud's subjects. In addition Duwish himself must surrender unconditionally and in person to Ibn Saud.

Duwish accepted the conditions and was carried on a stretcher from his settlement at Artawiya into the camp of Ibn Saud and laid at his feet. For some moments Ibn Saud looked down at him sternly and in silence. The old warrior gazed back up at him, unflinching as ever. At that moment Ibn Saud might have ordered his instant execution. The *ulema* had not forbidden it and Duwish probably expected it. But instead Ibn Saud, probably convinced that Duwish was going to die from his wound, forgave him. 'You are no match for me,' Ibn Saud said looking down at him. 'I am too powerful for you. I pardon you. You may go wherever you wish and I will give you whatever you need. But your future actions and behaviour, good or bad, will be judged by me and dealt with accordingly.'[15] Ibn Saud then ordered his own doctor to tend to Duwish and afterwards sent him home with his wives and other womenfolk. A few days later Ibn Saud issued a public statement to his people saying that he did not like 'killing even one Muslim' but that obedience to God was necessary and that Duwish and Ibn Bijad's Ikhwan had become 'fanatics', who had acted 'against the instruction of Shari'a'.[16]

The fighting at the Battle of Sibilla had probably lasted for barely half-an-hour and yet it marked a decisive turning point. Although Ibn Saud later claimed that he had captured the majority of Duwish's men, that some had been beheaded and others imprisoned, it was not to be the last battle of the Ikhwan rebellion. But after Sibilla there was never again any real possibility that the rebels would succeed in overthrowing Ibn Saud. Still more significant perhaps, the Battle of Sibilla turned out to be the last great traditional Bedouin battle ever fought on Arab soil, fought from the backs of camels and horses and on foot under essentially the same rules that had governed Bedouin warfare for more than three thousand years. The Battle of Sibilla was in essence little different from battles fought in the days of King Solomon or by Gindibu the Arab and his thousand desert warriors and their camels alongside the armies of the Syrians and Palestinians. Sibilla was the last battle fought under the ancient Bedouin rules of chivalry in warfare, by warriors many of whom still regarded warfare as a kind of sport. After Sibilla mechanisation finally began to enter into desert warfare and to prove decisive.

15 Ibn Saud's words as recorded in Leslie McLoughlin, *Ibn Saud: Founder of a Kingdom*, Macmillan Press, London, 1993.

16 Christine Moss Helms, op. cit.

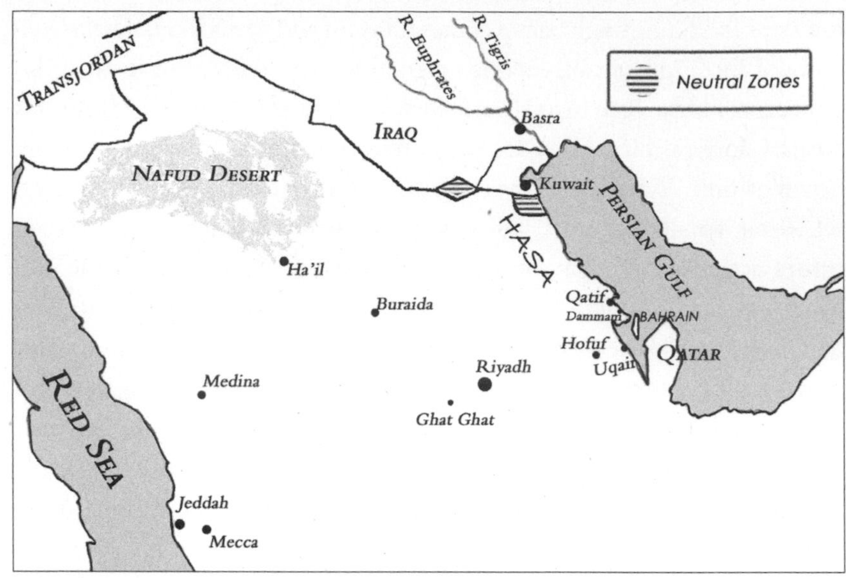

CHAPTER 11

Hard Times and the Coming of the Oil Men

After the Battle of Sibilla, Ibn Bijad had managed to make his way back to his Ikhwan settlement at Ghat Ghat. But Ibn Saud, having pardoned Duwish, sent his brother Abdullah to Ibn Bijad with a message asking him to give himself up as well. Perhaps lured by the forgiveness Ibn Saud had shown to Duwish, Ibn Bijad surrendered to Abdullah. However, Abdullah, acting on Ibn Saud's orders, immediately had Ibn Bijad taken to Riyadh and thrown into gaol along with other leaders of the uprising. Abdullah then ordered the inhabitants of the Ghat Ghat settlement to be turned out into the surrounding desert and all their weapons to be confiscated. The settlement itself was utterly destroyed and remained in ruins for the next seventy years as a warning to anyone else who might contemplate rebellion. A few years after Ibn Bijad had been thrown into jail in Riyadh a rumour began to circulate about a plot to free him. As a consequence Ibn Saud had him moved to Hofuf and incarcerated in a particularly appalling underground dungeon built by the Turks from which he never emerged again.

Believing the rebellion was now over, Ibn Saud returned to Buraida, thanking the people of the areas he travelled through for their loyalty and taking a bride from a prominent loyal tribe. He then travelled on to Mecca to undertake the *Hajj* of May–June 1929. But hardly had he arrived than news reached him that the desert had risen in arms against him once more. The cause of this fresh uprising was a particularly grisly murder committed by the son of one of his most trusted and dependable lieutenants, his cousin Jiluwi. On Ibn Saud's instructions Jiluwi, who was still the governor of Hasa, had sent his son Fahd to Dhaidan Al Hithlain with a message from Ibn Saud. The message thanked Al Hithlain for not taking part in the Battle of Sibilla and invited him to meet with Fahd to discuss terms for ending the differences between them. Many of Dhaidan Al Hithlain's followers suspected that the invitation was in fact a trap and warned him not to accept it. But Al Hithlain ignored their warnings and agreed to go to Fahd's camp for discussions. A day or so later, accompanied by a dozen attendants and carrying a safe conduct signed by both Ibn Saud and Fahd's father, Al Hithlain made his way to Fahd's camp. He was well received and the two men drank coffee together and then got down to negotiating. After some hours Al Hithlain, making it clear he intended to return to resume their discussions the next day, rose to leave. But Fahd, seemingly put out by Al Hithlain's words, invited him to stay the night in his camp. But Al Hithlain refused, saying that if he failed to return to his own camp that night his followers would fear the worst and come looking for him. For some reason Fahd interpreted Al Hithlain's words and actions as some kind of threat and ordered his attendants to seize him and his followers and clap them in chains. But one of Al Hithlain's followers, spotting the danger just in time, succeeded in evading Fahd's attendants, leapt onto his camel and galloped back to Al Hithlain's camp to raise the alarm. Immediately fifteen hundred of Al Hithlain's Ajman followers grabbed their weapons, mounted their camels and set out for Fahd's camp. In the early hours of May 1st they burst in Fahd's camp, hunting for their amir and slaying every one of Fahd's men they saw. Realising that he could not beat off the Ajman warriors Fahd ordered his father's African slave executioner to cut Dhaidan Al Hithlain's throat, mounted his horse and made to escape. But one of Fahd's own body-servants, shocked at his master's breach of Bedouin chivalry and duty towards a man who he had entertained in his tent as his honoured guest, grabbed the horse's bridle and drawing his gun, shot Fahd in the head.

News of what had happened and Fahd's scandalous abuse of the most fundamental rules of Bedouin honour and hospitality spread across the desert like wildfire, re-igniting the rebellion and bringing fresh adherents to the rebels' cause. The blame for what Fahd had done was widely put on Ibn Saud himself. Fahd was his trusted lieutenant Jiluwi's son, in inviting Al Hithlain to meet him he had been acting on Ibn Saud's instructions and Al Hithlain had been carrying a safe conduct signed by Ibn Saud himself when Fahd had had him murdered. Al Hithlain's tribe the Ajman, even many of those who had previously remained loyal to Ibn Saud, now rose against him. Duwish, who had not died from the wound he had received at Sibilla, again led his men out against Ibn Saud and sent his son Azaiyiz with a force of six hundred warriors to raid tribes in the north that were still loyal to Ibn Saud. The Ataiba, whose leader Ibn Bijad had been imprisoned and whose settlement at Ghat Ghat had been destroyed, also rose in revolt.

Upon hearing what had happened, Ibn Saud collected together all the motor vehicles he could find and set out to return to Riyadh. But his arrival was delayed because much of the route back from Mecca to Riyadh lay across Ataiba territory where he and his party would face the constant threat of ambush. As a result he was forced to make a detour of hundreds of miles to the north.

Meanwhile by the summer of 1929 Glubb had, in the face of much obstruction and delay by his superiors, managed to organise and train an effective fighting force to take on the Ikhwan raiders. Called the Southern Desert Camel Corps, it was made up of seventy camel soldiers, thirty machine gunners travelling in six open cars and trucks equipped with mounted machine guns and two wireless vans. This force could, when flying conditions were suitable and aircraft available, be supported by planes of the RAF. Although operating over huge areas of rough desert and sand in temperatures often in excess of 120°F, Glubb's Southern Desert Camel Corps, with its combination of radio communications, manoeuvrability and fire-power could find, overhaul and out-gun the Ikhwan raiding parties. Although at first the guns were mounted in such a way that they were only able to fire over the tailboard, with the result that the trucks had to race up after the enemy and when they got within shooting range slew round in the sand and come to a halt facing away from the enemy before opening fire, by the summer of 1929 they and the rest of Glubb's force were proving so effective that the Ikhwan were coming to fear them.

When Ibn Saud at last managed to get back to Riyadh with his fleet of assorted motor vehicles, many severely battered, their springs and suspensions broken by the hundreds of miles of rough terrain they had had to cross, he set about getting them fitted with machine guns and acquiring radio communications for them. Always a keen student of developments in Western military equipment and tactics, he had no doubt heard about the recent successes achieved by Glubb's mobile columns. At the same time he sent fresh appeals to the British to make sure that any of the rebels who sought refuge in Iraq or Transjordan were denied it and to prevent Shaikh Ahmad, the ruler of Kuwait, from supplying them with arms or offering them asylum.

Nevertheless by August 1929 the rebels seemed to be gaining the upper hand. Away from the towns the rebels seemed free to roam at will, raiding, killing and terrorising those loyal to Ibn Saud, stealing their possessions and driving off their livestock. Even a force of warriors and armed vehicles which was carrying fresh arms and supplies to Jiluwi in Hofuf, under the command of Ibn Saud's eldest son Saud, was ambushed by Ajman rebels. Fourteen of the lorries and other vehicles were destroyed and, according to reports, Saud only succeeded in escaping by being driven at breakneck speed across the desert and away from the fighting in a Mercedes. At the same time well to the north, close to the frontier with Transjordan and Iraq, Duwish's son Azaiyiz and his six hundred and fifty warriors were not only terrorising the local shepherds and Bedouin, capturing thousands of camels belonging to loyal Shammar and Amarat tribesmen, they also seized a convoy carrying ten thousand *rials*' worth of taxes which were in transit back to Ibn Saud in Riyadh.

Late in August Azaiyiz turned for home with his loot, intending to present it proudly to his father. But to have raided hundreds of miles out into the desert and away from the safety of his own home territory during the hottest period of the summer had been a foolhardy enterprise which an older and less hot-headed leader than Azaiyiz would never have embarked upon. Sandwiched between the Iraqi frontier and the Nafud desert he was forced to make his way from one deep well to another along a route which anyone with a knowledge of the region could predict. On Ibn Saud's instructions his governor in Ha'il had sent out parties of fighting men to each well and dug themselves into strong defensive positions around them. As a result as Azaiyiz and his warriors with their thousands of captured camels approached each well they came under a barrage of well aimed rifle fire from men in unassailable positions. So they were forced to travel on for day after day in temperatures well above 100°F, the men becoming thirstier and thirstier and the camels ever thinner, wasting away and dying in greater numbers as each day passed. With their condition now becoming desperate one of Azaiyiz's lieutenants, Faisal Al Shiblan, came to him and suggested that they change course and attempt to cross into the Iraq Neutral Zone. But Azaiyiz refused. He was determined to head by the shortest route back to his father. So Al Shiblan and one hundred and fifty of the warriors and several hundred of the captured camels split from Azaiyiz's force and headed north-eastwards into Iraq and eventually to Kuwait, where some months later, after making more raids he surrendered to Harold Dickson. Later, on Dickson's advice, he threw himself on Ibn Saud's mercy. Ibn Saud, recognising his bravery, not only pardoned him but took him into his service.

Meanwhile Azaiyiz with his remaining five hundred warriors and looted camels hurried on south-eastwards as best they could until, some thirty miles south of the Iraq Neutral Zone, they neared the wells at a place called Umm ar Rudhuma. It was midday, the temperature, according to Dickson, was probably approaching 170°F, and the need of Azaiyiz's men and camels for water was now desperate. Their last reserve water-skins had long ago been emptied and the men had not had anything at all to drink since the previous day. They must drink now or die. Azaiyiz's scouts had told him that the wells were defended by one thousand five hundred of Ibn Saud's loyal Shammar, Harb and Hadhar tribesmen, but Azaiyiz marched on until they were within sight of the wells and their defenders. Azaiyiz then halted his men and ordered the call to prayer. The five hundred thirst-crazed and exhausted men fell to their knees and prayed in the prescribed manner. When they had finished Azaiyiz rose and addressed them. 'Are we not of the brotherhood, and the elect of God? We must go on and win the water. The Almighty will help his children.'[1] Then, he turned and quietly told his slave to save his mare if it was at all possible. After that Azaiyiz remounted his camel and gave his Ikhwan warriors the order to charge.

Although met by a hail of rifle fire the desperate charge of Azaiyiz's five hundred thirst-maddened warriors almost succeeded. Because of the intense heat of the day the desert and everything in it danced in a mirage. As a result a lot of the wells' defenders' bullets missed their intended targets and many of Azaiyiz's charging warriors reached the defenders' lines and got in amongst them. The battle became a desperate hand-to-hand struggle. Hundreds on both sides died until, as the sun began to dip into the west, the greater numbers of the defenders began to tell. At last, with more than three hundred and fifty of his five hundred men now dead, Azaiyiz allowed five of his own bodyguards to lead him away from the last groups of blood-smeared, sweating, struggling, slashing, exhausted men and made his escape. By the end of that terrible day when all the fighting was at last done just thirty-eight of Azaiyiz's five hundred men were still alive. Two months later Azaiyiz's dried-up body and those of his five servants were found deep in the heart of the desert lying beside their dead riding camels. All had died of thirst.

In October, having received an undertaking from the British that they would prevent the rebels from finding sanctuary in Iraq or Kuwait, and with his vehicles hastily repaired, many only with wire, string or leather thongs, but with radios fitted to some, machine guns to others and the rest crammed with riflemen, Ibn Saud once more took to the field. Setting out westwards he quickly achieved a major victory over the

1 H. R. P. Dickson, *Kuwait and Her Neighbours*, George Allen & Unwin, London, 1917.

Ataiba, eliminating them for good as serious opponents, and then headed eastwards for the Hasa to confront Duwish.

With Glubb and the Shaikh of Kuwait's mobile columns now harrying any rebel groups who crossed into Iraq or Kuwait and driving them back into Najd, and Ibn Saud's mobile column out-pacing, surprising and out-gunning any groups of rebels it encountered, more and more of the tribes who had sided with Duwish began to re-join Ibn Saud. As ever greater numbers joined Ibn Saud in hunting down the rebel gangs, Duwish and the other rebel leaders seemed to lose heart. Duwish's own willingness to continue the struggle was probably also seriously undermined by the loss of his much-beloved son Azaiyiz. The result was that late in October Duwish crossed the border into Kuwait with a small escort of men and sent a messenger to Shaikh Ahmad, the ruler of Kuwait, and to the British Political Agent, Harold Dickson, to enquire if there was any chance of them allowing him, his tribesmen, their families and livestock to take sanctuary in Iraq or Kuwait. Acting on the instructions of the British Government, Dickson turned down Duwish's request. His reply made it clear that he held out little hope of Britain letting up in its operations against him in either Kuwait or Iraq nor even over the border in northern Najd. He ordered Duwish to withdraw out of Kuwait immediately. Duwish responded that, as it was clear that Britain was on the side of Ibn Saud and would not even offer protection to his womenfolk, he had no option but to try to make terms with Ibn Saud.

From that day on, although Duwish and the rebels still had ample munitions and men with which to carry on, Duwish made no further effort. He told his allies to leave him and try to make their own separate peace with Ibn Saud. Those who did not approach Ibn Saud but tried instead to cross into Kuwait or Iraq were driven out again or else captured and interned by the British. Any who resisted were slaughtered by a combination of British air power and the British-armed and -officered Iraqi and Kuwaiti armies and police forces. Having dismissed his allies and with Ibn Saud continuing his inexorable advance upon him from the south, Duwish sent a messenger to the King asking to open negotiations for a surrender. Terms were soon agreed but before Duwish went to hand himself in to Ibn Saud he went to see Dickson. He asked

Dickson to take all the women and children of his household into his protection. Duwish's last words to Dickson before he left to go to Ibn Saud and accept whatever punishment Ibn Saud had in store for him were: 'I hand my ladies to your personal charge, O Dickson, and from my protective honour to your protective honour.' Dickson accepted the responsibility and on January 10th 1930 he and Duwish rode out alone to the camp of Air Commodore Sir Charles Stuart Burnett, commander of the RAF in Iraq. There the old warrior, now a sorry but dignified shadow of his former fierce self, handed his sword hilt first to the Air Commodore and made his formal surrender. He and two other lesser Ikhwan leaders were then put on board an RAF plane and flown to Basra where they were transferred to the British warship, HMS *Lupin*, which was waiting at anchor in the Shatt al Arab.

On January 23rd Dickson, together with the British Political Resident in the Persian Gulf Sir Hugh Biscoe, Air Commodore Burnett and the Shaikh of Kuwait flew the ninety miles south to Ibn Saud's camp to negotiate terms for handing over Duwish and the other rebels who were in British and Kuwaiti hands. After three days of bargaining Ibn Saud agreed to spare the lives of the leaders and their followers and to prevent any future raids by his subjects into either Iraq or Kuwait. Then, on January 28th Duwish and the two other rebel leaders, fitted out with new clothes by Dickson, were transferred from HMS *Lupin* to an RAF plane in Kuwait and, in Dickson's charge, flown to Ibn Saud's camp. Upon landing Dickson and the three rebels were led to a large *majlis* tent where they found Ibn Saud sitting surrounded by members of his family and loyal tribal leaders. Tears were rolling down Ibn Saud's cheeks as in turn Duwish and the two other rebel leaders approached him and were allowed, as in the traditional greeting between Bedouins, to kiss him on the nose. Ibn Saud then sat Dickson down beside him and thanked him for all he had done on his behalf and for taking Duwish's womenfolk into his care. 'Verily, O Dickson,' he said, 'we appreciate your good deeds, for although Al Duwish did indeed rebel against his King and did fight us, yet his ladies are of pure and noble blood and are entitled to the fullest consideration and protection. It will be our special duty to continue to care for them, as soon as we are able to send cars to Kuwait and take them away from you.' Dickson then gave Ibn Saud a personal message from his wife in which she, as a mother, begged Ibn Saud to show mercy to all his 'erring children'.[2]

Ibn Saud kept his word. He did not cut off Duwish and the other rebels' heads as many of those around him, and probably Duwish himself, expected. Instead he placed Duwish in protective custody in Riyadh where he died eighteen month later of a haemorrhage of the throat which was probably the result of cancer. When he realised he was dying, rather than sending Ibn Saud a deathbed apology, Duwish sent him a message in which he forgave him. The rebels' loot was confiscated and the remnants of the *al Shuruf*, the honoured herd of black camels of the Mutair tribe, was taken into Ibn Saud's keeping. The descendants of the remnants of that herd of black camels survive to this day among the herds of the Saudi royal family.

Dickson and his wife looked after Duwish's children and womenfolk, thirty-seven in all, in Kuwait for six weeks, feeding, re-clothing and nursing them all back to health after the privations they had endured during the last phase of the rebellion. They were then taken to Riyadh in a convoy of cars sent to collect them by Ibn Saud, where they were given houses and treated with honour by the King for the rest of their lives. Ibn Saud kept the other leaders of the rebellion in prison in Riyadh until 1934. Ikhwanism did not die out, but from then on it took a less militant form. Even so Ibn Saud never regained his former popularity among some former Ikhwan members in the northeast who continued to feel that he had betrayed the Ikhwan's ideals. Traces of militant Ikhwanism survive to this day, troubling not only modern Saudi Arabia but the wider world.

* * *

During their negotiation with Ibn Saud in January the British delegation had proposed that a meeting take place between Ibn Saud and the King of Iraq, Husayn's son Feisal, to try to resolve the dispute between them. However, Ibn Saud refused point blank to visit Feisal in Iraq and Feisal refused to go to Najd to see Ibn Saud. The British, who were eager to

2 The account of Duwish's surrender is based on Dickson's own eye-witness account in *Kuwait and Her Neighbours,* op. cit.

end the continuing threat of war between the two monarchs, then suggested that they meet on neutral ground, a British warship out in the Gulf. Eventually, it having been agreed that the ship should be out of sight of land so that neither side could be said to have an advantage, Feisal and Ibn Saud agreed. The British also calculated that by holding the meeting out at sea on the deck of a warship neither participant would be in a position to outdo the other through displays of wealth or magnificence.

On the evening of February 21st 1930 three ships rendezvoused out of sight of land near the northern end of the Persian Gulf. Next morning the two monarchs were transferred from their ships to the deck of HMS *Lupin*. Feisal and Ibn Saud greeted each other politely enough and made affable conversation although throughout it remained perfectly clear to their British hosts that they did not like each other. However even this semblance of peace was shattered when the British proposed that the two monarchs should exchange letters agreeing to enter into a treaty of good neighbourliness. Feisal, who like the other Hashemites continued to believe that the Hijaz remained part of his family's historic birthright, refused to sign any letter to Ibn Saud which addressed him by any title which included the words 'King of the Hijaz'. Ibn Saud responded in kind, refusing to receive any letter which did not give him his new full title – 'King of the Hijaz and Najd and its dependencies'. Faced with this seeming impasse the British representatives hastily set about trying to smooth both kings' ruffled feathers. After much to-ing and fro-ing a resolution was found: it was agreed by both kings that they would employ no titles but address each other simply as 'Dear Brother'. While the small talk continued and a number of petty disagreements between the two monarchs were sorted out, below decks officials of all three sides hammered out an agreement of friendship and good neighbourliness between the two kingdoms. This was initialled by Ibn Saud's and Feisal's representatives in Baghdad a fortnight later. As a result, although relations between the two monarchs were never to become good, there were no further hostilities between their two countries during their lifetimes.

* * *

By 1930, following the Wall Street Crash and the onset of the world-wide economic depression, Ibn Saud's enlarged but still fragile state was in financial trouble. The cost of suppressing the Ikhwan rebellion in payments and gifts to his allies, together with the import of modern western inventions such as wireless, motor vehicles, guns and ammunition, had drained Ibn Saud's reserves of gold – held as they always had been by his treasurer, Abdullah al Sulaiman, in a portable tin trunk. The ravages of civil war had also seriously reduced stocks of animals and interfered with the cultivation and harvesting of crops such as dates. In many areas this was greatly exacerbated by two years of serious drought. The fighting, followed by the world economic crisis, also greatly reduced the number of overseas pilgrims entering the country to undertake the annual *Hajj*. 126,000 foreign pilgrims had entered the country in 1926 but by 1930 the number had fallen to 40,000 and was to continue to drop, reaching only 20,000 in 1933. The result was that while Ibn Saud's administrative costs had risen greatly owing to the enlarged size and complexity of his kingdom, the country's income from exports and taxes had fallen even further, from an estimated £5 million to under £2 million. By 1930, with his treasurer's tin trunk effectively empty, the wages of Ibn Saud's officials began to be withheld for months on end, the subsidies paid to tribal shaikhs began to cease and repayment of debts to foreign companies were delayed. In parts of the country there was famine. The corruption, extortion and dishonesty practised on the people by officials in the Hijaz before Ibn Saud had conquered it started to reappear and spread insidiously through the administration. It was a sorry departure from the puritanical standards of behaviour and financial probity normally expected of Wahhabis. The truth was that at heart Ibn Saud cared little about money and, although he did genuinely care about the well-being of his subjects, was too ignorant about matters of financial administration to take effective action. So, even if he knew about what was happening, he appeared to do little about it. Instead he came to depend ever more upon his treasurer al Sulaiman, trusting him to look after financial matters and save him from having to deal with them. He could then devote his energies to those things that really interested him. But al Sulaiman with his tin trunk and large ledger, wily and loyal though he was, was not up to the task of controlling the financial affairs of an emerging modern state. So, although to outsiders visiting Ibn Saud's court the King still appeared to entertain his guests, feed his subjects and give presents as generously as he ever had, out of sight new forms of opposition began to stir.

Shortly after Ibn Saud had completed his conquest of the Hijaz some of the leading Hijazi shaikhs who remained loyal to Husayn had fled to Egypt and set up an organisation dedicated to the re-conquest of the Hijaz, the League for the Protection of the Hijaz. Encouraged by Husayn's son Abdullah, the King of Transjordan, leaders of the League had toured the Arab world trying to drum up support. By 1930 they had succeeded in gaining the support of King Fuad of Egypt and émigré Hijazis in Egypt and Aden. Now they were also beginning to gain new adherents inside Ibn Saud's kingdom itself. Faced by all these problems, Ibn Saud knew that if he was to hold on to his new kingdom, bring it into the modern world and improve the lives of his subjects he desperately needed to find a new source of income. But where?

The answer came from Harry St John Philby, the junior civil servant on Sir Percy Cox's staff who had travelled to Riyadh with Colonel Hamilton in 1917 to negotiate the agreement under which, in return for a monthly subsidy and being supplied with British arms and ammunition, Ibn Saud had agreed to take a more active part in the war by attacking Turkey's allies the Rashids. The love of Arabia and admiration for Ibn Saud kindled in Philby during that first visit to Riyadh had never left him and in 1924, disillusioned with British policy in the region and feeling that his talents were under-appreciated, he had resigned from the British Indian Civil Service and set out to survive by his own efforts. After setting up his wife and young children in London and negotiating contracts to act as the agent in Najd and the Hijaz for a number of British and American companies, including Ford and Marconi wireless, Philby had travelled to Jeddah and set about working his way into Ibn Saud's confidence. By 1930 Philby, who one of his British colleagues had described a few years earlier as having a 'streak of madness' to run alongside 'his immense energy and real ability',[3] had

3 Reader Bullard's 'Report for July 1924' included in *Two Kings in Arabia: Sir Reader Bullard's Letters from Jeddah*, edited by E. C. Hodgkin, Ithaca Press, Reading, England, 1993.

formally embraced the Muslim faith and succeeded in becoming one of Ibn Saud's closest advisers and confidants. Ibn Saud even gave him one of his female slaves to comfort him during his long separations from his wife.

So it was that Philby happened to be with Ibn Saud in one of his motorcars returning from a hunting trip one afternoon in the autumn of 1930. The King seemed sunk in a mood of deepest gloom. When Philby asked the cause Ibn Saud sighed wearily and then went on to tell Philby about his serious worries over the state of his kingdom's finances. He told Philby that he could see no way of making ends meet and saw himself as beset on all sides by increasing problems. Philby responded boldly, chiding Ibn Saud and telling him that he and his Government were 'like folk asleep on the site of buried treasure, but too lazy or frightened to dig in search for it'. The King asked him to explain what he meant and Philby told him that he had no doubt that the enormous area that the King now controlled must contain huge amounts of mineral resources. But, he pointed out, those resources were of no use to him or anyone else while they remained buried deep in the ground. What the King needed was an expert geologist to explore the area, conduct a search and then tell him what was there. Once the minerals had been located he would then need foreign capital and expertise to exploit them. But, Philby chided, the King and his Government seemed to have turned their faces against granting any foreign companies concessions to enter the country to help to unlock its potential wealth. Instead, Philby scolded, you simply sit back and bemoan your poverty. Philby ended his admonishments by quoting one of his own favourite verses from the Qur'an: 'God changeth not that which is in people unless they change that which is in themselves.'

'Oh, Philby,' Ibn Saud replied almost imploringly, 'if anyone would offer me a million pounds, I would give him all the concessions he wanted.' Philby told the King that no one would just give him a million pounds for the concession without first carrying out an initial investigation into the country's potential deposits. But, he continued, there was at that moment a man in Egypt, an American, who Ibn Saud had refused to meet eighteen months earlier at the height of the Ikhwan rebellion. Philby told Ibn Saud that this man had recently visited Yemen and done much to help that country and 'He could help you too, for this is a very rich man, with important contacts in the American industrial community.'[4]

The man was Charles Crane who had been the other American in the car when the missionary Henry Bilkert had been killed by the Ikhwan during a raid into Kuwait in January 1929. Crane was a millionaire philanthropist who had inherited a family fortune made from a firm which manufactured and supplied bathroom fittings and plumbing materials. A proven friend of the Arabs, Crane had been a member of the Commission of Investigation sent to the Middle East in 1919 by President Woodrow Wilson to inquire into the British and French proposals under the terms of the Sykes-Picot Agreement to carve up the region between themselves into a series of mandates and the Balfour Declaration's promise to establish a Jewish national homeland in Palestine. The Commission's task had been to report to the President on how these arrangements could be squared with Article XXII of the Covenant of the League of Nations which required that the prime consideration in all such matters must be the wishes of the local population. In its findings the Commission had come down against the Anglo-French proposals, particularly the proposed national Jewish homeland in Palestine which, they said, because of the pressure on the Arabs already living there to surrender their land to the Jewish immigrants, would amount to 'a gross violation' of their rights. Since then Crane had helped the ruler of Yemen by providing him with a harbour and the first modern roads and bridges. He had also set about improving the country's agriculture by organising surveys to search for sources of artesian water. Crane had twice visited the Hijaz while Husayn was still on the throne for the same purpose. Philby told Ibn Saud that he was certain that Crane would be happy to meet him – 'He would willingly give one of his eyes to see you with the other!' All Ibn Saud had to do was to tell Philby when he would next be in Jeddah and he would make arrangements for Crane to travel there to meet him.

Ibn Saud agreed and a series of meetings took place over the week of February 25th 1931. After discussing a whole range of economic issues

4 Our account of Philby's conversation with Ibn Saud is based on a number of accounts given by Philby over the years, but principally the one in Philby's book *Arabian Jubilee*, Robert Hale, London 1952.

with Ibn Saud and his advisers, Crane offered to provide the King with the services of a well-qualified water and mining engineer for six months to carry out a survey of the country's potential water and mineral resources.

Five weeks later a frugal but energetic American mining engineer who had been working for Crane in Yemen, called Karl Twitchell, landed with his wife in Jeddah and, after meeting Ibn Saud and being provided with a guide and bodyguard, set off in a small convoy of cars to survey for sources of water close to the main towns of the Hijaz. After fifteen hundred miles of bouncing across all kinds of rough terrain, with frequent stops because of minor breakdowns and shredded tyres, the results of their endeavours were deeply disappointing. Apart from being able to recommend the installation of a modern American windmill and auxiliary diesel pump near an existing well outside Jeddah, the Twitchells had found very little evidence of other major untapped sources of water in the region. However, while carrying out their water survey the Twitchells had also taken note of various long-disused mine workings which they had come across during their travels. One in particular, about 3,000 feet up in the hills outside Medina, seemed particularly promising. The large nearby spoil heaps suggested that ancient miners must have worked the site intensively and for a considerable period. Known locally as Madh al-Dhahab (The Cradle of Gold), the area was reputed to be the site of the legendary King Solomon's Mines – in fact subsequent modern carbon dating has shown that the site must have been being worked as much as three thousand years ago. During their visit the Twitchells concluded that Madh al-Dhahab probably still contained gold in sufficient quantities to be commercially workable. So as well as reporting back to al Sulaiman in Jeddah at the end of their 1,500 mile trip their disappointing findings about potential additional water supplies, the Twitchells were able to offer the prospect of something more promising in the field of mineral extraction and of gold in particular.

After going home on leave for the summer of 1931, the Twitchells returned to Jeddah in the autumn to begin work on improving the town's water supply. During Twitchell's first meeting with Ibn Saud one of the subjects discussed had been the possibility of there being oil, especially in the Hasa. A few years earlier a major new oil field had been discovered in Iraq and the oil companies had become excited by the possibility that there might be other major fields to be discovered in other parts of the region. Local tribal legend in the area of the Hasa close to the Kuwait Neutral Zone told of a family imprisoned for eternity a long time ago in a deep underground cavern by a magic formula, their escape barred by a bubbling, vile-smelling, tar spring pool which, if anyone approached it intent on rescuing the family, erupted in violent sulphurous, oil-charged bubbles which re-activate the magic spell and repelled the would-be rescuers.

So, in December 1931, leaving his wife to supervise a team of some twenty-five Arab workmen who were to conduct test drills and, if they were successful, install the new windmill and diesel water pump outside Jeddah, Karl Twitchell set out to cross Arabia to the Hasa, on his way passing through Riyadh for a further meeting with Ibn Saud. As he set off, now kitted out in Arab robes and accompanied by a bodyguard, guide and a number of servants, officials from the British Legation were looking on. Secretly they were glad to see the back of Twitchell and resentful that he was present in the country at all. To them the whole of Arabia still belonged exclusively within Britain's sphere of special influence. After he had gone they sent a dismissive report back to the Foreign Office in London: 'It seems fairly clear that nothing of much importance will result from Mr Twitchell's investigations. He appears to be something of a busybody.'

Six days later Twitchell met Ibn Saud in his camp fifty miles north of Riyadh. As well as carrying out surveys for water and oil in the Hasa, the King asked Twitchell to cross over to Bahrain and deliver letters to the Sultan and other Bahraini notables. Having reached the Hasa Twitchell concentrated his search on the coast, especially in the area around Uqair and Qatif, the region of sand dunes in which ten years earlier Harold Dickson had searched in vain for traces of the oil seepage known years earlier to the Turks and where that mysterious employee of the Eastern and General oil-prospecting syndicate, the New Zealander Frank Holmes, had told Dickson and his wife he hoped to find a specimen of the extremely rare butterfly called the 'Black Admiral'. Twitchell failed to find traces of any oil seepage either. But his crossing to deliver the letters entrusted to him by Ibn Saud to the Sultan of Bahrain, that supposed site of the legendary pristine paradise where the gods had settled the Sumerian Noah after the flood, gave Twitchell the opportunity to take a look at how the oilmen then engaged in a hunt for oil on the island were getting on. They, knowing that Twitchell was also a geologist and oil man, were very suspicious of him, suspecting he was a spy from a rival company. Nevertheless, Twitchell picked up enough information to conclude that they had grounds for being optimistic about their chances of striking oil.

Three weeks later, on his return journey to Jeddah, Twitchell stopped off in Hofuf to report his findings to Ibn Saud. He found the King eager for news. He had heard about what was happening in Bahrain and Kuwait, and, more importantly that the rulers of these two tiny states were receiving large sums of money from the oil companies for doing nothing more than granting them concessions to search for oil. When Twitchell told him that if oil was found in Bahrain he thought that it was likely that there would also be oil in the Hasa, Ibn Saud asked Twitchell to arrange for oil geologists and well-drillers to go to Hasa and start exploring at once. But Twitchell, with the detachment of an experienced geologist, counselled caution. Ibn Saud should wait for the oil men in Bahrain to complete their test drill and see whether they found any oil. If they did, the geology of Bahrain and the Hasa mainland being similar, there would probably also be oil under Hasa. But if there was no oil on Bahrain then it was very unlikely that there would be any in Hasa either. Oil exploration and drilling, Twitchell told Ibn Saud, was very expensive, so it would be wiser to wait until he knew the results of the test drilling on Bahrain before he did anything at all. Ibn Saud, who after ten years was still smarting from being let down by Frank Holmes and the Eastern and General Syndicate, remained deeply suspicious of oil companies and oil men, so he accepted Twitchell's advice.

The six months of Twitchell's services which Charles Crane had said he would pay for were now up and because of the continuing economic depression he could not extend Twitchell's time in Arabia any further. So early in March 1932 Twitchell and his wife, who during her husband's absence in Hasa had successfully installed the windmill and diesel pump outside Jeddah, so adding an additional forty gallons of fresh water per minute to the town's antiquated and over-taxed water supply, departed. However, back in America Twitchell set about trying to interest a number of big corporations in the mining and oil possibilities in both the Hijaz and Hasa. At the same time Philby also set about trying to get companies interested.

But as 1932 progressed and the Depression continued to show no sign of letting up, the rumbles of unrest in the Hijaz continued to grow louder. Ibn Saud's anxieties grew. In spite of the visit by Crane and explorations of the Twitchells, the 'buried treasure' which Philby had held out to Ibn Saud as the means of his financial salvation, remained as 'buried' as ever. The number of pilgrims making the *Hajj* dwindled still further and the value and number of his country's few exports continued to decline. But then suddenly, in June 1932, news arrived that the oil men on Bahrain had struck oil in large quantities. At last it seemed that Ibn Saud might have something that he could sell.

Because of the Red Line Agreement, the private deal made in Ostend four years earlier between the four leading British, French, Dutch and American oil companies to carve up all the oil in the Middle East between themselves, the competition between oil companies for concessions in the region was likely to be limited. So Ibn Saud was still probably going to find it difficult to sell the Hasa concession for a good price. To make matters worse, ever since oil had been discovered in Persia back in 1908 Britain had done everything it could to prevent the oil companies of countries other than Britain from acquiring oil concessions in the region. During the First World War Balfour had made it clear that Britain would do all in its power to ensure that Britain and its dominions kept control of all the region's oil. As a consequence, in 1930 when the ruler of Bahrain had been on the point of selling the Bahraini oil concession to an American company, Standard Oil of California (SOCAL), the British Government had hastily dispatched a representative to him and reminded him of his obligations under a treaty he had signed with Britain 1914 under which he was provided with protection by Britain but in return had accepted certain conditions, one of which prohibited him from entering into any contracts with companies not registered in Britain or the British Dominions without the prior consent of the British Government.

However, SOCAL and the ruler of Bahrain had got round this obstacle by creating a subsidiary called the Bahrain Petroleum Company (Bapco) and registering it in Canada. It was this company, Bapco, owned by SOCAL, which had struck oil in Bahrain. Although the British had no similar treaty with Ibn Saud they nevertheless continued to regard his country as being within their own sphere of special influence and would try to frustrate any agreement over the concession which Ibn Saud attempted to make with any company which was not British. So, in late 1932, as it became known that Ibn Saud and his advisers were trying to sell the Hasa concession, the British Government, through its interest in the Anglo-Persian Oil Company, prepared to move in on any potential deal. In fact Anglo-Persian, with its fields in Persia and other parts of the region, had as much oil as it could sell and so had little real interest in acquiring the Hasa concession. That, however, did not mean that it would not try to stop any other company from acquiring it, or, failing that, do its best to keep down the price that Ibn Saud might get for it.

So it was that when, in February 1933, two representatives of SOCAL, accompanied by their wives, landed at Jeddah and moved into rooms on the top floor of a newly built hotel, they were quickly followed by a representative of Anglo-Persian. These two competitors for the concession were soon followed by a third, the mysterious 'butterfly collector', Frank Holmes of the Eastern and General Syndicate, the company which ten years earlier had had the concession but let it lapse. The fact that representatives of all three companies arrived at the same time, apparently set on staging a bidding war, was largely due to some hard work and clever fixing by Philby.

While in London visiting his family the previous summer Philby had been approached by two representatives of SOCAL and asked, as an intimate of Ibn Saud, what he thought were the chances of SOCAL being able to persuade Ibn Saud to grant them the Hasa oil concession. Over lunch at Simpson's in the Strand, Philby had encouraged their hopes, telling them that whatever the eventual terms of any deal, an important element in it was likely to be the payment of a lump sum up front in gold. Later, having conferred with Ibn Saud, Philby had wired SOCAL an outline of the terms on which Ibn Saud would be prepared to enter into negotiations for the concession and at the same time secured for himself a contract with SOCAL to act as their consultant. Philby, who was still receiving a small British Civil Service pension and so was still expected not to act against British interests, also made sure that the British Government knew of SOCAL's interest. What he did not tell the British Government, however, was that he was also receiving a fee of $1,000 per month as a consultant to SOCAL.

Frank Holmes did not stay in the bidding for long. A few days after his arrival in Jeddah Philby visited him and pointed out that in order to be taken seriously as a bidder he would have to pay the outstanding arrears in concession fees dating back to 1927, from when Eastern and General had ceased making their rental payments for their original Hasa oil extraction contract until the date when the concession had formally lapsed – a sum which amounted to £6,000 in gold. If Holmes failed to pay he would not only fail to be taken seriously as a bidder, he might find that he had incurred Ibn Saud's extreme displeasure. Holmes decided to beat a hasty retreat.

With Holmes gone, the people left in the bidding were, for SOCAL, their concessions lawyer, Lloyd N. Hamilton, supported by Karl Twitchell, who had been taken on by SOCAL because of his unrivalled knowledge of the territory, and for Anglo-Persian an outstanding Arabist and oil expert, Stephen H. Longrigg, who would later write one of the standard works on the history of the Middle Eastern oil industry. Longrigg was supported by the head of the British Legation in Jeddah, a career diplomat, Sir Andrew Ryan. Ibn Saud himself did not take much part in the actual negotiations, leaving those mainly to the man who was in effect his finance minister, al Sulaiman.

Before the negotiations began Sulaiman, Philby and Ibn Saud agreed between themselves that they should try to get the successful bidder to pay a lump sum of £100,000 in gold up front against future royalties of four shillings (20p in today's money) per ton of oil produced, payment also to be in gold. But once the negotiations started it soon became obvious that getting the upfront sum that Ibn Saud and Sulaiman wanted was going to be difficult. Nevertheless Philby worked as hard as he could to get the bidders to raise their price, continuously beating his way back and forth between them, conferring here, dropping a hint there and generally trying to get each in turn to raise their bid. For week after week the negotiations went on, into the start of the strength-sapping heat and humidity of the Arabian Red Sea summer, with Philby still shuttling unflaggingly between the three sides, between al Sulaiman and Ibn Saud, sometimes in Jeddah, sometimes in Riyadh or Mecca, and then either the British team in their base at the British Legation or the American team in their rooms on the top floor of their Jeddah hotel. Both bidders fairly quickly agreed to al Sulaiman and the King's proposed royalty rate of four shillings per ton of oil produced and to the condition that they must carry out their searches without interruption. From then on the negotiation turned on the size of the down payment, the thing which to Ibn Saud mattered most. Ibn Saud and al Sulaiman insisted on their £100,000 in gold up front, but the British stubbornly refused to offer more than £10,000, saying repeatedly that there probably was not any oil to be found anyway. But still Philby went back and forth, trying repeatedly to get the sum increased.

Eventually he persuaded SOCAL to up its offer to £50,000 against the agreed 4 shillings per ton royalty. Ibn Saud hesitated. He needed more than £50,000. Also, he had never dealt with the Americans before. Were they, or any oil company, to be trusted? On the other hand his immediate need for gold in-hand was now more urgent than ever. Also he knew the British of old, the way in which over the years since he seized power they had repeatedly let him down and belittled him, their tendency to interfere in the countries with which they had dealings, to treat the Arab countries as their colonies. The Americans, being further away, might be less inclined to interfere in his country's internal affairs. In a private interview Ibn Saud told the chief American negotiator, Hamilton, that he would prefer to give the concession to an American company. But in another private interview, with Stephen Longrigg, he said that he would rather award it to the British. Englishmen like Cox and, above all, Shakespear had been true friends.

Ibn Saud seems to have been genuinely undecided. However, in the end it was the size of the down payment that proved decisive. He needed the money and, with al Sulaiman and Philby both advising him to go with the Americans, he made his decision. Yet even so, right up to the last moment he hesitated. Throughout the weeks of negotiations Ibn Saud had studiously kept in touch with the British diplomat Sir Andrew Ryan. Now, right at the point of decision he consulted him for one last time. Should he accept the American bid? Ryan, it seems, replied that he should, saying once more that there probably was not any oil under the

Hasa anyway. So, after calling together all the members of his council and making al Sulaiman read out the full terms of the proposed agreement to them and allowing them to comment, he told al Sulaiman: 'Put your trust in God and sign.'[5]

The contract was finally signed by al Sulaiman on behalf of Ibn Saud and by Lloyd Hamilton on behalf of SOCAL on a blazingly hot day, May 29th 1933, in the new Khuzam Palace, constructed for the King just outside the old southern wall of Jeddah by an engineer called Muhammad bin Laden, the son of a poor Yemenite who had emigrated to the Hijaz before the First World War and established a successful building company. Karl Twitchell was there to witness the signatures and take a photograph of the signing. The terms of the deal stipulated that SOCAL would pay a sum of £30,000 in gold, plus £5,000 for the first year's rent immediately, followed eighteen months later by a second sum of £20,000 in gold, plus a rental fee of £5,000 per year against a royalty of 4/- per ton of oil produced. The agreement was to last for sixty years and the area covered by the concession was to include almost the whole of the eastern part of the kingdom. For SOCAL it was to turn out to be one of the most advantageous deals ever signed. That they had won themselves such a good deal was due in no small measure to the obstructionist and self-defeating intervention of the British Government and its proxy the Anglo-Persian Oil Company. Far from derailing the deal, the British intervention had resulted in the Americans paying even less than they would have had to had the British either themselves competed seriously to win the contract or allowed other companies which were not parties to the Red Line Agreement to take part in the bidding. The award of the concession to SOCAL marked the beginning of the end of the Red Line Agreement and of Britain's dominant influence in Ibn Saud's Arabia and the start of his country's special relationship with America.

But even the signing of the deal by al Sulaiman and Lloyd Hamilton on May 29th did not end the drama and problems surrounding the contract. On March 9th, shortly after negotiations towards the deal had

5 Philby suggests in his autobiography *Arabian Days* that it was he who told Ryan of Ibn Saud's decision and that Ryan was furious when he learned of it.

begun, the newly sworn-in American President, Franklin D. Roosevelt, as a part of his 'New Deal' programme to revive the American economy, had signed into law the Emergency Banking Act providing for the re-opening of America's banks, more than 5,000 of which had gone to the wall since the 1929 Wall Street Crash. He quickly followed the bank re-opening by going off the gold standard and embargoing gold exports, his aim being to put money back into the American economy and halt the disastrous outflow of gold from the United States to Europe and other parts of the world. The result was that SOCAL's head-office team in America could not get hold of the £35,000 in gold coins that it needed to pay to Ibn Saud to honour its side of the concession agreement. The result was an agonising hiatus lasting for most of the long, hot summer of 1933 until at last SOCAL officials found a way, by operating through a Dutch company with an office in Jeddah, of purchasing 35,000 British gold sovereigns on the London market and having them shipped out to Jeddah. There, on August 25th, in the Dutch company's office, the 35,000 shining gold coins were counted out one by one by Karl Twitchell and handed over to al Sulaiman. The coins were, reportedly, then put into al Sulaiman's portable tin trunk and transported back to Riyadh.

Just weeks later SOCAL set up a new subsidiary, The California Arabian Standard Oil Company (CASOC), through which to work the Hasa concession and dispatched a team of six geologists to Hasa. Escorted by guides and soldiers provided by Jiluwi, the Governor of Hasa, these geologists set about methodically mapping the whole area around Qatif and Uqair where Twitchell had said that oil might be found if it had been discovered in Bahrain. A few months later the CASOC geologists identified one particularly promising area a little south of Qatif, close to a small port village called Dammam. In the spring of the following year, 1934, the company sent an aeroplane to the area to conduct aerial surveys and increased the size of its team. Shortly after that they began sinking the first test drill. A further two years passed and more test drills were sunk, reaching down to depths of more than 3,000 feet. But none of them produced anything beyond a few smudges of oil and gas, some salty water and a quantity of a tar-like substance – similar to the material that had been used by Neolithic Gulf fishermen to caulk their reed boats and by Babylonian builders in the construction of the walls and towers of the city of Babylon. Perhaps, after all, the British had been right to be so pessimistic.

Twitchell's other promising report to Ibn Saud, on the possibility of there being gold in the mines of King Solomon, led in the autumn of 1933 to the resumption of gold mining in the region. But it too proved a disappointment. In the twenty years between 1933, when operations were resumed, and 1953 when they were discontinued, just £10 million worth of gold was recovered, most of it from the slag heaps left by earlier generations of miners, but at a cost considerably greater than the value of the gold recovered. It seemed that King Solomon's miners had been a lot more efficient than the 1930s Western experts had given them credit for!

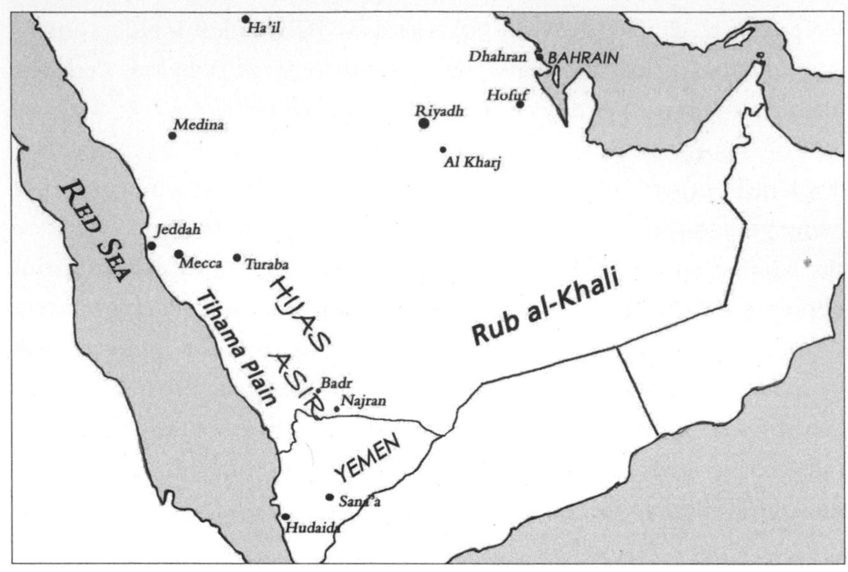

CHAPTER 12

New Ways, New Wars

The Asir region in the south west had for centuries before the coming of Gallus's Roman legions lived in peace as an independent nation so as the better to concentrate on trade. However, in modern times, and especially since the rise of the Ottoman Empire, it had become a source of numerous wars and disputes between the rulers of Yemen, the Turks and the Hashemites. Since 1919, when the Ikhwan had taken Turaba and pushed on into the south-west, Ibn Saud had been content to let the border between Asir and Yemen remain ill-defined, subject to the kind of shifting tribal loyalties that decreed that 'the only frontiers were those in men's hearts'. But in April 1932, while Ibn Saud was in the midst of trying to negotiate the agreement for the Hasa concession with the British and American oil companies, fresh trouble had flared on the border between Asir and Yemen. Ali Al Idrisi, a member of a family of Asiri shaikhs who had long sought independence for their region, led a

1 The old royal palace and square in Riyadh, photographed by Harold Dickson in the 1920s. The colonnade, and above it the enclosed passageway which leads from the family quarters inside the palace to the mosque, can be seen at the rear. Close to the palace door a small crowd of people sits waiting to be fed inside the palace.

2 One of the streets of old Riyadh through which the Saud family made their escape from the town in January 1891.

3 Newborn baby camel being carried in a saddlebag similar to the one in which the boy Ibn Saud and his sister Nura were carried during the Saud family's escape from Riyadh in January 1891.

4 Part of the walls that encircled Riyadh during most of Ibn Saud's lifetime, photographed in the early 1930s by the British diplomat Gerald de Gaury.

5 An old well in Wadi Hanifah, close to Riyadh, part of the system of irrigation for the surrounding palm gardens.

6 Chamber entrances carved into the rock face at Meda'in Saleh, the ancient city on the south to north trade route which ran up the western side of the Arabian Peninsula.

7 Part of the ruins of the old Saudi capital Diriya, destroyed by the Ottoman Egyptian army in 1818.

8 Bedouin tents similar to those that Ibn Saud lived in as a boy when he and his father were given refuge by the Al Murra tribe in the 1890s.

9 Bedouin mother holding baby wrapped in swaddling clothes.

10 The ancient well at Ain Hit – two modern pick-up trucks parked in front the entrance which is a gash in the rock-face at the foot of the limestone cliff. Here, at the end of Ramadan in January 1902, Ibn Saud and his small party of warriors broke their fast on the evening before going on to recapture Riyadh.

11 A shaft of sunlight falls on to the water deep inside the ancient well at Ain Hit. Here Ibn Saud and his warriors cleansed and refreshed themselves at the end of Ramadan 1902 before their daring recapture of Riyadh. The inside of the well is also associated with another important event in Ibn Saud's story – the discovery of oil.

12 Ibn Saud in 1911, aged about 30.

13 The Mismak Fortress in Riyadh, where Ibn Saud and his forty warriors surprised and killed Ajlan, the Rashid governor, on 15th January, 1902.

14 Jiluwi's spearhead still buried deep in the wood beside the postern door in the main gate to the Mismak Fortress.

15 Ibn Saud's army on the march. Photographed by Captain Shakespear in March 1911.

16 A bedouin shaikh's desert *majlis*.

17 A desert execution. The condemned man holds the dish into which his severed head will shortly fall.

18
Captain William Henry Irvine Shakespear.

19 The British Residency in Kuwait during Shakespear's time as Resident. His Union Jack can be seen flying at the top of the flag mast and his yacht rides at anchor in front and to the left of it.

20 The first photograph of Ibn Saud, his brothers and Shaikh Mubarak taken by Captain Shakespear at the British Residency in Kuwait in February 1910. Ibn Saud sits left, one of his children next to him and Mubarak third from the left.

21 Ibn Saud (sitting centre) in 1911 with his brothers. His three eldest sons sit in front of him, Turki on the left, Faisal centre and Saud right.

22 The walls of Hofuf, the capital of Hasa. Early in the summer of 1913 Ibn Saud sat on a sand dune outside the town looking down on the walls 'heavy with indecision' about attacking it, when thoughts of his beloved wife Jauhara inspired him to compose a poem to her. Then, with his mind made up, he attacked the town.

23 Sayyid Talib, the untrustworthy, murderous and grasping Basra politician whose unwanted presence proved a serious embarrassment to Ibn Saud and Captain Shakespear during their discussions in December 1914 and January 1915.

24 Sir Percy Cox greets Ibn Saud on his visit to Basra in November 1916.

25 Ibn Saud and Sir Percy Cox watch a British military flying display in Basra in November 1916.

26 Ibn Saud is shown the cockpit of a British bomber during his 1916 visit to Basra.

27 A street in Riyadh in 1914, photographed by Shakespear.

28 Ibn Saud's son Prince Faisal, aged about thirteen, at the time of his 1919 visit to Britain and Europe representing his father.

29 Prince Faisal and his party are shown over a Welsh steel works during his 1919 visit to Britain.

30 Prince Faisal's car mobbed by curious onlookers during his visit to Swansea in 1919.

31 Prince Faisal and the Mayor of Swansea, 1919.

32 Prince Faisal and party walk through the streets of Swansea. Wherever Faisal and his Arab companions went in Britain they drew large crowds.

33 The Cairo Conference in March 1921, chaired by Winston Churchill (*seated centre*). Sir Percy Cox sits beside and to the right of him and T. E. Lawrence stands behind Cox. Gertrude Bell stands in the second row one in from the left.

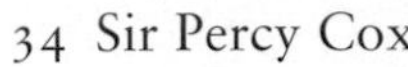

34 Sir Percy Cox.

35 Ibn Saud and Sir Percy Cox at Uqair, November 1922.

36 The mysterious, perspiring New Zealand oil prospector and butterfly collector Frank Holmes standing, his suit tight-buttoned as always, behind and between Ibn Saud and Sir Percy Cox during their meeting at Uqair in November 1922. Holmes's unexpected presence at Uqair caused Cox considerable embarrassment.

37 Sharif Husayn in 1917.

38 Mecca and the Ka'aba early in the twentieth century, before the conquest of the Hijaz by Ibn Saud or the extension of the Grand Mosque and modern growth of the city of Mecca.

39 The RAF attacking a group of Duwish's Ikhwan rebels in 1929.

40 Some of the Ikhwan.

41 Ibn Saud (*seated centre*) with Air Commodore Charles Burnett (*seated right*), the British Political Resident in the Gulf Sir Hugh Biscoe (*seated left*) and Harold Dickson (*standing behind and between them*) during the hand over of the Ikhwan rebel leaders to Ibn Saud outside Kuwait in January 1930.

42 H. St J. Philby

43 Charles R. Crane

44 Abdullah al Sulaiman and Karl Twitchell sign the SOCAL agreement in the Khuzam Palace, Jeddah, 29th May 1933.

45 Ibn Saud in his mid-50s.

46 Ibn Saud with President Roosevelt during their meeting on board the *USS Quincy* in the Great bitter Lake, Egypt on 14th Febraury 1945. Colonel William Eddy kneels beside Ibn Saud translating.

47 Ibn Saud having lunch with Winston Churchill at the Hotel Auberge du Lac beside Lake Karoun, Egypt, 17th February 1945.

48 Part of the Buraimi Oasis which in 1949 became the subject of a long running dispute between Ibn Saud and the British as a result of evidence of there being oil in the area.

49 Faisal, King of Saudi Arabia from 1964 until his assassination in March 1975. He had represented his father, Ibn Saud, on missions abroad since the age of thirteen.

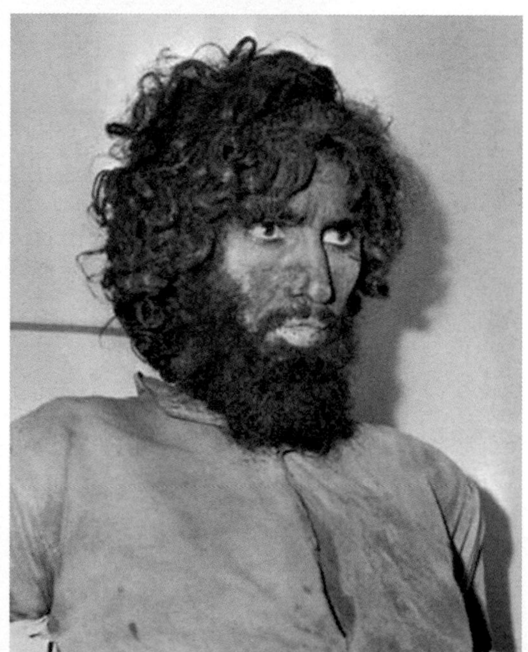

50 Juhayman Ataiba, leader of the rebels who seized the Grand Mosque in Mecca in November 1979, shortly after his capture by Saudi security forces.

51 Sun rising through mist over the mountains of southern Iran photographed from the Arabian side of the Straits of Musandum, the strategically vital channel at the southern end of the Persian Gulf through which much of the world's oil has to pass. An Omani gunboat can be seen on patrol in the left foreground.

52 King Abdullah meets Pope Benedict at the Vatican on 6th November 2007.

53 Dr Maha Al Muneef, Executive Director of the National Family Safety Programme, an organisation started by women to curb the level of violent abuse suffered by Saudi women, children and other vulnerable groups. Today the Programme is strongly supported by King Abdullah. In many offices in modern Saudi Arabia women work alongside men as equals although most still cover their hair and many still choose to cover their faces with the *niqab* as well.

54a and 54b Two photographic works by Manal AlDowayan, "I am a Petroleum Engineer" and "The Choice", which were among works shown in the 2008 exhibition of works by contemporary Saudi artists at London's Brunei Gallery. In her work Manal deepens perceptions of the contradictions in the position of women in modern Saudi Arabia.

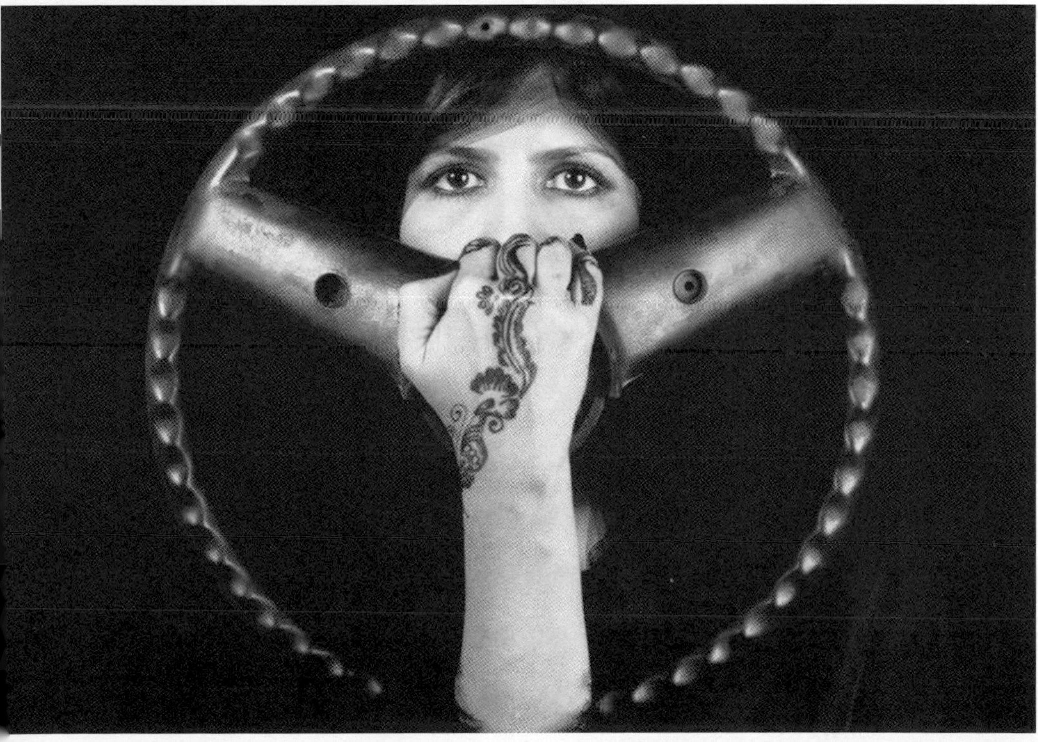

55 Modern Riyadh at night. Today a city of some 4 million people, it is virtually unrecognisable from the small, sleepy desert town of barely 20,000 known by Ibn Saud throughout most of his life.

successful uprising against his brother Hussayn, the Governor of Asir appointed by Ibn Saud. Ali's uprising had been supported by the ruler of Yemen, the Imam Yahya, who moved his troops into the south of Asir and seized the town of Najran close to the western end of the Rub al Khali Desert, claiming that Hussayn had been giving support to rebels in North Yemen.

Ibn Saud, warned by radio of what had happened, mobilised his troops while at the same time dispatching a delegation to Imam Yahya to try to settle the dispute. But the peace negotiations failed and in October, secretly encouraged by the British and Italians who wanted to increase their influence in the region, Ali Al Idrisi resumed his offensive and seized a small town called Badr to the north west of Najran. Ibn Saud responded by dispatching yet more troops to the region and sending Imam Yahya an ultimatum demanding that he and the Idrisis withdraw back into their own territory and that he must arrest the Idrisi brothers and hand them over to him. Yahya's response was to end his dispute with Britain over control of the important southern port of Aden and enter into a treaty of friendship and mutual assistance with her. Realising that if he attempted to drive the Yemenis out of Badr and Najran he now risked coming up against the British, Ibn Saud attempted to reach a compromise by proposing that a neutral zone, like those in the disputed areas between Kuwait, Iraq and Najd, be established in the disputed area around Najran. But Imam Yahya refused to give a definite answer. So in March 1934, having used some of the gold he had received from CASOC to purchase additional modern weapons, Ibn Saud ordered his two sons Faisal and Saud to lead a two-pronged advance towards the Yemeni capital Sana'a.

Unlike during their conquest of the Hijaz a decade earlier, the Saudi force was not dependent on the Ikhwan. There were contingents of Ikhwan warriors from the Turaba region amongst Faisal and Saud's columns, but they were not in the majority. Also their zeal for the fight was muted by the fact that, unlike in earlier battles where they had seen themselves as fighting a holy war in the name of Allah against infidels and in the sure belief that if they were killed fighting they would go to Paradise, in this campaign they were fighting against other good Muslims and only in the name of their King. The majority of the troops were levies sent from

Riyadh by Ibn Saud. Many now travelled not on camels but in the back of lorries, armed with machine guns and communicating by radio.

The advance started in a tremendous sandstorm which lasted for three days, severing all radio communications. But once the storm had blown itself out the column led by Faisal, driving south down the flat Tihama coastal plain, advanced rapidly. The terrain suited their vehicles and with their greater speed and superior firepower they easily overpowered their Yemeni opponents. Within three weeks they had smashed through the Yemeni defensive line just south of the disputed border and swept on more than one hundred miles into Yemen. On May 2nd they captured the port town of Hudaida. However, further inland the second column, under the command of Saud, which was attempting to drive south through the mountains towards the Yemeni capital Sana'a, after quickly recapturing Najran, ran into trouble. In the mountainous terrain the Yemeni fighters employed classic guerrilla tactics, fortifying each mountain village, repeatedly ambushing Saud and his men as they passed through narrow mountain defiles and swooping down from well-concealed hiding places upon his vulnerable supply lorries as they twisted and turned their tortuous way along the valley bottoms. The modern motor transport in which Ibn Saud had invested at such expense was wholly unsuited to warfare in this kind of terrain. More than once the column of lorries had to be painstakingly lowered one by one on ropes down the face of some sheer cliff. Within weeks Saud's army had been reduced to the same parlous state as the Roman army of Augustus Caesar's luckless general Gallus when it had tried to advance into the same region two thousand years earlier. Saud's army was reduced to a shadow of the force that had re-taken Najran just weeks earlier and its advance came to a halt.

But more serious still for Ibn Saud's hopes of expanding his domain into Yemen, British, French and Italian warships appeared in the Red Sea close to Hudaida. An Italian warship even began to put ashore troops – Mussolini, the Italian Fascist dictator, had set his heart on creating an Italian empire and was sizing up areas around the Horn of Africa and the south west of the Arabian peninsula for this purpose. His show of support for the Yemenis seemed intended to improve his chances of achieving his goal.

The sudden show of strength by the imperial powers convinced Ibn Saud that they would not tolerate a Saudi conquest of Yemen, so when Faisal, who had by now advanced well to the south, radioed his father to ask for permission to turn inland and advance up into the hills to attack Sana'a, he ordered him to halt. Ibn Saud had decided that he had better call off the attack and settle for the land he had regained. He therefore instructed Faisal to approach Imam Yahya and offer peace terms. On May 15th the terms of an armistice were agreed and a week after that a full Treaty of Muslim Friendship and Arab Brotherhood was drawn up under which both leaders recognised each other's independence and national sovereignty. Ibn Saud agreed that, in return for a payment by Yahya of £100,000 towards the costs of the Saudi campaign and Yahya relinquishing all claims to the territory in Asir which had been claimed by the Idrisis, he would withdraw all his forces from the areas of Yemen that Faisal and Saud had conquered. When Philby heard about the treaty and that Ibn Saud was planning to withdraw from Yemen and renounce all claims upon it, he wept. But Ibn Saud reprimanded him: 'You fool! Where will I get the manpower to govern Yemen? Yemen can only be ruled by its own ruler.'[1] The war fought by Ibn Saud against the Yemenis and Idrisis would be the last territorial war he fought. It was also the first of his wars in which Ibn Saud himself had not led his warriors into battle.

As could be seen from the way in which Ibn Saud took command of the war against the Yemenis by radio while himself staying behind in Riyadh to continue overseeing the government of the rest of his state, from the range of modern weapons and motor transport he had provided for his sons to fight the war, and from the unchallenged arrival in the country of the growing number of CASOC geologists with their aircraft, surveying and drilling equipment, Ibn Saud's kingdom was changing. After millennia of isolation the vast impenetrable heart of Arabia was starting to open up and become subject to outside influences. As well as the obvious potential benefits to the peninsula's people, such fundamental change was also fraught with danger. It could not be

1 Leslie McLoughlin, *Ibn Saud: Founder of a Kingdom*, Macmillan Press, London, 1993.

rushed and must be handled with care. People with long-set habits of life, ways of doing things, familiarity with their environment – no matter how harsh – with habits of thought, systems of social, family and tribal relationships, codes of justice, patterns of rule and strongly held religious belief could not be made to think, feel and behave differently overnight, no matter what the potential benefits. People confronted with change, particularly such profound change and fundamental challenges to their most deeply held core beliefs, can easily feel threatened. Feeling threatened they will resist and that resistance can rapidly descend into unreasoning violence. Ibn Saud, although he had seen the benefits of change and modern technology during his visits to Kuwait and Basra and knew that in order to survive and prosper his kingdom must embrace modern technology and many of the changes that it would bring with it, also shared many of the most deeply held beliefs and attitudes of his people. He remained at heart the same boy who had been raised through his early childhood in Riyadh in the deepest and most remote heart of Wahhabi Arabia, who had learned the Qur'an by heart by the time he was ten years old and had then spent his early adolescence hunting and living the tribal life of the desert Murra Bedouin. He had been born, brought up and remained a sincere, believing Wahhabi Muslim. He often spoke of his total commitment to his religion and reliance upon it and the Qur'an. In 1935, touching upon the potential clash between the rational and the religious in his life and decisions, he told his closest advisers during a discussion about importing foreign coinage to make good a catastrophic imbalance in the national budget which seemed to fly in the face of a Qur'anic injunction against changing silver against silver, 'In all things, surely it is well known to you, I am reasonable: in all things will decide on the merits of the case, save only where my religion is touched. By God – I have it here, close to my heart – without it I die – none shall take it from me. By God above I swear it!'[2] So Ibn Saud, while he knew that change must come to his kingdom and would ensure that it did, nevertheless not only understood the need for caution

2 Gerald de Gaury, *Arabian Journey and Other Desert Travels*, George G. Harrap, London 1960.

in managing that change, he shared many of the fears and reservations of those who would try to resist it.

In September 1932, while the country's financial situation was becoming desperate, a proclamation was issued that henceforth the country was to be known by a new name: The Kingdom of Saudi Arabia. This might seem an odd announcement to make at a moment when the country faced seemingly much more pressing problems. But it was much more than merely a nominal change. It was meant to mark an important shift and a new beginning, the start of a change from old and inefficient ways to new ways of running the country, and to herald the beginning of a shift from being a host of separate, often competing, tribes and regions into one coherent, centrally administered state.

When Ibn Saud conquered the Hijaz he conquered a kingdom that had been administered in accordance with Turkish post-revolutionary practice, that is to say along lines much closer to those by which modern European states were governed. It would not have been practical, even if Ibn Saud had wanted to, for him to return the Hijaz to the model of government still practised in Najd. To the citizens of the Hijaz that would have been provocatively old-fashioned. Therefore, if Ibn Saud was to succeed in making his kingdom into one unified and efficiently functioning whole, he had no alternative but to modernise it and bring the administrative system in all the other parts of his kingdom more into line with that already operating in the Hijaz. However, this did not mean that Saudi Arabia was to become democratic in the sense understood by Europeans and Americans, nor that real power would be devolved beyond Ibn Saud himself and a small circle of carefully chosen and trusted members of his family and advisers. His two eldest surviving sons were made viceroys. Saud, who had been officially proclaimed Ibn Saud's heir a year earlier, would exercise his father's powers in Riyadh during his increasingly frequent absences, and Faisal was to be his viceroy in the Hijaz. Ibn Saud also set up a council which, although it exercised no formal powers, acted in some ways rather like a cabinet. However, as one of Ibn Saud's most trusted advisers once confided: 'The King asks us all our advice and sometimes even when we are all agreed he does the opposite and proves to be right.'

None of the innovations introduced by Ibn Saud entailed Saudi Arabia adopting a constitution. A constitution was deemed unnecessary since government was based on a literal reading of the Qur'an. Of course, in practice this left lots of room for interpretation as the Qur'an contains very little specific legislation relevant to the day-to-day government of a country. Ibn Saud, like his forebears back to the time of Al Wahhab, had always laid claim to being the heir to the pure Islam of the Wahhabi revival. The *ulema* had bestowed legitimacy upon his state and in return he had enforced strict conservative religious values.[3] Traditional punishments were administered, women remained shrouded from sight and subject to their husbands and fathers and so on, even though in other Muslim states such traditional practices were beginning to be seen as unnecessary and in some eyes as contrary to Qur'anic teaching.

The growing centralisation of the administration, facilitated by the introduction of radio, meant a corresponding reduction in the power of the regional governors who had hitherto been able to exercise autocratic and effectively independent powers. One of the effects of the increased centralisation of the Kingdom's administration was to make the collection of taxes more efficient and reduce the scope of governors for siphoning off money for their own uses. The result was a measurable increase in the funds that flowed into al Sulaiman's treasury.

Abdullah al Sulaiman was, with the possible exception of his sons and a very few members of his closest family, Ibn Saud's most powerful minister. His critics would later claim that he had become 'the uncrowned king of Saudi Arabia'. The son of a merchant who had been born in Anaiza, he had visited India and lived in Bahrain and other Gulf states before settling in Riyadh. He had been his father's bookkeeper and later inherited his business. Ibn Saud had taken to the young man because of his good handwriting, intelligence and active nature. He had given him responsibility for some of his court's funds and then increased his responsibilities to include the important matter of the funds spent on his court and guests. His responsibilities had continued to grow until, in 1924, Ibn Saud had put him in charge of all the Kingdom's finances. At heart Ibn Saud had little interest in money

3 See Karen Armstrong, *Islam: A Short History*, Phoenix Press, London, 2001, pp. 137–8.

with the result that as Ibn Saud emptied the treasury's tin trunk it became al Sulaiman's responsibility to re-fill it. By the 1930s al Sulaiman had his own staff of officials, guards and slaves, said to number 400 in all.[4] Al Sulaiman had privileged access to Ibn Saud and was one of the few people he allowed to visit him when he was alone. By 1932–3, with the World Economic Depression at its deepest, the number of foreign pilgrims making the *Hajj* at an all-time low and income from exports more or less non-existent, Ibn Saud was more dependent on al Sulaiman's efficiency and ingenuity than ever. *Zakat*, or compulsory almsgiving which is the third of Islam's 'five pillars', was the main form of taxation in the country. Its payment was both a religious duty and a demonstration of loyalty to the ruler. *Zakat* is an obligation laid upon all believers by the Prophet in the Qur'an, where it is mentioned more than twenty times. It is both a religious duty and a demonstration of brotherhood towards one's fellow Muslims and thus a means of purifying one's wealth and limiting its accumulation – accumulation of wealth is repeatedly condemned in the Qur'an. Indeed, the word *zakat* connotes purification.

Ibn Saud and al Sulaiman set the levels of *zakat* in accordance with Qur'anic tradition. So all of a person's accumulated wealth above a certain level, with the exemption of a number of essential items such as a person's dwelling, was taxed at a rate of 1/40th, or 2.5per cent. It could be levied in kind on an owner's livestock and was paid at a higher rate on the value of all crops. The provincial governors were responsible for the collection of *zakat*, but they and their teams of collectors frequently embezzled much of what they collected. Ibn Saud once told Philby that he thought that only a third of the tax collected reached his treasury. One of the goals of Ibn Saud's centralisation of his administration in the 1930s was to make the collection and transmission of *zakat* back to the treasury more efficient.

The principal sources of income available to Ibn Saud other than *zakat* were customs duties, the proceeds of such things as the oil and mineral concessions and, above all, the taxes levied on pilgrims entering

4 See Alexei Vassiliev, *The History of Saudi Arabia*, Saqi Books, London, 1998, p. 299.

the country to make the *Hajj*. However, even in 1927, following the conquest of the Hijaz and the great influx of pilgrims after Ibn Saud had improved the security and conditions for pilgrims, the total amount of taxes received by the Treasury had only amounted to £1.5 million. Since the start of the Great Depression the country's income from pilgrims and customs duties had fallen off dramatically. Even by the mid-1930s, after the world economy had started to pick up and the country's income had started to improve, it still did not amount to much more than £2 million.[5]

In 1934, as part of Ibn Saud's modernisation programme, a national budget was drawn up for the first time. Each of the state agencies attempted to draw up a detailed account of their expenditure, list their priorities for the next year and estimate their likely expenditure. The biggest source of expenditure was Ibn Saud's army. As we have seen, he had spent liberally on motorised transport, up-to-date weapons, ammunition and wireless equipment. As well as giving money to those who were still serving him he also made grants to the widows of those killed or injured. A campaign such as the one he waged in Asir and Yemen between 1932 and 1934 was a big drain on his already straitened finances. On top of these costs al Sulaiman was also expected to find considerable sums of money to pay for state and court officials, the governors and staff of the different provinces and towns, for things like improving the roads and irrigation schemes. From the 1920s onwards al Sulaiman had also had to find funds for Ibn Saud's newly created Directorate of Education which, following the conquest of the Hijaz, began building new schools, bringing in trained foreign teachers and providing training for young people. Ibn Saud, advised by foreigners attached to his court, also started taking the first steps towards providing medical services and reducing the incidence of disease among his subjects. Last and by no means least among the calls on the funds in al Sulaiman's treasury was providing for the pay and work of the *ulema*.

In practice the budget was not adhered to. The shaikhs, and above all Ibn Saud himself, continued to believe that they were entitled to draw upon the *zakat* and other tax income as they deemed expedient. Ibn

5 See Vassiliev, op. cit., pp. 304–5.

Saud continued to spend freely upon his own needs. As we have seen, even at the height of the World Depression when year after year his income kept decreasing, he had the lavish new Khuzam Palace built for himself outside Jeddah. A whole host of poor people continued to live in Riyadh at his expense. Up to 2,000 still received two meals daily from the Riyadh Palace kitchens. Almost 100 of the families of his former enemies lived at court or in Riyadh totally at the King's expense. He also had between 500 and sometimes, according to some estimates, as many as 10,000 people living around him as his permanent guests. Bedouin travelled long distances to where the King was just in order to receive one of his generous gifts. Although his ministers and advisers did not receive salaries they did receive annual gifts, lived in special sections of the royal palaces and were fed at the King's expense, so tying them ever closer to him.

Ibn Saud still regularly moved around the country so that he could be seen by his people, listen to their complaints, settle their disputes. Everywhere he went he entertained huge numbers of people, distributing food and bestowing gifts. It was an essential part of strengthening his subjects' loyalty and maintaining his reputation as not just their ruler but as their caring and accessible father. Despite the obvious innovations, such as motor cars, this traditional way of ruling remained for a proud people steeped in many generations of desert custom and command, a vital link maintaining the connection between their Bedouin past and the new reality of the emerging centralised Saudi state. Ibn Saud's ongoing progresses around his kingdom contain obvious echoes of the royal progresses of European medieval kings and England's Queen Elizabeth the First at a similar stage in their countries' development, but with the important difference that any shaikh whose domain Ibn Saud decided to visit did not find themselves broken by the cost of having to entertain him. Colonel Harold Dickson tells of an occasion in the late 1930s when Ibn Saud had to set out hurriedly on a journey from Riyadh to an outlying district on the road to Mecca and, because of his haste, was travelling in only one car instead of his usual fleet of cars. Unfortunately his car became stuck in a sand-drift and while those travelling in the car with him tried to dig the car out he got out and went to rest in the shade of a nearby bush. Spotting him, a passing Bedouin walked over and asked him if the

Imam had recently passed that way or if, perhaps, he might be passing by later. Ibn Saud asked the Bedouin why he was so anxious to know and the Bedouin answered that he would greatly like to meet the Imam 'who all men praised and who was said to give money to Muslims'.

'Moreover,' the Bedouin added, 'the Bedouin say that the king gives little to persons when he meets them in a crowd, but when he meets poor persons in the desert, he sometimes gives them as much as twenty-five rials or even thirty.'

To this Ibn Saud replied, 'My friend, if you must know the truth, the Imam has gone on ahead. We whom you see are his servants and are following him as soon as we can get out of this accursed sand-drift.' But, he added, as he was a good Muslim, feared God and was anxious to do a good deed that day, he would give the Bedouin twenty-five rials out of his own pocket and give him another twenty-five rials in the name of the King.

The Bedouin's face lit up and he seized Ibn Saud's hand, and bending down kissed him on the nose in the usual Bedouin greeting. '*Sala'am alaikum, Ya Abdal-Aziz!* [I know that I am addressing the Imam himself!'][6]

Another similarity between the methods employed by Ibn Saud to bolster his hold on power and those employed by European monarchs during the medieval period was the use of marriage, except that being a Muslim Ibn Saud was not restricted to being married to only one woman at a time. Even though in 1930 Ibn Saud told Philby that from then on he intended to marry no more than two new wives per year, throughout the 1930s he continued to use marriages, both by him and by leading members of his family, to bolster his and his family's hold on power.

The Ikhwan rebellion had shown that Ibn Saud's reliance on a combination of the Ikhwan and levies from among the Bedouin tribes and the people of the major towns would no longer suffice. Although the system of levies was not entirely abandoned, after the conquest of the Hijaz the rudiments of a regular army began to be put in place. The advantages of having a disciplined and trained military force had been shown by the

6 H. R. P. Dickson, *Kuwait and her Neighbours*, George Allen & Unwin, London, 1956.

way in which the British had employed trained Iraqis and Indians in dealing with Ikhwan incursions across the Iraq, Kuwait and Transjordan borders. So after the fall of the Hijaz Ibn Saud invited all the officers of the Hashemite army to join a local police force, a force which in time came to form part of the nucleus of a regular army. In 1930 Ibn Saud created three regular regiments, modelled on the regiments in European armies. One was an infantry regiment, another artillery and the third were machine gunners. Uniforms and badges of rank were introduced, the regiments were divided up into separate brigades and posted to each of Saudi Arabia's provinces. In 1931 ten of Ibn Saud's brightest young men were chosen and sent to Italy to learn to fly and a number of aeroplanes were bought.

In the early years of his reign managing Ibn Saud's relations with foreign powers had been largely a matter of him holding meetings or exchanging correspondence with the representatives of those few countries that impinged on his territory or internal affairs. However, as the area that he controlled had increased, and especially after the conquest of the Hijaz, the running of his foreign relations became more complex. As we have seen, there were already a number of foreign legations or agencies in Jeddah and he now also had to have regular dealings with the governments of all those Muslim countries whose citizens undertook the *Hajj*. By the end of 1932, following the creation of Saudi Arabia, no fewer than ten countries had established diplomatic relations with the Kingdom – Soviet Russia, Britain, the Netherlands, France, Turkey, Germany, Persia, Poland, the USA and Egypt. In 1930, faced with a growing number of foreign diplomats establishing legations in Jeddah and his increasing contacts with other foreign countries, Ibn Saud had established an embryonic Ministry of Foreign Affairs and made Faisal, as the person who, after himself, had the most experience of dealing with foreigners and as the Viceroy of the Hijaz, the region in the kingdom which had the greatest amount of contact with foreigners, Foreign Minister.

Ibn Saud had long recognised the potential importance of radio, telephones and the telegraph in a country as far spread as his. He had used radio to good effect in dealing with the Ikhwan rebellion and during the war with Yemen. But he also understood its value in allowing him to keep up with what was happening elsewhere in the world. However, he had to overcome considerable opposition to such 'devilish' devices from many conservative-minded clerics. They held that these infidel inventions must be the work of the devil as there was no mention of them in the Qur'an. Their objections were only overcome when, on a pre-arranged day, Ibn Saud himself took one of the leading Mecca *ulema* to the wireless room in his palace and asked him whether, if these devices were the work of the Devil, the Devil would permit them to carry the word of God? The cleric angrily replied that of course he would not. Then, on a pre-arranged instruction from the King given over the wireless to his operator in Riyadh, the leading Riyadh imam, who was well known to the Meccan cleric, began to read the opening verses from the Qur'an:

> In the name of Allah, Most Gracious, Most Merciful.
> Praise be to Allah the Cherisher and Sustainer of Worlds;
> Most Gracious, Most Merciful;
> Master of the Day of Judgement.
> Thee do we worship and Thine aid do we seek.[7]

The Meccan cleric was convinced. If the wireless could carry the word of God all the way from Riyadh to Mecca it could not be the work of the Devil because the Devil would never countenance carrying the word of God. From that day on the religious opposition to the radio and, after a similar demonstration, to the telephone came to an end.[8]

Ibn Saud not only equipped his armed forces with radio but over the succeeding years built a network of radio stations across the country which both broadcast news and information to the people and allowed him to keep in regular touch with events and his governors in the provinces. He employed a small group of men to monitor radio news bulletins from around the world and prepare digests for him of the world's news. These he had read to him each evening after prayers. He

7 Surah 1 Al Fatinah, in the Wordsworth Classics translation by Abdullah Yusuf Ali.

8 Some commentators have doubted the veracity of this story, suggesting that it is a western invention. However it is often repeated and widely believed.

also began installing a telephone network in the country. One of the first lines he had installed in Riyadh connected him to his favourite sister Nura and from that day on even if they did not see each other they spoke daily on the phone. He continued, as he had from his earliest days, to seek her advice about all the most difficult decisions he had to make.

Yet in spite of his enthusiasm for adopting modern western inventions such as motor vehicles and radios in his quest to secure his country and improve the lot of his subjects, and despite his occasional disagreements with conservative clerics, Ibn Saud remained what he had always been, a sincere and devoted Wahhabi Muslim. Each week he had a formal meeting with the *ulema* at which he informed them about important events and sought their advice about policies that he intended to introduce. He not only listened to what they had to say, but often acted on their advice. He also invited senior clerics to attend and speak at his *majlis*. He left the imams, the *ulema* and the Committees for the Propagation of Virtue and the Prevention of Vice, the religious police, *mutawwa* or 'Zealators', who Palgrave had found so oppressive during his visit to Najd in 1862, to rule on matters of faith, religious practice and morals and in return they generally gave him a free hand in all other matters.

Ibn Saud's new kingdom, Saudi Arabia, was governed by *shari'a* law and its constitution, in so far as it had one, was the Qur'an. But in many of the more remote Bedouin tribes the courts were presided over by experts in the rules and customs of the particular tribe rather than *shari'a* law. The result was that what might be considered a crime among one tribe might not be seen as a crime in another. Similarly the customary punishments meted out for specific offences often varied from tribe to tribe. There were also great differences between the beliefs and legal practices of the settled and the nomadic peoples. But as Ibn Saud's new, enlarged state started to become more centralised that had to change. During the nineteenth century many tribes had largely forgotten Wahhabi teaching and reverted to many of their old pre-Islamic beliefs. With the spread of Ibn Saud's rule that had begun to change, particularly with the rise of the Ikhwan. Nevertheless even as late as the late 1920s there remained great differences between the legal practices and codes of the different regions. But, following the conquest of the

Hijaz, Ibn Saud instituted reforms designed to consolidate the legal codes and practices of all the different regions into one uniform, nationwide judicial system, based on the treatises of the early Hanbali theologians that had formed the basis for Al Wahhab's own strict brand of Islam.

Nevertheless, despite the division of spheres of responsibility between Ibn Saud and the religious authorities, clashes still occurred over particular policies. One such clash occurred in the newly established Directorate of Education, where the *ulema* exercised a very great degree of control. It was they who appointed the teachers. Ibn Saud had been impressed by the system of education that he had found functioning in the Hijaz and decided to establish a nationwide system of education. The clash with the *ulema* arose over the proposed curriculum. They objected to the inclusion in the syllabus for secular secondary schools of subjects such as technical drawing, geography and foreign languages, even though 22 out of the 28 lessons per week in primary schools and 25per cent of the time in secondary schools were to be devoted to religious studies. The *ulema* objected that teaching the young how to draw might tempt them into the sin of attempting to draw the human face or body. Geography, despite the proud record of the Muslim geographers and cartographers who a thousand years earlier had studied the work of Greek classical scholars, philosophers and scientists in accordance with Qur'anic command to look, see, learn and understand, was regarded by Ibn Saud's narrow-minded and fearful Wahhabi *ulema* as suspect because it might encourage in the young a dangerous curiosity about the infidel outside world. Similarly, if they acquired foreign languages they might be tempted into studying the infidels' religions, sciences and cultures. However, Ibn Saud countered these narrow, paranoid attitudes with logic and sound Islamic reason. Drawing was necessary for the making of maps of their own country and of the rest of the Muslim world. Similarly, knowledge of foreign languages, such as English, was needed in order to be able to communicate with the Muslims of other lands and had been useful to the Prophet's companions in their conquest and suppression of the lands bordering their own. Geography dealt in facts, and the pursuit of knowledge and facts was a specific duty laid upon Muslims in the Qur'an. According to the Qur'an all knowledge, even human knowledge, comes from God and is related to wisdom. Eventually a compromise was reached and Ibn Saud got most of what he wanted.

Rather than argument Ibn Saud would employ gentle mockery to counter some of the *ulema*'s more petty or silly attitudes. When a leading *ulema* chided Ibn Saud for the vanity of wearing a robe which was longer than the prescribed length and dragged upon the ground behind him, Ibn Saud ordered one of his slaves to bring a pair of scissors immediately. When the slave handed him the scissors Ibn Saud handed them on to the *ulema* and told him in front of the assembled courtiers to there and then cut off as much of his cloak as he deemed necessary. The *ulema* knelt down at the King's feet and did so, but he could not fail to notice that he had been made to look slightly ridiculous in the eyes of all those around Ibn Saud who had stood watching.

But maintaining the balance between creating a strong modern country, furthering the well-being and education of his people and at the same time ensuring that Saudi Arabia remained a devoutly Wahhabi state required continuous vigilance. As the 1930s progressed and the taste for freedom and progress took hold, especially among the young, Ibn Saud felt bound to try to rein it in to within what he regarded as bounds consistent with Wahhabi teaching. In April 1937, following news that some children had acquired dolls and a scandal in which some Egyptian women were alleged to have walked in the streets of Mecca without wearing veils, he issued a proclamation, printed in official newspapers and proclaimed through the streets by criers, condemning women who, under the pretext of being progressive, sought to mingle with men and so risked failing in their duties as wives, mothers and mistresses of the home. The local Mecca newspaper put a more palatable gloss on this condemnation of women, reminding them that 'the woman who rocks the cradle with her right hand rocks the world with her left'.[9] In the same proclamation Ibn Saud also attacked young men who he believed were pressing for freedoms which went beyond the bounds permitted to a good Muslim. Those young men who pressed for

9 Sir Reader Bullard, *The Camels Must Go: An Autobiography*, Faber and Faber, London, 1961, p. 199 and *Two Kings in Arabia: Sir Reader Bullard's Letters from Jeddah*, edited by E. C. Hodgkin, Ithaca Press, Reading, England, 1993.

'modernisation, progress, civilisation, liberty and what not' had, he said, 'been misled by the devil'. All such people were taking the path to moral ruin.[10]

Ibn Saud maintained a strict daily routine, no matter whether he was in Riyadh, Mecca, Jeddah or in camp out in the desert. Always punctual himself, he expected his court to be punctual as well. He always rose up to two hours before dawn and said his dawn prayers with intense devotion. He would often say additional prayers over and beyond the prescribed minimum and was frequently heard to sob, so intense was his religious feeling. He would then return to sleep for an hour before rising in time to start seeing relatives before starting work strictly at 8 a.m., at which time he would start seeing important visitors. Following that his young male secretaries would file in carrying sheaves of paper and, after greeting him, sit waiting for him to start dealing with the day's correspondence. Sometimes, except for a formal exchange of greetings when they entered, he would ignore them for some time, but then, on the command 'Begin', each would read out some piece of business or a letter that he needed to deal with. Often, at the same time as this was going on he would continue seeing less important visitors. The visitors would often be struck by his ability to maintain his conversation with them while dictating two or more letters on different subjects at the same time without losing the thread of any of them.

This session was followed by the day's main *majlis* which would open with a recitation from the Qur'an followed by a general discussion on a topic usually chosen by Ibn Saud himself and about which he would make an opening pronouncement before inviting general discussion. Visitors to his *majlis* were invariably presented with a gift before departing. Ibn Saud was noted for his extraordinary generosity and the cost of gifts was a major drain on his exchequer; as the court official responsible for the stores where the King's gifts were kept testified: 'Every king in the world is supported by his people but the people of Najd are supported by their king.'[11] The British Army officer and

10 Leslie McLoughlin, *Ibn Saud: Founder of a Kingdom*, Macmillan Press, London, 1993.

11 Quoted by Gerald de Gaury in *Arabia Phoenix*, Harrap, London, 1946.

distinguished Arabist Gerald de Gaury, who spent a considerable time at Ibn Saud's court in 1935, has left a description of Ibn Saud as he was at that time and the way in which he spoke to visitors in his *majlis*. Ibn Saud, he said, ' ... is well over six feet tall and robust in proportion. His left eyelid droops somewhat over an eye which is sightless. His nose is fine but prominent. His beard is pointed on the chin and small and close-clipped at the side ... His smile is very sweet and reveals well-made teeth. His hands and feet are fine and small for so large a man ... His right hand is scarred from an old wound.'[12] De Gaury was particularly struck by the forcible way in which he spoke, decorating his conversation with old Arab proverbs, Bedouin sayings and quotations from the Qur'an, and by how clear his arguments were. Sometimes he would speak 'sweetly, with gentle sidelong smiles and pertinent similes culled from Bedouin speech', at others he would scold. 'Then, point by point, indictment by indictment, he would build up his case. In this year of grace there was speaking before me an Abraham or a Job, the voice of the old Semite wrath. The swirling current of his talk swept one away, cling as one might to the banks of Western thought.'[13] His rebukes to his officials could be blistering. A group of provincial governors were told, 'You are like slaves, the older they become the less their value.' A senior customs officer was told that, 'To me you are nothing but a strayed beetle' and another addressed as 'O Swollen whore!' A Shaikh was warned, 'I swear by Almighty God, who raised up the sky without pillars, that if you do not cease your mischief ... '[14]

The morning *majlis* would end strictly at noon with the midday prayers after which Ibn Saud would hold a meeting of his small inner committee of advisers at which they would discuss whatever topics he determined. This was followed by lunch, after which Ibn Saud would often go to the women's quarters. In the afternoon there would often be some kind of a short outing, around the town or into the desert with his retainers and closest companions. People have commented on how Ibn Saud seemed content to spend so much of his time with the same small

12 Ibid.
13 De Gaury, *Arabian Journey* op. cit..
14 Ibid.

circle of his most trusted companions, people who had been with him for many years. With them he would relax, sitting on the ground in the desert, laughing, joking, re-telling old tales.

There would be afternoon prayers followed by a less formal evening *majlis* with readings from a religious work by a leading *ulema* and religious discussion. Time would be found each day, usually in the evening, for the digests of world news from the radio monitors to be read to him and, especially in Riyadh, a tour of the court, including his Foreign Affairs department. There would be evening prayer and usually a visit to some close relative before, late in the evening, Ibn Saud retired to bed.[15]

* * *

On May 15th 1935 Ibn Saud was in Mecca with his son Saud to perform the *Hajj*. As they walked bare-headed among the crowds making the prescribed seven counter-clockwise circumambulations of the Ka'aba three men with knives sprang out of the crowd and made to attack Ibn Saud. He would almost certainly have been killed had it not been for the quick thinking of his son, Saud, who thrust his own body between the would-be assassins and his father. Ibn Saud's bodyguards, who were also walking among the crowds close by, drew their guns and shot dead all three of the attackers. Saud had suffered serious wounds in the back and shoulder but the King had received nothing more than some grazing on the shins from fragments of the marble floor thrown up by his bodyguards' bullets. Ibn Saud completed the sacred rites and then went on to join his guests in celebrating the *Eid al-Adha* thanks-giving feast that marks the end of the *Hajj*. Meanwhile investigations had revealed that the three would-be assassins had all been members of the Yemeni army. It so happened that among the guests waiting to greet Ibn Saud at the *Eid al-Adha* feast was a representative of Yemen. Ibn Saud had given orders that there was to be no retaliation against the Yemen or Yemenis and he greeted the man as though nothing had happened. Another of Ibn Saud's guests that day, shocked by the assassination

15 Ibn Saud's daily routine is based in the main on first hand accounts by de Gaury and a summary in Leslie McLoughlin, *Ibn Saud: Founder of a Kingdom.*

attempt on the King, approached him weeping to offer his congratulations. Ibn Saud's response was to command his guest to 'Act like a man!'[16] From this time onwards relations between Saudi Arabia and Yemen began to improve. The motives of Ibn Saud's attackers were never discovered. Ibn Saud's survival was widely taken to be a good omen and accounts of his miraculous escape and Saud's bravery quickly spread through the towns, tribes and deserts of Arabia, becoming ever more exaggerated and wondrous with each re-telling.

However, throughout 1935, 1936, 1937 and 1938 Ibn Saud's kingdom remained as poor and al Sulaiman's Treasury as near empty as ever. The oil men drilling in the Hasa, in spite of now having drilled seven wells, had still found no oil and the effects of the worldwide economic depression were still almost as severe as ever. Discontent among his subjects remained and from time to time rumbled into open life. When a group of Hijazi merchants was discovered spreading damaging stories about Ibn Saud he called them together and issued them with a terrible warning: 'O people of Mecca, I am very angry with you. In spite of all the favours I have shown to you you ungrateful creatures are still engaged in mischievous propaganda against me ... I warn you to abandon your evil machinations or by Allah I will bring the might of the merciless Najdis and there will be nothing left in Mecca but decapitated heads.'[17]

The international scene darkened as well, not only in Europe following the rise of Hitler but in the countries around Saudi Arabia. On October 3rd 1935 the Italian Fascist dictator Mussolini (whose name Ibn Saud found it difficult to pronounce and so always referred to in conversation as 'Miss O'Looney'), still determined that Italy should have an empire, launched an assault on Abyssinia. The League of Nations instituted sanctions against Italy, but although they caused the Italians some economic hardship they proved ineffective. Germany and the United States were not members of the League of Nations and so ignored them, while the governments of other countries that were

16 Quoted by Leslie McLoughlin, op. cit. from K. Zirikli, *Arabia in the Time of Ibn Saud* (Arabic) 1970.

17 Quoted by Leslie McLoughlin, op. cit. from report by British Legation in Jeddah.

members of the League failed to act effectively. The onus to act therefore fell upon Britain, whose navy claimed control of the Mediterranean, which was the dominant power in the Red Sea and which still exercised enormous power in Egypt through a series of military bases and control of its economic and strategic policy. But Britain, now in the grip of appeasement, failed to take any effective action. In concert with France, she proposed a partition of the country, under which Mussolini was to get all the valuable fertile land and Haile Selassie, the Abyssinian emperor, be left with only the mountains. But Mussolini refused to accept even this compromise and ordered his armies to press on until, on May 1st 1936, Haile Selassie was forced to flee his country and go into exile. A week later Mussolini proudly proclaimed the birth of a new Roman Empire. With the death of Abyssinia the League of Nations, which had proved completely ineffective at stopping this act of open aggression, effectively died too. As the tragedy in Abyssinia had unfolded Ibn Saud, kept informed by his radio monitoring service, had watched with growing dismay. From the start of the crisis he had believed that Britain, with its powerful fleet and bases in Egypt, would step in to stop Mussolini. So when Britain failed to act, his faith in her, which Britain herself had so often seemed to seek to undermine, took another serious blow. At the same time Mussolini tried to increase his influence in the Arab world by making a series of gifts to the rulers of various Middle Eastern countries. His gifts to Ibn Saud included six aeroplanes and courses of flying instruction for a group of young Saudis. However, Britain's senior representative in Jeddah, Reader Bullard, doubted that Mussolini's gift would do him much good with Ibn Saud: 'Ibn Saud is no fool and he must know as well as anyone that the Italians are not disinterested.'[18] Later Ibn Saud endeavoured to get the Italians who had come to Saudi Arabia to service the planes removed and get the British to take over their maintenance.

A further blow followed a year later, in July 1937, with the publication of the report of a Royal Commission, chaired by Lord Peel,

18 Letter from Reader Bullard to his family, November 12th 1936 included in *Two Kings in Arabia: Sir Reader Bullard's Letters from Jeddah*, edited by E. C. Hodgkin, Ithaca Press, Reading, England, 1993.

into the future of Palestine. The rise of anti-Semitism in Europe and the increasingly repressive measures against Jews being introduced by Hitler in Nazi Germany were leading to a great increase in the number of Jews seeking new lives in Palestine. As the numbers of immigrants rose, the Palestinian Arabs, both Muslims and Christians, felt increasingly threatened and started to resist. Charged with investigating the causes of the recent violence between the Arabs and Jews, the Peel Commission found that the causes of the violence were the Palestinians' desire for national independence and their hatred and fear of the establishment of a Jewish National Home in their land. These had been exacerbated by the increased amount of Jewish immigration, alarm over an increasing number of Jewish land purchases, distrust of the British Government and its exercise of the Mandate and by growing Arab nationalism outside Palestine. The Commission found that the promises previously made to both the Arabs and the Jews were fundamentally irreconcilable. They therefore recommended that Palestine should be partitioned into a Jewish state which would occupy the western coastal area of the country from south of Tel Aviv to the Lebanon and Syrian borders and an Arab state, which would occupy the eastern side of the country from south of Nazareth along the river Jordan down to the Dead Sea together with the whole of the southern Negev desert between the border of Transjordan down to the Gulf of Aqaba and north-west to include a length of the Mediterranean coast running from Khan Yunis through Gaza to south of Jaffa and Tel Aviv. One small lozenge of the British Mandate was to remain which was to include Jerusalem, Bethlehem and a corridor through to the Mediterranean immediately south of Tel Aviv. Jewish immigration was to be restricted to 12,000 per year for five years and a plan for population transfer into the Jewish and Arab areas agreed with the populations. However the plan got nowhere. Both sides rejected it and the partition proposal was found to be unworkable.

Ibn Saud had strong emotional and religious sympathies with the Palestinians and started clandestinely sending arms to the Palestine Arab rebels. At the same time he knew that he could still not afford to antagonise the British. So while supporting the Palestinian fighters he also put his name to a joint statement with the rulers of Iraq, Transjordan and the Yemen calling on the Palestinians to moderate their rebellion. When Harold Dickson and his wife visited Riyadh, late in 1937, shortly after Dickson's retirement from government service, Ibn Saud told him how troubled he was over the issue of Palestine and the British Government's attitude. He and his subjects, he said, were 'deeply troubled ... over the ... strange hypnotic influence that the Jews, a race accursed by God according to his Holy Book, and destined to final destruction and eternal damnation hereafter, appear to wield over them [the British Government] and the English people generally. ... Our hatred of the Jews dates from God's condemnation of them for their persecution and rejection of 'Isa [Jesus Christ], and their subsequent rejection later of His chosen Prophet. It is beyond our understanding how your Government, representing the first Christian power in the world to-day, can wish to assist and reward these very same Jews who maltreated your 'Isa [Jesus Christ] ... It were far preferable from every point of view, if Great Britain were to make Palestine a British possession and rule it for the next hundred years, rather than to partition it ... such partition cannot possibly solve the difficulty, but must only perpetuate it and lead to war and misery.' He went on to suggest that the Jews were playing 'on the minds of the sentimental British masses by telling them that the Old Testament prophets foretold how they, the Jews would eventually return to their Promised Land' and they, the persecuted and wandering Israel, 'should not be denied a small place in the world, where to lay their weary heads. How, O Dickson, would the people of Scotland like it if the English suddenly gave their country to the Jews? But no, it is easier to give away other peoples' countries and not so dangerous.'[19] He told Dickson that the British government should stop all further Jewish immigration into Palestine but leave alone those Jews who were already there. A few months later he told Reader Bullard that the influx of Jews and partition of Palestine would be 'ruinous' to Britain and therefore dangerous to himself.

In the spring of 1938, six months after the Dicksons' visit, Ibn Saud received another important British woman visitor, Princess Alice, a cousin of King George the Sixth. A year earlier Ibn Saud's sons, Saud

19 H. R. P. Dickson, *Kuwait and Her Neighbours*, George Allen & Unwin, London 1956.

and Muhammad, had represented their father at George the Sixth's coronation and during their stay in London had invited Princess Alice and her husband, the Earl of Athlone, to visit Saudi Arabia. She and her husband had long wished to make an expedition to Arabia and so, after being received in Jeddah by Ibn Saud – the first time he had received a woman in public – she and her husband had gone on to Riyadh and then, after being both charmed and impressed by Ibn Saud and spending time with some of his wives and children, they travelled on to Hasa and the Gulf coast. One of the things that most delighted Princess Alice was the way in which Ibn Saud behaved towards his children. In one of her letters home she wrote: 'It appears the king adores his small children and takes them everywhere and even nurses them to sleep.'[20]

One of the places which Princess Alice and her husband visited while they were in the Hasa was Dhahran where the American oil men were still drilling for oil. By chance they arrived at an important moment, March 20th 1938. Almost five years had passed since al Sulaiman and Lloyd Hamilton had signed the Hasa oil concession. Since then the Americans had drilled seven wells into the fold of impervious rock at Dhahran, the area they had determined was the most geologically promising, but still found no substantial quantities of oil. Ibn Saud had never really believed that there was a fortune in oil under his kingdom and in the intervening years he had been too taken up with other problems to pay much attention to what the oil men were up to. However, of more interest to Ibn Saud was the possibility of the Americans being able to drill wells that would add significantly to his country's water supply and the drilling of artesian wells had been included in the agreement with Crane and the original report given to the King by Twitchell. As a result a group of the oil men had been sent to Riyadh to start looking for water.

On a storm-lashed day in April 1937 two of these American geologists, Max Steineke and Floyd Meeker, had gone exploring in the fertile area called Al Kharj an hour or two's drive south of Riyadh. One of the places they chanced upon that day was Ain Hit, the great gash in

20 Letter of Princess Alice, Countess of Athlone dated March 2nd 1938 quoted in *The Kingdom* by Robert Lacey, Hutchinson, London, 1981.

the limestone cliff where, at the end of the Ramadan fast in January 1902, Ibn Saud and his small band of warriors had washed and refilled their water bottles before their assault on Riyadh. The two Americans, like Ibn Saud and his warriors before them, had ducked under the low entrance to the cave and climbed down the steep zig-zag path inside. One hundred and fifty feet down, close to the deep pool of gently running fresh water from which Ibn Saud and his men had drunk, they had suddenly realised that the stratum of rock that they were looking at was the same as the enormous impervious rock sheet under which the huge reservoir of oil was trapped on Bahrain and was the same as the fold of rock where they and they colleagues had been drilling around Dhahran and out to Al Kharj. If this was part of one uninterrupted sheet of impervious rock that ran from under Bahrain and through Dhahran then it seemed almost impossible that there were not also large pockets of oil trapped under it in folds such as the one at Dhahran. Ain Hit was outside the area covered by the oil concession so there was no question of drilling for oil there, but nevertheless their spirits rose. As they explored further in the same area they found many other holes and outcrops of the same rock stratum. But by the time they had returned to Dhahran CASOC, the subsidiary company created by SOCAL to work the oil concession, had become so discouraged by the continuing failure to find oil and, with the American economy reeling under a fresh series of setbacks, was close to the point of giving up. However, armed with the detailed notes that Steineke and Meeker had made during their explorations around Ain Hit, the men running the oil exploration at Dhahran were able to persuade their bosses back at HQ in California to allow them to have one more go at finding oil by drilling their latest test well, Well Number 7, even deeper.

On the March 4th 1938 the drill sunk deep into Well Number 7 had reached a depth of 4;727 feet when suddenly the well 'blew'. Oil burst out and continued to gush in a great flood. No fewer than 1585 barrels' worth gushed out on that first day alone. The drillmen had nowhere to store the oil and were not yet ready to pipe it into barrels or storage tanks. Neither the pipework nor the storage containers had yet been installed on the site. So in order to store it somewhere they hastily rigged up a system of pipes to allow the oil to flow back into one of the abandoned unproductive wells that they had drilled earlier and abandoned. Over the succeeding days the volume of oil gushing from the well had increased still further until, on the day that Princess Alice and her husband visited the site, the volume had reached more than 3,000 barrels a day. As she wrote back home: 'We British were awful juggins's as we were offered the concession for this remarkably rich oilfield and turned it down as being no good; the Americans came along, ... found the oil – and we can't even have any of the share.'[21]

But while the oil men had been searching for oil the world beyond Arabia had continued to darken. In July 1937 Japan had renewed the unprovoked assault on China that it had begun in Manchuria in 1931. The so-called 'Great Powers' again did nothing and nor did the League of Nations. In March 1938, just one week before Princess Alice's visit to Dhahran, Hitler had moved unopposed into Austria and incorporated it into Germany. A month later he and his generals began sizing up Czechoslovakia. Meanwhile Mussolini, following his seizure of Abyssinia, had increased the number of Italian warships patrolling the Red Sea and started to take an unwelcome interest in the affairs of Yemen. Saudi Arabia had always been important because of its strategic position commanding the Persian Gulf and Red Sea astride the trade routes linking Europe with the Far East, but following the discovery of oil in the Hasa each of the great powers started to take an even greater interest in Saudi Arabia and in making friends with Ibn Saud. At the same time he, realising that there might well be another war, began making strenuous efforts, as he had in the years before the First World War, to make friends with each of the possible protagonists without committing himself to a binding alliance with any of them.

His relations with America presented no problem. With the oil men in the country preparing to start exporting large amounts of oil from his country and others nearby, and the American people gripped by isolationism and a determination not to become embroiled in foreign quarrels, America's prime interest in the region for the moment was to maintain the peace and secure an unimpeded flow of oil. Britain, on the other hand, posed a much more difficult problem. Ibn Saud had always

21 Ibid. Letter dated March 20th 1938.

tried to remain friends with Britain no matter how often she had appeared to brush him off. He had admired and been genuine friends with a number of distinguished British officers from Shakespear onwards. Britain was still the dominant power in the region and the largest source of his country's overseas trade. As he had told Dickson and his wife when they had visited him in Riyadh in October 1937, 'We definitely shall not wage war against you English.' He regarded the British as 'old friends' and 'the one potential ally we now have'. Yet at the same time there was the problem of Britain's policy in Palestine and her repeated failure to stand up to Mussolini or Hitler. A further glaring example of this occurred in September and October 1938 with the Munich Conference and Hitler's unopposed annexation of half of Czechoslovakia.

For her part, Britain was increasingly concerned about Mussolini's growing presence in the region and indications that Germany was putting out feelers towards Ibn Saud. In sanctioning the visit to Saudi Arabia of Princess Alice the British Government had been eager to demonstrate its goodwill towards Ibn Saud and, indeed, in issuing the invitation through his son Prince Saud, Ibn Saud had aimed to give a demonstration of his own ongoing goodwill towards Britain. The two senior Foreign Office officials who had visited Ibn Saud shortly before the visit to prepare the ground had had this confirmed when Crown Prince Saud had told them that 'The keystone of Saudi policy is friendship with Britain.' The Princess and her husband had themselves concluded from discussions they had had with Ibn Saud during their visit that he probably regarded Britain as 'the least dangerous of the foreigners with whom he had to deal'. British officials had always been particularly struck by Ibn Saud's 'political wisdom', regarding it as his most remarkable quality. 'He managed to be better informed on international affairs than many educated Europeans.'[22] The official who wrote those words, Sir Reader Bullard, was with Ibn Saud in his desert camp a few months later for the inauguration of the BBC World Service's Arabic Service, a further Foreign Office demonstration of the importance

22 From Sir Reader Bullard, *The Camels Must Go, An Autobiography*, Faber & Faber, London, 1951.

they attached to the Arab world. Unfortunately, however, the occasion nearly degenerated into a disaster when the Service's opening news bulletin featured a story about the hanging of a young Palestinian for possessing arms by the British Mandate authorities. After hearing the story Ibn Saud's eyes had filled with tears and the next morning he told Bullard, 'If it had not been for the Zionist policy of the British Government that Arab would be alive today.' Bullard hardly knew where to put himself, reflecting later that Britain's policy in Palestine would probably be used as an ongoing weapon in the armouries of his country's enemies in the region.[23]

The British Government was becoming increasingly concerned at German efforts at winning friends and influence in the region and in particular by the activities of Germany's representative in Baghdad, Fritz Grobba, who they knew also headed Hitler's intelligence network in the region. A number of Ibn Saud's trusted advisers, including his private physician and his private secretary, Yusuf Yasin, one of the two officials that Clayton and Antonious had found so difficult to deal with while negotiating the Bahra Agreement back in 1925, were strongly pro-German. In the months following the Munich Crisis Grobba had a number of private conversations with Ibn Saud during which, according to the reports Grobba sent back to Berlin, Ibn Saud made clear his deep hatred for Britain. He also sought Grobba's help in an effort to obtain German arms and smuggle them to the Arab resistance fighters in Palestine who were trying to foil Britain's plans for setting up a Jewish national home on their land. He also indicated to Grobba that he hoped that one day King Abdullah would be removed from the throne of Transjordan and replaced by one of his own sons. In January 1939 Saudi Arabia formally opened diplomatic relations with Nazi Germany and in February Ibn Saud wrote a personal letter to Hitler telling him that it was his 'foremost aim to see the friendly and intimate relations with the German Reich developed to the utmost limits'.[24]

23 Ibid. and *Two Kings*, etc., op. cit.

24 D. C. Watt, 'The Foreign Policy of Ibn Saud 1930–39', *Journal of the Royal Central Asian Society*, April 1963 quoted by Robert Lacey in *The Kingdom*, op. cit.

Meanwhile, in the months following their successful oil strike in Dhahran, CASOC had rapidly built up the number of men it had working on the site from about 50 to over 300. The wells had been deepened, additional wells drilled, and a forty-three mile long 10-inch pipeline laid from Dhahran to a point on the coast just north of Dammam where there was a low spit of land jutting out into the Gulf, called Ras Tanura, where it would be possible to construct a jetty capable of handling large oil tankers. A large camp, complete with modern health-care and leisure facilities, started to be built for the oil workers and their families, roads laid, water and sewerage plant and pipes put in, radio, telegraph and telephone systems installed. By the end of April 1939, with the help of British Admiralty charts, equipment and personnel, a safe navigation channel into Ras Tanura suitable for use by ocean-going tankers had been surveyed, laid out and marked, an oil jetty, storage tanks and all the necessary piping and pumps installed and constructed.

On May 1st, amid considerable ceremony, Ibn Saud swept into Dhahran in a convoy of cars to pay the site an official royal visit. He and his entourage inspected the installations and then he was filmed as he performed the official opening ceremony by starting the loading of the first tanker to dock at Ras Tanura and have her cargo tanks filled with oil ready for export from Saudi Arabia. The arrival of the Americans in Dhahran, and with them many of the features of the American way of life, was to mark the beginning of a profound change in the life of Arabia, triggering new aspirations and social changes among Ibn Saud's people which continue reverberating and causing tensions that are still on-going today. However, to Ibn Saud and his companions on May 1st 1939, it looked as if Philby's promise had at last been realised and that all his Kingdom's money troubles were over. By the end of 1939, 3.9 million barrels of oil, equivalent to almost 150 million US gallons, had been exported from the CASOC site at Dhahran, worth more in royalties to Ibn Saud than all the money he had received from CASOC since they had first signed the concession contract.

But that summer, as Ibn Saud's financial prospects soared, in the world beyond Arabia events were conspiring to dash them again. In March 1939 what remained of Czechoslovakia was swallowed by Hitler and he began to turn his attention to Poland. In April Mussolini invaded Albania; Britain and France moved to offer guarantees to Poland and at the end of April Britain announced her intention of instituting compulsory military service. In May Germany and Italy announced that they had entered into a military alliance – the so-called 'Pact of Steel'. President Roosevelt earnestly counselled all sides to disarm and refrain from aggressive acts but it now looked as if a new war was inevitable – the only question that remained was when would it start? In Riyadh Philby was repeatedly warning Ibn Saud that if war did come Britain would be defeated. That summer Philby returned to England to fight a by-election campaign in Hythe in Kent on behalf of a tiny, extreme right-wing party on a strongly anti-war pro-appeasement platform. Philby polled just 700 votes and lost his deposit.

Meanwhile Ibn Saud had entered into an arms agreement with Mussolini and was making a deal with the Germans to buy 4,000 of their rifles. In the event, a continuing shortage of cash meant that he never made his down payment and so never took delivery of any of the arms. That summer he was also approached by the Japanese who were interested in his oil. He rejected this approach but did eventually enter into a trade agreement and a treaty of friendship with them.

In August Germany and Russia signed the Nazi-Soviet Pact and on 1st September Hitler invaded Poland from the west, followed less than three days later by the Soviet Union from the north and east. Acting on the guarantees they had given to Poland, on September 3rd 1939 Britain and France declared war on Germany and the Second World War began. Ibn Saud responded by declaring himself neutral and, as a precaution, dispatched troops to the borders of Iraq, Kuwait and Transjordan.

CHAPTER 13

War and Meetings of Great Men

Ibn Saud was determined not to get drawn into the war, or at least not until he could be certain which side was going to win it. So he spent much of it adjusting his policies and his closeness to the protagonists depending upon their fortunes.

Through the rest of 1939 and 1940 the production of oil continued to increase but after that it fell and did not return to the same level until 1944 with the result that the wealth that had seemed within Ibn Saud's grasp in the summer of 1939 did not materialise. Worse, the war resulted in huge reductions in the number of pilgrims undertaking the *Hajj* and of the kingdom's exports. On top of which in the winter of 1939-40 the rains failed.

One novel solution to Ibn Saud's financial problems was put forward by Philby. He suggested that in return for a payment of £20 million Ibn Saud would support the creation of Jewish Homeland in Palestine and organise the resettlement in Saudi Arabia and other Arab lands of all the Palestinians who would be displaced as a result. However, when he put it to Ibn Saud he rejected the idea out of hand. Did Philby really think, he asked, contemptuously, that he could be bribed to sell out Palestine and the Palestinians to the Jews for £20 million?[1]

In April 1940 Hitler invaded Denmark and Norway. On May 10th Hitler invaded Holland, then France. Chamberlain resigned and Winston Churchill became Britain's Prime Minister. A month later, after Holland, Belgium and Norway had all surrendered and France was about to fall, Mussolini came into the war on Hitler's side. On June 22nd France surrendered and the next day Hitler made a triumphal tour of Paris. Britain now fought on alone. In July the Battle of Britain, intended by Hitler to be the prelude to his invasion of Britain, began.

Throughout the early months of the war and on into 1940 there could be no doubt about where Ibn Saud's sympathies lay. When news was brought to him of the sinking of the British battleship *Royal Oak* in October 1939 he had said 'I felt as though I had lost one of my sons.'[2] With each new report of a British defeat he would become more downcast and increasingly bewildered by Britain's apparent lack of fighting spirit. 'What has happened to you English?' he would demand of Philby. 'You should strike, and strike now!'[3] Sometimes it was Philby himself, rather than Ibn Saud's radio monitoring team, who was the first to bring news of a fresh British defeat to the King, having heard it in a German broadcast

1 Philby later claimed that Ibn Saud's reaction was quite favourable, however Philby was a notoriously unreliable reporter of events, especially if they reflected unfavourably upon himself. However the idea did later reach Roosevelt and Churchill, but was never taken any further.

2 See Reader Bullard, 'Ibn Saud' in *The Listener*, February 4th 1954 and *Two Kings in Arabia,* op. cit.

3 Quoted by Leslie McLoughlin, *Ibn Saud: Founder of a Kingdom*, Macmillan, London 1993, from K. Zirikli *Arabia in the time of Ibn Saud* (Arabic) 1970.

from Berlin. Thus it was that in April 1940, while he was encamped in the desert, Philby was the first to hear on the radio in his tent that Germany had invaded Norway and went straight over to Ibn Saud's tent to tell him the news. He was also the first to bring him news of the British withdrawal from Norway and, on May 10th 1940, to tell him that Germany had invaded Holland. There could not fail to be a certain note of 'I told you so' in Philby's successive reports of bad news and he came to be regarded by those around the King as a 'bird of ill-omen'. So much so that on the one occasion that summer when he brought the King good news – the rescue of more than 300,000 British troops from Dunkirk – Ibn Saud refused to believe it.[4] Yet there continued to be little doubt about where Ibn Saud's sympathies really lay. When the British battlecruiser HMS *Hood* was sunk in May 1941 Ibn Saud told those around him, who by that time believed that final British defeat was inevitable and seemed to welcome the prospect, that they should wait a little. When some days later news was brought that the British had sunk the German battleship *Bismarck* he made those same courtiers stand and clap.

The summer of 1940 brought Saudi Arabia tragedies of its own. The failure of the rains in the previous winter meant crops were now failing and the number of deaths among livestock was increasing. People were starting to go hungry and, as they always had done in times of trouble, they turned to Ibn Saud, the great shaikh and imam of all their tribes, for help. But this time Ibn Saud was in no position to help. His food stores were empty and al Sulaiman's tin treasury chest was bare. Signs of unrest began to grow, especially in the north, where tribesmen began crossing the borders into Iraq and Transjordan in search of food. Ibn Saud turned to Britain for help. And even now, in her own darkest hour and facing the threat of a German naval blockade, Britain provided it. Churchill ordered that wheat and flour should be shipped from Egypt and Canada, rice from India and coins from the Royal Mint. When the aid started to arrive Ibn Saud still faced the problem of how to get it from the coast to the places deep inside the country where it was needed. Much of his own small fleet of lorries was out of action, damaged by driving over rough desert tracks, and many of the baggage camels were

4 See Philby, *Arabian Days: An Autobiography*, Robert Hale, London, 1948.

dead or suffering from the effects of the drought and so in no condition to carry heavy loads hundreds of miles into the country's desert interior. So Ibn Saud turned to the oil men and it was CASOC lorries and drivers that carried the food inland to the starving people.

Until the summer of 1940 the war had seemed remote. Unlike during the First World War Turkey remained resolutely neutral and the fighting had so far all taken place on the far side of Europe or in distant oceans. But with the fall of France and the entry into the war of Italy on Germany's side all that changed. The Italians had 300,000 troops in Libya and a further 200,000 in Abyssinia, together with warships and aircraft in the Red Sea and Mediterranean. The fall of France and the creation of the collaborationist Vichy French Government meant that there was a likelihood that Syria and the French possessions in North Africa, together with all the French army units, aircraft and warships based in the region, might become available to the Germans. Against this the British had fewer than 100,000 troops and a small number of aircraft in the whole region, most of them based in Egypt. So it looked as though any defence of her interests in the region that Britain might attempt would have to rely heavily on the use of her navy.

On August 3rd Italy started moving troops from its bases on the coast of the Horn of Africa into British Somaliland. With Italian forces outnumbering British forces by more than three to one, after less than three weeks and one indecisive battle, Britain withdrew her troops, leaving the territory to Italy.

Although Ibn Saud had formally established diplomatic relations with Germany back in January 1939 he had, at Britain's behest, resisted Fritz Grobba's requests to be allowed to open a German diplomatic mission in the country. But following the German successes in 1940, he changed his position and granted Grobba permission to establish a large German mission in Jeddah. Since the start of the war Germany had been playing on anti-British and anti-imperial sentiment across the region, portraying herself as 'the friend of the Arabs', proclaiming that victory for Germany and her allies 'will liberate the Middle Eastern countries from the British yoke'.[5] Now, after

5 See Alexei Vassiliev, *The History of Saudi Arabia*, Saqi Books, London, 1998.

establishing himself in Saudi Arabia Grobba and his agents began spreading anti-British pro-Nazi propaganda among pilgrims making the *Hajj*. He and his agents also started covertly encouraging disaffected and dissatisfied Saudis, and anyone who harboured a grudge against Ibn Saud, to set up subversive groups which Grobba then supplied with arms and money. Shortly after the start of the war Grobba had been thrown out of Iraq for trying to engineer an armed uprising. So now, as he set about trying to do the same thing in Saudi Arabia, he took great care to keep his intentions hidden. Not long after his arrival in the country he asked Ibn Saud for a concession to extract mineral resources in the area bordering the Red Sea, but Ibn Saud refused him. To grant Grobba the concession risked becoming too closely involved with the Germans and might antagonise the Americans – something that Ibn Saud was certainly not going to risk. In August Ibn Saud also made a small gesture of support towards the British. Hearing that Philby was about to embark on a trip to America to give a series of defeatist anti-British lectures, he tipped off the British authorities, advising them to examine his bags. As a result, when Philby arrived in Karachi on the first leg of his journey he was arrested – or as Philby put it later in his own rather aggrieved account, 'kidnapped' – taken to London and interned.

On September 13th, at the time when the German Luftwaffe was starting its massive Blitz on British towns, a large Italian army massed on the eastern border of Libya launched an all-out offensive against the much smaller British army which was defending the frontiers of Egypt. Over the next four days the Italians fought their way fifty miles eastwards along the Mediterranean coast into Egypt. But with every mile they advanced their casualties mounted, with the result that when they reached the small town of Sidi Barrani they came to a halt.

As the autumn advanced Germany attracted further allies. In late September Japan joined Germany and Italy in the Tripartite Pact – 'The Axis'. In early October German troops invaded Romania and three weeks later Italy invaded Greece. In November Romania and Hungary joined the Axis. But that autumn also, because of Britain's success in the Battle of Britain, Hitler was forced to postpone his planned invasion of Britain. In November British dive-bombers sank or crippled most of the Italian fleet at Taranto and the Greeks defeated the Italian army which had invaded their country and drove it back into Albania. In December the British and Australians began a counter-attack against the Italians in Egypt and over the next two months drove them back some 300 miles into Libya, capturing Tobruk and Benghazi, took more than 100,000 Italian prisoners and 1,000 guns at a cost to themselves of fewer than 1,000 lives. The British also began recapturing all the ground the Italians had taken in the Horn of Africa, retaking all of Somaliland, Eritrea and advancing into Abyssinia. By May 1941 the British army and Abyssinian guerrillas had driven the Italians out of Abyssinia and the Emperor, Haile Selassie, returned from his exile in England.

However, responding to the series of Italian defeats and an anti-German coup in Yugoslavia, in the spring of 1941 German forces entered the region in strength and dramatically shifted the fortunes of war there in Germany's favour. In April 1941 a newly arrived German army commanded by General Erwin Rommel drove the British back out of Libya and left them surrounded at Tobruk. German troops attacked and defeated Greece and Yugoslavia, leaving only resistance groups in those two countries to carry on the fight. At the beginning of April a pro-German government took over Iraq, expelled King Abdullah and prepared to attack the RAF bases there. The British responded rapidly, sending troops and aircraft from India and Palestine. After a few days of intense fighting, during which one young British officer led a group of Palestinian Bedouin in a traditional Arab cavalry charge against the Iraqi usurpers, they succeeded in occupying Iraq before the Germans and Italians were able to deploy sufficient of their own forces to provide their Iraqi protégés with effective help.[6] British and Australian troops also entered Syria and by the middle of July had succeeded in overpowering and disarming all the Vichy French troops there. By these moves, undertaken, as Churchill later recorded, 'to meet a desperate need' Britain 'with pitifully small and improvised

6 The young British officer who led the cavalry charge was Captain David Smiley, later a member of the S.O.E., MI6 and commander of the Sultan of Oman's forces in the war against communist rebels during the 1950s.

forces [had] regained mastery of the wide regions involved.'[7] The British thus succeeded in putting an end to what they perceived as the German threat to their communications route through the Gulf to India and to the Persian, Iraqi, Bahraini and Saudi oilfields. They also removed the danger of the Germans being able to mount a pincer movement simultaneously from North Africa, the Russian Caucasus, Syria and Iraq on Egypt and the Suez Canal.

Called on by the Iraqi coup leaders for help, Ibn Saud refused, saying that to provide them with help would be an act of treachery against the British with whom he had long-standing ties of friendship. Even when he received a personal message from Hitler offering to make him 'King of all the Arabs' in return for attacking Britain he rejected the offer.[8] However, when the defeated leader of the short-lived pro-German Iraqi Government, Rashid Ali al-Gailani, fled following the British invasion, Ibn Saud offered him asylum. The British responded by demanding that Gailani be handed over to them as he had been sentenced to death by an Iraqi military court. But Ibn Saud refused and instead treated him as his honoured guest. Similarly, when the crew of an Italian motor torpedo boat fleeing the British entered Saudi waters in the Red Sea and was captured, Ibn Saud had the crew interned rather then handing them over to the British.

In August 1941, by which time Hitler had launched his attack on Russia and was diverting the majority of his war effort to that front, Britain and America announced the signing of the Atlantic Charter. Under this, although the United States was still officially neutral, Britain and America proclaimed their joint commitment to 'the final destruction of Nazi tyranny', to the right of all peoples to self-government, economic advancement and freedom from the threat of outside aggression. They also undertook to 'seek no aggrandisement, territorial or other' as a result of victory in the war.

In September, British and Russian troops entered Persia, took control of the oil installations, threw all the German agents out of the country,

7 Winston S. Churchill, *The Second World War: Vol II Alone,* Cassell, London, 1959.

8 Vassiliev, op. cit.

captured Tehran and forced the Shah, whom they regarded as dangerously pro-German, to abdicate, replacing him with his twenty-two-year-old son, Mohammad Reza. By this step the British and Russians opened a direct overland supply route through which the British could supply the Russians with arms and supplies and secured for themselves the oil resources. Just days later, Ibn Saud annulled the treaties he had entered into with Nazi Germany before the war and expelled Dr Grobba and the members of his German mission.

On December 7th 1941 the Japanese attacked and sank most of the American fleet at Pearl Harbor, bringing the United States into the war. Until America entered the war the US State Department had regarded Ibn Saud's kingdom as of only minor importance. Although the USA had formally recognised Ibn Saud's new state back in 1931, the American Government had never thought it worthwhile, even after CASOC had discovered the major oil field at Dhahran, to station an official representative in the country. But with America's entry into the war all that changed. Not only Saudi Arabia's geographic importance astride the routes linking the European and North African theatres of war with India and the Far East was recognised but its major importance as a source of oil. In the months following Pearl Harbor the oil fields and reserves of the United States, the Gulf of Mexico and the Caribbean were having to meet not only all of America's own domestic and military needs but most of those of Britain and her other allies. As the rate of depletion of the reserves rose it quickly became apparent that this could not go on for ever. On top of which the supply routes over which American oil and armaments had to be ferried across the Atlantic from the USA to her European allies were both long and dangerously exposed to the depredations of German U-boats. The Battle of the Atlantic, which had begun in 1941, would steadily grow in the months after America came into the war to reach a climax in the summer of 1943. In these circumstances the importance of the Middle East's oil and CASOC's huge fields in Saudi Arabia as an alternative source of supply not only for the United States but for her European and Far Eastern allies, quickly came to be recognised. Just three months after entering the war America set up its own official mission in Jeddah and appointed a dedicated attaché specifically to deal with oil affairs. A year later President Roosevelt sent his own special envoy, Brigadier General

Hurley, to study the position of American oil interests in Saudi Arabia and Ibn Saud sent no fewer than three of his sons, Saud, Faisal and Khalid, to the USA to meet President Roosevelt, members of the government and Congress.

In the months following the outbreak of the war the number of American staff based in Dhahran had been reduced from 370 to little more than 100. But following America's entry into the war, and the increasing demand for oil, new plant and wells in the Hasa were brought on stream and the number of American and local staff employed by CASOC again began to grow.

In 1940 Ibn Saud had invited Karl Twitchell to return to the Kingdom to carry out surveys into the possible construction of modern roads to replace the tracks in the Asir region. While he was staying in Riyadh during this visit Ibn Saud had one day asked Twitchell what chances he thought there might be of interesting an American commercial enterprise in exploring the possibilities for improving the water supplies in the Al Kharj area south of Riyadh with a view to increasing the area's agricultural production, and of getting them to bring in the drilling, pumping and agricultural equipment necessary to achieve this. Twitchell had promised to make inquiries on his return to the United States but, despite having a number of meetings with various American Government departments and companies, had failed to find any takers.

However, all that changed within weeks of America entering the war. Now the US Government itself offered to send a party of agricultural experts from the parched southern states of the USA to Saudi Arabia to undertake the work, funded out of the emergency funds of the President himself. Ibn Saud immediately accepted the offer and the agricultural experts, now dressed in Arab robes, arrived on May 11th 1942 with Twitchell and a party of about twenty American diplomats and technicians who had come to set up America's first official mission in Saudi Arabia. Their plane landed, after travelling from America via Cairo and Bahrain, on an airstrip improvised by two CASOC engineers in a boulder- and brush-strewn wadi north of Riyadh. The CASOC engineers had brought with them a radio with which to keep in touch with the plane on its flight from Bahrain and talk the pilot down onto the improvised airstrip. A number of the soldiers who had come with

Ibn Saud to meet the plane had become curious about the radio and asked the two American engineers what they had in 'the box'. The engineers had told the soldiers that 'the box' had a voice which told them that a 'great bird' would arrive in about twenty-five minutes bringing guests from America to see the King. When the plane had landed, and the party of twenty-plus Americans had climbed down out of it, one of the engineers asked the soldiers who had asked about 'the box' what they thought of it now? The Saudis were, as expected, full of awe and wonder at both what 'the box' had said and at 'the bird' and what it had brought. 'But', said one of them, 'The box was wrong. The bird arrived in twenty minutes, not twenty-five as it had said!'[9]

Ibn Saud had set up a large camp close to the airstrip and intended to receive his guests in style. A guard of honour and al Sulaiman were drawn up at the side of the airstrip to greet them on behalf of the King and conduct them to their tents. The Americans were then taken to a square some twenty-five yards across laid out with Persian rugs strewn on the sand and lined with comfortable armchairs in front of a great tent for an informal audience with the King, Crown Prince Saud, Prince Faisal and senior members of the King's Council. With his American guests sitting in chairs on the King's right and the princes and members of his council seated to his left, Ibn Saud formally welcomed his guests and the first American Minister to the Sovereign Kingdom of Saudi Arabia, Mr Alexander Kirk, formally presented his credentials. Cardamon-spiced Bedouin Arab coffee was then brought round in long-spouted, gracefully curved brass Najdi coffee pots by two of Ibn Saud's servants, one dressed in a brilliant-scarlet robe, the other in deep vivid blue, each crossed-strapped with bandoliers of ammunition and holsters with automatic pistols. After the tiny cups had been collected, incense was passed round among the guests in a burner, after which the audience was over. To the Americans, for most of whom this was a new experience, the charm and simple, dignified magnificence of the scene, was truly wonderful and an unforgettable introduction to a traditional Arab way of life which was shortly to begin to disappear.

9 See Twitchell, K. S., *Saudi Arabia: With an Account of the Development of Its Natural Resources*, Princeton University Press, 1953, pp. 167–9.

The following day the American party was driven in cars the three hours to Riyadh to stay in the palace of Prince Saud, be entertained by him and Faisal, and shown sound films in Arabic of the recent meeting of President Roosevelt and Winston Churchill on board HMS *Prince of Wales* off Newfoundland. The next day Ibn Saud himself entertained them to a traditional Najdi feast in the new palace he had had built a mile to the north of the old city. As a concession to western eating habits the feast was laid out on a large table, with Ibn Saud towering over his guests at its head, but otherwise conformed to the traditions of an Arab feast. Arrayed down the centre of the table for the King's thirty-two guests were eight great platters piled high with boiled rice and raisins and each crowned by a whole cooked sheep. Around these platters was spread a generous variety of other dishes holding chickens, other meats and vegetables.

The following day Twitchell and the agricultural experts were driven the fifty-odd miles south to Al Kharj to start work on developing the area for agriculture. Picking up from where work begun by a British team in the 1930s had stopped, they began digging wells, installing pumping equipment, laying out irrigation systems, levelling and improving the land. Helped by Saudi labour, engineers and other specialists from CASOC, over the next few years more than 2,000 acres of the land in Al Kharj was brought into high-yielding agricultural production, producing wheat, corn, hay, alfalfa, a wide range of vegetables, dates, melons, grapes, poultry and other livestock sufficient to meet most of the needs of Riyadh and regions beyond.

However, during the first two months after Twitchell and his agricultural experts arrived in Riyadh, Ibn Saud's radio monitors brought him news of further German military successes. On June 20th the British garrison holding Tobruk surrendered and 33,000 British and South African troops were taken prisoner, a defeat for British arms which Churchill himself described as 'a disgrace'. By the end of June, Rommel's Afrika Korps had advanced eastwards into Egypt to within 160 miles of Cairo, reaching a place called El Alamein. Mussolini hurried from Rome to North Africa in readiness to ride on a white charger at the head of his victorious army as it entered Cairo. At the same time as the German army in North Africa was scoring its successes the German armies in

Russia had also resumed their advance. By the first week of July they had crushed the last Russian resistance in the Crimea and begun to advance towards Stalingrad. Faced with these reverses, the British High Command in Egypt, fearful of a German pincer movement developing between Rommel's Afrika Korps from the west and the German forces in the Caucasus and Crimea from the north, secretly prepared plans to abandon Egypt and the Suez Canal completely and concentrate all their forces on the defence of the Abadan oil fields and Persia. However, the Americans responded by rushing reinforcements of the most modern American tanks to the British in North Africa and Churchill flew to Cairo and changed the army leadership in the region, putting General Alexander in overall charge and bringing General Sir Bernard Montgomery out from England to take command of the Eighth Army.

Shortly afterwards Ibn Saud sent his twenty-one-year-old son Mansur to Montgomery's headquarters at El Alamein to help rally the Muslim Indian troops fighting with the Eighth Army as it prepared for a major counter-attack against the Germans. This was a particularly important gesture of support for Britain as at this time the Congress Party in India was conducting a disobedience and non-co-operation campaign against the continued British presence in India and if the Muslims in India had risen up against the British at that moment it could have caused the British forces both in North Africa and in the Far East extremely serious problems. Ibn Saud's continued support for Britain throughout the war was important for Britain because, as probably the most important leader in the Muslim world at that time, if Ibn Saud had come out against the British in support of the Axis many millions of Muslims across the globe might have joined Germany, Japan and Italy in fighting Britain and her allies.

However the autumn and winter of 1942–3 saw a transformation in the war situation. On the night of October 23rd 1942 Montgomery began his counter-attack against Rommel at El Alamain and by 4th November Rommel and the Afrika Korps were in full retreat. Three days later the Americans began landing in French North Africa and a fortnight after that the Russians began their counter-offensive at Stalingrad, leading in January 1943 to the surrender of an entire German army and the first truly significant German defeat of the war. From then on, although the Germans would achieve some major successes, the eventual outcome of the war was never really in serious doubt. In February 1943, President Roosevelt himself came to the conclusion that Saudi Arabia's oil was going to be essential not only to the Allied war effort but for America's economy after the war was over. He therefore determined that under the terms of the American Lend-Lease Act the security of Saudi Arabia was 'vital to the defense of the United States' and that Saudi Arabia was therefore eligible for American government aid. As a result over the next two years between $33 million and $100 million dollars' worth of cash, gold bullion, equipment and goods of many types flooded into Saudi Arabia under the terms of the Lend-Lease Act, adding up in value to many times the total income that the Kingdom had received since the outbreak of the war. The difference between the many millions of dollars' worth of American aid supplied in this way and the £1 million annual subsidy provided by the British during the war was that the British subsidy was given to the country as aid and could therefore be treated as a 'gift', whereas much, though far from all, of the value of the aid provided to Ibn Saud by America under the Lend-Lease Act had to be treated as a loan that would have to be re-paid at some future date.

But it was not only money and materials that now started flowing into Ibn Saud's kingdom, it was also British and, above all, American personnel and expertise. As a result, although Saudi Arabia had not formally entered the war and remained firmly neutral, by 1943 Britain and the USA were not only working together as allies in Saudi Arabia, they were competing with each other for influence with Ibn Saud. In doing so, they were looking as much to their positions and influence in the country after the war as to their immediate war interests. Britain had been the dominant power in the region since at least the fall of the Ottoman Empire and Churchill had no intention of surrendering that position to America once the war was over. Roosevelt and the US Congress, on the other hand, were deeply committed, both by their own political ideals and because of their country's history, to bringing an end to imperialism and colonialism. However, they did not see, or at least did not admit to seeing, any contradiction in attempting to replace imperial rule over a country with their own economic dominance of it.

As for Ibn Saud, he wanted to secure the continued friendship of both

Britain and America. At the same time, however, he was quite happy to play one off against the other to his own financial and political advantage. So when the Commander-in-Chief of US Forces in the Middle East, General Roys, visited Saudi Arabia in December 1943 to make arrangements for the construction of two American airbases, the most important near the CASOC oil plant at Dhahran, and for the sending of a US military mission to train the Saudi army, Ibn Saud was careful also to invite the British to send in a team of instructors. The result was that military experts from both countries arrived in Saudi Arabia during 1944. The American team concentrated on teaching Ibn Saud's young soldiers military surveying, how to operate machine guns and how to drive and maintain motor transport, while the British specialised in training them to use light armoured vehicles.

The development of the oil industry, the introduction of modern agricultural methods, the increase in modern engineering and construction works such as road building and irrigation schemes, and above all the great increase in the number of Americans working in the country marked the beginning of a massive change in Saudi Arabia and in the lives of its people. These Americans did not travel in ones and twos and by traditional means. They came in large numbers, bringing with them cars, lorries, aircraft, radios, all manner of other modern equipment and, in many cases, their families. They did not live as earlier travellers to Arabia had, like the indigenous people. The Americans brought with them their own lifestyles. The biggest single influx of Americans was, of course, in and around the oil and military installations in the vicinity of Dhahran, Ras Tanura and Qatif. In less than two years between 1944 and 1945, CASOC, now renamed The Arabian-American Oil Company, or Aramco, built a major oil refinery, new storage tanks, loading lines, services, a pier, wharf, all the marine installations for handling large modern oil tankers and a permanent camp with homes, accommodation and air-conditioning for all its staff.[10] The camp

10 CASOC formally became Aramco, the Arabian-American Oil Company, in 1944, when more US oil companies became partners in the venture, so increasing the capital available to the company, widening its sales network and increasing the company's leverage with the US Government.

provided up-to-date medical facilities, schools, public services, leisure facilities, even shops. Within a very few years it had become, as one commentator described it, 'a town' where 'one may buy stamps and post a letter, get a hair cut or a beauty treatment, buy groceries, household supplies, and essential personal items'.[11]

In time it, and Aramco, became like a mini-state within a state. Aramco took on an increasing number of local workers and after a while began to provide training for the brightest of them so that they could progress within the company. Although the local workers worked for and often alongside the Americans and so began to become familiar with the American lifestyle, they remained in many ways segregated from them. Inside the camp itself there operated what amounted to a kind of apartheid, imposed by the Americans who still practised strict colour separation even among their serving armed forces and in public places such as diners, where even German prisoners of war could be served but not black American servicemen. The separation between Saudi workers and Americans was also tacitly encouraged by Ibn Saud and his officials, who feared the possible moral and spiritual 'contagion' that might arise from social contact with American 'unbelievers'. So the area where the Americans lived was separated from the area where the Saudi workers lived by a barbed wire fence. The 'Saudi Camp', as it was called, was unfenced and open to the surrounding countryside. It consisted not of modern air-conditioned homes like the American camp, but of breeze-block and concrete tin-roofed shacks and barracks, plus a small market where the workers could buy food and a few other basic items. Unlike the American camp, with its swimming pools, shops, hair salons, sports facilities and cinema, the Saudi camp lacked even basic services such as water, sewerage and electricity.

Most of the Saudi workers at Dhahran were Shia Muslims from the surrounding area and Hasa. But over the months word spread across the desert to other regions of Arabia. Desert Bedouin and townspeople from many regions of the kingdom and different tribes were attracted by the

11 A. Brown, *Oil, God, and Gold: The Story of Aramco and the Saudi Kings*. Houghton Mifflin, Boston, USA, 1999 quoted in Madawi Al-Rasheed *A History of Saudi Arabia*, Cambridge University Press, New York, 2002.

prospect of paid work. As one peasant from the Qasim region recalled: 'During the second war we almost starved in Qasim ... We heard from people that some *nasrani* [Christians] were offering jobs in Hasa for cash. My father decided I should go and try my luck.' After travelling with a Bedouin caravan to Dhahran this man was offered a job as a labourer. Over the next few years he lived in the Saudi camp at Dhahran and did all sorts of menial jobs, coming into contact for the first time in his life with people from other parts of Saudi Arabia: 'For the first time in my life I found myself with other tribesmen from Ataiba, Shammar and Qahtan, each had their stories and dialect. We worked together. I met people from Asir and other parts of Najd. It was amazing. We had a communal kitchen, it was our "restaurant". We called it *mat'am abu rub'* because they charged a quarter of a rial for the meal. The food was awful. But the Najdis would not say anything. They were shy; they would not complain. They would not ask for any more money or food.'[12] This unnamed worker listened to a radio for the first time while he was in the Aramco camp at Dhahran and as well as sending money home to his family in Qasim, he saved up to buy a radio of his own. It was, he said, all that he wanted – to be able to hear the news from other parts of the Arab world.

As can be seen from this story, and from the reaction of the two Saudi soldiers to the 'box' radio of the Aramco engineers who set up the improvised landing strip when Twitchell and his American agricultural specialists flew in to meet Ibn Saud, although modern western inventions had been present in the Kingdom for well over a decade and foreigners had been coming to the country with increasing frequency for even longer, the impact of the outside world and foreign influences upon the ordinary people of the peninsula had remained extremely limited. Although all of Saudi Arabia had on paper been one united country for almost twenty years, ever since Ibn Saud had completed the conquest of the Hijaz, the different regions of the country, their people and tribes, remained almost as completely cut off from and unknown to each other as they had been for thousands of years. Since proclaiming Saudi Arabia a single kingdom, Ibn Saud and his entourage had continually moved

12 Interview with an unnamed worker by Madawi Al-Rasheed quoted, op. cit.

about the country, asserting his authority and consolidating his rule. Yet any sense among his subjects of sharing in a common national identity, other than through him as their Amir and through their common Wahhabi faith, was non-existent. But the influx of Americans and the changes that they were to bring with them were to change all that for ever, and in doing so threaten the very foundations of Ibn Saud's young kingdom. Ways of life that had remained virtually unaltered since Biblical times were now set to change or disappear, resulting in uncertainty, social and spiritual tensions, and the threat of dissension and conflict.

One of the most immediate effects of Saudi Arabia becoming eligible for assistance under the Lend-Lease Act was to replenish the cash in al Sulaiman's tin treasury chest. Another was to relieve the cash shortages experienced since the start of the war by Ibn Saud and the members of his immediate circle. Of course, they had suffered nothing like the near starvation suffered by the family of that young Qasim peasant who had gone to work for Aramco or the rationing and shortages in many of the combatant countries. But with the coming of millions of dollars' worth of Lend-Lease many of those closest to Ibn Saud began to indulge themselves as they never had before. Ibn Saud, who had throughout the 1930s and the early years of the war continued building himself new palaces in the regions that he had conquered, now increased the pace of this building. The huge, rambling, bow-windowed and pre-stressed-concrete palace he started to build in the Al Kharj area south of Riyadh in particular attracted adverse comment from British officials in Whitehall responsible for supplying his country with aid.

Still worse, in the eyes of the Whitehall mandarins, was 'the extravagance of the royal princes', which they saw as 'an abuse of His Majesty's Government's generosity'.[13] Although the frequency with which Ibn Saud married new wives had slowed by this time (he is believed to have married five new wives between 1938 and 1945) and the number of new children he was having decreased (eight sons in the same period), his generosity towards his children remained as great as ever. More than a dozen of his sons had now grown up and were

13 Foreign Office Papers quoted by Robert Lacey in *The Kingdom*, Hutchinson, London 1981.

producing children of their own. Each of them was provided with money to build a palace of his own, to buy fleets of motor cars and live in the style expected of an Arab royal prince. Unlike their father, the royal princes had not experienced the frugal life of the desert, nor learned through personal experience the virtues of self-restraint. So, while Ibn Saud was never greedy for himself, his children grew up to expect to be able to indulge their taste for luxury. The money and aid that flowed into the country from Ibn Saud's western allies was not viewed as Saudi Arabia's money but as belonging personally to the King, to be dispensed as he, as the ruler and embodiment of the state, saw fit. Ibn Saud himself continued to rule in the traditional way, to entertain lavishly, to make generous provision for the members of his enormous extended family, pay subsidies to the heads of various tribes, provide housing and sustenance for the host of vanquished enemies he had brought to Riyadh and to provide daily meals and gifts for the hordes of his subjects who flocked to his palaces or to his desert camp when he was out on the march.

A further, and even greater source of concern to Saudi Arabia's British and American aid providers was corruption, the amount of money that seemed to stick to the hands of Ibn Saud's officials and never reach its intended recipients. American officials were as aware of the problem as their British counterparts, but less prepared to try to do anything about it. The fact was that the amounts of money and aid now flowing in, and the growing size and complexity of the Saudi state, were too great to be effectively controlled and administered by al Sulaiman, with his tin treasury chest, his ledgers, elementary book-keeping and small team of often inept or dishonest book-keepers. An American internal government report in 1944 described the kingdom's financial controls and accounting as 'inadequate' and 'chaotic'.[14] However, when the Head of the British Legation in Jeddah, Stanley Jordan, an Australian and an old-hand in Arab affairs who had served in Jeddah during the dying days of Hashemite rule, raised the matter directly with Ibn Saud and offered him the services of an Indian Muslim official to overhaul the

14 See Lacey, op. cit.

Saudi government's financial management, the King cheerfully acknowledged that there was a problem but politely declined to accept any help. Nevertheless, a little later he did get al Sulaiman to get rid of one of his most notoriously corrupt aides. However, when the Americans got wind of this they jumped to the conclusion that the corrupt official had been fired on the say-so of Jordan and, putting this together with the fact that Britain was then considering opening a bank in the kingdom, concluded that the British were using the leverage provided by the aid they were giving to Ibn Saud not merely to maintain their own influence in the country but to shut out the Americans. The Americans protested to the British and took up the matter directly with Ibn Saud. Ibn Saud, who seems to have been deliberately playing off the British against the Americans in an effort to get them to try to outdo each other in the amount of aid they were giving him, told the Head of the American Mission in Jeddah that Jordan was the enemy both of his country and of America. Jordan, said Ibn Saud, had tried as hard as he could 'to prevent our good relations and to injure my country'.[15] The upshot was that the British Government felt compelled to re-assign Jordan to another post and replace him with an official called Laurence Grafftey-Smith. Grafftey-Smith was soon providing Ibn Saud and his family with the kind of assistance that they evidently appreciated rather more than advice on how to run their financial affairs. Among the services he provided was the expertise of his own dentist who came to Riyadh from Cairo for three weeks to attend to the royal family's teeth.[16] The Americans meanwhile promised Ibn Saud a new post-war aid package running into several tens of millions of pounds, a sum with which the British could not hope to compete.

Ibn Saud was now in his sixties and suddenly all the war wounds he had received and all the years of hard living seemed to start to tell. He seemed to start ageing rapidly. He developed arthritis and by the latter

15 Leslie McLoughlin, op. cit. quoting B. Rubin, *The Great Powers in theMiddle East 1941–7*, London, 1981, p. 61.

16 A medical report on Ibn Saud made at about the same time by a Western doctor said that Ibn Saud's own teeth were still very good, so it must have been other members of his family who received most attention from Grafftey-Smith's dentist.

years of the war could only walk with difficulty, becoming unable to climb up stairs unaided. The warrior who throughout his life had stood out on account of his physical strength and endurance, now spent his days largely sitting, listening to the latest radio reports of the war and discussing them with those around him. With the lack of physical activity he began to put on weight. His sexual potency seemed to drop off too. The man whose sexual potency had been a major factor in his hold on power, who had said that there was no pleasure a man could enjoy to match putting his lips to a 'woman's lips, his body on her body and his feet on her feet' had now become pathetically eager to learn about any new aphrodisiac that might offer a return to his former virility. It was perhaps telling that at about this time he started dyeing his hair. Yusuf Yasin, one of Ibn Saud's two close advisers who had given Sir Gilbert Clayton such a hard time during the negotiations for the Bahra and Hada treaties twenty years earlier, had for many years provided Ibn Saud with a plentiful supply of younger and younger and ever more beautiful concubines, perhaps out of the common belief that sex with a much younger woman can revive an old man's sexual potency. But now not even the youngest and most beautiful girls that Yasin could provide were capable of reviving Ibn Saud's sexual powers.

Fortunately, however, the most vital of all Ibn Saud's faculties, his mind, remained as sharp as ever. So when, in October 1944, by which time the Italians and Germans had been driven out of North Africa and the Italians had pulled out of the war, the British and Americans had liberated much of Western Europe and the Russians were pushing into Poland and the other countries of eastern Europe towards Germany itself, Colonel William Eddy, the Head of the American Legation in Jeddah, approached Ibn Saud about arranging a secret meeting with President Roosevelt, Ibn Saud readily agreed. President Roosevelt's reasons for seeking the meeting seem to have been to secure the future of America's influence in Saudi Arabia, especially *vis-à-vis* the British and in respect of oil, and to try to persuade Ibn Saud to support America's position over Palestine and the creation of a Jewish homeland. Ibn Saud's motives in agreeing to the meeting were to achieve even closer and more favoured relations with his country's most generous and uncritical benefactor, and to secure the on-going protection of not only the world's most powerful country, but a country which, unlike Britain, had publicly eschewed all forms of imperialism. Roosevelt had repeatedly condemned imperialism and committed his government to bringing all forms of imperialism and colonialism to an end after the war. By contrast, in Ibn Saud's eyes Churchill remained the same unreformed imperialist who had divided up the Middle East at the Cairo Conference after the First World War and surrounded him with his enemies without so much as consulting him.

The meeting with Roosevelt had to be arranged in the utmost secrecy for reasons of security. A date was set for mid-February 1945. It was to be held on board an American battleship in the Great Bitter Lake on the Suez Canal when Roosevelt was scheduled to be making his return journey to America through Egypt after the Yalta Conference. So secret was the meeting that only Yusuf Yasin among those around Ibn Saud knew about it in advance and only a few of those close to President Roosevelt. Not even Churchill, who was present with Roosevelt and Stalin at the Yalta Conference, knew anything about it in advance. He only got wind of it during the final stages of the Yalta conference when Roosevelt told Stalin and Churchill that he would have to leave the next day to go to Egypt for meetings with 'three kings', Farouk of Egypt, Haile Selassie of Abyssinia and Ibn Saud. Churchill was horrified and immediately put his officials to work to arrange meetings for him with the same three kings in Egypt during his own return journey to London.

Early in February 1945 Ibn Saud gave orders for his court to set out for one of their routine visits to Mecca. However, heavy rain meant that the enormous royal caravan of two hundred assorted vehicles got stuck in soft ground near the ruins of a fort beside an oasis called Marat some eighty miles west of Riyadh. Lorries and motor cars were far less efficient at crossing the desert than camels had been and the royal party was bogged down for a whole week until the rains stopped. It was there that Daniel van der Meulen, the young Netherlands consul who had first served in Jeddah in 1926 and had now returned to Arabia to represent the Dutch Government in exile, chanced to find them. The royal caravan that van der Meulen and his companions came across was in many ways different from the caravans in which Ibn Saud had travelled in his early years. Not only had the number of people got far greater and the camels been replaced by lorries and cars, but the caravan was now guarded by red lorries, posted one at each corner, each one mounted with a machine gun and manned by royal bodyguards.

As in earlier times, near the centre of the camp a huge audience tent connected to Ibn Saud's own tent had been erected, close to which lay the kitchens, with large piles of firewood stacked nearby and flocks of bleating sheep and goats. As in the old days, the women's camp, with some seventy wives, family members and concubines stood a little distance away, with the women's cars, each with darkened windows, black window curtains and driven by carefully selected drivers specially imported for the purpose from Java, parked nearby. Another innovation was the two mobile radio stations which had been set up not far from the King's tent and were continuously on the air, both sending and receiving messages and monitoring broadcasts from foreign stations. Van der Meulen had a number of conversations with the King during this chance meeting and noted that unlike on earlier occasions, their conversation was frequently interrupted by a succession of male secretaries who would enter the tent, kneel before the King and pass him a new telegram, message or letter to read, which would be answered, signed and dispatched. In the old days before the advent of the radios and the small army of secretarial staff, the arrival in the camp of a messenger was an event worthy of note, but by 1945 the intrusion of the outside world, the advent of radio and Ibn Saud's greatly enlarged kingdom had changed all that. As van der Meulen noted, the King was as cordial as ever in his welcome but he now seemed continually distracted.[17]

At last on the evening of February 11th the rain stopped and Ibn Saud gave the order to be ready to move off the next morning. But the next morning, after the camp had been struck and all the courtiers, wives, cooks, other attendants and hangers-on, together with the flocks of sheep and goats had clambered or been lifted aboard the 200 lorries, cars and other vehicles, Ibn Saud gave the order that just 48 members of the party, plus part of the flock of sheep, were to accompany him while the rest were to make their way to Mecca as planned.

17 D. van der Meulen, *The Wells of Ibn Sa'ud*, John Murray, London, 1957.

At that same moment the destroyer USS *Murphy* was heading at top speed and in the utmost secrecy across the Red Sea from Suez to Jeddah on a mission coded '*Murphy* Mission to Mecca'. Ibn Saud and his reduced party now also headed for Jeddah. During the preliminary discussions about the meeting between Colonel William Eddy, the recently appointed first US Minister Plenipotentiary to the Kingdom of Saudi Arabia, a former US Marine and decorated war hero in the First World War who had been born in the Lebanon and spoke fluent Arabic, and al Sulaiman a compromise had had to be reached about the number of people who would travel with Ibn Saud. The US Government had instructed Eddy that Ibn Saud's party must consist of no more than twelve people for reasons of secrecy and because of shortage of accommodation on the *Murphy*. Al Sulaiman had responded that many more people would have to accompany the King as he could not be considered as travelling in state unless accompanied by his men and his harem, a total of about 200 people. The demand for the harem to make the voyage with the King was killed off by Eddy when he explained to al Sulaiman that it would be impossible to arrange for the seclusion of the womenfolk aboard the destroyer because the ship's ladders and companionways would have to be kept open at all times for sailors to use in going about their duties of keeping the ship running and manning its armaments and other equipment. In any case, Eddy pointed out to al Sulaiman, the King would not want his ladies trying to negotiate their way along and up the ship's companionways and ladders, which were very steep and narrow and where a sudden lurch of the ship might throw them off their balance. Al Sulaiman was, Eddy later recorded, both 'shocked and disappointed', but Eddy and the Americans got their way. No women would accompany the King and his party would consist of no more than 48 people, Ibn Saud and his closest family members being given use of the cabins of the captain and three other of the ship's officers.

As cover for the real purpose of the USS *Murphy*'s appearance in Jeddah it had been given out that she was making a courtesy call as part of a routine cruise through the Red Sea. Shortly after the *Murphy* had dropped anchor in Jeddah harbour several large Arab dhows sailed out to her loaded with sacks of grain and rice, tons of vegetables and one hundred fat sheep – provisions for both Ibn Saud's own party and the destroyer's crew for the whole voyage. As those who accompanied the dhows explained, the King expected, in accordance with Bedouin custom, to feed at his own expense all those who travelled with him and that they must eat freshly killed, *halal* meat. The captain of the *Murphy* stalled, waiting for Eddy to arrive with Ibn Saud, pretending in the meantime that he did not understand what was being requested. When he did arrive Eddy saw the nature of the problem at once and explained to Ibn Saud that the ship had plenty of food already, enough to feed everybody for sixty days. But, Ibn Saud responded, that didn't make any difference. His American guests must eat each day from his table the produce of his country, and in particular freshly killed lamb. Eddy and the American naval officer replied that the meat and other food on board was already safely stored in refrigerators. But Ibn Saud, having never encountered a refrigerator, simply did not understand. Coming from a country where meat went bad within twenty-four hours of slaughter, he insisted that he and his companions must have meat that had been freshly slaughtered each day. Eddy explained that this could not be – US Navy regulations stated that if a sailor ate anything but Navy rations he would be put in prison. Did he want all these good sailors dishonoured and imprisoned unnecessarily? Shaking his head in disbelief at the strange ways of these Unbelievers, Ibn Saud accepted a compromise. His companions must as good Muslims obey the dietary laws, but there was no need to take on board enough live sheep to feed the entire American crew as well. As a result just seven live sheep were hauled up from the dhow on to the stern deck of the destroyer where they were tethered by one of Ibn Saud's slaves to stanchions to await their turn to be dragged to the bows of the ship, hauled up the short flag-mast on the point of the bow by their feet and have their throats cut in preparation for butchering and cooking. Mrs Eddy later spotted ninety-three sheep returning to the land aboard their dhow, reprieved to live a little longer.

A further difficulty arose from the fact that by this time Ibn Saud was too weak to climb up from a barge or dhow on to the deck of the destroyer. This problem was overcome when a bright member of the *Murphy*'s crew suggested that the ship's whaleboat be lowered, Ibn

Saud lifted into it and then the whole whaleboat be hauled aboard the *Murphy*. So Ibn Saud was taken aboard the *Murphy* by being winched up in a US Navy whaleboat, his chequered headcloth and deep-blue cloak fluttering in the gentle sea breeze. As he rose, he was greeted by a royal salute fired by the *Murphy*'s guns. The salute was returned by Saudi batteries on shore.

Fortunately, by 1945 Ibn Saud had had the foresight to acquire his own Saudi interpreter, Abdullah Abal-Keir, a graduate of the American University of Beirut. So after some further sometimes slightly intense and potentially embarrassing negotiation, together with a lot of hectic and diplomatic translation by both Eddy and Abal-Keir plus some creative use of pointing and gestures by members of the crew of the *Murphy* and Ibn Saud's entourage, all the rest of the paraphernalia the King and his party had brought with them, and all the members of the King's entourage were got aboard and stowed. The members of Ibn Saud's entourage for whom there was no accommodation were quite content to sleep on the destroyer's deck and in any other nooks and crannies they could find, in gun turrets, curled up against bulkheads and near the feet of the lookout on the bridge.

The king had brought with him his brother Saud, his son Crown Prince Saud, together with Princes Muhammad and Mansur, al Sulaiman, Yusuf Yasin, another of his counsellors, his personal physician, his astrologer, his fortune teller, his official food taster, the chief *ulema* responsible for palace prayers, his chief radio monitor and radio operator, a chamberlain, a purse bearer, chief ceremonial royal coffee server and his assistant, ten dagger-wearing guards, three valets, nine slaves, kitchen staff and porters. Once on deck and safely lifted out of the whaleboat, Ibn Saud walked around as though inspecting the ship and then asked the ship's captain if a large tent could be erected on the forecastle for him and his entourage to use for eating and for the five daily prayers. A large white awning was procured from on shore and after it had been rigged on the forecastle deck the *Murphy* set sail, looking, according to one eye-witness 'as though she had grown a great white boil on her bow'.[18]

18 See Jim Bishop, *FDR's Last Year: April 1944–April 1945*, Hart-Davis, MacGibbon, London, 1975.

As the destroyer left harbour Ibn Saud confided to the captain that this was his first trip away from his own country (he clearly did not count his adolescent sojourn in Kuwait or his brief trip to Basra during the First World War). So the captain appointed a petty officer to point out the sights of interest as the ship made its way close in-shore northwards up the coast of the Hijaz. He also had a chart brought for the King with their course marked out so that he could see where he was at any one time, where they were headed and where President Roosevelt would be. After a while he lost interest, explaining that he was a simple warrior and nothing more, so the captain had the ship's large guns fired for him, had depth-charges dropped and had him shown around the torpedo tubes.

As the ship gained speed the awning on the forecastle blew down and had to be put back up. Nevertheless, carpets were laid out on the deck and a large golden chair, carried on board from one of Ibn Saud's dhows, set upon them for the King to sit in. Here throughout the voyage Ibn Saud held his *majlis* just as he would on shore. Five times each day at the appointed hours one of the king's servants would ask one of the ship's navigation officers which direction Mecca was in and Ibn Saud's party would all assemble on deck and facing in the direction of Mecca, kneel and prostrate themselves in accordance with the solemn, time-honoured ritual. Ibn Saud himself forewent sleeping in the captain's cabin at night, preferring to join the rest of his party sleeping under the stars on the *Murphy*'s deck. He had left Prince Faisal in charge in Mecca during his absence and each half hour, both day and night, his radio operator would go to the ship's radio room and signal to Faisal in Mecca 'OK?' and back would come the coded answer 'OK'. This continued to perplex the Americans who never could understand what was going on. In fact Ibn Saud was simply checking that in his absence everything in the country remained peaceful and that Faisal did not require his immediate return. This seems curiously paranoid behaviour considering that Ibn Saud had now ruled for over forty years and had not faced any serious opposition since he had put down the uprising in Asir almost ten years earlier. Yet it shows perhaps the lingering insecurity of a traditional ruler used to being on the spot and dealing with every problem himself.

In fact Faisal had faced one problem after his father had sailed away. The womenfolk who had not joined him on board and people in Jeddah who had seen their King taken out to the American warship and winched aboard and then seen her sail away had jumped to the conclusion that he had been kidnapped by the American Christians. They began to wail loudly and lament his loss. Faisal acted swiftly, assuring all those around him that his father had wished him farewell only a few hours ago and commanded him to rule until his return.

Despite the steady breeze that blew through the ship because of the speed she was making, the whole destroyer steadily became infested with the slightly sweet and increasingly putrid smell of drying sheep's blood and their disembowelled entrails. With the smell came the flies. The Arabs on board were used to this but for the American crew, many already dislodged from their normal bunks and hammocks, this added to their discomfort.

For the King's diversion, on the second evening of the voyage the Americans rigged up a projector and screen on deck and showed a recent one-hour Technicolor documentary called *The Fighting Lady*, narrated by Charles Boyer and Robert Taylor and detailing the heroic story of an American aircraft carrier, the USS *Yorktown*, operating off the Marianna Islands in the Pacific, as it is attacked from low level by Japanese torpedo bombers, its aircraft engage the Japanese air force in aerial combat and attack the Japanese Imperial Fleet. The film included lots of exciting cockpit camera footage of dogfights, shots from on board as the Japanese torpedo planes swoop over the *Yorktown* at barely mast height and hair-raising shots as badly shot up American airmen crash-land their planes on the flight deck. It also included the burial at sea of some of the American sailors and naval airmen featured earlier in the film. Asked what he thought of the film after seeing it, Ibn Saud replied guardedly, that it was a wonderful film but 'I doubt whether my people should have moving pictures even like this wonderful film because it would give them an appetite for entertainment which might distract them from their religious duties.'[19]

19 William Eddy, *F.D.R. meets Ibn Saud*, America-Mideast Educational & Training Services, Washington DC, USA, 1954.

Later that evening, after Ibn Saud had safely retired to bed, there was the usual evening showing of a recent Hollywood movie for the destroyer's crew in the wardroom. The film that evening was to be the 1943 Lucille Ball musical comedy, *Best Foot Forward*. Word of the showing had leaked out in advance and Eddy had been approached by Prince Muhammad wanting to know why he had not been invited. Eddy reminded him that his father would strongly disapprove of any of his subjects, particularly one of his own sons, attending a showing of such a godless exhibition of half-naked ladies, and begged him to forget about it. But Muhammad insisted – which would Eddy prefer, Muhammad asked in a low voice, to die instantly with one swift thrust or be chopped up into small pieces bit by bit. On the other hand, continued the prince, if he did see the film he would make sure that his father never found out about it. Faced with such an unappetising choice Eddy capitulated. Muhammad and his brother Mansur were sitting in the front row as the opening titles began to roll. The film was a technicolor musical, centred around Lucille Ball as a movie star visiting a military cadet academy as part of a publicity stunt and getting caught up in a series of escapades which included a sequence in which she is let loose in a men's dormitory and has her dress ripped off. There were also lots of dance numbers, scenes of close-quarters dancing by men and women in each other's arms and hit blues, swing and bebop numbers. The film was greeted with outbursts of whoops, whistles and applause by the crew in which the two princes appeared to join. At a later showing of the film at least twenty-five Arab members of Ibn Saud's party turned up and enjoyed it as much as the princes had. Happily Muhammad proved as good as his promise and word of these misdemeanours never reached the King.

The Arabs and the American sailors got on very well together throughout the voyage, fraternizing, as Eddy later said, without words but 'with a success and friendliness which was really astonishing. The sailors showed the Arabs how they did their jobs and even permitted the Arabs to help them; in return the Arabs would permit the sailors to examine their garb and their daggers, demonstrate by gestures how they are made and for what purposes. The Arabs were particularly puzzled by the Negro mess-boys on board who they assumed must be Arabs and to whom they insisted on speaking Arabic since the only Negroes whom they had ever known were those who had been brought to Arabia as slaves many years ago.'[20] Eventually the Arabs were, with considerable difficulty, persuaded that the mess-boys were American citizens and as much a part of the US Navy as anyone else.

The King too got on very well with the members of the crew. It was his first encounter with American food and he took a particular liking to American apple pie, later ordering that apple trees be planted at the Al Kharj experimental agriculture station. On the last night of the voyage Ibn Saud insisted on hosting an Arab meal for all twenty-one of the ship's officers, all of whom sat around him on carpets on the deck to eat heaped platters of spiced rice and boiled meat, fruit and sweetmeats. The King held them in thrall with stories of the battles of his youth, of hand-to-hand fighting and his various wounds and escapades. He showed them his broken finger, still paralysed by the fragment of a Turkish cannon ball.

Eddy had his work cut out for almost every minute of the voyage. When he was not translating for Ibn Saud or the Americans he would find himself being called on to stop the Arab cooks from lighting their charcoal burners to brew up coffee over boxes packed with dynamite charges or beside shell racks in the gun turrets, to keep the Arabs out of the engine and chart rooms or stop the American sailors as they went about their duties passing in front of the Arabs while they were praying – the rule requires that no non-believer must cast his shadow between a Muslim at prayer and Mecca. Eddy also had to retrieve members of Ibn Saud's retinue who got lost in various parts of the vessel's labyrinthine hull. One evening as the sun set it was Prince Mansur who was lost and Ibn Saud, spotting his absence from evening prayer demanded to know where he was, sending Eddy to find him. When Eddy eventually retrieved Mansur and brought him to Ibn Saud, still surrounded by his retinue on the forecastle deck after the completion of their sunset prayers, the king was furious. He made Mansur, who had recently been appointed Saudi Arabia's first minister of defence, go through his devotions in full and twice in succession in front of the whole assembly. No one, no matter how lofty his rank, was exempted or excused from the performance of

20 Ibid.

their duties towards God, for all men, prince and slave, were equal in the eyes of the Almighty – and, in this matter, before the King as well.

Early in the second morning of the voyage, St Valentine's Day, the destroyer entered the Suez Canal and began sailing northwards up the canal and Ibn Saud and his party began preparing to disembark. In accordance with Arab custom and his own long-established practice, Ibn Saud gave gifts to all of the American crew. The captain and commodore received gold daggers and Arab costumes, the other officers Arab costume and watches inscribed with Ibn Saud's name and every single member of the 279-man crew a sum of money in sterling – fifteen pounds for the petty officers and ten pounds for the other ranks. In return the captain and commodore presented Ibn Saud, after seeking Eddy's advice on the matter, with two sub-machine guns and a pair of Navy binoculars of a type he had admired during the voyage.

By this time the thirteen and a half thousand tons US heavy cruiser *Quincy*, which nine months earlier had taken part in the American landings in Normandy, had dropped anchor in the Great Bitter Lake. On board President Roosevelt was having breakfast with his daughter Anna (Mrs Anna Roosevelt Boettiger) when the deck officer knocked and came in to report that the USS *Murphy* was approaching from the south. Smiling, the President offered his daughter a choice – either she could confine herself to her stateroom or she could go shopping in Cairo. Why couldn't she stay to meet King Ibn Saud, she asked her father? 'This king,' Roosevelt replied, 'is a Muslim, a true believer. He has lots of wives. However, the Muslim will not permit women in his presence when he is talking to other men. Sis [his pet name for Anna], when he sees such a woman he confiscates her,' he said, and slipped a spoonful of peaches and cream into his mouth. Anna promptly opted to go shopping and within half an hour had left the ship and was on her way in a launch to the shore and thence by road to Cairo.[21]

Later that morning Roosevelt was sitting in his wheelchair relaxing in the sunshine behind one of the gun turrets when Harry Hopkins, his personal assistant, and a secret service agent appeared round the turret and said, 'Mr President, come around the other side and take a look.'

21 Jim Bishop, op. cit.

Roosevelt wheeled himself round to the other side of the turret and, with the two other men crouching and peering round the side of the turret like naughty schoolboys, saw an extraordinary sight. There, slightly below them, was the destroyer *Murphy* inching up alongside the much larger cruiser, a white awning flapping gently in the breeze in the bows, its foredeck covered in rich oriental rugs and a freshly slaughtered sheep swinging idly from the short foremast where a flag should have been. One or two others still bleated, tethered to the stanchions on the stern deck. Ibn Saud was sitting majestically high up on the superstructure in a gold, throne-like chair, all around him and lining the ship's rails stood his attendants, guards and courtiers, armed with rifles, scimitars and daggers, their robes and head-cloths fluttering mildly in the wind. 'Boss,' said the President's secret service agent, wiping the tears of laughter and wonder from his eyes, 'that's a sight to see!' At that moment the *Murphy*'s heliograph began to flash a signal, 'Going nuts here. What does OK? OK mean?' No one on board the *Quincy* knew either. The President quickly wheeled himself back behind the turret, not wanting to be spotted spying as the timeless east, having in effect taken over the *Murphy*, prepared to meet the most powerful man of the West.

A few minutes later Ibn Saud, the three princes and two ministers made their way down a gangplank onto the deck of the *Quincy*. This time no salutes of guns were fired as secrecy was vital and no one wanted to attract the attention of people on shore. The King and the President greeted each other and then sat talking informally on deck for more than an hour, with Eddy interpreting. Once the initial greetings, introductions and pleasantries were over Ibn Saud came straight out with a question that had clearly been troubling him. Just before embarking on the voyage to Egypt he had received a message inviting him to meet Churchill after his meeting with Roosevelt. Should he accept the invitation? 'Why not?' replied Roosevelt. 'I always enjoy seeing Mr Churchill and I'm sure you will like him too.'

Ibn Saud seemed relieved and the conversation turned to other things. Roosevelt asked if all the arid land in Saudi Arabia could be made to bloom and produce food. Ibn Saud replied respectfully that it was not a subject that interested him, he was now too old to become a farmer. He was a warrior and nothing more, nor less. He was now infirm and could now only walk with difficulty. 'No,' said the President, 'You are luckier than I because you can still walk on your legs and I have to be wheeled wherever I go.' 'No, my friend,' responded Ibn Saud, 'you are the more fortunate. Your chair will take you wherever you want to go and you know you will get there. My legs are less reliable and are getting weaker every day.' Roosevelt responded that if the King thought so highly of his chair he would give him the second, identical chair, which he had on board as a spare. Shortly afterwards the chair was wheeled across to the *Murphy* and, although it proved to be a good deal too small for Ibn Saud to use (Roosevelt was relatively slightly built), was kept by him as a treasured possession in his palace for the rest of his life. Ibn Saud told Roosevelt that they were really twins. Both were of roughly the same age, they were both heads of state responsible for feeding, defending and protecting their people, they were both farmers at heart, although he, Ibn Saud, was a simple warrior above all else, and both bore grave physical infirmities.

It was now time to break off and go below for lunch. At the end of their first hour together it was clear that the two leaders were getting on extremely well together. Roosevelt, although by now a very sick and tired man, was that day on fine form, full of his legendary, winning charm, courtesy and ever-ready smiles for his royal guest. Ibn Saud, too, was at his most genuinely respectful, entertaining and solicitous best.

The two heads of state descended to the private mess hall in separate lifts, the President pressing the red emergency button to stop the lift between decks so that he could quickly smoke two cigarettes. Roosevelt, a chain smoker, was taking good care not to offend Ibn Saud's strict Wahhabi principles. The lunch, which consisted of grapefruit, curried lamb, rice, eggs, coconut, chutney, almonds, raisins, tomatoes, olives, pickles and such other suitable accompaniments as the cook was able to rustle up from the cruiser's stores, was enjoyed by Ibn Saud so much that he asked to be given the cook as a gift, a request which when Eddy translated it caused considerable consternation amongst the Americans. But Roosevelt, always canny in a jam, swiftly explained that the cook, as a serving member of the US Navy, was under an obligation to serve out a fixed period of service and that his contract could not be broken.

Perhaps, suggested the President, His Majesty would allow us to train one of his own cooks?

Once lunch was over and everyone but Ibn Saud, Roosevelt and Eddy had withdrawn, the King and the President returned to the cruiser's deck to continue their conversation. Roosevelt immediately turned to the important political issues that he had wanted to discuss with Ibn Saud when he called for their meeting. Saying that he was confident that Germany would soon be defeated, Roosevelt said that he was particularly interested in the question of Palestine and had one serious problem over which he needed the King's advice and help. Ibn Saud immediately leaned forward on his elbows and said: 'You mean Jews?' Roosevelt replied that he felt it was shameful that these unwarlike people had suffered indescribable horrors at the hands of the Nazis, eviction and the destruction of their homes, torture and mass murder. He had information that suggested that as many as three million Jews had been murdered in Poland (Auschwitz had been liberated by the Russians just three weeks earlier). He told Ibn Saud that he felt a personal responsibility and that he had made a commitment to help to solve the problem of their future. He was looking to the King for his help in the rescue and rehabilitation of Europe's surviving Jews. Ibn Saud's voice was soft and laconic as he replied, but what he said was absolutely firm. He had stated his views clearly in *Life Magazine* and *The Times* almost two years earlier: he knew nothing of any 'justification' for the Jews 'claims in Palestine on the grounds that centuries before ... Palestine was a Jewish land. The Romans conquered the Jews, killing and scattering them so that no trace of their rule remained. The Arabs conquered Palestine over 1,300 years ago, freeing it from the Romans, and since that time it has remained Muslim. The Jews therefore have no right to the country, because all countries in the world have been conquered by people who have made undisputed homes in such lands. If we were to follow the Jewish theory, many settled people of the world would have to leave their homes. ... If the Jews need a place in which to live there are countries in Europe, America and elsewhere that are larger, more fertile and more convenient to their interests. This is justice.' Resettling lots of Jews in Palestine would only create another problem. Rather than that, suggested Ibn Saud, a more just solution would be to 'Give them and their descendants the choicest lands and homes of the Germans who oppressed them.'[22]

Roosevelt responded by explaining to Ibn Saud that the surviving Jews understandably feared returning to Germany where they might be oppressed again and that they had a 'sentimental' desire to settle in Palestine. But Ibn Saud refused to accept that argument. The Jews might well fear the Germans, but surely the Allies were going to totally destroy German power forever and in victory would be strong enough to protect the Jews. If not, why were they fighting this war, if they were going to leave Germany in a position to strike back? 'Make the enemy and the oppressor pay; that is how we Arabs wage war. Amends should be made by the criminal, not by the innocent bystander. What injury have the Arabs done to the Jews of Europe? It is the "Christian" Germans who stole their homes and lives. Let the Germans pay.'

Roosevelt objected that Ibn Saud had not helped him with his problem at all. The number of Jews was small compared to the number of Arabs. If the Jews settled in Palestine, they would present no problem to the Arab world. To that Ibn Saud replied by simply looking the President in the eye and quietly uttering one world, 'No.' But, argued the President, the Jews were industrious and would make good neighbours. But Ibn Saud was having none of it. The Jews might say they only wanted one narrow strip of land along the shores of the Mediterranean, but already they were buying up land all over Palestine and were creating a Jewish army in Palestine which was not intended to fight the Germans but to fight the Arabs. With the help of millions of pounds and dollars of British and American money they would soon be building farms and cities. Give the same money to the Arabs, said Ibn Saud, and they would do just as well.

Roosevelt then raised an idea that he said he had heard from Churchill – settling the Jews in Libya, which was much larger than Palestine and thinly populated. That, Ibn Saud objected, would not be fair to the Muslims of North Africa. The whole Arab world was watching, he warned. If the Jews went on adding to the amount of land they held and

22 The *Life Magazine* article which Ibn Saud referred to was also reprinted in shortened form in *The Times* on June 30th 1943.

went on to establish a culture entirely different from that of the Arabs in the region it would inevitably lead at some future date to war. And if that happened he, Ibn Saud, would have to fight on the side of his brother Arabs. But, he added, he could not understand this American over-solicitude for the Germans. It was simply incomprehensible, he said, to an uneducated Bedouin with whom friends got more consideration than enemies. The Arab custom, Ibn Saud told the President, was to distribute the survivors and victims of a battle among the victorious tribes according to the tribes' size and supplies of food and water. Fifty countries were members of the Allied camp among whom Palestine was just one small, poor country, yet already it had been assigned far more than its fair share of European refugees. 'The hope of the Arabs', he said, 'is based upon the word of honour of the Allies and upon the well-known love of justice of the United States and upon the expectation that the United States will support them.'

Roosevelt seemed won over by Ibn Saud's arguments because he now made Ibn Saud what Ibn Saud would come to regard as a historic and binding promise. He undertook personally, as President, that he 'would do nothing to assist the Jews against the Arabs and would make no move hostile to the Arab people'. The US Government would make no change in its basic policy in Palestine 'without full and prior consultation with both Jews and Arabs'.

Roosevelt would later confirm his promise to Ibn Saud in writing. He would also tell his colleagues and the US Congress that he had learned more about the whole Palestine problem, 'the Muslim problem and the Jewish problem' and the problem of Arabia, from his one conversation with Ibn Saud than he could have learned from any number of briefings or 'an exchange of two or three dozen letters'. Ibn Saud had told him that the Arabs had considered sending a mission to the United States and Britain to explain the position of the Muslim world and Roosevelt later told Harry Hopkins that he thought this would be 'a very good idea because so many people in England and the United States are misinformed'.

The conversation now began to wind down and turn to other things. Ibn Saud raised the issue of the French and whether after the war they might reassert their control over Syria and the Lebanon and Roosevelt assured him that the French had given him their word that those two countries would be granted their independence and that he would hold them to that promise. Ibn Saud re-stated his desire for the President's friendship because Roosevelt was known to be the champion of the Four Freedoms and 'of every freedom'. He had seen how 'the USA never colonizes nor enslaves'.

It was now 3.30pm and the Captain of the *Quincy* appeared and told the President that it was time for the ship to leave. Ibn Saud was appalled. That was impossible, he said, the President must first come over to the *Murphy*, his temporary home, to be his guest for an Arab meal. To seal a friendship it was essential that his friend be his guest and eat his food under his roof. Sadly, said the President, that was not possible. For security reasons the ship's movements were fixed and the schedule must be adhered to to the minute. Ibn Saud seemed very put out, turned to Eddy and told him off soundly for not having warned him in advance. Eddy replied, truthfully, that he had known nothing of the ship's schedule in advance. So Ibn Saud turned to Roosevelt and said, 'Will you at least drink a cup of Arabian coffee?' Roosevelt assented, Ibn Saud gave orders and within minutes the king's two magnificently dressed coffee-servers appeared brushing past the US Navy guards and poured the King and the President cups of dark, cardamom-scented Arabian coffee. Later the President told Eddy that no incident during the meeting had touched him so much as the pleasure that Ibn Saud so obviously derived from serving his new friend the coffee of Arabia. Gifts were exchanged, Ibn Saud presenting Roosevelt with four complete sets of Arab robes, a solid-gold knife and a vial of scent. Roosevelt presented Ibn Saud with a gold medal and told him he had made arrangements for him to be given a twin-engined DC3 aircraft complete with an American crew. When the plane arrived it was found to contain a throne that would swivel so that Ibn Saud could face Mecca whenever he needed to. That plane was later to become the first aircraft in the fleet of Saudi Arabian Airlines. Roosevelt's own physician, Admiral McIntire, also stepped forward and said that with the President's permission he would like to present a small box containing a wonderful new medicine called penicillin to His Majesty's doctor. Ibn Saud's physician asked McIntire if this drug was useful in curing venereal disease and McIntire said that it was. Both Ibn Saud and his doctor appeared to be very impressed.

Minutes later Ibn Saud and Roosevelt said their farewells. They had been together for more than five hours. Throughout all that time Roosevelt had been on his best form, alert, attentive and interested in all his guest had to tell him. But Eddy had noticed that in unguarded moments the President's extreme fatigue had showed in his eyes which would fleetingly 'fade in helpless fatigue'. The serious heart and pulmonary disease that was only a few weeks later to kill him, and the years of massive strain, were now taking their inexorable toll.

After parting from the President, Ibn Saud and his small party returned across the gangplank to the *Murphy* and moments later the *Quincy* weighed anchor and steamed swiftly away northwards, up the Canal towards Port Said and the Mediterranean.[23]

When she returned from her shopping trip Roosevelt's daughter found that several enormous parcels, addressed to her and to Mrs Franklin D. Roosevelt, had been delivered to her stateroom and she had to call in Colonel Eddy to explain their contents. There were several beautifully embroidered, brightly coloured silk Arab women's dresses, beautiful vials of coloured glass and alabaster containing a range of traditional Arab perfumes, huge pieces of uncut amber, pearly rings and earrings, pearl-studded bracelets, anklets and belts of superbly woven gold thread.

Late that same afternoon the *Murphy* put Ibn Saud and his party ashore at a point where a fleet of cars provided by the British were waiting for them. They were then driven away to the southwest to beyond Cairo and over the Nile to the Fayoum Oasis where Ibn Saud

23 The account of Ibn Saud's meeting with President Roosevelt is based mainly on the 1954 account by William Eddy, op. cit. who was with Ibn Saud throughout and of two others who were present at various times during the meeting, Captain John S. Keating, the commander of the *Murphy*, who wrote a magazine article in 1976 about his experiences and William M. Rigdon, Roosevelt's naval aide, who wrote a memoir entitled *White House Sailor*, Doubleday, New York, 1962, and as told by Jim Bishop in *FDR's Last Year,* op. cit. and *The Day FDR Met Saudi Arabia's Ibn Saud* by Thomas W. Lippman, *The Link*, Volume 38, Issue 2, April–May 2005 published by Americans for Middle East Understanding.

was to meet Churchill. The meeting took place three days later at the Hotel Auberge du Lac on the shores of Lake Karoun fifty miles south west of Cairo. Originally built by King Farouk as a hunting lodge, the hotel was by 1945 a favourite rendezvous for couples sneaking off for an illicit weekend. With the hotel cleared of other guests, the meeting, hosted by Churchill, took place over lunch in a room overlooking the waters of the lake. Splendid though the setting was, Lord Moran, Churchill's private physician who was present at the lunch, recorded in his diary that evening that it provided an inadequate background for the splendour of the Arab actors who took part in the spectacle. 'The King, Ibn Saud, himself appeared, wearing ceremonial robes, gold and brick red; he has a fine face with brown, benevolent eyes, a high hooked nose and expressive lips.' Ibn Saud was accompanied, as he had been on the *Murphy*, by his brother, three sons and three trusted counsellors 'with their brilliant robes and curved swords', his personal physician, astrologer, fortune teller, food taster, *ulema*, radio operators, purse bearer, ceremonial coffee servers, guards, valets, slaves and servants. 'During the luncheon the Food-Taster stood behind the king, holding a glass of water, a grim, dark-faced figure. On his left the interpreter stood, leaning forward with animation to interpret what the PM said to the King and what the King said to the PM. Behind the interpreter stood two armed guards, who looked the part. Their faces were unpleasant and contrasted with the open, intelligent countenances of the many sheiks. ... Ibn Saud is made after the pattern of when kings were kings. He has led armies in the field with unfailing success and is the master of the Arab world; he was not in the least overawed now by his English visitor, whose Zionist sympathies were no doubt known to him.'

The lunch got off to a decidedly uneasy start. Laurence Grafftey-Smith, the British Minister to Saudi Arabia, had warned Churchill that because of Ibn Saud's religion no one could smoke or drink in his presence but Churchill had reacted by saying 'No! I won't pull down the flag. I feel as strongly about smoking as His Majesty feels about not smoking.' As for alcohol, Churchill's solution was to order that the glasses used at the luncheon should be made of opaque glass. Nevertheless, the effect of Grafftey-Smith's warning had, as Moran put it, 'induced in the PM a mood not particularly receptive to the visit'.[24] The result was that Churchill opened proceedings by, in his own words, telling Ibn Saud that as 'I was the host I said that if it was his religion that made him say such things, my religion prescribed as an absolutely sacred rite smoking cigars and drinking alcohol before, after, and if need be during, all meals and intervals between them.' The King's reaction according to Churchill was 'complete surrender'. However, Ibn Saud had his own cup bearer offer Churchill a glass of water from Mecca's sacred well. 'Most delicious water I ever drank in my life,' Churchill commented later. Churchill could not help admiring Ibn Saud. Despite his age he had 'lost none of his warrior vigour. He still lived the existence of the patriarchal king of the Arabian desert with his forty living sons and seventy ladies of his harem and three of the four official wives, as prescribed by the Prophet, one vacancy being kept.'[25] Afterwards Churchill noted in his diary that 'All passed off well' and added that 'We were given something to drink. Did not know what it was. It seemed a very nasty cocktail. Found out afterwards it was an aphrodisiac.'[26]

It seems hardly surprising that the meeting produced no tangible results. In fact it probably says quite a lot for Ibn Saud's statesmanship that, despite Churchill's provocative behaviour he remained pleasant and polite throughout rather than simply getting up and walking out. Later Ibn Saud complained that Churchill had puffed cigar smoke in his face, was alternately devious and bullying and that when Ibn Saud

24 Extracts from the diary of Lord Moran for February 17th 1954 published in *Winston Churchill – The Struggle for Survival 1940–1965. Taken from the Diaries of Lord Moran*, Constable and Company, London 1966.

25 Churchill, Winston S., *The Second World War, Volume VI: Triumph And Tragedy*, Cassell, London 1948.

26 *Churchill Papers 9/206* from *Winston S. Churchill* by Martin Gilbert, Vol VII 'Road to Victory 1941–5', Heinemann, London 1986. There are discrepancies between Churchill's two accounts of the lunch and Laurence Grafftey-Smith's, *Bright Levant*, John Murray, London, 1970. Grafftey-Smith says that Churchill did not drink the water proffered by Ibn Saud, but passed it to Anthony Eden to drink. Grafftey-Smith does not mention Churchill telling Ibn Saud that his religion required him to drink alcohol and implies that the opaque glasses used at the lunch disguised the fact that Churchill drank alcohol during it. The other, 'aphrodisiac' drink is mentioned only in a diary note written by Churchill on February 23rd 1945 included in Gilbert's *Churchill Papers 9/206*.

wanted to discuss important topics would change the subject. The British Cabinet minutes later simply recorded that on the subject of Palestine Ibn Saud had '... explained his anxiety about the situation that was developing' and that Churchill had expressed '... the hope that he might count on His Majesty's assistance to promote a definite and lasting settlement between the Jews and the Arabs'.[27]

In fact Ibn Saud played his part in the proceedings so well that afterwards the people around Churchill judged the meeting to have been an unqualified success. Churchill, whose Zionist sympathies were by that time so well known that Ibn Saud would undoubtedly have been aware of them, probably did not really have his heart in the meeting and probably only arranged it out of a determination not to be outdone by the Americans in a part of the world that Britain still regarded as her special sphere of influence. He certainly did not really press Ibn Saud over Jewish immigration into Palestine – a considerable relief to Grafftey-Smith and the other British officials as beforehand Churchill had said that he intended to tell Ibn Saud that because Britain had done so much for the Hashemites, making Abdullah King of Jordan and Feisal King of Iraq, 'that it was for the Arabs now to do something for us'.[28] Churchill was in any case tired after having in quick succession gone through the strain of the Yalta Conference with Stalin and Roosevelt, at which he had been forced to make concessions over Poland and the future of Eastern Europe, and then paying a visit to Greece during which he had been greeted in the streets of Athens by huge cheering crowds. To Churchill, therefore, the meeting with Ibn Saud probably seemed like little more than a chore and his behaviour was probably simply an attempt to be mischievous and lighten matters up. If so, it backfired.

The meeting ended with an exchange of gifts. Ibn Saud presented Churchill with a sword and dagger in-laid with jewels. There were ropes of pearls and purple and gold robes for Mrs Churchill and a large diamond, with lesser presents for the other members of the British party.

27 War Cabinet No. 22 of 1945, Confidential Annex: Cabinet Papers, 65/51. See Gilbert, Martin *The Churchill Papers, Volume IV, Companion, Part 2,* William Heinemann, London, 1977.

28 Grafftey-Smith, op. cit.

The gifts presented to the British party were worth in total some thousands of pounds. The British government had also arranged for a gift to be presented by Churchill to Ibn Saud – a case of perfumes, concentrated amber, musk, mimosa and jasmine – the total value of which was just £100. Churchill, seeing that the British appeared 'rather out-classed in gifts' interjected to say to Ibn Saud, 'What we bring are but a token. His Majesty's government have decided to present you with the finest motor-car in the world, with every comfort for peace and security against hostile action.'[29] In fact Churchill's spur-of-the-moment gift was greeted with consternation back at the Ministry of Supply in London. Charged with supplying the car, a Rolls-Royce, they were stumped as to how to do it. Rolls-Royce had produced no new cars during the war and had none in stock. However, the day was saved when someone from the Ministry found a firm of coachbuilders who had had one new silver-grey Rolls on their hands since just before the outbreak of war. So, having received advice from the British Legation in Jeddah about the coachwork, other embellishments and fittings that would suit Ibn Saud's tastes, the car was despatched to Jeddah and then on by road to Riyadh. When Ibn Saud saw it he was loud in his admiration. But then he noticed that it was right-hand drive. No one in the British Legation at Jeddah had told London that Ibn Saud liked to travel in the front passenger seat. Convention in the Arab world said that to travel on the left of the driver would amount to a serious humiliation. As the member of the legation staff who had driven the Rolls to Riyadh was leaving he overheard Ibn Saud say to his brother Abdullah that he could have the car.

Ibn Saud had no wish to linger in Egypt after his meetings with Roosevelt and Churchill and rejected the idea of a sight-seeing tour. As his motorcade headed towards Cairo it passed close by the Pyramids, but when they were pointed out to him, and something of their history and construction explained, he said but one word: '*israf*!' ('A terrible waste of money.')[30]

29 Churchill, Winston S., *The Second World War, Volume VI: Triumph And Tragedy*, Cassell, London 1948.

30 See Leslie McLoughlin, op. cit.

Ibn Saud returned to Jeddah in a British cruiser, a bigger ship than the American destroyer that had brought him to Egypt. He had to be hoisted aboard by a crane. Although the British cruiser was more spacious he seems to have enjoyed the voyage home much less than the voyage out on the USS *Murphy*. Life on the ship seemed to be ruled by British formality. Although a large compass was set up on the deck so that Ibn Saud's party would always know the correct direction in which to face for the five daily prayers, there were no gunnery or other weapons demonstrations, there was no tent on deck, little fraternization between the Arabs and the British members of the crew and certainly no clandestine film shows.

On his arrival back in Jeddah Ibn Saud was greeted by large crowds of cheering people. There were speeches and formal welcomes and an outburst of spontaneous joy among the ordinary people. Their beloved leader and revered king had been away for over a week and they had feared he might never return. Although the *ulema* remained angry because the King had left the country without consulting them, the people danced and sang in the streets, beat drums and clapped their hands rhythmically as they had in the days before the Wahhabis arrived in the Hijaz. The religious police did not stop them.

Two weeks after his return Ibn Saud formally declared war on Germany and Japan, thus earning his country the right to become one of the founder members of the United Nations. On April 5th Roosevelt wrote to Ibn Saud reiterating the promise he had made to him over Palestine during their meeting. He promised Ibn Saud that 'He personally, as president, would never do anything which might prove hostile to the Arabs' and that 'the US Government would make no change in its basic policy in Palestine without full and prior consultation with both Jews and Arabs'.[31] To Ibn Saud there was no real difference between Roosevelt as President of the United States and himself or one of his shaikhs as the ruler or leader of a tribe. So Roosevelt's promises seemed to him to amount to being a treaty between their two countries. But one week after he wrote that letter, on April 12th 1945, Roosevelt died. The promises that he had made to Ibn Saud effectively died with him. In November

31 William Eddy, op. cit.

1945 Truman, Roosevelt's successor as President, spelled this out when the US representatives in Egypt, Lebanon-Syria, Palestine and Saudi Arabia were summoned to Washington to explain to the new President the deterioration in relations between these countries and the USA and attributed the deterioration to US policy with regard to Palestine. Faced with the prospect of future Congressional and presidential elections, Truman told them bluntly: 'I'm sorry, gentlemen, but I have to answer to hundreds of thousands who are anxious for the success of Zionism; I do not have hundreds of thousands of Arabs among my constituents.'[32]

On April 30th 1945 Hitler committed suicide and on May 7th Germany surrendered unconditionally. On August 6th the US. Air Force dropped the first atomic bomb on Hiroshima followed by a second bomb on Nagasaki on August 9th and five days later Japan, too, agreed to surrender unconditionally. The Second World War was over.

32 William Eddy, op. cit.

CHAPTER 14

Riches and the Dying of the Light

The war was over. Roosevelt was gone and so was Churchill, swept from power in the July 1945 general election by Clement Attlee's Labour Party. Ibn Saud and his country was now on the threshold of a wealth beyond anything that he could have previously imagined. Saudi oil production, which in 1941–2 had been less than 600,000 tons, had started to increase steadily during the last years of the war. But with the war over, restrictions removed and ships again moving freely, exports of Saudi oil began shooting upwards. Production more than doubled between 1945 and 1946 and in the six years after that multiplied a further six-fold. By 1952 Saudi oil production had risen to 41 million tons.[1] Ibn Saud's income from oil royalties multiplied by similar amounts. But such a sudden influx of such huge amounts of money into a country which for centuries had known nothing but hardship and austerity, whose social and religious structures were based on mutual support, tribal loyalties and the daily fight for survival, was bound to produce not only massive material changes but alterations in the expectations of its people and social tensions. Ibn Saud had conquered and created a unified kingdom, but now in his sixties and in deteriorating health, was he equipped to manage these changes?

Throughout his life Ibn Saud, unlike many of those around him, had embraced those technical and mechanical innovations from the developed world which could help him and his people while rejecting others that he believed would cause harm or he saw as clearly contrary to the teachings

1 Source: Longrigg, Stephen Hemsley, *Oil In The Middle East: Its discovery and development*, Oxford University Press, 1954.

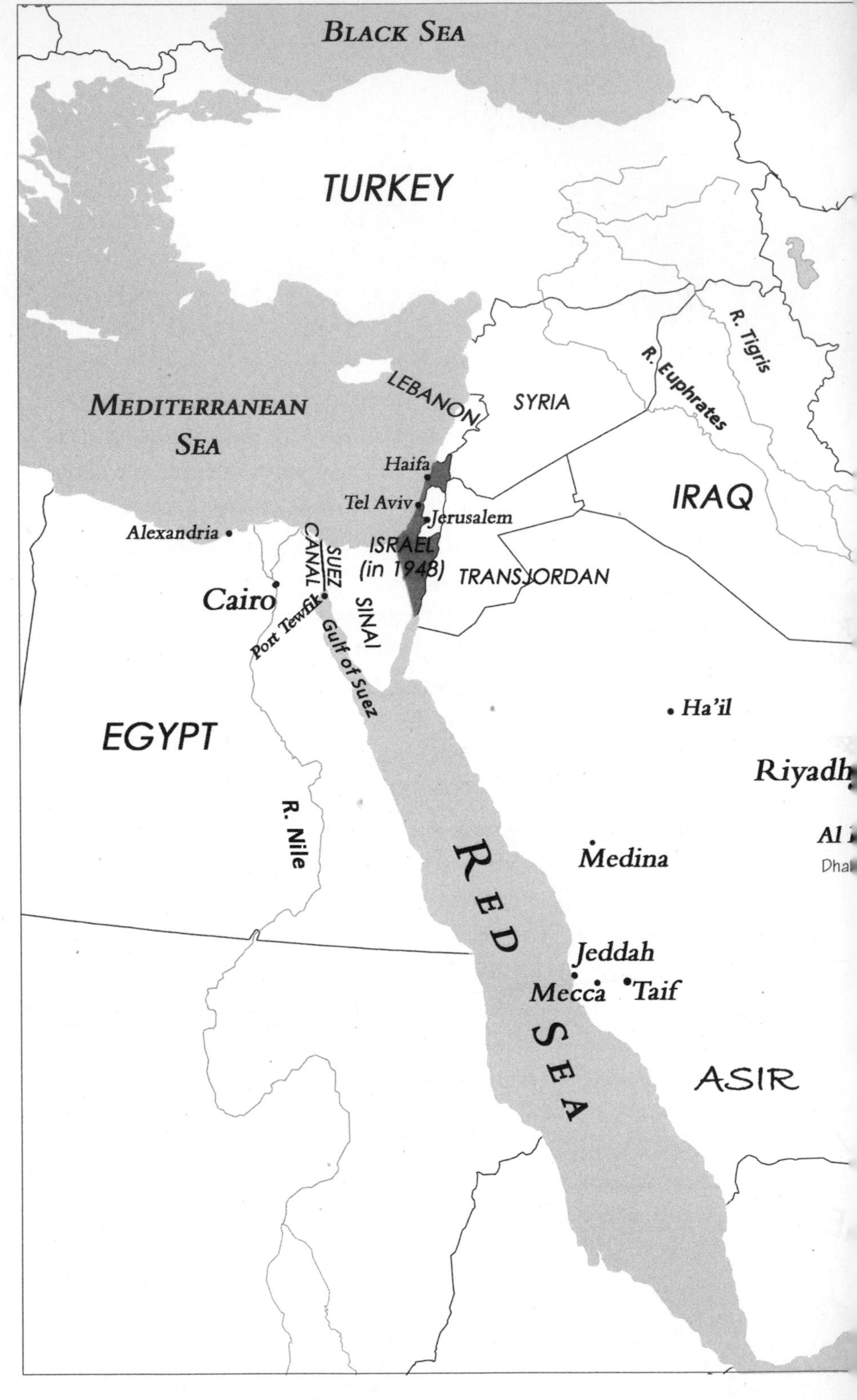

Black Sea
TURKEY
Mediterranean Sea
LEBANON
SYRIA
IRAQ
R. Tigris
R. Euphrates
Haifa
Tel Aviv
Jerusalem
ISRAEL (in 1948)
TRANSJORDAN
Alexandria
SUEZ CANAL
Cairo
Port Tewfik
SINAI
Gulf of Suez
EGYPT
Ha'il
Riyadh
R. Nile
Medina
Red Sea
Jeddah
Mecca
Taif
ASIR

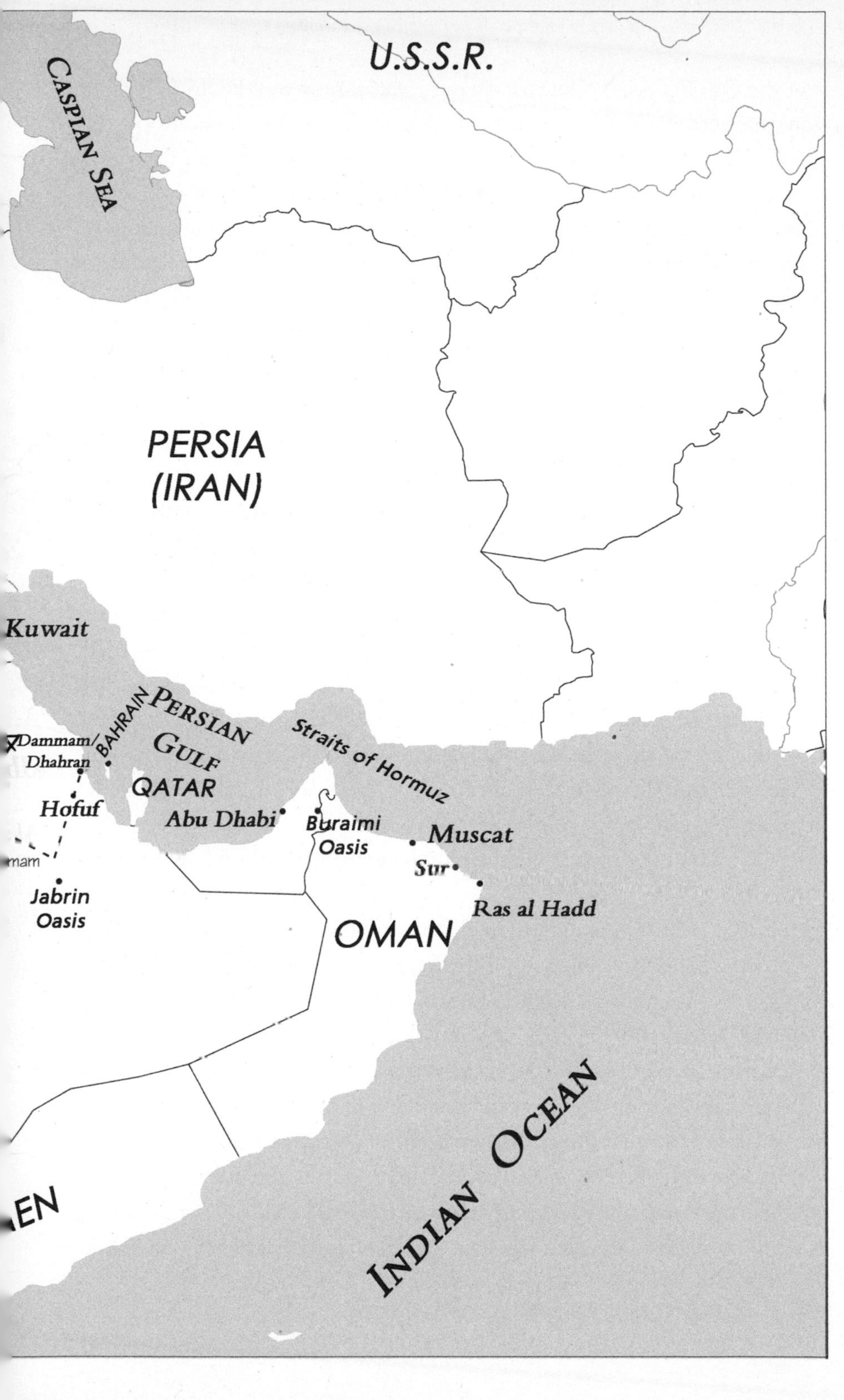

U.S.S.R.
CASPIAN SEA
PERSIA
(IRAN)
Kuwait
BAHRAIN
PERSIAN
GULF
Dammam/
Dhahran
QATAR
Hofuf
Abu Dhabi
Straits of Hormuz
Buraimi
Oasis
Muscat
Sur
Ras al Hadd
Jabrin
Oasis
OMAN
INDIAN OCEAN

of the Qur'an. So, in October 1945 he was happy to take his first flight in the aeroplane sent to him on the orders of President Roosevelt following their meeting. From that time onwards, although he would never become happy about being flown at high altitudes, he frequently used the plane to make his visits to the peoples of the far-flung regions of his vast kingdom. Similarly, in early 1947 when he visited the Aramco site at Dhahran to inspect progress he and his entourage travelled to the site not by camel as they had on earlier visits to the region nor in a fleet of cars as they had in May 1939, but in a flight of aircraft. But the use of aircraft did not alter other, more traditional, parts of the visit where Ibn Saud believed it was incumbent upon him to act in accordance with the time-honoured Arab ways expected of a ruler. So he entertained 500 American oil workers to a feast at which, reportedly, not only was a whole camel served up, head and all, but also 280 sheep, 2,000 chickens and 6,000 eggs, all on huge mounds of rice, plus an estimated 10,000 side dishes of fruit, vegetables and sweetmeats. After the first five hundred had eaten their fill the citizens of the surrounding area were let in to polish off what was left. Each of his guests received a gift, its size and value determined by the recipient's rank and status. Yet, as van der Meulen noted, he seemed tired, as if life was becoming a burden to him. 'He seemed to have lost his sparkle ... The glory of manhood of the Sultan was passing'. Van der Meulen feared that 'the great work' that Ibn Saud had performed 'might now begin to wither in his weakening hands'.[2]

In the years immediately after the war foreign matters as much as domestic issues pressed in upon Ibn Saud. For decades his relations with Egypt had been frosty but had improved following the accession of the young King Farouk. Farouk was British educated (at the Royal Military Academy in Woolwich), and by turn a thorn in Britain's side, a British protégé and a British puppet. Ibn Saud and Farouk had shared concerns over Britain's intentions for the future of Palestine. Farouk had made a state visit to Jeddah for talks about the issue during the war and, early in January 1946 Ibn Saud embarked on a reciprocal visit to Egypt. Farouk sent three ships, including his own royal yacht, to pick up Ibn Saud and

2 D. Van der Meulen, *The Wells of Ibn Sa'ud*, John Murray, London, 1957.

his party and take them to Port Tewfik at the head of the Gulf of Suez. The two kings met and were then taken by the royal train to Cairo. It was the first time that Ibn Saud had travelled on a train apart from a brief journey during his visit to Basra in 1916 (rumour has it that for part of the journey on the royal train in Egypt he travelled on the engine's footplate). He was so impressed by this and other train journeys he made during his two weeks in Egypt, that on his return home he put in hand plans to build a line to run from the Hasa, near Dhahran, through Hofuf to Riyadh.

Everywhere that Ibn Saud went in Egypt he was greeted by exultantly cheering crowds. Philby, who had been allowed to return to Riyadh at the end of the war and was with him during the visit, described his reception. 'The people of Egypt took him to their hearts: thronging the streets wherever he passed and often barring his passage to get a closer view of the great man of Arabia, or just to touch the car in which he rode. The enthusiasm was tremendous: women held up their babies to bask in the monarch's smile; girls lined the pavements to watch the passage of a modern Solomon; and Solomon himself was not blind to their charms. "There are some nice girls in this country", he said one night ... "I wouldn't mind picking a bunch of them to take back to Arabia, say a hundred thousand pounds' worth of the beauties!" ' Yet, as Philby noticed, Ibn Saud often seemed to pass through all the cheering, jubilant crowds with a passive face as if he was 'merely enduring an ordeal thrust upon him by his fame'. He did not make a single speech during the whole visit, nor give one interview to a journalist. Ibn Saud was in a difficult position. Farouk was becoming increasingly unpopular in his own country because of what the opposition and increasing numbers of his own people saw as his humiliating subservience to the British and because of his growing corruption. The Muslim Brotherhood, founded in Egypt in 1928, had become a powerful force calling for reform, based on a return to Muslim values and the Qur'an. They called for an end to subservience to the West and the establishment of a Muslim state in Egypt, taking as their model the state created by Ibn Saud in Saudi Arabia. Farouk and his government, in part in answer to this call, had demanded the withdrawal of British troops from Egypt. But for Ibn Saud to have been seen to give any encouragement to this call or to too openly acknowledge the enthusiasm of the crowds risked giving offence to either his unpopular host, King Farouk, or to his British and American allies. He had probably therefore decided that it was politic to say as little as possible and remain impassive. But as banquet followed banquet and visits of all kinds followed each other in bewildering succession – the Pyramids, the new university, the al Azhar Mosque, a new hospital in Alexandria and a modern cotton mill, Philby says that he realised for the first time that Ibn Saud 'had crossed the threshold of old age'.[3]

Ibn Saud seemed relieved to get back to Riyadh and the familiar ways of his own court. But any respite was short-lived as problems crowded in upon him from all sides. Just weeks after his return he was visited by three members of the Anglo-American Committee of Enquiry regarding the problems of European Jewry and Palestine. The end of the war had left hundreds of thousands of Jewish refugees, many of them cooped up in refugee camps, scattered all over Europe. Survivors of the Holocaust, they were fearful of returning to what had been their homes and sought somewhere to settle and build new lives. Ninety-eigyt per cent of them, when asked, said that given the choice their preferred destination would be Palestine and the Jewish National Home promised to the Jews in the Balfour Declaration. But in 1940, following the Arab uprising in Palestine, fearful of antagonising opinion in the wider Arab world and of jeopardising its strategically vital position in Egypt and the Middle East, Britain, which still exercised the Mandate over Palestine, had severely restricted Jewish immigration and banned Jews from purchasing land in 95 per cent of Palestine. The majority of the Jews in Palestine had supported Britain and her allies during the war, but there had also been small armed groups, the Stern Gang being the most notorious, which had mounted a campaign of murders and bombings against British rule and the harsh restrictions imposed by Britain on illegal Jewish immigration into Palestine. As the war neared its end increasing numbers of Jews in Palestine started to support those using force against the British. At the end of the war, when the full horror of the Holocaust, the six million dead and millions

3 H. St John Philby, *Arabian Jubilee*, Robert Hale, London, 1952.

more persecuted and uprooted, became known, a Zionist fervour swept across Europe and much of the rest of the world. Nowhere was that fervour greater than in the United States. It had been in this atmosphere that, in November 1945, President Truman had told the heads of the American missions to the Arab countries that he had 'to answer to hundreds of thousands who are anxious for the success of Zionism' and repudiated the commitments made by Roosevelt to Ibn Saud about Palestine.

An Anglo-American Committee of Enquiry was given the task of finding a solution to the Palestine problem, Jewish immigration and the displaced Jews in Europe. It was hoped that the committee could resolve, once and for all, the differences between the British and Americans over policy in Palestine, the Jewish refugees and immigration. Starting work in January 1946, the Committee were given just four months to carry out research, hear evidence in Europe, America, Palestine and other countries of the Middle East, write their report and publish their findings.

The Committee was made up of twelve men, six American, six British, headed by a High Court judge from each country. All of its members were laymen rather than specialists, with little or no prior knowledge of the countries or issues involved. One, the young newly elected socialist MP and British journalist, Richard Crossman, was typical. Only days before being asked to serve on the committee he had told his wife that 'There are two subjects I shall always be totally ignorant about, India and Palestine.' He had studied German, worked in Germany before the war and witnessed the coming to power of the Nazis. During the war he had worked at Eisenhower's headquarters as part of a team putting out Allied propaganda aimed at the German population. He had visited Dachau concentration camp shortly after it was liberated and been deeply shocked by what he witnessed. But, on his own admission, he 'knew nothing of the Arabs'.

Forced to work at speed, the Committee visited and heard evidence in America, Germany, Austria and other parts of Europe, in Cairo and then Palestine, arriving in Jerusalem aboard the High Commissioner's white-painted special train in early March. Heavily guarded against possible terrorist attack, they were put up and heard evidence in the King David Hotel, which was also home to Britain's military headquarters in

Palestine. The Committee heard evidence from both Arab and Jewish witnesses as well as paying visits to a range of Jewish and Arab communities in towns and villages around Palestine. After visiting one so-called 'show village' Crossman noted in his diary 'Arab conditions are abominable ... It actually has a school, which is unusual ... Many of the boys had ringworm and looked undernourished.' Later Crossman concluded from all he had seen and heard in Palestine: 'No, it is no good. These two people just don't mix, and the more you mix them, whatever the material benefits to the Arab, the more they hate each other and each other's way of life. ... All this sounds as though I were anti-Jewish, but I am not. ... I admire what the Jews are doing here and regard it as something which will develop into the first piece of western Socialism since Vienna. But no one suggested that the Vienna socialists should go out and occupy the mountain homes of the Greeks in the Peloponnesus.'[4]

In the third week of March three members of the Committee flew to Riyadh to interview Ibn Saud, who was even more outspoken than he had been when he met Roosevelt. By now his patience and trust in the successive promises made to him by both the British and Americans was wearing thin. He told the members of the committee that the Jews were the enemies of the Arabs in every place and every country to which they came. 'They create trouble and they work against our interests ... If the immigration of Jews continues and their possessions in Palestine increase, they will become one of the most powerful governments, equipped with arms and wealth and everything else. This will be against the Arabs and at the same time difficult for them. The proof of this lies in what the Committee has seen during its visit to Palestine.'[5] Ibn Saud also told the committee members that he had done everything he could to help the Allies during the war but what was now happening in Palestine placed him in a very difficult situation with his own people and the wider Arab community. If the United Kingdom now intended to go back on the promises it had made to him and his brother Arabs then he would have no choice but to say to the Muslims: 'Kill me. Depose me. Because

4 *Palestine Mission: A Personal Record*, by Richard Crossman, MP, Hamish Hamilton, London, 1947.

5 Crossman, op. cit.

that is what I deserve.' He also told the members of the committee that Roosevelt had told him during their meeting in Egypt that he had 'neither ordered nor approved the immigration of Jews to Palestine, nor is it possible that I should approve it'. What, Crossman wondered in his diary, did his American colleagues make of this?

On schedule, in late April 1946, the committee delivered their unanimous report. They recommended that a further 100,000 Jewish displaced persons from Europe be allowed to enter Palestine as soon as possible and that the 1940 order restricting Jews from purchasing land in 95% of Palestine be annulled. They said that the country should be neither Jewish nor Arab and called for the indefinite continuation of the 'trusteeship' – amounting in effect to an indefinite continuation of the Palestine Mandate. They called for equality as between Arabs and Jews in the standards of economic, agricultural, industrial and social development and stated that Palestine was 'a Holy Land ... [that] can never become a land which any race or religion can claim as its very own'.[6]

Faced with an intractable problem the committee had come up with a politically impractical solution. The committee's recommendations satisfied no one, either inside Palestine or in the outside world. President Truman, facing an emotionally pro-Zionist electorate and a crucial set of mid-term elections, immediately endorsed the committee's recommendations but offered no assistance in getting them implemented. Attlee, the British Prime Minister, faced with the on-going policing of Palestine, swiftly rejected the committee's call for further Jewish immigration. Inside Palestine itself increasing numbers of Arabs began taking up arms while the Jewish resistance groups combined to step up their attacks on the British. Their campaign culminated in July 1946 when a group of terrorists led by Menachem Begin, a future Israeli prime minister, blew up the King David Hotel, the British army's Jerusalem headquarters, killing ninety-two people, most of them civilians. In response, as a wave of anti-Jewish feeling and demonstrations spread across Britain, the British police and military units in Palestine stepped up their efforts to suppress the Jewish resistance groups and halt the

6 *Report of the Anglo-American Committee of Enquiry*, p. 3, April 1946.

flow of illegal Jewish refugees from Europe into Palestine. Thousands of Jews were detained without trial and tens of thousands more, men, women and children survivors of the Holocaust, were interned. British and American relations over the issue deteriorated rapidly, to the point where they were becoming openly antagonistic towards each other. On October 4th, just one month before the Congressional mid-term elections, President Truman, who was trailing badly in the polls and facing a fierce Zionist backlash, stepped up the pressure on Britain still further. In a speech on the eve of Yom Kippur, he called for even more Jewish immigration into Palestine than the Anglo-American Committee had recommended.

As long ago as the summer of 1945, during the last days of his administration, Churchill had suggested to members of his cabinet that perhaps it was time for someone else to take their turn at dealing with the unrewarding problem of Palestine. By early 1947 Attlee had come to much the same conclusion. With British troops in Palestine facing growing numbers of attacks from both Jews and Arabs, with Britain broke as a result of the costs of the war and facing even harsher rationing than at the height of the Battle of the Atlantic in 1942, having decided to pull British troops out of Egypt and grant India independence, Ernest Bevin, Attlee's Foreign Secretary, referred the problem of Palestine to the United Nations. The UN responded by setting up its own UN Special Committee on Palestine (UNSCOP), according to some counts the seventeenth inquiry, committee, special report or investigation into the future of Palestine since the Sykes-Picot Agreement and Balfour Declaration thirty years earlier.

Back in Saudi Arabia Ibn Saud was also facing growing popular feeling over Palestine. But increasingly dependent on American money from oil, there was little he could do apart from warn people such as the members of the Anglo-American Committee on Palestine of the dangers of Jewish immigration. He had been one of the prime movers in establishing the Arab League, an organisation founded in 1945 by Saudi Arabia, Egypt, Iraq, Lebanon, Syria, Transjordan and Yemen, to foster unity among the Arab states. One of its first actions had been to declare its opposition to the establishment of a Jewish state and the ceding of any part of Palestine to the Zionists. With his growing oil wealth, Arabs increasingly looked to Ibn Saud for a lead over the problems facing the Arab world, not least the problem of Palestine. So in 1946, at the end of his state visit to Egypt, he and King Farouk had issued a joint statement reiterating their support for the Arab League and commitment to the territorial integrity of Palestine as an Arab state. He reiterated his support for the Palestinians again in 1947 to the British journalist George Bilainkin, demanded freedom for the Palestinians and accused the Jews of 'invading' Palestine and 'making the policy of Britain'.[7] Yet at the same time, ever more fearful of antagonising his American benefactors, his real support for the Palestinians, except in such statements and gestures, remained little more than nominal. As a result discontent inside Saudi Arabia over the problem, and with his response to it, grew.

Palestine was far from the greatest of Ibn Saud's problems. Despite the rapidly escalating amounts of American oil money flowing into the country, Saudi Arabia was getting steadily further and further into debt. Ibn Saud's treasurer, al Sulaiman's book-keeping skills had never been better than rudimentary, based as they were on a few years' experience working for an Indian merchant, but were by now wholly inadequate to the task of keeping track of the huge sums that he had to deal with. A number of attempts had been made to re-organise the Finance Department. In one a Dutch banking expert had been called in by Ibn Saud to examine the country's finances, but when, after carrying out a thorough review, he started to explain to the King that the basis of any sound system would have to start by instituting a strict separation between the income of the Royal Family and the income of the state, the King had refused to hear him out. He remained resolutely opposed to submitting himself to any form of control or to allowing anyone else to know what he chose to do with his money. During the war the British had also tried to get some reforms instituted but had also been thwarted.

The result was that by the late 1940s the country still had no banking system. Instead more trunks and boxes had gone on being constructed to hold the steadily increasing quantities of silver and gold that flowed in to al Sulaiman's coffers. But at least the American oil royalties were

7 See Leslie McLoughlin, op. cit.

by this time being paid direct into an account in a New York bank. Unfortunately, however, this account also held al Sulaiman's own personal fortune. On top of which, as time had passed, such skills as al Sulaiman did possess had deteriorated, undermined by age, years of stress and a secret but growing dependence upon alcohol – Grafftey-Smith described him as 'the only Finance Minister I ever met who drank methylated spirit'. Presumably this was not the product which we might buy in a hardware store but rather the product of one of a growing number of illicit stills hidden away in the homes of the rich and powerful. By the late 1940s al Sulaiman was only capable of working for an hour or two a day before the effects of drink overcame him.

Al Sulaiman had never been able to stand up to Ibn Saud. So as the money coming in from oil rose to more than forty times as much as it had been in 1939, the demands made upon it by Ibn Saud, his enormous family and the filching of those around the King, resulted in al Sulaiman every year, for year after year, having to borrow a third more money than the treasury received. Even if al Sulaiman had fully understood the state of the country's finances, he would almost certainly not have apprised Ibn Saud of them. In his early days Ibn Saud had often been acutely aware of the precarious nature of his finances, but now with huge sums flowing in and even larger sums flowing out, he was kept largely in the dark and seemed happy not to have to bother about them. He had never been greatly interested in money and so long as he had enough for his own needs and to meet what he had always accepted as the traditional obligations laid upon an Arab ruler towards his guests, those subjects who sought his help and the exorbitant and ever-growing demands of his huge family, he was content to leave the day-to-day management of his finances to those whom he regarded as his trustworthy and loyal servants.

However, in the last resort Ibn Saud retained all power over money, as over everything else in the Kingdom, and even in those areas where he did allow some delegation of power, such as to the governors of the various provinces, the power he delegated was strictly limited. As a result, where al Sulaiman's financial decisions could often seem wayward, Ibn Saud's could sometimes be positively wilful. Thus, when shortly after the end of the war the American Government offered Saudi

Arabia $25 million worth of aid in kind, in food and silver, al Sulaiman turned the offer down and opted instead for $10 million in cash to be spent on hospitals in Riyadh and Taif, street lighting for Riyadh and a new harbour jetty for Jeddah. However, when al Sulaiman told Ibn Saud of his decision, he vetoed it and directed that all the money must be devoted to his own pet project – the Dammam to Riyadh railway. When his own advisers and American experts tried to tell him that railways were out of date and that building a modern highway and employing a fleet of trucks would be a much cheaper and more efficient way of moving large quantities of supplies and construction materials inland from the coast, Ibn Saud would have none of it. The truck drivers, he pointed out, were likely to be former Bedouin and they would always be stopping or turning off the road to go and visit friends. He also probably had in mind that lorries, like camel trains, would be much more vulnerable to raids by robbers or modern variants of the *ghazzu*, whereas a train once rolling would be much more difficult for robbers to attack. So construction of the railway went ahead.

Ibn Saud continued to see all the money now flowing into his treasury's coffers as his, rather than being in any sense the Saudi state's, because, as the King and accepted leader of his people, he was the state. But as growing numbers of Saudis came into contact with other countries and learned about the state provision and public works undertaken by foreign governments for the benefit of their citizens they began to press for similar provision at home. Some of Ibn Saud's sons, like Faisal, had by this time gained quite a lot of experience of life in other, more developed countries. Also some of his sons had been sent for part of their education to schools and universities in neighbouring countries such as Egypt and Lebanon. As a result, by the late 1940s some of them too began to put pressure on Ibn Saud for an increase in state welfare provision, for public works, education and a modernisation of the system of government in Saudi Arabia. But he resisted these calls. The concept of state welfare provision was meaningless to him. As a traditional ruler, he was, in his own eyes at least, the equivalent of a kind of welfare state. His subjects when they were in need came to him for help, he supported them, arbitrated in their disputes and they in turn gave him their loyalty. His *majlis* was open to all his subjects great and small, to lay their requests before him and to have their grievances heard. He still fed thousands of his needy subjects every day.

After conquering the Hijaz he had taken steps to improve water and sanitary provision in the province and control the risk of epidemics among pilgrims making the *Hajj*. As American oil money started to flow in he had, with American assistance, instituted schemes to drain water-logged areas around the Jabrin oasis and north of Medina to eradicate mosquitoes and with them malaria. He also welcomed researchers working on the prevention of locusts. But beyond such limited measures, the wider provision of state welfare seemed impractical. His country totally lacked people with the skills necessary to operate a wider system of welfare – trained nurses, doctors, health workers, engineers, administrators, teachers. He had made a start on the provision of elementary education back in the 1920s and 1930s, but it had remained, because of pressure from the *ulema*, firmly based on the teaching of the Qur'an, the *shari'a* and other Islamic texts. The total numbers of pupils receiving any education still remained pitifully small, barely 20,000 boys by the late 1940s and, of course, no girls. Ibn Saud took care to have his own sons educated, but this was done privately, inside the palace out of sight of the *ulema* in what became known as 'The Princes' School'. As explained earlier, some of his sons went on to university or further education outside the country. Ibn Saud put no obstacles in the way of other wealthy families who wished to have their sons educated, either in 'private schools' set up by themselves inside the country or by sending their sons abroad. Aramco also started providing training and technical education for some of its Saudi employees. As a result some hundreds of young Saudis, nearly all the sons of wealthy Saudi families, attended universities in Egypt and the Lebanon.

However, beyond such limited provision Ibn Saud would not go. Had he been younger he might still have had the energy and flexibility of mind to tackle the huge demands of introducing greater welfare provision, the social upheaval, the conservative and religious opposition and the importation of large numbers of foreign professionals to provide the experts and train native Saudis to operate such systems. There were also those who urged the King not to make such provision, arguing that the provision of a wider system of state welfare would bring with it alien elements and threatened to undermine the traditional Wahhabi Muslim way of life, its core teaching of personal responsibility, of the duty of each Muslim towards other, brother Muslims, the ideal of the Muslim *ummah* and shared Muslim identity. Philby, who had returned to Riyadh after the war, had even argued with Ibn Saud against the further education of his own sons.[8]

By 1947 Ibn Saud had thirty-six living sons (seven others had died, all but one in infancy or childhood), sixteen of whom were over twenty. No one knew how many daughters he had. His adult sons became increasingly quarrelsome, falling out over how the country was to be run and their future inheritance. His two eldest sons, his designated heir Saud, and Faisal, to whom he regularly assigned the task of dealing with foreign powers, had long jockeyed for favour with their father and competed to succeed him, so much so that a number of foreign diplomats had reported to their governments that if Ibn Saud were to die without the succession being clearly decided there might be civil war between them. During the Second World War Ibn Saud had ordered a truce between them and tried to bring about a reconciliation by arranging a marriage between Saud's eldest son Fahd and one of Faisal's daughters. But the reconciliation had been short-lived. When Ibn Saud's twelfth son Mansur, who was the son of a slave girl and had long been seen as one of his father's favourites, was appointed Minister of Defence in 1944, the competition between Ibn Saud's sons had widened still further.

Although those around him tried to hide what was happening, as the amount of oil money flowing into the country multiplied so too did the levels of corruption among the officials and trusted advisers who were closest to him. Everyone in Saudi Arabia and the neighbouring countries, it seemed, knew what was happening except for Ibn Saud. His officials and various members of his family had become familiar figures, high-rollers living the high life in the fashionable resorts of the Middle East. In cities like Damascus, Cairo and Beirut high officials who served Ibn Saud were buying up swathes of the most expensive buildings. Some of his sons were particularly notorious, both because of their flagrant disregard for the values of frugality practised by their father and

8 See Leslie McLoughlin, op. cit.

their transgressions of strict Wahhabi morals. With Ibn Saud's greatly increased wealth, and the generosity their father showed towards them, they becamc like children let loose in a toyshop, building themselves lavish palaces, buying fleets of the latest luxury cars and living lives of increasingly ostentatious luxury. When in their father's presence all would sit submissively at his feet. Even Ibn Saud's chosen heir, Saud, and the son to whom he entrusted important foreign assignments, Faisal, both by then in their forties, when in his presence would sit on the floor at his feet rather than in chairs beside him.

But no matter how submissive Ibn Saud's sons might appear in his presence nor how much people tried to hush up some of their more extreme transgressions, some were so gross that they could not fail to come to his attention. In June 1947 during a wild drinking party given in his palace by his twenty-seven-year-old ninth son, Nasir, who Ibn Saud had made governor of Riyadh, seven people died as a result of drinking alcohol made in an illicit still. One of the dead was a son of one of the Rashid ruler of Ha'il's sons who had been spared after the town's surrender to Ibn Saud in 1921 and brought back to Riyadh to live out his days as his honoured guest. Most of the others were women. Word of what had happened spread rapidly and when it reached the Hashemite rulers of Iraq was gleefully broadcast around the world. Nasir, who was already notorious for his womanising, had been involved in a drinking scandal nine years earlier, but had eventually been forgiven by his father. This time, however, there was no forgiveness. Stripped of his governorship, he was brought before Ibn Saud in the presence of all his sons and other members of the court. Ibn Saud then publicly sentenced him to death. As Nasir knelt cowering before him, Ibn Saud furiously rained down blows upon him with his stick and then, with tears filling his eyes, harangued his assembled family upon the evils of departing from the strict moral code of Wahhabism, the code which underpinned the Kingdom and had brought their family greatness. With the beating over, Nasir was thrown into prison to await his execution. Some time later, following intercession from Ibn Saud's other sons and people around him, Nasir was reprieved. Ibn Saud immediately instituted a total prohibition on the import of alcohol even by foreigners working in the country.

Later he said to Philby, 'Who would have thought even a few years ago that I should live to see liquor and drugs coming into Riyadh, when we used to condemn even tobacco? The fault lies not with others', he said bitterly, 'but in myself. If it were in my power to choose, I would have doomsday now!'[9]

Two months later, in August 1947, UNSCOP, the committee set up by the United Nations to look into the problem of Palestine reported back, recommending that a further 150,000 Jews be allowed to enter Palestine over the next two years and that the country be partitioned, giving the Jews 55 per cent of Palestine and the Arab population the remaining 45 per cent. On November 29th the United Nations General Assembly endorsed the Committee's recommendations by 33 votes to 13, with the United States and the Soviet Union supporting the resolution and thirteen states, including the Arab states and the Arabs in Palestine voting against. Britain, along with nine other countries, abstained. Prince Faisal, who was in New York to represent Saudi Arabia during the UN General Assembly's debate on the UNSCOP recommendations, was spat at by Jewish demonstrators, something he would never forgive or forget. When the USA voted for the UNSCOP recommendations and the partition of Palestine he urged his father to break off diplomatic relations with the USA, but Ibn Saud ignored him.

As soon as the result of the vote in the UN General Assembly became known, fighting between the Jewish and Arab communities in Palestine began and, as the British started to withdraw their troops, spread with more and more Palestinians being driven from their homes. Six months later, on May 14th 1948, as the last British High Commissioner left Jerusalem, David Ben Gurion, standing under a large portrait of Theodore Herzl in Tel Aviv, publicly declared the establishment of the State of Israel. The next day troops of the Arab League from Egypt, Syria, Transjordan, Lebanon, Iraq and Yemen invaded from the north, south and east. But Ibn Saud, having repeatedly threatened the British and Americans that if the Jews were allowed to establish a state in Palestine

9 See H. St John Philby, *Sa'udi Arabia*, Ernest Benn, London 1955. Also Lacey, op. cit., Howarth, op. cit., McLoughlin, op. cit., Alexander Bligh, *From Prince to King: Royal Succession in the House of Saud in the Twentieth Century*, New York University Press, New York, 1984.

he would join the other Arab countries in going to war against Israel, sent only a token force of a thousand men, less than any other Arab League country. However, he did instruct all of his provincial governors to open registers to help co-ordinate the efforts of volunteers who wanted to go to Palestine to fight alongside their fellow Arabs and authorise the creation of a fund to support the Palestinians in their struggle against the Jews.[10] But when he was urged by the leaders of other Arab countries and by people inside his own court to cut off the supply of Saudi oil to the Israelis' most important backer, the United States, he refused. By now totally dependent upon US oil dollars, he could no longer dare to do anything that might risk offending the Americans. Deeply frustrated by his own powerlessness, he wept in front of his advisers, explaining to them, 'I was thinking about the state my community and nation has been reduced to, and what is to be its fate.' Increasingly he was coming to be seen, both in the wider Arab world and inside his own country as an American stooge. These years were probably the most humiliating, frustrating and unhappy of his entire life.

The war in Palestine had begun as a fairly equal struggle, with both the Israel Defense Forces and the Arab League having about 50,000 troops each. But as the months passed and Jewish refugees and volunteers flowed into the new state the Israel Defense Forces doubled in size. Also the Jews, fighting as they believed for their survival, were much better armed. Where many of the Arab troops had to make do with pre-First World War weapons, the Israelis were supplied with the latest military equipment by supporters around the world and friendly governments such as Czechoslovakia. As a result the Israelis steadily gained the upper hand and began driving back the invading Arab armies. In March 1949, after both sides had committed atrocities against unarmed civilians but with the Israelis now in possession of 25

10 There is some disagreement over the extent of Ibn Saud's level of support for the Palestinians during the war, Philby claiming in his books *Sa'udi Arabia* and *Forty Years in the Wilderness* that Ibn Saud encouraged volunteers and the giving of money, Said K. Aburish, on the other hand, in *The Rise, Corruption and Coming Fall of the House of Saud*, Bloomsbury, London, 1994, claiming that Ibn Saud put obstacles in the way of volunteers.

per cent more land than had been originally assigned to them under the UN General Assembly resolution, a permanent ceasefire was called. Although Transjordan had occupied East Jerusalem and a fistful of mainly hilly and infertile land west of the River Jordan in Judaea and Samaria and Egypt had seized a narrow strip of land around Gaza at the southern end of the Mediterranean coast, Israel had conquered a large block of land along the Lebanon border north and east of Haifa, a much wider strip of land along the Mediterranean coast than had originally been assigned to her, had seized most of the land assigned to the Arabs along the coast south of Tel Aviv and the border with Egypt, had taken all of west Jerusalem and cut off Arab east Jerusalem from the sea. 750,000 Palestinian Arabs had been driven from their land and homes, some seeking refuge in neighbouring Arab countries but the majority living under appalling conditions in refugee camps in the Gaza Strip, the Jordanian-occupied West Bank and Israel. By 1950 the UN estimated that more than 900,000 Palestinian Arab refugees were living in camps administered by them dotted around Israel and the neighbouring countries of the Middle East. These camps were to become the recruitment centres for future Arab resistance groups and fertile breeding grounds of future Arab terrorism.

The Arab countries' response to what they saw as the disaster in Palestine – the *Nakba*, catastrophe – was to expel all the Jews from their own territories. Ibn Saud's response to the Palestinian refugee problem was to tell Aramco that he wished them to employ at least 1,000 Palestinian refugees. Aramco agreed and when their officials visited Beirut almost 6,000 Palestinians applied for jobs. By December 1949 Aramco was employing 100 Palestinians and a year later more than 800. However, when Abdullah, the son of the former ruler of the Hijaz, who was now king of Jordan, came to Jeddah in May 1948 to seek Ibn Saud's agreement to incorporate into his own kingdom the block of land in Judaea and Samaria which he had taken during the Palestine-Israel war, Ibn Saud absolutely refused to give Abdullah's plan his blessing.

On December 10th 1948 the United Nations General Assembly, meeting at the Palace de Chaillot in Paris, adopted the Universal Declaration of Human Rights. No countries voted against it but eight abstained and refused to sign up to the Declaration – six Communist countries, the newly elected Apartheid Afrikaner Nationalist Government of South Africa and Saudi Arabia. In Saudi Arabia the Universal Declaration's clauses granting human rights and religious freedom to all citizens were incompatible with the strict Wahhabi laws and prohibitions on other religions.

A few months later Ibn Saud was being driven in his limousine through heavy traffic in Jeddah when another car accidentally bumped into his. Ibn Saud flew into one of his terrifying rages, had the offending car driver dragged before him and ordered that he be put to death. The poor driver was thrown into jail and Prince Mansur was ordered to have the execution carried out. Mansur, who was as we have seen a special favourite of the king, was probably the only one of his sons or other senior officials who would dare to disobey such an order. So Mansur, treating his father's order as a passing outburst, waited for a few days and then had the offending driver quietly released. Nothing more was heard of the matter.

Since 1945 the American oil men had continued to find new oil fields in Hasa and south and east along the coast of the Persian Gulf. By 1949 they had come to suspect that there were substantial deposits to the east of the Qatar peninsula, around the Buraimi Oasis and under the land which had been at the centre of the dispute between Britain and the Ottoman Empire in 1913. Under the Anglo-Ottoman Treaty of July 1913, agreed just months after Ibn Saud had seized Hasa, it had been agreed that Britain should have exclusive rights to explore for oil in Persia, that Kuwait, Bahrain and Oman were British Protectorates but that Hasa remained a part of the Ottoman Empire. Control over this area of land had also been a major topic during the inconclusive discussions held between Shakespear, Major Trevor and Ibn Saud in Riyadh in December 1913. The area had been the subject of further abortive negotiations between Ibn Saud and the British Government in the mid-1930s. Now, prompted by the American oil men and probably also motivated by a need to assert himself at a time when for so long he had felt frustrated and powerless, Ibn Saud lodged a claim to a huge swathe of mainly arid land in the south east of the peninsula. The claim included 80 percent of the shaikhdom of Abu Dhabi, including the area which was the ancestral home of the shaikhdom's rulers, and a large area around the Buraimi Oasis which was claimed by the Sultanate of Oman. These were territories which were under British protection. Now, for the first time in his long reign, emboldened by his powerful new American allies, Ibn Saud appeared to issue a direct challenge to Britain. Ibn Saud based his claim on the fact that in 1795 the area had been conquered by the direct successors of the founders of the Saudi state, the sons of Muhammad ibn Saud and Muhammad Ibn Abd al-Wahhab. Ibn Saud probably calculated that with the British actively engaged in withdrawing from their empire around the world, they were unlikely to stage a showdown with Saudi Arabia over this stretch of what they probably considered miserable desert. Hitherto this area had been valued only for the major slave trading market in Buraimi itself, from whence convoys of slaves were still regularly sent to Riyadh and many other parts of Arabia. But far from simply acquiescing to Ibn Saud's claim, the British responded by firmly pointing out that the Saudi conquest of Buraimi had been no more than a passing episode in the history of the area and that its true owners were Abu Dhabi and Muscat.

The Buraimi Oasis consisted of a series of nine villages spread over an area of about 750 square miles. It is the convergence point of a number of ancient routes leading out from the coast of the Gulf and the foot of the Jabal Akdar range of mountains in Oman to Muscat, Yemen, Sur and Ras al Hadd on the extreme eastern tip of the Arabian peninsula. Even in the mid-1970s one could stand a mile or two from Buraimi and watch a continuous stream of lorries trailing clouds of dust that hung in the air behind them occasionally interspersed by long camel trains or parties of Bedouin plodding along the skyline or away over the distant horizon. The lights of the lorries, many of them driven by former Bedouin camel drivers who had forsaken the nomadic life, flared and then receded into the distance all night long as they fanned out to all points of the compass, south, west, north and east, before disappearing over the horizon or converged on Buraimi and were swallowed up in the villages of the oasis. No one who watched could fail to understand why Buraimi remained an absolutely vital axis to many of the ancient but continuingly important trade routes of the Arabian Peninsula. Any claim upon it was bound to raise issues of great strategic and economic importance not only for Saudi Arabia but for all the smaller eastern and southern countries and shaikhdoms of the peninsula.

Ibn Saud followed up his claim by allowing American geologists to enter the area and start exploring. Britain responded by warning that to allow the continuation of oil exploration in the territory might lead to an armed clash between Abu Dhabi and Saudi Arabia and proposed a meeting to determine the ownership of the region and precise borders. Ibn Saud, deciding that to escalate the confrontation at this point might be unwise, ordered the American geologists to be recalled until the borders of the disputed region were determined. An intense exchange of notes between Britain and Saudi Arabia then ensued, but in May 1950 while this exchange was still going on and exactly one year after Ibn Saud had lodged his original claim, the British inflamed the dispute by allowing geologists from the Anglo-Iranian Oil Company (the future British Petroleum) to start prospecting inside the territory which was the subject of the dispute. Ibn Saud responded by lodging a strongly worded protest. The Buraimi dispute was to continue in this way, with repeated provocations by both sides, angry notes, meetings and negotiations which ended in failure for the rest of Ibn Saud's life and for many years after his death.

At the same time Ibn Saud began another, more successful, attempt to assert himself. The oil-producing countries around him, such as Iran, had begun to demand a greater share in the profits of the foreign oil companies operating in their countries, but in Saudi Arabia, despite the fact that the amount of oil Aramco pumped and with it the company's profits had continued to grow exponentially, Ibn Saud was still only receiving the same small percentage of profit on the oil produced as agreed under the terms of his original contract with SOCAL. In 1950 he was angered to learn that the rulers of Venezuela had succeeded in negotiating a 50–50 profit-sharing agreement with the oil company operating in their country. Ibn Saud determined to get a similar deal for himself with Aramco. So he began to look for ways to apply pressure. In October 1950 he instituted a levy on the profits of all companies operating in his kingdom. Aramco protested, citing the clause in its original contract which exempted it from all Saudi taxes. However, Ibn Saud held firm and Aramco decided that it should negotiate. The result was a new contract, signed by officials of Aramco and a team of Ibn Saud's ministers in Jeddah on December 30th 1950, under which Ibn Saud would receive 50 per cent of the price of every barrel of oil produced after the deduction of production and marketing costs. This was probably the greatest victory, apart from those on the battlefield, that Ibn Saud ever won. Yet in spite of this apparently generous settlement, Aramco still succeeded in increasing its profits by 300 per cent between 1949 and 1951.[11]

In happier times Ibn Saud might have been buoyed up by his triumph over Aramco, but in the winter of 1950 to 1951 he was prostrate with grief over the death of his beloved elder sister and soulmate, Nura, who had died peacefully of old age in Riyadh during the previous summer. Just one year older than he was, Nura had been his closest companion through all the years and ups and downs of fortune ever since their childhood together in the home of their father Abd al-Rahman. It was Nura with whom as a ten-year-old boy he had ridden in the saddle bags strapped to either side of a camel when he and his family made their hurried escape from Riyadh and the approaching Rashids in the dead of that January night sixty years before. It was to Nura that he had turned for advice and comfort during all the great crises of his life. It was to the home of Nura that he had ordered the first telephone line from his palace in Riyadh to be connected so that he would be able to speak to her every day. Colonel Dickson's wife Violet, who met Nura a number of times, described her as one of the most charming and lovable women she ever met. She had 'all the magnetism and nobility of her great brother, and was clearly one of the most important personages in the whole of Arabia'. She was, according to Colonel Dickson himself, 'Undoubtedly one of Arabia's fairest, greatest and most famous daughters of all time', loved by the people and especially by the members of the noble Ajman tribe whose leader, Saud Al Kabir, she had married in a famous love match, and who Ibn Saud had spared from execution outside the walls of Layla in 1910. The women of the Ajman were famous for their beauty, but

11 See Aburish, op. cit. and K. S. Twitchell, *Saudi Arabia: With an Account of the Development of its Natural Resources*, Princeton University Press, New Jersey, 1953.

Nura had matched them. It was for one more glimpse of Nura's great beauty that her husband, Saud Al Kabir, was said to have slipped away at night from Ibn Saud's army on the eve of battle on more than one occasion. Among the people of Saudi Arabia, said Dickson, Nura's name was 'rivalled only by that of the mighty King Ibn Saud'.[12]

In May of the following year Ibn Saud suffered another grievous loss, the death of his favourite son Mansur during an operation for a kidney complaint in Paris.[13] Amid so much grief there was one success a few months later which he could enjoy, the realisation of his ambition that Saudi Arabia should have a railway. Constructed for him by the Americans, the cost deducted from his share of Aramco oil revenues, and equipped with locomotives and rolling stock from the New York, Newhaven and Hartford Railroad, the line ran south from the oil terminal at Dammam through Dhahran and south to Hofuf, then curving south and west in a great arc through the Al Kharj agricultural area for a total of 357 miles to Riyadh. The journey time for the whole distance was about ten hours, a lot quicker and more convenient than the ten or more day trek by camel so frequently undertaken by Ibn Saud in the past. Ibn Saud performed the opening ceremony himself in October 1951 at the newly constructed Riyadh station. During it he revealed to the people who were present that the new station stood on the very spot where almost fifty years earlier he and his forty warrior companions had left their camels on the night when they broke into the town before slaying Ajlan and restoring the Saud dynasty. The railway proved a great success and in its first year of operation carried four times the number of passengers expected and hundreds of tons of freight of all kinds.

But, just weeks later, fresh troubles came to haunt Ibn Saud. On a hot Sunday afternoon, November 16th 1951, Ibn Saud's moody, nineteen-year-old, eighteenth surviving son, Mishari, the son of an Abyssinian slave girl, got roaring drunk at a party given by the British pro-vice-

12 H. R. P. Dickson, *Kuwait and her Neighbours,* George Allen & Unwin, London, 1956.

13 There were some who suggested that he had been murdered at the instigation of one or more of his brothers, jealous of his favoured position and anxious to improve their own position in the succession. However it seems that the official explanation for his death is the most likely.

consul and his wife in Jeddah, Cyril and Dorothy Ousman. A dispute broke out and Mishari left the Ousmans house in a rage, only to return a little later with a tommy-gun. He fired wildly through an open window into the room where the Ousman's had been entertaining their guests. Ousman was shot dead where he stood and his wife only escaped by hiding behind a wardrobe. Mishari was immediately flung into prison and only spared from the death penalty because of his royal status. Cyril Ousman, who with his wife had befriended Mishari, was buried the next day in Jeddah's non-Muslim cemetery and his wife, Dorothy, given compensation by the Saudi Government sufficient to allow her to live out the rest of her life in retirement, quietly left the country shortly afterwards.[14]

Attempts were made to hush up what had happened but inevitably the story leaked out, spreading across the country and around the outside world, adding to Saudi Arabia and its ruling family's reputation for wild living, extravagance and immorality abroad and to discontent at home. A year earlier, Harold Dickson, for so long a uniquely knowledgeable friend of Saudi Arabia and by then living in retirement in Kuwait, had written, 'As far as one can visualize things from the Kuwaiti end of Arabia, Wahhabi doctrines and influence have now been discarded by Ibn Saud as political aids to an end.' He based his assessment on the frequent reports reaching him from Saudi Bedouin and other travellers he met in Kuwait. He recorded a 'growing dislike of the Saudi regime' that was spreading throughout tribal Arabia, a regime that was now increasingly losing touch with the feelings and concerns of the ordinary people. The people had come to bitterly resent the visits of members of the royal family to Europe and America where, the people said, 'they consort with wine-drinking Christians, acquire evil habits and forget their duty to God'. The people longed for a return to the personal rule of their King, directly accessible to even his humblest subjects as he had been in the past. Ibn Saud remained personally popular, but people increasingly feared 'the coming of the white man's civilisation, which means to them irreligion, forgetfulness of God and eventual slavery. Better than this, they say, would be a complete return

14 See Laurence Grafftey-Smith, *Bright Levant*, John Murray, London, 1970 and Robert Lacey, *The Kingdom*, Hutchinson, London, 1981.

to the tribal system in all its strength and glory, with their own tribal leaders and no one else to direct them.' Dickson commented that in the deep desert life was still as it was in Abraham's time in all its details and that the Bedouin nomad still relived the scenes of the Old Testament. 'His thoughts too are much the same as in the days of Job. His arrogance, independence, pride and self-sufficiency have only been intensified by Islam.' However, with the Bedouin now increasingly coming into contact with the Western way of life, as he frequently did when visiting the towns for supplies, he looked at the changes being brought about 'with unmistakable scorn and returns to his desert home more contented than ever with it and the life there. Yet the wheels of progress grind on inexorably, and the sons of the desert cannot escape.' Dickson noted how the acquisition of luxury Western goods, such as expensive motor cars and aeroplanes by members of the royal family, palace advisers and wealthy merchants was changing the psychology of all Arabs. As competition to own the latest and most expensive luxury goods escalated among the royal princes and rich merchants, discontent increased among the middle and lower classes. The new materialism, suggested Dickson, meant that whereas in the past Islam came to grips with many other religions and was never overthrown, it now seemed 'about to dissolve and break up in the home of its birth'.[15]

The discontent that Dickson recorded was further fanned by an increasingly militant Arab nationalism in other Middle Eastern countries. Lebanon, Jordan and Syria had all gained their independence from European control during or shortly after the war. Libya won its independence from Italian and then British and French mandate control in 1951 and late in the same year the Iranian Government, under Prime Minister Muhammad Musadeq, nationalised all British holdings in the Anglo-Iranian Oil Company. Also late in 1951 there were a series of brutal riots in Egypt targeted at foreign control of the Suez Canal and the on-going presence of British troops. The riots were followed in July 1952 by a group of nationalist army officers, led by Colonel Gamal Abdel Nasser, seizing control of the country and forcing King Farouk into exile. Stirrings of nationalism were also beginning to be felt in other

15 H.R.P. Dickson, op cit., Part Four.

Arab countries and at around this time a new element began to make itself felt – a specifically Islamic nationalism.

One of the major political elements in the growing political unrest that had led to the seizure of power by Nasser in Egypt was the teaching of the Muslim Brothers, who proclaimed that social justice could only be achieved under a government which took Islam as the basis for its policies and laws. After the fall of King Farouk the Muslim Brothers were the only political organisation exempted by the Colonels from a ban on all political parties. In the late 1940s and early 1950s the Muslim Brothers had begun to derive particular inspiration from the writings of one Sayyid Qutb, a former official in the Egyptian Ministry of Education who had gone for further study in America. In 1949 Qutb, disillusioned with what he saw as the materialism, racism and moral degeneration of American society, had published his most famous book *Social Justice in Islam*. He argued that for Muslims, as opposed to Christians, there was no gap between faith and life. All human acts should be seen as acts of worship. The Qur'an, Qutb maintained, laid upon all men a responsibility for everyone in society, all human beings being fundamentally equal in the eyes of God. Although all had different responsibilities depending upon their position in society, men and women were spiritually equal. It was just that they had different functions and responsibilities. Rulers too had special responsibilities: to uphold the law, enforce morality and maintain a just society. The right to property, Qutb argued, must be maintained, but the ruler had a duty to see that it was used for the good of society. Wealth should not be used dishonestly, for a life of luxury or usury, and should be taxed for the benefit of society. The necessities of the community's life should not be owned by individuals but owned in common. So long as the ruler upheld a just society the ruler must be obeyed, but if he ceased to uphold a just society the citizen's duty of obedience was ended.[16]

Although Qutb's ideas did not flow directly from Wahhabism, the similarity between the ideals which he preached and the ideals espoused by Al Wahhab is striking. Many of the sources of Qutb's inspiration

16 See Albert Hourani, *A History of the Arab Peoples*, Faber & Faber, London, 1991.

among the early Islamic writers and jurists were the same as those that inspired Al Wahhab. Although the ideas of the Muslim Brothers and Qutb reached Saudi Arabia initially mainly through intellectuals, as they began to percolate down through society they found ready listeners among all classes, especially among the growing numbers of those disaffected by the greed, sins and corruption of members of the royal family and the court elite. They had a particular appeal to former members of the Ikhwan and their descendants.

Another source of discontent among Islamists was the June 1951 extension of the US lease on the huge American military base and airfield at Dhahran. In agreeing the extension of the lease the Americans agreed to supply the Saudi armed forces with modern aircraft and tanks. In 1952 there was a further influx of American military 'advisers' and instructors to Saudi Arabia, who among other duties took over the training of Saudi military pilots. All of this amounted to a huge expansion of the American military presence in the country, effectively supplanting Britain and her post-war influence in the country's military affairs. At the same time as increasing its military presence in the country America also stepped up its level of assistance in developing agriculture, sending experts to help create a model farm and further irrigation schemes in the Al Kharj and Asir provinces.

However, far more money was by now being spent by the royal princes and wealthy merchants on creating huge, idealised gardens and palaces for themselves than was being spent on schemes intended to benefit the public at large. In the year 1950–1 no less than two-thirds of the country's entire budget was earmarked for expenditure on 'State Palaces, Princes' expenses and royal Establishments'. At the same time the country had run up enormous debts, estimated to total between $150 million and $200 million when the total income from oil was only just over $100 million. Ibn Saud had had elaborate gardens created around his new royal palaces but many of his sons were now comfortably out-doing their father in the amount they spent on their gardens. In 1952 Van der Meulen and a colleague were invited by Prince Saud to visit the new palace and garden he had had created for himself in the desert outside Riyadh.

Prince Saud's new palace stood surrounded by the garden at the end of a long avenue of young tamarisk trees planted in still-bare land. This avenue of trees had replaced an avenue that Prince Saud had hastily had planted four years earlier to show off to King Abdullah of Jordan when he had visited Saudi Arabia in an unsuccessful attempt to end the long feud in relations between the Sauds and the Hashemites. Just a few days before Abdullah's visit Saud had called in the American experts working on the Al Kharj agricultural scheme and asked for their assistance in getting the avenue of tamarisk trees planted in time for the visit. The Americans had told Saud that uprooting a set of mature trees at that time of year and transporting them, even at night, through fifty miles of desert from Al Kharj where they grew in profusion, would kill most of them. But Saud had replied that he did not care so long as they survived just long enough for Abdullah's visit. So the trees had been moved and the avenue hurriedly created. Sure enough, within days after Abdullah's visit almost all of them had died. Later, at a more suitable time of year they had been replaced by an avenue of younger trees and it was down this avenue that four years later van der Meulen and his colleague were driven to Prince Saud's palace.

Van der Meulen was met at the inner gate to the palace by one of Prince Saud's officers and asked to get out of his car and walk the rest of the way to the palace. The reason for the request was so that his guests should have a chance to properly admire the new garden that Prince Saud had had created for himself. Walking through this newly created garden, adorned with ornamental fountains and irrigated by a continual flow of water pumped, with the help of American engineers, from the underground sources which for so long had fed the palm gardens, wells and waterwheels of the Wadi Hanifah surrounding Riyadh, van der Meulen says he came to understand why Arabs use the same word for garden as for paradise. Under the expert care of a team of Indian gardeners imported to the country by the prince, a great profusion of flowers, bushes and lawns had been made to flourish out of the recently barren land of the desert – it was, as van der Meulen commented 'a real garden', modelled and fashioned upon the lines of famous gardens that Saud had seen and admired on visits to lands which rainfall and climate had made naturally green and verdant, such as America and Europe. Close to the palace van der Meulen and his colleague were offered comfortable chairs on a area of decorative mosaic paving beside a large, blue-tiled swimming pool filled to the brim with fresh, clean water. Because the trees and bushes in the garden were still relatively immature wild birds would not yet come to them to nest, so Saud had had a range of different kinds of birds kept in cages hung on long poles close to the pool so that his garden would be filled with birdsong.

When Prince Saud joined them in the late afternoon, with the sun already descending in the west, the air filled with the sound of gently gurgling water and the song of caged birds, he asked van der Meulen if he remembered what he had seen on this spot during his last visit to Riyadh in 1944. Van der Meulen replied, 'Nothing but sand and gravel, not even a single blade of grass.'

'You are right,' replied Prince Saud triumphantly, adding that it had been the same only a year ago. 'But', he continued, 'now look around you and you see this palace and garden. Do you like them?'

Van der Meulen told Prince Saud that he did indeed like them and that they were so magnificent that they were beyond his powers of description. Prince Saud was clearly delighted.

After eating a sumptuous meal at which an array of the finest European and Middle Eastern cooking was served, with evening drawing on Prince Saud's Christian visitors rose to leave in order to enable their Muslim hosts to make their sunset prayers. Whereupon Saud asked his guests to stay just a little longer and gave a servant an order which van der Meulen did not understand. Moments later hundreds and hundreds of coloured electric lights began to twinkle in the bushes all over the garden. At the furthest end from where they were sitting floodlights and more little fairy lights lit up Saud's private mosque, its minaret bathed in a great range of colours: blue, yellow, green and red. Nearer to them, the wall of the palace was now bathed in orange. More and more lights continued to come on until it seemed that van der Meulen and his companions were 'sitting in a garden covered with flowers of light. The amir sat there, himself radiant with satisfaction at the impression made on us.' From the top of the minaret 'a modern loudspeaker started to rend the air with a metallic roar that Allah was most great'.

But as van der Meulen later commented, Saud's palace and garden, far from being as perhaps Prince Saud intended, 'a return to an Arabian

Night of Harun ar-Rashid' was instead 'a demonstration that what should have been a last bulwark of Wahhabism was in full retreat from advancing materialism. And not a fighting retreat either! Here in the desert, where the West was breaking through the Wahhabi defences that had protected the last remnant of romantic Arabia, the future ruler of the country still seemed to believe in the methods of days that were irrevocably gone. His style was a copy of that of his father with its weaker sides magnified.'

Returning to their cars outside the palace's inner gate van der Meulen and his fellow guests became aware of groups of Bedouins – 'Dozens of them distinguishable in the glare of the thousands of electric light bulbs and the flood-lit walls of the palace and mosque. Light enough to shine on their wasted nomad bodies and on the dirty threadbare mantles that clad them so thinly in the cold desert night. Light enough to see their startled faces. There was amazement on those faces but not only that: there was scorn too.' These Bedouins, van der Meulen saw, had been awakened, had seen their own misery and begun to see what life might be for others and to hope that they too might enjoy another way of living, a way of living 'far from fear and poverty, an existence fit for human dignity'. For how long, van der Meulen wondered, would those Bedouin be content to stand in the desert at the outer gates and have only a distant view of the luxury inside? For how long would they be content to let their rulers take all the money from the oil and use almost all of it for themselves? How long before they would start to demand their share?[17]

Back in Riyadh, which only a few years previously had still been a place of great austerity and silence, everything now seemed to be bustle and activity, of new palatial homes and palaces being built for the wealthy, not out of the mud bricks of old but largely from new hewn and cut rocks, of new schools and mosques. In just a few years its population had multiplied from about 50,000 to 200,000. But just beyond the town and its rush of new building, bordering the empty desert, was a wide circle of densely populated Bedouin tented shanty towns, where the occupants had difficulty in scraping together a living. Lured to the town by stories of abundant well paid work, thousands of

17 D. van der Meulen, op. cit.

these desert nomads had been reduced to scraping a bare subsistence from labouring and other menial tasks, while others, even less fortunate, finding abundant water nearby and enabled to survive by the King's free food, had settled into a life of squalid idleness. Bereft of sanitation the camps had quickly become a vast, unsavoury, fly-blown latrine. Yet many of these men were the descendants of Ishmael, son of Abraham, the nomadic Arabs who had gained a reputation as formidable warriors in the armies of the Assyrians a thousand years before the birth of Christ. Many, too, were the sons and grandsons of men who had ridden with Ibn Saud when he had conquered the kingdom. For how long would they be willing to put up with lives of hunger and humiliation before they rose up and once more took to arms?

The ring of fly-blown camps and the quantities of waste food thrown out by the town's wealthier citizens had attracted a great horde of stray, mongrel, scavenging dogs, many maimed and limping as a result of being stoned by the Arabs whose scraps they had come to live off. In Islam the dog is unclean and a strict Muslim will not touch it, even to give it a kick. Instead, they will drive it away by hurling stones or lumps of earth at it. As the numbers of these dogs had risen their fights and barking, especially during the night, had begun to make life unbearable for the citizens of Riyadh. So the authorities, unwilling to kill them simply because they barked and fought, had erected a series of enclosures in the desert beyond the tented shanty towns and begun paying people three rials for every dog delivered to them. By the time van der Meulen visited Riyadh in 1952 these pens held between four and six thousand dogs. Van der Meulen looked in through a crack in the walls of one of them and could not drag his horrified eyes away from what he saw – thousands of fly-pestered, diseased and slowly dying animals. When he asked one of the officials who guarded the pen about the dogs he was told that they were given water and old dates 'and would doubtless die when their time came'.

And what of the poor, ill-clothed, ill-fed men trapped in their tented shanty towns between the pens of mangy, dying dogs and the bustling prosperous town? Would they be content just to lie down and die 'when their time came'? Van der Meulen visited the ruins of Diriya, the former capital of the first Saudi Wahhabi state destroyed by the guns of the

Egyptians one hundred and thirty years earlier. He saw its impressive ruins as a fitting memorial to the defeat of the men who had set out from there to create a new Islamic moral empire and compared their defeat to the much greater moral defeat he was witnessing now in Riyadh, infinitely wealthier than Diriya ever was and far richer in palaces than any town in Central Arabia had ever been before. Modern, prosperous Riyadh, he concluded, was in reality witness to the ruin of Wahhabism, 'a ruin that was greater, immeasurably greater, than that first ruin because this time the ruin was spiritual'.[18]

In 1951 Ibn Saud had authorised the creation of a regular army, drilled and uniformed after the manner of the armies of Europe, to replace 'Wahhab's rebel horde', the force that had done so much to win the country but had then turned upon him when he sought to prevent them from entangling him in battles with the colonial powers. It was intended that the new army should become a fourth pillar of the state, alongside the Royal Family, the *ulema* and the leaders of the great tribes. Garrisons were established in each of the larger towns and a limited amount of military band music began to be permitted to accompany parades and relieve the tedium of repetitious drilling, and, in this still otherwise almost musicless land, to encourage recruitment and entertain the populace.[19]

Just how much of what was going on in his kingdom, of the decisions being made and the plight of his people, Ibn Saud by this time understood is hard to gauge. Probably very little. The 'fire', as Philby said, 'had gone out of him'. When van der Meulen was shown into the audience chamber to meet the King for the last time in 1952 he saw an immediate change from the warrior king he had known in earlier years. Ibn Saud no longer rose to greet his guests as he had always done in former years. He stayed sitting in an invalid carriage, no longer able to walk and in perpetual pain from a combination of arthritis in his knees and the effects of old battle injuries. The sparse beard and bits of straggly hair that could be seen poking out from under his head-cloth were still black, but now no longer naturally black but dyed. The once strong and slender hands had become stiff and wrinkled, 'the face more set, the gaze

18 Ibid.
19 See H. St John Philby, *Sa'udi Arabia*, Ernest Benn, London 1955.

weak and lustreless'. The voice, that had for so long commanded men, struck fear into them or been the instrument of his special charm and poetic utterance, was faded to little more than a harsh whisper, indistinct and often hard for even those close to him to understand. Van der Meulen had met the King many times, but now he was not sure if he even remembered who he was although he averred that he did. It was reported that Ibn Saud had in recent years been seen to fall asleep during meetings. He no longer asked sharp questions of those who came to see him, but now often seemed to lose the thread of a conversation. Van der Meulen noted that while his replies to questions were still polite and to the point, they seemed tired. The one point at which Ibn Saud seemed to come back to some semblance of his former self was when one of the American oil men present told the king that he had recently been seriously ill but had recovered and now for the first time saw 'how great were God's gifts to men', how wonderful the world was, 'how beautiful the fair sex' and now understood that what mattered in life was not money, or success, but religion, above all religion. Ibn Saud seemed unimpressed and said to his interpreter, 'Tell him that if he had been a Muslim he need not have fallen ill in order to understand what matters in life. We knew that long ago!'[20] When van der Meulen left the audience chamber he felt for the first time unsatisfied by a meeting with Ibn Saud: 'The unfailing spring had failed.'

At a meeting with American oil men to discuss their next tactical ploys in the ongoing dispute with the British over the Buraimi Oasis Ibn Saud seemed to lose the thread of the conversation completely and was reduced to a beaming smile and the repetition over and over again of the words 'You are my friends, you are my friends. You can count on me. Anything you want, anything you want.'[21] The same reply was given over and over again to the insatiable demands of his many sons, his brothers, the members of his extended family, the members of his inner circle and the many others who came to see him with their requests. So the extravagance of those around him grew without bounds, squandering the resources which in a Muslim Wahhabi state

20 D. van der Meulen, op. cit.
21 Robert Lacey, *The Kingdom*, Hutchinson, London 1981.

true to its founding ideals would have been put to the use of the whole community, the Muslim *ummah*.

Ibn Saud himself still lived simply, drinking warmed and lightly curdled camel's milk as he always had in the past, sipping coffee from the old chipped mug he had used since his youth, keeping a seven foot long spear beside his simple bed. Ramps had been built to each floor of his palace so that he could be driven up to any level that he wanted to be on and could even hold his *majlis* in the open air on the roof as he often had in the past. Now nearly blind even in his one good eye, and virtually immobile, he would sit for hours on end in his wheelchair, his feet clad in thick woollen socks and western-style slippers in order to try to ease the poor circulation in his feet and ankles. Although he continued to urge his doctors and any quack who seemed to promise results to come up with remedies that would restore his virility, his sexual powers were now spent, his last surviving son had been born in 1947 after an interval of four years.[22] Yet he passed more and more of his time in his harem, especially with his favourite Umm Talal, no longer performing prodigious sexual feats, but quietly and companionably reminiscing about the past or gently dozing.

Three months after van der Meulen's visit to the King an incident occurred that provoked one of his last great rages. Since the introduction of radio around the country it had become even easier than in earlier years for anyone with a complaint, a dispute he wanted settled or in need of help to bring their problem to the King for settlement in his *majlis*. Now supplicants no longer had to make the journey to Riyadh as they could simply go to one of the many radio telegraph stations set up in all the major towns and provinces and bring their problems to the King's notice or seek his advice and help by that means. The result was a great increase in the number of people bringing their complaints and problems to Ibn Saud. However, some well-meaning members of his staff in an

22 Burke's *Royal Families of the World*, Vol II, London 1980 records a last son, his 64th child, as having been born in June 1952, but dying in infancy. However, the number of girl children Ibn Saud had is generally acknowledged to be unknown and the total number of children that he fathered seems likely to be quite a lot higher. In *The Kingdom* Robert Lacey lists the names of 43 sons and it therefore seems probable that Ibn Saud fathered a similar number of daughters.

attempt to reduce his workload began to try to discourage people from seeking his advice and to deal with some of the more minor complaints themselves without bothering the King with them. When Ibn Saud learned of this he flew into one of his formidable rages, berating the well-intentioned officials who had been trying to ease some of the burden upon him. In June 1952 he issued a royal decree. It read: 'Whereas we have been informed that some complaints addressed to us through wireless or post offices are withheld from us, we hereby order that any complaint submitted to us by any person whatsoever shall be sent to us literally without any change. Those concerned shall not delay it or reveal its content to the person complained of, whether he be a governor or a minister, of high or low rank.' It went on to threaten punishment for anyone who delayed or prevented the delivery of any complaint to him and ended by saying that 'we are always ready to receive any complaints' and that anyone who had been done an injustice would be given his full rights and the person who caused such an injustice would be punished as they deserved. It was signed simply 'Abd al-Aziz'.[23]

By 1953 performing the annual *Hajj* pilgrimage to Mecca in the intense mid-summer heat was beyond Ibn Saud's powers of physical endurance. However, he did perform one last official act by setting up a Council of Ministers. For years he had worried about the rivalry between his sons, especially between his eldest surviving sons Saud and Faisal. He had repeatedly tried to end the rivalry, but by 1953 it was again as intense as ever. By this time most of Ibn Saud's other surviving sons had been drawn in, either advancing rival claims of their own for preferred positions in the order of succession or for additional governmental powers and positions of responsibility. By the 1950s the sons had divided into five more or less distinct rival camps. So in 1953, by establishing a Council of Ministers, something his sons had for years been urging him to do, he hoped to be able to use it as a tool through which to put an end to their rivalries. But on August 8th 1953, immediately after signing the decree formally establishing the Council but before calling its first meeting, Ibn Saud gave instructions for his private aeroplane, the Dakota

23 See David Howarth, *The Desert King: The Life of Ibn Saud*, William Collins, London, 1965.

given to him by President Roosevelt, to fly him to his summer palace high in the cool of the hills near Taif, the site twenty-nine years earlier in 1924 of the infamous massacre by the Ikhwan.

An observer who witnessed him being transferred from the aircraft to his car upon landing at Taif noted that 'his gaze was frozen and that he recognised no one around him'.[24] Something was seriously wrong. His sons and members of his extended family rushed to be at his side. Yet he continued to cling to life and even seemed to recover somewhat. Later that month he bolstered his eldest son Saud's position in the hierarchy by giving him effective command of the newly created army. But by October he had become worse again and was confined to bed in Prince Faisal's palace in Taif. On October 11th he at last handed over some real executive power to his official heir Prince Saud, appointing him Prime Minister and granting him full authority.

The appointment of Prince Saud as Prime Minister coincided with the start of a bitter strike by Arab workers at the Aramco site in Dhahran. The disparity between their pay and conditions had remained almost as great as it had been a decade earlier. The Arab workers, who now included Palestinians and Syrians, were still confined to living in breeze-block and corrugated iron roofed huts in the Bantustan-like quarters of the Arab camp beyond the barbed wire fence separating it from the area where the American workers and their families lived. The lives of the Americans and their families at Dhahran were now almost identical to the lives of Americans living in prosperous small towns and suburbs back home in the United States. The official Aramco Handbook of the period includes pictures of the area where the American workers and their families lived which seem almost indistinguishable from pictures of small-town middle-class America at the same period. Well appointed single-storey family homes, each surrounded by its own well-tended and -planted garden, laid out on broad, gently curving roads and avenues, communal areas complete with swimming pools, sports grounds, cinemas, shops and even a 'hobby farm' where whole families could spend their weekends, ride, keep their pets and animals, stable the

24 Leslie McLoughlin, op. cit. based on account by Khair al-Din al-Zirikli, *The Arabian Peninsula in the Era of King Abd al-Aziz*, Beirut, 1970.

splendid Arab horses they bought for themselves locally, tend farm animals, relax and enjoy themselves. The letters home of one Aramco worker's wife, Mildred Webster, provide a graphic picture of life for one typical expat family, wife, husband and two teenage daughters, in the American Aramco community during this period. Their life seems almost idyllic – dinner parties with colleagues and friends, days spent at the hobby farm, tending their horses, bathing, going to the cinema, attending Aramco sports-club softball games, plays, minstrel shows and parties.

There is almost no mention in the letters of the Arabs with whom her husband worked and who lived so close-by until a letter home from Mimi Webster on October 21st which begins, 'This has been a very upset week ... I am sure there must have been some garbled reports of all sorts of things, but the sum and substance of it is that the Arabs went on strike.' In fact some workers representing the Arab workforce had been trying to negotiate improvements in conditions and wages on the site for some weeks, but with no union recognition by Aramco and trade unions banned under Saudi law, the negotiations had got nowhere. When some Arab workers downed tools in protest, the Governor of the Hasa province, a son of Ibn Saud's cousin Jiluwi, the hero of the 1902 seizure of Riyadh, maintaining his father's record for harsh government in the province, moved in and had all the negotiators thrown into jail in Hofuf. The result was that all 13,000 Arab workers at Dhahran promptly walked out on strike in sympathy, bringing the whole oil field to a standstill. The governor of Hasa's response to this was to move thousands more troops into Dhahran, beat up and start arresting the strikers. Hundreds were soon in jail and being tortured.

In her letter home Mimi Webster told her family that the problem had arisen because there had been 'some agitators among the Arabs and the funny thing', she explained, was that these 'agitators' came from among a specially selected group of men who had been sent by Aramco for advanced training in America. 'The stay in the States seems to have given them some advanced ideas,' she says, and on their return to Dhahran they had started 'stirring [up] the lower class to rebel'.

Mimi Webster continued: 'We have had practically martial law in that we have all stayed inside our own fence just to keep out of the way. There have been some rough treatments by the soldiers – they aren't very gentle.' Yet to her apparent surprise, the strikers still held out. 'I do not know what the out come will be, but it does not concern me personally. Of course we haven't been able to go to the hobby farm [where the Websters and their daughters kept their horses] or anywhere else.' She continued, 'Of course the poor ignorant [Arab workers don't] even know what is what about anything, so [are] very easily led in things – mostly Bedu from the desert.'[25] A week later, with the strike still continuing, the American community held their annual Halloween dance as usual.

The strike lasted for three full weeks and afterwards did eventually lead to some improvement in the Arabs' wages and conditions, although union organisation remained prohibited.[26] The 'advanced ideas' which the Arab workers had 'picked up', although some of them may have come from their time in the States, came mostly from Syria and Egypt and the socialist and nationalist movements that were gaining ground in those countries and other parts of the Middle East.

On October 20th the New York Times, in its report on the strike, had said that Ibn Saud was somewhat better and had regained control over the strikers, but by early November when the strike finally ended, he had relapsed. A week after that, by which time he had not left his bed in Faisal's palace for a month, in the early hours of the morning of November 9th 1953 Ibn Saud died peacefully in his sleep. Prince Faisal was at his bedside.

Later that same day, he was wrapped in a simple shroud, loaded aboard the plane given to him by President Roosevelt and flown to Riyadh. There, in accordance with strict Wahhabi custom, he was buried in an unmarked grave and his clothes were sold in the market place. He died as he had lived, a devout Muslim. His last words were: 'There is no power and no strength save in God.'[27]

25 *Dear Folks: The Webster Letters from Arabia 1944–59*, edited by Ken Slavin © 2002–9 Aramco Expats Corporation. Released April 1 2008. 3065. aspx.

26 See Fred Halliday, *Arabia Without Sultans*, Penguin Books, London 1974 and *The Rise, Corruption and Coming Fall of The House of Saud* by Said K. Aburish, Bloomsbury, London 1994.

27 See Leslie McLoughlin, op. cit.

CHAPTER 15

Legacy

SAUD TO FAHD

In the introduction to his book *Saudi Arabia*, written only months after Ibn Saud's death, H. St John Philby, who had been at Ibn Saud's side for much of the previous thirty years, suggested that his reign had marked perhaps the most brilliant chapter in the entire history of the Arab peoples, other than the period of the Prophet Muhammad's own lifetime. Like The Prophet, Philby said, Ibn Saud had been a 'man of destiny'. But in the immediate aftermath of Ibn Saud's death, while most people with a knowledge of the Middle East and the Arabs might have been willing to grant that Ibn Saud had been a fine and courageous leader of men, a wily politician-negotiator who had succeeded against daunting odds in forging a single kingdom out of a vast, unruly, largely unknown and arid landmass peopled with warring and untrustworthy minor shaikhdoms and tribes, probably few would have been willing to accept Philby's assessment of Ibn Saud as a 'Man of Destiny', let alone his judgement that he had been perhaps the greatest Arab since Muhammad.[1] To such people he had had serious weaknesses, the greatest of which was probably, in the words of one who had known him well, that until the end he had remained 'simply a benevolent tribal chieftain, on an immensely enlarged scale'. As a result he had made inadequate provision for Saudi Arabia's future entry into the modern world.

In the months immediately after Ibn Saud's death most outside

1 *Sa'udi Arabia*, H. St John Philby, Ernest Benn, London, 1955.

observers expected that with his death the rivalries between his sons, together with their many excesses and growing unpopularity, plus the ever-widening discrepancy between the huge wealth of the country's rulers and the deepening poverty of its poor and dispossessed, would lead to strife, civil war and the kingdom's disintegration. Ibn Saud's failure during his declining years to deal with these barely concealed fissures in his kingdom, together with the rising tide of Arab nationalism elsewhere in the Middle East and the increasingly strident voices of growing bands of radical Islamists, such as Sayyid Qutb's Muslim Brotherhood in Egypt, seemed certain to lead to the Kingdom's dissolution, just as the deaths of earlier charismatic Saudi leaders had led to the collapse of earlier Saudi states. To such pessimists the real test of Ibn Saud's greatness would lie not in his past achievements but in whether the kingdom he had created could endure and prosper without him to hold it together in a fast-changing world, a world that was already coming to impinge on Saudi Arabia to an extent that the outside world had never impinged on the heartland of the Arabian Peninsula in over 3,000 years.

It so happened that on November 9th 1953, the day that Ibn Saud died, Prince Saud, his eldest surviving son and designated successor, had been away from Taif on official business. So it was Ibn Saud's second son, Faisal, and not Saud who had been beside him when he died. Those who had forecast an immediate outbreak of hostilities between the two sons perhaps expected Faisal to use Saud's absence to grab the throne. But he did not. Instead, immediately Saud returned to Taif and entered the palace where Ibn Saud had died Faisal greeted his brother as King and pledged him his absolute loyalty. In return, Saud re-confirmed Faisal's position as Crown Prince, Viceroy of the Hijaz and Foreign Minister, while himself remaining President of the Council and thus, Prime Minister.

Just weeks before his death Ibn Saud, extremely worried about the rivalry between his two eldest sons, had summoned them. He had reminded them of the history of their family and of how disputes between its members had repeatedly led to its downfall. He warned them of the dangers that might arise from disagreements between them, especially if those disagreements became known to other members of the family or outsiders. He had made them solemnly swear to him that they would not quarrel, had made Faisal swear to accept Saud's

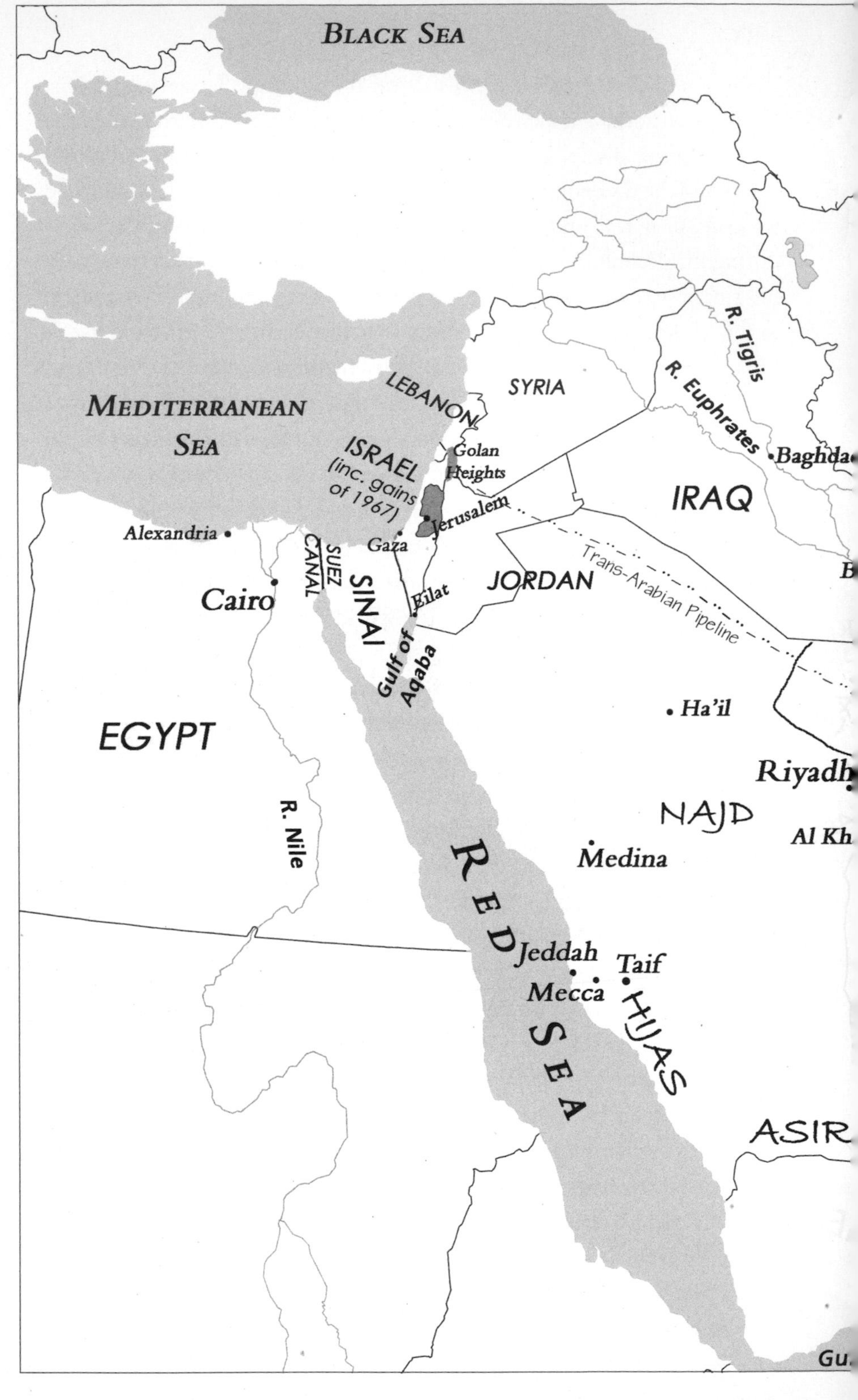

BLACK SEA
MEDITERRANEAN SEA
LEBANON
SYRIA
R. Tigris
R. Euphrates
Baghda
ISRAEL (inc. gains of 1967)
Golan Heights
IRAQ
Jerusalem
Alexandria
Gaza
SUEZ CANAL
Trans-Arabian Pipeline
SINAI
JORDAN
Cairo
Eilat
Gulf of Aqaba
Ha'il
EGYPT
Riyadh
NAJD
R. Nile
Al Kh
Medina
RED SEA
Jeddah
Taif
Mecca
HIJAS
ASIR
Gu

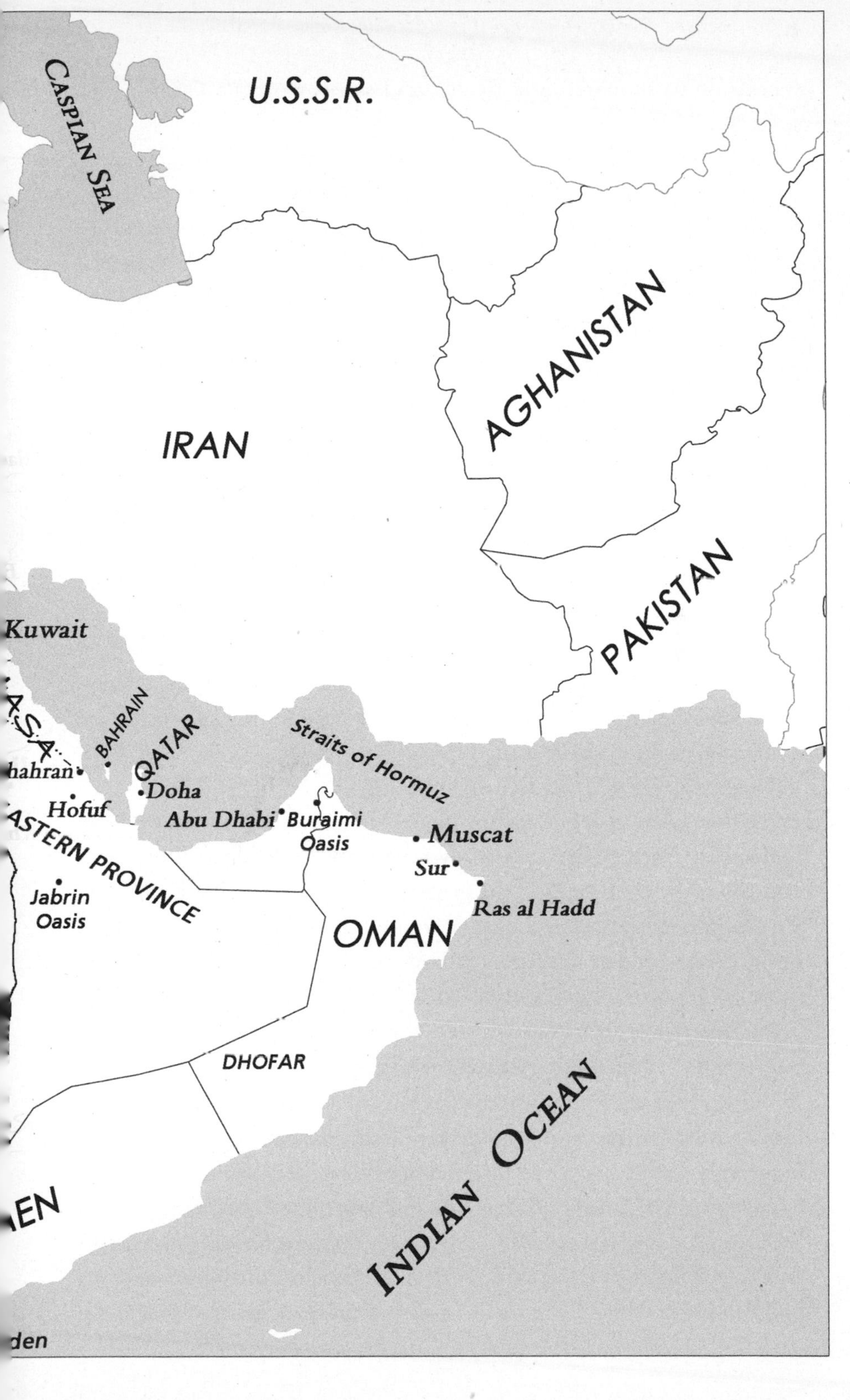

CASPIAN SEA
U.S.S.R.
AGHANISTAN
IRAN
PAKISTAN
Kuwait
BAHRAIN
QATAR
Straits of Hormuz
Doha
Hofuf
Abu Dhabi
Buraimi
Oasis
Muscat
Sur
Ras al Hadd
Jabrin
Oasis
OMAN
DHOFAR
INDIAN OCEAN

succession as monarch and made Saud swear to name Faisal as his successor.

So the first danger facing Saudi Arabia after the passing of its founder passed without mishap. But other dangers remained. The first centred on the new King's life-style, his extravagance, administrative incompetence and dependence upon a small clique of corrupt advisers. The Ministerial Council, although set up by Ibn Saud some months before his death, did not hold its first meeting until March 1954. When it did at last meet King Saud used the first meeting to set out his intentions as monarch. Proclaiming his total commitment to the established religious principles of the Kingdom, he told his assembled ministers that he intended to continue his father's policies and his methods of government. He would strengthen the army, tackle poverty, disease and hunger, increase healthcare provision and establish new ministries to oversee the development of agriculture, education and communications, would improve the nation's system of local and regional government and get the country's financial affairs in order. To this end, al Sulaiman, Ibn Saud's long-serving, if inadequate, Finance Minister was stripped of most of his responsibilities. The Finance Ministry was re-organised and customs duties reduced on items such as food and clothing.

However, King Saud's own spending on both himself and his immediate circle remained as profligate as ever. The hungry Bedouin that van der Meulen had spotted two years earlier gazing in amazement and contempt from outside the grounds of Saud's garishly lavish new Riyadh palace together with tens of thousands of others who had ended up in disease-ridden, mangy, dog-infested shanty towns, became ever more aware of the gulf between their lives and the extravagance and sinful lifestyles of their rulers. Every new enormity or scandal involving one or other of the legion of Saudi royal princes – every drunken brawl in a European nightclub, sexual lunge at a tart, failure to pay bills for luxury goods or piece of outrageous extravagance – was increasingly likely to be broadcast across the Arab world by the radio stations of the emerging republican and Arab nationalist governments of countries such as Egypt and Syria. As a result the chasm between Saud's promises to end the suffering of the poor, halt government corruption and his and other members of the royal family's profligacy became ever more glaringly obvious. Opposition to Saud's rule and that of the Al Saud family, latent during the last years of Ibn Saud's reign and only held in check by his own personal popularity, began to mushroom.

As well as the still-simmering discontent among the local oil workers in the Hasa, further fomented by covert Marxist-inspired trade union groups, a range of new opposition groups emerged. One, led by groups of school children, demanded that the curriculum and teaching methods be brought into line with those in the newly emergent Arab republics in Egypt and Syria. They called for the dissolution of the League for the Encouragement of Virtue and the Denunciation of Sin (the League of Public Morality, the body responsible for the *Mutawwa* or religious police), for an end to its control over education and the establishment of institutions of higher learning. After clashes in Buraida between students and members of the League of Public Morality dozens of the leaders of pupils and student groups were arrested and whipped, denounced as being 'infected with Communism'. To counter such secular ideas Saud instituted an annual 2,000 rial prize to be awarded to children who learned the Qur'an by heart.

Another movement, calling itself The Front for National Reform, brought together young army officers, government officials and educated Aramco workers. Professing anti-Western and Arab nationalist ideas, together with some mild tenets of Marxism, the group demanded the liberation of the country from imperialist domination and the economic yoke of the oil companies, a democratic constitution and elected parliament, freedom of the press, improvement of the lot of the poor and education for girls.

Other opposition groups arose among the urban middle-class in the Hijaz, among people living traditional tribal lives in Asir and northern Najd, among Shi'ites in Hasa and young army officers who had received training in Egypt and become infected with ideas of Arab nationalism and anti-monarchism. It was perhaps fortunate for Saud that the demands of these groups were so disparate and so never coalesced into a single unified opposition. In response Saud's government instituted a series of harsh crackdowns. In 1955 the leaders of a group calling themselves The Free Officers were executed and leaders of other groups thrown into prison.

One early victim of the crackdowns was Ibn Saud's old and trusted friend H. St John Philby. By then white haired and in his seventies, in February 1955 Philby had gone to Dhahran at the invitation of Aramco to talk to company employees about his long years of experience of living in Arabia. Speaking off the cuff, Philby had talked about how the country had changed since he first knew it, of the social revolution that had taken place since the war, of the almost complete transformation from a theocratic state into what he viewed as a secular state, of how the morals and laws of Islam and *shari'a* were giving way to an absorption in materialism, of how the government's emphasis had in recent years shifted from being focused primarily on the things of God to being focused primarily on the things of Caesar.[2] Shortly after returning to his home in Riyadh, Philby was visited by three of King Saud's close aides who told him that his criticisms had deeply displeased the King who required him to leave the country forthwith. So, unwilling to retract his criticism, after almost thirty years of loyal service to the Al Sauds, Philby left Saudi Arabia for ever.

Although by 1955 the Saudi government's income from oil had reached $300 million a year, due to King Saud's ongoing incompetence and profligacy the country was massively in debt. Despite his declared intention of ameliorating the lot of the poor and modernising the conduct of the country's financial affairs, Saud still regarded all of the country's oil income as belonging to him and his family to do with as they thought fit, to spend on cars, ever more lavish palaces and foreign luxury goods. As a result the Kingdom's finances continued to spiral further and further out of control.

Visiting Dhahran in July 1956 Saud was confronted by a mass demonstration. Inspired by the recent takeover of power in Egypt by Gamal Abdel Nasser on a programme of Arab nationalism and socialism, redistribution of income and state ownership of the means of production, the crowds that confronted King Saud waved placards bearing anti-imperialist slogans and calling for the closure of American military bases. They handed the King a list of demands which included

2 See Philby, H. St John, *Forty Years in the Wilderness*, Robert Hale, London, 1955.

the official recognition of their committee, higher wages, a shorter working day, an end to arbitrary sackings and equality between the conditions of themselves and American workers. The King responded by issuing a decree banning all strikes and having the ringleaders arrested and beaten. Uncowed, the protesters declared a general strike and upped their demands to include a national constitution. On the orders of the King the Governor of Hasa then dispatched a mixed force of Bedouin from the remaining Ikhwan *hijras*, his personal guard and freed slaves to break up the strike. Hundreds of protesting workers were arrested, jailed, tortured and the foreigners among them deported.

However, Saud did now introduce some reforms, for instance a weekly women's *majlis* to which women could for the first time themselves bring their complaints, grievances and disputes. He began a school development programme, built new roads and hospitals, looked into the possibility of introducing television to the Kingdom and, mainly at the instigation of his brother Crown Prince Faisal's wife, Effat, sanctioned the opening of a few carefully regulated and controlled girls' schools in Taif, Jeddah and one inside the grounds of his own palace for his own daughters. However, even in cosmopolitan Jeddah initially few families were willing to send their daughters to such schools. Nevertheless when the *ulema* and members of the League of Public Morality got wind of what was happening and scrutinised the proposed curricula they demanded the elimination of almost all the classes devoted to science and their replacement with Qur'anic studies.

In July 1956, with the last British troops about to pull out of the Suez Canal Zone in response to Egyptian pressure, President Nasser of Egypt paid a visit to Saudi Arabia. By this time acknowledged across the Arab world as the leader of an increasingly confident and assertive brand of republican, broadly socialist, Arab nationalism, he was greeted everywhere he went in Saudi Arabia by huge crowds of wildly cheering people. Even in normally staid, traditionally conservative and religious Najd and Riyadh he was hailed by tens of thousands of hysterically cheering people who broke through the police cordons in their enthusiasm just to touch this Arab conquering hero. The people of Riyadh had never shown such enthusiasm for any Saudi leader, not even Ibn Saud when he returned from his many military successes. Saud and those around him were both delighted and alarmed. For the republican Nasser to be given such a reception by their own subjects was clearly symptomatic of the growing unpopularity of the royal family and a clear sign that the tide of republican Arab nationalism that had been sweeping across the Middle East had made deep inroads into Saudi Arabia.

Days after returning to Egypt Nasser, in a two-hour speech to a vast crowd in Alexandria, announced his intention to nationalise the Suez Canal in order to finance the building of a huge dam, irrigation and hydro-electric power project in the Nile Valley at Aswan. A few months later, Britain and France, in secret collusion with Israel, invaded the Suez Canal Zone in an attempt to regain control of the Canal. King Saud immediately declared his support for Egypt, made Saudi airfields available for use by Egyptian warplanes, announced his readiness to help Egypt with military assistance, broke off diplomatic relations with Britain and France and, despite it damaging his already desperate finances, imposed an embargo on exports of Saudi oil to them. America refused to support Britain and France, interpreting their action as a piece of naked old-style colonialism. As a result Britain and France were forced into a humiliating withdrawal of their troops. Hailed around the Arab world as a new Arab hero, Nasser's popularity with the Arab masses soared, in Saudi Arabia no less than anywhere else.

Yet in spite of repeated protestations by the leaders of both countries of friendship between Egypt and Saudi Arabia, plus Nasser's continuing need of Saudi oil and financial support, Nasser continued to allow his radio stations to pour out material hostile to Saudi Arabia and to highlight stories of corruption, profligacy and sinful goings-on among members of the Saudi royal family. The result was to heighten discontent inside Saudi Arabia and with Saud and the royal family in particular. Two fresh plots by Saudi army officers against the royal family were uncovered during 1956 and another came to light early in 1958. All led to executions. The loyalty of the Saudi army was now in serious question.

Early in March 1958 Nasser revealed details of an alleged plot, masterminded according to the Egyptians by King Saud and his closest advisers, to assassinate him and derail the recently announced union between Egypt and Syria. So great was Nasser's popularity inside Saudi Arabia by this time that members of the royal family feared the revelation might lead to a full-scale popular insurrection. So, already alarmed by Saud's mishandling of the nation's finances, resentful of his increasingly autocratic rule and reliance on a small circle of his cronies and young, inexperienced sons, members of the Saudi royal family who were outside Saud's closed circle turned to the family's one acknowledged elder statesman, the one person with sufficient authority both to command the respect of other royal princes and admonish the King himself. That elder stateman was Ibn Saud's younger brother, Abdullah, the brother to whom he had given the Rolls-Royce sent to him by Churchill after Ibn Saud had noticed that it had right hand drive.

Over four days during the Ramadan fast in March 1958 Abdullah convened a series of private meetings in his palace with all the surviving sons of Ibn Saud, except for Saud and Faisal, the most important religious leaders and tribal shaikhs. By the end of their deliberations they had reached a clear decision: Adbullah was to call upon the King and demand that he abdicate in favour of his brother Faisal. Faisal was at that moment away from Riyadh in camp out in the desert convalescing after a major operation for a non-malignant stomach cancer. So Prince Talal, the leading liberal among the royal princes, was dispatched to find Faisal and summon him urgently back to Riyadh.

But when Faisal returned to Riyadh and the royal princes told him of their decision he demurred. Mindful of the advice given to him and Saud by their father on his deathbed and of the solemn promise that they had made their father, he told them that although he was willing to take over day-to-day responsibility for all the Kingdom's foreign and domestic affairs Saud must remain King with the right to play a major role in government. In making this condition Faisal, in addition to honouring the promise he had made to his dying father, was aware that Saud still retained considerable support among traditionalists and the religious and tribal leaders and that if he was to reform the government and repair the Kingdom's battered finances he would need to avoid antagonising the traditionalists or causing an open split within the royal family.

Later that same day Faisal and his uncle, Abdullah, with ten of the other royal princes, went to see Saud in his palace. When all were seated, with the elderly Abdullah on one side of Saud and Faisal on the other, and when all Saud's guards and other courtiers had left the room, Ibn

Saud's son Prince Fahd, looking around all the others to include them in what he was about to say, said to King Saud: 'We have sworn to save you and in doing so to save ourselves and the Kingdom.'

Bewildered by this gnomic statement, Saud turned to his uncle and brother Faisal for an explanation. But they said nothing. Then, after a short, uneasy silence, he turned to the others: 'What do you want me to do?'

Then Muhammad, the eldest of the brothers after Saud and Faisal, speaking for them all, said, 'We decided to demand your abdication, but your brother Faisal opposed the idea and said that you should remain King. We have accepted what he said, but on one condition – you hand over all your powers to Faisal.'

There was a barely perceptible pause, then Saud said quietly, 'I accept.'

The tension evaporated at once. Over the next hour the princes together drew up a decree, Saud signed it and later that evening a formal broadcast of solemn Ramadan readings from the Qur'an was interrupted by an announcer who informed the country that King Saud, although he would remain King, was handing over the day-to-day government of the Kingdom to his brother, Crown Prince Faisal.[3]

Deeply embittered for the rest of his life, Saud died in exile in Greece eleven years later. Until the end he continued spending just as he had while he occupied the throne. In the last year of his life alone, it was estimated that by his lavish spending and profligate lifestyle he added no less than 1 per cent to the annual foreign currency earnings of the Greek economy.[4]

Laurence Grafftey-Smith, the British diplomat who had known both Saud and Faisal since they were young men, has left a description of the two eldest royal princes as they had been a few years before Ibn Saud's death. Saud he said, having always lived 'rather dimly' in the shadow of his overwhelming father, was himself 'something of a shadow of Ibn

3 The conversation between the royal princes and King Saud is based on accounts of and quotations from the conversation included in De Gaury, *Faisal*, op. cit., Alexander Bligh, *From Prince to King: Royal Succession in the House of Saud in the Twentieth Century*, New York University Press, 1984, and others.

4 See Lacey, Robert, op. cit.

Saud, such as a flickering lamp might throw on a wall: as tall or taller, as large or larger, with blurred edges of outline and no clear angles; fleshily soft and insecure'. Faisal on the other hand, according to Grafftey-Smith was 'a very different man, fine-drawn and cautious; his hawk-face sardonic with a twist of constant pain [who displayed] a refreshing common-sense and tolerance (within limits), and an unfailing courtesy'.[5]

Ever since his first visit to Britain and Europe as a thirteen-year-old in the autumn and winter of 1919, Faisal had spent a lot of his time handling foreign assignments for his father. He was, therefore, a great deal more open to modern liberal ideas and methods of government than his brother Saud. Now, vested with the full powers of government, he started applying that knowledge to dealing with the array of major problems that beset Saudi Arabia. Just three weeks after taking over he made a major broadcast on foreign policy. Expressing his desire for friendly relations with all states not hostile towards Saudi Arabia, he said he intended to pursue a policy of positive neutrality, not joining any military bloc. Referring to the principles of the United Nations and Islamic law, he immediately set about repairing Saudi Arabia's relations with other countries, notably Britain and France.

Years later Faisal would say that if he had known the full depth of Saudi Arabia's financial problems beforehand he would probably never have accepted the job of running the country. On taking over he found that the Kingdom was broke, the Treasury absolutely empty and capital was fleeing the country at a truly alarming rate. $100 million was owed by the Treasury to local banks and merchants, one bank was on the point of becoming insolvent and the value of the Saudi rial against other currencies had collapsed. He immediately instituted new banking rules, brought in a proper, balanced national budget for the first time and over the next six years progressively slashed royal expenditure by two thirds. At the same time he progressively increased expenditure on education, health, major infrastructure projects and industrial development. The import of all non-essential goods was prohibited and vigorous steps taken to reduce corruption and extravagance among members of the royal family and government servants. Faisal himself led by example. He

5 Grafftey-Smith, Laurence, *Bright Levant*, John Murray, London, 1970.

had always lived modestly by comparison with Saud and he now cut his expenditure still further. Unlike Saud, with his enormous new palace surrounded by high walls, lavish gardens, private mosque and long tamarisk-tree-lined drive, Faisal lived in a relatively modest house that faced onto a Riyadh street. He often drove himself into his office in the mornings and dispensed with the huge escorts of soldiers, guards and motor cycle outriders that had accompanied Saud's motorcade wherever he went.

Within a year the Saudi rial had been stabilised and was on the way to becoming one of the most reliable currencies in the world. Within two years restrictions on imports began to be eased and, despite ups and downs, within five years the national budget had been brought back into balance.

Of course not everyone was pleased with Faisal's reforms. There were those whose opportunities to make huge sums out of royal contracts and corruption had been curtailed and princes whose peculations had been curbed. There were traditional tribal leaders and conservative *ulema* who condemned the liberal reforms of Faisal in areas such as education as deviations from the true path of Islam and there were some princes, such as Faisal's thirty-year-old younger brother Talal, who had spent a lot of time in Egypt, who were dismayed that Faisal was not going further and converting the Kingdom into a full, democratic, constitutional monarchy, committed to Arab nationalism and even a degree of socialism. To people such as Talal, Faisal's reforms amounted to no more than an attempt to make the regime of the Al Sauds more secure. This group, who became known as The Free Princes and of whom Talal was the most prominent, Faisal attempted to buy off by giving some of them important jobs in the Government.

In 1960, with the economy repaired and much of the opposition silenced or out-manoeuvred, Faisal began strengthening the powers of central government and enlarging its responsibilities while at the same time reducing the powers and functions of the traditional, more conservative and narrow-mindedly religious leaders. All cabinet posts, except the ministries of religious and foreign affairs and the department responsible for the country's security, were entrusted to commoners. Faisal's drive to modernise and develop the Kingdom, improve welfare and health services for his subjects, develop the nation's infrastructure, agriculture and industry, overhaul and make more efficient the central state and regional government administration required the recruitment of an army of foreign trained technicians, instructors, teachers, medical staff, administrators and experts of all kinds. The result was that in a space of just a few years expatriate foreigners came to make up about 20 per cent of the total Saudi population and no less than one third of the country's workforce. It was not only highly skilled and trained expatriate professionals and technicians who flooded into the country, but also unskilled or semi-skilled workers, mostly from neighbouring Arab and Muslim countries, to fill the jobs that Saudis could not or would not do. In some urban areas expatriates came to account for more than a third of the population.

As well as importing the labour and expertise he needed to fulfil his ambitious development programme, Faisal instituted a further massive increase in education and training. By the mid-1970s one million Saudis, 20 per cent of the population, were in some form of education in addition to the traditional Islamic and Qur'anic studies. Twenty-five thousand Saudi students were studying at Saudi universities and another five thousand were studying abroad.

Many of the development programmes put in hand by Faisal achieved impressive results. The number of companies, approximately 80 per cent of them entirely Saudi owned, operating in the country tripled over a ten year period from the mid-1970s to the mid-1980s while their value multiplied almost thirty-fold. In the twenty-year period from 1970 agricultural production made similar advances, the production of fruit and vegetables quintupling, dairy products quadrupling and poultry meat production increasing more than thirty-fold. The result was that by the end of the 1980s Saudi Arabia was to be in a position not only to meet its domestic demand but to make exports to neighbouring countries and even to countries in western Europe – a transformation that would have seemed impossible in Ibn Saud's lifetime.

However, such rapid social and demographic changes were bound to cause tensions, especially in a society which had been shut off from the outside world for most of its previous history and where the social and religious order had remained virtually unchanged for well over a thousand years. At the same time as foreign labour was flowing into the Kingdom Saudis, sometimes with their families and sometimes without, were moving in huge numbers into the bigger, developing towns from the oases, deserts and villages. The result was escalating social, housing and public health problems and unemployment. At the same time those who had been displaced from lucrative positions by Faisal's drive to modernise and those who believed that the changes and influx of foreigners and outside influences threatened to undermine the Kingdom's traditional moral and religious values started to resist. In 1965 when Faisal authorised the start of a television service the first broadcasts were greeted with violent riots in Riyadh instigated by conservative Wahhabi clerics and those who believed that by broadcasting moving images of people, television contravened the Islamic injunction against graven images. One of the leaders of the demonstrations was Khalid, the religious zealot son of one of Faisal's own younger brothers, Musaid. When Khalid, at the head of a mob, turned up outside the TV station intending to stop the broadcasts, he and his followers were met by a body of armed policemen. Fighting broke out and shots were exchanged. Khalid and his mother were both killed by police rifle shots. The opposition to television only abated when some clerics started to see that, as earlier with radio, television could be utilised to promote the values and teachings of Islam.

Meanwhile fresh trouble was looming on Saudi Arabia's borders. Jewish immigration into Israel had continued, displacing more and more Arabs and putting ever more pressure on those who remained. In response Palestinian resistance organisations inside Israel and in neighbouring countries, especially Egypt, Syria and Iraq, mounted a growing number of attacks. With tensions growing between Israel and its neighbours, on June 5th 1967 Israel launched simultaneous bombing raids on airfields in Jordan, Syria and Egypt, followed by ground assaults. Their purpose, in the words of Israel's Defence Minister Moshe Dayan, was 'to demonstrate to the Arabs that Israel could stand up for itself' and was no longer an 'imperialist implant' but 'a lasting deed'.[6]

After six days of fierce fighting and sweeping Israeli advances the war

6 Dayan, Moshe, *Moshe Dayan, The Story of My Life*, Morrow, New York, 1976.

ended. By then Israel had seized all of the predominantly Arab old city of Jerusalem, including the Temple Mount, the one remaining wall of the original Jewish Temple of King Solomon – The Wailing Wall – at the base of the Mount and the two holy Islamic sites on top of it – the Al Aqsa Mosque and The Dome of the Rock, built more than a thousand years earlier to house the rock from which Muhammad was reputed to have begun his visionary night flight to heaven. Israel had also seized all the Jordanian territory on the West Bank right down to the River Jordan, driving the Jordanian army, and with it thousands of new Palestinian refugees, over the river on to the East bank and back into what remained of Jordan. Israel had also captured the Golan Heights in south-eastern Syria and taken all of the Sinai desert right up to the banks of the Suez Canal and down to Eilat and the Gulf of Aqaba at the north-eastern end of the Red Sea. By these advances Israel had trebled the area of land it held. It was an astonishing victory, hugely boosting the self-esteem and military arrogance of the Israelis and inflicting an extremely deep humiliation upon the Arabs. Unlike US President Eisenhower, who after the 1956 Suez Canal war had put pressure on the Israelis and made them withdraw from the banks of the Suez Canal and Sinai, President Johnson, heavily under the influence of American pro-Israeli lobbyists, allowed the Israelis to retain the territory they had seized. In doing so he removed any last remaining doubts in Arabs' minds about whose side the Americans were on in the Middle East. At the same time he undermined one of the fundamental founding principles of the UN Charter, that conquest was not to be allowed as a means of settling disputes and that no nation should be allowed to gain territory from another through aggression.

The Six Day War and the American, and to a lesser extent European nations', support for Israel provoked massive anti-American and anti-Western demonstrations in many regions of Saudi Arabia, especially in Riyadh, the Hijaz and the oil-producing districts of the Eastern Province. There were attacks on the US airbase and US consulate in Dhahran, sabotage attacks on oil installations and at several points along the major trans-Arabian oil pipeline carrying oil from Dhahran in the east across to the Mediterranean. Saudi Arabian oil production was brought to a halt for a whole week.

King Faisal, who saw it as his duty to protect Islam's Holy Places and whose country's constitution was proclaimed to be the Qur'an, felt the humiliation inflicted upon the Arabs by the Six Day War, and especially the Israelis' seizure of the old city of Jerusalem and the Dome of the Rock, particularly deeply. To him it became a personal challenge. It greatly strengthened his enmity towards Israel and left him with a determination that Islam's Holy Places in Jerusalem must be regained.

The 1967 Six Day War was a watershed in other even more significant ways. As a result of the War what had been a local Middle Eastern problem became an international problem affecting the major powers and all the other countries which identified with the Arabs or Israelis. The Heads of the Arab states, meeting in Khartoum three months after the War, agreed that there would be no recognition of the Israeli conquests and no negotiations. In November 1967, after much wrangling, the United Nations adopted Resolution 242 calling for 'a just and lasting peace in the Middle East ... withdrawal of Israeli armed forces from the territories occupied in the recent conflict' and the 'acknowledgement of the sovereignty, territorial integrity and political independence of every State in the area and their rights to live in peace within secure and recognised boundaries free from threats or acts of force' and for a 'just settlement of the refugee problem'.[7] The War induced a new determination among the Palestinians that their future fate was now in their own hands and provoked a new wave of terrorist attacks on Israel, Israelis and Israeli interests both inside Israel and beyond. The War provoked an upsurge in anti-American and anti-imperialist activity, plots and attempted coups throughout the region, led by both pro-Marxist, Arab nationalist and Ba'athist groups.

Inside Saudi Arabia itself there was a fresh wave of plots and attempted coups, not only by groups inspired by Marxist and Arab nationalist movements which flourished elsewhere in the region, but also by educated Saudi technocrats and air force pilots. The Saudi authorities responded by greatly expanding their military and security forces and by conducting a series of purges, led by Faisal's younger brothers, Prince Abdullah, commander of the National Guard, and Prince Sultan, the Minister of Defence.

7 UN Security Council Resolution 242, November 22nd 1967.

Threatened from the south by new revolutionary Marxist governments in South Yemen and Aden, by an increasingly successful Marxist guerrilla insurgency in the eastern, Dhofar region of Oman led by PFLOAG (the Popular Front for the Liberation of the Occupied Arab Gulf), by the appearance of a Russian naval flotilla in the Arabian Sea, by the Iranian seizure of strategically vital islands in the Straits of Hormuz at the entrance to the Gulf, and by Ba'athist regimes in Iraq and Syria, Faisal turned to the USA and Europe for help. In a move aimed at massively strengthening his military capability he signed huge arms deals and brought in lots of military pilots and instructors to train young Saudis.

Faisal had repeatedly promised to form a National Consultative Assembly but throughout the early 1970s had repeatedly deferred setting it up. Despite having greatly expanded the government and increased the number of government ministers, he continued to take all the really important decisions himself and to interfere whenever he thought fit in the decisions of his ministers. Although he had brought in reforms, liberalised in a lot of areas and greatly increased the levels of education and welfare, he had at the same time publicly sought a renewed 'Islamic authenticity'. So at the same time as expanding practical and conventional education, he had also greatly expanded religious education. While modernising, Faisal continued to rule in essentially the same paternalistic style and tradition as his father, opposing any genuine democratisation. In clinging to Arabia's paternalistic, Islamic and traditional welfare system and style of government Faisal claimed to be saving the country from the woes of both 'corrupt material Western democracy' and of 'atheistic Communism'. He countered the demands of those who demanded faster progress towards social equality by telling them that: 'True socialism is the Arab socialism laid down by the Qur'an.'[8]

Although increasingly dependent on American arms, as the 1970s advanced Faisal increased his pressure on the United States to make the Israelis more amenable to a just and lasting settlement of the Palestinian problem. In the summer of 1973 Faisal warned Aramco that he would freeze oil production unless the USA changed its policy towards Israel. He indicated that in the event of a fresh outbreak of hostilities between

8 De Gaury, *Faisal: King of Saudi Arabia*, Arthur Baker, London, 1966.

Egypt and Israel, Saudi Arabia would support Egypt. However, the American National Security Advisor, who was shortly to become Secretary of State, Henry Kissinger (a strong supporter of Israel whose own parents had fled Nazi Germany shortly before the Second World War), responded by secretly agreeing contingency plans with the Shah of Iran. Apparently with President Nixon's full knowledge and support, Kissinger and the Shah agreed that in the event of serious instability or a radical takeover in Saudi Arabia they would jointly seize control of the Kingdom and its oil installations. Kissinger was firmly of the view that 'backward' nations, like Saudi Arabia, must not be allowed to hold 'the industrialised West hostage by threatening to restrict oil supplies'.[9] So when that autumn Saudi Arabia again called on America to put pressure on Israel to implement UN Resolution 242 and withdraw from the occupied territories the Nixon administration did nothing. Remembering earlier Saudi threats to oil supplies in 1956 and 1967 that had come to nothing, they did not take the Saudi warning seriously.

At 2 p.m. on Saturday, October 6th 1973, Yom Kippur, the holiest day in the Jewish calendar, the Egyptian army launched one of the heaviest artillery barrages in modern history along the entire one-hundred-mile length of the Suez Canal. Almost 200 artillery shells per second rained down on Israeli army positions. Simultaneously Syrian artillery began a barrage against Israeli army units dug in on the Golan Heights and Egyptian planes bombed Israeli airfields. By the fourth day of the attack the Egyptian army was across the Suez Canal and advancing through the Sinai desert, Israel had lost five hundred tanks, fifty military aircraft, was suffering heavy casualties and her commanders believed their country was in danger of defeat. Golda Meir, Israel's Prime Minister, put Israel's nuclear forces on immediate standby to attack Egypt or Syria.

On the day after the start of the attack Henry Kissinger, who was now the US Secretary of State, sent King Faisal a telegram calling on him to persuade Egypt and Syria to halt their assault. But Faisal responded that he supported Egypt and Syria and instead called on Kissinger and

9 See Patrick Tyler, *A World of Trouble: America in the Middle East*, Portobello Books, London, 2009.

Nixon to put pressure on Israel to withdraw from the territories they had seized in 1967. Five days after that Faisal sent Saudi troops to fight alongside the Syrians attacking the Golan Heights and followed this up by leading a move by ten Arab oil-producing states to reduce oil production by at least 5 per cent every month until the conflict in the Middle East was resolved. Saudi Arabia and Kuwait went even further, immediately reducing their oil production by 10 per cent. But ignoring the Arab oil producers' action, the Americans organised an 'air bridge' and began supplying the Israelis with large quantities of arms of all kinds. By this move the Americans had finally abandoned all semblance of neutrality and were now openly supporting the Israelis But uncowed, the Arab oil producers responded by upping the stakes still further. They completely cut off all oil supplies to the USA and the Netherlands (Holland had also adopted a strongly pro-Israeli policy). The Arabs reinforced the freeze on oil supplies to America by placing an embargo on supplies of oil to any processing plant that normally sold its products to the USA. Simultaneously the oil producers also raised the price of crude oil by 70 per cent and, when that did not produce an immediate result, doubled the new increased price.

By now the Russians were threatening to intervene on the Arab side. So finally, three weeks after the war had begun, after high-level talks between the United States and the Soviet Union plus an emergency resolution in the UN Security Council calling on both sides to end all hostilities immediately, a halt to the fighting was agreed. However, by the time the resolution actually came into effect and the shooting finally stopped, six days after the passing of the UN resolution, the Israelis had inflicted heavy losses on the Syrians and not only regained most of the ground they had lost in the Golan Heights but actually extended it. The Israeli army had also regained the majority of the ground it had lost in Sinai and established a substantial bridgehead on the western side of the Suez Canal towards its southern end. However, elsewhere along the Canal Egypt had regained and now held long strips of the land it had lost in 1967 on the eastern side of the Canal. So, unlike in the 1967 war, the Arabs had this time achieved considerable military successes and had definitely not been humiliated. Their battered pride had been restored. In contrast the Israelis, although they had repulsed the Arab assault and demonstrated that they could not be defeated militarily, had received a shock. The result was that they would never again allow themselves to be left so unprepared.

The chief effect of the war, however, was the way in which it changed the relations of the two superpowers with the Middle East. The war had shown that, while the Americans would always ensure that Israel could not be destroyed, the Russians had shown that they would not allow their Arab allies, Egypt and Syria, to be defeated either. The result was to draw both great powers even more deeply into the affairs of the region. At the same time the war had demonstrated to the Israelis that, no matter how resolute an American president might plan to be about imposing a solution to the Palestinian issue upon the Israelis or forcing them to make concessions, co-ordinated action by the Israeli lobby in Congress could always be relied upon to deflect that US president from those intentions.

As a result of Faisal's resolute action, his popularity and authority both inside Saudi Arabia and among the more conservative Arab states was greatly increased. The use of the 'oil weapon' had swiftly produced the desired result for the Arabs. Within days of the war ending the EEC countries and Japan had announced that they were in favour of the implementation of UN Security Council Resolution 242 in full and of the withdrawal of Israel from the territories it had occupied during the 1967 war. In December the Arab oil-producing countries decided to resume supplies to all the European countries which had adopted a favourable attitude towards the Arab nations. But the embargos against the USA and the Netherlands continued. However, in March 1974, at Saudi Arabia's insistence, the embargo against the US was also lifted. The unpalatable fact for the Saudis was that, as Faisal knew full well, Saudi Arabia was dependent on the USA both for its economic development and for its military defence. It was a dependence that was to lead to escalating trouble with the Islamic conservatives and the substantial anti-Western elements within the Saudi population.

The other striking effect of the oil embargo and price hikes was the massive increase in Saudi Arabia's income, which by January 1974 had multiplied five-fold in just one year. The result was that all of Faisal's development programmes and his procurements of arms and military know-how could now proceed unchecked. As a consequence the volume of mismanagement, more or less blatant fraud, greed and bribery among the Saudi elite also grew virtually unchecked and Saudi Arabia acquired a reputation for greed and bribery unrivalled in the outside world.

But Islamic-fundamentalist nemesis was already waiting for Faisal and it came from an unexpected direction. On the morning of March 25th 1975 Faisal was receiving guests at his *majlis* in the royal palace in Riyadh at a ceremony to mark a religious festival. One of those lining up to congratulate the King was a namesake, Prince Faisal ibn Musaid, a brother of Prince Khalid ibn Musaid, the protestor shot by the police ten years earlier during the demonstrations against the start of the Saudi television service. As the King bent down to kiss him the young prince drew a small pistol from his robe and shot King Faisal three times in the head at point-blank range, shouting that he was doing it to avenge the death of his brother. The King, bleeding profusely, was rushed to hospital but died shortly afterwards.[10]

Khalid, Ibn Saud's seventh son and Faisal's named heir, became King by the unanimous agreement of the other royal princes in an untroubled transfer of power. Muhammad, the one surviving son of Ibn Saud who was older than Khalid, had years before voluntarily given up all interest in the succession. Ibn Saud's eleventh son Fahd was named as Khalid's heir and his younger brother Abdullah second deputy prime minister. Two other surviving sons of Ibn Saud, both older than Fahd, had also renounced any interest in the throne.

The Kingdom which Ibn Saud had created had now survived three changes of monarch in the twenty-two years since his death. Saudi Arabia had managed each of these changes of ruler with apparent ease, at a time when other monarchies all over the Arab world had been crashing and giving way to various kinds of republics. Furthermore,

10 There have been a range of speculations about Musaid's motive for shooting King Faisal ranging from it being part of a CIA plot in revenge for the oil embargo, it having to do with the fact that the assassin was engaged to a daughter of one of the Rashids or that the assassin was mentally unstable. However, the motive ascribed to his crime at the time (namely that he was doing it in revenge for the death of his brother – making it in effect an act in an ongoing old-fashioned blood feud) seems the most probable.

Saudi Arabia had so far relatively easily withstood the successful rise elsewhere in the Middle East of a whole range of different forms of militancy, of Arab nationalism, Islamic fundamentalism and Marxism. On top of which, following the huge rise in its oil revenues, Faisal's championing of liberalising reforms and a whole range of development programmes, the country now seemed securely set on course to make its successful entry into the modern world in a condition of unrivalled prosperity.

However, the new king, Khalid, was soon beset with a host of problems and Saudis soon came to look back on Faisal's reign as a golden age. Khalid was Ibn Saud's eldest son by his favourite wife Jauhara, the wife whose love had so inspired Ibn Saud before his successful assault on Hofuf in 1913. He was sixty-three years old and by the time he ascended the throne in March 1975 already in ill-health. In a little-publicised move, two months after becoming King he handed full responsibility for the day-to-day running of the Kingdom to his nominated successor Prince Fahd, while retaining to himself ultimate authority for all major decisions. The effect of this decision was that while Khalid reigned, it was Fahd who ruled. Khalid meanwhile became the patient, kindly face of the Saudi regime. Like Faisal, he lived unostentatiously and seemed happiest when out in the desert amongst the Bedouin. Like his father, he received hundreds of his subjects in his *majlis* every day, listening to their problems, rectifying wrongs, dispensing judgement and feeding them.

Khalid's policy as ruler, implemented by Fahd, was to continue and accelerate still further Faisal's development and welfare programmes, while at the same time endeavouring to placate the religious and more conservative elements in Saudi society. Later, as these plans started to come to fruition, the emphasis shifted towards making the country even more self-sufficient in agriculture and towards developing industries which could supplement the income from oil in preparation for a time when the country's oil reserves became seriously depleted.

In spite of Faisal's education drive, the country was still desperately short of skilled manpower to realise all these new plans. Even those Saudi men who were not illiterate mostly had little or no knowledge of science, mathematics or technical subjects. The labour shortage was exacerbated by many Saudis' refusal to do labouring and unskilled jobs. This was more than the product of Saudi pride, real though that was. Nor was it primarily the result of the Government's generous welfare system, which provided free education and health care for all, generous financial assistance for widows, the poor, needy, aged and infirm, and help with housing and the purchase of items such as motor cars.

The roots of many Saudis' refusal to take up the abundant less-skilled jobs that were available lay in something deeper than either pride or laziness. The pure desert Arab, especially the Bedouin, had always regarded his way of life as far superior to any other. To people who for millennia had depended for their very survival on the community, the tribe and their extended family, the concepts and values embodied in 'the protestant work ethic' were completely alien. The pursuit of personal self-advancement, maximisation of wages, even 'wages' themselves, and individual competition in the workplace had no place in their lives. These were people for whom sharing, hospitality, celebration of the achievement or good fortune with other members of the tribe and extended family were, with their religion, the highest values and pinnacles of life. For such people, accustomed and conditioned for generations to living from day to day off what the desert, providence or Allah might provide, to driving animals in accordance with the dictates of the changing seasons, to tracking and reading the vagaries of the landscape and skies, the routines, regular time-keeping and demands of the workplace, office or construction site made little sense. For people who so often thought and spoke in imagery and poetry, who had always gloried in the sound of words as much or more than in their precise meaning, for whom the sheer beauty and sound of the original Arabic words and language of their sacred text, the Holy Qur'an, were an essential element of its power, things such as commercial or employment contracts and legal agreements, let alone development or business plans, or worse, 'the language of business' and the ghastly linguistic contortions of 'management-speak' or the management school, were simply so much meaningless imported gibberish.

The early years of Khalid's kingship marked perhaps the period of the country's greatest development chaos and financial waste. Both resulted from too much development being attempted too fast by too many different enterprises with too little co-ordination and too few honest, adequately trained and experienced people running them. The scenes in Saudi Arabia at this time were similar to scenes in other suddenly rich oil-producing Arab countries, only more so because Saudi Arabia was both bigger and richer and even less developed than others. Sandra Mackey, the political scientist and journalist wife of an American doctor working in Riyadh, has left a series of graphic descriptions of Saudi Arabia in this period.[11] She describes the thousands of foreign businessmen, 'con artists and hucksters' who poured into a Riyadh that was totally unprepared for the onslaught 'to solicit every Saudi who could read as a business partner'. She described the daily and nightly scenes in the one and only hotel in Riyadh that 'could be called habitable'. Situated in a narrow street between the town and the airport, bookings were effectively meaningless: 'It was essentially first come, first served. Bribery helped, of course, but even if a room were obtained, it still meant sharing it with three other men. The lobby was like a pilgrims' rest, as exhausted businessmen from a dozen different countries sprawled on the sparse furniture or stretched out on the floor, their luggage spread around them defining their space.' There they tried to grab some much-needed sleep or huddled in small groups with others in the hallways and the toilets 'plotting strategies to win contracts or cut the price of the Saudi "agent" or middleman'.[12]

Getting around was near impossible. There was no public transport. Although there were taxis their drivers were so reckless and inept that to use them was to risk life and limb. Rental cars did not exist. So to get around many businessmen, even though they might be staying for only a few days or weeks, were compelled to buy a car if, by any chance, they could find one. Even then the roads were often impassable in anything

11 Sandra Mackey, *The Saudis: Inside the Desert Kingdom*, W. W. Norton, New York, 2002. (Although the original edition of Mackey's book was not published until 1987, she first arrived in Saudi Arabia in May 1978 and started writing the articles on which it is largely based shortly afterwards under a series of pen names, necessary because of Saudi censorship and restrictions on women.)

12 M.D. experienced similar scenes in the same period in a smaller but at that time still equally wild and untouched Arab country just across the border to the south, Oman.

other than a four-wheel drive. This applied even to the main highway between the capital and the centre of the country's wealth, Dhahran. As a result foreign businessmen (business women were, of course, still out of the question in Saudi Arabia) were forced to try their luck with Saudia, the country's national airline which ran commuter services between Riyadh, Jeddah and Dhahran. But that, like the hotels, was overbooked and chaotic. A final alternative way of getting from Riyadh to Dhahran was by the by now wheezing and dilapidated railway. That, however, entailed a twenty-five-mile journey south to al-Kharj to catch the train and then eight hours of jolting trundle through the arid countryside. The advantage of the train journey, if the businessman could endure the heat and discomfort, was that he could see some of the still-striking Arabian landscape.

The rapid influx of people into the towns from the rural and desert areas as well as from overseas – the population of Riyadh had more than quadrupled in the preceding ten years – had resulted in serious housing shortages and led to the introduction of a massive domestic housing programme to add to the legion of hugely ambitious infrastructure projects. These problems were exacerbated still further by Saudi Arabia's rapidly accelerating birth-rate and fall in infant mortality due to improved health and maternity services.

Because of the sheer volume of construction work, the shoddy workmanship, harsh climate and corrupt and dishonest practices of some of the businessmen responsible for the work, the average life of a new building put up in the 1970s was said to be only seven years, after which it had to be demolished and a new one put up in its place.

The chaos and confusion that resulted from so much rapid change and the continuing inherent contradictions present throughout Saudi society became apparent to anyone entering the country from almost the moment they landed at Riyadh airport. On leaving the plane the passengers, mostly westerners but also a few better-off middle- and professional-class Saudis, were herded down the steps into waiting buses clutching their hand baggage and the women gathering up their long, unfamiliar, billowing skirts in order not to trip. Having been driven the short distance to the one small terminal building, distinguishable only by a light on top of it, they were thrust straight into the confusion and noise of the tiny, ill-organised airport arrival hall. Having retrieved their luggage from the pushing, shouting scrum around the one conveyor belt, passengers queued for hours in the minute customs hall while three abusive Saudi customs officers went through every passenger's luggage piece by piece, hurling out not only clearly forbidden items such as pork, alcohol or pornography, but a wide range of books, especially those about Western art containing pictures of people by painters such as Leonardo da Vinci and Botticelli. Reproductions or photographs of the *Venus Di Milo*, *David* and even the *Mona Lisa* were confiscated. On her arrival Sandra Mackey watched as one family who had tried to bring an artificial Christmas tree and decorations into the country had the Christmas tree confiscated, the decorations dropped one by one on to the floor and ground under his foot by the customs official. Little girls arriving in Saudi Arabia with their parents would have to watch in mounting distress as favourite dolls were torn limb from limb by customs men who regarded them as idols. Mackey concluded that the Saudis, both the people and their leaders, were labouring under the delusion 'that they could buy the physical development that they wanted without disturbing the stability of their traditional society'.

Yet for all the Saudi authorities' draconian safeguards, both in the customs hall at the airport with its hunt for alcohol, pornography and graven images, and its draconian efforts at censorship across all reaches of the realm against insidious, blasphemous and seditious ideas, the 'dangerous influences' still made their way across the borders and through the airwaves into the Kingdom. They entered not only from the heretic Christian West and godless Communist East, but from much nearer to home in the Middle East. These influences from closer to home were soon to endanger the health of the Saudi regime and the Kingdom's traditional social order more than the spread among the population of either the West's materialism or its lax morals.

The same power which Ibn Saud and his successors had for so long harnessed to unify the Kingdom, bind their subjects to them and check the influence of seditious ideas: fundamentalist Wahhabism, the *ulema* and the clerics, was to prove the source of a succession of challenges. Saudi Wahhabism was by its nature conservative and some of its older and most senior figures sometimes ridiculously so. In the 1960s, centuries after men had first circumnavigated the world, decades after aircraft had begun routinely circling it and years after satellites had gone into orbit around it, one of the Kingdom's most revered religious scholars and Islamic judges, Abdul Aziz bin Baz, Grand Mufti and Head of the Council of *Ulema* since 1962, had ruled that the sun revolves around the earth, rather than the earth around the sun, and that the earth was flat. Writing on what he saw as a heresy about the solar system being taught in Riyadh University, bin Baz had said: 'I say the Holy *Qur'an*, the Prophet's teaching, the majority of Islamic scientists, and the actual fact prove that the sun is running in its orbit, as Almighty God ordained, and the earth is fixed and stable, spread out by God for his mankind and made a bed and cradle for them, fixed down firmly by mountains lest it shake.'[13]

Bin Baz epitomised the conservative pole of the schizophrenic delusion Sandra Mackey described the Saudis as living under. Orphaned as a boy and blind since his teens, Bin Baz had by his mid-twenties grown into a noted Islamic scholar and been appointed an Islamic judge in the Al Kharj region of Najd, south of Riyadh. He had first come to prominence in the 1940s when he had opposed Ibn Saud's employment of Americans to develop agriculture in the area. This bin Baz had condemned as being against the teachings of the Prophet and *shari'a*: 'The presence of infidels, male or female, poses a danger to Muslims, their beliefs, their morality, and their children's education.'[14] Angered, Ibn Saud had brought bin Baz to Riyadh and thrown him in jail for a short while. Then, having explained to bin Baz that such statements could undermine the Islamic foundations of the Wahhabi Saudi state and lay it open to the even greater dangers of atheism and Communism, Ibn Saud had co-opted bin Baz by progressively promoting and encouraging him as a conservative

13 See Holden, David, and Johns, Richard, *The House of Saud*, Holt, Rinehart & Winston, London, 1981, etc. Years later bin Baz claimed that he had been traduced by those who interpreted his words as meaning that he believed the earth was flat. However, according to one account it was not until 1985 that he accepted that the earth was round, and then only after one of the royal princes who had taken a trip aboard a satellite explained to him that he must be wrong because he had seen with his own eyes from the satellite that the earth was round.

14 Bin Baz quoted in Trofimov, Yaroslav, *The Siege of Mecca: The Forgotten Uprising*, Penguin, London, 2007

religious voice speaking with the authority of his Islamic learning in support of the ruling house of Al Saud. Bin Baz had, at the same time as supporting the Al Sauds, retained the respect of the most conservative and fundamentalist elements in the population by speaking out against the most blatant of the Al Sauds' sinful practices. He had condemned the hanging of royal portraits in official buildings, saying that they might lead to the worship of the picture or of the royal personage portrayed. He had attacked the existence of barbers shops and the practice of clapping because they aped western ways. Similarly, he had spoken out against Saudi men wearing western suits and condemned foreign travel. He hotly opposed even the smallest easing of the restrictions applied to women.

Appointed Deputy Rector and then Rector of the new Islamic University of Medina, bin Baz came to exert a powerful influence on successive generations of committed young Muslims, many of them also heavily influenced by the fundamentalist teachings of political Islamist movements such as the Muslim Brotherhood and other movements which called for 'a return to the pure values of Islam' as the heart of nations which should be governed by the principles of Islam and the *shari'a*. The Muslim Brothers recognised as legitimate only those rulers who, unlike the Saudi rulers, rejected all forms of foreign, non-Muslim domination or influence. Although Sayyid Qutb, the most articulate and outspoken of the leaders of the Muslim Brotherhood, had been executed by the Egyptian regime in 1966 because of his repeated calls for revolution, he continued to exert a powerful influence upon devout young Muslims across the whole of the Middle East.

Qutb's calls for 'the wiping of human kingship from the face of the earth' and the establishment in its place of the rule of God[15] appealed particularly to those students of bin Baz's who were discontented with the Saudi regime on account of its headlong embrace of Western morals and materialism or because they themselves were too poor to fully partake in such material advances. There were others who harboured generations-old grudges against the Al Sauds. One Islamic student and young cleric who attended bin Baz's question and answer sessions after

15 Sayyid Qutb, *Milestones*, quoted by Delong-Bas, Natana J. *Wahhabi Islam: From Revival and Reform to Global Jihad*, I. B. Tauris, London, 2004.

evening prayers in the mosque at Medina was the son of one of the warriors who had fought beside Ibn Bijad, the great Ikhwan leader and head of the Ataiba tribe who had risen in revolt against Ibn Saud in 1929. That young Islamic student and cleric was Juhayman Ataiba. Born seven years after the Battle of Sibilla, he had been named by his father Juhayman, meaning 'the scowler', because he seemed to grimace such a lot. During his childhood his father had brought up young Juhayman on heroic stories of the great Ikhwan revolt, of Ibn Saud's betrayal of the 'pure Islam' and of the indignities heaped upon his tribe. His father had drilled into young Juhayman the final words of the great Ikhwan warrior Ibn Bijad as the battle of Sibilla was drawing to its close in abject defeat: 'Never give up.'[16]

Events outside Saudi Arabia in the late 1970s conspired to inflame the passions of fundamentalist young men like Juhayman Ataiba to fever point. In November 1977, in an act that was seen by hardline Islamists across the Middle East as a betrayal, President Sadat of Egypt had flown to Israel at the urging of US President Jimmy Carter, met the Israeli leaders, visited the Temple Mount in Jerusalem, the holy site of the three great Abrahamic religions, prayed at the Al-Aqsa Mosque, paid his respects to the victims of the Holocaust at the Yad Vashem Memorial and laid a wreath on the tomb of Israel's Unknown Soldier. By these acts Sadat appeared to signal his willingness to recognise the legitimacy of the Israeli Zionist state. So although Sadat had aimed to achieve an eventual Middle East peace, the immediate result was an increase in tensions across the region and a spate of terrorist attacks by extremists.

At the same time a huge wave of demonstrations and strikes against the repressive, pro-Western regime of the Shah began sweeping across Iran. Their main inspiration was an exiled Muslim cleric and scholar, Ayatollah Khomeini, who accused the Shah of undermining the Islamic foundations of the Iranian state. Denouncing American and Western influence in the country, he called for the Shah's overthrow. As 1978 progressed the numbers of protestors on Iran's streets responding to Khomeini's call became so great that not even the combined might of the

16 See Trofimov, Yaroslav *The Siege of Mecca: The Forgotten Uprising*, Penguin Books, London, 2007.

Shah's army and his brutal, torturing secret police, Savak, could clear them and in January 1979 the Shah and his family fled the country. On February 2nd 1979 Ayatollah Khomeini returned to Tehran in triumph to be greeted as a national hero by millions of wildly cheering Iranians. After winning a national referendum by a landslide, Khomeini was appointed Iran's religious and political leader for life and the country was declared an Islamic republic ruled by *shari'a* law.

Meanwhile, in strictly Muslim Afghanistan a modestly modernising President Daoud, who had been attempting to improve relations with India and the West, was overthrown in a pro-Soviet coup. At the same time on the south-western border of Saudi Arabia itself the President of North Yemen was assassinated by a diplomat from Marxist South Yemen who set off a briefcase bomb in his office. Alarmed by these events and growing calls from Islamic fundamentalists all over the region to depose all Muslim monarchs and to cleanse Muslim lands of non-Muslims and Western influences, the Saudi royal family turned urgently to the Americans for military assistance. But President Carter, who was still trying to bring about a lasting peace between Israel and her Arab neighbours, was anxious not to upset either side. So while he agreed to the sale of some additional F-15 fighters to Saudi Arabia, he refused to offer anything beyond that.

Now fearful that their American allies were no longer to be relied upon, the Saudi regime started looking elsewhere for ways of bolstering its security. They gave financial and logistical assistance to other regimes in the Arab world who were fighting Islamists and Marxists and in 1979 began a major crackdown on groups throughout Saudi Arabia which were suspected of pro-Iranian, Islamist, Marxist, Arab nationalist, republican or other radical sympathies. Nevertheless, later that year anti-government leaflets began to appear, calling for everything from reform to the overthrow of the regime, the institution of an Islamic republic and the expulsion of all foreigners. Insurrections flared in the Hijaz and other tribal areas where members of the royal family had seized land. Yet even after this string of precursors of trouble, when the real blow landed the regime still appeared almost wholly unprepared.

Early in the morning of November 20th 1979 an event occurred which would transfix the whole Muslim world and shake the Saudi royal family to its very foundations. It was the first day of the Muslim year 1400. The Grand Mosque in Mecca was crowded with worshippers for the dawn prayer. Many of them had slept in the mosque overnight huddled up on the floor, some of them accompanying coffins bearing the bodies of relatives upon whom they hoped the imam would bestow a blessing of the kind that could only be obtained in such a sacred place. Just as the imam completed the dawn prayer with the sacred call for the blessing of peace, shots suddenly rang out from within the crowd. As the people turned in amazement and fear – to fire a weapon within the precincts of Islam's holiest site was a grave sin – gunmen brandishing automatic weapons and clad in the simple white robes of pilgrims, began to emerge from the edges of the crowd. More and more of them, all converging on the sacred *Ka'aba.* Members of the sacred mosque's own police force, who were armed only with sticks, rushed forward to intervene but were unceremoniously gunned down. Turning in panic towards the mosque's gates to flee, the tens of thousands of worshippers found that all the gates were barred, each one chained shut with groups of wild-haired, ruffian-looking, gun-wielding fanatics guarding them. Meanwhile yet more wild-eyed, ragged-haired, bearded men were unloading yet more guns from some of the coffins – coffins which they had carried into the mosque the night before under the pretence of being mourners.

Now a slender man with dark burning eyes, flowing black hair and a beard, his head bare and wearing the simple white robe of a pilgrim, appeared from deep among the shadows of the mosque. With an obvious air of authority and purpose he strode through the crowd, across the open marble-floored courtyard to the *Ka'aba.* He was Juhayman Ataiba, the son of the former Ikhwan warrior who had fought alongside Ibn Bijad at the battle of Sibilla in 1929, the one-time student who had attended lectures given by bin Baz. Over the intervening years Juhayman had turned into a fiery Islamic preacher and founded a small, militant, fundamentalist reform movement – The Movement of Muslim Revolutionaries of the Arabian Peninsula. Snatching the microphone from the elderly imam who had been conducting the dawn prayers, Juhayman barked a set of military orders to his followers, instructing them to immediately shoot down any government soldier or policeman who attempted to intervene. Then, with his voice booming over the

Grand Mosque's loudspeakers into every corner of the building and out from the loudspeakers at the top of the almost three-hundred-feet-tall minarets over the surrounding city of Mecca, Juhayman began to address the crowd. 'Mecca, Medina and Jeddah are all now in our hands', he told them. He and his fellow rebels had come to cleanse the Kingdom of materialism and corruption, to end the rule of the sinful and unjust Al Sauds, and to terminate the country's relations with 'infidel powers'. Then Juhayman handed the microphone to one of his fellow rebels. Addressing the crowd with obvious authority and in the cadences and tones of the classical Arabic of a learned Muslim scholar, this new speaker told them that the wicked ways of the House of Saud were a clear sign to all true believers that the world was coming to an end and that, in accordance with prophecy, Islam's final triumph over unbelief was at hand. The preacher listed a whole catalogue of sins and corruptions for which the Saudi state was responsible: the debauchery of many of those who ruled over them – the governor of Mecca, a brother of the present King, was singled out for special opprobrium; the corruption fuelled by television, the pollution of minds brought by infidel Westerners to the very cradle of Islam, the desecration of the moral purity of women caused by their employment, the pagan scourge of the newly introduced game of soccer, the fact that the royal family had become the mere pawns of infidel foreign powers.

All these things and many more rendered the Al Sauds no longer worthy to rule over true Muslims in the birthplace of Islam, the land of the Prophet Muhammad Himself. The people's oaths of allegiance to the Saudis were therefore no longer valid. They were null and void. But, he was proud to tell them, relief was now at hand! Citing relevant *Hadith* and other prophesies dating back to the centuries immediately after the Prophet Muhammad's death, the rebel preacher announced that the Mahdi had arrived and was here in the Grand Mosque with them. At that moment the gunmen started pushing back the crowd of worshippers to open a corridor through them to the *Ka'aba*. Then from within the deep shadows of the mosque's encircling arches there emerged a tall, pale, fair-haired young man, his head loosely covered in a red chequered headcloth and carrying a sub-machine gun. With no outward show of emotion 'the Mahdi' approached the *Ka'aba*, the crowd gasping at his youth. Having reached the *Ka'aba* he turned and stood impassively as one after another the gunmen knelt before him and in turn kissed his hand, pledging their allegiance in the same words with which the first Muslims are reported to have pledged their allegiance to the Prophet Muhammad: 'We will obey you in weal and woe, in ease and hardship and evil circumstances ... except in what would disobey God.'[17] The 'Mahdi' then launched into an hour-long sermon denouncing the House of Saud and the corruptions, sins and deviations from the true path of Islam of the Kingdom they had created.

The figure of the Mahdi (literally 'the Guided One') is common to all branches of Islam but also controversial, especially among Sunnis. He is not mentioned in the Qur'an although he does appear in one *Hadith* and later prophecies and learned Muslim texts. He is prophesied to be going to appear at the end of time, just prior to the Day of Judgement. He will bear the name Muhammad and, in a time of strife, when 'the princes have corrupted the earth', will be sent to 'bring back justice'. Throughout history there have been people who have claimed to be the Mahdi, perhaps the best known being the 'false' Mahdi who led an uprising against the British during the 1880s which resulted in the humiliation of a British and Egyptian army and the death of the charismatic General Gordon – Gordon of Khartoum.

The 'Mahdi' that Juhayman Ataiba and his fellow rebels presented to the crowd in the Grand Mosque in Mecca on the morning of November 20th 1979 was Muhammad Abdullah al-Qahtani. Young Qahtani came from Asir, the poor region in the south west of the country. He had met Juhayman a few years earlier while he had been studying Islamic law at the Islamic University of Riyadh where the writings and sermons which Juhayman had begun to deliver had started to attract a considerable following among the most ardently Islamic students. It was Juhayman and his followers who first convinced the rather dreamy and impressionable young Qahtani that he was the Mahdi who, as promised in the *Hadith*, would come to cleanse Islam and redeem all true Muslims. As Juhayman pointed out to the worshippers in the Grand Mosque on that November morning, young Muhammad Abdullah al-

17 ibid.

Qahtani fulfilled the specific prophecies made about the coming of the Mahdi: after all the wars and revolutions that had wracked the Muslim world in recent decades he did indeed come 'in a time of great discord', at the start of a new Muslim century, at a moment when the princes were 'corrupting the earth' and Muslims had been drifting away from the faith; he bore the first name Muhammad and had features similar to those attributed in the *Hadith* to the Mahdi – he was tall, had a fair complexion, a large birthmark on his cheek, and claimed descent from the family of the Prophet Muhammad. He came now, Juhayman and his fellow rebels assured the crowd in the mosque, to fulfil the prophecy, to lead the true Muslims in a cataclysmic encounter with the forces of evil, to overthrow those forces of evil and to 'fill the Earth with peace and justice as it will have been filled with injustice and tyranny before then'.[18]

When Qahtani finished speaking some hundreds among the thousands-strong crowd were convinced. Falling to their knees, they hailed him as the Mahdi and volunteered to join the rebels in the fight. The rebels then opened more coffins and handed out yet more guns to these new followers. The rebels then allowed most of the able-bodied worshippers who had not volunteered to join them to begin making their escape through the mosque's narrow windows, while keeping back a few as hostages.

In the streets around the mosque, as word of what had happened spread, people started to flee. When a police car approached the mosque to investigate, it was riddled with well-aimed fire by rebel gunmen stationed in the Grand Mosque's minarets and most of the policemen in the car were killed. Throughout the rest of that day other armed policemen or soldiers who approached the mosque were also summarily gunned down.

As news of what had happened reached Riyadh members of the royal family came together in anxious huddled conference. What should they do? Crown Prince Fahd, responsible for day-to-day rule in the Kingdom, was not even in the country. He was in Tunis attending a conference of Arab leaders. Prince Abdullah, the Head of the National Guard, was

18 The words of the prophecy about the coming of the Mahdi as quoted in Trofimov, op. cit.

holidaying in the south of France and the prince who headed the security service was with Fahd in Tunis. A total blackout of information was ordered on broadcasting stations and all lines of communication out of the country were disconnected. It was the following day before Crown Prince Fahd discovered the details of what had happened. Meanwhile the rebels continued broadcasting their demands out over the city of Mecca from the Grand Mosque's loudspeakers, while on the streets of the country's major towns leaflets mysteriously began to appear detailing the rebels' accusations and demands. The rebels demanded the dismissal of named corrupt high-ranking princes, the end of sales of Saudi oil to Western countries, a return to the true canons of Islam and the expulsion of all foreign military advisers from the Kingdom.

Back in Riyadh King Khalid and the senior princes had decided that they could not negotiate with the rebels: their demands were wholly unacceptable. The rebels had to be overpowered and control of the Grand Mosque wrested back. By seizing Islam's holiest site and issuing their demands and accusations the rebels were challenging the very foundations of the Al Sauds' claim to the right to rule. The rebels posed the most serious threat to the Al Sauds that they had faced since Ibn Saud had put down the Ikhwan rebellion fifty years earlier.

But dare the Sauds order their forces to attack the Grand Mosque? The rebels had already committed one of the gravest of sins by shedding blood in it. So dare the Al Sauds, who claimed to be the true guardians of Islam's Holy Places, now desecrate the holiest site of all by risking damaging it with gunfire and killing perhaps many hundreds of worshippers? Not even a bird was allowed to be killed inside the precincts of the Grand Mosque, nor a plant uprooted. Khalid issued an urgent summons to bin Baz and the Kingdom's other senior *ulema*.

It took until the next day to assemble the *ulema*, many from the farthest corners of the Kingdom. But once they were gathered they concluded, after careful consideration of all the known facts about the rebels and their actions, that not all the preconditions set forth in the prophecies about the coming of the Mahdi had been met. Al-Qahtani, the young man being hailed by the rebels as the Mahdi, could therefore not be the true Mahdi. So he must be just another impostor, like all the previous impostors who down the centuries had claimed to be the Mahdi.

King Khalid asked the *ulema* to issue a *fatwa* against the impostor, officially declaring him not to be the Mahdi, condemning the rebels and sanctioning the retaking of the Grand Mosque by force. Without such a *fatwa* the call by the rebels for the ending of corruption in the state and a return to the full rigours of the Islamic moral code might prove very attractive to many Saudis disillusioned with the behaviour of some of the royal princes and what they saw as the growing moral laxity that was sweeping the Kingdom.

Bin Baz was quite happy to issue a *fatwa* denouncing Qahtani's claim to be the Mahdi and condemning the rebels' actions in seizing the Grand Mosque and shedding blood. However, the rebels' call for an end to corruption and return to the true path of Islam was very attractive to him and his fellow *ulema*. The rebels were in many ways true Wahhabis and their movement was one which bin Baz and his fellow conservative clerics had done much to help to inspire. So bin Baz and the *ulema* drove a hard bargain. They would give the King what he wanted. They would permit the King and his forces to drive the rebels from the Grand Mosque, would issue a *fatwa* proclaiming that al-Qahtani was not the true Mahdi and reaffirm the regime's Muslim legitimacy, but in return they required the King and the state to live up to its Islamic obligations. The policies of liberalisation must be halted and where possible rolled back. There must be an end to licentiousness and the drinking of alcohol, to women appearing on TV and gaining employment, and to the screening of 'lewd' western films. And a greater part of the billions of dollars of oil money flowing into the country must be put to shoring up Wahhabism in the Kingdom and spreading the faith around the world. As some of the royal princes who were present at the negotiation put it, it amounted to the *ulema* demanding that King Khalid adopt Juhayman's agenda in return for their help in getting rid of him.[19]

But even after the *ulema* had issued their *fatwa* and their condemnation of the rebels as 'renegades' and 'deviationists from Islam' had been broadcast across the country on Riyadh Radio, the regime's forces were still faced with the serious practical problem of how to retake the mosque and overcome the rebels. They could not just go in 'all guns

19 See Trofimov, op. cit.

blazing', smashing up the Grand Mosque and killing hundreds of people in the process. It was clear that the rebels were well prepared and skilled in using firearms. In fact, many of the rebels were disillusioned former National Guardsmen from Bedouin tribes which, like Juhayman's own tribe, had been involved in the Ikhwan rebellion in 1929. There were somewhere between two and three hundred of these rebels well embedded in good positions throughout the mosque. They had been joined by some hundreds of volunteers from among the original worshippers, making a total opposition force of perhaps one thousand. The regime's forces were therefore going to have to attempt to retake the mosque by unconventional means, a fact which became more obvious when their first attacks were easily repulsed by the rebels.

Although they deeply disapproved of Shi'ism and the teachings of Ayatollah Khomeini, the rebels had concluded that if Khomeini and the Iranian students could overthrow a regime as powerful as that of the Shah they could achieve a similar revolution in Saudi Arabia. Days passed and the rebels repeatedly beat off ineffective sorties by Khalid's forces. But the rebels suffered one major disappointment. Although there were some small scattered risings against the regime elsewhere in the country and a more serious uprising and rioting by Shia in the oil-producing Eastern Province, there was no widespread general revolt such as had occurred in Iran. The fact was that Saudi Arabia was not Iran. The Saudi rulers, for all their faults, were not as unpopular as the Shah, nor were they as brutal.

After days of unsuccessful attempts to dislodge the rebels the Saudi authorities realised that their troops simply did not have the necessary know-how and specialised equipment to dislodge the rebels from the Grand Mosque on their own. However, they could not simply call in foreigners to do it for them. To do so would not only amount to a very humiliating public admission that the Saudi regime and their armed forces were not up to dislodging a few hundred fanatics from Islam's holiest site, but to allow non-Muslims to enter the Holy City of Mecca, the Grand Mosque and even approach the sacred *Ka'aba* itself, would be totally *haram* – strictly forbidden under the most sacred laws of Islam. So a top-secret channel was opened between the highest levels of the French Government and one of the senior Saudi princes. As a result three French specialist commando officers with a great deal of experience of dealing with terrorist attacks and hostage crises were flown in the utmost secrecy to Saudi Arabia, together with a large amount of specially selected equipment and munitions, to devise a strategy, train one hundred and fifty of Saudi Arabia's best and most fearless troops and supervise the operation.

The final assault on the mosque, exactly two weeks after the rebels had seized it, was fought out mainly in the maze of cellars below the mosque. After almost twenty-four hours of close-quarters fighting, in which large quantities of gas and chemicals were used as well as guns, the last of the rebels were either killed or captured. Qahtani was killed early in the operation, but Juhayman was captured alive. Asked by his captors, pointing to the desecrated shrine, 'How could you do this?' Juhayman is reported to have replied, 'It was God's will.'

The official casualty figures were 12 Saudi officers killed, 115 other ranks, and 450 seriously injured, 117 rebels killed, 26 worshippers killed and 110 wounded, many of them foreign nationals. The real figures were almost certainly a lot higher than this – American government sources suggested around 1,000. On January 9th 1980 Juhayman was executed in Mecca while those of his fellow conspirators who had been captured were executed at the same time in Saudi Arabia's other eight most important cities. The Saudi authorities were determined to leave Saudis across the Kingdom in no doubt about who ruled.

Although he had dealt with the insurrection, events outside Saudi Arabia continued to add to King Khalid and his government's problems. Late in December 1979 the Russians, alarmed by what had happened in Iran and fearful that Islamic opposition movements, inspired and backed by the Iranians, might begin liberation campaigns in the largely Muslim southern Soviet republics, invaded Afghanistan to prop up the new pro-Soviet government which had seized power eight months earlier.

In April 1980 came the transmission by ATV in Britain, in the face of Saudi government protests, of a dramatised documentary made by the distinguished British documentary maker Anthony Thomas. 'Death of a Princess' depicted events three years earlier in which a married Saudi royal princess, one of Ibn Saud's great-granddaughters, had fallen in love with a man who was not her husband, had an adulterous relationship with him and, while attempting to flee the country disguised as a man, had been apprehended by the authorities at the airport with her lover. Condemned to death in accordance with *shari'a* law, the pair had been publicly executed in a car park in Jeddah, she by six pistol shots to the head and her lover by beheading, an act which it took no fewer than five separate hacks at the neck to complete. The Saudi government had done its best to prevent the story from leaking out, but it had and Anthony Thomas had investigated it. Although he changed the names of both the princess and her lover, and described the country where the events had taken place simply as 'somewhere in Arabia', when the impending ITV transmission was announced the Saudi government had brought pressure on the British government and the ITV company to stop the transmission. But ATV and the British broadcasting authorities had held firm and the programme was transmitted in an atmosphere of greatly heightened interest on April 9th 1980.

After the transmission the Saudi authorities vented their anger on the British government by barring British companies from being awarded contracts in Saudi Arabia and demanding the withdrawal of the British ambassador. They also took steps to try to prevent the transmission of the programme elsewhere in the world. Shortly after the British transmission two American-based Saudi lawyers announced that they were suing ATV and its chief executive for $20 billion on behalf of '600 million Muslims', claiming that the programme was 'part of an international conspiracy to insult, ridicule, discredit and abuse followers of Islam throughout the world'.[20] These Saudi actions, far from helping the regime, simply added to Saudi Arabia's already bad image in the Western media and heightened Muslims' sense of grievance against the outside world.

In 1980 the coming of the Reagan and Thatcher administrations in the USA and Britain marked the beginning of a major economic recession and downturn in world trade, leading to a series of sharp falls in Saudi Arabia's oil income. This limited the possible options available

20 See Darlow, Michael, *Independents Struggle: The programme makers who took on the TV establishment*, Boa MS & Quartet, London, 2004. The lawsuit eventually came to nothing.

to the Saudi regime for dealing with the myriad of problems that now beset it both inside the country and out. Badly shaken by the Mecca mosque seizure and scale of the uprisings in Hasa, the Saudi government took a number of steps to shore up their own position and at the same time to assuage the criticisms of the many more conservative Saudis. In accordance with the undertakings they had given to bin Baz and the other senior *ulema*, the government ordered the removal from Saudi TV screens of women announcers, the strict enforcement of prohibitions on the employment of women, even by western companies operating in Saudi Arabia, the removal or blacking out of female images in magazines and other publications – in one instance the face of seventy-one-year-old American movie star Bette Davis was obliterated from a photograph in a prominent Jeddah magazine. Screenings of American and other western films were reduced, the prohibition on the consumption of alcohol, even by westerners, which had in recent years been quietly relaxed, began to be enforced again with renewed vigour, and additional funding was given to the religious police, the *mutawwa*, who went around in increased numbers stamping out behaviour and forms of dress which they deemed un-Islamic, inappropriate or not in accordance with *shari'a* or the commands of the Qur'an. Funding for the religious universities was increased, resulting, according to some estimates, in one quarter of all of the university students in the Kingdom being students of religious studies. Additional funding was also given to the *ulema* and Department of Religious Affairs, for the setting up of *madrasas* – religious schools and institutes of Muslim learning and legal sciences – both inside the Kingdom and overseas, where their mission was to spread and promote adherence to the Wahhabi brand of Islam.

Over the course of the next decade some of these institutions would develop into new centres for the incubation of Islamic extremism and fundamentalist opposition to the Saudi regime. One of the leading princes would later say that in dealing with the seizure of the Grand Mosque in Mecca and its aftermath, he and his Saudi colleagues had 'eliminated the individuals' who had committed the crime 'but overlooked the ideology that was behind the crime' and so permitted its spread.[21]

21 See Trofimov, op. cit.

When, late in September 1980, Saddam Hussein's Iraq launched a war against Iran, following a dispute over the Shatt al Arab, the last length of the combined rivers Tigris and Euphrates before they flow into the Persian Gulf, Saudi Arabia started to pour millions of dollars into Iraq to support Saddam Hussein's war effort. At the same time refugees who had flooded out of Afghanistan into Pakistan following the Soviet invasion began to organise an armed resistance movement, the *mujahidin*, and the Saudi authorities started supplying them with large amounts of money for the purchase of arms. When the *mujahidin* split into two wings, one traditionalist and the other fundamentalist, the Saudi Government directed its funds towards the fundamentalist wing and encouraged a new and eager generation of Saudi young men, who had been educated in traditional Wahhabi religious schools and were now eager to join the worldwide struggle for Islam, to enlist in the ranks of the fundamentalist *mujahidin* fighting in Afghanistan against the army of the atheistic Soviet government.

Among those who joined the fundamentalist *mujahidin* in Pakistan was a bright, earnest young Saudi in his twenties who had moved since his earliest childhood among the highest in the land. He was Osama, one of the many sons of the poor Yemeni-born engineer who had set up a construction company and in the 1930s built Ibn Saud's Khuzam Palace just outside Jeddah. Muhammad bin Laden had gone on to fulfil many major construction contracts throughout Saudi Arabia and the wider Arab world, including the renovation and enlargement of the Grand Mosque in Mecca, and amassed a fortune. Young Osama had accompanied his father on many of his business trips around the Middle East and as he grew up had attended numerous meetings and dinner parties held by his family with senior members of the royal family and leading clerics. When his father Muhammad had been killed in a plane crash in 1967 he had left his fortune, amounting to some $11 billion, to his almost five dozen children, making Osama a very rich young man. During his time studying business management at Jeddah University, Osama had attended lectures given by Mohammed Qutb, the younger brother of Sayyid Qutb, who in his writings had done so much to articulate the beliefs of the Muslim Brotherhood. Osama had become fired up by the teachings of the Brotherhood and their Saudi followers, and by their belief in the necessity of an Islamic revolution that would take in all spheres of life, religious, personal, political, economic, national and international, that would recognise as legitimate only those rulers who acted in accordance with the *shari'a*, would work to liberate Palestine, defeat America and Israel and oppose all forms of foreign rule that threatened the *shari'a* and the community of true believers.[22] Osama bin Laden, with his access to his family's fortune, his contacts and knowledge of business and management, was able to supply the *mujahidin* with much-needed money, contacts and know-how. He quickly became one of their most effective tacticians and fighters.

On June 12th 1982 the ailing King Khalid died and, in accordance with the previously agreed order of succession, was succeeded by his sixty-one-year-old brother, the eldest son of Ibn Saud's wife Hassa Sudairi, Crown Prince Fahd. Fahd was the first of the seven sons of Ibn Saud by Hassa Sudairi, the so-called Sudairi Seven, to become king. Intensely loyal to each other, the seven full Sudairi brothers, all of whom had held high office in the Kingdom's government, had long been thought to present a threat to the continued unity of the Al Saud family – the fear being that they might act in concert with each other to exclude other sons of Ibn Saud from the succession, setting off a conflict, like Al Saud family conflicts in the nineteenth century which had led to their demise as the ruling house. But in 1982 no such conflict occurred. Fahd became King with the full agreement of the rest of the family and Abdullah, two years younger than Fahd and the next eldest surviving son of Ibn Saud by a wife other than Hassa Sudairi, was immediately named as Crown Prince and First Deputy Prime Minister, while another of the Sudairi Seven, Prince Sultan, became Second Deputy Prime Minister and next in line of succession after Abdullah.

However Fahd, who had undertaken much of the day-to-day business of running the Kingdom's government during the reign of Khalid and was known as the chief proponent of Saudi Arabia's rapid modernisation, would never enjoy the popularity and prestige of Faisal or even

22 See Riedel, Bruce, *The Search for Al Qaeda: Its Leadership, Ideology and Future*, Brookings Institution Press, Washington DC, 2008 and Hourani, Albert, *A History of the Arab Peoples*, Faber & Faber, London, 2002.

Khalid. Ordinary Saudis still expected their rulers to possess the qualities of the traditional tribal shaikh, elected to rule over his people by the consent of the tribe and for his qualities of leadership, courage, generosity, piety and identification with the tribe. Fahd in no way lived up to this ideal. Far from appearing hard and virile, able to withstand long days in the saddle and survival on little food, Fahd was seriously overweight, obese even. If required to walk more than a few steps he had to resort to a wheelchair. Identified with technocrats, he rarely visited the desert or the Bedouin, and if he did he travelled with a huge entourage in a procession of eighteen-wheel Mercedes trucks complete with his own operating theatre and clinic. His reputation was mired in his image as a playboy, drinker and high-roller among the international luxury resorts of the seriously rich, chasing after blondes and playing the gaming tables – *Stern* magazine in Germany had once reported him as losing DM20 million in a single evening's gambling in Monte Carlo.

Unlike Ibn Saud or Faisal, who had lived unostentatiously among their people following simple tastes and pleasures, Fahd had seven huge palaces shut away behind massive fortified walls and gardens in various parts of Saudi Arabia, a 100-room palace in Marbella, others in Geneva and Paris and a house outside London reputed to have cost £30 million to refurbish. He also built himself a house in Riyadh designed to resemble the White House, but he never moved into it as this aping of the Americans produced such an outcry among his people that he deemed moving into it would be too risky. In addition to his many houses he had a liner-sized luxury yacht anchored in the Red Sea where he could escape prying eyes and live in the manner that he chose, plus a private Boeing 747 jet, fitted with sitting rooms, a sauna and large pink decorated master bedroom, with a cabin crew of eight comely, mostly Western, women to attend on him.[23]

Yet for the next few years Fahd, supported by Abdullah, who in contrast to Fahd was tall, lean and known as a traditionalist, pursued policies that were broadly similar to the policies that had been pursued by Khalid. Much of the construction work and modernisation

23 See Aburish, K. Saïd, *The Rise, Corruption and Coming Fall of the House of Saud*, Bloomsbury Publishing, London, 1994 and Mackey, Sandra op. cit.

undertaken in the previous decade was now complete. Modern four-lane highways had replaced the camel tracks linking the Kingdom's main cities. Modern steel and concrete buildings, identical to those to be seen all over America and western Europe, had sprung up around all the major towns, replacing the old, mud-brick houses and market places – only a few of the most notable old buildings were still preserved. The new buildings stretched far out into what had only two to three decades earlier been desert. These buildings had replaced the shanty towns that had so shocked van der Meulen in the 1940s, and now housed the huge influx of Saudis who, with the continuing urbanisation, rising Saudi birthrate and de-Bedouinisation programme, had continued to flow into the towns in search of work. The Saudi government built more than 2.5 million housing units during the 1980s and more than 30 per cent of the men of the leading Bedouin tribes, tribes such as the Al Murra which had played such an essential role in the development of Ibn Saud's character and skills, had now left the desert to serve in the army, police, frontier or National Guards.

In and around these unrecognisable towns cars flowed day and night along the modern boulevards, beneath garish streetlights and between glaring, blinking neon signs above international chainstores bearing names familiar in the West – Safeway and Euromarché. Luxury western goods and electronics were everywhere – Cartier, Chanel, Toshiba, Sony. The public scribes who could still be found in small shops and arcades now had typewriters and men who ten years earlier had herded goats now carried briefcases down the sidewalks. Among the throngs on modern streets the women still moved in pairs or were shepherded by their husbands and young male relatives amid all the modernity. They were still firmly shrouded and invisible as they always had been under and behind folds of encasing black material. In 1983 the new King Khalid International Airport had opened outside Riyadh. It replaced the cramped airstrip and terminal buildings where Sandra Mackey had arrived just five years earlier to meet her first rude taste of the realities of Saudi life. Now at the airport, said to be the largest in the world, instead of one small cramped terminal building, there were four, one of which had to be mothballed because there were not enough passengers to use it, all housed in one massive, beautifully designed airport building. Now after emerging from the well-ordered arrivals halls where the seething, pushing scrums of five years earlier were no more than an unpleasant memory, passengers found themselves not in the dark desert night to begin a long wait for a taxi to take them to Riyadh's one 'habitable' overcrowded hotel, but on a well-lit concourse where taxis glided up in a well-ordered continous flow to pick up passengers and take them to whichever of the selection of new hotels belonging to the major international chains they had booked. However, the accident rate on Saudi Arabia's roads was still horrendous as drivers, still more used to the overtaking and closing speeds of camels, grappled with the complexities of a mass of modern cars moving on modern tarmaced roads at speeds many times those of a camel on a desert track.

By 1990 the number of hospital beds in the country had more than quadrupled, rising from 9,000 in 1960 to 41,000. The number of doctors had multiplied twenty-fold and other medical personnel were increasing by similar amounts. Life expectancy had gone up from 49 years in 1965 to over 63 years. However, there were still millions of more menial jobs which the Saudis could not or would not take on. Used to being able to live largely on the generous provisions of the Saudi welfare state, which provided free education, health care and housing, many Saudis still refused to do the kinds of work that they considered beneath them. The shortfall was still made up largely by workers from other, less prosperous Muslim countries. During the early 1980s, despite the decrease in Saudi oil revenues, which dropped by 31 per cent in 1982 alone and continued to drop, the number of overseas workers as a percentage of the total workforce rose from 41 per cent in 1975, to 46 per cent in 1980 and 48 per cent in 1985.

Yet despite all the rapid changes, the outside pressures and deterioration in the Kingdom's finances – the price of a barrel of oil dropped to below $10 in 1986, forcing King Fahd to admit that it was no longer possible to formulate the nation's economic plans with any accuracy – and the resultant cuts in the levels of welfare benefits, the 1980s generally were marked by a period of relative calm and stability in the Kingdom. At the same time as continuing to support religious institutions and crack down on behaviour likely to offend the religious conservatives, Fahd quietly instituted further measures of modernisation.

Previously, Qur'anic injunctions against interest or usury – *riba* – which precluded the lending of money or commercial loans to enterprises undertaking development – had prevented Saudi Arabia from establishing any conventional banks with the result that all kinds of ingenious schemes and scams had appeared, designed to get round the prohibition. But in 1983 two brothers were allowed to open Saudi Arabia's first Islamic bank. In 1986 a 365-day fiscal year was introduced for the first time.

On the international front Saudi Arabia worked to further increase its own security. It took the lead in trying to broker international peace deals to end the conflict over Palestine and conflicts in other regions. Fahd repeatedly pressed the Reagan administration to do something to curb Israel's continuing oppression of the Palestinians and her repeated incursions against her neighbours. But his efforts continued to be rebuffed. To shore up their own defences against attack by Iran, other neighbours or internal insurrection, the Saudis entered into a new series of massive arms deals. The most notorious was the series of Al Yamamah deals – Al Yamamah meaning The Dove in Arabic. Beginning in the mid-1980s, and over the following decades the Al Yamamah arms contracts were to be worth many tens of billions of pounds to British defence contractors. The deals involved the sale by British armaments contractors, led by British Aerospace (BAE), of aircraft, military equipment, spares, training and servicing contracts. Hailed by the British press as 'Maggie's bonanza' for British jobs, securing the deal for Britain in the face of strong competition from France and vocal opposition from Israel had involved senior British ministers, officials and intermediaries, reaching right up to Mrs Thatcher herself. Allegations of corruption surrounding the deal began to circulate almost from the moment that it was signed. These alleged that in return for awarding the contract to Britain rather than her French competitors, senior members of the Saudi royal family and their officials had demanded and received hefty payments in the form of commissions paid to off-shore companies in which they had controlling interests, slush funds paid into Swiss banks, artificially inflated price tags on items of equipment and lavish hospitality.

During Fahd's reign the continued lavish lifestyles, corrupt dealings and sinful personal lives of some Saudi princes, senior businessmen, arms dealers and contract negotiators, fuelled a further alienation and discontent with their leaders among many ordinary Saudis.

By 1989, with the Soviet Union starting to implode, the *mujahidin*, supported and encouraged by the American and Saudi governments, had defeated the Soviet Army in Afghanistan. As a result thousands of foreign fighters who had enlisted in the *mujahidin* began to return to their own countries, leaving the two Afghan *mujahidin* factions, traditionalist and fundamentalist, to sort out between themselves who was to rule the country. The Saudi government was estimated to have helped as many as 20,000 young Saudis to join the *mujahidin* struggle in Afghanistan. Now these young Islamist zealots began to return home, with their confidence and Islamist ardour boosted by their military success. These ardent young men, having been encouraged by their government to fight in what was hailed as a pure Islamist cause, were now unlikely to be content to simply settle back into the dull, and to them increasingly impure, routine of Saudi life. As a result they soon came to present the Saudi regime with a new threat, a threat not unlike the threat presented to Ibn Saud after he had completed his conquest of Saudi Arabia with the help of the Ikhwan. All that was now needed was a spark and the Kingdom might face a blaze every bit as serious as the rebellion of 1929.

At that same moment Saddam Hussein who, with the continued support of the Americans and in the face of clear evidence that he had used chemical weapons, had forced the ailing Ayatollah Khomeini to sue for peace, also began looking for fresh fields to conquer. Flushed with success and with his army substantially strengthened as a result of the war, confident of continued US backing because of the Reagan administration's ongoing fixation on the Cold War struggle with the Soviet Union, Saddam Hussein accused Kuwait of stealing oil from Iraq by 'slant drilling' from its own territory into an Iraqi oil field and of keeping world oil prices artificially low by flooding the market. On August 2nd 1990 he launched an invasion. Bombing raids were followed with a ground assault by more than 100,000 soldiers and 700 tanks. The Kuwaiti ruling family fled and took refuge in Riyadh, and on August 8th, Saddam Hussein declared that he had annexed Kuwait and that from now on it was to be the 19th province of Iraq.

Having completed his conquest of Kuwait Saddam Hussein now started massing troops on the border with Saudi Arabia. The Saudis, fearing that Saddam Hussein was about to attack their oil fields, appealed to America for help. As a massive American troop build-up began in north-eastern Saudi Arabia, close to the border with Kuwait and Iraq, King Fahd voiced suspicions that King Hussein of Jordan was secretly siding with Saddam Hussein, hoping that he might use him in a bid to restore Hashemite rule over Islam's Holy Places. Fahd's suspicion seemed confirmed when Jordan voted against an Arab League motion condemning the Iraqi invasion of Kuwait and told a Mossad envoy that Saddam was a re-incarnation of the sixth-century BCE Babylonian conqueror of Jerusalem, Nebuchadnezzar.[24]

However, to many Saudi clerics and religious conservatives the rapid build-up of American forces on Saudi soil was deeply disturbing – these were infidels in the Prophet Muhammad's own land. Why was Fahd seeking protection from foreigners, non-Muslims, to fight Muslims? Osama bin Laden, who had himself recently returned from Afghanistan, sought an urgent audience with the King. Failing to get it, he met with the Defence Minister, Prince Sultan. Long a vocal critic of Saddam Hussein and his Ba'athist Party, who he condemned as secular socialists allied to the Soviet Union and enemies of Islam, bin Laden offered to raise a guerrilla army, based around a core of his own fellow former *mujahidin* fighters in Afghanistan, to drive Saddam Hussein out of Kuwait. But Prince Sultan seemed uninterested in bin Laden's offer. Pointing out that Kuwait was very different from Afghanistan, Sultan said, 'You cannot fight them from the mountains and caves. What will you do when he lobs missiles at you with chemical and biological weapons?'

'We will fight them with faith,' replied bin Laden.[25]

Feeling snubbed by Sultan, who had made it clear that he preferred to place his faith in the power of America's modern arms and experience, bin Laden went away to help the new government of Sudan create what they intended to be a new model Islamic state. But by his rejection of bin

24 See Patrick Tyler, op. cit.
25 Tyler, op. cit. and Riedel, op. cit.

Laden's offer Prince Sultan had started a new and dangerous rift between bin Laden and the Saudi royals.

On January 16th 1991 the battle to liberate Kuwait started with a prolonged series of air attacks. This was followed six weeks later by a ground assault led by hundreds of thousands of Americans supported by smaller contingents of British, French and Italians, and units of Muslim troops from Egypt, Morocco, Syria and Saudi Arabia. 'Operation Desert Storm' was the first time, with the exception of the action to retake the Grand Mosque in Mecca, that the Saudi armed forces had been engaged in a real war since the death of Ibn Saud. Four days after the ground assault began, by which time the Iraqis, both combatants and civilians, had suffered horrendous casualties, Kuwait had been liberated and the fighting stopped.

In Saudi Arabia the war marked an important turning point. The presence of over a thousand foreign journalists in the country to cover the war, in addition to almost half a million American servicemen, induced a new mood of openness among many ordinary Saudis and emboldened those seeking reform. At the same time it produced a corresponding backlash among traditionalists and religious conservatives, deepening still further the divide in the Kingdom between progressives and conservatives. A dramatic manifestation of this occurred during the run-up to 'Operation Desert Storm'. A group of 46 women, all wearing the traditional black from head to toe, staged a demonstration by driving cars onto one of Riyadh's main streets and blocking the traffic, demanding the lifting of the prohibition on women driving cars. The reaction of the authorities was both swift and angry. The women were promptly arrested, taken to a police station and held there until their fathers or husbands came to collect them. All those who had jobs were sacked and their passports were confiscated. The senior clerics, headed by bin Baz, followed these moves with a strongly worded public condemnation of the idea of women driving. However, six months later King Fahd held a meeting with four of the women and told them that he was ready to consider their demands and six months after that all the women were given their jobs back, received compensation and had their passports restored. The driving ban, however, continued. As one of the women commented fifteen years later, the results of the protest were disastrous, delaying the advance of women by years on account of the conservative backlash it prompted from people who wanted the country 'to go back to the fourteenth century'.[26]

The contradictory reactions of the authorities were all the more confusing because the number of women in employment had been rising for over a decade and the percentage of women among Saudi university students had been over 40 per cent since the mid-1980s and was continuing to grow. For years economists had been urging the Saudi authorities to lift the driving ban on women because of the billions of rials it was costing the country's economy for women to be chauffeured around.

Nevertheless the calls for reform from both liberals and religious conservatives continued unabated. One group of leading public figures, including former ministers, writers, businessmen and university professors, wrote an open letter to the King calling for the formation of a consultative council drawn from qualified and knowledgeable people, for municipal councils, a modernisation of the legal system, a commitment to 'total equality among all citizens', greater freedom of the media, reform of the *mutawwa* and a larger role for women in public life 'within the scope of the *shari'a*'.[27] Such calls were answered by counter-calls from groups of preachers and clerics demanding a return to a stricter adherence to the requirements of Islam.

The war also marked the start of a substantial continuing American military presence in the country. Despite the fact that before the war King Fahd had said that the American presence would be 'temporary', after the fighting was over the security threat to the Kingdom remained. Much of Saddam Hussein's army had survived and he continued to refuse to comply with UN resolutions requiring him to disarm and destroy his weapons of mass destruction. The Americans continued to fly armed reconnaissance patrols over Iraq and there was also the possibility of armed raids by the Iranians and their supporters. Five years after the war ended there were still over 5,000 American military

26 See BBC report 'From Our Own Correspondent' by Bridget Kendall, April 29th 2006.

27 Madawi Al-Rasheed, op. cit.

personnel in Saudi Arabia. Despite oil production increasing by about 50 per cent, the cost of the war, of more new defence contracts – a further 72 F-15 fighter jets purchased from the Americans in 1992 and a further phase of the Al Yamamah arms contract with Britain – plus the continued extravagance of members of the royal family (estimated by the mid-1990s to cost the country at least $4,000 million per year) combined to push the country deeper and deeper into debt.

The reaction of many young Saudi religious fundamentalists, people who had come under the same kind of influences as Osama bin Laden, was a hardening in their hostility towards the Al Sauds. Once again some started secretly plotting ways in which they might overthrow the Al Sauds and force the Americans to leave.

King Fahd's response was to publish a series of decrees entitled 'The Basic Law of Government', amounting in effect to a formal setting out of a national constitution. The first decree proclaimed that 'the Kingdom of Saudi Arabia is a sovereign state with Islam as its religion; God's Book (The Qur'an) and the Sunnah of His Prophet ... are its constitution'. It went on to state that the country was ruled by the sons and grandsons of Ibn Saud, that the judiciary would be independent and follow the *shari'a*, and that the King had the right to hire and fire all government ministers, appoint deputies and declare war. He also announced that he was setting up a consultative council (*majlis al-shura*) of sixty members, to be selected by himself, with a term of office of four years. It was to advise him and make recommendations although he would retain the power to make final decisions on any matters where there was no agreement between the council and himself.[28] This council, long promised, finally came into existence in 1993. The Council, although far from turning Saudi Arabia into a democracy in the Western sense, did at least open up the making of important government decisions to a far greater range of influence and opinion and could, optimistically, be seen as the Kingdom's first small, tentative step in the direction of representative government. In 1999

28 *The Basic System of Governance*, Kingdom of Saudi Arabia Ministry of Foreign Affairs 2005 and Alexei Vassiliev, *The History of Saudi Arabia*, Saqi Books, London, 1998.

twenty women attended the Council for the first time. However, a year later Amnesty International was still describing Saudi Arabia's treatment of women, especially foreign domestic workers, as 'untenable' by any legal or moral standard.[29]

Late in 1995 King Fahd, who had been ailing for some time, had had a stroke and his younger brother Crown Prince Abdullah had taken over the day-to-day government. Although six months later Fahd had recovered sufficiently to take back the reins, from this time onwards Abdullah played a much bigger part in running the country. Known as a traditionalist, he had for many years headed the elite National Guard and had much closer links with the tribes than Fahd. Unlike the King and so many other members of the royal family, Abdullah lived relatively modestly and was popular with the people. He had consistently tried to get other members of the royal family to do something to reduce the amount of corruption.

However Abdullah's increasing role in the country's government had done little to assuage the anger of the fundamentalists. On November 13th 1995 a group calling itself the Islamic Movement for Change planted a bomb in a Saudi National Guard compound killing five American officers, several Saudis and people of other nationalities. Seven months later a huge lorry bomb exploded in the US military complex near Dhahran, killing 19 and injuring over 300 American and other service personnel. There had been terrorist attacks attributed to Islamic extremists in other parts of the world for some years, most of them linked to the struggle in Palestine or events in Lebanon, Libya, Syria, Iran and various other 'liberation' struggles. There had also been attacks on specifically American targets – a car bomb in the World Trade Center in New York in 1993 and bombs in American embassies in East Africa in 1998 – but this was the first time that there had been terrorist attacks of this sort inside Saudi Arabia itself specifically targeted at state institutions and the country's American allies, attacks perpetrated mainly by Saudis. The name of Osama bin Laden began to be linked to some of these attacks. In the years since the rejection of his offer to raise a *mujahidin* force to drive the Iraqis out of Kuwait bin Laden's attitude towards the

29 See BBC News *Saudi Arabia: Chronology of Key Events,* © BBC 2009.

Saudi government had changed from one of criticism to one of outright hostility. In 1994 he had been stripped of his Saudi citizenship because of his increasingly outspoken verbal attacks on the royal family and their relations with the USA. At the urging of the Saudi government bin Laden's own family had disowned him. In December 1994, while still in the Sudan, bin Laden had written an open letter to the country's leading cleric bin Baz. In it he criticised the royal family, bin Baz and his fellow clerics for inviting the Americans into the country to fight Saddam Hussein and for supporting the American-brokered Oslo peace process between the Palestinians and Israelis. He called a recent decree of bin Baz's justifying the latest peace efforts as 'astonishing', 'a disaster for Muslims' and described the royal family's part in these events as 'nothing but a massive betrayal ... by traitorous and cowardly Arab tyrants'. He advised bin Baz to distance himself from 'these tyrants and oppressors who have declared war on God' and called for a *jihad* to recover every Islamic land 'from Palestine to al-Andalus'.[30]

9/11, KING ABDULLAH AND THE FUTURE

Having returned to Afghanistan from Sudan, in 1998 Osama bin Laden founded a new revolutionary, jihadist organisation – The Base, *al Qaeda*. To bin Laden, like many of the Taliban and other fundamentalists, the whole history of the previous century was to be seen as a sustained campaign by the Christian West, principally Britain and France but later America, in a conspiracy with Zionists, to undermine the Arab countries, divide the Muslim *ummah* and overthrow Islam. Bin Laden and those who thought like him found their evidence for this in the actions of the imperialist powers a century earlier, in the secret Sykes-Picot Agreement of 1916 that divided the Arab lands between Britain and France and in the Balfour Declaration which made the first promise of a homeland for the Jews in Palestine. They blamed what they saw as the continuing success of these western policies on a whole series of weak and complicit Muslim and Arab governments. To bin Laden and those who thought like him the last legitimate Islamic government, until the recent

30 Quoted in Riedel, op. cit.

emergence of the fundamentalist Taliban government in Afghanistan, had been the Ottoman Caliphate. On August 23rd 1996, from a cave high in the Tora Bora mountains of Afghanistan, bin Laden issued what amounted to a declaration of war against the United States, Israel and the Saudi royal family.

On October 12th 2000, some men in a small dingy full of explosives attacked the US destroyer Cole in the Gulf of Aden killing 17 US sailors and injuring many more. On 11th September 2001, in a well-concerted plan, hijackers seized four airliners and deliberately crashed two of them into the twin towers of the World Trade Center in New York. A third hijacked plane was flown into the Pentagon in Washington while a fourth was only prevented from reaching its target when its passengers fought the hijackers and caused the plane to crash into a field in Pennsylvania. A total of more than 3,000 people were killed in the 9/11 attacks.

In the days that followed, as the world reeled under the impact of what had happened and world leaders rushed to offer America their sympathy and support, it emerged that fifteen out of the nineteen hijackers had been Saudi nationals and that those behind the attacks were Osama bin Laden and Al Qaeda. Almost overnight the attitude of people around the world towards Saudi Arabia and Saudis changed. Where before Saudi Arabia had been a far-off, mysterious land with a lingering aura of romance and Saudis either corpulent princes and businessmen making multi-billion-dollar arms deals, arbitrarily hoisting or lowering the world oil price while gambling fabulous amounts on the tables of world's capitals of pleasure, now Saudis and Saudi Arabia became a source of fear, of unpredictable terror and a centre of evil. Millions of people who did not know where Saudi Arabia was other than being somewhere vaguely in the Middle East rushed to find it on the map.

The hatred and fear directed towards Saudi Arabia in the months following 9/11 by the foreign media and their governments, and the venom and discrimination suffered by individual Saudis at the hands of Westerners, had the effect of bringing Saudi Arabia together as a nation as never before. Whereas before the Saudis had always seen themselves primarily as members of a particular tribe or family rather than as Saudis they now found themselves being hated and discriminated against not as members of a particular tribe but as Saudis. Attacked by outsiders for being Saudis, they began to react as Saudis, to come together with their fellow countrymen as Saudis and to have a fellow feeling for those around them not just as members of the same tribe but as fellow Saudi Arabians. In this sense the Al Qaeda attacks of 9/11 began to bring Saudi Arabia together as a nation in a way that all the efforts of Ibn Saud and his successors had never done.

Just days after the 9/11 attacks US President George W. Bush promised the frightened American people that his administration would 'rid the world of evil-doers' and, in a remark which would inflame Muslims around the world, described the campaign he intended to mount as a 'crusade', a 'war on terrorism'. Although Bush, alerted by his advisers of the reaction that his use of the word 'crusade' was likely to provoke across the Arab world, subsequently dropped it, the damage had already been done. To millions of Arabs, steeped in the history of the Crusades and the bloody wars of conquest waged by the Christian West against Islam, Bush's use of the word 'Crusade' signalled that the West intended to launch a new war of conquest against them and their faith.

Four weeks after the Al Qaeda attacks on the World Trade Center the US, supported by Britain, Canada, Australia and other NATO countries, invaded Afghanistan. Their aim was to capture bin Laden, defeat Al Qaeda and remove the Taliban government that had harboured them. By December they had overthrown the Taliban and replaced them with a friendly government. However they had failed to catch bin Laden or most of the other Al Qaeda leaders. As the hunt for bin Laden continued, Bush and his aides turned their minds to where their 'crusade' to rid the world of 'evil-doers' might turn next. In his annual 'State of the Union Address' on January 29th 2002 Bush told the American people that he would not 'wait on events while dangers gather' but would act pre-emptively to remove governments which help terrorism and seek to acquire weapons of mass destruction. He named three countries as an 'Axis of Evil' that threatened world peace – Iraq, Iran and North Korea. Bush's 'War on Terror' had begun.

As the build-up to war on Bush's first chosen target, Iraq, began, America, with the help of her principal ally Great Britain, tried to enlist allies and persuade the UN to authorise an invasion on the grounds that

Saddam Hussein was developing weapons of mass destruction and was 'a threat to peace'. Saudi Arabia, which for years had been trying to broker a peace settlement between Israel and the Palestinians, tried to deflect Bush and get him to concentrate instead on achieving lasting peace in the region by applying pressure to the Israelis to make concessions over Palestine. But, to Crown Prince Abdullah's fury, Bush refused to budge – in any forthcoming conflict in the region Bush was going to need Israel's continued support. Since 9/11 Saudi Arabia had been suspect to many senior figures in Bush's administration. The Kingdom's earlier funding of bin Laden and fundamentalist elements in the Afghanistan *mujahidin* made Saudi Arabia in their eyes a 'supporter of terror'. In the months immediately before 9/11 some senior advisers had even speculated about the desirability of a US invasion of Saudi Arabia to secure the Saudi oil fields and break up the Kingdom into a series of smaller regional and tribal states.[31] In the same period one adviser, Bush's speech writer David Frum, had written in the *New York Times Magazine* that the overthrow of Saddam Hussein and his replacement with a new government in Iraq 'more closely aligned with the Unites States, would put America more wholly in charge of the region than any other power since the Ottomans, or maybe even the Romans'.[32] To anyone who read Frum's words America's aims in the region seemed clear.

As it became obvious that Bush, with his British allies, was going to press ahead with their invasion of Iraq whether or not they could get a UN resolution directly sanctioning such an attack, the Saudis were placed in a difficult situation. While still needing the protection of American arms they were fearful of the reaction of fundamentalist elements inside the Kingdom if American troops started launching assaults or air-strikes into Iraq from bases inside Saudi Arabia. Crown Prince Abdullah and the Saudi ambassador to Washington, Prince Bandar, repeatedly urged the Americans not to launch an invasion of

31 The idea of a US-led or -backed invasion of Saudi Arabia, the seizure of the oil fields and division of the Kingdom into smaller states, seems to have recurred among senior advisers in successive United States administrations from Nixon and Kissinger's time onwards. See Tyler, op. cit.

32 *New York Times Magazine*, February 2001.

Iraq without the specific sanction of a UN resolution. But it was no use. America and Britain were intent on invading Iraq no matter what anyone said. So as war moved closer during the opening months of 2003, the Saudis told the Americans that if they did attack without the authorisation of a UN resolution Saudi Arabia would deny them permission to use bases in Saudi Arabia.

Even when UN arms inspectors reported that they could find no evidence of weapons of mass destruction in Iraq Bush and British Prime Minister, Tony Blair, refused to back down. To bolster their claims that an attack was justified the Americans produced a 'flawed intelligence report' and the British a 'dodgy dossier', both purporting to show that, despite what the UN arms inspectors said, Saddam Hussein did possess weapons of mass destruction or the capacity to produce them in the very near future.

So on March 20th 2003, still without the legal authority of a UN resolution sanctioning an invasion and against a background of massive anti-war demonstrations around the world, Bush and Blair, with small contingents from Spain, Poland and Denmark, launched their massive assault on Iraq. Although the Saudis did secretly allow US operations from at least three air bases, permitted US special-forces to mount attacks on Iraq from inside Saudi Arabia, and continued to supply the Americans with cheap fuel, they at the same time publicly refused to allow the Americans permission to use bases inside Saudi Arabia and urged them to remove all their remaining forces from the Kingdom.[33] Late in April, just days before Bush, standing on the deck of an American aircraft carrier in the Gulf, declared 'Mission Accomplished' and the end of all major combat operations in Iraq, the Americans withdrew their last major military unit, an operational HQ and command and control facility, from Saudi Arabia to Qatar. Relations between the Americans and Saudis reached a new all-time low.

On the eve of the American assault on Iraq bin Laden had delivered a sermon from his secret mountain hiding place on the borders of Afghanistan and Pakistan in which he ordered the start of an uprising

33 See *Saudi Arabia Exposed: Inside a Kingdom in Crisis* by John R. Bradley, Palgrave Macmillan, New York, 2005.

aimed at the overthrow of all the monarchies in the Arabian peninsula, in particular the monarchy of Saudi Arabia, for their betrayal of the Muslim *ummah* and delivery of the Palestinians to the Jews and Americans. On May 12th 2003 Al Qaeda suicide car bombers carried out three simultaneous attacks on compounds used by foreign workers in Riyadh killing 26 people, including 9 US citizens, one from the UK and 7 Saudis, and injuring hundreds of others. Al Qaeda's declaration of war also encompassed countries which bin Laden saw as America's accomplices. In Spain, one of the countries which had sent a contingent to fight alongside the Americans in Iraq, on March 11th 2004 suicide bombers exploded ten bombs on four crowded rush-hour commuter trains, killing 191 Spaniards and injuring another 1,800. A year later, on July 7th 2005, British-born Islamist suicide bombers with suspected links to Al Qaeda detonated bombs on London Underground trains and a London bus, killing 52 people. There were also bombs in night-spots frequented by western and Australian tourists in Bali. Although not all carried out by Saudis, almost all of these attacks were believed to have been carried out by Muslims inspired by bin Laden, fundamentalist Islamic preachers and other teachers and Islamic theorists with a similar world view. Many of these fundamentalists had been associated with *madrasas* based in the countries where the terrorist outrages occurred, *madrasas* which had been funded by Saudi Arabia following the agreement reached between clerics and the Saudi royal family in the aftermath of the 1979 Mecca mosque siege.[34] As a result governments and newspapers around the world began accusing Saudi Arabia of being 'the kernel of evil' and of 'exporting terror'.

In Saudi Arabia the Al Qaeda attacks continued, building into what was to prove the most serious and prolonged internal struggle in Saudi Arabia since the Ikhwan uprising of the late 1920s. In just two years there were 30 major terrorist incidents in Saudi Arabia. The Saudi security forces reacted immediately with determination and, to some outsiders, surprising success. Between 2003 and 2005 as attacks, hostage

34 During the reign of King Fahd alone Saudi Arabia claimed to have set up or paid for more than 1,300 mosques in foreign countries, 400 colleges and Islamic centres and 2,000 schools.

takings and murders continued, the security forces arrested or killed about one hundred terrorists. Raids, arrests and running gun battles between the security forces and terrorists took place in almost every major city in the Kingdom. As quickly became apparent, most of the terrorists came from among the young, urban poor who had lost out in the recession and rising unemployment in the years after the first Gulf War in 1991. Official Saudi Government estimates suggested that by 1999 the overall unemployment rate in the country stood at 9.6 per cent and by 2002 had risen to 11.9 per cent. Unofficial estimates suggested that the true figure among males was 15–20 per cent and might well be as high as 30 per cent.

Until the attacks inside Saudi Arabia itself bin Laden had remained something of a popular hero in the Kingdom on account of the part he had played in driving the Soviets out of Afghanistan. But the attacks in Saudi Arabia changed that. Many Saudis, probably the majority, now turned against bin Laden and his supporters.

The Iraq war also gave rise to further demands for liberalisation inside Saudi Arabia. Led mainly by intellectuals and academics, a new series of reform petitions began circulating and were presented to the King. In 2003 alone there were separate petitions calling for a constitutional monarchy and other liberalisations to the system of government, for the right to peaceful assembly, for a larger role for the Shia in the country's political life, for an independent judiciary, statutory protection for basic legal and constitutional freedoms, for the establishment of trade unions, for recognition of women's full legal and civil rights, an end to a woman's need for a male legal guardian, for an extension of general education to both sexes, the launch of new university courses for women and the recruitment of women into all sectors of the economy.

Some of these reforms were enacted – late in 2003 thousands of Shi'ites across the Eastern Province were allowed to come out onto the streets to mark *Ashura*, the day in the Shia calendar marking the martyrdom of the Imam Hussayn, and Crown Prince Abdullah met a Shi'ite delegation. However, the reaction to this of some Sunnis was violent. Shi'ite mosques were firebombed and there were attacks on Shi'ite communities. Crown Prince Abdullah held meetings with leading signatories of many of the other petitions and in October 2003 plans were announced to elect half of the members of the kingdom's local councils. Additional powers were also given to the National Consultative Council, the *Shura Al-Majlis*. A 'National Dialogue Forum on Excess and Moderation' was held at the end of 2003 to look at ways of reforming the education system, at 'opening the doors to free speech, spreading the spirit of tolerance and developing a spirit of innovation'.

However, a large group of leading religious scholars and university professors responded to these moves by warning that changing the school curriculum risked taking 'the Kingdom along the path of infidels'. Similarly, when the liberal Saudi newspaper and voice of liberal Islamist reformers, *Al Watan*, which was supported by Crown Prince Abdullah, launched a campaign against the religious police its editor was fired by the Minister of the Interior, Prince Nayif, who was one of the group of Sudairi princes. Petitioners who called for a constitutional monarchy were arrested and briefly jailed, sending them a clear warning not to push their calls for reform too far. The fact was that Saudi Arabia's rulers, like their father Ibn Saud, knew full well that, the survival of their Kingdom depended on them maintaining the delicate balance between traditional Islamists and progressives. As the editor of *Al Watan* told David Gardner, the author and *Financial Times* leader writer, some years later, 'Saudi Arabia has to be an Islamic state; it is the birthplace of Islam. The question is *which* Islam?'[35]

The Iraq war had one clear positive effect for Saudi Arabia: it pushed up the world oil price and ended the country's succession of budget deficits. Suddenly Saudi Arabia had the money to pay for reforms and at the same time to increase the protection provided for Saudis by the social security system and to enter into new arms deals to safeguard its security. Plans were launched for a new round of large-scale public works and commercial developments worth billions of dollars in water supply and power generation. New mobile phone services, hospitals, clinics and educational facilities, with the potential to create thousands of new jobs, were announced. Talks began over a fresh phase of the Al Yamamah arms deal, by this time believed to be the most valuable arms

35 David Gardner, *Last Chance: The Middle East in the Balance*, I. B. Tauris, London, 2009.

contract in British history. A massive new arms contract was also agreed with France for the supply of helicopters, armoured ground assault vehicles and a range of other weapons. It has been estimated that between 1990 and 2004 alone Saudi Arabia spent $268.6 billion on arms purchases, equivalent to more than $12 million for every man, woman and child in the country.[36] However, allegations of corruption continued to dog the Saudi arms deals, further discrediting the Saudi royal family in the eyes of their own citizens and of the public around the world. In 2003 a British newspaper, *The Guardian*, carried the first of a series of stories alleging that a British arms manufacturer at the centre of the Al Yamamah contract, BAE, had created a 'slush fund' worth £60 million from which they had bribed Saudi princes to ensure that they got the contract. It was alleged that over the years millions of pounds had been transferred from it into the Washington bank accounts of Prince Bandar and Swiss bank accounts linked to agents of Saudi royals. In 2006 a British Serious Fraud Office investigation into these deals was halted by the British Government on the grounds that to continue it threatened the national interest. This, it was alleged, followed threats from senior members of the Saudi royal family to the British Prime Minister, Tony Blair, that unless the investigation was called off Saudi Arabia would sever intelligence links with Britain so rendering the country liable to further terrorist attacks and loss of life on Britain's streets.[37]

On May 27th 2005 it was reported that King Fahd had gone into hospital for unspecified medical tests. Since suffering a severe stroke ten years previously, Fahd had been little more than a figurehead, monarch in name only, seen in press photographs receiving visitors from his wheelchair or holidaying in the south of France, while Crown Prince Abdullah had got on with running the country. On August 1st Fahd died. Abdullah, aged eighty-two, was proclaimed King and his half-brother, Prince Sultan, another of the 'Sudairi Seven', became

36 *When will the House of Saud feel safe? Saudi Arabia and Military Expenditure*, by Dr Abbas Abbas Bakhtiar, Information Clearing House.

37 *Guardian*, September 2003, June 2007, January 18th 2008, February 15th 2008, April 15th 2008. In March 2010 it was reported that BAE Systems had pleaded guilty in a US court to making false statements in realtion to arms contracts and agreed to pay a substantial fine.

Crown Prince and First Deputy Prime Minister.[38] Despite the previous predictions that once Fahd, a member of the Sudairi clan, was ensconced on the throne the Sudairis would never let anyone other than a Sudairi rule, the succession of Abdullah, not a Sudairi, went smoothly. In spite of reports that Abdullah and Sultan did not get on, Saudi Arabia had survived another potential crisis point without apparent dissent inside the royal family or the Kingdom's disintegration. A year after coming to the throne Abdullah, in a move aimed at reducing the possibility of any future internal family power struggle, delegated powers to decide the way in which the country chooses its future monarchs to his brothers and nephews, through a new creation, The Allegiance, or *bay'a*, Council. Made up of all Ibn Saud's surviving sons and a grandson of each of Ibn Saud's sons who had died, were medically incapacitated or 'otherwise unwilling to assume the throne', plus one son of both Abdullah and the Crown Prince Sultan, its task will be, on the death of a King and accession of the Crown Prince, to determine who will become the next Crown Prince.[39]

One of Abdullah's first acts on succeeding to the throne was to free the editor of *Al Watan*, the newspaper which had criticised the religious police, and four reformers who had been jailed for criticising the slow pace of change. Abdullah, with the reputation of a traditionalist, was at the same time a reformer. Before coming to the throne he had been hampered in his reforms by more cautious or corrupt members of the royal family, notably the Sudairis who were widely believed to be deeply mired in much of the worst corruption and personal extravagance. But with the added authority and prestige of being King, plus his close links with the tribes, the Bedouin and popularity among the ordinary people –

38 Sources give a range of different ages for Abdullah, as for most of the other children of Ibn Saud. Lacey states the year of his birth as 1923. Other sources suggest 1925.

39 The *bay'a* was the sacred oath of loyalty, with roots dating back to the pact between Muhammad ibn Saud and Muhammad Ibn Abd al-Wahhab, sworn by the religious leaders and heads of familes to Ibn Saud after his recapture of Riyadh in 1902. The description of the make-up and functions of the Council, plus the quotation from the words of the decree, are taken from the translation of the Allegiance Institution Law published by the Saudi–US Relations Information Service.

he was admired by poor town-dwellers, whose slums he had visited and whose grievances he had listened to – his simple and unostentatious life-style and reputation for speaking his mind, Abdullah was now in a uniquely strong position to accelerate the pace of reform. He also had the benefit of a continuing sharp rise in the oil price. By the time he assumed the throne the price of a barrel of oil had increased over the previous seven years six-fold, from around $10 a barrel to around $60. Although the rate of increase would slacken briefly during the second half of 2007, by the summer 2008 it had touched almost $150 and forecasters were talking of it reaching $200 by the end of the year and even $500 over the next few years. However, in the second half of 2008, with banking failures in the USA, the coming of the 'Credit Crunch' and a worldwide recession, the price fell to about a quarter of its summer peak only to recover again by the middle of 2009 to about $70 per barrel, a level substantially higher than at any time during Fahd's reign.

Yet in spite of the country's improved financial position on coming to the throne Abdullah faced a host of formidable problems. The average real income of Saudis had fallen to about one third of what it had been twenty years earlier. Almost two-thirds of indigenous Saudis were under the age of twenty-five and unemployment was rife – from polling evidence it appeared that unemployment was people's biggest single worry. At the same time military expenditure remained out of all proportion for a country of Saudi Arabia's size and population, and the royal family, now believed to number 5,000 princes, still devoured a huge proportion of the country's national income. On top of all this there still remained a substantial internal threat from Islamist terrorists. Barely a month after Abdullah's accession a gun battle between terrorists and police close to the key oil facility at Dhahran resulted in the death of five terrorists and arrest of eleven more. A further attack on the country's oil facilities occurred six months later but was foiled by police. Abdullah responded by stepping up efforts to halt the attacks and undermine the terrorists. He pledged $1 billion to the rebuilding of war-ravaged Iraq and announced the construction of a 520-mile electrified fence along Saudi Arabia's border with Iraq to prevent terrorists from crossing undetected between the two countries. More than 40 per cent of the foreign insurgent fighters in Iraq were believed to be Saudis. In the last three months of 2006, 136 terrorist suspects were arrested in Saudi Arabia and the following April another 172 and $32 million dollars were seized. More than 200 more arrests followed over the next six months and in June 2008 the authorities announced the arrest of a further 520. In the six months after that another 208 were arrested, making a total of almost 1,250 suspected terrorist arrests in little more than two years, and the drive continues. At the same time the country's recognised religious leaders stepped up their condemnations of the use of terrorism as a means of achieving change.

Abdullah also pushed ahead with a succession of reforms and other moves aimed at helping those hit by falls in the value of their incomes. Within weeks of becoming King he granted all government employees a 15 per cent wage rise, the first they had had for 22 years. In the early months of 2005, immediately before Abdullah came to the throne but largely due to his efforts, the first ever elections had taken place in Saudi Arabia. Held in response to the demands of the liberal reformers, the elections were for half the seats in each of Saudi Arabia's 178 municipalities, the remaining half of the seats continuing to be filled by government appointment. The franchise had been restricted to men over 21 years of age. Although voter registration was low – only about one third of those eligible – the turnout among those who had registered was high, over 80 per cent, and foreign observers who witnessed the election said that it appeared to be fair and conducted in a calm spirit. Political parties were forbidden but voters had a huge array of different candidates to choose from. Those elected were overwhelmingly Islamists. Subsequently it was announced that from 2009 onwards women would be allowed to vote. However, under pressure from conservatives, this was later rescinded. In November 2005, following an order from Abdullah's government, two women were elected to the Jeddah Chamber of Commerce and allowed to sit and debate in the same chamber with the men: an important first step in the on-going struggle for women's emancipation. Yet, at the same time, the secret police continued to enforce the ban on the right to assemble, even in private homes, to discuss political issues. So, such small advances as Saudi Arabia has made in recent years still fall far short of marking anything like the achievement of full democracy. Yet such small steps do represent important milestones in the Kingdom's slow, often contested, advance towards becoming a modern state.

In November 2005 Saudi Arabia was at last admitted, after a negotiation which had dragged on for twelve years, to the World Trade Organisation. This is widely seen by reformers and outsiders as being an important catalyst for change in the way Saudi enterprises are managed and run, a change which is expected to spread beyond business to bring forward modernisation in many other parts of Saudi society.

Unemployment, and the disenchantment which it brings, is recognised as a powerful recruiting sergeant for Islamist extremists. So simultaneously with liberalising moves, Abdullah has instituted a further series of massive new development schemes, this time designed specifically to create new jobs and tackle the unemployment problem among young Saudi men. The largest development, The King Abdullah Economic City near Jeddah, is planned to cover 100 square miles, create 1 million new jobs and be home to 2 million people by 2016. A second scheme, The Knowledge Economic City near Medina, is planned to create 20,000 new jobs and a third, the Prince Abdul Aziz Mousaid Economic City near Ha'il, is intended to become Saudi Arabia's most important centre for industries related to agriculture. Three other similar schemes are also planned. Abdullah has also instituted an overhaul of education, the re-writing of textbooks, changes in teaching methods and vetting of teachers. He initiated a scheme, agreed with President Bush, for 15,000 Saudi students to be enrolled at colleges across the United States. Abdullah takes as his inspiration and justification for such polices the great age of Muslim scholarship: the centuries when, while Medieval Christian Europe was in the grip of what we know as the Dark Ages, it was Muslim scholars, building on the example of the ancient Babylonians and taking their command from the Qur'anic injunction to look, see, learn and understand, who not only preserved the learning of the ancients, but oversaw huge advances in subjects ranging from astronomy to engineering, mathematics to medicine, and geography to philosophy. Similarly, many young men who have joined the terrorist extremists, having been arrested, are persuaded by Abdullah's security forces to abandon their Islamist activities not by threats and maltreatment but by being offered a stake in the community.

They may be provided with a job, a new car and in some cases even a new wife.

Abdullah has continued bridge-building towards Shia Muslims, inviting Iran's President Ahmadinejad to visit Saudi Arabia and reaching an agreement with him to fight the spread of sectarian strife. But at the same time there continue to be tensions between the two countries, especially over alleged Iranian support for Shia rebels in the border area between the Asir province of Saudi Arabia and Yemen. He has convened and taken part in inter-faith forums with Jews and Christians. However, places of worship for other faiths continue to be banned in the Kingdom.

Aramco, now wholly Saudi owned, has long been widely regarded as one of the most technically advanced oil companies in the world. Another company, set up by royal decree in 1976 with mainly Saudi government money, the Saudi Basic Industries Corporation (SABIC), has been developed into one of the world's leading petro-chemical companies, with headquarters in Riyadh and plants across the country and in other parts of the world, developing and producing petro-chemicals, plastics, metals and fertilisers. Now a world-class enterprise, its Saudi personnel are today sent around the world to receive the best possible specialist training. This has been achieved without confrontation and Abdullah intends to build on that experience to develop a range of other industries which will both improve his subjects' economic fortunes and reduce the Kingdom's dangerous over-dependence on oil production.

In the same vein, in the autumn of 2007 the government announced a drive to attract western tourists to Saudi Arabia. While highlighting the Kingdom's almost unbroken sunshine, unusual wildlife – animals such as desert oryx and monitor lizards – ancient monuments like Meda'in Saleh, scuba diving in the Red Sea, 'the wonderful shopping experience' in traditional souks, camel and horse racing, they also had to warn westerners about such things as the strict dress code, especially for women, limited entertainment, ban on alcohol, gambling and women driving.

In another liberalising move shortly after Abdullah came to the throne, a tentative return, after a thirty-year absence, of film shows was permitted when a children's film was screened in a large hall in a Riyadh hotel for women and children. Late in 2008 there were screenings in Taif and Jeddah of a locally produced comedy. Shown in a hall seating 1,400, with men and women segregated – women in the balcony and men and boys in the stalls – the film proved so popular that eight screenings a day had to be held for the whole of the film's ten day run. The religious authorities promptly condemned the showings but, following protests and pressure from the royal family, modified their opposition, denying that they had said that all films were bad, only those that distracted people from their faith. A few months later plans were announced by Aramco to build a purpose-built cinema in a cultural centre in Dhahran. Recently stand-up comedians have been permitted to perform, even one female comedian. However Mufi, as she calls herself, cannot use her real name for fear of bringing disgrace upon her family. In the autumn of 2008 a group of 16 Saudi artists, men and women, working in all regions of the country staged an exhibition at the Brunei Gallery in London. Working in all kinds of media, their works ranged from re-explorations of traditional Arabian forms to examinations and expressions of some of the contradictions in modern Saudi society. By 2009 Abdullah was being hailed in the western media as 'The Monarch Who Declared His own Revolution'.[40]

Abdullah has also been active on the international stage. As the world oil price surged towards $100 a barrel in late 2007 Saudi Arabia signed up to the Kyoto climate change protocol, announcing that it wanted to play a positive role in dealing with problems related to the earth's environment. The Saudi oil minister argued that the way forward lay not in policies that discriminated against petroleum and fossil fuels, but in developing new technologies.

Significantly, perhaps, Abdullah's first overseas visit after becoming King was to China, not the United States. In another departure from past practice, Abdullah's official delegation included a number of women rather than only men. Since that first visit to China there have been increasing signs that Saudi Arabia has been drawing closer to China in a number of areas, notably trade and arms supply.

In November 2007, during an official tour of Europe, King Abdullah

40 *Newsweek*, 30th March 2009.

met the Pope at the Vatican to discuss Muslim/Jewish and Christian relations. Abdullah held the meeting in spite of the fact that a year earlier the Pope had delivered an extremely controversial theological lecture at Regensburg University in Germany which had given great offence to millions of Muslims around the world. During his lecture the Pope had quoted an obscure 1391 medieval religious dialogue between a Persian Muslim scholar and the Byzantine Emperor Manuel II Paleologus in which the Emperor had challenged the Muslim scholar to 'Show me just what Muhammad brought that was new, and there you will find things only evil and inhuman, such as his command to spread by the sword the faith he preached.' Although the Pope had quoted from the medieval dialogue in the context of a much longer discussion of the proper relationship between faith, reason and the use of force, by quoting the Byzantine Emperor's pejorative words about the Prophet Muhammad and his preaching Pope Benedict had provoked a storm of protest. Across the Muslim world there had been riots, street protests and threats by extremists of terrorist attacks on the Vatican. Although the Vatican had issued a statement saying that the Pope deeply regretted offending Muslims, he had still stopped short of issuing an apology. As a result, a year later when King Abdullah elected to meet Pope Benedict, the sense of grievance among Muslims still remained strong. So by deciding to meet the Pope during his European tour specifically to discuss Muslim/Jewish and Christian relations, Abdullah seemed to be sending a signal of his determination to achieve a Middle East peace agreement and a just settlement of the Palestinian problem by means of patient and persistent dialogue rather than through a resort to violence.[41]

In 2002, while still Crown Prince, Abdullah had persuaded the Arab League countries meeting in Beirut to adopt a comprehensive Middle East peace plan under which Israel would be offered full recognition in

41 Quotation from Pope Benedict's lecture from official Vatican version of full text. Of course, it might reasonably be said that in their remarks both the Emperor Manuel II and the Pope had chosen to overlook the Christians' own long history of choosing faith over reason and pursuing conversion by the use of the sword, whether in the Crusades, the burning of those deemed to be heretics, the wars of the Reformation or in the more recent 'crusades' of the likes of President George W. Bush and Tony Blair.

exchange for returning all the Arab lands it had captured since before the 1967 war and returning to its pre-1967 borders, recognising a Palestinian state and agreeing to a just solution to the Palestinian refugee problem.[42] Abdullah also tried to mediate between Syria and Lebanon and between the two Palestinian factions, the PLO and Hamas. In March 2007 he intensified his efforts, hosting a meeting of Arab heads of state in Riyadh, which renewed the 'land-for-peace' offer to Israel. In 2009, after Israel's assault on Gaza in which many innocent Palestinian men, women and children were killed, injured and made homeless, as well as condemning Israel's assault and methods, Abdullah donated $1 billion towards the reconstruction of Gaza, more than any other country, and advanced efforts to get all the Muslim nations to adopt the Saudi peace plan. Abdullah also intensified his pressure on the United States and other western governments to push Israel into accepting the Saudi peace plan and stopping their maltreatment of Palestinian civilians.

In the autumn of 2008 Abdullah initiated talks between representatives of the Karzai government of Afghanistan and moderate members of the Taliban aimed at brokering an end to the Afghan war.

Back at home in Saudi Arabia a touchstone issue in King Abdullah's programme of domestic reform remains the treatment of women. In October 2007 the King laid the foundation stone of a new science and technology university being built from scratch on the Red Sea coast about 50 miles north of Jeddah. Primarily a centre for postgraduate science and technology, education and research, it was opened by the King in September 2009. The groundbreaking feature of this new university is that it is the first in Saudi Arabia to take both male and female students; men and women are allowed to mix freely on the campus and women are not required to be veiled in the mixed-gender classes. This was condemned by some hard-line clerics, but nevertheless the religious police do not operate on the campus and women are permitted to drive and take part in sports. The university aims to become a world leader in science, technology, alternative energy resources and

42 The Oslo Accords, signed in 1993, had similar aspirations but allowed the Israelis to impose so many conditions that since then no progress has been achieved on the ground.

environmental research, spearheading Saudi Arabia's drive to escape its economic over-dependence on oil production. Abdullah hopes that his new university, forecast to grow to a total population of 20,000, will become a beacon lighting his Kingdom's advance towards becoming a more progressive, liberal and united country.

In January 2008 new rules were announced permitting women to stay in mixed-gender hotels provided that they had their male guardians' permission and the hotel proprietor registered their presence with the police. However the bureaucratic hurdles put in the way of the initiative and continuing conservative male attitudes meant that few women were able to avail themselves of this new-found freedom. In response, in March 2008 Saudi Arabia's first women-only hotel opened just outside Riyadh. Early in Abdullah's reign female shop assistants were allowed for the first time in women's clothes shops, meaning that now Saudi women no longer needed to buy their underwear from male shop assistants. In 2009 King Abdullah for the first time appointed six women to serve on the 150-member *Shura Al-Majlis*, or National Consultative Council. Sometimes described as the Kingdom's legislature (the Council became a member of the Interparliamentary Union in 2003), the Council's role nevertheless remains essentially advisory. Executive power remains almost exclusively in the hands of the King and his appointed ministers.

On the surface reform often seems to be moving at a snail's pace, yet out of sight profound changes are occurring. In some cafés in Jeddah there is now a section where men and women, although the women are still swathed from head to toe in black, are allowed to sit together. At Durat Al Arous, a Red Sea resort a few miles outside Jeddah, men and women mix almost as they might in a western resort, even swimming together from the same beaches.

Nevertheless Saudi women still caution that, in order to avoid a conservative backlash, it remains vital not to push the pace of reform too fast.[43] Saudi Arabia's first woman TV announcer appeared in 2001. However, although she was swathed in black with no trace of hair or

43 Bridget Kendall, BBC Radio 4, 'From Our Own Correspondent' April 29th 2006.

neck visible, the conservative clerical establishment still insisted that it was a sin for women to show their faces on TV at all because it could lead men into temptation. Interestingly, in 2006 one of Saudi Arabia's most prominent women TV announcers debated the issue with a leading Saudi cleric on a Turkish TV channel. She insisted that her face was an important part of her identity and that if men were permitted to show their faces on TV women should be permitted to do so as well. The Qur'an, she argued, said that men and women had been created equal, with equal duties and responsibilities. To deny her the right to show her face was to deny her her equal rights as a professional woman. However, in 2009 shortly after King Abdullah appointed a woman to serve in his cabinet as vice-minister of education, the woman concerned declined to appear in a TV interview, saying that she would not unveil her face to appear in front of the cameras unless specific permission was given to her to do so.

In what may be a sign of a continued yearning for old certainties and pleasures, one of the most popular of today's TV shows throughout the Arabian peninsula is a talent contest, the Million's Poet competition, broadcast by Abu Dubai TV. In it contestants from all over the Arab world recite their own poetry composed in a traditional Bedouin style called Nabati dating back to a time before the Prophet Muhammad. The hit of the series in 2010 was a Saudi housewife, Hissa Hilal, dressed from head to toe in a full, face hiding *burqa*. In her fifteen verse poem, *The Chaos of Fatwas,* she condemned the extremist clerics and suicide bombers who 'sit in the position of power', frightening people with their religious edicts, 'vicious in voice, barbaric, angry and blind, wearing death as a robe cinched with a belt'. Extremists and people sympathetic to *Al Qaeda* responded by issuing death threats against Hissa Hilal and her family.[44]

One particularly notorious incident occurred in 2002 when a fire started in a Mecca girls' school. When the blaze began at eight o'clock in the morning on the top floor of the school, girls, many suffering from burns, started streaming out of the building. But a group of religious

44 See *The Guardian* March 30th 2007, *The Times* and *The Independent* March 24th 2010.

policemen turned up and started pushing the girls back into the burning building because they did not have their heads covered and were not correctly dressed according to the strict dress code. The policemen also tried to prevent the rescue services from intervening. In the end fourteen of the girls were killed and another fifty seriously injured. In a break with normal practice, the Saudi press published the story and criticised the action of the religious police, helping to provoke a nationwide outcry and widespread demonstrations. Crown Prince Abdullah responded by removing control of girls' education from the clerical establishment and giving it to the state.

In another case, in 2006, a nineteen-year-old woman from Qatif was raped fourteen times by a gang of seven men. The men were sentenced to between ten months and five years in prison but at the same time the young woman was sentenced to 90 lashes because she had been riding in a car with a man who was not a relative. When she appealed against her sentence and the lenient sentences given to the men, the court as well as increasing the rapists' sentences also increased the woman's sentence to 200 lashes because, the judge said, she had tried to 'aggravate and influence the judiciary through the media'. And her lawyer, a prominent defender of women's rights, had his licence to practise revoked. After an outcry from human rights groups around the world and criticism from President Bush, King Abdullah stepped in to pardon the woman, but in a manner that appeared to be aimed at both meeting the criticism of Bush and the outside world and, at the same time, not offending his own conservative judiciary. In a statement the Saudi justice minister said that the king had issued the pardon out of his concern to alleviate undue suffering among his subjects but that the King remained 'convinced and sure that the verdicts were fair'.[45]

The need to trim the drive towards reform and liberalisation to avoid provoking a destabilising backlash from still-powerful conservative elements in Saudi society is to be seen across a wide range of economic, social and foreign policies. So in 2006, the year in which Saudi Arabia got itself elected to the UN Human Rights Council and committed itself to observing the UN Charter on Human Rights, King Abdullah instructed

45 Associated Press, 18th December 2007.

Saudi newspapers to stop publishing pictures of women. Human rights bodies such as Amnesty International and Human Rights Watch continue to chart the Kingdom's multiple abuses of human rights. Although admitting that the Kingdom has been making some progress, these bodies repeatedly highlight the continuing use of the death penalty – over one hundred executions in 2008 – arbitrary arrest, imprisonment without trial, frequent use of torture, abuse of foreigners working in the country, restrictions on open debate, censorship, lack of democracy, discrimination against women and children. A Human Rights Watch report in 2008 found that Saudi Arabia's continuing laws on male guardianship over women and segregation of the sexes resulted in women still being denied their full human rights. Treated as if they were children, women are unable to work, travel, study, marry or access health care without the written permission of their male guardians. So when the eight-year-old daughter of a divorced woman was married off to a fifty-eight-year-old man by her father in payment of a debt and her divorced mother appealed to a court in Qasim to have the marriage annulled, the court turned her plea down. The judge said that the girl's mother did not have the right to lodge the appeal and her daughter would have to lodge the plea herself 'when she reaches puberty'. A few months later, after a further appeal by the mother, the original judgement was confirmed. But following an outburst of protests inside Saudi Arabia and beyond, in the spring of 2009 the governor of Qasim Province, Prince Faisal bin Bandar, intervened and brokered a negotiated settlement between the girl's lawyer and the girl's husband.

In 1999 a group of women, concerned at the level of abuse by men against women throughout the Kingdom, created the National Family Safety Programme to provide services for the victims of abuse. King Abdullah gave the project his backing and appointed his daughter, Princess Adelah, to head the Programme. Today it provides services for a whole range of victims of abuse, sexual, physical and psychological, women, children and the elderly. It intervenes to protect victims against further abuse and provides therapeutic and educational services for abusers, with the aim of preventing further abuse. It also conducts research, training, education and community awareness programmes.

Through all the changes, advances and setbacks, one thing remains clear – the royal family's determination to do whatever it deems necessary to maintain its own unchallenged hold on all real power. Prince Nayif, the Interior Minister, has told reformers and dissidents seeking change, 'What we won by the sword we will keep by the sword' and Crown Prince Sultan said publicly in 2004 that the Kingdom was not ready to be ruled by an elected parliament because the electorate might choose 'illiterates'.[46]

Yet the Saudi Arabia of today is unrecognisable from the kingdom of Ibn Saud at the time of his death almost sixty years ago. To outsiders it may still be a distant country of which they know little: hot, dry, strange, secretive, dangerous and terrible. But to Saudis old enough to remember the land of Ibn Saud it is massively changed. The endless burning deserts are still mostly there, but the Bedouin nomads no longer ride their camels across it or live in black-camel-hair tents as they drive their flocks from one small rock-strewn oasis to another under an unrelenting sun. Those few who are still nomads today nearly all drive air-conditioned four-wheel drives while the rest of the former nomads live in the newly constructed cities and, if they work, it is often in refineries and processing plants amid endless stainless steel piping and flaring gas vents or in air-conditioned factories and offices. The towns they work in are no different from the 'new-build' towns of the United States and Western Europe, a garish jungle of steel, concrete and glass stores and office buildings where life goes on without ceasing for twenty-four hours a day amid a sea of blinking neon signs, electric light, endless noise and moving, foul-smelling, pollution-producing traffic. The only timeless note is the call of the muezzin which five times a day still calls the faithful to prayer above the din. But now the voice rings, curls and echoes from metallic loudspeakers perched high on the local neighbourhood mosque and through the shopping malls, bouncing the unchanging centuries-old words incongruously off and between the reflective surfaces of modern buildings. And the call is still answered. The stores close, the shopping malls empty and are stilled, the traffic thins and for a few blessed minutes the incessant din is reduced.

In Ibn Saud's childhood Riyadh probably had a population of barely

46 David Gardner, op. cit.

20,000. Today it is a mega-city of some four million; and some recent estimates suggest that the figure is now nearer six million. Since Ibn Saud's death the population of the Kingdom he created has multiplied seven-fold, from about four million to approaching thirty million. Whereas in Ibn Saud's time most of the population lived outside the towns today over 80 per cent are town and city dwellers. Saudi Arabia has one of the highest birth rates in the world and life expectancy has increased from an average of less than fifty years to over seventy. Although tribal affiliations remain important and family links with a Bedouin past are still a source of pride, the rapid decline in the importance of the Bedouin nomadic way of life has been highlighted by Saudi Arabia's 2005 decision to construct an electrified fence along the country's border with Iraq to prevent terrorists and insurgents from moving freely between the two countries. Eighty years ago Ibn Saud struggled with the British to keep that same border open to permit the continued free movement of the Bedouin with their flocks to and from their traditional wells and summer pastures on either side of it. Because of the high birth rate more than 60 per cent of Saudis are now aged under twenty-one and 75 per cent under thirty. Whereas in Ibn Saud's youth few people could read, today 85 per cent of men and 80 per cent of women are literate. In Ibn Saud's day most people knew little beyond the life of the tribe, the small town or oasis in which they lived, but today, in spite of heavy state censorship (Saudi Arabia ranks twelfth from the bottom of the world's nations as regards freedom of its media), homes have access to the internet and satellite TV and Saudis are well aware of the life, ideas, brand names and fashions of the world beyond their own country.

One feature of Saudi urban life that would particularly shock Ibn Saud is the rocketing crime rate, especially among the young. In his day the country was regarded as effectively crime free. In 1999 the Islamic courts dealt with over 600 murders, the largest number of them in the Holy City of Mecca.[47] In its report for 2008 Amnesty International lists 158 people as being executed for murder, rape, drug offences, witchcraft, apostasy and other offences. Reporters have told of drugs being widely

47 See Bradley, op. cit.

available on the streets, of prostitution and armed robberies. Riyadh police recorded 13,000 serious robberies in the city in 2003 alone, while nationally the number of people arrested for possession of drugs was over 17,000 by 2001. The numbers of Saudis using drugs has almost certainly risen since then. During two months in the summer of 2009 the Saudi police seized more than three tons of hashish, millions of amphetamine tablets and quantities of pure heroin.

Groups of bored, listless, rowdy young men, frustrated by the lack of satisfying outlets for their energy and sources of entertainment in a patriarchal society ruled by Wahhabi tradition, roam the streets causing mayhem – hurling lighted fireworks into crowds at football matches, disguising themselves as women to gain admittance to women-only venues, luring police officers into 120-mile-an-hour chases along freeways. Young men and women now regularly approach each other and make dates without their parents' knowledge by using their mobile phones and text messaging. Traditionalists respond by condemning the west for what they see as the moral rot and disintegration of their society.

In the of face such enormous demographic and social changes it seems almost inevitable that Saudi Arabia's political regime must soon undergo some fundamental changes. The question remains, will this occur peacefully or through violent upheaval? Can the Saudi monarchy established by Ibn Saud, indeed the Kingdom, survive that change? Liberal reformers, both women seeking equal rights and opportunities with men, and social modernisers, have in recent years turned to the Qur'an and religion as a source and argument for such change. By revisiting the sacred texts and Islam's long and distinguished history in the pursuit of knowledge and innovation in the sciences, mathematics and technology, and their beneficial application, they have found a new weapon in their struggle with the conservative clerics and traditionalists. They have turned again to the Qur'an's teachings on the equality of all human beings under God. Today, as well as the official clergy, paid by the state, living in large houses and driving around in comfortable cars, there is also a burgeoning unofficial, popular clergy. Many of them are the same religious scholars, university professors, judges, and other respected people who have been signing the reform petitions since the 1990s. They may, with their call for a return to the true tenets of Islam, turn out to be the saviours of the country. It is they perhaps, by their use and knowledge of the sacred texts, who may succeed in neutralising the dead hand of the Wahhabi fundamentalists and unblock the path to popular but stable change in Saudi Arabia.

But even if these reformers succeed the threats from outside forces and terrorism, from division inside the royal family, will remain. For over a century, from the time Ibn Saud captured Riyadh, for the rest of his life and repeatedly over the more than fifty years since his death, commentators have been forecasting the imminent disintegration of the state which he created. Yet his state has endured while all around other states have disintegrated, been brought down by civil war and revolution, or been overrun. Since Ibn Saud's death, which commentators had confidently predicted the Kingdom would not survive, Saudi Arabia has survived the accession and incompetent rule of his son Saud, the peaceful transfer of power from him to his brother Faisal, the assassination of Faisal, the seizure of the Grand Mosque in Mecca by the successors of the Ikhwan, numerous wars in the Middle East, the long reign and illness of Fahd, the attacks and designs upon the Kingdom of Islamist followers of Osama bin Laden and foreign powers, the passing of Fahd, a member of the Sudairi Seven, and his succession by Abdullah who is not one of the Sudairis. In the last fifty years it has survived massive social, economic and demographic change.

Yet to say that the Kingdom has survived thus far is not to say that it always will. All five kings since Ibn Saud's death have been his sons. But sons of Ibn Saud can not go on succeeding each other for many more years. All are getting older. Abdullah was over 80 when he came to the throne and Sultan, the Crown Prince, is more than 80 already and reputed to have health problems. Even Ibn Saud's youngest surviving sons are already well into their sixties. If the monarchy is to survive, at some point the throne is going to have to pass to a member of the next generation. What happens then, when one line of direct descent from Ibn Saud takes precedence over others? Despite the creation of the Allegiance Council, has the next generation of the Al Sauds really absorbed the lessons of their family's history, of how dissension inside the family led to successive downfalls? Have they sufficiently taken to heart Idn Saud's warning to his quarrelling sons that in order to retain their kingdom they must not let differences within the family lead to open dissension?

Outside observers warn that to survive Saudi Arabia must bring about real social and political change as a matter of urgency; that the power of the conservative clergy and traditionalists must be curbed and that the influence of fundamentalist Wahhabis who resist change must be reduced. However, Western commentators and political leaders who are so quick to tell Saudi Arabia what to do should perhaps reflect on the fact that Saudi Arabia is a very different country from their own countries, with a different history, traditions and beliefs. Perhaps they should be reminded of how long it took their own countries to make the changes that they now urge upon Saudi Arabia, and reflect on how long it took them to emerge as modern democratic states. In Britain women did not get the vote until after the First World War, nearly three hundred years after Parliament chopped off the head of Charles I and even today the members of one chamber in our Parliament remain unelected. Perhaps Americans might reflect on the fact that in the 1960s, one hundred years after the end of the Civil War, African-Americans were still having to fight for their rights and that it has taken until 2009 for the first African-American to enter the White House as President.

History shows that countries that try to force through change too fast, before the people are really ready, frequently end up in chaos and civil strife. Perhaps the great powers should show a little humility and consider how many of the Middle East's current problems are the result of their own meddling and mismanagement, whether in the imperial past through such initiatives as the Sykes-Picot Agreement, the Treaty of Versailles, the Cairo Conference and the Peel Commission or their own recent interventions in places such as Egypt, Iran and Iraq. Recently the British Foreign Secretary, David Miliband, told a conference at the Oxford Centre for Islamic Studies that the ruined Crusader Castles of the Middle East remain a poignant reminder that 'you can't teach morality with a sword'. Yet his former boss, Blair, had routinely mocked such views as 'benign inactivity'. As Blair's former constituency agent explained in a recent book, Blair's willingness to launch armed interventions, or 'Crusades', in Muslim countries was easily explained in terms of Blair living out his faith. In his eyes it 'was all part of the

Christian battle; good should triumph over evil'.[48] If that was his motivation was he really acting so differently from an Islamic jihadist? Western statesmen with Christian supremacist attitudes that hark back to the Middle Ages are surely among the least desirable people to determine or advise on the fate of countries such as Saudi Arabia. Perhaps the election of President Obama, the first leader of the West or a major world power since the fall of the Ottoman Empire to show a real appreciation and sympathy for the Muslim world, offers new hope for the Middle East. Obama appears to have a real appreciation of the values and history of the Muslim world and to understand the debt that the world owes to Islam, its scholars, scientists and innovators down the ages. So when he talks of making a new beginning between the Muslim world and the West for the first time in generations perhaps there really is cause for hope.

For the moment Saudi Arabia is sitting on more than one-fifth of the world's known oil reserves and so its immediate economic future seems assured. But what happens when the oil runs out or the world invents its way out of its dependence on oil and gas? Will Saudi Arabia have used its time and current prosperity to diversify sufficiently to ensure its survival after oil? Until that time Saudi Arabia's huge oil reserves give it a pivotal position in the world's affairs and even after oil has ceased to be important Saudi Arabia's history as the birthplace of Islam and its geographical location astride so many of the world's strategic trade and communications routes are likely, even in an age of easy air travel, electronic communications and dwindling faith, to render the future of Saudi Arabia a central concern of other countries.

When, a few months after coming to office, President Obama set out to make his historic speech in Cairo outlining his vision for a new relationship between the Muslim and Western worlds, he travelled first to Riyadh to confer with King Abdullah. In 1945 Roosevelt was the first American President, quickly followed by Prime Minister Churchill, to travel to the Middle East to meet a king of Saudi Arabia, Ibn Saud. But then it was as something of an after-thought in order to secure America's

48 *We Don't Do God* by John Burton and Eileen McCabe, Continuum, London, 2009.

interest in Saudi Arabian oil and the King's help over the issue of the Jewish homeland in Palestine. Today Saudi Arabia is no afterthought, it is an essential player in finding solutions to many of the world's most pressing problems. Today, and for the foreseeable future, a knowledge of Saudi Arabia, of its history and how it came to be as it is, is essential not only to understanding Saudi Arabia and its actions, but to understanding the Middle East, the Muslim world and much of what is happening in the world today.

As we hope we have made clear over the preceding pages, Saudi Arabia is a very different society, enjoying a very different history and culture, from those of most Western societies. For that reason we should perhaps judge the successes and failures of Saudi society rather differently from the way in which we judge the successes and failures of our own. The delicate balance so skilfully achieved by Ibn Saud between its different elements and traditions has, despite some hiccups, continued to serve the Kingdom well in the near sixty years since his death while all around it other states have collapsed. So, while in no way condoning human rights abuses or terrorism, it surely behoves outsiders to accept that Saudi Arabia must be allowed to develop in its own ways and at a pace which suits Saudis themselves. Left to determine its own destiny Saudi Arabia may evolve into a state and society both very different from ours in the West and very different from the Saudi society of today. If so, and provided that they do not threaten others, who are we to criticise or deny them that?

And what about Saudis themselves, their lives, their happiness? What of those Saudis who still refuse to take up the less skilled of the jobs created by Saudi Arabia's embrace of the modern world? What have the West and Saudi modernisers to say to those former Bedouin and others who continue to believe that the life of the pure desert Arab was far superior to any other on offer today? Is modern Saudi life, the life in the cities lived by so many of today's Saudis, especially the young, really so superior to the lives once lived by their grandfathers? Is it really more meaningful than a life which depended for its very continuance upon a shared spirit of community, on the tribe and the extended family? Does the modern pursuit of money for oneself, plus perhaps one's immediate family, and an over-arching belief in the benefits of competition really produce greater happiness and fulfilment than a life where sharing, hospitality, celebration of achievement and good fortune with other members of the tribe and extended family and of one's religion were the highest values and pinnacles of life? Is a life in offices and air-conditioned factories, and rush-hour car journeys to work, better than one of driving your animals on camelback from well to well and seasonal feeding ground to feeding ground, of hunting and depending on what Allah might provide? Are modern entertainment, passive consumption, television, computer games and industrially distributed popular music really more fulfilling than the sound and beauty of spoken Arabic verse, the Holy Qur'an, or the age-old stories of one's tribe told around the desert camp fire? The old life was certainly shorter. It was certainly harder. But worse? Who dare say so?

However, Saudi Arabia cannot go back to what it was even if it wanted to, nor can Saudis turn back the clock and return to what they once were. Saudi Arabia and Saudis have to go forwards to whatever future they map out for themselves, fate or Allah decrees. But no matter what that future may hold, the story of Ibn Saud and of his achievements will, in spite of his faults and failings, continue to be told and to have something to say to Saudis and to outsiders. It will continue to inspire and remind people of the vital role and power in life of individual personality and courage, of personal determination and belief, no matter how irrational, cruel, selfishly protective of its own familial or social group, that belief may sometimes be, nor how noble and enlightened. Philby was surely right to say that Ibn Saud was a great man, a 'man of destiny' even. Just how great, in some imagined league table of greatness, is irrelevant.

Bibliography

The Holy Bible: Authorized Version, Oxford University Press, Oxford.

The Holy Qur'an, translated by Abdullah Yusuf Ali, Wordsworth Classics of World Literature, Ware, UK, 2000

The Koran, translated by N. J. Dawood, Penguin Classics 50th Anniversary Edition, Penguin Books, London, 2006

Aarts, Paul & Nonneman, Gerd (eds), *Saudi Arabia Exposed: Political Economy, Society, Foreign Affairs*, C. Hurst, London, 2005

Abir, Mordechai, *Saudi Arabia: Government, Society & the Gulf Crisis*, Routledge, London, 1993

Aburish, Saïd K., *The Rise, Corruption and Coming Fall of the House of Saud*, Bloomsbury, London, 1994

Ahmed, Feroz, *Turkey: The Quest for Identity*, Oneworld Publications, Oxford, 2003

Alangari, Haifa, *The Struggle for Power in Arabia: Ibn Saud, Hussein and Great Britain, 1914–1924*, Ithaca Press, Reading, 1998

Ali, Kecia, and Leaman, Oliver, *Islam: The Key Concepts*, Routledge, Milton Park, Oxon, 2008

Armstrong, H. C., *Lord of Arabia: An Intimate Study of a King*, Penguin Books, Harmondsworth, Middlesex, 1938

Armstrong, Karen, *Islam: A Short History*, Weidenfeld & Nicolson, London, 2000

——— *Muhammad: A Biography of the Prophet*, Victor Gollancz, London, 1991

Asad, Muhammad, *The Road to Mecca*, Max Reinhardt, London, 1954

Bayly Winder, R., *Saudi Arabia in the Nineteenth Century*, Macmillan, London, 1965

Bell, Gertrude, *The Arabian Diaries 1913–14*, Victor Gollancz, London, 1991

Bell, Gertrude, *The Letters of Gertrude Bell, 2 Vols.*, edited by Lady Bell, E. Benn, London, 1927

Bishop, Jim, *FDR's Last Year: April 1944–April 1945*, Hart-Davis, MacGibbon, London, 1974

Bligh, Alexander, *From Prince to King: Royal Succession in the House of Saud in the Twentieth Century*, New York University Press, New York, 1984

Blunt, Anne, *A Pilgrimage to Najd, the Cradle of the Arab Race: A Visit to the Court of the Arab Emir, and our Persian Campaign*, John Murray, London, 1880

Blunt, Wilfrid Scawen, *My Diaries: Being a Personal Narrative of Events, 1888–1914, Part Two 1900 to 1914*, Martin Secker, London, 1920

Bradley, John R., *Saudi Arabia Exposed: Inside a Kingdom in Crisis*, Palgrave Macmillan, New York, 2005

Brent, Peter, *Far Arabia: Explorers of the Myth*, Weidenfeld & Nicolson, London, 1977

Bullard, Sir Reader, *The Camels Must Go: An Autobiography*, Faber and Faber, London, 1961

——— *Two Kings in Arabia: Letters from Jeddah 1923–5 and 1936–9*, edited by E. C. Hodgkin, Ithaca Press, Garnett Publishing, Reading, England, 1993

Burgoyne, Elizabeth, *Gertrude Bell from her Personal Papers*, London, 1961

Burton, John & McCabe, Eileen, *We Don't Do God*, Continuum, London, 2009

Burton, Captain Sir Richard F., *Personal Narration of a Pilgrimage to Al Madinah and Mecca*, Dover Publications, New York, 1964

Çetinsaya, Görkan, *Ottoman-British Relations in Iraq and the Gulf, 1890–1908*, Turkish Review of Middle East Studies, 2004 – 15

Churchill, Winston S., *The Second World War, Volume VI: Triumph And Tragedy,* Cassell, London, 1959

Clayton, Sir Gilbert Falkingham, *An Arabian Diary*, edited by Robert O. Collins, University of California Press, Los Angeles, 1969

Commins, David, *The Wahhabi Mission and Saudi Arabia*, I. B. Tauris, London, 2006

Crossman, Richard, *Palestine Mission: A Personal Record*, Hamish Hamilton, London, 1947

Darlow, Michael, and Fawkes, Richard, *The Last Corner of Arabia*, Namara Publications & Quartet Books, London, 1976

Dayan, Moshe, *Moshe Dayan, The Story of My Life*, Morrow Publishers, New York, 1967

De Gaury, Gerald, *Faisal, King of Saudi Arabia*, Arthur Baker, London, 1966

——— *Arabian Journey and other Desert Travels*, George G. Harrap, London, 1950

——— *Arabia Phoenix*, George G. Harrap, London, 1946

Delong-Bas, Natana J., *Wahhabi Islam: From Revival and Reform to Global Jihad*, I. B. Tauris, London, 2004

Dickson, H. R. P., *The Arab of the Desert: A Glimpse into Badawin Life in Kuwait and Sau'di Arabia*, George Allen & Unwin, London, 1951

——— *Kuwait & Her Neighbours*, George Allen & Unwin, London, 1956

Dickson, Violet, *Forty Years in Kuwait*, George Allen & Unwin, London, 1971

Eddy, William, *F. D. R. meets Ibn Saud*, America-Mideast Educational & Training Services, Washington DC, USA, 1954

Elon, Amos, *Herzl*, Schocken Books, New York, 1986

Fandy, Mamoun, *Saudi Arabia and Political Dissent*, Palgrave, New York, 1999

Al-Farsy, Fouad, *Saudi Arabia: A Case Study in Development*, KPI Limited, London, 1982

Fisher, H. A. L., *A History of Europe – Volume II: From the Beginning of the Eighteenth Century to 1935*, Eyre & Spottiswode, London, 1935

Gardner, David, *Last Chance: The Middle East in the Balance*, I. B. Tauris, London, 2009

Gibbon, Edward, *Decline and Fall of the Roman Empire*, Dent, London, 1954

Gilbert, Martin, *Winston S. Churchill, Volume VII 1941–5*, William Heinemann, London, 1981

——— (ed.), *The Churchill Papers, Volume IV, Companion, Part 2*, William Heinemann, London, 1977

Gilmour, David, *Curzon*, John Murray, London, 1994

Glubb, Sir John Bagot, *War in the Desert: An RAF Frontier Campaign*, Hodder and Stoughton, London, 1960

Goldberg, Jacob, *The Foreign Policy of Saudi Arabia: The Formative Years, 1902–1918*, Harvard University Press, Cambridge, Ma., USA, 1986

——— *Captain Shakspear & Ibn Saud: A Balanced Reappraisal*, Middle Eastern Studies 21 (1985), Routledge, London, 1985

Grafftey-Smith, Laurence, *Bright Levant*, John Murray, London, 1970

Graves, Philip, *The Life of Sir Percy Cox*, Hutchinson, London, 1941

Halliday, Fred, *Arabia Without Sultans*, Penguin Books, Harmondsworth, Middlesex, 1974

Herodotus, *History*, translated by A. D. Godley, Cambridge, Ma., USA, 1926

Hobsbawm, E. J., *The Age of Revolution: 1789–1848*, Weidenfeld & Nicolson, London, 1962

——— *The Age of Empire: 1875–1914*, Weidenfeld & Nicolson, London, 1987

Holden, David, and Johns, Richard, *The House of Saud*, Sidgwick & Jackson, London, 1981

Hourani, Albert, *A History of the Arab Peoples*, Faber & Faber, London, 2002

Howarth, David, *The Desert King: The Life of Ibn Saud*, William Collins, London, 1965

Howell, Georgina, *Daughter of the Desert: The Remarkable Life of Gertrude Bell*, Macmillan, London, 2006

Hoyland, Robert G., *Arabia & the Arabs from the Bronze Age to the Coming of Islam*, Routledge, London, 2001

Kay, Shirley, and Basil Malin, *Saudi Arabia: Past & Present*, Namara Publications, London, 1979

Kennedy, Paul, *The Rise and Fall of the Great Powers*, Unwin Hyman, London, 1988

Lacey, Robert, *The Kingdom*, Hutchinson, London, 1981

——— *Inside the Kingdom*, Hutchinson, London, 2009

Lawrence, T. E., *Seven Pillars Of Wisdom*, Jonathan Cape, London, 1935

Lee, Christopher, *This Sceptred Isle: Twentieth Century*, BBC Worldwide Ltd, Penguin Books, London, 2000.

Liddell Hart, B. H., *History of the First World War*, Book Club Associates, London, 1973

Lippman, Thomas W., *The Day FDR Met Saudi Arabia's Ibn Saud*, Americans for Middle East Understanding, New York, USA, 2005

Longrigg, Stephen Hemsley, *Oil in the Middle East: Its Discovery and Development*, Oxford University Press, Oxford, 1954

Mack, John E., *A Prince of our Disorder: The Life of T. E. Lawrence*, Harvard University Press, Cambridge, USA, 1998

Mackey, Sandra, *The Saudis: Inside the Desert Kingdom*, W. W. Norton, New York, 2002

Makovsky, Michael, *Churchill's Promised Land: Zionism and Statecraft*, Yale University Press, USA, 2007

Mantel, Hilary, *Eight Months on Ghazzah Street*, Viking Press, London, 1988

Mayer, Karl E., and Brysac, Shareen Blair, *Kingmakers: The Invention of the Modern Middle East*, W. W. Norton, New York, 2008

McLoughlin, Leslie, *Ibn Saud: Founder of a Kingdom*, Macmillan, London, 1993

Moran, Lord, *Winston Churchill: The Struggle for Survival 1940–1965*, Constable, London, 1966

Morrison, Samuel Elliot, *The Oxford History of the American People, Volume Three: 1869 through the Death of John F. Kennedy, 1963.* First Meridian Printing, Penguin Books, New York, USA, 1994

Moss Helms, Christine, *The Cohesion of Saudi Arabia: Evolution of Political Identity*, Croom Helm, London, 1981

Nanji, Azim (with Nanji, Razia), *The Penguin Dictionary of Islam*, Penguin Books, London, 2008

Nolde, Eduard, *Reise nach Innerarabien, Kurdistan und Armenien*, Vieweg, Braunschweig, 1895

Palgrave, William Clifford, *Personal Narrative of a Year's Journey through Central and Eastern Arabia (1862–63)*, Macmillan, 1871

Pelly, Lieutenant Colonel Lewis, *A Visit to the Wahabee Capital, Central Arabia*, Journal of the Royal Geographical Society No. 35, 1865

Philby, H. St John, *Sa'udi Arabia*, Ernest Benn, London, 1955

——— *Arabian Days: An Autobiography*, Robert Hale, London 1948

——— *Arabian Jubilee*, Robert Hale, London, 1952

——— *Forty Years in the Wilderness*, Robert Hale, London, 1957

Probert, Henry, *Bomber Harris: His Life and Times*, Greenhill Books, London, 2000

Al-Rasheed, Madawi, *A History of Saudi Arabia*, Cambridge University Press, New York, 2002

Raunkiaer, Barclay, *Gennem Wahhabiternes Land paa Kamelryg*, Nordisk Forl., Copenhagen 1913

Riedel, Bruce, *The Search for Al Qaeda*, Brookings Institution Press, Washington DC, 2008

Rihani, Ameen, *Ibn Sa'oud of Arabia: His People and His Land*, Constable, London, 1928

Rutter, Eldon, *The Holy Cities of Arabia: Volume 1*, G. P. Putnam, London, 1928

Safran, Nadav, *Saudi Arabia: The Ceaseless Quest for Security*, Cornell University Press, 1988

Salameh, Ghassene, and Steir, Vivian, *Political Power and the Saudi State*, MERIP Reports (Middle East Research and Information Project), 1980

Sampson, Anthony, *The Arms Bazaar: The Companies, The Dealers, the Bribes: From Vickers to Lockheed*, Hodder & Stoughton, London, 1977

Schwartz, Stephen, *The Two Faces of Islam: Saudi Fundamentalism and its Role in Terrorism*, Anchor Books, New York, 2003

Slavin, Ken (Ed.), *Dear Folks: The Webster Letters from Arabia 1944–59*, Aramco Expats Corporation, © USA 2002–9. Released on Worldwide Web, April 1st 2008.

Sorkhabi, Rasoul, *The Emergence of the Arabian Oil Industry*, Geo Publishing Ltd, GEO ExPro, London, 2008

Taylor, A. J. P., *English History 1914–1945*, Oxford University Press, London, 1965

Thesiger, Wilfred, *Desert, Marsh and Mountain: The World of a Nomad*, William Collins, London, 1979

Thornton, A. P., *The Imperial Idea and Its Enemies*, Macmillan, London, 1959

Troeller, Gary, *The Birth of Saudi Arabia: Britain and the Rise of the House of Sa'ud*, Frank Cass, London, 1976

Trofimov, Yaroslav, *The Siege of Mecca: The Forgotten Uprising*, Penguin Books, London, 2007

Twitchell, K. S., *Saudi Arabia: With an Account of the Development of Its Natural Resources*, Princeton University Press, 1953

Tyler, Patrick, *A World of Trouble: America in the Middle East*, Portobello Books, London, 2009.

Van Der Meulen, D., *The Wells of Ibn Saud,* John Murray, London, 1957.

Vassiliev, Alexei, *The History of Saudi Arabia*, Saqi Books, London, 1998

Westrate, Bruce, *The Arab Bureau: British Policy in the Middle East, 1916–1920,* Pennsylvania State University Press, USA, 1992

Winstone, H. V. F., *Captain Shakespear: A Portrait*, Jonathan Cape, London, 1976

——— *Gertrude Bell*, Jonathan Cape, London, 1978

——— *The Illicit Adventure: The Story of Political and Military Intelligence in the Middle East from 1896 to 1926*, Jonathan Cape, London, 1982

——— *My Travellers in Central Arabia and the Gulf*, a talk delivered at the opening of an exhibition of British Travellers in Arabia at the embassy of the Kingdom of Saudi Arabia in London on September 29th 2004

Zirikli, K., *Arabia in the Time of Ibn Saud* (Arabic), Beirut, 1970

Report of The Anglo-American Committee of Enquiry regarding the problems of European Jewry and Palestine, April 1946

King Abdul Aziz (Ibn Saud) Information Resource, Saudi Arabia, 2008

Newspapers, periodicals, internet and other sources drawn upon are referenced individually at relevant points in the text

Index